SOCIOLOGY:

a systematic introduction

Harry M. Johnson

SIMMONS COLLEGE

Under the General Editorship of

ROBERT K. MERTON

COLUMBIA UNIVERSITY

ALLIED PUBLISHERS PRIVATE LIMITED
NEW DELHI MUMBAI KOLKATA CHENNAI NAGPUR
AHMEDABAD BANGALORE HYDERABAD LUCKNOW

ALLIED PUBLISHERS PRIVATE LIMITED

1/13-14 Asaf Ali Road, **New Delhi**–110002
Ph.: 011-23239001 • E-mail: delhi.books@alliedpublishers.com

87/4, Chander Nagar, Alambagh, **Lucknow** - 226005
Ph.: 0522-4012850 • E-mail: appltdlko9@gmail.com

17 Chittaranjan Avenue, **Kolkata**–700072
Ph.: 033-22129618 • E-mail: cal.books@alliedpublishers.com

15 J.N. Heredia Marg, Ballard Estate, **Mumbai**–400001
Ph.: 022-42126969 • E-mail: mumbai.books@alliedpublishers.com

60 Shiv Sunder Apartments (Ground Floor), Central Bazar Road,
Bajaj Nagar, **Nagpur**–440010
Ph.: 0712-2234210 • E-mail: ngp.books@alliedpublishers.com

F-1 Sun House (First Floor), C.G. Road, Navrangpura,
Ellisbridge P.O., **Ahmedabad**–380006
Ph.: 079-26465916 • E-mail: ahmbd.books@alliedpublishers.com

751 Anna Salai, **Chennai**–600002
Ph.: 044-28523938 • E-mail: chennai.books@alliedpublishers.com

Hebbar Sreevaishnava Sabha, Sudarshan Complex - 2
No. 24/1, 2nd Floor, Seshadri Road, **Bangalore** - 560009
Ph.: 080-22262081 • E-Mail: bngl.books@alliedpublishers.com

3-2-844/6 & 7 Kachiguda Station Road, **Hyderabad**–500027
Ph.: 040-24619079 • E-mail: hyd.books@alliedpublishers.com

Website: www.alliedpublishers.com

First Indian Edition, 1966
Reprinted, 2016
ISBN 81-7023-137-X

Published by Sunil Sachdev and printed by Ravi Sachdev at Allied Publishers Private Limited, Printing Division, A-104 Mayapuri Phase II, New Delhi - 110064

Foreword

The historian of science Donald Fleming once noted that the textbook ideally records "a consensus of informed opinion, intended not to repress innovation but to give it point and zest and a prospect of general acceptance." In effect, Fleming has described this book by Harry M. Johnson, a book that is at once a manual of instruction and a significant treatise in its own right.

In describing Mr. Johnson's book as a treatise, I do not intend to make it sound forbidding. I mean only that it presents a methodical account of the basic principles of the subject and makes systematic but not extravagant use of these principles to illuminate a vast diversity of sociological data. I know of no other introduction to sociology that does this so effectively. Yet the book does not slavishly conform to a single "system" of sociology. Instead, it uses the core ideas that today constitute an appreciable working consensus among sociologists, whether these ideas are called structural-functional analysis or by some other name. The book achieves intellectual coherence, but not at the expense of neglecting intractable facts. Mr. Johnson refuses to force data about social structure, function, and change into the mold of a particular theory in those cases where the theory is not yet adequate to account for them. He treats sociological theory as both an instrumental convenience and an eventual goal. He does not employ it as a Procrustean device designed to bend recalcitrant facts to its shape.

Mr. Johnson has brought together the results of a great amount of empirical investigation through field observation, surveys, experiment, and historical and cross-cultural comparisons. These materials are not provincial in the sense that they are drawn only from sociological sources or confined to American society. Mr. Johnson's unobtrusive erudition has enabled him to make critical use of materials from such neighboring fields as anthropology, psychology, political science, economics, and history—always from the standpoint of their relevance to sociological problems and sociological thought. The book is consequently anything but a grab-bag of disparate and unconnected facts. But, I must say again, the facts are marshaled to exhibit their theoretical meaning; they are not dragooned to support flimsy speculations.

The student who would undertake to study on his own all the hundreds of sources drawn upon by this book would be buried in an avalanche of learning. Mr. Johnson has saved him from this fate. He has sifted these materials, related them to his theoretical framework, and reported enough of their substance for the student to know not only what sociologists have found out but how they have gone about finding it out. Probably not every instructor or student will judge every one of Mr. Johnson's interpretations entirely acceptable. That is as it should be. Some of these matters are still in dispute, and, rather than exclude them altogether, Mr. Johnson has tried to indicate their currently tentative character.

Throughout, Mr. Johnson has avoided that excess of facts which keeps us from seeing "the wood for the trees, or the trees for the twigs." He has done most of the hard work needed to help us see the wood, the trees, and, on suitable occasion, the twigs too—each in its fitting perspective. I say that he has done most, not all, of the hard work because, as a genuinely educational book should, this one leaves some of the work for the instructor and the student. The book provides sociological food for thought, not mere sociological pap, complete with spoon and bib. The undergraduate student will probably find that it makes about the same demands upon his capacities as the better introductions to biology or history or psychology. For effective use, it requires some industrious study, the application of trained intelligence and the learning of sociological knowledge rather than the repetition of sociological cant. It is not a recondite book, only an instructive one. It is the kind of book that Whitehead evidently had in mind when he observed,

> Whenever a textbook is written of real educational worth, you may be quite certain that some reviewer will say that it will be difficult to teach from it. Of course it will be difficult to teach from it. If it were easy, the book ought to be burned; for it cannot be educational. In education, as elsewhere, the broad primrose path leads to a nasty place. This evil path is represented by a book or a set of lectures which will practically enable the student to learn by heart all the questions likely to be asked at the next examination.

There is no danger that this book, with its multiple uses, will lead anyone down that primrose path. Instead, the student who has mastered its substance will have acquired a thoroughgoing orientation to sociology even if he were never to take another course in the subject. For the student majoring in sociology, it provides a solid foundation for more specialized courses. And for the occasional student who goes on to graduate work in sociology, it provides the kind of methodical grounding on which he can later base his own independent studies. For them all, it gives a sense of the development of sociology by periodically tracing continuities of sociological thought and investigation.

Now that this book exists, sociologists can give a responsible and eminently satisfactory answer when they are asked to name the single text that will best introduce the serious general reader to contemporary sociology. Not, of course, that every part of sociology is fully treated in the book. It is no longer possible for a single text to encompass in detail every department of sociological knowledge. Mr. Johnson has comparatively little to say, for example, about demography. But he has much to say about other important matters that usually receive little attention in introductory textbooks—for example, the subject of ideology and the functional analysis of authority systems and of bureaucracy. In any case, there are no perfunctory chapters in the book, included merely for the record. Indeed, there are few if any perfunctory paragraphs and, as a breather, only an occasional perfunctory sentence. It is, in short, a serious and closely written work sustained at a high intellectual level.

On more than one occasion, the book makes an independent contribution to our knowledge about a particular subject. Mr. Johnson's analysis of the sources of social conformity, for example, builds upon and extends other systematic treatments of this subject (which remains an important one despite currently popularized mistreatments of it). And his concluding chapter, on social change, which of course only introduces the student to this large subject, nevertheless casts new light on a complex set of murky problems.

Because they are set apart at the end of each chapter, Mr. Johnson's recommendations for further reading might easily be passed over with little attention. This, I believe, would be a mistake. In composite, these annotated bibliographies afford a critical and informed introduction to major sources of sociological findings and ideas.

With this book, Mr. Johnson joins the small circle of such masters of sociological writing as Kingsley Davis, George Homans, and Samuel Stouffer, whose command of language, both technical and vernacular, enables them to say just what needs to be said, clearly and often gracefully. Mr. Johnson writes to the student without writing down to him. Close-woven as it is, his prose is never opaque.

There would have been no point in trying to hide my enthusiasm for this book, for I could not possibly have succeeded in the attempt.

ROBERT K. MERTON

New York, New York
February 1960

Author's Preface

My chief goal in writing this book has been to present a systematic account of the foundations of contemporary sociology in such a way as to make it both understandable and interesting to readers with little or no previous knowledge of the subject. This goal has to a large extent dictated the coverage of the book. No doubt there will not be perfect agreement among sociologists concerning which topics should and which should not have been chosen for extended treatment. As compared with other available textbooks the book gives an unusual amount of space to social structure, functional analysis, socialization, ideology, the sources of conformity and deviation, and social change. More attention than usual is also given to institutional variation in society as a whole; thus there are rather long chapter sequences on kinship, economic and political institutions, religion, and stratification. A topic of growing theoretical and social importance treated in considerable detail is bureaucracy. On the other hand, the book touches only briefly upon such topics as population theory, the sociology of the community, formal systems of education, and the sociology of small groups. But enough is said to direct the interested student to specialized sources on these subjects as well as on those treated in more detail.

Although I have attempted to make *Sociology: A Systematic Introduction* a unified work, any experienced teacher will nevertheless be able to omit some chapters or parts of chapters in order to adapt the book more closely to his own needs. Thus, for a short course stressing, let us say, the social structure of the United States, he might with little difficulty omit certain of the more theoretical chapters.

It is a great pleasure to thank publicly some of those who have helped me. Several years ago Professor Bernard Barber, of Barnard College, and I thought of writing a text together and, although nothing tangible came of our efforts then and he is in no way responsible for this work, the book as well as its author has profited from our many conversations during the years of our friendship.

Professor Arthur K. Davis, now of the University of Saskatchewan, carefully read an early version of five or six chapters and made several useful suggestions concerning the order in which some ideas should be presented.

My greatest debt by far is to the general editor, Professor Robert K. Merton. He has made many valuable specific suggestions, but he helped me above all by being a severe critic, especially early in my work, and by encouraging me generously throughout. Needless to say, in neither substance nor style have I attained the high standard he has set, but I am grateful to him for making me work harder and to better effect.

The reader will discover for himself my indebtedness to published works. I have been impressed by the truth of a remark by Samuel Johnson, that the best way to find out about a subject is to write a book about it. I am aware that I have *not* referred to all the works on a particular subject. The choice has depended in part on the particular emphases of this book. Nevertheless, my neglect of some important books and articles may well be due to sheer ignorance. I shall be grateful to any reader who calls my attention to errors or serious omissions.

HARRY M JOHNSON

Boston, Massachusetts
February 1960

SURVEY TABLE OF CONTENTS

Contents

part one

THE FRAME OF REFERENCE

1. Sociology: The Study of Groups

What is a science and what is not? This question has often been the subject of fruitless debate, perhaps because "science" is a matter of degree. Many sciences have approached the ideal of systematization and predictive power more closely than sociology has. Nevertheless, sociology to some extent has the following characteristics of science:

1. It is *empirical;* that is, it is based on observation and reasoning, not on supernatural revelation, and its results are not speculative. In the early stages of their creative work, all scientists speculate, of course; but, ideally at least, they submit their speculations to the test of fact before announcing them as scientific discoveries.

2. It is *theoretical;* that is, it attempts to summarize complex observations in abstract, logically related propositions which purport to explain causal relationships in the subject matter.

3. It is *cumulative;* that is, sociological theories build upon one another, new theories correcting, extending, and refining the older ones.

4. It is *nonethical;* that is, sociologists do not ask whether particular social actions are good or bad; they seek merely to explain them.

In all these respects, sociology is far from having reached perfection; but progress is being steadily made.

A Definition of Sociology

Sociology is the science that deals with social groups: their internal forms or modes of organization, the processes that tend to maintain or change these forms of organization, and the relations between groups. So complex a subject as social groups requires, for scientific treatment, precise concepts and carefully defined technical terms for them. As we shall see, the very term "groups," although it has meaning enough in ordinary usage to serve our needs for the moment, will have to be examined carefully.

The value of a science of social groups should need little emphasis. Each of us is born into a family group, and most of our actions thereafter are performed in our capacity as a member of one group or another. All social problems, such as juvenile delinquency, "racial" discrimination, inadequate housing or education, and war, have to do with the functioning of groups or with the interaction of groups. Social policy has always been guided to some extent by more or less sound knowledge of particular groups, but it has also been guided by unexamined and even unconscious assumptions. Tested generalized knowledge about the processes that maintain or change the organization of groups will become a more and more valuable aid solving social problems. Further, as we shall see in greater detail, the m intimate ideals, goals, and beliefs of each individual are largely shaped the groups in which he has participated, is participating, or would like to participate. Sociology, therefore, should contribute something to one's self-knowledge. Finally, in addition to having practical value, sociology can be fascinating for its own sake, like any other serious attempt to discover facts and to explain them in terms of systematic theory.

Sociology, like any other science, abstracts from the concrete world of experience. In the first three chapters of this book, we shall deal with many facts, some of them new to beginners in sociology; but our main task will be to see in exactly what ways sociology is abstract. To do so, we must become familiar with certain technical concepts. These concepts are, of course, interrelated; together, they make up a frame of reference that will enable us to discuss our subject coherently. The frame of reference does not consist of facts; it consists of concepts with which we seek to order facts. Like any other frame of reference, the one we use here has the advantage that it makes explicit what we have decided to regard as relevant and helps us to communicate some of the facts that have been discovered. On the other hand, it also causes us to ignore certain aspects of reality. It is selective. Fortunately, the facts that emerge in the course of using the sociological frame of reference are complex enough to force sociologists to modify the frame of reference itself from time to time. Sociological *theory* consists of tested and systematic statements about social groups. These statements are expressed in technical terms which are names for the concepts of the frame of reference.

Other sciences, of course, are also concerned with human behavior. The psychology of personality, for example, consists of systematic theory about *individual* behavior. To be sure, the psychologist takes account of the fact that each individual's personality is formed in the course of his interaction with others—his father and mother, for example, and his brothers, sisters, teachers, and friends, as well as many other people. The psychologist is interested in interaction between people, however, only for the purposes of theorizing about its effects on individual personality; his focus is not on the interaction itself but on some of its effects. When he turns to the study of the mental processes involved in the combined acts of many people—for example, the study of mob behavior or of the formation of public opinion—he becomes a *social* psychologist; that is, he is applying psychology to problems that are essentially sociological, much as a biochemist applies chemistry to biological problems. Sociology is concerned with interaction itself. A social group is a system of social interaction.

When two persons "interact," each takes account of the other, not merely as a physical object, but as an individual with attitudes, expectations, and the capacity to pass judgment; the action of each is based, to some extent, on his attitudes toward the other and his expectations about the other's probable reactions to him. The action of each person is meaningful to himself, partly on the conscious level, partly on the unconscious level; and part of its meaning to him is his continuous assessment of what meaning it is likely to have for the person with whom he is interacting. We should perhaps note in passing that knowing the meaning of behavior does not in itself enable the scientist to *explain* that behavior satisfactorily. This is true in both psychology and sociology. Investigation of meaning, however, is one of the necessary steps leading to explanation. Indeed, this is a truism, since what is to be explained is not mere outward behavior but meaningful behavior.

In order to explain the concept of a group as a social system or as a system of social interaction, we shall begin by making a distinction between "groups" and "social relationships" in general. We shall say that a social relationship exists to the extent that two or more individuals, or two or more groups, or individuals and groups to any number of either, interact with one another. Social relationships vary from tenuous, transitory interactions, such as an exchange of greetings between two Americans abroad, strangers to each other and to the people around them, to "permanent" systems of interaction, such as a family or a close friendship. The parties to a social relationship may be friendly or unfriendly; they may cooperate with one another or they may strive to destroy one another. The relationship between opposing armies is a social relationship.

All groups are social relationships, but not all social relationships are groups. A group, in our usage of the term, involves some degree of cooperation among its members for the attainment of common goals. The degree of cooperation may be slight and may even be compulsory, as in a prison chain gang; but without some degree of cooperation, there is no group. The cooperative aspect of a group does not preclude some degree of antagonism among its members. A group may be a hotbed of rivalries and even settled hatred, as some families are; yet it remains a group provided that its members cooperate at times in their interactions in order to attain some common goals. For example, the family cooperates to keep a common household, to prepare meals, to defend its members against the outside world if necessary.

Further, at any particular moment of time, a distinction can always be made between members and nonmembers of any particular group. The line may be hard to draw in barely organized or short-lived groups, but, in general, members have rights that nonmembers do not have, at least within the particular interaction system being considered. More important, members have obligations or duties that are not binding upon nonmembers. These rights and obligations are essentially rules of behavior. They compose a complex *normative pattern,* in terms of which the members are oriented toward one another and, as representatives of the group, toward nonmembers or other groups. The members do not necessarily have exactly the same rights and obligations.

We must emphasize that the two characteristics of a group—cooperation, and the sense of belonging together that is involved in common membership—are highly variable. The members may cooperate for many purposes or for one or two; they may devote a small or a large proportion of their time to the system of interaction. Moreover, some members may be more tightly involved in the group interaction than others.

To some extent, whether we consider a particular social relationship to be a group is arbitrary. For example, we usually think of two football teams engaged in a game as two opposing groups. Each team is a cooperative unit acting *against* the other team. Each is trying to *prevent* the other from making its "goals." Yet, from another point of view, the two teams together compose a single group, for they are cooperating with each other to achieve a decision, to see which is the better team. They cooperate in following the same rules of fair play. If some third party were to interfere with their game and try to prevent it from going on, the two teams would suddenly become aware of their *common* goal and their *belonging together;* yet the common goal and the belonging together exist as aspects of their interaction whether they are fully aware of them or not.

In one sense, a group consists of people. This seems obvious. Yet, strictly speaking, a group consists of certain persons *in their capacity as members.* Every one of these members is also a member of many other groups. Thus the football player also belongs to a family, a fraternity, a church, a school; he is a citizen (member of the state); he works in the college dining room (and is therefore a member of a work group); he participates in many friendships; having "pinned" a girl from one of the leading sororities, he is a member of another two-person group which he considers rather important. His action in all these other groups is not part of his participation in the football team.

The football player is, of course, a single more or less well-integrated personality, and his various memberships affect one another; for example, if he stays out too late dancing with the sorority queen, his timing may suffer at football practice the next day. Nevertheless, his actions at the dance are not part of the interaction system of the team. Viewed in this light, a group is an abstraction. It consists of parts of the action systems of its members. Whatever superficial appearances may be, each member is actually oriented toward other members, not as concrete persons in all their activities, but only in their capacity as participants in the same one interaction system. Some relevant "parts" of the members' action systems are oriented not immediately toward other members but toward the common goals for which they are all striving.

There used to be some controversy about whether a group exists when its members are not gathered together in the same place, in one another's physical presence. According to the conception now prevailing, a group does not cease to exist when its members leave one another temporarily. If the football player goes home early from the dance in order to keep in training, he is acting at that moment as a member of the football squad. Thus the football team exists continuously, even though the duties of its members do not require their attention at every moment. At times a particular group membership is quiescent or dormant in one's personality, but during those times it is still ready to assert its claims, so to speak, if a proper occasion should arise.

In this abstract sense of "group," one never can observe a group in a flash of time, even when all its members are gathered together in the same room. Strictly speaking, the existence of a group must be inferred from observations made over a span of time. One must put together numerous observations of particular interactions, verbal and nonverbal, that are related to the same goal or goals. Some of the interaction of group members, however, is not directly related to their common goals; in their relationship of cooperation, they build up feelings of mutual liking, and sometimes of mutual animosity, which they express in interaction. As Homans puts it (1950, Chap. 5),[1] their sentiments spill over into actions that are not strictly necessary for the survival of the group.

If one wished to make a distinction in terms, one might use the word "group" to refer to the members as an aggregate of persons and the term "social system" to refer to the interaction system, in abstraction from the total action systems of the members. We shall not bother to make this distinction in usage consistently, but we must never forget that in sociology we are interested in human beings *only as participants in systems of social interaction.* As we shall see, this focus of interest makes some things about human beings more directly relevant than others.

Groups and Subgroups

In sociological literature, few small groups are more famous than the so-called "bank wiring group" which was carefully studied by a team of researchers.[2] The fourteen members of the group worked together in a room at the Hawthorne Works of the Western Electric Company, assembling switches for central-office telephone equipment. In this task, there were three interdependent "roles," or jobs: one was connecting wires in banks of terminals; one was soldering the connections; and the third was inspecting

[1] Dates following the name of an author refer to references listed in full (alphabetically by author) in the bibliographical index.

[2] The research was done by F. J. Roethlisberger and W. J. Dickson and is reported in Roethlisberger and Dickson, 1939. The present selective account, however, is based on Homans, 1950, Chaps. 3-6.

the results to see whether the wiring and soldering had been done properly. The entire group was divided into three four-man "teams," each consisting of three wiremen and one solderer. There were two inspectors (making fourteen men in all); each inspector worked with one team and shared the work of the third team with the other inspector.

Here we see that the fourteen-member group had within it three overlapping subgroups. Actually, the organization was more complex, for, in addition to these formal arrangements made by the company, there were two informal "cliques" which in membership cut across the three teams.[3] The members of a clique interacted with one another in several ways. For example, they helped one another in their work; they traded jobs (a wireman exchanging jobs for a while with a solderer); they played games; they pooled small sums to buy candy. Moreover, the integrity or unity of each of the cliques was somewhat dependent upon the existence of the other clique. Clique A regarded itself as superior to Clique B, and Clique B both resented A's claim to superiority and acted, at times, in such a way as to justify A's claim. At bottom, however, the differences between the cliques would probably have seemed rather trivial to an outside observer; this, of course, does not mean that they *were* trivial. The members of Clique A felt that their conversation was on a somewhat higher level than the conversation of Clique B. A bought a different kind of penny candy. A's games involved betting on various things; B members bet less often with one another but more often played a game called "binging," in which one man strikes another on the biceps, and the other strikes back to see whether he can inflict more pain than the first. There were some other differences between the two cliques, but we can disregard them in our present limited description.

One might ask in what sense these fourteen men were members of a single group. Three "teams" and two mutually opposed "cliques" obviously existed; how did they all compose a single group? The main reason for regarding all fourteen men as belonging to one group is that they cooperated in maintaining certain rules. These rules, or norms, were not known to company officials until after the research. In fact, the maintenance of the norms had the effect of maintaining the integrity of the whole group *vis-à-vis* the management. In this perspective, the management was part of the "environment" of the bank-wiring group. In order to survive as a group, the fourteen men had to perform their tasks well enough to satisfy the management. Three of the norms that arose in the group were as follows:

1. Each man must maintain, on the average, a certain established rate of output. This rate was set by the group itself, not by the management. In fact, the method of calculating wages, which management had devised, was intended to induce the men to produce as much as possible, not to produce at a fixed rate. This method made the earnings of each man dependent to

[3] Three of the fourteen men, however, did not belong to either clique, and another was a sort of fringe member of Clique B. These cliques were discovered only after careful observation.

some extent upon the output of the group as a whole. Within the group, any man who fell below the informal rate was known as a "chiseler."

2. The second rule or norm is implicit in the first, but it needs special attention. Each man must see to it that he did not *exceed* the informal rate of output set by the group. Anyone who violated this rule was known as a "rate-buster."

3. The third rule was that no member of the group was to report to a representative of management anything that would be detrimental to another member. To violate this norm was to be a "squealer."

The concept of norm is a central one in sociology. Every chapter of this book will have something to say about norms. A norm is an abstract *pattern,* held in the mind, that sets certain limits for behavior. An "operative" norm is one that is not merely entertained in the mind but is considered worthy of following in actual behavior; thus, one feels that one *ought* to conform to it. This feeling means that one "accepts" the norm. "Conforming" to the norm means guiding one's conduct in relation to it, keeping within the defined limits (which may be clearly or vaguely defined, according to the particular norm). Norms never do or could prescribe how one should behave down to the last detail of the concrete act. Every act is unique if regarded in all its concreteness. Whether a particular act violates a norm that is relevant to it depends upon one's interpretation of the norm; and one must apply this interpretation to the particular act, concentrating on the abstract form or pattern of the norm and ignoring many irrelevant details of the act. Thus, whether a member of the bank-wiring group spread his work out over the day or did most of it during the first few working hours, he might in either case hew rather closely to the norm for the daily rate of output. He might work with his right hand or his left: this detail would be irrelevant to the norm.

Sociologists are interested in *social* norms—that is, norms that, like the fixed rate of output, are accepted in a group. (Thus, private norms, such as most New Year's resolutions, are of little direct interest in the study of interaction groups.) Moreover, sociologists are mainly interested in *operative* social norms—that is, norms that are "sanctioned" in such a way that violators suffer some penalties in the group and those who conform are rewarded. By contrast, for example, most of the norms of the Sermon on the Mount, although they are often referred to, are not sanctioned; one is not punished socially for taking oaths or for refusing to "turn the other cheek." The norms operative in the bank-wiring group had more or less definite sanctions: A rate-buster or a chiseler was "binged" on the arm. He was ridiculed. He ran the risk of being ostracized.

In general, violators of accepted norms suffer the following kinds of (negative) sanction:

1. The persons with whom they are interacting retaliate by withholding from the violators cooperative acts and friendly expressions, the loss of which will be painful to the violators.

2. Violators of accepted norms suffer some loss of prestige. If they are

persistent violators and have therefore acquired a reputation for falling below the norms, then they have a relatively low prestige rank in the group. In the bank-wiring group, the members of Clique B ranked below those of Clique A partly because they cared less whether they fell short of output standards. In this way they were expressing their resentment against Clique A, but they were also confirming their low rank. The members of Clique B did not ignore the norms entirely; they were simply not quite so careful to conform.

3. Finally, violators are often subjected to specific penalties—"binging," ridicule, fines, imprisonment. These penalties are intrinsically unpleasant, but they also express and bring about loss of prestige. For example, a man who has never before been sent to prison suffers both from the imprisonment itself and also, sometimes much more, from his degradation.

By contrast, of course, those who conform continue to enjoy the expected cooperative performances of others; they maintain good standing in their group; and they receive rewards, or positive sanctions, such as praise, bonuses, and promotions.

In Chapter 2, we shall consider the fact that not all members of a group are subject to precisely the same norms. In the bank-wiring group, for example, the wiremen were not expected to behave, in all respects, in the same way as the solderers or inspectors. A complete description of a social norm would state (1) who is expected (2) by whom (3) to do what, or refrain from doing what, (4) in what circumstances. In addition, it would specify (5) what penalties will be forthcoming if the norm is violated, or what rewards if it is conformed to, (6) what circumstances surrounding a violation will be regarded as extenuating, and (7) who will administer the penalties or give the rewards. The laws of the state are easiest to describe in this way. But social interaction is governed by many other norms as well, explicit and implicit.

Returning to the bank-wiring group, we see that, despite internal friction, it was indeed a group, and one that contained several subgroups. A subgroup is a group entirely contained within some other group. All the members of the subgroup are also members of the larger group, and their interaction within the subgroup may be regarded as part of the interaction system of the larger group. Whether a particular interaction system is treated as a group or as a subgroup depends in part upon one's perspective. We have treated the bank-wiring group as the main group and the teams and cliques as subgroups; but in a larger perspective the bank-wiring group was itself a subgroup within the Western Electric Company. This company, in turn, is a subgroup within American society.

Characteristics of Societies

Although everyone has a rough idea what is meant by calling the United States a society, the concept of society is so important in sociology that we should examine it more closely. A society is a group with certain characteristics that we shall discuss briefly under these four headings: (1) definite territory, (2) sexual reproduction, (3) comprehensive culture, and (4) independence.

Definite territory

A society is a territorial group. Some nomadic societies move about within a much larger territory than they occupy at any one time, but they regard the whole range as "their" country. There are, of course, territorial groups within societies—for example, clans, neighborhoods, and political units, such as cities and counties.

Sexual reproduction

The members of a society are recruited, in large part, by means of sexual reproduction within the group. Many societies also obtain members by adoption, enslavement, conquest, or immigration, but sexual reproduction within the group itself remains a fundamental source of new members. Many groups other than societies, of course, also depend upon reproduction within themselves, but these other groups are excluded from the category of societies by some other characteristic or characteristics

Comprehensive culture

Sociologists use the term "culture" in the sense given it by the English anthropologist Edward Tylor. According to Tylor (1924, p. 1), culture is "that complex whole which includes knowledge, belief, art, morals, law, custom, and other capabilities acquired by man as a member of society." (By "society," Tylor obviously meant social life in general; "man as a member of society" means man as a participant in systems of social interaction of any sort.) Later in this book (Chap. 4), we shall consider this definition of culture in more detail and modify it slightly, but for the present it is enough to notice that "culture" in the technical sense of the social sciences is extremely broad in meaning. It is not confined to the knowledge and standards of a cultivated minority, nor is there any suggestion that all culture is necessarily "good." For example, by Tylor's definition, the art of cheating at cards is cultural, since it is "knowledge" and a "capability" learned in the course of associating with others in social life.

As in ordinary usage, however, so in technical usage we distinguish between culture in general and "a" culture, or "the" culture of some particular group. Thus we might speak of "pre-Columbian cultures," meaning the several, to some extent interrelated, cultures of the groups that existed in the Americas before the arrival of Columbus. Every group has a culture. The bank-wiring group, for example, could hardly have got along without a good deal of technical knowledge about wiring and soldering, without language (a "capability" learned in early social life), or without norms (what Tylor calls "morals" and "custom").

We must bear in mind, however, that a "group" is an abstraction. The members of the bank-wiring group were also participants in many other social systems (families, religious groups, political parties, and lodges, to suggest a few). Much of the culture they possessed and used in their capacity as members of these other groups was irrelevant to their interaction in the bank-wiring group. In short, "the" culture of the bank-wiring group includes only that part of the total culture of its members, as concrete persons, which was involved in their common interaction system.[4]

To return to our consideration of societies: "the" culture of a society is "comprehensive," not in the sense that it includes the totality of human culture, but in the sense that it contains cultural patterns sufficiently diversified to enable the group to fulfill all the requirements of social life. This societal culture is not entirely possessed, of course, by every member of the society, any more than the culture of the bank-wiring group was necessarily possessed in its entirety by each member. Typically, no one member of a group possesses the entire culture of that group. Every full member must possess enough of the culture to enable him to do his part in the interaction system, but only that much.

A society has a "comprehensive" culture in the sense that the group is culturally self-sufficient. A society may of course carry on trade with other societies, but the cultural patterns involved in this trade are part of the culture of the society itself. For example, the pattern of extending credit, the recognized rates of exchange, the means of payment, the form of contracts—all these cultural patterns, although they may be involved in the interaction between societies, are part of the culture of each.

There are borderline cases. For example, many American Indian tribes have highly distinctive cultures of their own, but it is a question whether some of these tribes could survive without the cultural patterns of the (non-Indian) Bureau of Indian Affairs, and without developing substitute cultural patterns (see Levy, 1952, Chap. 3). One of the important tasks of sociological theory is to determine exactly what kinds of cultural pattern a group must have to qualify as a society or, better, what kinds of cultural pattern are necessary to enable a group to fulfill all the requirements of social life. We shall see, for example, that every society probably requires norms governing the possession and use of scarce valuable things. Such norms, called "property rights" or simply "property," can and do vary in detail within wide limits, but every society must have norms of this *kind*.

Independence

A further characteristic of a society is that it is not a subgroup of any other group. This criterion does not exclude groups that are politically subject to some other group unless they have actually been absorbed by the other group. Japan was a society even when it was occupied by representatives of the United States.

The culture of a subgroup is sometimes called a subculture. Just as "groups" and "subgroups" are relative to one another, so are cultures and subcultures.

One case perhaps requires special comment. What about the United Nations? Is it a society? At first glance, it might seem to meet all the criteria. Actually, however, the United Nations is an organization of political units called *states*. A state is only an aspect of a society, not the society itself; nor is any organization of states a society (see Chap. 13). Americans as individuals do not belong to the United Nations in the same sense that they belong to the United States. Apart from the permanent staff of the United Nations, which of course fails to meet the other three criteria of a society, the individuals who take part in the discussions, debates, and agreements of the United Nations do so only as the representatives of states. The United Nations, on account of its permanent staff, cuts across several societies, but it does not *contain* any society.

It is obvious that societies, as defined by our four criteria, are social systems of an important type. Most people's entire round of social interaction occurs within a society. All other social systems have vitally important connections with societies, either as parts of them or as systems cutting across societies but dependent upon them. There are many religious organizations, for example, that cut across several societies. But these organizations do not attempt to provide for all the needs of their members. Their culture is not "comprehensive"; it is a subculture within each of the societies. The social interaction of their members is not confined to the religious fellowship as such; it is partly concerned with secular matters in the several societies. Various aspects of the more comprehensive type of group—society—will be treated in later chapters of this book.

In what we have just said, we have implied that there *are* such groups as societies. If we wished, we could treat society (as in the expression "a society") as a "construct," an "ideal type"—a neat concept that does not correspond perfectly to any actual group in the world. Most people spend their entire lives in one "society." We might define "society," in part, as a perfectly self-contained group, a group whose members *never* interact with outsiders. In that sense, of course, virtually all actual societies are only approximations to the concept *society*, although some primitive groups may still exist that are isolated enough to be entirely self-contained.

In theoretical reasoning, it is sometimes convenient to invent concepts for which there is no exact counterpart in nature. Physicists have the concept of a "vacuum." A sociologist might add to his concept *society* the idea of perfect integration. The integration of a society has to do with the relations between individuals and subgroups. In a perfectly integrated society, the normative pattern for the whole interaction system would be such that interacting individuals and subgroups would know what to expect from each other and would approve of one another's goals. Conflict would not disappear, but it would be much reduced.

If we defined "society" as a permanent, self-contained, perfectly integrated group, it might be interesting and scientifically valuable to ask what else must be true of such a group. A perfectly integrated society, for example, would have only one religion.

Needless to say, the concepts of science do not primarily evaluate phenomena. Thu perfect integration would not necessarily be desirable. Nevertheless, it is clear that notions such as "social conflict" and "deviant behavior" imply some *concept* of perfect integration. One of the theoretical tasks of sociology is to develop a better understanding of society in the sense of the construct that we have only touched upon in the foregoing remarks. The concept *society,* although unrealistic, might have as great scientific interest as, let us say, the concept of perfect competition in economics. We mention this possibility only in passing, however, for we shall do little in this book to develop it. In the next chapter we shall return to a less abstract plane.

RECOMMENDED READING

For a good discussion of the abstractness of groups, see C. K. Warriner, "Groups Are Real: A Reaffirmation," *Amer. sociol. Rev.,* Oct. 1956, v. 21, pp. 549-54. For an excellent treatment of the concepts of membership and nonmembership, see R. K. Merton, *Social Theory and Social Structure,* rev. and enl. ed., Free Press, 1957, pp. 284-97. Pp. 308-26 contain a useful discussion of twenty-six variable properties of groups.

For a "classical" study of norms, see W. G. Sumner, *Folkways: A Study of the Sociological Importance of Usages, Manners, Customs, Mores, and Morals,* Ginn, 1906, Chap. 1. The subtitle adequately indicates what Sumner meant by "folkways." The more binding folkways Sumner called "mores" (the plural form of the rarely used Latin word "mos," pronounced mo'-rez). He defined the mores as "the popular usages and traditions, when they include a judgment that they are conducive to societal welfare, and when they exert a coercion on the individual to conform to them, although they are not coordinated by any authority . . ." (Preface). Sumner's work shows in general that a great deal of our behavior is guided by cultural patterns that are socially binding to varying degrees. For a simple but useful classification of norms, see A. H. Barton, "The Concept of Property-Space in Social Research," in P. F. Lazarsfeld and M. Rosenberg, eds., *The Language of Social Research: A Reader in the Methodology of the Social Sciences,* Free Press, 1955, pp. 50-52. Barton lassifies norms according to three principles: (1) whether they crystallize gradually, without deliberation on anyone's part, or have a definite point of origin in time and a definite source, such as a legislature or a judge; (2) the degree of importance that people attach to conformity; and (3) whether sanctions are formal or informal. Formal sanctions are administered by specifically designated persons; informal sanctions are meted out by any member of a group, regardless of whether he has been given any special authority. A more elaborate typology of social norms is given in R. T. Morris, "A Typology of Norms," *Amer. sociol. Rev.,* Oct. 1956, v. 21, pp. 610-13.

Although in this text we shall call attention from time to time to the methods by which research results were obtained, on the whole we must unfortunately give less space to research method than we should like. A serious student should do a little reading on his own. The following suggestions will give him a good start. On the importance of carefully defined concepts, see the first section of Lazarsfeld and Rosenberg, eds., 1955. For an extremely clear and interesting essay which explains in detail the steps necessary to establish facts and confirm hypotheses, see S. A. Stouffer, "Some Observations on Study Design," *Amer. J. Sociol.*, Jan. 1950, v. 55, pp. 355-61. This paper describes and illustrates the fundamental reasoning involved in good research design and also some of the short cuts, legitimate and illegitimate, used by researchers. If the student has time to read only one paper on methodology, he should read this one by Stouffer. For a discussion, with illustrations, of the mutual influence of theory and research, see Merton, 1957, Chap. 2: "The Bearing of Sociological Theory on Empirical Research," and Chap. 3: "The Bearing of Empirical Research on Sociological Theory." These papers also emphasize the cumulative character of sociology. Among textbooks on research method, we recommend two for beginning students: W. J. Goode and P. K. Hatt, *Methods in Social Research*, McGraw-Hill, 1952; and C. Selltiz, M. Jahoda, M. Deutsch, and S. W. Cook, *Research Methods in Social Relations*, Holt, 1959, rev. 1-vol. ed.

General note

The reader who is interested in pursuing any special topic in sociology ought to become acquainted with certain periodicals and reference works. *The Encyclopaedia of Social Sciences* is often helpful. *Sociological Abstracts*, published quarterly, is extremely valuable. So is *Current Sociology*, published by the United Nations Educational, Scientific, and Cultural Organization (UNESCO); of the four issues each year, each of the first three is an annotated bibliography on a special topic—for example, the sociology of religion, or the sociology of bureaucracy—and the fourth is a classified list of books and articles in several languages. The official journal of the American Sociological Society is *The American Sociological Review* (*Amer. sociol. Rev.*). Another important American periodical is *The American Journal of Sociology* (*Amer. J. Sociol.*). In addition to articles, these two journals contain news items about the sociology departments of colleges and universities, announcements of meetings, book reviews, and exchanges of letters on controversial matters in sociology.

2. *Institutionalization*

Norms are so important in social-interaction systems that we shall devote a good deal of attention to them. In this chapter we shall consider certain ways in which norms cluster in complex patterns. In particular, we shall explain the concepts "social position" and "social institution." We implied in Chapter 1 that some norms are regarded as more important than others. In this chapter, we return to this point in our treatment of "institutionalization"—a term that can refer either to a certain process or to the result of that process. Roughly speaking (for the moment), an institutionalized norm is one that is both widely accepted in a group and deeply inculcated in the personalities of its members. As we shall see, however, there are degrees of institutionalization. In few if any social systems is there perfect conformity to even the most firmly institutionalized norms. In the final section of this chapter we shall consider some of the factors that may bring about imperfect conformity or outright violation. We shall return to this topic in Chapter 20.

Social Positions

As we pointed out in Chapter 1, the participants in a social system are not all expected to do the same things. Whether a norm applies to a particular person depends upon his social position in the system. One of the most important aspects of the organization, or "structure," of any social system is the fact that its members are differentiated according to the social positions they occupy.

This internal differentiation of the system is the second aspect of the structure of groups. The first aspect we encountered was the division of the group into subgroups. The members of the group as a whole are differentiated, first, according to which subgroups they belong to and, secondly, according to which social positions they occupy in the group as a whole and in any of the subgroups to which they may belong.

The content of a social position—that is, its complex of rights and obligations—is entirely normative. In the bank-wiring group, for example, a solderer (occupant of a particular social position) was expected to have and use certain skills: he had to know how to heat the soldering metal, how to handle the soldering iron, how much of the molten metal to apply to the wire connections. The content of his position was normative in a double sense. First, *technical* norms were involved in using the soldering materials correctly. Secondly, the expectation that the solderer, in performing his work, would conform to the technical norms was a *social* norm: if the solderer made a mistake (deviated from the technical norms), his inspector would reject his work.

At the same time, a solderer had the right to expect certain performances from others. For example, he could not do his work unless the wiremen in his team made the wire connections for him to solder. Moreover, within the larger system of the Hawthorne Works (for the bank-wiring group, remember, was a subgroup of the Western Electric Company), the solderer had the right to expect that a trucker would keep him supplied with the materials necessary for his work. These "rights" were also normative; they differ from the solderer's "obligations" only in this respect, that his obligations were norms that applied to him as an *agent* in the social system, whereas his rights were norms that applied to certain other persons in their interaction with him within the system. The solderer's rights were other people's obligations. As one possessed of rights, the solderer was a social *object* (rather than an agent); but he had to be aware of both his rights and his obligations in order to do his part properly in the social system.[1] The smooth functioning of the system required that each participant in it know and accept a considerable part of the whole normative pattern of the system.

It appears, then, that a social position has two parts, one consisting of obligations and one consisting of rights. A person is said to "occupy" a social position if he has a certain cluster of obligations and enjoys a certain cluster of associated rights within a social system. These two parts of a social position we shall call its *role* and its *status*, "role" referring to obligations and "status" referring to rights. Thus, every social position is a status-role. When the context would prevent misunderstanding, however, we may use either "role" or "status" to mean the entire social position. The role structure of a group is the same thing as its status structure, because what is role from the point of view of one member is status from the point of view of the others.[2]

A social position may be occupied, of course, by more than one person. There were three solderers in the bank-wiring group. A few social positions are occupied by only one person at a time—for example, the presidency of the United States. It is also important to note that the same person occupies

---

[1] The distinction between the actor as agent and as object is made and explored in Parsons and Shils, eds., 1951, Part II.

[2] This discussion of status and role follows Parsons and Shils, eds., 1951, Part II. Ralph Linton, 1936, pp. 113-14, offers a different distinction, but his is not helpful or even clear.

many social positions. A man may be a doctor, a husband, a father, a member of the American Medical Association, a citizen, and a Republican.

We can bring out certain other aspects of the concept of social position by considering another example. A master artist in Italy in the early Renaissance belonged to a guild and was subject to its strict regulations regarding quality of work and terms of payment. These regulations, then, defined the role of master artist, at least as a member of the guild. In addition, he had more detailed obligations to his clients, who for the most part were noblemen and rich merchants and bankers. These men gave him commissions. Every such commission was a contract, which specified in some detail what the artist (or his shop) was to turn out. Since every work was intended for a particular purpose and place, the contract might specify such things as the thematic content, medium, colors to be used, and size of the finished work. Any large piece of work was likely to be a joint product. The master in the shop, as part of his role, might make a sketch of the grand design; his assistants, the better-trained ones, might execute some difficult parts under his direction; and his apprentices, according to their experience, might do easy parts or merely wash brushes and sweep the floor. The master would probably give the final touches to an important work. This division of labor was common for both painting and sculpture (Hauser, 1951, v. 1, pp. 266-353).

A fifteenth-century master artist had a status as well as a role. His status included the authority to direct the work of assistants and apprentices; the right to receive fees for completed commissions; the right to make use of a shop or studio, with all its tools and materials; and a certain amount of prestige. (The term "status" is sometimes used to mean prestige alone: "So-and-so wants more status.") Artists in the early Renaissance were on a footing with tradesmen (petty bourgeoisie). Indeed, they were not known as "artists," with all the connotations that term has for us; they were craftsmen—goldsmiths, painters, stonemasons—and they worked not only on great projects but also on small commissions, such as designs for carpet weavers and even shop signs. Since these craftsmen were under strict guild regulation and worked according to the minute specifications of their clients, they had no exalted status, and almost all were men of humble origin.

The prestige of a social position may change in time. The prestige of artists gradually changed in the course of the fifteenth century. Leonardo da Vinci helped to establish the idea that art is based on unusual talent and on science as well: to be an artist, one had to know perspective and anatomy. Artists began to sign their works. They often included self-portraits in their paintings. The idea of intellectual property had arisen, with its emphasis on originality. Instead of commissioning a specific work, art patrons became collectors and bought whatever the artist of their choice turned out. They even saved sketches and unfinished works, since it was supposed that such works gave a more intimate glimpse of the artist's personality. By the time of Michelangelo's death, in 1564, the great artists, at least, were regarded as geniuses, divinely inspired.

As our brief description of the activities of fifteenth-century artists illustrates, an occupant of a particular social position ordinarily, by virtue of his position, interacts not only with many other persons but with persons occupying many different positions. In other words, it is an important aspect of social structure that social positions are interrelated. The term "role-set" has been coined to refer either to the total complex of other social positions with which any particular social position is characteristically connected or, when a particular occupant of a particular position is taken as the point of reference, to the total number of occupants of the correlative social positions with whom he must ordinarily interact (Merton, 1957, pp. 368-70). A fifteenth-century artist interacted with fellow artists, with shop assistants, some of whom were apprentices, with guild officials, and with clients. Ignoring the fact that this list is no doubt incomplete, we can say that the positions of fellow artist, apprentice, other shop assistant, guild official, and client constituted the role-set for the position of master artist. For any particular artist, the persons who occupied these positions constituted his role-set in the more concrete sense. His role in relation to the various positions in his role-set involved, of course, somewhat different patterns of behavior for each—as some writers would say, different routine performances or, simply, different routines. At the same time, his own position was undoubtedly not perceived in the same way by the occupants of all the various positions in his role-set. Some of these other persons, for example, were his status equals, some were inferiors, and some were superiors. The status of artist was a different object of regard according to the role and status of the beholder. Later in this chapter we shall consider briefly some of the consequences of the fact that members of a role-set, occupying varying positions, may make conflicting demands and exert pressure in different ways.

For the moment, note that the varying "routines" that a person performs by virtue of occupying a particular position and interacting with his role-set are technically not different roles; they are different "faces," so to speak, of the same role. As we have noted, every person occupies many roles, and for *each* of them he has a particular role-set.

Our master artists afford us an especially good opportunity to call attention to an important distinction: the distinction between a *role* and the *role performance* of a particular occupant of that role. The role is much the same for all artists at any given time, but the achievement of all artists is, of course, not the same. Closely related to these facts is the distinction between the prestige aspect of the artist's status and the prestige of any particular artist. By Michelangelo's time, artists in general had greater prestige than the artists of the early Renaissance, but only the greatest artists, such as Raphael, Michelangelo, and Titian, were able to associate intimately with kings and popes.

The enormous variety of activities required by all the roles in complex social systems makes it difficult to specify role content ("obligations") for roles in general. There is necessarily a corresponding variety in the content of statuses; yet we can say, in general, that a status often (but not always) includes the following: (1) some kinds and degrees of authority over others; (2) the right to remuneration (some reward for role performance); (3) certain privileges and immunities, such as the right to use certain premises, the services of a secretary, or other means necessary or convenient to the position occupants if they are to carry out their role obligations; and (4) some degree of prestige, symbolized in the privileges and immunities already mentioned, and in general expressed by certain marks of respect from those with whom the status occupants interact. Some appurtenances of a social position are part of both the status and the role. Thus, a military officer is obliged, on certain occasions, to wear a uniform and certain insignia of rank; at the same time, these things are marks of prestige, and it may be said that the officer has the privilege of displaying them.

We have been considering social positions in connection with social groups—e.g., the bank-wiring group, a guild of craftsmen, a master artist's "shop" or studio. Often, however, we speak of a position independently of any particular organization. Thus a man may be called a lawyer whether or not we specify the law firm to which he belongs, or whether or not he is actively engaged in practicing law. All occupants of the same social position, regardless of the particular groups to which they may belong, are said to belong to the same "status group." Clearly, a status group, such as "domestic servants," "employed domestic servants," or "unmarried adult men," is not the same thing as an interaction group; it is not a social system but a social category, including all those of whom certain things are objectively true.

Finally, such are the vagaries of sociological terms, "status" is sometimes used to refer to an individual's total standing in society. In that sense, it embraces all his particular statuses and all the prestige he may have for his personal qualities and attainments. The apprentice sociologist must learn to expect some inconsistency in the use of sociological terms, especially from one writer to another. The context usually helps to make it clear what sense is intended.

Institutionalization [3]

Now that we understand the concept of social position, we can see a little more clearly how social norms operate in a group. A social norm operative in one social system may not be operative in another. Thus, Mohammedan societies permit polygyny, but Christian ones do not. A social

[3] The concept of institutionalization, which is basic in sociological theory, has been most elaborately explained and consistently used in the work of Talcott Parsons. One of his most recent formulations is in *The Social System* (1951), Chap. 2, a rather difficult work for a beginner in sociology to follow.

norm is said to be *institutionalized* in a particular social system when three conditions are met:

1. A large number of the members of the social system accept the norm.
2. Many of those who accept the norm take it seriously. In psychological terms, they have *internalized* it.
3. The norm is sanctioned. This means that certain members of the system are expected to be guided by the norm in appropriate circumstances.

Certain other aspects of institutionalization should be clearly understood. First, institutionalized norms apply to members of the social system according to their social positions within the system. As we have seen, the wiremen, solderers, and inspectors in the bank-wiring room were not expected to do exactly the same things—although some norms did apply to all, regardless of social position. Yet all the members knew and supported the entire normative pattern; even though some of the norms that applied to wiremen did not apply to solderers, still the solderers knew and sanctioned the norms for wiremen, and the wiremen knew and sanctioned the norms for solderers. In other words, the entire normative pattern of the group was part of their *common* culture. This was possible in the bank-wiring group because the group was small. We shall see that institutionalization does not always go so far in a group.

Secondly, the internalization of a norm by the "average" members of a social system is a matter of degree. The obligation of parents to protect their child is deeply internalized—taken very seriously indeed. So is the responsibility of a government official to keep official secrets, especially to keep them out of the hands of foreign agents. In American marriage, the expectation of mutual sexual fidelity is more binding than the expectation that the wife will get the husband's breakfast.

Thirdly, "widespread" acceptance of a norm in a social system is also a matter of degree. What proportion of the members of a social system must know about and accept a norm before the norm can be said to be institutionalized? This question cannot be answered precisely. The necessary proportion varies from case to case, depending upon the norm and the size and complexity of the social system. In a large-scale social system, it is not necessary for everyone to know about, let alone accept, all the norms operative in the system. For example, the functioning of the stock market in the United States requires institutionalization, but many people have only a vague conception of the norms that govern participation in it. What is necessary is that most of those who participate in the stock market in any way know and accept that part of the total pattern of rights and obligations that affects, or is relevant to, their actual interaction with one another. Beyond that, a more generalized acceptance of the rule of law and the authority of the courts ensures that the wider public will support the norms at a distance, so to speak. Thus, a stock-market scandal will reduce the prestige of a broker even among people who do not understand precisely what his offense has been.

Finally, note that beliefs as well as patterns of overt behavior may be institutionalized. A dogma, for example, is a religious belief that members of a particular religious group "must" accept.

SOCIAL INSTITUTIONS[4]

Norms may be institutionalized in a group of any size and complexity. Particularly when speaking of a total society or other territorial group of considerable size, sociologists sometimes refer to a *complex* of institutionalized norms as a "social institution." Marriage, for example, is a social institution to the extent that there exists a body of widely known and supported expectations (operative norms) governing the relationship between "husband" and "wife" (two recognized status-roles).

An institutional pattern may exist even though it does not have a name. For example, there is a recognized set of norms governing the relationship between a medical doctor and his colleagues. An obstetrician has given us a glimpse into this pattern:

> A ticklish problem arises when a doctor has left the city for a while and turned his practice over to other doctors temporarily. Recently, a young woman came to me whose chosen obstetrician was out of the city. I took care of her confinement and everything went smoothly. The next time she became pregnant she came to me and said that she had been so pleased with her former treatment at my hands that she wanted me to take her on as a patient. I had to tell her that she could go to any other obstetrician in town in preference to her old one, but that she couldn't have me. A person just can't be too meticulous in such cases [O. Hall, 1948, p. 333].

Wherever we look in history or in the contemporary world, whether at civilized peoples or the most primitive, we find that social life is molded to a large extent by social institutions. Another example, taken from a study of certain English villages of the thirteenth century, is the rule of primogeniture. The boundaries of a village were often the same, or nearly the same, as the boundaries of a manor (a lord's estate). A villein (a tenant of a certain kind) held his land according to a pattern that was supported by common sentiments and upheld in the manorial courts, presided over by the lord of the manor or by one of his stewards. The rule by which the heir to a parcel of land was determined varied from manor to manor, but in each case the rule tended to be generally known and accepted. This is shown by extant "custumals" (manorial records of land holdings and rents) and by "court rolls" (records of the cases brought before the manorial courts).

> The most familiar [of these rules] . . . was primogeniture: According to primogeniture, a tenement descended to the eldest son of the last holder. He was the son and heir. If there were no sons, the custom of some manors

---

[4] The discussion of social institutions given in this chapter seems to be in rough agreement with Sumner's rather brief treatment (1906, section 61). However, we follow Talcott Parsons more closely.

> was that it descended to the eldest daughter, but more commonly, it went to all the daughters as coheiresses: only in this case was the tenement divided. If there were no children to inherit, then the tenement descended to the eldest brother of the last holder, and so on, according to well known canons [Homans, 1942, p. 123].

If the rightful heir paid various fines, swore fealty to the lord, and thereafter paid his customary rent and performed his customary services, he could keep the land and ensure the title to it for his own heir.

A social institution is thus a recognized normative pattern. As such, it applies to a particular category of relationships. Thus the institution of marriage is a complex normative pattern that applies to all marriages in a particular social system or a particular segment of a social system. These marriages (relationships) conform to the pattern in varying degrees, of course; but married partners all *know* the pattern itself, if it is truly institutional, and they regard it as morally valid and binding.

In this book we shall continue to use the term "social institution" for a complex normative pattern that is widely accepted as binding in a particular society or part of a society. We must recognize, however, that some sociologists and many laymen use the term "social institutions" to refer to particular groups. A good reason for distinguishing between the normative pattern and the social systems to which it applies has already been given: namely, that particular social systems may not conform to the pattern in all respects. Indeed, one important kind of sociological problem is to account for behavior that deviates from the accepted norms. There is another reason for making the distinction between pattern and group: a particular social institution seldom exhausts the normative patterning of any relationship. Primogeniture was not the only pattern binding upon a villein's descendants in thirteenth-century England. The interaction between a particular husband and wife may conform perfectly to the institution of marriage, but they will always develop some additional private norms for their relationship.

Despite these facts, both laymen and sociologists often speak of schools, churches, business organizations, prisons, and the like as "the institutions of the community." This usage is so frequent that we should be foolish to condemn it. It is an easy extension of the technical meaning, for all these organizations, in a particular community, have in common the fact that they are subject to fairly well-recognized patterns of norms: in other words, to social institutions.

INSTITUTIONALIZATION, CONFORMITY, AND SOCIAL CONTROL

Conformity to institutionalized norms is, of course, "normal." The actor, having internalized the norms, feels something like a need to conform. His conscience would bother him if he did not. Further, regardless of his own attitude, other people stand ready to disapprove of him if he violates the established pattern. Consider the remarks of the obstetrician quoted earlier. A doctor's career depends not only upon his knowledge and skill but also upon his relations with other doctors. This is especially true of specialists. There is a well-established convention (part of an institutional pattern) against "stealing" patients. If a doctor should ignore it, he would run the risk of destroying the network of cooperation upon which he depends. His personal relations with his colleagues would suffer; so would his prestige and, ultimately, his income.

The fact that both internalized "need" and external sanctions are effective in bringing about conformity was shown in an exploratory experiment conducted at Harvard and Radcliffe Colleges (Stouffer, 1949). The "subjects," 196 students, were asked to assume, in imagination, the role of a proctor:

> Imagine that you are proctoring an examination. . . . About half way through the exam you see a fellow student openly cheating. The student is copying his answers from previously prepared notes. When he sees that you have seen the notes as you walked down the aisle and stopped near his seat, he whispers quietly to you, "O.K., I'm caught. That's all there is to it." *You do not know the student*. . . .
>
> If you knew that, *except for your action*, there could be very little chance that either the authorities or your student friends would hear about your part in the incident, which of the following actions . . . would you as proctor be most likely to take? Next most likely? Least likely? Next least likely?
>
> * * *

A. Take away his notes and exam book, dismiss him and report him for cheating.
B. Take away his notes, let him finish the exam, but report him for cheating.
C. If he can be led to withdraw from the exam on some excuse, *not* report him for cheating; otherwise, report him.
D. Take away his notes, but let him finish the exam, and *not* report him for cheating.
E. Act as if nothing had happened and *not* report him for cheating.

After making this decision, the students were asked to choose among the same alternatives but assuming different conditions, as follows:

> Now, assume that *except for your action*, there could be very little chance that your student friends would hear about your part in the incident. But assume that, for some reason, there is a good chance, whatever you do, of the authorities finding out about it.

After making their choices for these two situations, the respondents were asked to make new choices assuming somewhat different conditions:

> Now suppose the facts in the case . . . are exactly the same as in the first case, except for one difference. The student you as proctor see cheating is *your own roommate and close friend*. You know that your roommate is a hard working, though not a brilliant, student and desperately needs a good grade in this course.

The respondents were then asked which of the five courses of action they would choose—first, when the choice was to be "private" ("If you knew that, *except for your action*, there could be very little chance that either the authorities or your student friends would hear about your part in the incident") and then when the choice was to be "public" ("If you knew that, *except for your action,* there could be very little chance that your student friends would hear about your part in the incident, but that there is a good chance, whatever you do, of the authorities finding out about it"). The respondents' choices for all four situations are summarized (in part) in Table 1.

In all four situations, the respondents were faced with a possible conflict between duty to the "authorities" and loyalty to a fellow student or, worse, a roommate-friend. This conflict helps to account for the considerable deviation from proctoral duty, especially when the culprit was the roommate-friend, and for the wide range of variability among the respondents. Table 1 shows, among other things, that at least some of the respondents, although willing to deviate from their proctoral duty when they ran no risk of external sanctions, said that they would conform more closely when there was such a risk.

We have already noted, however, that sanctions are not equally effective for all violators of the norm. They always have some effect but not always the same degree of effect. In the bank-wiring group, the "inferior" clique, which we called Clique B, did not conform so scrupulously to some of the group norms as Clique A, and the members of Clique B had less prestige than the members of Clique A. But this loss of prestige did not cause Clique B members to strive to conform more strictly. They had adjusted themselves to their lower prestige and, for the pleasure of annoying the members of Clique A, they were willing to forego the pleasure of higher prestige. Their level of conformity had become stabilized below perfection. Their only concern was not to lose any more prestige. In general, failure to conform, when it is known, brings a penalty, but the effectiveness of the penalty varies

TABLE 1

Hypothetical actions which the respondents say they would be most likely to take as proctor (N = 196) *

Action	*In case of ordinary student*		*In case of roommate-friend*	
	PRIVATE	PUBLIC	PRIVATE	PUBLIC
A	21%	30%	4%	6%
B	47	48	12	34
C	16	13	18	31
D	15	7	38	18
E	1	2	28	11
	100%	100%	100%	100%

* Adapted from S. A. Stouffer, "An Analysis of Conflicting Social Norms," *Amer. sociol. Rev.*, 1949, v. 14, p. 713, Table 2.

according to the social rank of those on whom it is imposed. Those of low rank can lose prestige on account of a drop from their established standard of conformity, and the same is true of higher-ranking persons; but the higher-ranking start from a higher level of conformity and consequently suffer more from a relatively slight departure from full conformity.[5]

The same idea can be expressed a little differently. The members of a group evaluate one another's conduct and performances, using the norms of the group as standards. In the course of long association, every member becomes the object of more or less stable sentiments on the part of all those with whom he interacts. In addition, he acquires a more or less stable reputation and a degree of popularity or unpopularity, even with people whom he may never have seen. Once these sentiments have become established, the norms of the group are to some extent modified for each person to whom they apply. That is to say, a man with a reputation for being incompetent is no longer expected to be perfectly competent; he is only expected to be no less competent than he has ordinarily been. Consequently, those with whom he interacts will not impose heavy penalties or sanctions for his every lapse from perfection; they will simply treat him as usual—with somewhat less deference than they give to people with a better reputation. For this reason, sanctions should not be thought of necessarily as definite rewards and punishments meted out for particular acts; a certain level of sanctioning is continuously operative in the form of "frozen" reputations.[6] This means that the group is not so much expecting conformity to a normative pattern as it is expecting and maintaining a particular and unique degree of conformity from each member of the group. Perfect conformity remains an ideal, attainment of which brings a higher level of prestige. But fear of lowered prestige is, for most people, a stronger motive than desire for higher prestige.[7]

To the extent that an institutional pattern has become part of the moral consensus of the members of a group, it is a relatively disinterested element in their motivation. That is to say, they will tend to conform, or try to conform, regardless of immediate advantage or disadvantage. This non-expedient element in their motivation does not preclude their having "selfish" or expedient motives as well; the institutional pattern is simply a moral framework within which the elements of calculated expediency are normally confined. (As in all cases of orientation to norms, a particular actor may, of course, violate the pattern at times.) The two elements, self-interest and

---

5 This point is very well made by Homans (1950, pp. 140ff.). Homans mentions a qualification of this general rule: very well-established members of a group may depart slightly from group norms with impunity, because they no longer have to prove their basic loyalty to the group.

6 Parsons treats the distribution of "rewards" as analytically distinct from the distribution of "possessions" and as an aspect of the structure of social systems. (See Parsons, 1951, pp. 127ff. *et passim.*)

7 Both Homans (1950) and Barnard (1946) have made the point that the "average" person fears a lowering of prestige more than he desires to gain more prestige. Barnard points out that this fact is important for the maintenance of authority.

disinterestedness, are well illustrated in contractual relations. Ordinarily, a person makes a contract only when he has something to gain from it, and he presumably tries to make the terms of the contract as advantageous to himself as possible; yet the *institution* of contract is, in itself, a perfectly neutral or disinterested framework to which he subscribes.

The institution of contract, of course, is not the same thing as a particular agreement. For example, the institutionalized rules for industrial relations—rules established by "collective bargaining"—exist independently of any particular agreement between a company and a worker or group of workers. The institution does not specify detailed terms (although it may set precise limits within which detailed terms must fall if they are to be valid). Yet, in another way, the institution may be more detailed than any particular contract: for example, it is a guide to what must be done in case of contingencies unforeseen by either party.

The rules of the institution of contract, as Emile Durkheim showed in detail (1893, trans. 1933), are various. Parsons (1937) explains them as follows:

> They regulate, in the first place, what contracts are and what are not recognized as valid. A man cannot, for instance, sell himself or others into slavery. They regulate the means by which the other party's assent to a contract may be obtained; an agreement secured by fraud or under duress is void. They regulate various consequences of a contract once made, both to the parties themselves and to third persons. Under certain circumstances a party may be enjoined from enforcing a contract quite legally made, as when the holder of a mortgage is sometimes prohibited from foreclosing when interest payments are not made. Similarly one party may be forced to assume obligations which were not in his contract. They regulate, finally, the procedures by which enforcement in the courts is obtainable. In a society like our own this nexus of regulations is exceedingly complex.
>
> For convenience Durkheim lays the principal stress on the body of rules which are formulated in law and enforceable in the courts. But this must not be allowed to lead to misunderstanding of his position. . . . Durkheim's main stress is on the existence of a body of rules which have not been the object of any agreement among the contracting parties themselves but are socially "given." . . . Of course if the rules were not to some degree enforced, they would be unimportant, but it is on their independence of the process of *ad hoc* agreement that Durkheim lays his emphasis. Secondly, while he discusses mainly legal rules, he is careful to point out that these stand by no means alone, but are supplemented by a vast body of customary rules, trade conventions and the like which are, in effect, obligatory equally with the law, although not enforceable in the courts [pp. 312-13].[8]

When circumstances make conformity to an ideal pattern difficult, there are often second-best patterns to follow. For example, in China, a family of good reputation ordinarily expects to have to pay a fairly large sum, in

---

[8] In footnotes, Parsons remarks, "There may also be rules enforced on themselves by occupational groups such as the professions." He quotes Durkheim's "most succinct formula": "Tout n'est pas contractuel dans le contrat" (Not everything in contract is contractual).

the form of gifts and expensive wedding arrangements, for a bride for one of its sons. But a poor family may avoid some of these expenses by taking in a very young girl as a foster-child and marrying her to one of the sons when she grows up. During the depression that followed the T'ai P'ing Rebellion (1848–65), many families resorted to this pattern. But the prestige attached to matchmaking, marriage gifts, and "the sending of the meeting-boat and sedan chair"—not to speak of the satisfaction to be derived from conformity for its own sake—restored the traditional form of marriage when the depression was over (Fei Hsiao-T'ung, 1939, pp. 53ff.)

However well-institutionalized a norm may be, many persons who are subject to it are tempted on occasion to depart from it. This is shown by the existence of sanctions. Sanctions are involved in all forms of social control—that is, mechanisms by which tendencies to deviate from institutionalized norms are held in check. We must not suppose, however, that sanctions derive their effectiveness mainly from being applied. One of the most important aspects of social interaction is that each actor is able to foresee in imagination the probable response of others to alternative courses of action on his part. We may infer, therefore, that many persons who are tempted to deviate from expected behavior patterns check themselves. They do not try to find out experimentally how others would react to a violation; they can imagine vividly enough. This inner check is no less a form of social control than the direct application of sanctions.

Conformity and Specificity of the Norm

Let us return for a moment to the experiment discussed above, concerning students' hypothetical actions in the role of proctor, assumed in imagination. We noted that more students would conform to the norms for proctors when they were sure that their actions would be known to the university authorities than when they could act without fear of any sanctions except their own conscience. But we must now take into account another influence on their action. For many norms, there may not be complete agreement about the range or "band" within which an act can be regarded as conforming. Yet widespread objective conformity to a norm depends, of course, upon agreement as to just what the norm demands. Without that agreement, we should expect a wide range of behavior, regardless of whether sanctions are feared or not. In the proctor-student situation, there was, as a matter of fact, considerable disagreement among the respondents as to what courses of action the university authorities would approve of—that is, what courses of action could be regarded as modes of conformity to the role obligations of a proctor. The harshest actions, it will be remembered, were A ("Take away his exam book, dismiss him and report him for cheating") and B ("Take away his notes, let him finish the exam, but report him for cheating"). In the case of the ordinary student, as distinguished from that of the roommate-friend, thirteen of the 196 respondents thought that the authorities would approve of A only; five thought that the authorities would approve of B only; and 134 thought that the authorities would approve of either A or B. But forty-four had a different interpretation of the norm; three even professed to believe that the authorities would approve of any one of the five courses, including E ("Act as if nothing had happened and *not* report him for cheating"). Such lack of agreement is perhaps unusual: the respondents were students and presumably knew and accepted the norm "Don't cheat," but they had had no indoctrination as proctors.[9]

Yet, one of the ways in which social norms may vary, certainly, is in the degree of agreement among those who are subject to them concerning the exact range of permissible behavior. It is conceivable that "cheating" might be variously defined. Using prepared notes is presumably cheating, but suppose that a student has been studying desperately right up to the examination and, anxious lest he forget some key points, writes them down, without consulting friends or books, while he is waiting for the examination questions to be handed out. If he uses those notes during the examination, is he cheating? Opinions might differ.

In considering the problem of agreement or disagreement about the range of acceptable conforming behavior, there is another source of difficulty. The students were not asked to state the norms for proctors; they were asked to state which of several particular actions would be approved of in concrete circumstances. This form of the question permitted the respondents to assume that the authorities, in passing judgment, might regard the circumstances as extenuating, or might even regard the proctor's "obligations" as a friend as decisive. Thus while thirteen of the respondents thought that the authorities would approve of nothing but the most drastic action (A) in the case of an "ordinary student" caught cheating, only four said that the authorities would approve only of A when the cheater was a roommate-friend of the proctor.

Role Conflict and Deviation

It will be remembered that the student respondents in all the hypothetical situations, but especially in the ones involving a roommate-friend, were placed in a potential role conflict. As proctor, responsible to the university and to the impersonal norm of fair play, the respondent presumably had to report a case of cheating, no matter who might be involved. According to this view, only actions A and B could be regarded as modes of conformity. But as a roommate and a close friend, the respondent might have felt an

9 There was a slight fault in the design of the experiment. Before being asked what their own action would be in the hypothetical situations, the respondents should have been asked, in general, which of the alternative actions the authorities would approve of on the part of a proctor who had caught a student using prepared notes during an examination. After making a difficult choice of a course of action, some of the respondents may have rationalized it by pretending to themselves that their choice was actually in line with their duty.

obligation to be lenient, especially in the "private" situation, when to retrain from reporting the friend would actually have kept the friend out of trouble with the authorities.

In order to see how the respondents interpreted their obligation as a roommate-friend, the investigator asked them to say which of the possible courses of action their friends in the student body would approve of. As one might expect, there was even less agreement for this norm than for the norm of proper conduct from the point of view imputed to the university authorities. Of the 196 respondents, 120 said they thought that the university authorities would approve of either A or B but of no other course of action for a proctor. These 120 students, however, had widely varying opinions about what course or courses friends in the student body would approve of.

As one might expect, the respondents on the whole thought that their student friends would expect leniency (Stouffer, 1949, p. 715, Table 5). Only one respondent thought that students would be more harsh than the university authorities; he thought that the students would approve of A only. Only eleven respondents thought that the students would agree exactly with the authorities. The rest of the respondents thought that the students would, to varying extents, be more tolerant. In their hypothetical actions, the 120 respondents tended to decide the conflict of expectations in favor of the students. Only twenty-four chose A or B in the private situation; only fifty-eight chose these courses in the public situation.

There is evidence, moreover, that the role conflict went beyond a conflict in normative expectations. Seventy-five respondents believed that the range of decisions of which the students would approve overlapped with the range of actions of which the authorities would approve. For example, thirteen of the respondents thought that the students would approve of either B, C, or D, and that the authorities would approve of either A or B. These respondents, by choosing B, could have satisfied both groups. Of the seventy-five who perceived some overlap, however, only twenty-two in the private situation and forty-seven in the public situation decided in such a way as to satisfy both the authorities and the students. Of the seventeen respondents who decided in such a way as to conform to the normative expectations of neither the authorities nor fellow students, every one in the private situation decided on a course less harsh than those of which he thought his student friends would approve. It is not likely that these respondents had very different moral attitudes from those of their fellow students. We must conclude, therefore, that a large number of respondents deviated from the normative expectations of both roles as they perceived them. Presumably they experienced a role conflict not only in the technical sense of normative conflict but in the sense of conflict between duty and feeling.

The power of negative sanctions is also revealed in this part of Stouffer's results. In the private situation, only twenty-four respondents conformed to the expectations imputed to the authorities—that is, they chose one of the more drastic acts, A or B. But in the public situation fifty-eight chose either A or B. Of the seventeen who decided to conform to neither authorities nor students in the private situation, only eight kept to this course in the public situation. Here is an interesting detail: whereas the seventeen "absolute" deviants in the private situation—those who chose outside both approved ranges—all chose to act more leniently than they thought the students would approve, in the public situation two of the remaining eight sentimentalists, though still refusing to choose A or B as the authorities would wish, did choose a more drastic course of action than they thought the students would approve. Fear of sanctions caused them to totter perceptibly in their convictions, but they did not topple over.

Objection might be made to the student-proctor study on the ground that the respondents were only saying what they would do in a hypothetical situation. The same objection could not be made, however, to a study conducted at the Air Command and Staff School of Air University, Maxwell Air Force Base (Getzels and Guba, 1954); but the Air School study showed a similar result: that role conflict tends to produce deviation.

Air University trains Air Force officers. The instructors are all officers in uniform. A sample of these officer-instructors were interviewed to see what role conflicts, if any, they felt in their assignments. Four problem areas were revealed in these interviews:

1. *Procedure.* Some of the officer-instructors interviewed seemed to think that there was some conflict between the typical military interaction between officers and the type of interaction that ought to prevail between colleagues in teaching, or between teacher and pupil. In military life, a subordinate in rank must defer to a higher-ranking officer, but in teaching the ideal is more "democratic." Note that this difference is one of norms or standards.

2. *Rank.* Some of those interviewed felt that it was unjust to give the same pay and rating to instructors who were high-ranking officers but had no teaching experience as to instructors who were lower-ranking officers but had a great deal of teaching experience or academic training. And yet this could happen because high rank in the Air Force depends mainly on flying duty, especially in combat, not on teaching.

3. *Career.* Some of those interviewed were troubled because their assignment to teaching would not advance their career in the Air Force. Only "field" experience could do that.

4. *Assignment.* Some were troubled because they had been assigned to teach courses that they did not feel qualified to teach. Some wished that they had not been assigned to teaching at all.

Using material drawn from these interviews, the investigators composed two "inventories," which were later given, as questionnaires, to a larger number of officer-instructors at Air University. The inventories took account of the fact that the University was divided into nine courses, known as "schools." Inventory I consisted of a number of statements, each followed by a list of possible opinions about the statement. For example:

37. Compared with a tour of duty in a field command, a tour at Air University is a gap in the career of a professional Air Force Officer.

The statement as made would be agreed to at my school by:
0—practically none of the instructors
1—a small proportion of the instructors
2—some of the instructors
3—a considerable number of the instructors
4—many of the instructors
5—very many of the instructors

Inventory I as a whole was designed to show, first, the extent to which officer-instructors at Air University thought that role conflict of certain types existed at the University; and, secondly, the extent to which the nine "schools" differed from one another in their appraisal of the amount of role conflict.

Inventory II was designed to find out how many officer-instructors, and which ones, actually felt role conflicts themselves, and which role conflicts. Thus the same statements or items contained in the first inventory were included in the second, but each item was followed by this list of alternatives to choose from:

The situation described in the statement troubles me:
0—not at all
1—to a small degree
2—to some degree
3—to a considerable degree
4—to a great degree
5—to a very great degree

In addition to Inventory I and Inventory II, a Personal Questionnaire was composed, designed to elicit descriptive information, such as age, rank, educational training, and current duties; attitudinal information, such as interest in the goals of Air University, feelings of adequacy or inadequacy in their work, and sentiments toward the educational procedures; and ratings of fellow-instructors as either below average or above average in teaching effectiveness. The investigators recognized that the ratings of fellow-instructors might not be the most valid possible index of teaching effectiveness, but on this point they have this to say: ". . . because of the policy at Air University that all instructors systematically visit each other's classes and try out all their lectures before their colleagues, the instructors were in particularly favored positions to make valid judgments of their fellows."

The over-all purposes of these three instruments were, among others, to find out which officer-instructors were most subject to role conflict, and whether these officers were also the least effective instructors. The results showed that two of the nine "schools" at Air University were distinguished by the fact that the officer-instructors, on the average, thought that there was little role conflict in their schools, while the instructors in two other schools thought that there was a great deal of role conflict in their schools. This result, obtained from Inventory I ("The statement as made would be agreed to at my school by: . . ."), is compatible with two facts: First, the schools in which little role conflict was perceived were primarily for military subjects, while the two schools in which much role conflict was perceived were primarily for nonmilitary subjects, such as bookkeeping and law. Secondly, a higher proportion of instructors in the "much conflict" schools were men who identified themselves with nonmilitary professional roles, such as accountant and lawyer. From these two facts, one might have expected that the officer-instructors in the second pair of schools would be more subject to role conflict in a military academy. They were compelled to play a "civilian" role and a "military" role at the same time, under circumstances in which the norms for neither role could be fully operative or fully met. This result and diagnosis was confirmed by the data on officer-instructors who most often reported (Inventory II and Personal Questionnaire) that they personally felt role conflict (Getzels and Guba, 1954, p. 172).

From these data on schools and on individual officer-instructors, it is clear that the basic conflict was between the role of officer and the role of teacher. For some this basic conflict was intensified by the fact that in their civilian roles they had internalized norms that were not quite in harmony with the norms operative in the officer-instructor role combination.

That the officer-instructors most subject to role conflict were also the least effective teachers is shown in Table 2.

TABLE 2

High- and low-conflict scores compared with role-ineffectiveness ratings *

		High-conflict group	*Low-conflict group*
INVENTORY I	Ineffective	15(20%)	4(13%)
	All others	60(80%)	26(87%)
INVENTORY II	Ineffective	12(34%)	8(12%)
	All others	23(66%)	60(88%)

* Adapted from J. W. Getzels and E. G. Guba, "Role, Role Conflict, and Effectiveness: An Empirical Study," *Amer. sociol. Rev.*, April 1954, v. 19, p. 173.

Relations Between Groups

These studies of role conflict illustrate the fact that institutionalization of norms may not result automatically in conformity. We can pursue the variable results of institutionalization by considering in some detail a series of possible relations between groups, of which role conflict is only one. Our purpose here is not to analyze all aspects of the relations between groups but, rather, to emphasize the fact that the attitude toward norms in any particular group is affected by the relations between that group and oth-

groups. We begin by summarizing briefly what we have already shown about the relation between role conflict and deviation from norms.

ROLE CONFLICT

In role conflict, two groups (or two subgroups of a single group) are brought into a kind of relation with each other through the fact that the same person occupies a role in one of the groups that to some extent is incompatible with a role he occupies in the other. In the hypothetical case studied at Harvard and Radcliffe, the proctor, as an agent and representative of the administration of the university, had a kind of membership in that group; but he was also in fact a member of the student body. (The student body may be regarded as either an interaction group or a status group.)

The role conflict at Air University was of two kinds. Some of the officer-instructors had not yet acquired field experience and were eager to do so in order to further their careers in the Air Force. This ambition, which it might be regarded as virtually a duty for them to have, came in conflict with their obligation to devote themselves to teaching. Other officer-instructors (or possibly the same ones, in some cases) were involved in another role conflict. They had to observe the hierarchical distinctions among military officers, but they felt that these distinctions were sometimes incompatible with good teaching and with their status as teachers well qualified in their "civilian" subjects. Here they were identifying themselves with a different status group—that of lawyers or accountants. The officer-instructors who were teaching courses in "weapons" or "tactics" felt this conflict much less keenly because they were more likely to be high-ranking officers with field experience.

The result of role conflict in all these cases was deviation—some departure from ideal conformity to some of the expectations of one or both of the roles. (Even compromise involves *some* deviation.)

There are, of course, many other examples of role conflict. As Americans imbued with the ideal of equality of opportunity regardless of color and with the ideal of fair play in competition, many "white" Southerners feel a conflict with their role as Southerners, loyal to the ideals of the Confederacy, which fought to maintain a social order in which Negroes and whites were not to be treated as equals in opportunity (Parsons, 1951, p. 281). (Role conflict is, of course, only one factor in the relations between Negroes and whites in the United States, but it is often neglected in discussion.)

REINFORCEMENT OF ROLES

If a person occupies two roles, the second of which reinforces his motivation to conform to the first, we have the opposite of role conflict. One of the best examples of this in contemporary society is the mutual reinforcement of occupational role and familial role, if both are occupied by an adult man. Indeed, most husbands-and-fathers cannot fulfill their obligations in the family unless they also perform adequately in an occupational role outside the family. Some writers (e.g., Parsons, 1955, p. 13) go so far as to assert that having an occupational role is *part* of the role of husband-and-father. The point, of course, is that a husband-and-father is expected to support his family. The obligation and wish to support a family presumably are strong incentives for a man to do well in his occupation.

One point needs to be added to the present discussion. We must remember that every role has more than one obligation. It is possible to fulfill one obligation—e.g., supporting a family—while neglecting others—e.g., spending some time with one's children. Any two roles occupied by the same person, although they may reinforce each other, may also conflict in practice if the incumbent fails to allot his time and energy properly between them. Such failure, however, is due not to role conflict but to deviation in role performance, which is always possible. Role conflict, properly speaking, is inherent in the normative patterns of the roles themselves, and this is more rare.

INTERACTION BETWEEN GROUPS

Perhaps the most common kind of relation between two groups is interaction. This, of course, must take the form of interaction between individuals in their capacity as members of the groups. For example, in the Deep South especially, but elsewhere in the United States as well to some degree, a Negro can hardly ever interact with a white person merely as one worker, let us say, with another; it is almost always pertinent to the interaction that the Negro and the white belong to two different ethnic groups, one socially superior to the other.

One of the most important kinds of interaction between two groups takes the form of a transaction between two or more *representatives* of the groups. A representative of a group is not an ordinary member; he has the right and obligation to act *for* the group, to commit the group to an agreement or otherwise to look after its common interests in some sphere of action. Political offices are an example of this kind of role.

Role-sets

Our present interest in the interaction between groups, as we have said, is limited to the effects of such interaction upon conformity to institutionalized norms. We can best approach this problem through the concept of role-set. For convenience, let us designate as "ego" any person who is taken as the point of reference in a discussion. (This is a fairly common practice in anthropology, clinical psychology, and sociology.) We shall here use "ego" to refer to a person in his capacity as occupant of a particular social position.

It will be remembered that a role-set consists of those social positions which are structurally related to ego's position, or of the persons who occupy those positions; ego's position together with its role-set, or ego together with his role-set, compose a complex whole. The institutionalization of norms ensures that, to some extent at least, the persons composing ego's role-set will agree on what ego's role obligations are. Nevertheless, this agreement is seldom if ever perfect. The persons composing ego's role-set occupy somewhat different positions from ego's and from one another's. Consequently their perspectives and their interests are not quite the same. While they may agree in principle on ego's role obligations, they are likely to stress different things and make different interpretations.

> The fact, for example, that the members of a school board are often in social and economic strata quite different from that of the public school teacher will mean that, in certain respects, their values and expectations differ from those of the teacher. The individual teacher may thus be readily subject to conflicting role-expectations among his professional colleagues and among the influential members of the school board and, at times, derivatively, of the superintendent of schools. What is an educational frill for the one may be judged as an essential of education by the other. These disparate and inconsistent evaluations complicate the task of coming to terms with them all. What holds conspicuously for the [position] of the teacher holds, in varying degree, for the occupants of other [positions] who are structurally related, in their role-set, to others who themselves occupy diverse [positions] [Merton, 1957, pp. 370-71].

To some extent the kind of disharmony illustrated in this quotation is virtually inevitable. We could say either that the obligations of ego's role are imperfectly institutionalized or (a somewhat better formulation in some cases) that the existence of institutionalized patterns, although it mitigates conflict within the role-set, does not prevent it entirely. Note that a poorly articulated or inharmonious role-set is not the same thing as a role conflict. A role conflict occurs when ego occupies two roles with incompatible role obligations. The kind of conflict we are discussing here—imperfectly articulated role-sets—also puts incompatible demands upon ego, but these come not from different positions that he occupies but from different "members" of the role-set connected with *one* of his positions. Both kinds of conflict, role conflict and imperfectly articulated role-sets, are relevant to our present subject in that both lead to deviation from institutionalized norms or at least to compromise, which is a kind of mild double deviation.

We may assume that disharmony varies in degree from one role-set to another. Where it exists to any significant extent, the members of ego's role-set are seeking to influence him in incompatible directions; we may think of them as engaged in a struggle for control of his role performance, whether or not they are aware that a struggle is going on. Some of the factors affecting the outcome of the struggle have been identified (Merton, 1957, pp. 370-80) and are worth describing briefly here. The first three factors are similar in that they require no special activity on ego's part; the last three factors are similar in that they do require such activity.

1. In some cases, ego's position is potentially so vulnerable to conflicting pressures from his role-set that an institutional pattern exists to protect his autonomy to some extent. A notable example of this is the position of university teacher. The role obligation of the teacher, recognized in principle

by "everybody," is to teach the truth to the best of his knowledge and belief. An important aspect of his status is known as "academic freedom"—a kind of privileged immunity from the cruder forms of retaliation, such as removal from office, to which he might otherwise be subject from persons in his role-set who disapprove of his opinions. Academic freedom, however, is notoriously hard to maintain. Patriotic groups, university boards of trustees, university administrators—even ego's colleagues—are sometimes tempted to violate his academic freedom by interpreting it narrowly or by asserting that some other value is more important. To some extent, such pressures are forestalled, however, by the mechanism of preventing some "members" of ego's role-set from being able to observe his activities readily.

> The norm which holds that what is said in the classrooms of universities is privileged, in the sense of being restricted to the professor and his students, has this function of maintaining a degree of autonomy for the teacher. . . .
>
> More broadly, the concept of privileged information and confidential communication in the professions–law and medicine, teaching and the ministry–has the same function of insulating clients from ready observability of their behavior and beliefs by others in their role-set [Merton, 1957, p. 375].

Here we see that the institutional pattern itself is such as it might be if it had been planned by someone who was determined to prevent role-sets from having too much influence. (We are not asserting that it *was* planned by anyone who had this in mind.) For short, we may call this the pattern of insulation. Its operation requires no activity on ego's part except routine assertion of the rights of his status and no activity on the part of the members of his role-set except routine refraining from intrusion; protection of ego's role performance is built-in.

2. The various members of ego's role-set usually have varying degrees of interest in his activity. Other things being equal, those with less interest can be relatively ignored.

3. One of the "other things" that are seldom equal, however, is the distribution of power in ego's role-set. This factor, unlike the first two, involves not so much the relation between ego and his role-set as the relations within the role-set itself. Ego is often allowed a certain degree of role autonomy by the fact that the members of his role-set to some extent neutralize one another. The weaker ones are often able to counteract the stronger by forming coalitions.

4. Another factor affecting the outcome of the struggle for control of ego's role performance—one that involves special activity on ego's part—is the common strategy of making known to the various members of the role-set that conflict exists among them, and playing one member off against another.

5. The fifth factor, ego's power to withstand pressure, is in a way complementary to the third (the distribution of power among the members of ego's role-set—power to control one another and to affect ego's role

performance). Just as the members of ego's role-set can combine in various ways, some against others and all against ego's role autonomy, so ego can join in combinations to protect that autonomy. The most likely kind of combination, in many cases, is an organization composed of all or some of those in ego's position (i.e., in his status group). Organizations such as this rarely or never confine themselves to protecting the common status of their members against the corresponding role-set; they also normally seek to improve their members' common status and to win acceptance for "progressive" redefinition of the members' common role. (See, e.g., Merton, 1958, 1958a.) An example of this mode of dealing with the role-set is the activity of the American Association of University Professors. This organization performs numerous services for its members as individuals, for the profession of teaching, and for the society as a whole, but most observers would probably agree that one of its most important services is the investigation of cases of alleged violation of academic freedom. If private correspondence does not succeed in rectifying the abuses discovered, the Association provides publicity, which is seldom ineffective. Indeed, we may safely assume that fear of such publicity deters many persons in the professor's role-set from seeking to destroy his academic freedom. (We are here conceiving of the Association's activity, which ego presumably supports, as a kind of countervailing power to the power of ego's role-set. It is only fair to remark, however, that the Association, true to the standard of impersonal truth which it professes to defend, also affords protection to certain members of the role-set who may be unjustly accused of violating academic freedom.)

6. The last in our list of factors affecting the outcome of the struggle for control of ego's role performance is ego's ability to eliminate "offensive" (or too aggressive) members from his role-set. This ability varies depending upon ego's position and also, to some extent, upon his personality. Ego can seldom eliminate a *position* from his role-set; he will sometimes be able to eliminate a particular individual from his role-set in the concrete sense; but, perhaps most often, if ego cannot bear the pressures directed toward him from his role-set, he will have to give up his social position if he can and leave the role-set to others to cope with.

Contemplating these six factors, we cannot say in general what the outcome will be for ego's conformity to the norms of his role. We shall be unable to say *anything* intelligent, however, unless we clearly distinguish between two levels of analysis. At the more abstract level, we analyze the relations between social positions or between types of group, disregarding the particular individuals who occupy the positions and disregarding particular groups. For example, we might ask what the position of university professor typically involves in the United States, how much agreement there is about its rights and duties, and to what extent professors in general conform to the norms of their role. At the more concrete level of analysis, we might analyze the position of Professor Jones in a specific university. At either level, we apply the concept of role-set and investigate the interplay of the six factors we have discussed. The general framework of the analysis would be the same, but the content would be different.

At the more abstract level, perhaps the first thing to note is that the power factors—especially the distribution and alignment of power in the role-set and the existence and relative power of organizations based on ego's status group—help to determine what the institutionalized norms of ego's role *are,* not only the degree of conformity to them. Social institutions are to some extent the relatively stabilized resultants of past power struggles. In that sense, the interplay of the six factors—with others, no doubt—will in general operate to establish institutional patterns and to maintain conformity to them. Stability, however, is always relative and always a matter of degree. Any marked change in any one of the six factors will, unless it is counteracted, bring about, first, a change in ego's degree of conformity to his role and, secondly, more gradually, a change in the institutionalized definition of that role. There is necessarily a close relation between *operative* norm and actual practice: if average practice departs too far from the norm, then mechanisms of social control tend to restore the original level of practice; if they do not so tend, then the operative norm has obviously changed.

The second thing to note at the more abstract level of analysis is that if there is very serious difference between ego and his role-set about ego's role (what he is normatively expected to do), then the role cannot be said, strictly speaking, to be institutionalized. But if we consider that institutional patterns are partly the resultant of past power struggles and, further, that it must be rare for all the factors involved to be in a perfectly stabilized interrelationship for any great length of time, then we must realize anew that the institutionalization of norms is a matter of variable degree. In the more unstable situations, the persons composing ego's role-set, who themselves occupy varying social positions, will have such widely different conceptions of what ego ought to do—different from one another's and different from ego's—that no matter what ego actually does do he will be violating someone's norms for him. We may repeat that compromise is also a form of deviation, a kind of violation, in that it necessarily falls short of the ideal expectations between which it is a compromise.

Before leaving this somewhat abstract discussion of role-sets, we must make one more observation, lest we unwittingly create a false impression. In discussing six of the factors that will affect the outcome of any struggle for control of ego's role performance, we recurred to the same example as a focus for the discussion: we took the role of university professor, and we paid especial attention to academic freedom. Academic freedom is an aspect of the professor's *status,* not of his role, although if academic freedom is violated the professor will not be able to perform his role. The point here is that academic freedom is more likely to be violated by members of the professor's role-set than by the professor himself; consequently, in our discussion we tended to think in terms of a struggle between the professor-hero and his role-set. The suspenseful question was, Will the factors operate in such a way as to allow the professor to maintain his integrity and conform to his role? It would be a gross error, however, to think, in general, that ego's conformity depends simply upon the degree of autonomy he is able to keep intact against his role-set. On the contrary, more often than not, ego's conformity to his role obligations depends in part upon the pressures from his role-set. The norms for ego's role are not determined by ego alone. Both he and the "members" of his role-set are involved in a complex normative pattern, and to some extent they press one another to conform to the pattern.

REFERENCE GROUPS

The reference-group kind of relation between groups has always been very common, but it has been neglected in sociological theory until rather recently. The concept of "reference group" arises essentially from the fact that any person acting in any situation may be influenced, not only by the positions he occupies in one or more interaction groups or status groups and by his conceptiors and expectations of the group or groups with which he may be interacting, but also by his conception of still other groups of which he is not a member and apart from any interaction he may be having with them. These groups—they may be interaction groups or status groups—exert their influence as reference groups in a purely passive way, simply by being thought of. (They do not exist solely as reference groups, of course, but we are speaking of their influence in this capacity.) Any group may be a reference group for a given person—a group to which he belongs or one to which he does not belong; an interaction group, a status group, or a statistical category; a group whose members are aware of their influence or one whose members are not; an actual group or even an imaginary one. Any group is a reference group for someone if his conception of it, which may or may not be realistic, is part of his frame of reference for appraisal of himself or of his situation, aspirations for himself, or appraisal of or aspirations for one of the groups to which he belongs. We take it for granted that the groups to which a person belongs will serve as reference groups for him; if they did not, he could hardly be said to be truly a member of them. Therefore, the concept of reference group is perhaps most useful in that it calls attention to the fact that groups to which one does not belong ("non-membership groups") also serve as reference groups.

For members of a particular group, another group is a reference group if any of the following circumstances prevail:

1. Some or all of the members of the first group aspire to membership in the second group (the reference group).

2. The members of the first group strive to be like the members of the reference group in some respect, or to make their group like the reference group in some respect.

3. The members of the first group derive some satisfaction from being

*un*like the members of the reference group in some respect, and strive to maintain the difference between the groups or between themselves and the members of the reference group.

4. Without necessarily striving to be like or unlike the reference group or its members, the members of the first group appraise their own group or themselves using the reference group or its members as a standard for comparison.

These four types will become clearer with some examples.

Striving for admission

One study (Stouffer *et al.*, 1949) found that Army privates who accepted the formal rules were more likely to be promoted than those who did not. Among privates generally, acceptance of formal rules was by no means complete and usual; in fact, the ambitious privates who were "bucking" for promotion by displaying their cooperativeness with superior officers were known as "brown noses." Their reference group was the status group of officers, in which they aspired to membership. This ambition helped to account for their deviation from the informal rules of the status group of privates as a whole, for whom "bucking" was wrong. That the privates in general had informal rules was shown in the unpleasant sanctions they applied to the ambitious. The epithet "brown nose" was one of the milder sanctions (Merton and Kitt, 1950).

Another study (Greenblum and Pearlin, 1953) showed that persons whose occupational position was either higher or lower than that of their fathers were more prejudiced against Negroes, Jews, and the foreign-born than were persons whose occupational position was at the same level as that of their fathers. In this study, a change from a manual to a nonmanual occupation in successive generations was treated as "upward mobility." Two manual occupations, or two nonmanual, were treated as being on the same level.

"Prejudice" was indicated in several ways. All respondents were asked the question, "Suppose a family from any of these American groups were about to move next door. Are there any of them you would prefer not to have as neighbors?" The list of American groups included Jews and Negroes, among others. Of the "upward mobile," 15 per cent would keep out Jews and 71 per cent would keep out Negroes. Of the "downward mobile," the corresponding percentages were 13 and 63. The "stationary" respondents (those whose occupation was at the same level as their fathers') were against Jews and Negroes by somewhat smaller percentages, 11 and 59, respectively. These differences are perhaps not striking by themselves, but they become more significant when we find that the "mobile" respondents gave more prejudiced answers to other questions as well. A higher proportion of the "mobile" than of the "stationary" thought that Jews, Negroes, and foreign-born persons are "getting too much power . . . in the U. S. than is good for the country." A higher proportion agreed that "although some Jews are honest, in general Jews are dishonest in their business dealings" and that "generally speaking, Negroes are ignorant and lazy."

We can see these responses more clearly as behavior in reference to a reference group if we realize that the relevant groups are probably social classes, of which the occupational categories "manual" and "nonmanual" are only rough indices. Many of the "upward mobile" were striving to gain admission into the middle class (a status group), of which they were at best marginal or insecure members. The "downward mobile" were still oriented to the middle class as a reference group to which they had once belonged (perhaps insecurely). Both mobile groups rejected Negroes, Jews, and the foreign-born in order to distinguish themselves more sharply from the class they were striving to leave, in the case of the "upward mobile," or the class to which they had reluctantly fallen, in the case of the "downward mobile," and from the less secure members of the middle class.

A similar finding was made in a study conducted in Israel (Eisenstadt, 1954). New immigrants who were socially ambitious—that is, eager to gain admission into high-ranking groups—were also the most prejudiced and aggressive toward low-ranking groups.

Emulation

Many examples of striving to be like a reference group are to be found in the study of "minority" problems.[10] The "dominant" group in the United States consists of white Protestants of Anglo-Saxon ancestry, with a fringe of white Protestants whose ancestors came from northern European countries other than England. Some members of ethnic and religious minorities are, of course, trying to gain admission to the dominant group, but this is not true of all those who are trying to be like the members of the dominant group. For example, Negroes who have their hair straightened are not necessarily trying to pass as whites; Jews who change their names or have plastic surgery done are not necessarily trying to pass as Protestants. The motivation, no doubt, varies from one individual to another. Some minority-group members, having internalized dominant-group standards, have become ambivalent or downright hostile toward the minority culture and now strive to be like the members of the dominant group. Other minority members strive to pass. Still others, although not striving to pass into the dominant group as such, are striving to be more acceptable to it so that they may be admitted into nonethnic and nonreligious groups in which dominant-group members participate and have power. Of this last category of minority members, some have also internalized dominant-group standards: they have a double motive for striving to be like members of the dominant group.

10 The literature on minority problems is vast. For one guide to it, see G. W. Allport, 1954

Conferral of superiority

The third kind of relation to a reference group requires little explanation. If whites as a status group are a reference group for Negroes, so, especially in the South, are Negroes a reference group for whites—with this difference, that the whites strive to remain *unlike* the Negroes. For some whites, there is a satisfaction just in being "white," but this satisfaction is possible only with reference to the nonwhite group. This kind of relation to a reference group merges into the next kind (simple comparison). The difference is that in the South, and in the North to some extent, whites not only compare their status with that of Negroes but also strive to preserve the difference. The status of being a "white" is not merely a matter of possessing "white" skin; it involves superiority in prestige ranking In this sense, the whites could lose their status without losing their white skin. Consequently, they strive to distinguish themselves from Negroes by retaining privileges.

Although it is reinforced by interaction between Negroes and whites, the "conferral of superiority" upon whites as a result of their taking Negroes as a reference group is analytically independent of interaction. A Negro in a small Southern town won a big new automobile in a radio contest. When he drove around town in it, many whites, including some with equally big cars, with old cars, or with no car at all, were indignant. The satisfaction they derived from merely *knowing* that Negroes are "inferior" was being threatened. Southern whites derive satisfaction from the flowery names that some Negroes give their children: this satisfaction is based on the mere knowledge that so "naïve" a group as the Negroes exists in the same society. If a white happened to like one of these names, he would avoid giving it to one of his own children: he would not wish to be like a Negro.

In the Coast Guard Academy, which trains officers in a four-year course, the "swabs" are warned against looking like "reserves." For Academy men, the reserve officers ("ninety-day wonders") are a reference group. (See Dornbusch, 1955, p. 33.)

Simple comparison

Even when there is no striving to be like or unlike a reference group, or to be admitted into it, contemplation of the reference group may have important consequences for the morale of the group whose action is being analyzed. For example, privates in units whose officers shared hardship with them were found to be less critical of officers in general than were men in units whose officers avoided hardship as much as possible (Stouffer *et al.*, 1949, v. 1, p. 181).

More noncombat troops still in the United States said they were "usually in good spirits" than did noncombat troops overseas. More noncombat troops still in the United States thought that "the Army is run pretty well" or "very well." The differences in response between the two groups, however, were slight, because both groups took as a reference group combat troops, in comparison with whom their own situation was good. Here we have an example of two reference groups with *conflicting* influences: with reference to noncombat troops at home, the noncombat troops overseas felt "worse off," but with reference to combat troops they felt "better off." [11]

One might expect Negro troops stationed in the North to have higher morale than Negro troops stationed in the South, where Negroes are generally treated as inferior. But the reverse was found to be true (Merton and Kitt, 1950, pp. 43-45). With reference to Negro civilians in the South, the Negro troops stationed there felt that they "had a position of comparative wealth and dignity" (Stouffer *et al.*, 1949, v. 1, p. 563). The corresponding reference group for Negro troops stationed in the North consisted of Negro civilians in the North, many of whom had relatively high-paying jobs in war industries, along with freedom from regimentation and combat risk. Since objectively the Negro troops stationed in the North were probably better off than those stationed in the South, we must conclude that the influence of reference groups was stronger than the influence of "objective" conditions.

A combination of types

One of the studies made by the Research Branch of the War Department during World War II, on certain aspects of morale, obtained results that at first seemed difficult to interpret. Three groups were asked the same questions. One group consisted of "green" troops in green outfits; the second, of green replacements in divisions with combat veterans; and the third, of the veterans in the latter divisions. In answer to a question, 45 per cent of the green troops in green outfits expressed willingness to go on combat duty. Only 15 per cent of the veterans, in answer to the same question, expressed a willingness for combat, as did 28 per cent of the green replacements in the divisions with these veterans. The replacements were no greener than the green troops in green outfits: why were fewer of them willing to go into combat?

Asked about their willingness to take charge of an outfit in combat, the veterans were most willing, the green troops in green outfits were next, and the green replacements were least willing. Why the reversal of position between the green troops and the combat veterans?

In answer to a third question—whether the men thought that they were in good physical condition—the green replacements and the green troops in green outfits showed no difference: a higher percentage of both groups than of the veterans' group said that they were in good physical condition. Was this result at variance with the results of the two previous questions?

The results on the third question were probably due in large part to an objective difference between the veterans and the green troops. After com-

[11] The concept of *conflicting* reference groups is taken from Merton and Kitt, 1950. They also discuss *mutually sustaining* reference groups, with examples.

bat experience, it is probable that fewer of the veterans *were* in good physical condition. But objective differences hardly account for the results on the first two questions: the replacements and the troops in green outfits were equally green, and yet they answered differently from each other and differently for the two questions.

By this time, the reader can probably apply the concept ot reference group for himself. If we assume that the green troops wanted to be like combat veterans (an assumption for which the Research Branch studies as a whole provide ample support); then we can explain the results on the first question (willingness for combat) without difficulty. The combat veterans, having proved their manhood and lost any romantic conceptions they may have had, were not eager to go into combat again. But the green troops in green outfits imagined that a "real soldier" would express willingness to go into combat. The green replacements, having had a better chance to learn the true attitude of combat veterans, answered more nearly like them than did the green troops in green outfits. It is also possible that the replacements had learned from the veterans what combat is like and had become less enthusiastic about it. This example illustrates the fact that conception of the reference group may or may not be realistic.

The results of the second question (willingness to take charge) can be interpreted as an example of two different kinds of behavior in relation to reference groups. The green replacements were influenced by a *simple comparison* between themselves and the combat veterans in their own divisions: in comparison with these seasoned men, the replacements felt themselves less capable of taking charge. Indeed, in so far as the replacements wished to gain acceptance by the combat veterans—whose prestige was relatively high—they had to be careful. In expressing a willingness to take charge when there were combat veterans in their own divisions, they would have been claiming, or seeming to claim, not merely equality with combat veterans but, worse still, superiority over them. Therefore, of the three groups, the replacements were the most modest about expressing willingness to take charge in combat.

For the combat veterans, in turn, the reference group was the group of green replacements in their own divisions. In comparison with these green troops, the combat veterans were conscious of their greater experience. They were also, perhaps, ready to claim superiority by emphasizing implicitly their dissimilarity to the green troops. The combat veterans, therefore, were the most willing of the three groups to take charge in combat.

The green troops in green outfits were in a different position. Their reference group was probably the general status group of combat veterans—seasoned men, "real" soldiers—whom, presumably, they wished to be like. At the same time, they were not inhibited by having combat veterans in their own outfits. The green troops in green outfits, therefore, emulating their conception of "real" soldiers but also conscious of their own lack of experience, were willing to take charge, but somewhat less so than the combat veterans.

The motive of showing appropriate modesty in relation to the reference group may have been involved in their answers to the question about physical condition. As we remarked, the green troops probably *were* in better physical condition on the average. But if so, the reason was that they had not been worn down in combat. These soldiers, then, might have regarded poor physical condition as a badge of honor. Green troops, both those in all-green outfits and those among veterans, might have been reluctant to claim that they were *not* in good physical condition lest they appear to minimize or deny the greater hardships of the veterans' experience (Merton and Kitt, 1950, pp. 70-78).

In all these examples of the influence of reference groups, the general hypothesis is borne out that "some similarity in status attributes between the individual and the reference group must be perceived or imagined in order for the comparison to occur at all" (Merton and Kitt, 1950, p. 61). The social structure itself largely determines which groups will have influence as reference groups in a particular situation. But this "determination" is not so obvious that an observer can in all cases predict, for a particular group, what other groups its members will take as reference groups. Indeed, a good deal of research remains to be done to find out what factors determine which of a person's *membership* groups serve as reference groups, and in what situations. The studies reported have not gone so far as one might wish, but they do open up problems that are not incapable of solution by known methods (Merton, 1957, Chap. 9).

In the present context, reference groups are interesting chiefly for their effects on the conformity and morale of groups. The study of reference groups shows how institutionalized patterns impinge differently upon different groups and how, in turn, these groups affect one another's attitudes toward their own group and its norms.

It will perhaps be helpful to compare the concept of reference group with the pair of concepts "in-group" and "out-group." As we have noted, a reference group may be either a membership group or a nonmembership group. Obviously there is some resemblance between the pair of concepts "membership reference group" and "nonmembership reference group," on one hand, and the pair of concepts "in-group" and "out-group," on the other. From the point of view of Negro troops, Negro civilians are a nonmembership reference group, and yet both groups belong to the status group "Negroes." In general terms, the members of one group and the members of one of its nonmembership reference groups may all belong to a third group. Similarly, Negroes and whites in an army division belong to the same in-group when they are fighting shoulder to shoulder against a common enemy; yet in many interactions between a white and a Negro in the United States, each is a member of the out-group from the point of view of the other.

There are also *differences* between the pair of concepts "membership reference group" "nonmembership reference group" and the pair "in-group" "out-group."

First, the members of an in-group are always relatively hostile, or at any rate less friendly, toward the members of the out-group. The term "in-group" stresses the "we-ness" or solidarity of the group as against outsiders. But, as we have seen, the members of one group may not be at all hostile toward their nonmembership reference group or groups. The green troops were probably not hostile toward combat veterans, whom they admired and tried to be like. In another example, we found that minority-group members are sometimes hostile toward their *own* group. The two pairs of concepts focus attention on different aspects of the relations between groups.

Secondly, a reference group is always a clearly defined interaction group or status group, but an out-group is frequently just a residual category. In relation to Christians (as in-group), *all* non-Christians belong to the out-group.

Finally, the terms "in-group" and "out-group" stress the fact that members of the first treat fellow members better than they treat "members" of the out-group, whereas there is not necessarily any interaction at all between a group and the members of one of its nonmembership reference groups.

RECOMMENDED READING

The best treatment of institutionalization and social institutions is to be found in the works of Talcott Parsons, especially *The Social System,* Free Press, 1951, pp. 36-45, and *Essays in Sociological Theory,* rev. ed., Free Press, 1954, *passim* (see the index). G. C. Homans, *English Villagers of the Thirteenth Century,* Harvard University Press, 1942, esp. Chaps. 8 and 9, is valuable because it gives details of concrete situations in which institutionalized patterns of inheritance were used as guides.

On role conflict, see the two articles referred to in the text: S. A. Stouffer, "An Analysis of Conflicting Social Norms," *Amer. sociol. Rev.,* Dec. 1949, v. 14, pp. 707-17 (on the proctor-student role conflict); and J. W. Getzels and E. G. Guba, "Role, Role Conflict, and Effectiveness: An Empirical Study," *Amer. sociol. Rev.,* April 1954, v. 19, pp. 164-75 (on Air University). These studies are also examples of good research design.

Our discussion of role-sets is based, with little change, on R. K. Merton, *Social Theory and Social Structure,* rev. ed., Free Press, 1957, pp. 370-80. For a good research report using the concept of role-set, see M. J. Huntington, "The Development of a Professional Self-Image," in R. K. Merton, G. G. Reader, M. D., and P. L. Kendall, eds., *The Student-Physician: Introductory Studies in the Sociology of Medical Education,* Harvard University Press, 1957, pp. 179-87.

On reference groups, see R. K. Merton and A. S. Kitt, "Contributions to the Theory of Reference Group Behavior," in R. K. Merton and P. F. Lazarsfeld, eds., *Continuities in Social Research: Studies in the Scope and Method of "The American Soldier,"* Free Press, 1950, pp. 40-105 (reprinted as Chap. 8 in Merton, 1957). For a concise account of the activities of the Research Branch of the War Department during World War II, with summaries of several important studies, see S. A. Stouffer, "A Study of Attitudes," *Scientific American*, May 1949, v. 180, pp. 11-15, reprinted in R. Freedman *et al.*, 1952, pp. 33-43. Merton and Kitt, 1950, is an analysis of parts of the Research Branch work.

The most detailed discussion of reference groups is Merton, 1957, Chap. 9. An excellent paper, somewhat abstract but clear, is R. H. Turner, "Role-Taking, Role Standpoint, and Reference-Group Behavior," *Amer. J. Sociol.*, Jan. 1956, v. 61, pp. 316-28. For an account of the effects of bilingualism among some minority-group members, describing attempts to conceal a foreign accent and become more like the dominant group in speech, see J. H. S. Bossard, *The Sociology of Child Development*, rev. ed., Harper, 1954, pp. 204-17. E. V. Stonequist, *The Marginal Man*, Scribner's, 1957 gives many examples of striving for admission into the dominant group as a reference group. (A "marginal man" is one who is not fully at home in either of two groups to which he belongs—partly because of his own ambivalence, partly because his membership in one or both of the groups is very insecure. Many minority-group members are marginal men). G. Myrdal, with the assistance of R. Sterner and A. Rose. *An American Dilemma: The Negro Problem and Modern Democracy*, Harper, 1944. v. 1, pp. 683-88, shows that "racial" traits are not the only barriers to "passing." For estimates of the number of Negroes who pass as whites in the United States, see J. H. Burma, "The Measurement of Negro 'Passing,'" *Amer. J. Sociol.*, July 1946, v. 52, pp. 18-22; and E. W. Eckard, "How Many Negroes 'Pass'?" *Amer. J. Sociol.*, May 1947, v. 52, 498-500.

3. *Structure and Function*

The social interaction of all the people of the United States during one minute would be impossible to describe and difficult to imagine. The welter of facts would be overwhelming. There are, however, various ways of simplifying without distorting very much. One way is to deal with *samples* of facts rather than with all the relevant facts. There is no escape from the necessity of using samples; we can only seek to become more aware of possible distortion and try to forestall it by making our samples as representative as possible. In this chapter, however, we shall be concerned with another way of simplifying the study of social interaction—namely, by using concepts that help to determine which facts are more relevant than others.

Two such concepts are "structure" and "function." Structure and function are complementary concepts: full understanding of either depends upon an understanding of the other. We shall begin with structure, which we have already considered to some extent.

Structural Aspects of Social Systems

The "structure" of anything consists of the relatively stable interrelationships among its parts; moreover, the term "part" itself implies a certain degree of stability. Since a social system is composed of the interrelated acts of people, its structure must be sought in some degree of regularity or recurrence in these acts. As we have seen, the participants in a social system can be thought of as occupants of roles. Note that in "permanent" groups roles persist beyond the occupancy of any particular person; that is, roles are more "stable" than the role occupants themselves. Moreover, role occupants are organized in subgroups within the larger system, and some of these subgroups persist longer than any particular members. Many other subgroups persist as *types* longer than any particular example of the type. This is true, for example, of families.

As we have pointed out, roles, and also subgroups to some extent, are normatively defined. It would be manifestly untrue to say that all the stability, regularity, and recurrence that can be observed in social interaction are due to normative patterning; nevertheless, we shall say that roles and subgroups of various types are the "parts" of social structure to the extent that stability, regularity, and recurrence in social interaction are due to the social norms that define roles and the obligations of subgroups.

This is a first approximation. We shall later consider certain quasi-structural aspects of social systems. But first we have to say a little more about the structural interrelations of roles and subgroups. As we have noted, the very concepts of role and subgroup imply interrelationship. Any role occupant is expected to fulfill obligations to other people (who are also role occupants), and the interrelations of subgroups are also subject to social norms. Social structure, however, includes more than the norms we have mentioned thus far.

The norms of a social system may be divided roughly into two classes. Some norms specify positive obligations. These norms usually differentiate among roles and among subgroups. Thus the positive obligations of a family are not the same as those of a business concern; the positive obligations of a father are not the same as those of a son. Norms of the other class specify the limits of *permissible* rather than obligatory action. A role occupant or subgroup "must" do certain things, "may" do certain others, and "must not" do still others.

Norms of the first class (obligatory) may be called "relational," since they specify the positive content of relations between role occupants and between subgroups. Norms of the second class (permissive) may be called "regulative." Regulative norms do not differentiate between roles and between subgroups to the same extent as do relational norms. In the United States, for example, more or less regardless of one's role, one "must not" seek to influence another by threats of violence, still less by violence itself. At least, use of these possible means of influence is normatively regulated rather strictly.

In addition to relational and regulative norms, we must include cultural values in social structure. Few concepts have been more diversely treated than the concept of value.[1] "Value" may be defined as a conception or standard, cultural or merely personal, by which things are compared and approved or disapproved relative to one another—held to be relatively desirable or undesirable, more meritorious or less, more or less correct. All kinds of "things" may be evaluated: feelings, ideas, actions, qualities, objects, persons, groups, goals, means.

All values are "cathected"; that is, the individual (or group, if the value is a cultural one) is emotionally committed to the relevant standards—i.e., accepts them and uses them, to some extent, in making choices and in judging things. In particular cases, however, there may be a conflict between values and other, more specific desires: "Disvalued activities are cathected

[1] For a survey of discussions, see Kluckhohn *et al.*, 1951; and Parsons and Shils, eds., 1951, pp. 159-89.

(despite values). People are strongly attracted to adulterous relationships. Conversely, a man goes to church on Sunday when (apart from the value element) he would strongly prefer to start his golf game early" (Kluckhohn *et al.,* 1951, p. 399). For conflict to take place, there must be cathexis of the value as well as of the activity with which the value is in conflict. Values help to integrate a personality or a system of social interaction. They provide a means by which conflicts tend to be forestalled or resolved, but some conflicts of course persist: probably no system of action is perfectly integrated.

There are different kinds of value, corresponding to different spheres of activity, different aspects of life. The Greeks distinguished the good, the true, and the beautiful; most classifications are similar to theirs. Without cognitive standards, we should not be able to decide between conflicting ideas, and we should be unable to agree on what is true. The "beautiful" is the aesthetic sphere in a broad sense: the sphere of the expression of feeling, of "feeling and form." [2] The "good" has to do with morality, with harmonizing the rights of others with one's own wishes.

All values imply a cognitive element, however, in that one's conception of what is desirable depends upon one's conception of what *is* and of what is possible.

> To take an almost absurd but clear example: In their conceptions of a desirable state of affairs people do not postulate conditions under which the law of gravity ceases to operate, the threats and irritations of climatic variations disappear completely, or food and drink appear spontaneously ready for consumption [Kluckhohn *et al.,* 1951, p. 392].

Obviously values are closely related to norms—so closely that one might ask what the difference is. A sufficiently broad sense of "norm" would eliminate any difference. In general, however, we shall use the term "norm" for a relatively specific pattern of expected behavior. Unusual intelligence, for example, is valued in the occupants of almost any social role, but obviously it can be required in relatively few. Women in our society are not expected to be very brave physically, but a brave woman is admired. Values are general standards and may be regarded as higher-order norms. Norms themselves may be evaluated; so may behavior conforming to two different norms, both of which are accepted. Being a foreman is "better" than being an ordinary worker, yet both jobs are respectable. "[A man] may turn down promotion to foreman because the job has too many 'headaches,' but he will concede that this job is somehow, on an absolute scale, better than his own" (Homans, 1950, p. 128).

In addition to social structure, there are cultural patterns of knowledge, belief, cathexis, evaluation, and overt action that may not be clearly normative but still are more or less standardized and stable and contribute to the regularity of social interaction. Some religious beliefs, for example, are

---

[2] The title of a book by Susanne Langer, 1953

clearly institutionalized within subgroups such as the Roman Catholic Church, but the same or similar beliefs affect the behavior of many people who are not members of any organized religious group, and there are other beliefs that are not sanctioned at all and yet are influential.

The structure of a social system, then, includes the following:

1. Subgroups of various types, interconnected by relational norms.
2. Roles of various types, within the larger system and within the subgroups. Each role system is also connected with others, of course, through relational norms.
3. Regulative norms governing subgroups and roles.
4. Cultural values.

Any one of these elements—a type of subgroup, a role, a social norm, or a value—may be called a "partial structure."

In order to prevent misunderstanding, we must emphasize the relative nature of social structure. Norms are never perfectly institutionalized, as we have pointed out. Moreover, even if a norm is accepted, it may not be followed on every possible occasion. Thus any description of social structure is likely to be a simplification of reality to some extent. To *what* extent will depend upon the care with which the description takes account of the quantitative aspects of institutionalization and the amount of deviation from institutionalized patterns. Not only is there deviation in role performance, but any large social system is likely to have within it some subgroups that are actually organized according to norms that violate the regulative norms of the larger social system. If we are describing the structure of the larger system, such criminal subgroups will be treated as deviant. (Criminality is not the only form of social deviation, but there is no need to distinguish other forms here.) All forms of deviation obviously have to be defined and analyzed in relation to some standard. The social structure, as we have defined it, is the standard by which we define social deviation.[3]

Functional Problems of Social Systems

In a famous passage in his *Leviathan* (1651), Thomas Hobbes wrote of the scarcity of some things relative to the number of people who would like to have them; although men are unequal in natural endowments and learning, he said, they are equal in hope. Hobbes meant that almost all men strive to gain possession of the scarce valuable things around them. In a "state of nature" (that is, in a hypothetical state of social life without regulative norms), the struggle for power, with individuals and coalitions pitted against one another to gain supremacy, would be rather bitter; as Hobbes said, the life of man would be "poor, nasty, brutish, and short." No one could feel secure in his possession of anything.

If organization and stability are to characterize social life at all, there

---

[3] For a more detailed discussion of social structure, see Parsons, 1951, pp. 114-50.

is a "need," we might say, for some mitigation of this inherent struggle for power. We do in fact find in all societies some norms defining property rights, limiting the means men may use to influence one another, and regulating the settlement of disputes. Just as *scarcity* and the *struggle for power* are universal, so are *property* rights and *authority*.

The "need" we are discussing as an example is a *social* need. It arises, not in the nature of the individual organism, but in social interaction. This point, although obvious, is sometimes overlooked; people speak as if property and government arose somehow from an inborn "drive" to power. It is no doubt true that some men seek power, and that some of them seek to enter (or become) the government; in that sense, a drive to power, whether inborn or not, is indeed related to the existence of government. But government, in the sense of a certain kind of organization, established and functioning to some extent according to norms, is not only an expression of a drive to power and a field for the exercise of power; it also serves to some extent to regulate the struggle for power, of governed and governors *both*.

The social "need" to regulate the struggle for power does not necessarily produce cultural patterns of property and authority. There are many cases of social interaction—between nations, for example—in which commonly accepted property norms and authority hardly figure at all. These cases of social interaction are not striking, however, for cooperation and stability.

The concept of "social need" is definitely not intended to explain the existence of cultural patterns. But if there were no scarcity there would be no property rights. In that sense, scarcity *is* a partial explanation of the existence of property rights. Moreover, if there were no recognized property rights, there would be no cooperative, organized, and stable social interaction. Only in that sense is there a "social need" for property norms. No scarcity, no property; no property, no society. The concept of social need does not necessarily imply a value judgment. To speak of the social need for recognized property rights is merely one way of asserting that *if* a society is to exist, there must be recognized property rights. The concept does not imply that any *particular* property norms are desirable or indispensable.

There are some needs that every group, whatever its type, must fulfill, and some that every group of a particular type—for example, the personnel of a library—must fulfill. The circumstances of any particular society present problems that to some extent are peculiar to that society, although they may be particularized examples of needs that every society must meet. Thus Israel cannot survive without help from other countries, whereas the United States conceivably could; yet the United States, like any other society, also has the general problem of adjusting itself to its environment, social and nonsocial.

Broadly speaking, every social system must solve four functional problems. They have been given the following names: (1) pattern maintenance and tension management, (2) adaptation, (3) goal attainment and (4) integration.[4] Also broadly speaking, the social structure of every system *does* to some extent solve these problems; if it did not, the system would cease to exist as an independent or distinctive entity. When we say that the social structure solves problems, we mean, of course, that action in conformity with a social norm or value makes some contribution toward meeting the "needs" of the system. When conformity to any partial structure makes such a contribution, that structure is said to have a "function" for the system. Before analyzing this concept of function, however, we must try to make clear what the four functional problems or "needs" of a social system are.

PATTERN MAINTENANCE AND TENSION MANAGEMENT

The patterns of a social system—its social structure—must be maintained in the sense that the units of the system, whether role occupants or subgroups, must learn the patterns and invest them with the appropriate attitude of respect. Thus any social system must have mechanisms of "socialization"—the process by which cultural patterns come to be incorporated in the personalities of system members (see Chap. 5). Moreover, once they are learned, cultural patterns have to be renewed, so to speak, through appropriate rituals and other symbols.

As for tension management, the units of any social system are subject to emotional disturbances and distractions, which must be "managed" if the units are to be able to carry on effectively. One of the functions of the family, for example, is to keep its members in good working order by relieving anxiety, providing encouragement, and caring for minor physical ailments.

ADAPTATION

Any social system must be adapted to its social and nonsocial environment. As far as the society is concerned, the economy meets this need. It partly controls the environment, partly adjusts to it. But every "permanent" social system, even one smaller than a total society, has its division of labor. For the production of goods and services, role differentiation seems to be necessary. Even if every person could acquire the knowledge and skill necessary for the performance of diverse tasks, there would still have to be role differentiation, for no one person could perform simultaneously all the tasks that have to be so performed. There is no need to insist upon the fact that role differentiation also makes possible a higher average degree of skill than would otherwise be possible.

GOAL ATTAINMENT

Every social system has one or more goals to be attained through cooperative effort. Perhaps the best example of a societal goal is national se-

---

[4] This list, in virtually the same form, was first developed by Robert F. Bales for the analysis of small groups. It has been further discussed by Parsons, Bales and Shils, 1953, pp. 183-86; Parsons, 1953, esp. pp. 395-97, 415-39; and Parsons and Smelser, 1956, pp. 46-51 *et passim*.

curity. Adaptation to the social and nonsocial environment is, of course, necessary if goals are to be attained. But, in addition, human and nonhuman resources must be mobil zed in some effective way, according to the specific nature of tasks. For example, there must be a process for ensuring that enough persons, but not too many, occupy each of the roles at a particular time, and a process for determining which persons will occupy which roles. These processes together solve the problem of allocation of members in the social system. We have already touched upon the "need" for property norms. The rules regulating inheritance—e.g., primogeniture—in part solve this problem.

The allocation of members and the allocation of scarce valuable resources are important, of course, for both adaptation and goal attainment. The difference between adaptation and goal attainment is a relative one. The economy of a society is that subsystem which produces goods and services for a wide variety of purposes; the "polity," which includes above all the government in complex societies, mobilizes goods and services for the attainment of specific goals of the total society regarded as a single social system. A business firm, for example, may have the *goal* of producing steel. This goal is *adaptive* for the society, since steel can be used for many purposes, including many that are purposes of other business firms, not of the total society. The adaptive problem of a particular steel company, as distinguished from its goal, is to adjust to the government and to competing firms and to provide itself with the necessary raw materials for its productive goals.

INTEGRATION

Whereas pattern maintenance and tension management have to do with the state of the units of a system, integration has to do with the interrelations of units. To some extent, the members of a system must be loyal to one another and to the system as a whole. This is a problem of solidarity and morale. Morale is important for both integration and pattern maintenance. Morale is closely related to common values. But it is more specific. It is the willingness to give oneself to specific undertakings. Poor morale is the lack of this willingness. In day-to-day routine living, the goals and interests of a whole society are less present in the minds of most of its members than are the goals of (smaller) subgroups. But there are sometimes crises, such as war, that demand widespread "giving" if the society is to survive as an independent group. The philosopher William Ernest Hocking has written about morale so fittingly that we shall borrow three short quotations.

> Morale is a character of the will in reference to a particular undertaking (either of one's own or of outside suggestion); it is a measure of one's disposition to give one's self to the objective in hand. It thus belongs to the region of the little-explored activity of "giving," in that deeper, idiomatic sense in which the producer of a play calls on an actor to "give" [1941, pp. 303-04].

> Even in a slave gang or in a prison shop where structural democracy is at zero there is a more-or-less of morale for the current performance; the amount and quality of the product depend on the level of that morale, quite as much as do the quality and amount of the product of a group of field hands. It is a democratic element because it cannot be compelled; it can only be offered by the workers. The modern dictator is dependent on it and knows that fact [p. 308].

> Giving implies intelligent teamwork, frictionless acceptance of division of labor with whatever subordination of one's own role is involved, and obedience to the agreed source of direction. With a good group morale, the members spontaneously use "we" as the author of the group action [p. 312].

Cooperative activities obviously require decision-making and a hierarchy of authority (legitimate power to give orders). The need for regulative norms is also fairly obvious. Among the most effective means of influencing others, in the short run, are force and fraud. If these means were not regulated, the "state of nature" imagined by Hobbes would soon be a reality. Property norms are also regulative to some extent (one must not infringe on others' property rights). Another area in which regulative norms are necessary is the expression of affects (feelings) of all kinds. The need for regulation is obvious for negative affects such as hate and envy, but regulation of positive affects is also necessary (one must not invade the rights of others in attachments such as marriage).

As we have seen, in almost every social system, and in every system as large as a society, some participants, including whole subgroups, violate the relational or regulative norms. So far as these norms meet social needs, violations are a threat to the social system. The need for "social control" is the need for standardized reactions to violations in order to protect the integrity of the system. When there is dispute concerning the interpretation of relational or regulative norms, or concerning the factual aspects of conflicts of interest, there is need for agreed-upon social arrangements for settling the dispute. Otherwise the social system would be subject to progressive splits.

In a broad sense, of course, all institutionalized patterns are integrative. The integrative problem, as distinguished from the pattern-maintenance problem, allows for the fact that some partial structures are more clearly and more nearly exclusively integrative than others. Patterns of authority, for example, obviously coordinate or integrate the social relations of a cooperative group, whereas patterns of socialization merely *prepare* individuals to fit into such groups. Even if the members of a group are fully socialized, their interaction from day to day will still have to be coordinated in relation to changing specific tasks and circumstances. Moreover, even if the primary relational or prescriptive norms of the group are well institutionalized, a problem—or, rather, numerous problems—of integration will still arise. In the first place, every social system permits its members some freedom to pursue "self-interested" goals within limits. Many transactions, while quite legitimate, involve more or less latent conflicts of interest, and there must be mechanisms for counteracting such elements of conflict with some emphasis on solidarity or on interests that transcend the conflict. We have briefly analyzed contractual relations, in which the integrative elements are perhaps especially important since the conflict of interest is especially and explicitly prominent.

Detailed analysis of social interaction shows that the pursuit of common goals inevitably produces, as a kind of cost or by-product, a considerable amount of personal friction. In focusing upon the task in hand, members of the group tend to subordinate whatever comfortable feelings of good fellowship they may have for one another; they forget to be tactful; they inevitably ruffle the vanity of some whose suggestions or contributions to the task performance have to be rejected or criticized. Here, then, with the best morale to begin with, we nevertheless find threats to integration as a normal accompaniment of cooperation itself. There must, therefore, be mechanisms for restoring solidarity. Such mechanisms are normally operative most of the time, but there is also a tendency for task performance to proceed in a cycle, with a phase of relatively great emphasis on adaptive problems, followed by a phase of relatively great emphasis on goal attainment, followed by an integrative phase, in which the members pick up the broken peace, so to speak (see Bales, 1955).[5]

Finally, no matter how well-institutionalized the norms are, there are virtually always deviant tendencies, which may be disruptive; consequently, there is need for "secondary" mechanisms of social control—secondary in the sense that they back up the fundamental structure of the group and would be meaningless without that structure to start with. In a modern state, the whole apparatus for apprehension and rehabilitation of criminals exemplifies secondary mechanism. In a religious context, confession and penance are examples of such mechanisms.

Levels of Social Structure

The structure of every social system can be analyzed in relation to these four functional problems. In any functional analysis it is important to bear in mind the fundamental rule that *partial structures have functions* (when they do) *for a system of which they are part*. If the only social system superordinate to a particular business firm is the total society, then the business firm, as a partial structure, must have functions (if it has functions)

[5] Homans has dealt with the same phenomenon in somewhat different terms. He speaks of the primarily adaptive and goal-directed activities as organized by the "external system," whereas the integrative, seemingly aimless activities are organized by the "internal" system. Much of the "horsing around" of the informal groups within the bank-wiring room was integrative (part of the so-called "internal system"). Moreover, there was a marked tendency, as Homans notes, for the work to be done intensively during the first part of the day, while the "playing" was done intensively for the rest of the day. Of course, the external and internal systems were interdependent. (See Homans, 1950, pp. 150-55 *et passim.*)

for the total society as the system of reference; it would be inappropriate to speak of the firm as having functions for one of its own parts. On the other hand, it would be quite appropriate to speak of the functions of the research department for the business firm of which it is a part; in this case, the business firm is the system of reference. If this principle of hierarchy is not followed, the functional analysis will run into hopeless confusion.

If the society is the system of reference, then the subsystems immediately subordinate are "functional subsystems of the society." Below that level would be particular groups. Cutting across these two levels are what might be called "structural subsystems of the society."

FUNCTIONAL SUBSYSTEMS

Since a society is a social system, it has the four problems of pattern maintenance and tension management, adaptation, goal attainment, and integration. For each of these problems there will be a corresponding "functional subsystem of the society." Such a subsystem, however, is exceedingly abstract; it is not a solidary social system in the sense we have understood thus far. For example, the "economy" is the functional subsystem that deals with the adaptive problem of the society. But this "economy" is not composed of a definite number of groups, each of which is exclusively an "economic" group. It is not, for example, made up of business firms exclusively; for if we define the economy as the subsystem that produces goods and services (more technically, the subsystem that produces "utility" for the society), then obviously families also produce goods and services and are thus part of the economy. Moreover, business firms are not exclusively economic organizations, for they also make contributions to the solution of the other three "problems" of the society. (Business firms are, however, *primarily* economic organizations, just as families, although partly economic and partly integrative and partly involved in the goal-attainment subsystem of the society, are primarily units in the pattern-maintenance system.) It should be clear that the "economy" is not a solidary group, even though it is in some sense a functional subsystem of the society. One may boast of being an American, but one does not go around boasting that one belongs to the economy.

The economy is the *adaptive* subsystem of the society in the sense that it produces goods and services that can be used for a wide variety of purposes—purposes of the government, of families, of business organizations, and of groups of other types. In this sense, the function of the economy is production of highly *generalized* "facilities." (In a primarily economic context, such scarce valuable things as factories, railroads, and raw materials are called "facilities." In a general sense, however, anything that is valued primarily as a means is a facility.) These generalized facilities produced by the economy solve the adaptive problem of the society by providing the society and its units with the means of coping with almost any exigency, of attaining any goal. Of course, the system problem of adaptation is never perfectly "solved," nor is any other system problem. In the adaptive subsystem, business firms have clear primacy.

With respect to the problem of pattern maintenance and tension management, the family is clearly primary. It is the main socializing agency of the society. It also plays a part, as we have noted, in the day-to-day management of tension, thus equipping and "freeing" its members psychologically for participation in a wide variety of roles in society. The responsibility for pattern maintenance is also borne, notably, by schools, religious groups, and recreational groups. Hospitals and other health organizations, as well as recreational and religious groups, play a part in tension management.

As for goal attainment, the government clearly has primacy in attempting to deal with this problem. A full analysis of the sense in which a society may be said to have goals would be rather complex. In our own society especially, there are few societal goals to which more than a minority of the population ever gives more than a passing thought—mainly because we delegate the task of goal attainment and even the responsibility for deciding what the goals shall be largely to the government. One of the basic functions of national election campaigns is to "engage" people in societal goal definition and attainment. Despite its primacy, the government is not *the* goal-attainment subsystem of society, for other groups also produce power for the attainment of system goals and even help more directly to attain them. Such, for example, are all pressure groups that mobilize public opinion or write model bills for Congress. The proper term for the goal-attainment subsystem is "the polity."

The integrative subsystem is the most diffuse of all. In our society, the legal profession is extremely important for its integrative function, but so are journalists and, to some extent, religious leaders. In general, it is likely that the action of every type of group in the society is functionally relevant to all four system problems; in some cases, the relevance to one or more problems may be slight.

According to theory, each of the functional subsystems of a society can itself be analyzed as a social system, with its own system problems. For each of these subsystems, the other subsystems are viewed as the most significant part of the "environment," and all the subsystems have systematic "interchanges" with one another.[6] Thus the households of the pattern-maintenance subsystem contribute labor to the economy in exchange for wages with which they can purchase goods and services and maintain a symbolically important style of life. If the system of reference for functional analysis is a *subgroup* within a society, then the rest of the society is treated as part of the "environment" to which the subgroup must adapt if it is to

---

[6] In *Economy and Society*, 1956, upon which this whole section is largely based, Parsons and Smelser analyze the economy as a social system and treat its interchanges with the pattern-maintenance system, the polity, and the integrative system.

survive and achieve its goals. It always happens that the cost of meeting societal problems is borne unequally by the subgroups of society. In our own society, for example, successful functioning of the economy requires that certain particular business firms must be allowed or "forced" to fail; otherwise the economy as a whole would be less adaptive than it is.

STRUCTURAL SUBSYSTEMS

A functional subsystem of society, as we have seen, is not composed of concrete groups; it is composed of all those aspects of the total social structure which have a bearing on *one* of the four functional problems of the society. A structural subsystem, on the other hand, is made up of concrete groups. The kinship system, for example, is made up of families, clans, lineages, etc. (see Chaps. 6, 7, 8); consequently, this system has a bearing on more than one of the functional problems of the society. It should go without saying that "concrete" groups may overlap with one another; consequently, although everyone participates in the kinship system, the kinship system is not the same thing as the concrete society. Many societies (but not all) have other structural subsystems in addition to the kinship system, such as a national educational system or a national church.

If a functional subsystem of society fails to coincide with concrete structures, the question might be asked, why go to the trouble of so much abstraction, why not simply analyze the functions of the concrete subgroups of the society? The answer is simple: it is precisely the abstractness of the concept of functional subsystem that makes the concept useful for comparing different societies. Most societies depend upon the kinship system for many more functions than does our society. In particular, kinship units are often the most important productive ("economic") units in the society. Our own society is remarkable for the degree to which the various functional subsystems are structurally differentiated from one another. Even in our society this structural differentiation, as we have seen, is far from complete. Analytically, however, every society—indeed, every interaction group of any kind—does have the four *functional* subsystems we have briefly described. One of the most important questions to ask about the structure of any society is, what kinds and degrees of structural differentiation and fusion does it have with respect to the four functional problems? The tendency, in primitive and so-called backward societies, to fuse pattern-maintenance and adaptive ("economic") functions in kinship groups is one of the basic reasons for economic traditionalism or stagnation in such societies. To take another example, the fusion of the polity and the economy in totalitarian societies means almost inevitably that economic production in those societies is subordinated to political purposes to a far greater extent than in our own society. Needless to say, it is not our purpose here to pass judgment on the relative merits of these different systems. They depend ultimately upon somewhat different value patterns. Consequently, one cannot rank them objectively as wholes; one can only compare them.

Quasi-structural Aspects of Social Systems

Earlier in this chapter we listed four elements in social structure: subgroups of various types, roles of various types, regulative norms, and cultural values. Five additional aspects of social systems are so closely related to social structure proper that we might call them quasi-structural.

1. *The number of subgroups of each distinct type, and the ratio between the number of subgroups of one type and the number of subgroups of closely related types.* For example, if we were describing an economic system, we should like to know not only what types of group it contains—proprietorships, partnerships, corporations, etc.—but also how many of each. (Needless to say, we might distinguish many more types and subtypes of "economic" group, but that is not our present concern.)

2. *The distribution of members among the subgroups of each type.* In analyzing a social system, we should consider not only the relative size of the various subgroups but also the overlapping of membership of different subgroups. If membership in one group is a prerequisite to membership in another, the resulting overlapping is, of course, a structural feature of the second group. But subgroups also overlap as a result of more indirect processes, and this overlapping may be important for each of the interaction systems involved. The activities of a political party, for example, are often affected by its religious composition, even though there may be no norm with regard to the religious affiliation of party members. Similarly, the activities of a religious group may be affected by the political affiliations of its members.

3. *The number of occupants of the various roles within the subgroups and within the system as a whole.* For some roles, of course, the number of occupants is normatively fixed; for example, the Supreme Court of the United States, when complete, has nine members by law. In other cases, however, the number of role occupants is determined by other factors. For example, why are there so many bachelors and spinsters in Ireland?

4. *The distribution of "facilities."* This aspect of social systems will require more explanation than the others. Among the most important norms of any society, as we have seen, are those commonly referred to as property rights (or "property" for short). Property is the whole pattern—often, as in our own society, extremely complex—of rights and obligations with respect to the possession, use, acquisition (and hence disposal) of scarce valuable things. (Note that the term "property" is used both for rights and for the things in which rights are held. The context should always make clear which reference is intended.) The relevant scarce valuable things are, of course, inherently transferable; one does not have a "right" to one's intelligence, for example. A moment's reflection will show that the complex of property norms is partly relational and at the same time wholly regulative. Note also, in passing, that the things in which an individual or subgroup may hold property

rights are not necessarily tangible. The right to intellectual property, for example, is recognized in most modern societies; this right is at the same time a regulative norm (thus, one "must not" plagiarize).

Property norms are partial structures in the strict sense that they are part of social structure proper. A compendium of the property laws of the United States would tell us nothing, however, about the actual *distribution* of property rights in scarce valuable "things" in the United States. The law would tell us what the rights of stockholders are, for example, but it would give us no idea how many individuals and subgroups, and which ones, actually own shares of stock. In the English villages of the thirteenth century, to which we have previously referred, the "custom of the manor" defined, among other things, the property patterns, or some of them; the *custumals*, or record books of the manorial stewards, contained a record of the distribution of landholdings among the villagers. John Smith, *villein*, was in rightful possession of such and such a yardland, for which he paid annual rent of such and such an amount.

This distinction between structural patterns and the distribution of specific property rights has to be refined still further. Some scarce valuable things are valued for their own sake, and some are valued merely as means for the attainment of other things. The ones that are valued primarily as means we have called facilities. The distribution of facilities, including intangible ones, such as the right to a certain job, is the fourth "quasi-structural" aspect of social systems. The distribution of the other kind of possessions is the fifth.

5. *The distribution of "rewards."* All the norms and values of a social system are standards by which people are judged. As we noted in Chapter 2, if a role occupant conforms to the norms for his role he tends to acquire a good reputation. Moreover, he is said to *deserve* a good reputation: he has a right to expect that others will approve of him. The same thing applies to subgroups.

People are valued, moreover, not only for what they *do* but for what they *are*, for the qualities they have. Thus a woman may be valued (admired or loved) because she is beautiful. As this example suggests, people and groups are not only evaluated, they are "cathected"—liked, disliked, loved, hated, respected, despised. All such specific valuations and cathexes, and all their tangible symbols, are "possessions." Such possessions (when they are positive) tend to be valued for their own sake, as distinguished from facilities, which are valued for their usefulness. The term "rewards" has been suggested for those possessions, tangible and intangible, that are intrinsically valued (Parsons, 1951, p. 127).[7]

The concept of "rewards" is similar to the concept of sanctions. Affection and respect (and their opposites) are partly sanctions of role perform-

[7] The term "rewards" may seem a little awkward, but it is difficult to think of a better one. "Reward" at least suggests something intrinsically valued and something that may be either tangible or intangible.

ance. As we noted in Chapter 2, however, a level of performance may be attained and stabilized, and with it a level of "reward." A mediocre physician may not receive great respect from his colleagues, but he may have come to take his status for granted. In this case, his colleagues' lack of respect is not only a sanction but a quasi-structural aspect of his relationship with them.

Moreover, some "rewards" cannot be regarded as sanctions at all A person who has "merit," in a narrow sense, has presumably put forth some effort and has performed well; but, in a broader sense, a perfect profile, for example, has "merit," even though it is hardly an achievement in most cases. The admiration aroused by native endowments is no less a "reward" than the admiration aroused by meritorious effort.

Rewards and facilities are not necessarily concretely different. The furnishings of a house have market value but they may also symbolize the attachment between husband and wife; in the latter sense, they are rewards. Despite the concrete overlapping of facilities and rewards, it is important to distinguish between them, for the elements in motivation differ according as the actor is interested in something as a facility or as a reward. Disguised as a male lawyer, Portia has just saved Bassanio's friend Antonio from death; now she maliciously puts Bassanio in a quandary by asking him to reward her with the very ring, in itself of little value as a "facility," that she in her proper person had given him as a token of her love, and that he had sworn never to part with.

Both facilities and rewards may be bases of power, which Weber has defined as "the probability that one actor (individual or group) within a social relationship will be in a position to carry out his own will despite resistance, regardless of the basis on which this probability rests." He goes on to say, "All conceivable qualities of a person and all conceivable combinations of circumstances may put him in a position to impose his will in a given situation" (Weber, 1947, pp. 152-53).

These statements show how broad a concept "power" is. Money and all more specific facilities, such as a newspaper or instruments of force, are bases of power. A person has power if someone loves him, for he will be able to induce the other to do things the other might prefer not to "have" to do: in other words, in this case, the loved person is "in a position to carry out his own will despite resistance." All sentiments and emotions, in oneself and others, are therefore in relevant circumstances bases of power. Power is broader than possessions (rewards and facilities). Not all bases of power are inherently transferable, whereas possessions are. One's physical strength, for example, is not transferable, but it is obviously a basis of power.

Putting together our lists of structural and quasi-structural aspects of social systems, we get the following composite list:

1. The number and size of subgroups of all types;
2. The overlapping of subgroups;
3. The number of occupants of roles of each type;

4. The distribution of facilities and rewards among types of subgroup among types of role, among specific subgroups of each type, and among specific occupants of each type of role;

5. Regulative norms (apart from the regulative aspects of relational norms);

6. Cultural values.

Social Functions and Dysfunctions

Any partial structure—a type of subgroup, a role, a social norm, or a cultural value—is said to have a *function* if it contributes to the fulfillment of one or more of the social needs of a social system or subsystem; any partial structure is said to have a *dysfunction* if it hinders the fulfillment of one or more of these needs.

Note that "function" is to be distinguished from purpose (see Merton, 1957, pp. 23-24). A purpose is something subjective—that is, something in the mind of the participant (or participants) in a social system. But a function (or dysfunction) is an objective consequence of action. When we attribute functions to a partial structure, we mean that action conforming to that partial structure has certain consequences for a social system, whatever the motives of the actor or actors may be. Motives are, of course, never irrelevant to action, but they are not the same thing as functions or dysfunctions.

Let us take the Chinese family as an example of a social system. In this system, a man upon marrying brings his wife to live in his father's already established household. The man's brothers and their wives and his and their children will also live in this household, although his sisters and daughters, when they marry, will have to leave to live with their husbands' families. A partial structure of this system—called a "patrilocal extended family," for reasons to be explained in Chapter 6—is the norm that the oldest male has authority over the other men in the group. Another partial structure is the norm that the men should contribute their earnings to the general coffers of the extended family and entrust them to the management of the family head. These norms are functional, for a goal of the extended family is to keep its lands intact and to increase its power; they help the family head to carry out his chief task, which is to manage things for the long-run interests of the family. Note that function and purpose here coincide, but only in the sense that the purpose is often fulfilled; many purposes, of course, are not.

In large-scale formal organizations of the "bureaucratic" type (see Chap. 12) occupants of high positions are ordinarily not removed before retirement age except for flagrant misconduct. (Sometimes they are "kicked upstairs.") We should make it clear that this pattern is not absolutely binding; it is a strong informal expectation rather than a formal rule of governmental or business bureaucracy. It may be taken as an example of a pattern that has both functions and dysfunctions.

Some of the dysfunctions are not hard to imagine. We shall mention only two. (1) In the course of time, many officials become less competent than they were when they were first appointed. Family troubles, sickness, and diminished energy due to increasing age tend to cut down efficiency gradually. The result is that at any particular moment a large organization does not have the most efficient distribution of available ability; there are younger men of superior ability who are not in the best position to use it. (2) The security of high offices tends to reduce the initiative not only of the holders of those offices but also of subordinates; merely routine administration may not be given the highest rewards, but it is not greatly discouraged. The combination of these and other consequences of permanent tenure of office makes the organization less adaptable to its environment than it might be. In business, for example, a company may continue in its old routines, fail to take advantage of new opportunities presented, say, by technological advance, and ultimately fail altogether.

As against these dysfunctions, security of tenure has at least three positive functions. (1) High status in an organization is an incentive to career men. But if high status were insecure, it would be less effective as an incentive. Men do not like not being promoted, but they like being demoted even less. (2) When a man is promoted to a high position in an organization, the promotion is given a good deal of publicity. There may be impressive ceremonies, in which the values and goals of the organization are prominently celebrated. Thus high offices tend to symbolize the organization as a whole. If there were frequent removals from high office, the prestige of the organization would suffer in the minds of the public; hence the competitive position of the organization would suffer. (3) Frequent removals of high officials would also adversely affect the morale of subordinates. If high officials symbolize the organization, and if high officials are frequently, in effect, declared incompetent, a general feeling might arise that the organization is not a good one to work for. This feeling would lower the self-esteem of subordinates and hence their morale.

More could be said about the difficulty of maintaining a net favorable balance between security of tenure and swift promotion of talent. Any change in the top executive staff of an organization involves at least a temporary diminution of efficiency. The new man, though possibly superior in ability to the old, will often be less effective at first. He will have to take time to learn the details of operations in progress, and he will have to establish social relations with his immediate superiors and subordinates. The system of communication will be disrupted. Moreover, the morale of any man who has been removed from high position is likely to be permanently crippled. Finally, although an ambitious man might feel a sense of injustice when he sees an inferior man in a higher position, his feeling will perhaps be tempered by the fact that, looking *down* the line of command, he will see at least one man more able than himself. Whether the net balance of functions and dysfunctions is favorable or unfavorable to the organization will depend upon circumstances. The need for adaptability is greater in some cases than in others. Moreover, we have considered only a few of the variable patterns of organization itself.[8]

Many partial structures of a social system have consequences for other partial structures of the same system. In this way, a partial structure may have indirect functions or dysfunctions. For example, to a large extent in our society the selection and advancement of personnel in government and industry are guided by the value that objective merit should be the main consideration. This value presumably has something to do with the efficiency of organizations. If objective merit is to play an important part in the allocation of personnel in the occupational system, obviously it is necessary that our society permit a great deal of freedom of mobility from place to place: mobility increases the field of choice for those who are making appointments. The wider the field of choice, the greater the scope for consideration of objective merit. At the same time, from the point of view of those seeking placement, the greater the competition, the greater must be their efforts to excel objectively.

In the light of these facts, we must conclude that the expectation in our kinship system that a newly married couple should, if possible, establish their own household—a rule technically known as "neolocal residence"—is a partial structure that helps to sustain the pattern of appointment on the basis of objective merit, for neolocal residence helps to make freedom of mobility possible. Thus a kinship pattern has an indirect function for the efficiency of "economic" and "political" groups.

A functional or dysfunctional partial structure may be called a "mechanism." Since a partial structure may be indirectly functional or dysfunctional, by sustaining or weakening some other partial structure that is functional or dysfunctional, obviously a partial structure may be in one aspect a mechanism, bringing about certain consequences for the social system, and in another aspect it may itself be a consequence (in part) of some mechanism or mechanisms.

We must be careful not to overgeneralize on the basis of the example involving neolocal residence, social mobility, and efficiency in the occupational sphere. Some anthropologists have asserted that societies are functionally integrated to such an extent that every partial structure contributes to the maintenance of the total structure. Merton, 1957, pp. 25ff., has pointed out the inadmissibility of this *a priori* assumption. In the first place, we cannot assume that every partial structure is functional or dysfunctional. Secondly, we cannot conclude that all the partial structures of a social system reinforce one another. Finally, a partial structure may sustain a second partial structure that is functional and also a third that is dysfunctional.

---

[8] Permanent tenure is much more common in nonprofit organizations than in business. In universities it helps to safeguard academic freedom. In addition, it partly compensates the personnel of nonprofit organizations for the relatively low salaries they receive. See Parsons and Smelser, 1956, pp. 154ff. Most of our analysis of tenure, however, has been taken from Barnard, 1946.

Another way in which a partial structure may have functions or dysfunctions for a social system or subsystem is by affecting any one of the quasi-structural aspects of the system (see pp. 60-62). A system of "regressive" taxation, for example, will tend to maintain the existing distribution of facilities; a system of "progressive" taxation will tend to change it. Obviously such effects will be functional or dysfunctional to the total social system in various ways, depending upon often conflicting needs.

Manifest and Latent Functions and Dysfunctions

"Manifest" functions are those that are intended and recognized; "latent" functions are unrecognized and unintended (Merton, 1957, p. 51). The incest taboo is a good example of a partial structure with latent functions. Perhaps the most common explanation of the taboo among non-sociologists is that it prevents biological degeneration. This explanation, however, seems to have little merit (see Lévi-Strauss, 1949, Chap. 2; and Murdock, 1949, p. 290). Primitive societies show no interest in genetics, and anthropologists have even doubted whether some of them are aware of the elementary fact of biological paternity; yet the incest taboo is universal. (We are speaking here of the so-called "primary incest taboo," which prohibits marriage and sexual relations between father and daughter, mother and son, and brother and sister—that is, between all cross-sex relatives in the immediate, or "nuclear," family except husband and wife. The incest taboo is always extended to relatives outside the nuclear family, but these extensions are not universally the same—a point to which we shall return in a moment.) As for the threats of congenital deformity that are a common sanction of the incest taboo, no great importance can be attached to them since such threats are a common sanction of all sorts of norms, including ceremonial taboos. Moreover, if genetic considerations were involved, then the extensions of the incest taboo would be different from the ones we actually find.

> . . . incest taboos, in their application to persons outside of the nuclear family, fail strikingly to coincide with nearness of actual biological relationship. Regulations vary widely in different cultures; relatives with whom intercourse and marriage are strictly forbidden in one society are often privileged or preferred mates in another. Even within the same society, taboos frequently apply certain distant relatives but not to other kinsmen who are genealogically . . [Murdock, 1949, pp. 286-87].

Finally, inbreeding is not generally harmful anyway: nonhuman species do not have the incest taboo. And we must remember that marriage outside the family would still be possible in the absence of the incest taboo.

Other erroneous explanations of the incest taboo are that it is based on instinct and that the close association of nuclear family members apart from husband and wife causes them to grow sexually indifferent to one another.

If there were an instinct against incestuous relations, then presumably incest would not occur; but of course it does. And if brothers and sisters were instinctively or spontaneously indifferent to each other, there would be no incest taboo, for there would be no need to have a social proscription. The hypothesis of spontaneous indifference is also incompatible with the intensity of moral revulsion with which violators of the incest taboo are universally punished.[9]

Obviously, any functions the incest taboo may have must be latent.

For the family, the taboo tends to prevent conflict. The sex drive is, of course, strong. Rivalries over sex objects, where they are permitted to break out, tend to be especially disruptive. As a result of the incest taboo, the father does not have to compete with his sons as a lover, nor the mother with her daughters, nor brother with brother.[10]

For society as a whole, the incest taboo has the function of binding the society together by a network of marriages, each of which connects two families directly and many more indirectly. This network results, of course, from the positive aspect of the incest taboo, which requires a person, if he marries at all, to marry outside his own nuclear family (Fortune, 1932; Lévi-Strauss, 1949). Further, the incest taboo helps to tie a society together culturally as well as socially. Every family develops its own little cultural innovations. The joining of families through marriage helps to diffuse these cultural innovations; families are prevented from becoming too "ingrown" culturally (Parsons, 1954a, p. 117n; Murdock, 1949, p. 296).

The incest taboo has still another latent function for both the family and the wider society. One aspect of the taboo is that it reinforces the sexual union between husband and wife. This strong sexual union helps to make possible a "coalition" of the parents in their dealing with the children; thus the children are less able to play one parent off against the other, and the parents are better able to perform their function of socializing the children (Bales, 1953, p. 149). In Chapter 5 we shall discuss another way in which the incest taboo is functional for socialization.

Sometimes a partial structure has both manifest and latent functions. For example, a manifest function of the romantic-love pattern, common in the United States, is its contribution to the mutual loyalty of husband and wife and hence to the stability of their marriage despite the relative social isolation of the neolocal household. A latent function of the romantic-love

---

[9] This revulsion is evidence that sexual attraction within the family is strong. Once the incest taboo is inculcated, the child tends to repress wishes not in conformity with it; that is, he tends to become and remain unconscious of such wishes, so that he will not be tempted to act upon them. (But note that the taboo does not spring from repression. Repression results from the taboo.) The horror of incest is a "reaction-formation," which arises to back up repression. By the mechanisms of repression and reaction-formation, which were analyzed by Freud, people are doubly protected against any tendency to express their "natural" sexual interest in tabooed members of the family.

[10] Murdock gives credit for this point to Seligman, 1929, pp. 243-45.

pattern is also a contribution, but less direct, to marital loyalty and stability: being institutionalized, the pattern affords the young adult, before marriage, a legitimate basis upon which to resist undue pressures that parents, in their "natural" anxiety, may exert to influence his choice of marriage partner. In our system, it is primarily the "child," not his parents, who will have to get along with the prospective husband or wife. The romantic-love pattern helps to ensure relative independence of choice.

Another latent function of romantic love for marital stability is that it counteracts to some extent the girl's inevitable interest in the relative "success" of her prospective husband in the highly competitive, highly mobile occupational system. Romance glosses over or modifies the fact that she is competing for status in an open marriage market; and, in the future, romance may both compensate her for her husband's relative "failure" and forestall a sense that she herself has "failed" in not having chosen "better."

The distinction between manifest and latent functions is obviously somewhat relative. A function may be manifest for some participants in the social system and latent for others. It is safe to say, however, that awareness of the functions and dysfunctions of most of the partial structures of society must be rare. Why, then, do we try to distinguish explicitly between manifest and latent functions and dysfunctions? First, if the sociologist were not explicitly sensitized to the possibility of latent functions, he might think that certain partial structures have no functions at all, or he might rest content with discovering their manifest functions. Failure to push his analysis far enough to discover latent functions would be unfortunate, since his best chance of going beyond "common sense" is in the field of latent functions and dysfunctions. Further, proposals for social reform are likely to be ineffectual if the reformer does not take account of the latent functions and dysfunctions of the partial structures he is seeking to change. Knowledge of the way in which society actually "works" is the only sound basis for social planning. Naive moralizing can be not only ineffectual but wasteful and otherwise harmful.[11] Finally, the distinction enables us to pose the question, what difference does the manifestness or latency of a mechanism make to the effectiveness of the mechanism for "good" or "bad"? "Basic query: what are the effects of the transformation of a previously latent function into a manifest function (involving the problem of the role of knowledge in human behavior and the problems of "manipulation" of human behavior)?" (Merton, 1957, p. 51).

Equivalent and Alternative Mechanisms

No mechanism is indispensable to a social system. That is to say, we can always conceive of the system achieving its goals and meeting its needs

[11] A good example of somewhat blind effort is the perennial crusade against so-called "corrupt" political machines in some of our large cities. See Merton, 1957, pp. 71ff.

without that particular mechanism, for some other mechanism might have the same function. It is perhaps rare for a social system to depend upon one mechanism alone to fulfill a given need. There are usually functionally "equivalent" mechanisms. For example, in polygynous marriages (a system in which a man may have more than one wife at the same time), the danger of jealousy or rivalry between the wives of the same man is fairly great. There is, then, a "need" in such systems for mechanisms that will forestall or reduce disruption due to jealousy or rivalry. As we shall see in Chapter 6, there are at least five such mechanisms. Some of them are found together in the same society. Others are to some extent "alternatives." To cite a few more examples, hereditary monarchs can be dispensed with as long as it is possible to elect chiefs of state. Elected judges can be substituted for appointive judges, or *vice versa*.

The existence of functional alternatives is too obvious to dwell on. Yet we are obliged to recognize that such expressions as "equivalent mechanisms" and "functional alternatives" are somewhat loose. Every social structure imposes some limits on the structural innovations that would be compatible with it.

> It would, for instance, be absurd to speak of the effects of introducing polygamy into a model of the English marriage system unless one included among the "effects" all the changes in attitude and behaviour which must occur before the introduction of polygamy would be possible. And these changes would produce a new society requiring a new model [Marshall, 1956, p. 64].[12]

Moreover, two different mechanisms might not fulfill the same need to the same degree. The relative merits of elected and appointed judges, for example, have been debated. In any case, the threats to competence in appointive systems are somewhat different from those in elective systems (see Weber, 1946, pp. 200-03).[13] Finally, as we have noted, any partial structure may have both functions and dysfunctions, for different needs of the social

---

[12] On "structural constraint" and functional alternatives generally, see Merton, 1957, pp. 33-36, 52-53.

[13] The mechanisms of election and appointment obviously work out differently in different situations. Tocqueville feared that the election of judges in the United States would open the way to political influence in a bad sense, and Weber asserts that the greater competence of American federal judges, who are appointed, over state judges, who often are elected, is well known; but the most recent American editor of Tocqueville, Phillips Bradley, has this to say: "There is a vast literature on the relative merits of the two systems of selection. Little evidence exists, however, to indicate that the electorates in states where judges are elected wish to change to an appointive bench. Nor is there an observable difference in the respect with which the decisions of elective and appointive supreme courts are received by their colleagues of the bench and bar. The decisions of several elective courts are cited, for instance, about as frequently by the Supreme Court of the United States as are those of the most respected appointive courts. The record is different in many lower courts . . ." (*Democracy in America*, Vintage Books, 1954, v. 2, p. 456: Bradley, "Historical Essay"). A definitive answer to the question, even for a particular set of circumstances, would obviously be difficult to obtain.

system. It is probably rare for any two "equivalent" mechanisms to have exactly the same complete set of functional and dysfunctional consequences.

Functional Analysis and Social Change

A change in any distributional (quasi-structural) aspect of a social system is one kind of social change. The other kind is change in some *structural* aspect of the system—for example, a change in the regulative norms or in the types of subgroup. A change from capitalism to socialism, say, or from parliamentary government to dictatorship, is a structural change. A change in the ratio of married women to unmarried women of marriageable age, or in the ratio of family-controlled business corporations to corporations not controlled by a family, or in the proportions of voters supporting three political parties in a three-party system, would be a distributional change. The total disappearance of one of the parties would be a structural change, for a two-party system is different from a three-party system. It is easy to see why the distributional aspects of a social system are called "quasi-structural."

Since partial structures sometimes weaken other partial structures and sometimes change the distributional aspects of social systems also, and since many of these effects have functions and dysfunctions for the social system, obviously functional analysis is far from being static. It should be obvious, too, that any particular structural or distributional change may result in a more adequate net fulfillment of needs, or in a net weakening of the system. From this fact it follows, of course, that a partial structure that produces change may be functional or dysfunctional or both.

Perhaps the greatest difficulties in functional analysis arise from the fact that most changes affect different subgroups, favorably or unfavorably, more obviously than they affect the total system. Few changes will affect the survival of the total system, and the over-all efficiency of the system is exceedingly difficult, if not impossible, to assess. Moreover, the long-run effects of change are often strikingly different from the short-run effects. For example, there can be little doubt that in the long run racial integration of our public schools will strengthen our society in numerous ways; but the short-run effects of the famous Supreme Court decision (itself a structural change) are not so obviously good.

Another difficulty in functional analysis is that a change in the *setting* of a social system will make necessary a new assessment of the functional and dysfunctional consequences of some of the partial structures of the system. (For the term "setting" we can substitute "environment," provided that we understand by "environment" much more than physical things. A change in the political alliances of other countries, for example, may be an extremely significant change in the "environment." We must also keep in mind that for a subgroup taken as the system of reference changes *within* a society may be "environmental" changes. The rise of peaceful uses of atomic energy, for example, will no doubt affect coal companies.) Reassessment will also be necessary if the *goals* of the system itself change, for in this case the bearing of the setting on the system obviously changes. Mechanisms that were once adaptive may now be maladaptive. For example, the social needs of a country at war are somewhat different in detail from those of the same country at peace.

Functional Analysis and Causal Analysis

We have seen that some partial structures have functions for a social system or subsystem. Since functions are consequences of a certain kind, obviously these partial structures have causal force.

We cannot conclude from this, however, that a given partial structure was established because of its functions. In the first place, some functions are latent (unintended and unrecognized). Secondly, many partial structures are the result of a variety of historical events working more or less blindly; and the functions and dysfunctions of partial structures *change* in the course of time. The anthropologist Ralph Linton was perhaps the first to point out that every society has *potential* mechanisms—that is, existing partial structures which may become functionally more important in case of "need" (Linton, 1936, p. 418). Thirdly, many social systems lack certain partial structures that *would* be functional: we must remember that social "needs" do not automatically produce social mechanisms. In some cases, "needs" are simply not recognized. In others, "needed" mechanisms are available but members of the group cannot agree to adopt them, even to achieve internal harmony or to assure the survival of the group. In still other cases, "needs" are recognized but adequate mechanisms have not been found. The conditions that make solutions easy or difficult vary, of course, with the nature of the problems to be solved.

In Aristotle's terms, to assume that the functions of a partial structure are the causes of its existence would be to explain by "final causes" rather than "efficient causes" (Homans and Schneider, 1955).[14] This is no more admissible in sociology than it is in biology. Yet there are, of course, cases in which the connection between people's motives and the establishment of structural patterns is close. This is obviously true for some mechanisms having manifest functions: only a great cynic would maintain that legislatures never correctly forecast the effects of the laws they pass.

But there may also be a close connection between motives and the establishment of mechanisms with latent functions. A little earlier in this

---

[14] Cf. Merton: ". . . like the Christian theologians devoted to the argument from design, [the functional analyst] might be cozened by a Ben Franklin who demonstrated that God clearly 'wants us to tipple, because He has made the joints of the arm just the right length to carry a glass to the mouth, without falling short of or overshooting the mark: "Let us adore, then, glass in hand, this benevolent wisdom; let us adore and drink"'" (1957, p. 38).

chapter, in showing that the incest taboo is not intended and could not function to prevent inbreeding, we noted that in many societies the preferred type of marriage is one with a fairly close blood relative. An analysis of the motives and functions connected with one type of marriage joining biologically close relatives will show that at least in some cases the difference between final causes and efficient causes is not great even for patterns with latent functions.

In many societies the preferred marriage for a boy is with his mother's brother's daughter—that is, with one of the daughters of one of his mother's brothers. This type of marriage is called by anthropologists "matrilateral cross-cousin marriage" (Homans and Schneider, 1955). To simplify the discussion, we shall assume that when the boy marries his mother's brother's daughter, his wife will come to live in his parental home: this, in fact, is the usual pattern. Let us assume, further, that the *fundamental* pattern is this rule that the bride goes to live with her husband in his parents' household—whoever the bride might be, whether or not she is the groom's mother's brother's daughter. Now let us ask, given this fundamental pattern (known, incidentally, as "patrilocal residence," and common in classical China and traditional India), what *motives* might have been involved in the first marriages of the type in which the young man marries his mother's brother's daughter. Then we shall consider the *functions* of this type of marriage, and the relation between motives and functions in this case.

The probable feelings of the bridegroom—which of course are prominent in his motivation—cannot be understood unless we bear in mind that the relations between the young man, his father, and his father's brothers are probably rather close. This follows logically from the fundamental pattern: the boys continue to live in (or near) their parental home even after they get married. To understand the boy's feelings, we have to appreciate, further, that in such a society the boy probably learns his work role from his father; the father directs him in their joint work. The father's authority tends to create a certain distance between father and son; there may be affection between them, but the relationship is not free of constraint on either side. The boy's somewhat constraining respect toward his father is likely to extend to his father's brothers—the boy's paternal uncles.

On the other hand, the boy's relationship with his mother is likely to be affectionate and relatively free of constraint on either side; and this relative freedom is likely to extend to the boy's relationship with his mother's brothers. The warm relationship between a boy and his mother's brother or brothers is a recurring theme in the literature of several countries (Homans, 1950, pp. 252-56). The mother's brother is a great favorite and friend in Icelandic sagas, in *Beowulf* (Anglo-Saxon), in the *Chanson de Roland,* and in the famous ballad of *Chevy Chase*. In the English of Chaucer's time, the mother's brother was called by a different term ("eme") from that used for the father's brother ("uncle"). The point of all this is that since the boy's relationship with his mother's brothers is likely to be warm, the boy might well be attracted to a daughter of one of them for a wife. The boy's parents might also be expected to favor such an arrangement. They will be glad to welcome as son's wife a girl who is already related to someone in the household. The boy's mother, especially, is likely to be pleased. She came to the household from her own family as a comparative stranger among her husband's people. Now she sees the welcome possibility of being joined by someone from her old home; she may acquire an ally.

From the bride's point of view too the prospective marriage might well be relatively attractive. She must inevitably have some trepidation about leaving her parental home and going as an inexperienced bride to an established household, where she will be critically supervised by her husband's people, who are likely to favor him and at worst might be jealous of her relationship with him. Her natural trepidation could be calmed a little by the thought that at least the husband will be someone her father likes and someone who likes her father. Her father will be able to intercede for her, if necessary, in her new home, for he is the brother of the bridegroom's mother. We should note in passing that a man is likely to be able to look after her interests abroad much better than a woman would be, especially in a society that stresses male prerogatives as these societies obviously do. The girl would be less well protected, presumably, if she were to marry one of her *mother's* nephews on either side. A match with father's *brother's* son would serve her interest equally well, but such a match is precluded by the fact that she would in effect be remaining in her own home or village after marriage. The extensions of the incest taboo would probably have protected the solidarity of the village by prohibiting marriage within it. There would be a still greater likelihood that the incest taboo would be extended at least to cover the close cooperative group comprising her father and his brothers and their children. We may conclude that from the girl's point of view marriage with her father's sister's son is relatively favorable, and indeed this kind of marriage (between boy and mother's brother's daughter) is far more common, as an ideal pattern, than the opposite type of marriage (between boy and father's sister's daughter). The girl's parents will also be pleased. Her father will be glad to turn his precious daughter over to a boy he knows and likes and has helped in the past.

In short, such a marriage might have been agreed upon at first because people's affections rather "naturally" favored it in the circumstances in which they were all placed, and because all the people involved might have expected such a marriage to work out well both for the young couple and for the relations between their parental families. So much for the motives that might have been involved. Now if we ask what the functions of the *cultural pattern* of matrilateral cross-cousin marriage are we must arrive at a similar result. This mechanism has the function of stabilizing marriage in a situation made difficult by the fact that one of the partners has to go to a new household while the other one remains where he is. Another function is to strengthen the ties between somewhat distant families whose readiness to help each other in case of need provides a measure of security in life. In other words, motives and functions are not far apart. Indeed, they are so close that it might be asked whether the functions of matrilateral cross-cousin marriage are really latent. Are they not manifest? We have already noted the fact that the difference between manifest and latent functions is not absolute. A particular function may be latent for some persons and manifest to others.

Behind every institutionalized mechanism of the social system there are, of course, mechanisms of individual personalities. The repression and reaction formation that support the incest taboo are good examples. The problem of accounting for the origin of a structural pattern is different, however, from the problem of explaining conformity to it once it is established. Once established, a pattern is taught, sanctioned, and often sanctified. One follows it without necessarily being aware of its functions for the social system. It is easy to see, therefore, that the functions of matrilateral cross-cousin marriage in China may well be latent, despite the more or less convincing speculations concerning the motives that might have helped to produce these mechanisms originally.

It is important to note, however, that although the pattern of matrilateral cross-cousin marriage, once institutionalized, may have almost entirely latent functions as a mechanism in the social system, the typical motives that might have produced it in the first place are nevertheless still operative if the social-structural context apart from this pattern has remained the same. To put this point in another way, if matrilateral cross-cousin marriage has been institutionalized in China (or anywhere else), and if now for any reason the young Chinese man should *not* typically have a warm attitude toward his mother's brother (or if for any reason his mother's brother's daughter should have no great regard for her father's sister), then there would probably be a tendency to avoid matrilateral cross-cousin marriage. We may conclude, therefore, that the typical feelings of warmth that ego has for his mother's brother and the typical reluctance of a girl to enter a completely strange household support or, as it were, continually "cause" the pattern of matrilateral cross-cousin marriage. These feelings are conditioned by patrilocal residence—that is, by a partial structure other than matrilateral cross-cousin marriage itself. They may be regarded as socially conditioned and therefore typical personality mechanisms that "lie behind" the social mechanism of matrilateral cross-cousin marriage. Institutionalization of the marriage pattern has merely reinforced motives that are present anyway. Yet these motives are themselves, in part, structured by still other institutional patterns—among them, patrilocal residence.

Attributing Functions and Dysfunctions

In attributing a function to a partial structure, one is in effect saying that if the social system in question did not have that partial structure (or some alternative), then some need or needs of the system would not be so well fulfilled. And in attributing a dysfunction to a partial structure, one is in effect saying that without that partial structure the system would work better.

There seem to be three basic methods for arriving at knowledge concerning functions and dysfunctions.

MENTAL EXPERIMENT

The essence of the method called "mental experiment" is to "think away" the partial structure in question and ask what would happen in and to the social system without it. This method, supplemented by comparative analysis (see pp. 76-77), was used to analyze the functions of the incest taboo (pp. 66-67). It is obviously not without pitfalls, and one's reasoning should be checked against facts wherever possible. For example, the facts about *extensions* of the incest taboo are in harmony with the conclusions arrived at by considering the primary incest taboo itself.

In using this or any other method, it is desirable to give a "complete" description of the partial structure to be analyzed, including at least the following items listed and discussed in greater detail in Merton, 1957, pp. 56-60:

1. A statement of what the pattern is exactly.
2. A statement of what roles and subgroups are involved, and of what persons participate. For example, it is striking that in China extended families are found almost exclusively among the rich. This fact is a clue to the function of certain patterns in the extended family.
3. A statement of what the pattern excludes—that is, of possibilities of action or thought that the pattern in effect shuts out. For example, the pattern of romantic love shuts out parental arrangement of marriages.
4. A statement of the motives people have for participating in a subgroup or following a norm. Membership in many groups is voluntary. The subjective reasons for joining are, of course, not the same as the functions or dysfunctions of the group, but they may provide a clue.
5. The characteristic feelings, or sentiments, and beliefs connected with the pattern in the minds of those who follow it. These may or may not contain a clue to functions and dysfunctions, but whatever hypothesis one comes up with should be compatible with these facts. The horror with which incest is contemplated fits in with the functional interpretation of the incest taboo.
6. A statement of regularities of behavior "surrounding" the partial structure under investigation. These regularities may or may not be associated with the pattern in the minds of the participants. Obviously one can never make a complete statement of the regularities accompanying a particular pattern, but one might, in the course of investigating them, turn up facts relevant to the goal of uncovering functions and dysfunctions.

COMPARATIVE ANALYSIS

Another basic method of discovering functions and dysfunctions is to compare cases that are similar except for the partial structure in question. This method is well illustrated in a study of the social structure of twelve Chicago restaurants (W. F. Whyte, 1949). During rush periods in a restaurant, emotional tension rises so high that some waitresses break down in tears. One of the many sources of friction is the fact that men, at least in our society, do not like to take orders from women. If many customers are in a hurry and are putting pressure on the waitresses, the waitresses tend to nag the bartender and the countermen, who have to fill the orders for food. The bartender and countermen sometimes get so angry that they deliberately slow down. The waitresses are more frustrated than ever; tension mounts.

In some restaurants, however, there are patterns that may be said to have the function of forestalling tension between men workers and women workers, by keeping verbal exchanges between them at a minimum or by ensuring that a great deal of initiative is reserved to the men. These patterns may or may not have been worked out consciously, but observation and comparison show that they improve morale and efficiency. For example, (1) instead of giving orders orally to the countermen, the waitresses in some restaurants write the orders out on slips of paper and put them on a spindle. The spindle is on top of a warming compartment so high that only the tallest waitresses can see over it. The countermen then fill the orders and leave the dishes on top of the warming compartment for the waitresses to pick up. The high physical barrier and the pattern of writing orders tend to discourage oral exchanges between waitress and counterman. (2) In some restaurants, the waitresses give the orders to a male pantry supervisor, who then relays them to the countermen. The male supervisor is a kind of barrier. (3) Some bartenders and countermen do not fill orders in the same temporal sequence in which the orders come in. Instead, they sort out a number of order slips that come in at about the same time and then decide for themselves which orders to fill first. The bartender will make up several Martinis at once, then several Manhattans, and so on. This pattern has the effect of giving the initiative to the bartender and forcing the waitresses to adjust to his decisions. Both bartender and waitresses are happier with this arrangement. The function of preventing friction is latent, however: the bartender and waitresses notice only that the pattern saves time.

In using the comparative method, one need not confine oneself to cases so similar as Whyte's twelve restaurants. For example, we attributed to matrilateral cross-cousin marriage in China the function of binding extended families together and the function of redressing the balance of power between the husband and the wife. If we ask why the Bedouins can get along with patrilateral parallel-cousin marriage, we notice that for them the cohesiveness of the *band* is the main thing. The wife does not lose the protection of her kinsmen in her family of orientation, for she remains in the same band, which is small.

ANALYSIS OF DEVIATION

The third method of discovering functions and dysfunctions is to analyze what happens in the social system when the partial structure under consideration is not adhered to. If a deviation from a normative pattern is exposed, one result, of course, will be the application of negative sanctions to the deviant; but for functional analysis of the norm that has been violated one must note, not the disruption caused by the application of sanctions, but the disruption caused by the violation itself.

For example, one of the norms binding upon nurses is that they should regard the patient as a "case"; that is, they should be relatively uninterested in him as a person and should concern themselves with him only in his role as a patient. They can, of course, give him a certain amount of emotional reassurance, but this is strictly limited (normatively) and is part of their professional role. If this pattern is violated, any one of several consequences, all detrimental to the goals of a hospital, can result. If a nurse becomes emotionally involved with a patient, she will suffer too much in sympathy with his suffering; if he dies, she may break down. This sometimes happens, despite the norm of emotional neutrality which is part of the nurse's role. When it does happen, the nurse's efficiency is obviously impaired, and in extreme cases she is unable to work again till she recovers from grief.[15]

Functional Assessment and Evaluation

"Functional" does not mean "good," nor does "dysfunctional" mean "bad."[16] When we say that certain patterns are functional for polygynous families, the statement is not meant to indicate approval of the patterns or of polygynous families. When France was occupied by the Nazis, the activities of the Maquis (French "underground" resistance forces in France) were no doubt dysfunctional to the whole Nazi system, but this does not mean that the resistance movement was bad. In technical terms, a social revolution can always be shown to be both functional and dysfunctional; but different observers, even if they agree on the essential facts, may have directly opposing opinions on whether or not a particular revolution was "good." To take an extreme example, it is conceivable that certain patterns that strengthen the independence of modern national states may be hindering the establishment of a world government. Some observers, therefore, would be unhappy or ambivalent about the mechanisms that sustain any modern society as such.

The important point, for our purpose in this book, is to see that the

---

15 For a discussion of other functions of the pattern of emotional neutrality in the nurse's role, some of them less obvious than the one we have singled out, see Thorner, 1955.

16 On the ideological neutrality of functional analysis, see Merton, 1957, pp. 37-46.

concepts of structure and function are valuable tools for objective analysis of social systems, their stability, their efficiency, their changes. On the basis of the facts in any particular case, one can make one's own evaluations.

RECOMMENDED READING

T. Parsons, "The Position of Sociological Theory," *Amer. sociol. Rev.*, April 1948, v. 13, pp. 156-71, presents, in broad terms, an influential view of the divisions of sociological theory and its relation to psychology, anthropology, economics, and political science. Parsons has developed his attitude toward theory-building in the present state of sociology in his introduction to the revised edition of *Essays in Sociological Theory,* rev. ed., Free Press, 1954. For a somewhat critical discussion of Parsons' "Position of Sociological Theory," see R. K. Merton, "Discussion," in *Amer. sociol. Rev.*, April 1948, v. 13, pp. 164-68. Without denying that general concepts are desirable for sociological theory, this brief paper makes the point that it is also desirable to work out more limited theories to account for limited ranges of detailed empirical data, all the while being alert to the possibility of consolidating two or more limited theories; and that unless certain explicit concepts (some of which are mentioned) are included in general theory there is danger that sociological research will make complex societies seem more integrated and more static than they actually are.

The best general paper on the concepts of function and dysfunction is R. K. Merton, "Manifest and Latent Functions: Toward the Codification of Functional Analysis in Sociology," in Merton, *Social Theory and Social Structure,* rev. ed., Free Press, 1957, Chap. 1. For T. Parsons' functional theory, see *The Social System,* Free Press, 1951 Chaps. 1-5. Although Parsons has recently modified his approach somewhat, these chapters are still valuable. For a brief treatment of the four functional subsystems of society, see T. Parsons and N. J. Smelser, *Economy and Society: A Study of the Integration of Economic and Social Theory,* Free Press, 1956, pp. 46-51 *et passim.* The usefulness of the "four-problem" approach to social structure may also be seen in T. Parsons, "A Revised Analytical Approach to the Theory of Social Stratification," in R. Bendix and S. M. Lipset, eds., *Class, Status and Power,* Free Press, 1953. See esp. pp. 395-97, 415-39 of Parsons, *Essays,* in which this paper is reprinted. For a succinct statement showing how efforts to meet adaptive and goal-attainment problems lead to integrative problems, and how efforts to cope with integrative problems may produce problems of adaptation and goal attainment, see R. F. Bales, "Adaptive and Integrative Changes as Sources of Strain in Social Systems," excerpt from Bales, *Interaction Process Analysis: A Method for the Study of Small Groups,* Addison-Wesley, 1949, reprinted in A. P. Hare, E. F. Borgatta, and R. F. Bales, eds., *Small Groups: Studies in Social Interaction,* Knopf, 1955, pp. 127-31. For another discussion of structural-functional analysis, see M. J. Levy, Jr., *The Structure of Society,* Princeton University Press, 1952. The anthropologists A. R. Radcliffe-Brown and Bronislaw Malinowski were among the first structural-functional theorists. For a review of their ideas and also those of Parsons and Merton, see R. Firth, "Function," in W. L. Thomas, Jr., ed., *Yearbook of Anthropology 1955,* Wenner-Gren Foundation for Anthropological Research, 1955, pp. 237-58. Firth's article contains valuable references to recent functional research in anthropology.

On "final causes" and "efficient causes," see G. C. Homans and D. M. Schneider, *Marriage, Authority, and Final Causes: A Study of Unilateral Cross-Cousin Marriage,* Free Press, 1955. This study, which analyzes reports on thirty-three societies, raises the question whether a functional "explanation" of a partial structure may be regarded as a sufficient explanation of its existence and stresses the necessity of looking for efficient causes. In his review of the Homans and Schneider book (*Amer. sociol. Rev.,* June 1956, v. 21, pp. 402-03), F. Eggan presents some facts not considered by these authors.

For a survey of the place of the incest taboo in more than two hundred societies, see G. P. Murdock, *Social Structure,* Macmillan, 1949, Chap. 10, "Incest Taboos and Their Extensions," and Chap. 11, "Social Law of Sexual Choice." The best functional analysis of the incest taboo—which of course builds upon previous scientific work—is T. Parsons, "The Incest Taboo in Relation to Social Structure and the Socialization of the Child," *Brit. J. Sociol.,* June 1954, v. 5, pp. 101-17. Homans discusses the role of the mother's brother in a larger context of theory, in *The Human Group,* Harcourt, Brace, 1950, pp. 252-61.

Our brief treatment in the text does not do justice to the pithy article by C. I. Barnard, "Functions and Pathology of Status Systems in Formal Organizations," in W. F. Whyte, ed., *Industry and Society,* McGraw-Hill, 1946, Chap. 4. Barnard is an experienced executive.

I. Thorner, "Nursing: the Functional Significance of an Institutional Pattern," *Amer. sociol. Rev.,* Oct. 1955, v. 20, pp. 531-38, is an excellent structural-functional analysis, illustrating the concept of latent function, the concept of alternative mechanism, and the specific social "needs" of a particular kind of small social system.

Another good structural-functional analysis is W. F. Whyte, "The Social Structure of the Restaurant," *Amer. J. Sociol.,* Jan. 1949, v. 54, pp. 302-10, which illustrates, among other things, the comparison of cases as a method for discovering functional and dysfunctional mechanisms and the practical usefulness of structural-functional analysis. (No doubt many restaurants have improved morale and efficiency by applying the knowledge gained in Whyte's research, which was financed by the National Restaurant Association.)

part two

CULTURE AND SOCIALIZATION

4. Culture

Perhaps the most famous definition of culture is Tylor's, which we have quoted in an earlier chapter: "that complex whole which includes knowledge, belief, art, morals, law, custom and other capabilities acquired by man as a member of society." Culture consists of abstract patterns of and for living and dying. Such abstract patterns are cultural to the extent that they are learned directly or indirectly in social interaction and to the extent that they are part of the common orientation of two or more people.

Culture is abstract in the sense that it is manifested in behavior and in the results of behavior but is neither the behavior itself nor the tangible results. Since culture must be inferred from observation of uniformities in behavior, it is to some extent an imperfect, or approximate, construct of the observer. A language, for example, is part of culture, and a scientific description of a language must certainly be based on observation of the way in which people actually speak. Yet a scientific description of a language is not a complete description of the linguistic habits of any one speaker. Although pitch is less important structurally in English than in Chinese, the speech of educated persons in southern England nevertheless has culturally patterned "intonation curves" that distinguish it from the speech of, let us say, educated Midwesterners in the United States. But any particular British or American speaker of course has his own unique patterns within the cultural pattern that he shares with others. His idiosyncratic characteristics of pronunciation and intonation are not cultural and are ignored in any description of "the" language. The shared patterns must be abstracted from many concrete examples of the speech of many speakers. What is here said of a language is equally true of a norm, a value, a role, a belief, a technique, or any other item of culture.

Behavior, then, is to a large extent cultural, but it is not culture. It is also chemical, physical, genetic, and physiological. What about the results of behavior? Many sociologists and anthropologists make a distinction between "material" culture and "nonmaterial" culture. Material culture, in their sense, comprises tangible things that have been shaped to some extent by man—such things, often called "artifacts" or "culture objects," as houses, house furnishings, tools, and works of art.[1] This view should be modified somewhat. Like behavior, artifacts are indeed cultural, but *as concrete objects* they are not part of culture.

First, it is not possible to "learn" an artifact. One can learn certain things about it, or about certain things expressed in it, but one cannot learn the object itself. An automobile is, of course, an artifact. Its cultural aspect, which, like anything else cultural, exists in human minds, is intangible. It is composed of the knowledge of how to make such an automobile, how to make it work, what it may be used for. As a tangible object, the automobile would remain the same even if it were transported to central Brazil and abandoned among Indians who, never having seen such a thing before, would have no idea of its cultural meaning. During World War II some G.I.'s bartered away their alarm clocks to natives in the South Pacific, who wore them around the neck (Muzumdar, 1951, p. 717). In addition to its symbolic aspect, many things about Leonardo da Vinci's *Mona Lisa* are cultural—for example, the customary technique of using pigment mixed with oil; the custom of painting on canvas; the custom of painting portraits; the custom of hanging pictures in museums, to be viewed by many people; the ready-made, socially transmitted belief or evaluation that *Mona Lisa* is a great work of art. All these intangible patterns are shared through learning. They appear in behavior; they are not behavior itself. They contribute to the cultural form and meaning of artifacts; they are not the artifacts themselves. Culture is part of men, in a sense; but if we were to take seriously the idea that anything molded by man or anything "embodying" culture is itself part of culture, then we should have to regard men as part of culture, for, as we shall see in Chapter 5, to some extent men are molded by other men.

There is no harm in speaking of artifacts and domesticated animals and plants as part of culture, provided that we recognize that we are speaking somewhat loosely—treating something abstract as if it were concrete. We should also be aware of the ambiguity involved in speaking in this way. From the Spanish in New Mexico, the Plains Indians acquired horses, and from the English and the French they acquired guns, axes, steel knives, and cloth. We might say, then, that Plains Indian culture included horses, guns, axes, steel knives, and cloth. Such a statement, however, is ambiguous. The "horse complex" became independent in Plains culture in a sense in which guns did not: that is, the Plains Indians learned how to tame and breed horses and how to make their own riding gear—"saddles, bridles, stirrups, quirts, ropes, cruppers"—whereas they never learned how to make guns, steel axes and knives, and cloth; these they had to obtain ready-made from the whites. Moreover, the cultural meaning of all these items, from horses to guns, was not exactly the same for the Indians as for the whites. For example, the Indian tribes had a pattern of raiding one another to steal

[1] A survey of over 160 more or less formal definitions of the term "culture" shows that at least fifteen sociologists and anthropologists include "material culture" explicitly. See Kroeber and Kluckhohn, 1952, Part II.

horses, and they used knives and axes to build *tipis* (Lowie, 1954, pp. 40-41).

A second reason for not regarding concrete artifacts as part of culture is that although artifacts can be socially transmitted—for example, by gift, bequest, exchange, or seizure—they cannot be transmitted without loss to the original possessor. Frequently they cannot be "shared" without being divided up. But culture, when transmitted, is not lost to the original possessor, and all its possessors share it without having to divide it up.

To continue our commentary on the definition of culture with which this chapter opened, culture is learned "directly or indirectly" in social interaction. One can learn culture by reading a book as well as by interacting directly with others.

Culture is part of the common orientation of two or more people. If we focus attention on this quantitative aspect of culture, we might say that an object is cultural to a greater or less degree. Most of the words we use, for example, are clearly cultural objects (neglecting the personal idiosyncratic meanings they always have for us); but some words are "shared" by only a few persons in a family, and others may depend for their meaning on an incident in the interaction between two persons.[2] Every new idea is partly cultural and partly not. To the extent that it depends upon and incorporates well-known ideas, it is cultural; to the extent that it has original elements, it is noncultural until it is transmitted to someone else; and the more people to whom it is transmitted, the more clearly it becomes culture. The line between the idiosyncratic and the cultural is not absolutely clear cut. If we think of public opinion as the gradual crystallization of many private opinions, formed in the course of multitudinous direct and indirect contacts, we must admit that some parts of public opinion are more clearly cultural than others.

Although culture is abstract and intangible, its influence is far from superficial. A food taboo can be internalized so deeply that the digestive system will revolt if the taboo is violated. The involuntary physiological responses to embarrassment—blushing, stammering, and the like—are in effect controlled by culture, for the "proper" occasions for embarrassment are culturally defined (Goffman, 1956). Even an angry mob is acting in terms of learned and shared values and beliefs, activated under circumstances whose very meaning to the participants depends upon the culture they have. One sometimes hears the lynching of a Negro described as if some primitive aspects of 'human nature" had broken through the so-called "veneer" of culture; yet neither the emotions involved, the goal of the mob, their selection of a victim, nor the procedures they follow can be understood without reference to a cultural complex—an amalgam of false beliefs about "racial" superiority and inferiority, convictions about the social position Negroes

---

[2] A good example is "to do a cattleya" (in French, all one word), which to Swann and Odette (in Proust's *Swann's Way*) meant "to make love, to have intercourse." This usage arose from an incident that took place early in their acquaintance; a Cattléya is literally a certain genus of orchid.

"ought" to have, and deeply inculcated readiness to set to "rights" any state of affairs, real or fancied, that does not correspond to learned preconceptions. Such cultural factors are of course more intensely activated by the spiraling interstimulation and response of the participants, but even this sociopsychological process depends upon the fact that a large number of the participants share the same cultural complex. Before they can arrive at a common definition of the immediate situation, they must start with the same partly implicit premises.

By the distinction between *explicit* and *implicit* culture, sociologists and anthropologists take account of the fact that a particular individual, or most of the persons who share a cultural complex, may be unaware of some aspects of the complex. One of the best examples is the cultural possession we call language. Every language is a highly intricate and subtle instrument of thought, communication, and expression; yet a child of five can speak correctly without being at all able to state what the underlying patterns of pronunciation and syntax are. For him these patterns are implicit culture. He must "know" them on an unconscious level in order to speak correctly, and he might be able to "see" them if they were pointed out to him, but he cannot put them into words for himself. Despite the ubiquity of language, the science of philology, which makes explicit the structure of languages, has been independently developed only twice in human history, both times late. From India and Greece it has spread to other places (Kroeber, 1944, p. 234). Implicit culture, then, consists of those aspects of culture which its bearers (or possessors) are not able to describe very exactly, if at all. Explicit culture consists of those aspects of which the bearers are fully conscious.[3]

As we speak of "living" and "dead" languages, we may speak of "living" and "dead" culture in general. Culture is living if it is internalized; it is dead if it approaches being a mere *object* of orientation, like the Latin one learns for an examination but cannot speak without stumbling labor. Apparently we do have some imaginative power to penetrate "dead" cultures. But the Greek gods and heroes, for example, are less vivid to us than they were to the original audiences of Aeschylus, Sophocles, and Euripides. Undoubtedly many modern scholars "know" more about the Greek tradition than the Greeks did, but, in the nature of the case, this modern scholarship has to be "knowledge-about" rather than "knowledge of acquaintance."[4]

The terms "living" and "dead" as applied to culture are, of course, figurative. Unlike long-dead organisms, culture that is long dead can yet be

---

[3] The terms "overt" and "covert" are also used, but they involve a greater departure from ordinary usage. The terms "manifest" and "latent" are also sometimes used, but they should be avoided in this connection since their established technical use is different. Implicit culture is known unconsciously to its bearers, but latent functions are not necessarily known even unconsciously.

[4] The distinction between "knowledge-about" and "knowledge of acquaintance" is made by William James in his *Principles of Psychology*, 1890. It is possible to have both kinds of knowledge of the same thing, but not in the case mentioned above.

"resurrected"; that is, lost arts can be rediscovered and put into practice again. Moreover, our figurative terms treat the quantitative aspects of culture too violently. Aeschylus' plays are less "dead" for scholars of Greek than they are for freshmen in a forestry course. Now that Irish patriots have come into power and now that Israel is a state again, Gaelic and Hebrew are more "alive" today than they were a few years ago.

Although the concept of culture is one of the most important in sociology, sociology is not the science of culture. Changes in culture are of sociological interest only when they accompany, cause, or constitute changes in social relationships. Nevertheless, the connection between social systems and culture is so intimate that it is desirable for us to have a better idea of the content of culture.

Elements in Culture

Several kinds of culture are likely to be involved together in any social interaction. The several cultural "elements" listed below overlap to some extent, but the list at least will suggest the variety of culture.

COGNITIVE ELEMENTS

The culture of all peoples includes a tremendous amount of knowledge about the physical and social world. Even the most "primitive" peoples, such as the Andaman Islanders and the Eskimos, have to know a great deal simply in order to survive. Their knowledge is seldom knowledge for its own sake; it is practical knowledge—knowledge of how to obtain food, how to build shelters, how to travel and transport, how to protect themselves against storms, wild animals, and hostile people. Such knowledge is carefully taught to each generation. In advanced societies there are, of course, quite elaborate sciences and technologies, so numerous and so complex that any one person can hope to master only a small part of the whole. In addition to knowledge of the physical world (especially in its relation to man's activities), every society has in its culture many ideas about its own social organization and how it works. Such ideas, which are an important element in ideologies, are of course only partly true (confirmed or validated by strict logical and empirical methods). In this respect, cultural ideas about social life are similar to cultural ideas about the physical world.

BELIEFS

From knowledge and cognitive errors we may distinguish *beliefs,* which in empirical terms are neither true nor false. The Eskimo shaman uses fetishes and goes into a loud trance in order to chase the evil spirits out of the body of a sick person. The Christian missionary, in addition to giving medicine and prescribing warm broth and rest, says a silent prayer for the recovery of the patient; having built himself a rather crude jolly boat, he names it the

Santa Maria, to help keep it safe on the rough waters. The beliefs implicit in such actions are of course quite common. They are all alike in one formal respect: they are so phrased that in no conceivable way could they be confirmed or disconfirmed on the basis of empirical evidence. For example, if the patient dies despite the efforts of the shaman, the shaman will have an "explanation" that will make it possible for him to continue to believe in evil spirits.[5] Civilized men have been no less ingenious in creating similar beliefs and passing them on to succeeding generations. The social functions of such beliefs will be considered in Chapters 15, 16, and 17.

Tested empirical knowledge and untestable beliefs are "elements" of culture in the sense that they are often mixed together in the same concrete acts; a process of intellectual analysis is necessary to separate the different elements from one another. For example, the missionary says a silent prayer at the same time that he is taking his patient's temperature with a thermometer.

VALUES AND NORMS

Values are sometimes hard to pin down and catalog neatly. They are inseparable from attitudes, except perhaps analytically. And values tend to overlap with one another. A beefsteak is a value for most people in the United States (but not in India, for example); so is a certain kind of texture in beefsteaks; so are certain nourishing properties of food in general. In sociology, of course, we are most concerned with values that are directly or indirectly involved in social relationships: moral and religious values that have been to some extent institutionalized.

In attempting to define the values of a society and to see their interconnections, one promising approach is to examine the four functional subsystems of the society (Chap. 3).[6] These subsystems, it will be recalled, are not concrete groups, structurally differentiated from one another. Research into functional subsystems, in the analytical sense, is still so new and undeveloped that we cannot speak with confidence about many important questions. Yet it is clear that every society must have some arrangements corresponding to the four functional subsystems, even though these subsystems are likely to be interwoven in the concrete arrangements. It is also clear that the social activities implied in the very concept of function must be shaped to some extent by values, more or less stabilized culturally. It is unlikely,

[5] These examples are taken from De Coccola and King, *Ayorama,* 1956. This book about the Krangmalit, an Eskimo people in the Canadian Central Arctic, contains many excellent detailed descriptions of technology, erroneous ideas, and religiomagical beliefs.

[6] What follows is based on Parsons, Bales, and Shils, 1953, Chap. 5: "Phase Movement in Relation to Motivation, Symbol Formation, and Role Structure"; Parsons, 1953; and Parsons and Smelser, 1956, esp. pp. 46-51. See also Bellah, 1957, Chap. 1, which is based largely on these sources. Also relevant but less important because they have been superseded are Parsons, 1951, pp. 180-200; and Parsons and Bales, 1953. The section in *The Social System* (Parsons, 1951), differs in some important details from Parsons' later work.

however, that any society can stress all four subsystems equally at the same time. The values most characteristic of one subsystem (or perhaps two) must therefore predominate in any particular society.

This point has been illustrated by Bellah (1957) in his study of Japan of the Tokugawa period (roughly 1600 to 1868). During this period, "political" values seem to have been dominant in Japan. In other words, there was great emphasis on the attainment of system goals and on loyalty to the government. Prestige was based on power in its relation to the attainment of system goals. At the top of the hierarchy of prestige was the emperor, who symbolized the nation. Just below him in prestige was the *shogun,* an official who ruled in the name of the emperor. Then came the feudal lords (*daimyō*). Also very high in prestige was the class of *samurai* (warriors and officials), whose basic activities were of course political. All other classes or categories had much lower prestige. The farmers, then the artisans, outranked the merchants—partly because the farmers supported the nobles and the *samurai* and the artisans provided them with goods, partly because the merchants were regarded as "selfish" in that their work was least directly related to attainment of national goals. The low status of merchants is especially noteworthy since they were often richer than the *samurai.*

Throughout the social structure there was stress on loyalty: loyalty to the family; loyalty to the *han,* or feudal domain; loyalty to Japan. The lord of the *han* commanded such strict loyalty that a *samurai* was expected to give his life if necessary to further his lord's interests, to commit *seppuku* (mandatory suicide) if asked, to go into exile if the lord required it, to suffer injustice from the lord, to avenge any slight to the lord without mercy or thought of self-interest. The head of a family had similar prestige and authority in the family. Thus even this group was given a "political" cast.

The dominance of "political" values was further shown in Japanese religion. The peculiarly Japanese religion, Shinto, was from the beginning connected with the myth of the divine origin of the imperial line. Whereas in China filial piety, a religious as well as a social value, required a child to protect his parents under any circumstances whatever, in Japan filial piety, which was equally both a religious virtue and a social value, was subordinate to loyalty to the state. According to the Japanese Buddhist Nichiren, ". . . when a father opposes the sovereign, dutiful children desert their parents and follow the sovereign. This is filial piety at its highest" (quoted by Bellah, 1957, p. 82).[7] Zen Buddhism, which is a way to apprehension of the oneness of things—an austere form of mysticism—was practiced by *samurai* for self-discipline and steadfastness unto death in the service of their lords. Here "other-worldly" religious doctrine and practice were subordinated to

---

[7] Nichiren is describing an ideal pattern. How far this pattern was actually institutionalized is of course a question. The explicit reinterpretation of Confucian teaching is, however, symptomatic. Some writers attempt to make a distinction between "ideal" and "real" patterns of culture. It is better to distinguish different degrees of institutionalization.

"political" values. Ishida Baigan (1685–1744), founder of a religious movement especially influential in the cities, also reflects the dominance of political values.

> When [he was to] respectfully view the imperial palace, he always bathed to purify himself before approaching, and before the south gate he passed by with the feeling of worshipping the shrine of the Sun Goddess.
>
> * * *
>
> Before an official signboard he took off his hat and bowed at the waist as he passed. This was to show respect for the official decrees. In doffing his hat, he took it off more than 100 yards away. This was so as not to appear presumptuous.
>
> When inspecting an official notice he was deeply reverent.[8]

Ishida's exemplary conduct, which might strike an American as slightly ridiculous, was all the more remarkable in that he was a mystic, dedicated to communion with "God," to the transformation of his personal life through asceticism and study of Confucian, Buddhist, and Shinto classics, and to teaching the "Way" to others. It is worth remarking, to prevent misunderstanding, that Ishida's patriotism was not a naive quirk in a saint remote from practical life; it was based on principle (and Ishida was far from being out of touch with practical life)

We might ask how we can know what values are dominant in a society. The case of Tokugawa Japan affords some clues to general criteria. Without regard to Japan, however, and without regard to the four functional subsystems, one sociologist (Williams, 1951) has suggested the following criteria of dominant values:

> 1. *Extensiveness* of the value in the total activity of the system. What proportion of a population and of its activities manifest the value?
>
> 2. *Duration* of the value. Has it been persistently important over a considerable period of time? [9]
>
> 3. *Intensity* with which the value is sought or maintained, as shown by: effort, crucial choices, verbal affirmation, and by reactions to threats to the value—for example, promptness, certainty, and severity of sanctions.
>
> 4. *Prestige of value carriers*—that is, of persons, objects, or organizations considered to be bearers of the value. Culture heroes, for example, are significant indexes of values of high generality and esteem [pp. 382-83].

The Soviet Union is probably a good example of a modern society in which system goals and the associated "political" values are dominant. The differences between Tokugawa Japan and the Soviet Union remind us of the fact that in speaking of "political" values we are speaking of a broad class within which there is much variability. It is only in a highly formal sense that Tokugawa Japan and the Soviet Union have similar values. Moreover,

---

8 Quotation from a memoir of Ishida composed by his pupils. The entire work is translated by Bellah and given in an appendix to his *Tokugawa Religion* (1957).

9 Williams recognizes that this second criterion is less important than the others.

even in a particular society there may be change in the more specific content of "political" values.

> It must be noted that though goal-attainment is of primary concern in the value system, the content of the goals to be obtained is relatively variable. Naturally the goals chosen will, or it is thought that they will, increase the power and prestige of the collectivity. But the power and prestige of the collectivity may be increased through internal peace and prosperity, through victory in war, through imperialistic expansion, through becoming a model for other nations in peacefulness and a high level of culture, etc. [Bellah, 1957, pp. 14-15].

Every society probably has secondary values in addition to its dominant values. In Japan, for example, there is considerable stress on "aesthetic-emotional" values—the cultivation of pleasurable personal experience in art, the theatre, the tea ceremony, friendship, and the geisha quarters. The patterned activities in which such values are sought must be regarded as belonging to the subsystem of pattern maintenance and tension management. The personal strain generated by the demands of serious life in Japan might well seek relief in "aesthetic-emotional" values. Without such safety valves, the cumulation of personal anxiety could be a threat to the dominant values and to the performance of social roles. In Japan, even the family was no refuge from the demand for achievement and loyalty.[10] Although the expression of emotions and the enjoyment of pleasures were kept within strict cultural limits—were in general subordinate to "political" values—for some persons and groups they were the focus of life. There was "danger" that the culturally approved outlet of hedonism would become a floodgate; consequently asceticism was also highly valued.

> The strength of the hedonistic tendency, however, is illustrated in the development of a refined, sensitive, and often very expensive austerity, which serves rather to express than destroy its opposite, among certain circles [Bellah, 1957, p. 18].

Identifying the values of the dominant functional subsystem of a society is not the first step in analysis. It is necessary to examine the social structure in detail, with its more specific institutionalized norms. Going from details to the more abstract level of value analysis has two advantages. First, it helps to reveal the more pervasive coherence in norms that might otherwise seem unrelated.[11] Secondly, it helps to reveal the existence of an underlying con-

---

[10] Bellah gives a perhaps extreme example of this (1957, p. 57, n.5): "When starting off from his home village early one morning to attend the Confucian school in Edo, [Tomita] heard footsteps and turned around to see his mother running after him. He asked what was the matter and she replied, 'If you do not succeed, you need not return home.' [Armstrong, 1912, p. 153]." In general, however, one of the most important mechanisms of social control in Japanese society is the realistic threat that if a person is shamed, his own family will disown him.

[11] Compare, for example, Williams' "Value Orientations in American Society" (1951, Chap. 11) with Parsons' "A Revised Analytical Approach to the Theory of Social Stratification" (1953), esp. pp. 415-39. The latter more clearly reveals the existence of a *system* of values by showing the interrelations of the functional subsystems of American society.

tinuity in the midst of social changes, or of fundamental change in the midst of apparent continuity. The Meiji Restoration in 1868 seemed to be a great change in the social structure of Japan. And indeed it was: the emperor was restored to actual rule (over the *shogun*); the powerful *daimyō* were reduced to submission; Shinto was made a more prominent religious support of imperial power and national unity; and the system of taxation, from the domain of the emperor as chief feudal lord, was extended to the country as a whole. Yet underlying these changes was a strengthening of the basic political values that had characterized the Tokugawa period. In this sense, the Meiji Restoration was the logical expression of the dominant values of Japanese society. The slogans of the movement leading to the Restoration were essentially political in the sense that they specified system goals: restore the emperor (to actual power) and expel the barbarians (Europeans and Americans).

SIGNS

Signs are the next important "element" or class of elements in culture. Signs include signals and symbols. "A signal indicates the existence—past, present, or future—of a thing, event, or condition. Wet streets are a signal that it has rained. A patter on the roof is a signal that it is raining" (Langer, 1942, pp. 45-46).[12] A signal and its object are both parts of a more complex event or unit. We might have included knowledge of signals among the cognitive elements in culture, for to be able to interpret one part of a complex event as a signal of another part obviously requires knowledge of the interconnections of things.

In addition to the signals "given" in nature, there are artificial or invented signals, which may be of great importance in social life. "A shot may mean the beginning of a race, the rise of the sun, the sighting of danger, the commencement of a parade. As for bells, the world is mad with their messages" (Langer, 1942, p. 47).

A placard bearing the words "No Parking" is a signal; it indicates the presence of a place where one is not supposed to park. Words, however, are primarily an important class of *symbols*. Like a signal, a symbol is meaningful to some interpretant, but it serves to bring a concept of something to his mind rather than to announce the presence of the thing itself. "Dog" is said to *connote* such and such a concept. Words may also denote. Thus "dog" denotes any animal of a certain kind. In logical form, a signal is involved in a three-term relationship (interpretant, signal, object) while a symbol is involved in a *four*-term relationship (interpretant, symbol, concept, object)

Signals are involved in all our practical activities. Symbols are important

---

[12] In this quotation we have substituted the word "signal" for the word "sign," which appears in the original. In her later work, *Feeling and Form* (1953), Mrs. Langer adopts the term "signal." Her later usage has the advantage of freeing "sign" for use as the generic term, covering both signals and symbols.

in many kinds of communication and expression, including religion and art. In every human society, one of the most important symbol systems is language, of which the original and main form is speech.[13] There are populations, called "nonliterate," in which reading and writing are unknown and the language is entirely oral.

Without written records, a people must depend upon the memories of the aged, and knowledge of the past and of other places and peoples is necessarily meager and inaccurate. Without texts to study and compare, logical reasoning on complex topics is extremely difficult. The line between nonliteracy and literacy is such an important one that anthropologists are tending more and more to give up the rather vague terms "primitive" and "savage" in favor of "nonliterate" or "preliterate." The *il*literate person at least lives in a society where some people can read and write, and he shares in some of the results. Yet the mental horizon of the illiterate himself is likely to be low.

There is an understandable tendency for published statistics to underestimate the extent of illiteracy. These statistics have some value, however, and, as Table 3 shows, there are striking differences from one country to another. Furthermore, some languages open up a much vaster cultural field than others. Anyone who can read English, Spanish, French, or German has the key to an extremely rich culture. But this is not equally true for one who is literate only in Chinese or Hindi. The latter languages are not necessarily inferior in general, but fewer and less various books have been printed in them.

Speech consists of vocal gestures. There are other kinds of gesture too. Bowing, shaking hands, beckoning, saluting, and kissing are all conventional gestures. As with any other symbol in use, none of these gestures is necessarily connected intrinsically with the feeling it connotes. One must smile at acquaintances whether one is really glad to see them or not. Judas kissed Jesus. Nevertheless, gestures are often interpreted, and often correctly, as *signals* based on internalized symbols. That is to say, "spontaneous" gestures, even though they were originally learned and are essentially symbols, often do in fact express (often unwittingly) states of feeling, in the sense of being symptomatic of such states.

More generally: any stabilized social interaction depends or rests upon the fact that the participants share a common system of symbols—a cultural system—in terms of which they react to one another. This system of symbols includes speech, but it includes far more in addition. In reacting to another, we are continuously having to decide what the other's *intentions* are. In

---

[13] The so-called "language" of bees, by which a worker bee is able to inform other bees where food is located, is a system of signals but not of symbols. So far as we know, bees cannot "talk" about food without indicating its presence. This is only one of the differences between the significant movements of bees and true speech. (See Von Frisch, 1955, Chap. 11.) Strictly speaking, it is also a question whether the bees' movements should be called "dancing," since dancing as ordinarily understood is symbolic.

TABLE 3

Illiteracy in various countries *

Country	Per cent illiterate	Date	Test and other remarks
Australia	3	1944	Inability to read or write
Canada	4	1941	11% of persons over 10 years had less than 5 years of schooling
Chile	23	1940	Over 7 years and unable to read and write own name
Ecuador	60	—	Data incomplete
Egypt	88	1937	Total population
Greece	30	1938	Persons over 8 years
India	85	—	Data incomplete
Norway	—	1944	Practically unknown since 1850
Philippines	51	1939	Unable to read and write in any language
United States	4	1940	Persons 25 years of age and over having less than one year of schooling

* Adapted from L. W. Harding, "Illiteracy," *Encyclopaedia Britannica,* 1957 printing, v. 12, p. 94.

particular, we implicitly—the process is usually smooth and unnoticed—ask such questions as these: Did he intend to do what he has just done? What is he likely to do next? The second question implies that we interpret what the other has just done as a signal of what he is about to do. Our actions, then, cannot be arbitrary; they must conform to the largely implicit system of meaningful symbols in terms of which they will be interpreted. Thus, if we depart too far from the system, our actions will be misinterpreted. Strictly speaking, this means that even instrumental acts—practical acts carried out to accomplish some purpose—are at the same time expressive, and will be taken as expressive. That is to say, they *mean* that we have such and such feelings or attitudes as well as such and such practical goals. The implicit symbol system is internalized so well that we are constantly expressing feelings of which we are unaware, and the persons with whom we interact are to some extent reacting, perhaps unconsciously, to our implicit meanings. All this presupposes a common, or cultural, symbol system (see G. H. Mead, 1934 Chaps. 9-12).[14]

14 Mead's "significant gesture" is what we mean by cultural gesture, except that significant gestures are apparently always "explicit" in our sense. More difficult to read, but well worth the effort, is Parsons, "The Theory of Symbolism in Relation to Action," Chap. 2 in Parsons, Bales and Shils, 1953.

Any object or aspect of objects that is involved in a stabilized social relationship may acquire a cultural symbolic meaning for the interacting participants. Put in simple terms, this means that (1) any object may arouse conceptions and feelings associated with other objects or repeated acts involved in the same interaction complex, and (2) some of these symbolic meanings of objects may well become cultural (shared), since the objects are involved in a complex of interaction in which the participants, or some of them, have repeated experiences together and are constantly communicating thoughts and feelings. In the United States, skin color has acquired cultural symbolic meaning.

> As the color white is associated with everything good, with Christ and the angels, with heaven, fairness, cleanliness, virtue, intelligence, courage, and progress, so black has, through the ages, carried associations with all that is bad and low: black stands for dirt, sin, and the devil. It becomes understandable and "natural" on a deeper magical plane of reasoning that the Negro is believed to be stupid, immoral, diseased, lazy, incompetent, and *dangerous*—dangerous to the white man's virtue and social order [Myrdal, 1944, p. 100).

The symbolic meaning of "black" and "white" skin color is largely if not wholly cultural. This is shown by the fact that many white persons under certain conditions have come to think of dark skin color as "natural" and good and have even been somewhat repelled by white skin.[15]

Many artifacts are primarily symbol vehicles. Flags, pictures, and statues are good examples. In many of these artifacts, not only is the symbolic form cultural to some extent but the material vehicle of the form has been chosen by cultural standards. Architecture as an art (that is, apart from its obvious utilitarian purposes) is the creation of a kind of "virtual space"—a domain symbolic of culturally patterned activities and values (Langer, 1953, pp. 92-102). This is true of private dwellings, but it is perhaps more strikingly true of public buildings and areas for public activities (squares, camps).

> Actually, of course, a domain is not a "thing" among other "things"; it is the sphere of influence of a function, or functions; it may have physical effects on some geographical locality or it may not. Nomadic cultures, or cultural phenomena like the seafaring life, do not inscribe themselves on any fixed place on earth. Yet a ship, constantly changing its location, is none the less a self-contained place, and so is a Gypsy camp, an Indian camp, or a circus camp, however often it shifts its geodetic bearings. Literally, we say the camp is *in* a place; culturally, it *is* a place. A Gypsy camp is a different place from an Indian camp, though it may be geographically where the Indian camp used to be.
>
> A place, in this non-geographical sense, is a created thing, an ethnic domain made visible, tangible, sensible. As such it is, of course, an illusion [Langer, 1953, p. 95].[16]

---

[15] The white ethnologist Raymond Firth is an example: "For . . . nine months I saw no white man . . . and when the *Southern Cross* finally arrived I can say that the colour of white faces seemed less pleasant than that of brown . . ." (1936, p. 5).

[16] The whole context is worth looking up. See also the remarks and references by Levi-Strauss, 1953, pp. 533-34.

In terms with which we are already familiar, a building, a camp, a square, a ship, or a tomb, as a physical place, is in one aspect a symbolic form, the meaning of which is intangible and cultural. The cultural meaning of the symbolic form is not "illusory," however; what is illusory is the created feeling we have that the culture itself has been made "visible, tangible, sensible" in the "place." This is only a way of saying that the (abstract) form of the physical place is symbolic, and the symbol is a powerful one.

NON-NORMATIVE WAYS OF BEHAVING

If we include in culture certain ways of behaving that are not mandatory and are often unconscious, our list of cultural "elements" will probably be complete. That such patterns exist there can be no doubt. A good example is provided by the excellent and observant writer Isak Dinesen (Baroness Karen Blixen). She tells of Kabero, a Kikuyu boy who, having got into serious trouble among his own people, ran off to live with the Masai. After five years he came back:

> . . . the Masai Reserve had had from the farm a small lamb, and now gave us back a young leopard. . . . He had acquired the Masai carriage of the head, with the chin stretched forward, as if he were presenting you his sullen arrogant face upon a tray. He had also the general rigid, passive, and insolent bearing of the Moran [Masai warrior], that makes of him an object for contemplation, such as a statue is, a figure which is to be seen, but which itself does not see [Dinesen, 1938, pp. 134-35].[17]

Cultural Systems and Subsystems

Thus far we have been speaking of culture in general, with occasional references to particular cultural items. Now we must consider the fact that culture tends to form *systems* of varying degrees of coherence or integration. For example, a well-developed branch of science, such as organic chemistry, consists of logically coherent concepts and propositions; we could say that organic chemistry is a cultural system. Another example is a language or dialect. Every language is a highly articulated system, embracing rules for pronunciation, rules for the combination of sounds in meaningful units, rules for combining such units in longer utterances, and semantic rules. The technical vocabulary for describing such systems is beyond the scope

---

[17] For similar nonnormative cultural patterning of bodily behavior, see Bateson and M. Mead, 1942, v. 2, p. 19, and related plates. Nonnormative behavior shades over, of course, into normative behavior and symbolic behavior. For an excellent study of gestures accompanying speech, see Efron, 1941. Efron studied first-generation Jews from Eastern Europe and first-generation Italians from the southern part of Italy. The Italian gestures involve the whole arm, are expansive and symmetrical, and tend to express emotions. The Jewish gestures, relatively speaking, largely involve the hands, are close to the body, and tend to symbolize the subtle evolution of an argument, a train of thought. Both these symbol systems, since they are cultural and not hereditary, have tended to disappear in the United States in the second and later generations.

of this book; we are merely calling attention to the fact that a language is a complex cultural system (see Trager, 1957; and Whorf, 1940). What about a whole culture, such as the culture of France? The many systems and items that compose French culture are, of course, heterogeneous. Sciences and technologies, several dialects, several forms of religion, ideologies, kinship patterns, economic institutions—these and many other things are found in French culture. The question is, do all these various things make up a cultural system or are they merely a congeries of items that happen to be found within the boundaries of France?

One thing can be said immediately: such various components of a culture do not form a coherent system in quite the same sense as organic chemistry does. The coherence of a culture is "never" complete, and it cannot be analyzed apart from the interaction system to which it helps to give some degree of integration.

> Thus, if the question is raised, in abstraction from concrete cases of *behavior*, whether "pacifism" and "abolitionism" are compatible or incompatible, the answer must be indeterminate. . . . In the case of the Quakers, adherence to both these values involved integrated action for the abolition of slavery without resort to violence whereas Garrison and his disciples, initially advocates of non-resistance, retracted their pacifist views in order to get on with the war to abolish slavery. It should be noted that prior to the occurrence of this situation, there was little basis for assuming any conflict between the values of abolitionism and pacifism. If anything, the cultural analysi might be tempted to consider these values as components of an integrated value-system labelled "humanitarianism." Abstract cultural synthesis which seeks to reconstruct the "underlying unity of outlook" may thus lead to false inferences [Merton, 1941, p. 502; see also Merton, 1945].

Several factors make it possible for seemingly incompatible values and beliefs to coexist peacefully in the same society. Without attempting to be exhaustive, we may list at least the following five:

1. As we have noted, there is a tendency for potentially conflicting values to be reconciled by means of hierarchization. "Dominant" values take precedence over secondary values, except in particular situations.

2. Most societies have "safety valves" in the form of secondary institutions which enable anxiety to be drained off in a relatively controlled way. Frequenting geisha girls is a secondary institution in Japan. Secondary institutions shade over into near-deviant patterns.

3. "Incompatible" values and beliefs can coexist provided that their bearers are to some extent insulated from each other by having different social roles or by distinguishing appropriate occasions for expressing the different values and beliefs.

4. Although different religious groups, for example, may hold mutually incompatible beliefs or values to some extent, they may also hold some other value, such as religious tolerance, which permits them to get along with each other and even to cooperate within limits. On the whole, the religious groups in the United States approximate this state of affairs.

5. Contacts between two groups holding different values may be mediated by persons whose own outlook or cultural equipment is more flexible than that of either of the two "incompatible" groups.

> A Western ranch owner may share a set of values with respect to appropriate masculine behavior with his ranch hands, who may have a dislike for the "market mentality," and share another set of values with respect to the market with cattle buyers in Chicago, with whom he also maintains periodic face to-face relationships. The cattle buyer and the cowboy may have little in common in many ways. but their activities can be articulated. nevertheless, without unendurable tensions for the ranch owner. The roles he plays are separated in time and space [Aberle. 1950. p. 499].

Such cultural "middlemen" may be involved in those "safety-valve" phenomena, such as gambling, that have less than full legitimacy in the wider society and at least border on the deviant. In his study of a large Eastern city made during the depression of the 1930's, W. F. Whyte (1955) found that the police and other officials sworn to enforce the law were in fact "middlemen," well aware of the moral sentiments against gambling but also sympathetic to the very different needs and moral sentiments of a less "respectable" segment of the population. The law against the "numbers game" (a form of organized gambling) was supported mainly by a Protestant, Republican, upper-middle-class, more well-to-do segment; the numbers game was played, without pangs of conscience, mainly by a Catholic, Democratic, lower-class, financially unsuccessful segment. For a cut of the profits of the numbers racket, the police allowed the gambling to go on unmolested for the most part, provided that it was not flaunted. At the same time, the police sometimes conducted token raids in order to appease the morally strict part of the population. Since the numbers game was technically illegal, there was of course the possibility of disruptive gang wars for control of the illicit business. To a large extent, however, such conflicts were averted, for the police cracked down on interlopers, thus helping to maintain the peaceful monopoly of the established racketeers. Such activities show that the society was malintegrated to some extent; the culture was not so coherent as it might have been. On the other hand, "coherence" and "system" are relative concepts; it is worth noting that the police, as middlemen, were able to maintain a kind of *sub rosa* equilibrium between the divergent moral views within the population and were able to keep the malintegration from being as disruptive as it would have been if the police had attempted to suppress gambling rather than control it.

Just as it is possible for social arrangements to mitigate cultural diversity, so it is possible for social arrangements to intensify it. One cannot answer the question, in the abstract, whether it is possible for Hinduism and Mohammedanism to coexist peacefully in the same society?

> If, for instance, the British [in India] had established an electoral law which would have obliged every candidate for office to seek support from the members of two or more racial or religious communities. the communal issue would soon have disappeared from Indian political life.

> Instead, the British did just the opposite. They founded the electoral law upon the representation of communities, allotting each a set number of seats in the central and provincial legislatures, thus requiring Hindus to vote for Hindu candidates, Moslems for Moslem candidates, and so on. This system inevitably produced the politicalization of communal tensions, which the British aggravated by supporting personalities or parties as it suited the tactical needs of the moment [Taylor, 1947, p. 155].

It would be wrong, of course, to jump to the conclusion that *any* elements of culture can cohere provided only that social arrangements permit them to. The coexistence of two religions, for example, at best creates a problem of social integration. Moreover, it is likely that diverse parts of a culture (for example, religion and science, political institutions and science, religion and political institutions) are interrelated on the purely cultural level—that is, on the level of ideas and values—in such a way that each part influences the others. In Chapters 15, 16, and 17, we shall present evidence that religious ideas and values may in some cases help and in others hinder the development of science. It remains true, however, that the helping or hindering does not take place in a social void, that the social situation of culture bearers always determines to some extent which of the numerous logically possible outcomes of knowledge, beliefs, and values will actually emerge. For culture, although in a short-run perspective it is stable, is in reality always changing, though slowly, in response to the changing needs and experiences of successive generations of culture bearers. Probably no element of culture is transmitted with absolutely no change from a parent to a child, and the cumulation of numerous subtle changes can be considerable from one generation to the next (see Spiro, 1951).

The integration or systemic quality of a culture is not necessarily affected by the historical origin of its various items.

> . . . cultures can blend to almost any degree and not only thrive but perpetuate themselves. Classic Greek civilization was a mixture of primitive Greek, Minoan, Egyptian, and Asiatic elements. Of the Asiatic elements, the alphabet, the zodiac, and the system of weights . . . are only a few examples. Japanese civilization is partly autochthonous, whence its god-descended Emperor and Shinto ritual; partly Chinese, such as its writing and philosophy; Indian in its prevalent Buddhism; Western in its factories, export trade, telephones, and movies. It is needless to pile up examples: . . . the greater part of the content of every culture is probably of foreign origin, although assimilated into a whole that works more or less coherently and is felt as a unit [Kroeber, 1948, pp. 259-60].

Such expressions as "Western culture" (or "Western civilization") and "Moslem culture" are of course more arbitrary than such expressions as "Japanese culture." Western culture, although perhaps characterized by such things as Christianity, highly developed science and technology, democratic institutions, and the patterns of industrialization, nevertheless includes considerable religious, linguistic, political, and economic diversity. Numerous wars show that the more or less "common" culture has not succeeded in integrating the West politically. Even the "common" elements do not fit into the various national societies in the same way. Every element has been more or less bent in each society to fit it into a unique total configuration; Roman Catholicism is not exactly the same in Ireland, Spain, Italy, and France. Here again we see the necessity, in a sociological treatment, of relating cultural patterns to their setting in social interaction.

Culture and Race

Race is a matter of the distribution of genes in populations of the human species. The existence of different cultures is itself evidence that human populations of varying size have lived in relative isolation from one another over long periods of time. Each such population has tended to become relatively homogeneous biologically through the operation of such factors as selective adaptation to the environment, mutations, gradual "pooling" of original genes and mutations through the marriage system of the population, and, possibly, selection according to cultural standards of "beauty," such as preference for a certain skin color or for breasts or buttocks of a certain shape.[18] Migrations have brought about new physical types through mixtures of the old and through the continued operation of the other factors on the mixed "material." But almost all genes are the same for all human beings. Differences in physical type are due to differences in few genes only, in so far as they are due to genetic differences at all.

Physical anthropologists have come to see that the problem of delimiting subtypes of the human species is complex and difficult. Our knowledge of human heredity, apart from blood groups (a very small part of the problem), is meager. It is known that the same gene type, if combined with different ones, will produce different observed characteristics (so that genetic similarity is obscured), and that different combinations of gene types may produce similar observed characteristics (so that physical resemblance is not necessarily a sign of genetic closeness). As far as morphological traits (outward traits) are concerned, human beings can be arranged or ordered in many different continua of variation, according to the characteristic selected for measurement. Any selection is arbitrary. Any combination of measurements is arbitrarily selected. Moreover, mere change of physical environment produces remarkable changes in some observed characteristics *even in the same generation.* Although isolation, mutation, geographical adaptation, inmarriage, and cultural selection have undoubtedly been operative, migrations and crossbreeding have been frequent enough to forestall the development

[18] Culturally different preferences for certain physical characteristics are discussed in Ford and Beach, 1951, Chap. 5. With regard to marriage systems, the culture of every population includes rules of marriage, and although marriage rules vary from one culture to another, they all have one effect alike, achieved in different ways: each set of rules systematically ensures a diffusion of genes in the population. Culture *interacts* with heredity and environment.

of a neat mosaic of races. There is no identifiable human group with identical gene types. Some anthropologists have decided to define a "race" as a mere "ideal type" or construct, which particular individuals only approximate to varying degrees. Others treat a "race" as a rough statistical group and admit that any classification is therefore a somewhat arbitrary result of the characteristics that are selected for observation and measurement. Perhaps the simplest way of stating the facts is this: there exist a few large and broadly defined groups (white, yellow, and black) that roughly coincide with broad geographical areas; a few isolated, fairly stabilized smaller groups; and innumerable transitions and combinations.[19]

There are very few, if any, well-established examples of *adaptive* "racial" characteristics. Although some African groups and Mediterranean European groups apparently fare better in tropical climates than northern Europeans do, it is not certain that the causes are primarily biological (see Price, 1939, pp. 234-35). There is no valid evidence, either, that peoples who live in cold climates are *genetically* better adapted to them than other peoples are (see M. Bates, 1953, p. 704). In order to test the hypothesis of adaptive "racial" traits, one would have to rear different "racial" groups *in the same environment and with the same culture from infancy*. In any case, any examples of "superiority" would be relative to the particular environments concerned.

We are more interested, however, in possible mental differences among races. Such differences might, of course, be related to the capacity to learn, and hence to cultural differences. For a long time, even experts thought that the results of intelligence tests given to many sample groups of American Negroes and American whites proved that Negroes are inferior. Then it was discovered that on tests given by the Army in World War I, Negroes from certain Northern states attained higher scores, on the average, than whites from certain Southern states. Ingenious research showed that the superior performance of the Negroes was not due to the migration from the South of Negroes with superior genes. Since that time, psychologists have shown that scores on intelligence tests depend not only on innate factors but also on schooling, educational background of parents, presence or absence of social barriers, attitude toward the test situation, attitude toward the tester, and other factors. The scores of Negroes and whites tend to be about equal, on the average, if educational background and social class are about the same. At the very least, it can be said that if racial differences in innate capacities exist, they have not been found; and if they are found in the future, they will be slight (see Klineberg, 1944, 1944a; and Myrdal, 1944, v. 1, Chap. 6).[20]

---

[19] For good authoritative discussions, see Krogman, "The Concept of Race," 1945; Vallois, "Race," 1953; and Montagu, "The Physical Anthropology of the American Negro," 1944.

[20] Myrdal italicizes certain conclusions: ". . . the research literature on the subject indicates that even if future research should be able to establish and measure certain innate psychic differences between American Negroes and whites, on the average, *it is*

Culture and Environment

Whereas human heredity is a relatively constant factor (apart from *individual* variation), the nonhuman environment is highly variable and is therefore a much more important cause of variability in culture. Climate, soil, vegetation, animals, mineral resources, and topographical features such as mountains, rivers, lakes, oceans, and coastlines have obviously affected the life and culture of every group. The great floods of the Nile River, the alluvial soil, and the warm climate made possible the agricultural system of Egypt. The steppes of Russia and the great Middle Western plains of the United States, with their rich soil, obviously have something to do with agriculture in those regions. The Eskimos of the North, not the Tauregs of the Sahara Desert, developed snow houses. Wild maize (Indian corn) became the foundation, one could almost say, of the pre-Columbian civilizations in Central and South America. The natural harbors of Rio de Janeiro, Hong Kong, and New York probably helped to determine the very location of those cities and their growth as great seaports. The theme is inexhaustible.

The environment, however, did not *determine* these cultural developments, or any others. Until a certain level of culture is reached, the sea is a barrier, not a road, and a great natural harbor does not become the location of a great city. Coal existed in the Old World and the New for thousands of years before anyone thought of using it for fuel. Only recently in man's history has culture developed far enough to make uranium interesting. All the natural resources of North America did not enable the American Indians (who were not deficient in intelligence) to develop machine industry. Even "obvious" uses of the environment may not enter culture. The Eskimos build snow houses but the Chukchee, who live in Arctic Siberia, do not. Many American Indian tribes hunted the buffalo but none ever domesticated it, although many peoples, including the Indians' Asiatic relatives, have domesticated cattle. The ancient Chinese kept sheep and goats but never learned for themselves to use wool for clothing; they learned from other peoples.

In answer to earlier "geographical determinists," who made excessive claims for the influence of geography on human culture, many contemporary geographers and anthropologists have pointed to cases in which two peoples live in the same area but have widely different cultures—for example, the

---

highly improbable that such differences would be so large that—particularly when the overlapping is considered—they could justify a differential treatment. . . .

"For the theoretical study of the Negro problem in all its other branches . . . the negative results in regard to *milieu* are also of paramount importance. It means that *when we approach those problems on the hypothesis that differences in behavior are to be explained largely in terms of social and cultural factors, we are on scientifically safe ground. If we should, however, approach them on the hypothesis that they are to be explained primarily in terms of heredity, we do not have any scientific basis for our assumption*" (p. 149).

Tauregs and the Moors in the Sahara, the Navaho and the Hopi Indians in the American Southwest, the Bushmen and the Hottentots in South Africa.

Moreover, man's culturally shaped activities have profoundly affected the environment or its possibilities for human life. Bridges cross rivers, tunnels go through mountains, dykes hold back the sea. Maize became the food staple of large populations only after centuries of crossbreeding and cultivation of seeds. By inefficient methods of agriculture, men have caused the soil to erode in many places. Deforestation has affected "natural" water storage and in turn the productivity of soil. Now soilless agriculture (hydroponics) promises in some measure to make up for the waste.

Geographical determinism, like racial determinism, is now almost dead in scientific thought. Nevertheless, one hypothesis in particular has had many supporters. We mention it here, not so much because scientists still widely accept it, as because, like racial determinism, it has had a tenacious life among nonscientists This is the idea that climate—that is, temperature and humidity—has had more effect than anything else on the development of culture. Most exponents of this idea have believed that higher cultures had their beginnings in warmer climates but that "real" progress depends upon temperate climates. Tropical climates, it is said, provide too much abundance for little effort and thus offer no challenge; the coldest climates, on the other hand, are too severe and require the greatest efforts on the part of man merely to keep alive. Ellsworth Huntington (1945) thought that temperate climates are best, but he gave more emphasis to their energy-producing quality and the alleged enervating effect of the tropics. He also thought that the "center" of culture has always been in a temperate climate. To maintain this position, he had to attempt to show that the climate has changed in many places during the historical period.

Most anthropologists, sociologists, and geographers have rejected or greatly modified the "climate and culture" hypothesis. It does not seem to be true that civilizations generally considered superior have always risen in the temperate zone. For example, the Mayan civilization of Yucatan developed in a warm climate, while in most other parts of the Americas the Indians lived in supposedly more favorable climates but did not develop engineering and astronomy (for example) to so high a point. Some Southern cities in the United States today—for example, Dallas, Texas—are more "energetic" than some other cities in the same climate or more "favorable" climates. Further, many authorities do not accept the evidence advanced to show that climatic shifts occurred in accordance with the "climate and culture" hypothesis. In any case, culture and "energy" have often changed profoundly without any profound change in climate. Modern Japan is a good example. One critic comments as follows on the views of Gomperz, another environmentalist:

> His theory will not account for the fact that Greek civilization developed in the sixth and fifth centuries B.C., arts, sciences, and philosophies which culminated in a period of brilliancy never achieved previously nor sub-

> sequently. Geographical conditions in Greece have not changed in any note-worthy respect, if they have changed at all; meanwhile, in this land of brilliant sunshine, civilization has waxed and waned, has died and found new birth [Wallis, 1926, pp. 704-05].

Finally, even if we accept the argument that a temperate climate gives more energy to human beings and that other factors merely obscure this fact in, say, Dallas, the climate still does not determine the ways in which men will exert themselves.

From the foregoing discussion of the nonhuman environment, we may draw the following conclusions:

1. The environment presents to man many *possibilities* for the development of culture.

2. The environment always imposes some *limits* on the culture that may be developed or come into use in any particular place.

3. The effect of environment depends somewhat upon the state of culture, which in turn depends a great deal on other factors, such as diffusion ("borrowing" of culture from other groups).

4. We cannot state the ultimate limits of the possibilities presented by the environment, because science and technology are improving all the time (see Gilfillan, 1953, esp. pp. 265-66).

5. The advance of culture progressively frees man from the limitations of any particular place and at the same time makes him more dependent upon conditions, both environmental and cultural, in remoter places.

6. While "freeing" man, in one sense, from the direct and limiting effects of the environment, the advance of culture also binds him to the environment in more ways by revealing more of its aspects and making him more and more aware of its possibilities (see F. Thomas, 1940, pp. 143-211; and M. Bates, 1953, pp. 700-13).

Cultural Progress

Is there any objective basis for evaluating different cultures? Is there cultural progress, or merely change? Any question of evaluation immediately involves the prior question of standards of evaluation. Standards may be clear-cut or vague. The clarity of a standard is largely a matter of the extent to which different people can apply it and arrive at the same conclusions. But a standard may be largely useless if people cannot agree to use it in the first place. Cultures are difficult to evaluate objectively because it is hard to find clear and definite standards that all people would accept. However, the subject is worth going into a little. In our discussion we shall consider both definiteness and acceptability of standards.[21]

---

[21] Note, however, that the problem would be much simpler (though difficult enough) if we merely used clear, definite standards of comparison and ignored the question whether or not everyone would accept them.

The subject is best approached by considering different "parts" of culture in turn, rather than dealing with culture as a whole. The parts of culture that are most difficult to evaluate objectively are the ones we have called beliefs and values. Because religion involves beliefs and values to such a marked extent, it is perhaps the most difficult "part" or "area" of culture to evaluate objectively. Beliefs, being nonempirical, cannot be tested by scientific evidence. A religious belief often rests on faith in a "revelation." Since many religions claim valid revelations, how can one decide among them? Is that revelation best which is most consistent logically? Some of the most religious persons—for example, Tertullian and Pascal—have rejoiced in the apparent absurdity of their beliefs. As for values, the situation is no better. Religious beliefs and values are inextricably bound together; if one cannot evaluate the beliefs, neither can one evaluate the values. One might attempt to evaluate on the basis of the empirical *consequences* of holding various beliefs or values. From a religious point of view, such an attempt would be impertinent, because from a religious point of view some of the main consequences would be nonempirical ones (such as the salvation of souls).

No less than a social custom such as marriage, any work of art expresses values of its time, directly or indirectly, and tends to depend to some extent on a particular cultural tradition and a particular cultural context. Centuries after it was created, we may "appreciate" it to some extent, or imagine we do, even if we are ignorant of its context and tradition. We shall probably appreciate it better if we take the trouble to read up on the background. But if we remember that "living" culture is internalized culture, then we must see that the great works of the past cannot possibly have all the emotional resonance and other meaning for us that they had for the times in which they were written. No tolerably integrated (self-consistent) personality can internalize *all* cultures.

A few aspects of government and economic systems come closer than art to being objectively evaluable. This is true with respect to the rather narrow standard of efficiency in attaining fairly clear and definite goals. The use of money in exchange is obviously more efficient than barter. Large-scale rational organization, technically called "bureaucracy," has everywhere tended to replace older forms in government, military organization, and industry. The reason is that the essential features of bureaucracy can be used efficiently in organizations differing widely in purpose. Some other aspects of government, however, are largely matters of ultimate values—standards accepted for their own sake. Thus there is little genuine agreement about the relative merits of "democracy" and "autocracy."

More generally, empirical *techniques,* whether in organization or in art, medicine, or engineering, being comparable as to their efficiency in attaining empirical goals, have a good chance of being evaluated with wide agreement.[22] Mystical or other religious "techniques"—being directed toward *non*empirical goals such as union with God—are not empirically evaluable in terms of their efficiency or effectiveness. But there is little question about the merits of Western medicine as compared with Oriental medicine. The royalty of Thailand come to Boston and Baltimore when they need an operation.

When we come to science and scholarship, considered as systems of empirical knowledge, we are in the most objective areas of culture. Here the standards are on the whole clear and definite. By such generally applied standards as logical *consistency*, *simplicity* of necessary assumptions, *congruence* with empirical observations, and *scope* of empirical reference, scientific theories progress. No scientist expects his theories to stand up forever. Progress will build upon them. The same thing is true, though perhaps less strikingly, of empirical scholarship in such fields as history and textual criticism.

An aspect of science and technology closely related to definiteness of standards is the fact that they can be learned and reproduced easily. The formula for egg-tempera technique in painting is reasonably precise, so that any artist can learn and use it. It is not so easy, however, to make a formula for creating symbolic forms. The skill necessary to build an airplane can be taught. The skill necessary to create a masterpiece cannot.

The objective merits of science and technology, *in their fields*, probably account for the relative ease with which they can be diffused from one part of the world to another, provided, of course, that channels of communication are available. The best-known instance is modern Japan. After the Meiji Restoration in 1868, Japan soon took over Western science and technology, but it remained relatively unaffected by many other aspects of Western culture, such as forms of government and religion.

Moreover, even when forms of government and religion are diffused, they tend to be changed in the process. A subtle interplay occurs between the new forms and the old forms in the same sphere. But a rifle made in China is not much different from one made in the United States.

We have been considering different "parts" of culture. Some are apparently capable inherently of progress and easy transmission, and others less so. We should note, however, that in practice all these "parts" may be involved, in varying degree, in the same concrete acts and products of acts. Tools are made according to aesthetic as well as technical specifications. An artist has to develop purely technical skill as well as imagination in its exercise.

---

[22] Here we must distinguish between cultural patterns *per se* and culturally patterned habits. Once a technique has become habitual, it is often preferred to a superior but unfamiliar technique. In comparing the efficiency of two techniques, it is necessary in practice to compare the performances of persons who are skilled in one with the performances of persons skilled in the other.

We have decided that progress is possible within the range of empirical ideas, and that the question is more difficult of determination in other parts of culture. But if we ask whether a *total* culture, one in which science and technology are prominent, is as good as, better than, or not so good as another total culture, in which science and technology are much inferior, we should have to say that there is no objective answer to the question. The elders of the Hopi Indian tribe are not demonstrably wrong to resist the influence of modern science. Even if we know that their resistance will be futile in the long run, we cannot say that their judgment is wrong. They might legitimately prefer to go down fighting for a way of life they would be miserable without. In other words, progress in science is possible, but no one is obliged to regard progress in science as a good thing in itself. For this reason, it does not seem possible to say objectively that there is *general* cultural progress or that one total culture is better than another: we could not reach agreement on the complex criteria that would be necessary for such judgments.[23]

Ethnocentrism

The existence of groups and subgroups with differing cultures gives rise to the phenomenon known as ethnocentrism. Internalized standards tend to be taken for granted and regarded as "natural." Ethnocentrism is the partly conscious but largely unconscious tendency, when one comes in contact with "foreigners" (bearers of any strange cultural patterns), to take the culture of one's own group as the basis of one's emotional reactions, cognitive assessments, and aesthetic and moral judgments. Areas in which ethnocentric responses are likely to be particularly strong are food preferences, table manners, toilet habits, health practices, patterns of sexual behavior, and religion. Being ignorant of the inner meaning and total context of what we see among strangers, we misinterpret, project our own feelings or wishes inappropriately, or judge with naive harshness or naive approval.

In South Africa, some of the native tribesmen, such as the Lovedu,

---

[23] This whole section is based upon well-known sociological work. Robert M. MacIver, following the German sociologist Alfred Weber, has developed a distinction between "civilization" and "culture": they are different aspects of culture in the comprehensive sociological sense. In MacIver's treatment, the most important difference is that "civilization" is instrumental (has to do with means) whereas "culture" is an end in itself. The most important aspect of a typewriter, for example, is "civilizational"; the most important aspect of a painting is "cultural." Robert K. Merton, 1936, commenting upon Weber, MacIver, and others, lays stress on the objective precision and reproducibility of civilizational aspects rather than on the *motives* for producing them. We have not adopted the distinction between "civilization" and "culture" because the wider meaning of "culture" is too firmly established among sociologists and anthropologists. For MacIver's latest discussion, see MacIver and Page, 1949, pp. 498-506. For another original and interesting discussion of cultural progress, see Kroeber, 1948, pp. 128ff.

do day work for Dutch farmers. The sober, rather puritanical Dutchmen are annoyed and scornful because the Lovedu seldom keep appointments punctually, do not work very hard, and often tell patent lies. The Dutch control the tribes rather ruthlessly, but most of them, and certainly these farmers, know virtually nothing about Lovedu culture. The Lovedu feel no need to be punctual—the very idea of punctuality hardly has any meaning for them. They work, but they have no conception of the kind of dedication to work common in European Protestant culture; on the contrary, they are easily and without compunction diverted from a work party to join a beer party. Finally, their experience with the Dutch has not been without pain; they tell lies (rather unskillfully for the situation, one gathers) because they do not like or trust their employers. At the same time, the Lovedu are of course also ethnocentric. For example, in their society they do not customarily pay for things directly and explicitly, and they abhor anything that smacks of the impersonal commercial spirit; to most of them the Christian churches, which have sought to woo them, seem too much like a business, for in the churches one is expected to contribute money to a collection. To the Lovedu, nothing is more businesslike than money (Krige and Krige, 1943, esp. pp. 294-98).

It is often said that ethnocentrism strengthens one's loyalty to one's own group. It is just as true that loyalty to one's own group produces ethnocentrism. In a sense, loyalty to one's own group *is* ethnocentrism, since without its culture one's own group would have no existence as a group.

Obviously, the more extreme ethnocentric misinterpretations and revulsions are serious barriers to international cooperation. But of course ethnocentrism is not the sole barrier to cooperation. "Understanding" the other fellow may lead either to friendship or to conflict with him. In the first place, cultural differences are real, although ethnocentrism may distort or exaggerate them. Secondly, with or without great cultural differences, conflicts of interest tend to produce hostility and distorted conceptions of the intentions of one's opponent. On the other hand, cooperation reduces mutual antagonism and reduces that special type of antagonism which is called ethnocentrism or, in extreme form, xenophobia.

In attempting to cope with one's own ethnocentrism, the first step probably should be to try to see and accept the fact that the culture of one's own group is not necessarily "right"—that wider knowledge and perspective might cause one to reject or modify things one now takes for granted. Secondly, one must assume that one really knows little about a different culture, that first reactions are inevitably based more on ignorance than on knowledge. Thirdly, one must make a determined and sympathetic effort to "see" with the eyes of the bearers of the strange culture. One might still prefer one's own culture, but at least one will be able to develop an informed intellectual appreciation of other values, other beliefs. A sociological perspective might help us to see different cultures as, in part, alternative solutions to similar problems. As we have already acknowledged, however, it is impossible for any person to *internalize* more than a tiny fraction of the cultures of the world.

RECOMMENDED READING

For a learned and highly readable discussion of culture, see A. L. Kroeber, *Anthropology: Race, Language, Culture, Psychology, Prehistory*, rev. ed., Harcourt, Brace, 1948, Chap. 7, "The Nature of Culture." Although long and somewhat polemical, M. E. Spiro's article, "Culture and Personality: The Natural History of a False Dichotomy," *Psychiatry*, 1951, v. 14, pp. 19-46 (reprinted in W. E. Martin and C. B. Stendler, eds., *Readings in Child Development*, Harcourt, Brace, 1954, pp. 117-41), will help to fix certain important points in the student's mind. In particular, Spiro deals well with the shifting quantitative aspects of culture. What is idiosyncratic in the father becomes cultural when he passes it on to his son; but it may remain cultural only within a small group. No two persons have exactly the same culture.

On values, serious students should read T. Parsons, "A Revised Analytical Approach to the Theory of Social Stratification," in R. Bendix and S. M. Lipset, eds., *Class, Status and Power: A Reader in Social Stratification*, Free Press, 1953 (reprinted in Parsons, *Essays in Sociological Theory*, rev. ed., Free Press, 1954, Chap. 19). This essay relates the dominant and secondary values of a society to social structure, especially to the ranking of families. It is not easy to read, but pp. 415-39 (as numbered in *Essays*), being an application of the general ideas to American society, are somewhat easier than what goes before. For a review of several other attempts to specify the dominant values in American culture, see R. M. Williams, Jr., *American Society: A Sociological Interpretation*, Knopf, 1951.

On ethnocentrism, see E. J. Krige and J. D. Krige, *The Realm of a Rain-Queen: A Study of the Pattern of Lovedu Society*, Oxford University Press, 1943. The strangeness of Lovedu institutions to Western people makes this monograph a little difficult to read, but the effort required is well rewarded. The student will see, in this detailed and sympathetic report, that there is a tragic element in the ethnocentrism of both the Lovedu and the Dutch. Few studies, moreover, could serve as a better foil for bringing out the peculiarities of Western culture. Finally, Lovedu society is an excellent example of a society in which the main emphasis is on the integrative subsystem.

On signs, see S. K. Langer, *Philosophy in a New Key: A Study in the Symbolism of Reason, Rite, and Art*, Harvard University Press, 1942; also in a Mentor Book edition, 1948. Mrs. Langer's *Feeling and Form: A Theory of Art developed from "Philosophy in a New Key,"* Scribner's, 1953, is a fascinating study of symbolism in the arts. For an excellent article showing how culture is embodied in, as well as modified by, individual creative works of art, see M. Schapiro, "Style," in A. L. Kroeber, ed., *Anthropology Today*, University of Chicago Press, 1953, pp. 287-312. This article discusses the concepts that have been developed for analysis of such problems. For mention of several studies of spatial arrangements as symbols of social structure, see C. Lévi-Strauss, "Social Structure," in Kroeber, ed., 1953, pp. 533-34.

For a good introduction to the nature of language and differences between languages, see G. L. Trager, "Language," *Encyclopaedia Britannica*, 1957 printing, v. 13, pp. 696-703. B. L. Whorf, "The Relation of Habitual Thought and Behavior to Language," in L. Spier, A. I. Hallowell, and S. S. Newman, eds., *Language, Cul-*

ture, and Personality, Sapir Memorial Fund, 1941, gives examples of the misleading connotations of certain English words and shows how they may lead to inappropriate behavior, such as unwitting setting of fires; for example, "spunstone," on account of its ending, "-stone," suggests imperviousness to fire, but spunstone is flammable; "empty" oil barrels, despite the connotations of "empty," have a dangerous residue of flammable oil or vapor in them. Whorf does not say so, but probably every language has ambiguous words of this kind. Whorf also deals with structural differences between languages, but here, as in his other articles, he seems to attach much too much importance to such differences. For a learned critique, see J. Whatmough, *Language: A Modern Synthesis*, St. Martin's Press, 1956 (also in a Mentor Book edition, 1957), Chap. 12. For a brief comment on both Whorf and Whatmough, see R. K. Merton, *Social Theory and Social Structure*, rev. ed., Free Press, 1957, pp. 91-92, esp. p. 92, n. 9a.

For a discussion of the relations between man and the environment, see M. Bates, "Human Ecology," in Kroeber, ed., 1953, pp. 700-13. Bates gives a good bibliography. For a missionary's vivid account of twelve years with an Eskimo tribe, see R. De Coccola and P. King, *Ayorama*, Oxford University Press, 1956, which describes the ingenious technology of a primitive people in the context of use and social interaction and shows how human culture adapts to "extreme" environmental conditions. Father De Coccola's somewhat naïve and complacent ethnocentrism suggests the dangers of a nonfunctional, moralistic approach to the study of culture. At the same time, several passages are likely to arouse ethnocentric revulsion in any European or American reader.

For an excellent introduction to the anthropology of race, see W. M. Krogman, "The Concept of Race," in R. Linton, ed., *The Science of Man in the World Crisis*, Columbia University Press, 1945. A broader survey of diverse investigations and conceptions is given in H. V. Vallois, "Race," in Kroeber, ed., 1953, pp. 145-62. R. M. MacIver and C. H. Page, *Society: An Introductory Analysis*, Rinehart, 1949, Chaps. 4, 5, is a good treatment of race, environment, and culture.

5. Socialization

At birth the human infant is unable to take part in any human society. What its mental life is like we cannot know directly, but we do know that it has no interest in regulating its bowel movements, no sense of propriety about revealing the various parts of its body—indeed, no conception of its body as something distinct from other objects, or of its fingers and toes as distinct parts of its body. It has no conception of a "self" of its own, with wishes that may or may not be opposed to the wishes of other people. It is thus unable to distinguish between its own presumably vague inner life and the "reality" of objects independently existing; it has no idea that such a distinction is possible. Consequently, ideas of property rights, regulation of "aggressive" impulses, and logical reasoning are as foreign to the newborn infant as they are to sunflowers.

Yet not so foreign: for somehow human infants develop into more or less adequate members of human societies. As we shall see, this development is largely a process of learning. "Socialization" is learning that enables the learner to perform social roles. Thus, not all learning is socialization, since presumably some learning is irrelevant to the motivation and ability necessary for participation in social systems

Culture is what is learned in socialization. The extent to which seemingly inborn attitudes are cultural—and therefore learned—is not always appreciated. In a recent work on socialization in a collective farm (*kibbutz*), Spiro (1958, pp. 375-76) maintains that the *kibbutz* emphasis on collective property requires that the child be weaned away from his "natural" adherence to the institution of private property. Actually, however, private property has no more (or less) basis in original nature than collective property has. It is true that young children vigorously object to having "their" things taken away from them. But private property also involves recognizing other people's property rights, and this young children do no more readily than they recognize or understand collective property.

In this chapter, however, we are mainly concerned with the *process* by which individuals acquire the already existing culture of groups they come into. In many ways, this process is similar in all societies, but we shall pay some attention to differences as well as to similarities.

Preliminary Observations

BIOLOGICAL POTENTIALITIES

Although we shall say little about the biological characteristics of the human species, we must assume, of course, that human learning depends upon them. For example, the large size of the human brain as compared with the brains of other species is necessary for man's capacity to form and retain concepts and to develop speech. Man's upright posture, made possible by the structure of his body, frees the arms and hands for "manipulation" of tools. Prehensile hands and opposable thumbs are important for the same reason (see Huxley, 1939).

PLASTICITY OF THE INFANT

Within fairly broad limits, the same human infant is capable of growing into different kinds of adult. His potentialities cannot all be realized. His adult personality, formed in one society, will be more or less unfitted for participation in many others. He is *capable* of learning how to write a sestina, but of course he may never have the chance. If reared in the Masai tribe of Africa, he will eat nothing but meat, drink milk and blood, and grasp wild lions by the tail and hang on while his companions come in for the kill. There is a trustworthy account of an Australian aborigine who had had no chance to learn his tribal language; instead, he had been trained to speak English, which he did with a perfect Irish brogue, like that of his teachers (Slotkin, 1952, pp. 172-74).

The biological potentialities do not develop automatically. Socialization must be distinguished from that growing up and gradual changing of the organism which we call maturation, and which is inevitable provided that the organism survives without serious physical injury.

> The process [of learning] is *not* merely one of unfolding. Botanists tell us, for example, that microscopic examination of the tulip bulb reveals a blossom in miniature which, under proper culture, is merely elevated, enlarged, and colored until it assumes the familiar form of the spring flower. The development of social behavior is not of this sort; there is no miniature social response already present and waiting to be unfolded. There is nothing, to begin with, but biological imperatives and biological capacities. In being irritated, in responding, and in learning, the organism literally changes itself. It is necessary to say "changes itself" because it is only through *responding* that the changes occur. It is also true that it is "changed by" the environment, because without external stimuli the infant could not make the responses by which he changes himself [Newcomb, 1950, p. 51].

As this quotation implies, all learning involves some change in the organism—perhaps in the cells of the brain or in the paths by which nerves are activated. This aspect of learning is largely ignored in the present account, but if we keep it in mind we shall realize that the human infant, althoug plastic, is not infinitely so; his biological nature has limitations as well as potentialities. No amount of training will give him the qualities for which the springbok, the bloodhound, or the elephant is famous. Whether he grows up to be a Masai warrior or a Buddhist monk, he will still be first of all a human being.[1]

TIMING

Maturation could not produce fully human adults without socialization. But socialization and maturation proceed together in the early years of the life cycle, and attempts to teach will have varying effects depending upon the point reached in the maturation of the pupil. "Timing is important. It is foolish to expect successful bowel training before the neuro-muscular system is sufficiently matured to control the sphincters, or to expect the child to be quiet before he is capable of sustained inhibition" (White, 1948, p. 117).

What is learned early influences later learning in two ways. First, some learning depends upon prior mastery of other skills. For example, it would be impossible to learn the calculus without the ability to speak or read. Secondly, some early learning makes it *difficult* for some other learning to occur. This is particularly true of learned fears. Since fear often leads to avoidance of what is feared, the child may never allow himself the opportunity to test reality adequately and learn to make realistic discriminations. (We must remember that not all learning is "good.")

SOCIAL PATTERNING OF SOCIALIZATION

Since the infant at birth is largely helpless, he is dependent upon adults for his survival and for training. Moreover, the process by which adults train him is not left to their unguided ingenuity. On the contrary, ways of training children are part of the culture of every society, and the task is performed by occupants of definite roles. The family in particular is organized in such a way as to make socialization possible.

Internalized Objects

Before attempting to describe the process by which an infant becomes an adult, we must have some understanding of the contrast between the infant's organism and the adult's personality. We cannot speak of the infant's "personality" because the newborn infant does not have a personality in a strict sense. A personality, in one aspect, is a complex inner system "representing" the outer world. It depends upon a consciousness of self as against this outer world of objects, animate and inanimate. The adult's inner construc-

---

[1] In one sense, to be human is to be socialized. So-called "feral children" (brought up in relative isolation from human beings) do not become human in this sense. For example, they do not learn how to talk until after they have been trained by socialized human beings. For brief accounts of feral children, see K. Davis, 1949, pp. 204-08, and Newcomb, 1950, p. 49.

tion of the outer world will not be accurate in all details; yet even a psychotic's personality reflects, however imperfectly, some of the features of objective reality. But for the newborn infant there is no objective reality: no space, no time, no causality. The mother's breast, a bottle, a rattle are not things in themselves, existing independently of the infant's own existence; to him they are somewhat capricious comings and goings of sensory images, images not perceived as images of things nor distinguished, presumably, from the acts of sucking, seeing, hearing, touching. That is to say, at first the infant does not distinguish between his own perceiving and the things perceived. Having as yet no self-consciousness, he acts as if the whole world impinging upon him were part of himself (see Piaget, 1954, esp. Chap. 1).

According to Piaget (1954, Chap. 1), the infant goes through six stages before he convinces himself that there are external objects with an existence of their own. In the first stage, reflexes such as sucking "produce" sensations of a breast and a nipple; there is no evidence that the infant "thinks" of these sensations as anything other than his own act of sucking. In the second stage, simple motor habits, such as looking from a certain perspective, "produce" sensations or incipient perceptions; but the infant seems to think that his act of looking sometimes produces and sometimes does not produce the desired images: he will not search for them if they disappear. In the third stage, which appears sometime during the third to the sixth month, the infant grasps what he sees, if it is within reach. He is beginning to coordinate the information obtained through different senses: sight, hearing, touch, and perhaps smell. But during the fifth month, if an object is dropped directly in front of him, he will make no effort to follow it with his eyes; he continues to look hopefully at the spot from which it was dropped, or his attention lapses. If he is hungry and he is given a bottle with the wrong end toward him, he will not turn the bottle around so that he can put the nipple into his mouth. (He has not yet "constructed" the bottle.) During the fourth stage (ninth to tenth month), he learns to search for an object that he has seen an adult put under a cloth; he will remove the cloth. But he is not yet able to take account of a sequence of changes of position: if he twice discovers a toy parrot under cloth A and then before his eyes it is placed under cloth B, he will continue to look for it under cloth A. During the fifth stage (twelfth to eighteenth month), the child learns to take account of changes of position, but still imperfectly. During the sixth stage (fifteenth to nineteenth month), he apparently "constructs" the object so that he can imagine its existence when it is invisible and can find it readily although its position has been changed several times. We may say that the child now has the ability to have "internalized objects" corresponding, to some extent, to the external objects as they are perceived by adults.[2]

---

[2] Piaget is here interested in the stages by which the child develops the *concept* of external objects—the general idea that there are such things as external objects. He is not in this chapter interested in the process by which *particular* objects or classes of object come to be internalized, each with its personal meaning in the motivational sys-

What is an internalized object? On the physiological level, it may be conceived as a group of cell assemblies in the brain, a set of "traces" left by experience. Psychologically, it has two aspects. First, it is a "cognitive map" of an external object (or class of objects).[3] The object itself is "external" in the sense that it has a socially agreed-upon objective existence; it is not a figment of the imagination. The term "cognitive map" is appropriate. Like an ordinary map, the internalized object is a *symbol* of something else. As a map of Paris "represents" the various buildings and streets of the city, so the internalized object represents the external object (which of course may be a person or a thing, or a class of persons or things). Looking at the map of a city, one may go in imagination from place to place within that city; the parts of the city are represented in a way analogous to the way in which they are related in reality. So with the internalized object. One may "predict" with varying degrees of confidence and accuracy, according to the nature of the external object and the extent of one's experience with it, what one will find if one goes around the object, speaks to it under varying circumstances, touches it, manipulates it in certain ways, and so on. These "predictions" are made possible by the internalized object.[4]

In its first aspect, then, an internalized object

> . . . is a series or a system of "If A then B" propositions, hence the [internalized] object seems to be a set of implications.
>
> . . . an automobile is a thing which, (i) if you turn on the keys and step on the starter, gives out an engine noise, (ii) if you then engage the gears, gives a postural feeling of accelerating motion, (iii) if you then turn the wheel, gives visual and postural feelings of left or right turning, (iv) if you stand in its path when it is moving, gives you an injury, (v) if it gives an auto-standing-still-nearby type of configuration, and if you approach and touch, you get a cold, smooth, metallic sensation, and so forth [Olds, 1955, pp. 207-08].

In addition to the cognitive aspect of an internalized object, there is a motivational aspect. The internalized object is never an emotionally neutral concept. Even in its latent state (that is, when the external object is not being thought of, remembered, wished for, perceived, or enjoyed), the internalized object, as a system of cell assemblies, carries a potential of motivational energy, a set of positive and negative charges, so to speak. When the necessary cell assemblies are activated (that is, when the external object is thought of or perceived in some one of its possible conditions), the

---

tem of the developing personality. Because Piaget conducted his ingenious experiments with a small number of subjects (his own children), the specified ages at which the several stages are reached must be regarded as rough approximations for children in general. A larger number of subjects might show a wider range of variation.

[3] The term "cognitive map" is used by Edward C. Tolman in several publications. See, for example, "A Psychological Model," Part III of Parsons and Shils, eds., 1951.

[4] The present description of internalized objects is largely based upon Olds, 1955, esp. Chap. 5. His analysis deals with many complex problems for which we have no space.

cell assemblies are capable of mobilizing a certain amount of energy from the organism. Moreover, this energy has a certain direction of flow; it motivates the subject to "approach" or "avoid" the external object, to seek to change the aspect of the external object that is contemplated or presented, or otherwise to influence the relation between the subject and the external object. In short, the internalized object is more than a cognitive map; it is charged with "meaning" in the emotional life of the personality; it is related, through the deposits or "traces" of experience, to other internalized objects within the same personality; and the whole system of internalized objects is related to the "world" of persons and things outside the personality. If the subject thinks of Jones, whom he admires and whose approval he would like to have, and if his cognitive map of Jones has in it a "region" showing Jones disapproving of the subject, then this "region" of the internalized object will mobilize a certain amount of energy directed toward changing Jones's attitude, so that the subject may enjoy a slightly different internalized object—one with a "region" showing Jones approving of the subject.[5]

It will be obvious from what has been said that an internalized object "representing" another person is far more than a stored image of that person's physical appearance. Of course, the physical appearance of the external object, as seen from varying distances and perspectives, may well constitute a certain part of the cognitive map.[6]

Internalized objects are built up gradually in the course of interaction with the environment. This is obvious when the internalized object is a "social object" (a person), but it is no less true when the object is non-social. The coordinated sensory powers of the organism must accommodate themselves to the objective properties of the object; these properties interact, so to speak, with the organism. We shall return to this point below, when we consider in greater detail the process of internalizing objects. Note, however, that experience of the world ("interaction" with it) may be indirect as well as direct. A person may have an internalized object representing Jones even if he has never seen Jones but has only heard or read about him. Many sources of information contribute to the internalized object.[7]

---

[5] This example is paraphrased freely from Olds, 1955.

[6] Cooley had the complex internalized object in mind when he wrote: "Thus the face of a friend has power over us in much the same way as the sight of a favorite book, of the flag of one's country, or the refrain of an old song; it starts a train of thought, lifts the curtain from an intimate experience. And his presence does not consist in the pressure of his flesh upon a neighboring chair, but in the thoughts clustering about some symbol of him, whether the latter be his tangible person or something else" (Cooley, 1902, p. 82).

[7] "Now suppose . . . that I take up Froude's 'Caesar,' and presently find myself, under the guidance of that skillful writer, imagining a hero whose body long ago turned to clay. He is alive in my thought: there is perhaps some notion of his visible presence, and along with this the awakening of sentiments of audacity, magnanimity, and the like, that glow with intense life, consume my energy, make me resolve to be like Caesar in some respect, and cause me to see right and wrong and other great questions as I conceive he would have seen them" (Cooley, 1902, p. 99).

THE SELF

As we have noted, the infant at birth has no self-consciousness. But at the same time that he is building up internalized objects corresponding to other people and to things, he is also building up a concept of himself as an object. The "self" might be regarded as the internalized object representing one's own personality. Thus it includes one's own conception of one's abilities and characteristics, an evaluation of these aspects of one's personality, and certain feelings of pride, shame, and self-respect, any one of which can be activated under certain circumstances. The construction of the self and the construction of other internalized objects obviously go on together; if one's own being has not been distinguished as a separate entity, one cannot distinguish other beings or things as separate entities.

Many writers have emphasized that the self arises in interaction with the social and nonsocial environment. The social environment, of course, is especially important. The baby cries, and mother responds with milk or cuddling or a fresh diaper—with something good. If the mother continues to respond with care and love, the baby will eventually learn to distinguish between the state of affairs when the mother is present and the state of affairs when the mother is absent. The mother will be "internalized" as an object system. Primitive symbolic communication will be established. For example, the baby's crying will come to mean "I want mother." The mother's behavior will eventually come to mean to him "Mother is pleased with me, Mother loves me." Here we have the beginning of a self. ("I am lovable. I can influence Mother.")

The formation of the self thus involves "taking the role of the other"—seeing oneself, in imagination, as an object seen by someone else.[8] The child, putting himself in the place of another, not only forms a concept of himself but also evaluates that concept, invests it with feeling and worth. To a considerable extent, then, the self is, in Cooley's phrase (1902, pp. 151ff.), a "looking-glass self"—a reflection of the attitudes and evaluations of others. Needless to say, one's interpretation of the behavior of others is subject to error: the self must be revised as new evidence comes in, or as one actively "tests reality" to find out how others feel. The term "looking-glass self," although undoubtedly appropriate, can be misunderstood. There is no implication that one's conception of one's own being changes radically every time one confronts a new person (as a looking glass shows a new image if a new person confronts it). The deposits of experience build up a more and more definite and stable self, just as they build up more and more definite and stable "representors" for all the other external objects besides one's own personality. (One's own personality, of course, has certain characteristics

---

[8] "Taking the role of the other" is analyzed at great length in G. H. Mead, 1934, Part III. By an extension of the meaning of "role," Mead also speaks of taking the role of things: in manipulating nonsocial objects, one builds up expectations of the way in which they will "respond" in various situations—of the "role" they will play.

regardless of one's conception of it; in this sense, it is an "external" object.)

The self develops gradually. The "egocentricity" of the young child is due, paradoxically, to his uncertain grasp of the fact that he is a distinct being, located in a certain way relative to others. A child may reveal some ability to "take the role" of another, but for a long time he will be far from able to match adults in this respect. A child who can tell his own right hand from his left may not be able to tell someone else's right hand from the left. Adults often think that children are lying when in fact children are for a long time unable to distinguish between fiction, possibility, and observed reality (socially agreed-upon reality). (See Piaget, 1928, Chap. 5.)

ROLES

From a sociological point of view, social roles are among the most important "objects" that are internalized in the course of socialization. Later sections of this chapter will be concerned mainly with the social conditions in which the child learns the roles of himself and others. For the present we must notice that an internalized role is a little different from the role itself. In this respect, internalized roles are similar to all other internalized objects. The role itself is composed of norms, as we noted in Chapter 2. As an "establishment" in the personality, however, a role, like any other internalized object, is invested with *personal* meaning. Its character is determined in part by the place it has in that personality—its place among the other internalized roles, persons, and things. The motivation it commands in a particular personality will not be quite the same as the motivation similar establishments command in other personalities. For example, the role of boy in a particular society is part of the culture of that society, but the role object internalized in any particular boy is a particular variant of the cultural role, and it contains more than culture. In the same way, the internalized object "representing" the city I live in bears a close relation at many points to the actual city and, moreover, is similar in many ways to the corresponding object internalized in any other inhabitant fairly familiar with the city; and yet "my" city is also intensely personal and in some ways different from the "cities" of my fellow residents.

Conditions of Learning

If all our experience leaves "traces" in the brain and hence in the personality, then in a sense "learning" is going on all the time. For good or bad, "cognitive maps" are being constructed or confirmed, motives are being strengthened or weakened, and action patterns are becoming more (or less) habitual. This is a neutral sense of "learning." In this sense, as far as socialization is concerned, some learning is regarded as "good" or "successful," and some learning is regarded as "bad" or "unsuccessful." Socialization, being learning that contributes to one's ability to perform social roles, is learning with a particular direction and quality; from the point of view of some particular social system, it is desirable and desired learning. It is therefore appropriate to ask under what conditions "successful" learning takes place. We shall distinguish three conditions.

DISCRIMINATION

Successful learning of new behavior patterns, or successful internalization of new objects, requires that the person being socialized be able to distinguish between the new objects and behavior patterns and the ones with which he is already familiar. The socializing agent must present him with "cues" that will enable him to perceive the new object as something different from those that he has encountered hitherto. All students of learning recognize that there is a kind of inertia in the personality such that we tend to class new objects with old ones unless we are struck by differences great enough to arouse "testing" activity. Even then, the testing activity is designed to find out to what extent we can safely assimilate this new object to categories already established. A child who has been treated well by adults will tend to trust new adults he encounters, provided that they do not act in ways too strange. In general, if we are to react appropriately, we have to know what we are reacting to; we have to be able to define the situation correctly, for often the same manner of behaving is appropriate in some situations but inappropriate in others.

REWARD AND PUNISHMENT

We have already noted that internalized objects are always vested with some degree of latent or active motivational energy, and that this energy guides action in patterned ways. We can hardly speak of objects in the external world without suggesting behavior patterns appropriate in relation to them. If the socializing agent wishes a child to control his bowel movements, for example, he must first make it clear to the child in what situations it is "all right" to release and in what situations it is not. Placing the child on a pot will probably be the distinguishing cue in our society. But the socializing agent must also reward the child for "correct" performances and either withhold reward or punish for "incorrect" performances. Reward and punishment are said to "reinforce" the desired behavior pattern. Reward and punishment need not come in tangible form; a smile may be more effective than a piece of candy.

The effectiveness of reinforcement increases (1) the more often the "correct" behavior is rewarded, (2) the more consistently it is rewarded, (3) the greater difference there is between the satisfaction resulting from the correct behavior and the satisfaction (or dissatisfaction) resulting from incorrect behavior in the same situation, and (4) the sooner the reward comes after the correct behavior.[9]

---

[9] These statements about learning are not phrased with technical rigor. For an authoritative, more thorough, and more technical summary, see Olds, 1955, Chaps. 2, 3. Olds gives a brief summary on pp. 76-78.

The theory of reinforcement, which is based on numerous experiments, holds that both reward and punishment are effective in training. Some societies, however, depend more on one than on the other. The question arises whether reward and punishment are equally effective, or whether one is always better than the other, or whether some combination is best.

There is no doubt that reward can be quite effective and that it is less likely than punishment to produce undesirable side effects in the personality. In one study (Fales, 1937), nursery-school children were given some training in putting on and taking off their wraps, and they were praised for correct performances. A control group was given no training and no praise. At a later point, the members of the experimental group refused help more often than the members of the control group. In another study (Winterbottom, 1953), twenty-nine boys aged eight to ten were given the Thematic Apperception Test. This is a standard "projective" test, in which the subject is asked to tell a story for each of a series of ambiguous pictures; the stories reveal the relative prominence of different trends in the personality of the subject. The stories of the twenty-nine boys showed that the boys differed in their concern for achievement according to the training they had received. Those with the greatest interest in achieving had been most rewarded for their achievements in the past. Moreover, although these boys had been subject to more restrictions than the others tested, they had also been rewarded more for accepting restrictions. The mothers of the boys most interested in achievement had also made "demands" for achievement earlier than the other mothers. The same study contained other evidence that the rewarded boys were more interested in achieving than the other boys were.

Before considering the effects of punishment, we should be careful to make a distinction between punishment and the imposition of frustrations. The experience of frustration is necessary for learning to take place, even if the frustration is only relative: reward will not have the desired effect unless incorrect responses are *not* rewarded—in other words, unless the subject is rewarded for some responses and frustrated for others. Punishment, properly speaking, is some painful action that symbolizes the socializing agent's attitude of disapproval (as reward symbolizes his attitude of approval). There are at least two dangers in punishment. Both seem to lie in *excessive* punishment relative to some standard of justice, or relative to the level of tolerance for pain in the subject being trained.

The first danger is that punishment will produce hatred for the socializing agent and will either make the subject less sensitive to his disapproval or give the subject a motive for frustrating the socializing agent by disobeying in retaliation. The motive of frustrating the socializing agent can become stronger than the motive of avoiding punishment

Another danger in punishment is that the subject will "overlearn." He may develop so much anxiety in the behavior field in which he has been punished that he will be inhibited in "normal" and desirable behavior patterns. There is some evidence, for example, that punishment for "aggressive" behavior may produce anxiety about normal self-expression (see Child, 1954, p. 671). The precise effect of "excessive" punishment, as of any other experience, depends upon the subject's prior experience and the personality structure that has been developed. It also depends upon the nature of the punishment, what it is being administered for, what the punishment agent's motives are, and the general nature of the relationship between the punishing agent and the person being punished. It has been surmised that this second danger has perhaps led some societies to depend much more on reward than on punishment. Examples are the Comanche Indians (see Kardiner, 1945, Chaps. 3, 4) and the Eskimos. The avoidance of punishment in socialization in these societies is no doubt functional, for the conditions of life are so exacting that the ability to act autonomously, swiftly, and courageously is virtually necessary for survival.

Nevertheless, good reasons have been advanced for not eschewing punishment altogether in socialization. Some acts are dangerous, and it is not always possible or convenient to provide an environment in which the child will not be able to hurt himself. Better to train by punishing than to let the child take risks that he is not able to appreciate. Further, it is perhaps desirable to make a child sensitive to disapproval early, so that in later life he can be guided by hints of disapproval from others. Mild expressions of disapproval are among the most common means by which adults "control" one another's incipient tendencies to social deviation (see Mowrer, 1947, pp. 465-67).[10]

CONTROL OF THE EFFECTS OF FRUSTRATION

A third condition for learning is control of the effects of frustration. The feeling of frustration is the unpleasant response that one has to being thwarted in some activity, deprived of something one has been enjoying, refused something one wishes to have. Obviously, a great deal of frustration occurs in socialization. Frustration is likely to be especially severe during the early years, since the young child cannot understand the "reasons" for others' frustrating him, and since he has not yet learned how to cope well with his own feelings. The thwarting, depriving, refusing, and demanding by socializing agents must often seem arbitrary at best, and at worst, as we shall see, unjust. In any case, frustration tends to produce aggressive feelings and possibly indignation. If the frustrating agent—for example, the mother—is also loved, then the child may develop anxiety as well: anxiety lest the mother withdraw her love and care. From the point of view of the socializing agent, the danger in these feelings of aggression, indignation, and anxiety is that they make the child unable or unwilling to give his attention to the "task" of learning; he may not be able to make the discriminations necessary;

---

[10] Mowrer gives other reasons, but it is not clear that he distinguishes properly between punishment and the imposition of frustration. (Making a child go to school, for example, is not punishing him, and one might argue that it is better to reward him for going than to punish him for not going.)

he may develop a strong motive to thwart the socializing agent by refusing to cooperate. It is necessary, therefore, for the socializing agent to do something to counteract the effects of frustration, to reassure the child, to reward him whenever he does what is required. Here we see a good example of the fact that socialization takes place in social interaction.

In the "growth gradients" that Gesell and Ilg have published, showing at what age certain kinds of activity are "normally" manifested by middle-class American children, we can see evidence that frustration is common. We read, concerning the two-and-a-half-year-old child (who is trying to cope with new "demands" being made upon him): "Crying from temper. Stormy. . . . Whining." In the growth gradient for assertion and anger, we read: "Tantrums: extremely aggressive whole-body response. Caused chiefly by mother. . . . Anger chiefly aroused by interference with his physical activity or with his possessions." For the average child at five and a half, we read: "Abrupt onset of temper tantrums, with loud angry crying. . . . Some moodiness, whining, expression of resentment." Under "assertion and anger," we find: "Temper tantrums. Slams doors. Strikes parents or other children" (Gesell and Ilg, 1946, pp. 292-94).

In addition to such overt behavior, the dreams characteristic of five-and-a-half-year-old children also show anxiety: "Dream of things in their beds. Waken and go to mother's bed. . . . Wild animals (wolves, bears, foxes, snakes) chase or bite the child" (p. 306). Children whose mothers punish them for aggressive acts may become inhibited in expressing aggression directly, but they may reveal more aggressive fantasies in their doll play than other children (see Hollenberg and Sperry, 1951).

The amount of frustration the child must undergo in socialization varies considerably from one society to another. In one of the best relevant investigations (J. Whiting and Child, 1953), ethnographic reports on seventy-five primitive societies were analyzed in order to provide a statistical test of certain hypotheses.[11] The societies were rated with respect to degree of severity in the socialization of children. Five areas of training were rated: nursing and weaning, toilet training, sexual training, training for independence, and training with respect to aggressive behavior. Great variation was found, for example, in the age of weaning. The most indulgent society was the Chenchu tribe of India, who do not wean their children before the age of five or six. Middle-class Americans wean children at a little over half a year. Of fifty-two primitive societies for which the evidence on weaning was adequate, only one was more "severe" than ours.[12]

Training with regard to aggressive behavior varies from that of the Siriono (South American Indians), who are most permissive, to that of the Harney Valley Paiute (North American Indians), of whom it is written:

---

[11] The hypotheses tested have only peripheral relevance to the present chapter.

[12] American practices were rated according to the same system that was used for the primitive societies. The evidence for the United States was found in two works by A. Davis and Havighurst, 1946 and 1947.

"If siblings fight among themselves, the older ones are whipped. If a child strikes his parents, they hit him back" (B. Whiting, 1950, p. 68). Of thirty-one primitive societies for which the data were adequate for rating, only seven were thought to treat aggressive behavior more severely than the American middle class. Indeed, for all five "areas" of training, with respect to indulgence or severity in the early weeks and months, the average rating of the American middle class was the same as that of the two most severe primitive societies. In a contest between the forty-eight societies for which the data were considered adequate, the American middle class would be tied for second place in severity of socialization—that is, in imposition of frustration. Yet the United States may not be the most severe of modern Western societies. From a description of child training in a village in south-eastern France (Wylie, 1957), one gets the impression that in many ways the average French child experiences more frustration than the average American child.

In general, however, Whiting and Child found that all societies impose frustration, and that most societies are relatively severe in some areas of training and relatively indulgent in others.

> We may conclude for indulgence and severity, and with less certainty for age, that the practices of a society for one system of behavior are almost entirely independent of its practices with respect to other systems of behavior [p. 117].

Stages of Socialization

One of the most obvious things about socialization is that the socializing agent does not try to teach everything at once. He (or she) concentrates on one task or on a few tasks at a time. Moreover, the process of accomplishing any one of the aims of socialization is gradual. Especially during the early stages of life (infancy and childhood), socialization takes place within a "simplified" social world; that is, the social system in which the infant or child is being trained is much less complex than the society as a whole. This simplification makes it possible for the child to attend to relatively few things at a time. Thus he has a better opportunity to make the necessary discriminations, to cope with his negative reactions due to frustration, to establish new learning more firmly, to integrate new learning with old, and to reorganize his inner world slowly. He is not allowed to be overwhelmed with social stimuli. Gradually the social system within which socialization is going on is broadened to include more objects to be discriminated and internalized.[13]

Since socialization is learning to participate in social roles, the most important objects to be internalized are the social roles themselves. But, as we saw in Chapter 2, in order to perform any social role adequately, one

---

[13] This whole section is based largely on Parsons, 1955a.

must "know" the other social roles in the same social system. In the terms of the present chapter, the child must internalize the roles he will be expected to perform himself and also the roles of the other persons with whom he will interact. As the self grows concomitantly with other internalized social objects, so one's own roles grow in one's personality concomitantly with other roles. In fact, the internalization of roles is almost the same thing as the growth of personality, and those internalized roles with which one "identifies" (makes one's *own* roles) are at least the main focus of one's "self." At each stage of socialization, therefore, the child internalizes a *system* of roles, not just one role.

We shall describe briefly four stages of socialization from infancy to adulthood. The names given to the stages have become fixed in usage, and they are fairly appropriate although far from adequately descriptive. They are (1) the oral stage, (2) the anal stage, (3) the oedipal stage and latency, and (4) adolescence. (The third stage is sometimes regarded as two stages, but, as we shall see, the logical symmetry of the whole division into stages —which in any case is only a rough indication of the sequence of events in actual life—requires that the oedipal stage and the latency period be treated as substages of one main stage.)

In all these stages, but especially in the first three, the family is the main socializing group. Therefore, we must consider the structure of the family as it bears on socialization. The family varies in composition from one society to another, but the nuclear family is universal (except for the Nayars of India, discussed in Chap. 6). For our purpose, we shall ignore the variation in particular families and concentrate on the *institutional* structure of the nuclear family. There are four roles: husband-father, wife-mother, son-brother, and daughter-sister. In detail, these roles also vary from one society to another, but again there are all-but-universal features. One such feature is obvious: the division according to generation is also a division according to relative power to control interaction; father and mother are able to control son and daughter more than son and daughter are able to control parents. Another "universal" feature has to do with the division according to sex.

Zelditch (1955) examined ethnographic reports on a sample of fifty-six societies to test the hypotheses (1) that in all nuclear families "instrumental" leadership is differentiated by role from "expressive" leadership, and (2) that in all nuclear families the instrumental leader is institutionally the father and the expressive leader is the mother.

> Ego . . . [is] considered *instrumental* leader of the nuclear family if the ethnographer's report offers statements of the form:
>
> 1. Ego is boss-manager of the farm, leader of the hunt, etc. Ego is the final court of appeals, final judge and executor of punishment, discipline, and control over the children of the family.
>
> Ego . . . [is] considered *expressive* leader of the nuclear family if the ethnographer's report offers statements of the form:

2. Ego is the mediator, conciliator, of the family; ego soothes over disputes, resolves hostilities in the family. Ego is affectionate, solicitous, warm, emotional to the children of the family; ego is the "comforter," the "consoler," is relatively indulgent, relatively unpunishing [Zelditch, 1955, p. 318].[14]

Of the fifty-six societies, forty-six made a role differentiation for instrumental and expressive leadership. Careful study of the ten negative cases, however, throws considerable doubt on the ethnographers' reports, or at least on the conclusion that the cases should be regarded as inconsistent with the first hypothesis.

What about the second hypothesis? Of the fifty-six societies, forty-eight clearly made the husband-father the instrumental leader and eight did not. But here again the "negative" evidence was far from conclusive. (For example, some of the "negative" cases are societies in which the wife's brother is the provider for her children. As far as the *nuclear family* is concerned, however, there is no case in which there is clear evidence that the wife herself has "instrumental" superiority over the husband, and no case in which the husband clearly has "expressive" superiority over the wife. We are speaking, of course, of the institutionalized roles; "bossy" women probably exist in every society as deviants.) In experimental work with small task-oriented groups of the same sex, Bales and Slater (1955) had found a definite tendency for instrumental and expressive leadership to be separated. They also found, however, that the task leader and the "best-liked" leader often formed a coalition, and they pointed out that the stability of the family, as of their experimental groups, probably depends on such a coalition. The investigation by Zelditch checked and supported their analysis.

As for the younger generation, there is a universal tendency (no one will dispute) for the son's role to be more like the father's and for the daughter's role to be more like the mother's. We have been speaking of the four roles in their developed form; as we shall see, the child does not internalize any of these roles *in this form* until he is fairly well along in the third stage.

THE FIRST STAGE

In the womb the fetus is presumably warm and comfortable. At birth the infant faces his first crisis: he must breathe, he must exert himself to be fed, he is susceptible to cold, wet, and other discomforts; he cries a good deal. The essential goal of the first stage of socialization is to establish oral dependency. The infant builds up fairly definite expectations about feeding time, and he learns to signal his pressing needs for care. During this stage, the infant is not involved in the family as a whole. He is involved only in the subsystem consisting of him and his mother. For the other members of the family, as Parsons says, the baby is little more than a "possession." If

---

[14] Zelditch used four other "designation rules" for classifying his cases, but the two quoted give the basic meaning of "instrumental" and "expressive."

the father or anyone else shares with the mother the task of caring for the baby, no role differentiation is involved: that person will also be performing the role of "mother" (in its simplest form at this "oral" stage).

What does the infant internalize? He is so passive relative to the "mother" that it is questionable whether he internalizes two roles at all. This is the stage of what Freud called "primary identification." In the personality of the infant, by the time oral dependency has been established, his own role and that of the mother (or other provider of care) are probably not clearly distinguished. Mother and infant are "merged."

Some control over the hunger drive has been established, and the infant has been sensitized to the diffusely "erotic" pleasure of bodily contact with the mother.

THE SECOND STAGE

The time at which the second stage of socialization begins varies depending upon the society, the social class, and the particular family. In the American middle class it probably begins soon after the first year and is completed during the third year. The "anal" crisis, with which the stage begins, is caused by the imposition of new "demands," notably the demand for the child to take over some degree of care for himself. Toilet training is the main focus of *new* concern. During this stage, the child internalizes two roles—his own and that of his mother, now clearly separate. The child not only receives *care;* he also receives *love,* and gives love in return. Psychoanalysts have pointed out that to the child in this stage the feces are a gift, a symbol of the child's love for his mother. On the other hand, withholding feces or releasing at the "wrong" time is an expression of aggression (defiance). The positive sanction for correct performances is the mother's love. In the more "severe" societies, punishment is also used to discourage incorrect performances; but in all societies the child is enabled to discriminate between correct and incorrect, first by cues given by the socializing agent, and secondly by being rewarded for correct performance and not rewarded for incorrect.

In this second stage we see clearly the importance of a general fact about all socialization: the socializing agent always has a dual role. During this "anal" stage, for example, the mother participates, first, in the limited social system consisting of her interaction with the child; secondly, she participates in the family as a whole. In the subsystem she is the instrumental leader *relative to the child,* for she is still chiefly responsible for meeting his specific needs. The child's contribution to the system is mainly expressive: he helps to integrate the system by cooperating and giving love; he is still too young and dependent to contribute very much to task accomplishment.

The dual role of the socializing agent is important for several reasons. The task of the socializing agent, after all, is to train the child so that he will ultimately be able to participate in a more complex social system: obviously the socializing agent has to know the roles and common values of that larger system.

Secondly, socialization is an unpleasant task, to some extent, for the socializing agent as well as for the child. The mother does not enjoy seeing her child suffer through the process of weaning, toilet training, and the like. No doubt she can console herself (as the child cannot) with thoughts of the final accomplishment; but probably she is "forced," to some extent, by pressure from the larger social system of which she is a member. Her husband may feel sooner than she (probably too soon, as Gesell says) that it's about time his son were doing more for himself and whining less often. This pressure from the larger system is, of course, only one of the cues for the mother that she had better be getting along with her task.

The counterpart of this pressure is resistance on the part of the mother. Her dual role enables her to protect the child to some extent from the excessive pressure of other members of the family. Thus the mother "represents" the larger social system in relation to the smaller, and the smaller in relation to the larger. Viewed in another way, her dual representative role is an aspect of her "expressive" leadership in the whole family as a social system.

Finally, at the same time that the mother (as socializing agent) is mediating between the subsystem and the larger system—now yielding, now resisting—she is also supported by that larger system. Her husband especially (in the "normal" case we are using for the framework of analysis) will understand the strain she is undergoing, will relieve her of some other burdens (for example, by spending more time with the other children), and will back her up when she must be firm with the child being socialized.[15]

THE THIRD STAGE

The third stage (in the American middle class) extends from about the fourth year to puberty (the age of twelve or thirteen: the age varies somewhat, and puberty is merely a rough dividing line). The "oedipal crisis" occurs typically during the fourth and fifth years, and the so-called "latency" period follows.

In the course of the third stage, the child becomes a member of the family as a whole. He must internalize all four roles of the family, and he must above all identify himself with the social role ascribed to him on the basis of his biological sex. We shall discuss below what "identification" means.

The "Oedipus complex," as Freud named it, is the feeling of jealousy the boy is believed to have toward his father on account of their rivalry for the mother; and the boy's feelings are believed to be sexual. For the girl, the "Electra complex" is the corresponding set of feelings: she is believed to be in love with her father and therefore jealous of her mother.

It is perhaps desirable to distinguish between sexual and erotic feelings,

---

[15] The dual role of the socializing agent is discussed by Parsons, 1955a, *passim*, and also by Parsons and Olds, 1955, *passim*.

even though the two are closely related. In our own society at least (not necessarily in all others), the child of four, five, or six does not necessarily have a clear understanding of the fact that there are two sexes; he may have observed the anatomical differences between boys and girls, but he probably has no appreciation of their sexual function. His mother is not yet female in the sexual sense, nor his father male. Therefore the child at first is incapable of "sexual" feelings in a narrow sense. Yet there is no doubt that the child, and probably the infant, has a diffuse erotic attachment to his mother. He not only loves her in the sense that he wants to please her and would be desolate if she were taken away from him; he also derives bodily pleasure from contact with her (see, e.g., R. W. White, 1948, pp. 120-21). Indeed, this aspect of the child's attachment to his mother is important for socialization, since the mother can use bodily contact as a reward for "correct" performances on the child's part. The erotic attachment, moreover, is mutual. The danger that it might go "too far" (thus disrupting the family and making it difficult for the mother to keep love conditional upon the child's correct role performance) is prevented by the incest taboo, which restrains mother and child both.

The boy's feeling of chagrin at having to share his mother with siblings and father, and his jealousy, are quite understandable whether the boy has "sexual" feelings for his mother or not. The same is true of the girl, who is equally disturbed, at first, at having her "exclusive" relation with the *mother* disturbed. In the following remarks, Gesell and Ilg are not distinguishing between boys and girls:

> Fathers also come in for their share of a 5-year-old's affection. The father, however, is rarely the preferred parent. . . . In the insecurity of the middle of the night [the child] wants his mother most of all. If, however, the mother is sick, some FIVES who have been slow to build up a relationship with their fathers will now accept them [Gesell and Ilg, 1946, pp. 80-81].

The child at six is also chiefly concerned with his (or her) mother, although the mother as socializing agent, making and enforcing demands, is also the main target of aggression:

> Although Six is often described as being "embroiled with" his mother, he is actually extremely ambivalent in regard to her. He may say "I love you" at one minute and "I hate you, I wish you were dead" at the next. He is most loving with his mother, yet most of his tantrums are directed against her [p. 118].

When the proper stage of socialization has been reached, many social pressures are brought to bear on the child to identify with the appropriate sex. Boys begin to be rewarded for behavior appropriate to boys (according to the culture), and girls are rewarded for acting like girls. More and more, the toys given to boys are different from those given to their sisters. Fairly striking anatomical differences make the correct identification easy; yet the correct identification is largely an achievement of socialization. Moreover, despite social pressures, some children fail to identify with the correct sex for them, and others, as we shall see, make an ambivalent identification.

When the boy has successfully identified with his father with regard to sex role, it is understandable that he should be particularly jealous of his father. And when the girl has successfully identified with her mother, it is equally understandable that she should be jealous of her mother. Special interest in the opposite sex is not inborn; nor is interest in the opposite sex the cause of identification with one's own sex. On the contrary, identification with one's own sex is the cause of one's interest in the opposite sex. Failure to make the correct identification is a cause of homosexuality (see Mowrer, 1950, Chap. 21, esp. pp. 605ff.).

Following the turmoil caused by the "intrusion" of the father and possibly of siblings into the "romance" of mother and child, the child must settle down to mastering many new demands for independence. He has to go to school. He joins groups of playmates ("peer groups," as they are called). In many situations he must learn to get along without the immediate guidance and support of his family. In our society, this period is one in which interest in the opposite sex (particularly for boys) tends to be suppressed to some extent in favor of devotion to the problems of mastering skills. Boys are no doubt struggling with the task of being *boys,* hence of being unlike the mother and sisters; their rejection of girls, after a certain point, is probably a reaction-formation—a repression of "girlish" dependency needs and a somewhat ill-assured assertion of masculinity. In this period, interest in the opposite sex is relatively "latent" (hidden, inactive). However, the latency period, so called, seems to have no physiological basis and is not found in all societies (see White, 1948, p. 121).

The meanings of "identification"

The term "identification" has been used in different ways.[16] We shall use it to mean either of two closely related things: (1) One is said to identify with a social *role* if one not only internalizes the role but adopts it as one's own, striving to attain the necessary skills and to conform with the role norms. (2) One is said to identify with a social *group* if one internalizes the role system of the group and considers oneself a member of it. Identification in the first sense links a boy with his father and brothers, for example, but not with his mother. Identification in the second sense links a boy with his family, including both parents and all siblings. No new principles of learning are involved in the process of identification. The three basic conditions of all learning are of course necessary: cues for discrimination, relative deprivation (reward for correct performance, no reward for incorrect performance), and control of reactions to frustration.

According to the definition we adopt, the boy makes three identifications

---

[16] For an excellent analysis of the ways in which Sigmund and Anna Freud used it, see Mowrer, 1950, Chap. 21. In the text, however, we follow Parsons, 1955a, pp. 91-94.

during the third stage of socialization. First, he identifies with his father and brothers (sex-role identification); secondly, he identifies with all his siblings (role of child in the family); and finally, he identifies with the whole family as a member. (The last identification can hardly be made firm until the child has considerable experience with nonmembers of his family; school and peer group thus help him to identify with his family.) In this third stage, identification does not affect only the roles identified with. Identification with the sex role, for example, obviously requires a change in the internalized objects "representing" mother, father, and siblings of each sex. Up to this point, the difference between father and mother has not been clearly a *role* difference. Now the father appears clearly as the "instrumental" leader of the family, while the mother, who has hitherto been the instrumental leader in her relation with the child, now appears to him clearly as the "expressive" leader of the family.

The selective character of identification should be emphasized. In "identifying" with his father, a boy does not *become* his father (even in imagination); he wants to be *like* his father (and his older male siblings) in sex *role*. Moreover, the "sex role" at this point is far from being the same thing as the adult's "sexual role"; in his emphasis on generally masculine qualities, including interest in "instrumental" activities, the boy can successfully identify with his father at this stage even though the boy may still have a hazy idea of the nature of sexual intercourse.

The selective character of identification helps us to see how the mother can also help the boy to make the proper sex identification. Being a socialized adult, the mother has already internalized both the female and the male role, and she is able to reward the boy selectively for choosing the right one for him.

Nevertheless, the father is especially important in helping the boy to make the necessary discriminations, for the father can serve as a direct model in certain ways. Probably in every society the father helps his son by showing him how to do things. For example, of a father in Wogeo (New Guinea) we read:

> . . . when Marigum was making a new canoe he allowed his youngest son, Sabwakai, to take an adze and chip at the dugout. On my inquiring whether the boy did not impede his progress, the father agreed that he would be able to work much faster alone. "But if I send the child away," he added, "how can I expect him to know anything? This time he was in the way, but I'm showing him, and when we have to make another canoe he'll be really useful" [Hogbin, 1946, p. 152].

The Eskimo father makes small bows and arrows and carves toy animals for his son to play with, and the father shows the boy how to shoot; as the boy gets older, the father makes larger bows and eventually lets the boy try his skill on small game. In Bali, where the boy begins to learn how to dance before he can walk, the father stands behind him, holding him up, and guides the boy's arms and hands in the traditional movements (Bateson and

Mead, 1942, pp. 14, 86-87). In general, of course, once the boy has learned the goal of being like men, he will tend to imitate men, especially his father.

Identification with one's sex role may or may not be complete or "wholehearted." The likelihood of successful identification is greater (1) if the main model for a boy's sex role (the father) shows affection for the boy; (2) if the boy's acquaintance with the role model is intimate and prolonged; (3) if other important persons (notably the mother) encourage the boy to take his father as a model (in which case the boy will be doubly rewarded: first by the father and then by the mother); and (4) if the role model treats the boy's mother well (for then the boy, who presumably loves his mother, will *want* to be like him). Obviously, the reverse of any of these conditions will tend to have the opposite effect. For example, if the boy's mother has contempt for her husband, the boy will be in conflict about the goal of becoming a man, lest he become "contemptible," like his father.[17]

THE FOURTH STAGE

In general, adolescence, which begins roughly at puberty, is the stage during which the young boy or girl is ordinarily more and more "emancipated" from parental control. The "crisis" of the period is precisely the strain produced by much greater demands for independence. At the same time, in the middle class of our own society at least, the adolescent is still controlled to some extent by his parents in many activities in which he might like greater freedom. This is especially true, perhaps, of sexual activity. The physiological changes that accompany adolescence would not in themselves produce problems if full sexual activity were permitted, but since it is not, these changes, in our own society, may intensify the ambivalence with which the adolescent approaches adulthood—impatient of restriction desiring independence, yet fearing freedom at the same time.

In our society, the goal of adulthood is considered to be attained when a person can support himself or herself entirely independently of the parental family. Full adulthood also implies the ability to form a family of one's own. Here an explicit distinction should perhaps be made between the ability to do so and the decision to do so; on the one hand, certain persons marry and become parents without being very well prepared, and, on the other hand, there are others who would be competent in marriage and parenthood and who possess the necessary skills to approach the opposite sex successfully but who deliberately decide not to marry.

Whether adolescence is a period of great strain depends upon the cultural definition of adult roles. There seems to be considerable variation from one society to another in the ease or difficulty with which the transition is typically accomplished. Adolescence is probably unusually difficult in our society because the adult-to-be is required to make important decisions more

---

[17] On variables affecting the success or failure of sex identification, see Stoke, 1950, and Mowrer, 1950, Chap. 21. Both articles contain excellent descriptions of cases.

or less on his own. In many other societies the choice of a marriage partner is made by elders within conventional rules. The other great life-decision, for men especially, is the choice of an occupation. Here again, in our society the burden of choice is placed largely on the individual himself.

We are now in a better position to understand the functions of the incest taboo. In Chapter 3 we noted that the primary incest taboo prevents sexual rivalry within the nuclear family, ensures that the families composing a society will be interconnected through marriage, helps to ensure a larger common fund of culture than there would otherwise be, and helps to strengthen the "coalition" between husband and wife, which makes it possible for them to maintain a common front *vis-à-vis* the children. In this chapter, following Parsons, 1954a, we have been able to extend the analysis of the part played by the incest taboo in socialization. As we have seen, some degree of frustration is probably unavoidable if the child is to learn new roles. The mother or mother substitute is the most important socializing agent in the child's early years. As Parsons remarks, the mother must be able to frustrate the child rather seriously without losing control of him. Perhaps the most important condition of which the mother can take advantage is the fact that the child is capable of deriving a great deal of erotic pleasure from bodily contact with her (or with any other person close to him, including the father). The child's erotic gratification may be in some ultimate sense sexual, but it is not necessarily genital gratification. The sex drive is a particularly good foundation for the child's attachment to the mother because it *can* be frustrated without danger to life. Its diffuseness is the very thing about it that makes it useful in the process of socialization; in this respect, it is unlike the hunger drive, for example. But this attachment between child and mother is mutual; the mother, that is, also derives gratification from bodily contact with the child. In this fact lies a threat to the coalition between the parents and also to the development of the child, especially of the boy. Since sexual attachments, as Parsons says, have some of the characteristics of addiction, there is danger that the boy will be "stuck" in this early stage and will be unable to leave the family to learn new things and form new attachments. The incest taboo functions in part to prevent mother and son from continuing their erotic relationship.

In the normal course of development, the boy at some point tends to repress his attachment to his mother and even, in some societies, to repress for a while his sexual interest in all girls and women. He tends to put a good deal of his sentiment into a play group or gang of boys of his own age. This group helps him to establish the proper sex-role identification. At the same time, in this group he is better able to assert his new degree of independence, since in this group he is an equal of the other members. The emphasis on relative equality within the group is brought out in the name that is commonly given to it: the "peer group."

On turning from his mother, the boy cannot take his father as an erotic substitute for several reasons. Every society puts homosexuality below heterosexuality, presumably because the very survival of the society depends upon heterosexuality. A father-son erotic attachment would destroy the husband-wife "coalition" and would make it difficult for the boy to identify with the proper sex role.

The relation between mother (or father) and daughter is a little different from that between mother (or father) and son. Since girls are permitted—indeed, expected—to be more dependent than boys, there might seem at first glance to be less danger in the mother-daughter and father-daughter attachments. But any attachment between either of the parents and a child of either sex obviously is in danger of destroying the husband-wife coalition. Moreover, if the boy must turn away from his mother and father sexually and from other boys as well, then there must be girls available to whom he can turn. This necessity also precludes a parent-daughter attachment. Finally, this attachment is culturally precluded also, because the girl, in her later role as a mother, must be able to control her erotic attachments to her own children.

The boy cannot turn to his sister because, if in general boys are expected to leave their families, there must of course be unattached girls with whom they can form new families. In any case, if the mother is tabooed the sister would be dangerously close from a psychological point of view, and the taboo of the mother would almost automatically be extended to the daughter-and-sister as a matter of defense.

A More Detailed Analysis of Process

Implicit in what we have said so far is the fundamental idea that socialization involves a process of social interaction between a socializing agent and his or her "pupil." The socializing agent guides the process by presenting cues for discrimination, controlling the pupil's negative reactions to frustration, and rewarding the pupil for doing the new things that are expected of him. Throughout the process, the pupil's personality is gradually (and unevenly) changing in approximately the direction aimed at by the socializing agent.

Taking the third stage (oedipal crisis and latency period) as an example, let us follow in a little more detail the phases of the process.[18]

The socializing agent is the mother. The previous stage of socialization has ended with the establishment of a love-attachment between mother and child. The child is still dependent upon the mother. Other members of the family have no clearly differentiated roles from the point of view of the child. They are merely on the periphery of the all-important relationship

---

[18] This section is based on Parsons, 1955a, pp. 38ff.; and Parsons and Olds, 1955 pp. 216ff. Certain aspects of the original analysis are ignored here.

between him and his mother. The "crisis" introducing the new stage is the mother's requiring the child to take more responsibility for himself. The father, who hitherto has been only a "second mother," now enters the scene more prominently and insistently as one who also requires the child to do more things for himself. The father, an "intruder," seems to be in charge, and the mother "betrays" the child by seeming to side with the father. Thus, instead of the two "objects" the child has already internalized—himself as the loving dependent child and his mother as the nurturant parent—there are new objects to be internalized. There is the father of the family. There is the mother in a new role. Possibly there are siblings. Cues have been presented for the development of a new self also. In this learning situation, the child goes through some turmoil and must be treated with special consideration. According to Parsons and Olds (1955), the socializing agents typically do four things in their control of learning: they take a permissive attitude toward the inevitable reactions to frustration, they provide emotional support, they deny reciprocity to certain overtures, and they manipulate rewards.

The child's first reaction is a feeling of frustration. His existing needs are not being satisfied in the old way. Since he had been led to expect certain behavior from his mother, he now feels that he is being let down; he feels a kind of moral indignation. His very first reaction—perception of error (his existing expectations are seen to be unfounded)—is "adjustive." It is the first step in making the necessary cognitive discrimination for internalizing new roles. His first negative reaction is also adjustive: by aggression directed against the mother and father, he tries to restore the previous state of affairs, to remove the source of disturbance. His anxiety that his mother may not love him is also adjustive in the sense that it is a reaction to the external world. At the same time, certain shifts may take place within his personality—motivational shifts not directed toward the environment. For example, he may relieve tension to some extent by "regressive" fantasies or by a kind of easing of the restraints on aggression that he has already established in his personality. These reactions may be called "mechanisms of defense," to distinguish them from mechanisms of adjustment, the main object of which is to change the external world.[19] The mechanisms of defense are

[19] The term "mechanism," as in "mechanism of defense" or "mechanism of adjustment," refers to any process within the personality that has functional consequences for the personality. "Adjustment," as we have seen, has to do with the relation between the personality and the outside world. (The term "adjustment" is preferred to "adaptation" since the latter might suggest that the personality only passively accepts or submits to the environment.) "Defense" has to do with the relations of the parts of the personality to one another mechanisms of defense, therefore, have the function of maintaining, restoring, or creating integration within the personality; they "cover up" or resolve inner conflicts. A mechanism may be a relatively simple or a complex process, and its "function" may not be clear at once but may depend upon its place in a longer sequence of events within the personality. The functional "success" of any process is always contingent upon factors external to the process itself. See Parsons and Olds, 1955, pp. 187-89, 224n.

inner shifts whose function is to maintain some sort of integration in the personality. Toward these negative reactions to frustration the parents take a *permissive* attitude (they realize the child is under strain).

The mother is not only permissive. She gives the child more *emotional support* than usual, thus helping to relieve his anxiety about loss of love. Presumably the child's need for love is reactivated by the mother's demonstration of love. There is the implicit promise that he can continue to have his mother's love if he tries to learn the new things required of him. This perception of the mother's attitudes is also adjustive: it is the second step in cognitive discrimination (the first was the perception of error). The new reassurance and promise of love also make possible integrative mechanisms (mechanisms of defense). Thus, the child is now in a better position to inhibit his dependency and his aggression. He is also ready to make room in his personality for new objects cathected by his mother. In particular, he is ready to extend his love to include the father because the mother loves the father.

In the next phase, the child internalizes the new system of roles. This does not happen all at once. The parents *deny reciprocity* to his overtures based on the old system of expectations. Gradually he learns more than the fact that there is a changed situation: he learns more exactly how it has changed; he begins to generalize—that is, to see how many specific stimuli "belong to" the same object. This is the first step in cognitive generalization. The formation of new concepts is a mechanism of adjustment. The new concepts include, for example, a concept of father as the instrumental leader of the household, the disciplinarian, the one who primarily looks for adequacy and rewards with approval and esteem more than with affection. At the same time, the new internalized objects are invested with positive feeling. This "generalization of cathexis," paralleling cognitive generalization, is also a mechanism of adjustment, having to do primarily with the child's relation to the external world of "social objects." As denial of reciprocity for the old behavior patterns continues, the child also develops integrative mechanisms within his personality. These mechanisms of defense, in this phase, include "repression" of the old needs, which is presumably more far-reaching than inhibition; and also, to some extent, "extinction" or "unlearning" of old patterns, which is more far-reaching than repression. The culmination of this phase is the integrative mechanism of identification. The child identifies with his parent and siblings of the same sex.

As we have already suggested, this identification leaves room for the other internalized objects in his personality. He has a "mother" within him and a "sister" as well as a "father" and a "brother." What identification does in a boy is to establish a clear-cut supremacy for the more "masculine" behavior patterns and needs. "Feminine" patterns and needs are also there, but in a subordinate place. Because it establishes a hierarchy within the personality, identification is perhaps the most important of the integrative mechanisms.

The last phase is one of reinforcement, a phase in which the new internalized objects, including the ones identified with, are strengthened and sharpened. The socializing agents now *manipulate rewards* in such a way as to bring about this reinforcement; presumably the old patterns have by now been so well repressed or extinguished that the parents are seldom called upon to deny reciprocity to them.

In the child's personality in this phase, cognitive generalization is being strengthened by more active reality-testing. This reality-testing is of course a mechanism of adjustment. At the same time, the child is now receiving gratification for his new motives (for example, he enjoys being praised for being such a fine boy). His commitment to the beliefs and values of his "ego" (the core of his personality, composed of his identifications) is being confirmed. A "superego" is being developed. The superego is the existence in the personality of certain mechanisms of defense of integration, or of the structure already formed: mechanisms such as guilt and shame and rationalization. These mechanisms are the basis of self-control, which is thus seen to be a kind of inner social control of any temptation to deviation that may arise. At this point the personality is ready for the next stage of socialization.

Needless to say, our description of process has been simplified. In particular, we have not taken account of such variable factors as those we mentioned earlier in connection with failures, or partial failures, of identification. Nevertheless, the description in this section will serve as an indication of the *kind* of process that goes on in socialization.

Internalized Roles as Prototypes

The roles internalized during the early stages of socialization contain elements of motivation that will carry over to other roles in later life. For example, the "internalized father" contains a need for conformity to broad and basic social norms. At the same time, the child has been sensitized to the approval and disapproval of others. A need for adequacy in the performance of tasks requiring skill has also been developed. On the more "feminine" side of the personality, the child has developed a need for "response" (or affection), and some capacity for giving affection and help to others. He is thus sensitive to corresponding sanctions; that is, he will be guided to some extent by others' acceptance and response (or denial of acceptance and response). (See Parsons, 1955a, p. 82.)

The "social" nature of these needs should be emphasized. The personality has not developed mainly through extension of the scope of biological drives, such as hunger and thirst. On the contrary, the first task of socialization is to bring these drives under control and to substitute for them needs that bind the individual more closely to his fellows in social life: above all, the needs for approval and acceptance. In adult life, people are not ordinarily motivated strongly by hunger and thirst because these needs are usually provided for in a routine way; not so, however, the needs for approval and acceptance.[20]

Certain other characteristics of the roles internalized during early life are also important for later roles. In going through the four stages of socialization, the "pupil" in effect learns to make four fundamental distinctions—fundamental in the sense that they will be applicable to all subsequent role behavior. These distinctions have to do with the *kinds* of normative pattern that are involved in all roles. Needless to say, the distinctions are not explicitly formulated by either the socializing agent or the pupil.[21] Each of the four distinctions is a distinction between two possibilities. Hence each pair of possibilities may be regarded as the *values* of a *pattern variable*.[22]

DIFFUSENESS-SPECIFICITY

The first pattern variable is called "diffuseness-specificity" (the two possible values of the variable). The occupant of a role, in his interaction with another person, may have strictly limited and specific obligations toward that person or he may have an indefinitely large number of obligations, depending upon the requirements of the occasion and the limits imposed by obligations to other persons and groups. In adult role relationships, examples of relatively specific roles are the role of medical doctor in relation to his patient, the role of landlord toward his tenant, the role of mathematics teacher toward his pupils. Examples of relatively diffuse roles are the role of friend, the role of leader of a political movement, the role of husband or wife, mother or father. In these diffuse roles, the pattern of obligation is not defined, as it were, by a legal contract containing specific conditions and expectations. On the contrary, a "friend" (as opposed to a casual acquaintance) is expected to do whatever he can for his friend, if asked, and the only limits to his obligation are those imposed by his obligations to other persons and groups. There is a hierarchy of obligations and, psychologically, a hierarchy of identifications. (Thus, in the United States today, a man's obligations toward his wife and children and toward his country take precedence over his diffuse obligation toward a friend.) Psychologically, then, as occupant of a "specific" role, one has a limited scope of interest in the persons or groups with whom one is interacting, whereas the occupant of a diffuse role has a great, and always potentially greater, scope of interest

---

[20] Under great deprivation, the biological needs dominate the personality more imperiously than the social needs. See Sherif, 1948, pp. 75ff. On the whole, however, the sociologist W. I. Thomas seems to have been right in his attempt to name a few fundamental wishes that run through human adult behavior. He named four: the wishes for recognition, response, new experience, and security. His most extended discussion is in *The Unadjusted Girl* (1923), Chaps. 1, 2.

[21] We do not mean to imply in this analysis that these four are the only distinctions that one might make in classifying role patterns.

[22] This section is based mainly upon Parsons, 1955a, pp. 50ff., and 1955b, pp. 134ff. However, the pattern variables are discussed in many other works by Parsons. See especially Parsons and Shils, 1951, Chap. 1, esp. pp. 80ff.

in the occupants of reciprocal roles. The difference, though ultimately a relative one, should be fairly clear.

What does this have to do with socialization? The distinction just mentioned can hardly be made, *on the adult level,* within the family: all family roles are diffuse. Toward the end of the anal stage, however, the distinction can be applied to *the roles internalized in the child's personality*. In this stage of "the family romance," as it has been called, the child's role is diffuse, whereas by contrast in his eyes the mother's role is specific. The culmination of the stage is the three-year-old, celebrated in the pages of Gesell for his compliance and loving attachment to his mother. His role obligation is to show his love for his mother as well as he can, to cooperate in whatever ways she may wish. Her role, on the other hand, is relatively specific: if a button is hard to manage, she is the expert on buttons; her tasks on behalf of the child are specific tasks, and her love is not her *differentiating* contribution to the social system but essentially the reward she gives the child for his diffuse cooperation. To the adult, the role of mother is probably the very archetype of diffuse roles; but to the three-year-old child, his role involves diffuse interest in the mother and is thus the prototype of all his later diffuse roles. We have had other occasions in this chapter to point out the necessity of distinguishing between the "simplified" role system internalized by the child and the "actual" role system as it is perceived by the adult. The stage of oral dependency provides a more extreme example: the primary identification, or "merging," of mother and infant in the infant's personality prevents any role differentiation from his point of view: consequently there is no pattern variable for this stage.

AFFECTIVITY-NEUTRALITY

The pattern variable "affectivity-neutrality" has to do with the question whether a role permits certain kinds of expression of feeling ("affect") or requires that those kinds of expression be held in check. Expression of feeling is a form of self-gratification or enjoyment. Feelings may be positive or negative. The pre-oedipal child is permitted to indulge his feelings of anger or love with little or no restraint—at least he is not expected to have any *inner* restraint (self-control). During the so-called oedipal crisis, however, he is rewarded for certain kinds of self-control and not rewarded for the corresponding kinds of self-indulgence. Whereas earlier he was restrained, when necessary, "because he didn't know any better," now he has to submit to *discipline*. Discipline has the aim of inculcating *self*-control. In this sense, therefore, the role of the pre-oedipal child is characterized by permissiveness for affectivity and that of the oedipal child by "affective neutrality."

This distinction is highly relative. Any role whatsoever permits some immediate gratification, and any *adult* role whatsoever requires self-control (forbids the role occupant to take advantage of certain objective opportunities for gratification). The distinction is more strictly applicable, therefore, to behavior permitted or forbidden to the same role in different situations.

What the oedipal child learns, essentially, is that one must sometimes forego the pleasure of affectivity in the interest of attaining goals; one must sometimes do relatively unpleasant things for *deferred* rewards. All adult roles, of course, require their occupants to distinguish between occasions in which one may relax and have fun and occasions in which one must "tend to business."

But in some roles there are both unusual opportunities to indulge impulses and also a strong normative pattern of affective neutrality. Until the green salesman learns affective neutrality *for the role of salesman,* he is likely to have trouble suppressing feelings of boredom and personal dislike. The nurse new to the operating room must learn to control a "perfectly natural" feeling of nausea. Yet when the role of nurse is completely internalized, nausea will no longer seem "natural"—the relevant kind of affective neutrality will have been established in the personality. The role of oedipal child stresses affective neutrality in the sense that any suppression of affectivity, any discipline, is still relatively new to the child. The contrast with the previous stage is perhaps the important thing.

UNIVERSALISM-PARTICULARISM

Like "affectivity-neutrality," the pattern variable "universalism-particularism" may be thought of as applying to roles or merely to normative patterns within roles. The values of this pattern variable answer the question "Shall I, as occupant of this role, in this situation, treat the other person as a member or nonmember of some interaction group to which I belong, or as a person who has or does not have certain characteristics, regardless of his group membership?" To put the distinction in another way, some obligations derive from the fact that the other person has a certain social position, and other obligations arise from the application of general criteria having nothing to do intrinsically with social position. For example, the obligations of a son toward his father depend upon the social position the father occupies in relation to the son; they do not depend to any great extent upon the kind of man the father is. Such obligations are "particularistic." The *role* of son or father is particularistic. The role of judge in court, on the other hand, is strongly "universalistic." A judge is supposed to make decisions, not on the basis of the social position of the persons before the bench, but on the basis of strictly impersonal criteria of justice.

Up to the time he joins play groups outside the family and goes to school, the child has hardly any opportunity to make the distinction between particularism and universalism. All roles in the family being particularistic, no distinction between them is possible on this score. During the latency period, however, the child has to go to school, where he will be treated according to standards that apply equally to him and all the other pupils, regardless of the families they come from. All the pupils will be classified, for example, according to their ability to read. Even if there are no report cards, the pupils themselves will be conscious of differential approval according to universalistic standards. There are few schools that do not award prizes for merit. At the very least, the pupils will be concerned about promotion from grade to grade. In most American schools there is also a lively interest in athletic skill, which of course is judged according to universalistic standards (see Brookover, 1955, Chap. 7).

In the latency period, groups of age-equals (peer groups) also help to establish the distinction between particularism and universalism. According to Piaget's famous studies (1948) made in Switzerland, children below the age of seven or eight cannot participate in true "games." G. H. Mead (1934, pp. 150ff.) also distinguishes between "play" and "playing in games." We shall see that this distinction is essentially an instance of the distinction between universalism and particularism.

Children frequently play together without cooperating to achieve a definite outcome according to commonly accepted rules. A "true game" involves such cooperation. Each player in the game must "take" the roles of the other players as well as play his own. The other players, moreover, are not viewed as "Johnny" or "Jimmy"; they are viewed as occupants of clearly defined roles in the game. Thus it makes no difference whether Johnny or Jimmy is pitching—any occupant of that position is subject to the same rules. That is, the rules are universalistic. Before the stage of playing in games, children seem to feel that rules emanate from parents or older children; the children do not yet understand the function of rules in making a cooperative *group* possible. The rules, to them, exist in and for themselves, not for larger purposes. The rules are "sacred" particularistic obligations to parents or other persons in authority.

Piaget found that Swiss boys in their games of marbles are helped to see the universalistic character of the rules of the game by two things: First, the age differences between the players are not great; the boys are one another's "peers," and the rules are seen as securing that equality in the game. Secondly, the boys soon learn that there are many games of marbles, with slightly different rules. After a time, they are able to sense (implicitly) that all the different games have the same underlying constitutive rules, in the sense that particular variants always ensure fair play and always allow scope for skill as well as luck. The basic "rules of the game" guarantee that each player, *whoever he may be,* will have the same rights as the other players. This is the essence of universalism. Once the boys understand it, they freely invent their own rules and agree upon them, striving always to justify their legislation by showing that it ensures fair play. By the time they are eleven or twelve they are great experts and codifiers. It is as if they were glorying in the fact that they have a new measure of autonomy, freed to some extent from imposed particularistic rules.

The rules of logic are of course universalistic. In peer groups, the child soon learns that he cannot win an argument by appealing to the authority of his father, for among these equals from different families no particular father has authority for the whole group. To carry his point, he must argue according to rules equally applicable to all.[23]

QUALITY-PERFORMANCE

The pattern variable focused upon in adolescence is "quality-performance." The distinction has to do with the aspect of a role that one pays more attention to. A role pattern emphasizes "quality" if one reacts to some objective characteristics of the occupant, such as age, sex, or group membership, and takes it for granted that everyone with that objective "quality" will be able to do certain things. The role occupant, of course, may be oneself or another. A role pattern emphasizes "performance" if one pays particular attention to what the occupant can do and how well he can do it, relatively regardless of his age, sex, and group memberships.

This distinction is similar to a well-recognized technical distinction between "ascribed" roles and "achieved" roles.[24] A role is said to be "ascribed" if its occupants *acquire* it automatically as a result of certain objective characteristics or relations to others which are beyond their control. The most important bases of ascription are birth into a particular family, birth order, sex, and age. Son-in-law, for example, is an ascribed role because it is based on a relation over which one has no control—the membership of one's wife in a particular family.

Technically, any role is said to be "achieved" if it is not "ascribed." It is now easy to see the similarity between the quality-performance distinction and the distinction between ascribed and achieved roles. Although one may have certain "achieved" roles without having striven for them and even without having any great merit, nevertheless there is a tendency for distinctive *performances* to be stressed in achieved roles, and for the emphasis in ascribed roles to be placed on *not falling below a certain standard* in fulfilling traditional expectations.

It is this difference that we wish to emphasize. Interacting with a person in his capacity as occupant of an ascribed role, one acts toward him mainly on the basis of certain *qualities* (his sex, his age, his family), taking certain *performances* on his part more or less for granted; interacting with another in his capacity as occupant of an achieved status, one treats age, sex, and the like as secondary and tends to emphasize what the other can *do*—his presumed capacity for performances that one does not routinely expect every person of his age, sex, or kinship positions to have. The pattern variable quality-performance is somewhat more abstract than ascription-achievement, however, for some ascribed roles lay great stress on a high and distinctive level of performance. A good example is the role of hereditary king.

---

[23] Piaget, 1928, Chap. 5, analyzes the stages in the development of logical thought from prelogical beginnings. This, of course, is an important part of socialization.

[24] The distinction between ascribed and achieved roles was first made by Linton, 1936. See also K. Davis, 1949, pp. 97-113.

Before adolescence, all one's roles are ascribed, and the emphasis is on qualities rather than on performance. This is true even of early roles in school. At a certain age one is expected to be in a certain grade, and one's performances are ascribed with the role ("anyone in the sixth grade knows that"). There is opportunity to do unusually well, certainly, but the lines are laid down. Like everyone else of the same age, one is a pupil in school; one happens to be a good pupil, that's all.

Beginning in high school, however, one has to make important choices leading toward achieved occupational roles, in which, of course, the emphasis will be placed on performance and much less on age. In the United States, a basic decision is the one to enter the "college course" or the "commercial course." In adolescence, the other great area for "performance" is competitive dating.[25] This is ordinarily preparation for marriage, and Americans regard marrying the "right" person as an achievement.

It should be clear that the internalized roles of the four stages of socialization, incorporating basic norms and social needs, sensitivity to basic social sanctions, and all the values of basic pattern variables, may be regarded as prototypes for all later roles.

Socialization of Adults

The socialization of adults is easier than the socialization of children for at least three reasons: (1) the adult ordinarily is motivated to work toward a goal that he already envisions; (2) the new role that he is trying to internalize has many similarities to roles already existing in his personality; and (3) the socializing agent can communicate with him easily through speech. These advantages more than offset the disadvantage of relative inflexibility.

Nevertheless, the socialization of adults can be a prolonged and difficult process. This is especially true when the skills to be learned are complex and the responsibilities of the role are heavy; when the role requires the deep internalization of norms and attitudes that run counter, in some way, to norms already established in the personality; and when the socializing process has not been made routine.

Some of these points are well illustrated in a study of the training of cadets at the Coast Guard Academy (Dornbusch, 1955). We shall confine our attention to the inculcation of norms and attitudes and say nothing about the technical training. The Coast Guard officer must be able to give commands and to obey superiors without hesitation, for action at sea often requires speed and close coordination of the efforts of the group. He must have great self-respect for his role and pride in the service, for otherwise

[25] As Parsons points out, Waller almost satirized this aspect of college dating in his "The Rating and Dating Complex" (1937).

the sometimes harsh life might undermine morale. Finally, living at close quarters with his fellow officers, he will fit in better if he feels solidarity with them and has the same tastes.

How are the "proper" attitudes inculcated? Like the norms that guide socializing agents in one's early life, the norms at the Academy probably have partly latent functions. A trained sociologist, however, is able to analyze the system to some extent.

The inculcation of "automatic" obedience to superior officers, yet at the same time of the ability to give orders, is largely achieved through the system of hierarchical classes. The men in their first year—the "swabs"—are forced to submit to hazing at the hands of the men in the second and third years. But of course the swabs will eventually haze the class that follows them. The seniors have a large part in controlling the behavior of the classes below.

Self-respect and pride in the service are obtained in several ways. (1) The swab, who is not yet a full member of the organization, is defined as a nobody in comparison with the upperclassmen. Consequently he comes to feel that becoming an upperclassman and eventually an officer is an achievement to be proud of. (2) Submitting to hazing and harsh discipline without complaint is defined as proof that one is a man and can "take it." (3) The superiority of Academy men is constantly emphasized by comparisons with civilians and reserve officers (reference groups). (4) The cadets are made to feel that as cadets they are highly eligible for marriage. "No one is too good for them." They are watched to see that they invite worthy middle-class college girls to dances. (5) After this build-up, they are prepared, as seniors, against any let-down after graduation by being told that their position on ship will not be an exalted one immediately.

As for solidarity and compatibility with fellow officers, several mechanisms at the Academy help to create them. (1) For two months after coming to the Academy, the recruit is isolated from the outside world. For four years the Academy is the center of his life. (2) He is not permitted to receive money from home, and he must wear a uniform. Thus differences among the cadets tend to be minimized. (3) During his four years, one of the paramount norms is that the cadet must be loyal to the men of his class. He must not report them for anything. He must not embarrass any one of them by seeming to know more in recitations. With them he suffers the rough first year of hazing. (This common suffering probably helps him also to endure the hazing.) Although he suffers from upperclassmen, he knows that they have gone through the same thing themselves: all the graduates can look back on an essentially common experience, and they can look forward to a similar career. Moreover, there are informal relations between the classes that somewhat counteract the more formal hierarchical relations. (4) The Academy trains the cadets in etiquette and in other ways, as noted, seeks to create a kind of uniformity that will extend to their finding one another's wives socially acceptable.

RECOMMENDED READING

For a review of experimental work on socialization, see I. L. Child, "Socialization," in G. Lindzey, ed., *Handbook of Social Psychology,* Addison-Wesley, 1954, v. 2, Chap. 18. The best single book on socialization is T. Parsons and R. F. Bales, in collaboration with J. Olds, M. Zelditch, Jr., and P. E. Slater, *Family, Socialization and Interaction Process,* Free Press, 1955. In treating socialization we quite rightly tend to stress the role of parents. For interesting essays on the part played by brothers and sisters, guests, and domestic servants, see J. H. S. Bossard, *The Sociology of Child Development,* rev. ed., Harper, 1954, Chaps. 5, 11, 12. An unusually interesting study of adult socialization is R. C. Fox, "Training for Uncertainty," in R. K. Merton, G. G. Reader, M. D., and P. L. Kendall, eds., *The Student-Physician: Introductory Studies in the Sociology of Medical Education,* Harvard University Press, 1957, pp. 207-41. The medical student must be aware of his ignorance and personal inadequacy ever to master the enormous body of medical knowledge, and he must be aware of the inadequacy of existing medical knowledge itself; yet he must learn not to be overwhelmed by anxiety in the face of these inadequacies. This paper brings out the importance of the controlled sequence of experiences to which the student is exposed and the importance of reference groups, notably his fellow students and the doctor-teachers. It shows how research can focus on certain aspects of learning a role while fruitfully neglecting other aspects, leaving them for other research projects.

A classic work on the relation between the self and social experience is C. H. Cooley, *Human Nature and the Social Order,* Scribner's, 1902. One of the few research projects in which Cooley's concept of the looking-glass self is explicitly used, and perhaps the only one in which it is used systematically, is M. J. Huntington, "The Development of a Professional Self-Image," in Merton, Reader, and Kendall, eds., 1957, pp. 179-87.

For a clear review of experimental literature in the psychology of learning, see A. W. Melton, "Learning," *Annu. Rev. Psychol.,* 1950, v. 1, pp. 9-30. For later developments, see J. Olds, *The Growth and Structure of Motives: Psychological Studies in the Theory of Action,* Free Press, 1955. L. Wylie, *Village in the Vaucluse,* Harvard University Press, 1957, which is an untechnical study of a French village, contains a good deal of information about socialization; to an American perhaps the most striking thing is the emphasis on discipline and the "cruel" use of humiliation as a technique. Wylie describes many specific incidents to illustrate his points.

Mowrer's *Learning Theory and Personality Dynamics,* 1950, is interesting for its attempt to integrate Freudian theory and "behavior psychology" (in popular terms, "rat psychology"). See especially Chaps. 16, 19, 21, 22, 24. T. Parsons and J. Olds, "The Mechanisms of Personality Functioning with Special Reference to Socialization," Chap. 4 in Parsons and Bales, 1955, fuses learning theory, Freudian psychology, and sociology. It analyzes the phases of process in the third stage of socialization (1) within the personality of the socializing agent, (2) within the personality of the child being socialized, and (3) within the relevant social system and subsystems. This paper also contains some interesting speculation on the origins of personality deviations, relating them to the stages of socialization. H. Orlansky, "Infant Care and Personality," *Psychol. Bull.,* 1949, v. 46, pp. 1-48 (reprinted in part in W. E. Martin and C. B. Stendler, eds., *Readings in Child Development,* Harcourt, Brace, 1954, pp. 321-36), is a review of evidence on the effects of different bowel-training and feeding practices; it shows that the claims of some theorists have inadequate empirical support. Evidence in the

Kinsey reports shows that differences between men and women in sexual behavior are to a considerable extent due to socialization. For an article that brings out this fact more clearly than do the Kinsey reports themselves, see B. Barber, "The Three Human Females," in D. P. Geddes, ed., *An Analysis of the Kinsey Reports on Sexual Behavior in the Human Male and Female,* Mentor, 1954, pp. 49-61.

part three

KINSHIP GROUPS AND SYSTEMS

6. *Marriage and the Family*

A society is a system of interlocking groups more or less well integrated through institutionalized patterns. One of the most important structural subsystems of every society is its kinship system. A structural subsystem is made up of groups of certain types. A kinship system, for example, is made up of families and other types of kin group. Such groups overlap in membership with groups of other types; that is to say, families and lineages are not *segments* of society. As we shall see particularly when we deal with political phenomena, it is one of the most important facts about society that few groups, if any, are "segments" in the sense that they do not overlap with other groups.

The kin groups of a society compose a structural sub*system* in the sense that they tend to be focused on the same few problems for the maintenance of the total society; they tend to make similar contributions to the society as a going concern. Further, they are subject to institutional patterns so closely interwoven that they constitute a superordinate pattern. This superordinate pattern organizes kin groups in a larger social system, the kinship system, with typical problems that must be met if the kinship system in turn is to make its contributions to the total society. This does not mean, of course, that the kinship system is structurally independent of the rest of the society. It is a structural *sub*system: it has a certain unity of its own, yet at the same time it is and must be tied in with the other structural subsystems of the same society.

In this chapter and in Chapters 7 and 8 we shall attempt to show what a kinship system is, how kinship systems vary, and how they change from one type to another.

A Definition of Marriage

The essential thing about marriage is that it is a stable relationship in which a man and a woman are socially permitted, without loss of standing in the community, to have children. In some societies an unmarried girl may give birth to a child without loss of standing provided that she gets married soon afterward: sometimes, in fact, this proof of fertility is necessary before a girl can get a husband.[1] Whether every relationship in which a man and woman are permitted to become parents is to be called a marriage depends, of course, upon how narrowly one wishes to define "marriage." A society may make a distinction between a wife of full status and a concubine while permitting both to have children by the husband.

The right to have children implies, of course, the right to sexual relations. According to a narrow definition of marriage, two other conditions must be fulfilled; namely, regular or normal cohabitation in the same household, and some degree of economic cooperation (Murdock, 1949, pp. 4ff.). This definition, however, is probably too narrow. At least, in the socialist *kibbutzim* (collective farms) of Israel, although all adults who are able participate in the economy and all share in its fruits, there is virtually no economic cooperation between husband and wife as such. Yet most people would recognize that these *kibbutzim* have the marriage tie, and we should have to admit that their family groups are at least as close-knit as family groups in our own society. The socialist economy is so arranged that fathers, for example, see their children more often, for longer periods, and in more relaxed circumstances than is usually possible in the United States (Spiro, 1956, 1958).

It is true, however, that relationships with the full complex of rights and obligations specified by Murdock exist in almost all societies. At the same time, in virtually every society an adult couple of opposite sexes may live in the same house or cooperate in economic production without having sexual rights in each other; and there are very often recognized relationships with sexual rights but lacking either common residence or economic cooperation.

The amount of economic cooperation in marriage varies a good deal. In early American farm families the husband and wife were the managers and chief workers on the farm, and this is still so in most societies with large peasant populations. In modern urban societies, however, family economic cooperation, although it is seldom limited to joint consumption of goods and services entirely produced outside the household, is not the main form of economic cooperation in the society.

The right to sexual relations also varies in important respects. For example, it is not necessarily an exclusive right. Many societies have "privileged relationships," as they are called by anthropologists—that is, kinship relationships in which premarital or extramarital sexual relations are permitted. At least thirty-four societies permit a man to have sexual relations

---

[1] According to one report, the surplus of women and economic difficulties in postwar West Germany and West Berlin have brought about a more liberal attitude toward parenthood without marriage. Thirty-three per cent of a quota sample of men and women questioned said, without qualification, that an unmarried woman had a right to have a child; 53 per cent said that she had such a right if she decided to have a child—that is, decided before becoming pregnant, not merely decided to allow an unplanned pregnancy to come to term (Friedeburg, 1953).

with his brother's wife; twenty-eight societies, with his wife's sister; and six, with his mother's brother's wife (Murdock, 1949, p. 270).[2] Such privileges are not arbitrary phenomena. Careful examination of the social systems in which they occur will usually make them understandable. Typically, the sexual privilege cements a relationship that is close for other reasons. Thus, many societies have a pattern known as sororal polygyny: a man may have two or more wives at the same time, provided that they are sisters. (Sometimes sororal polygyny is only the *preferred* form of polygyny.) In such societies, privileged extramarital sexual relations with a wife's sister merely anticipate a future marriage relationship, or at least a potential marriage relationship. Again, in some societies a man is expected to marry his brother's wife if the brother dies, and this obligation, along with others, colors the man's relationship with his brother and with his brother's wife when all three are alive. Privileged sexual relations may be regarded as a reinforcement and symbol of social relationships with important nonsexual content (see Murdock, 1949, pp. 6, 268-72; Ford and Beach, 1951, pp. 113-15). More generally, it should be recognized that the attitude toward sexual relations that prevails in our society is extremely restrictive as seen in the perspective afforded by a comparative study of a large number of societies. We tend to think that sexual relations should be confined to marriage and that a person should have only one marriage partner at a time (monogamy).

In many societies, the so-called double standard is more explicitly and firmly institutionalized than it is in ours. In Japan, for example, a wife is expected to be sexually faithful to her husband, but a husband who is having sexual relations with women other than his wife need not conceal the fact (Winch, 1953, p. 60). Of 115 societies for which data were available, forty-nine permit premarital sexual relations (Murdock, 1949, p. 263).[3]

So far we have mentioned culturally permitted pre- and extramarital relations. In all societies with "stricter" rules, these rules are of course sometimes broken. The Kinsey reports (Kinsey *et al.,* 1948, 1953) show that a high proportion of American men and women have some premarital sexual intercourse. Of the sample of 5940 females of all ages, 50 per cent admitted to having had premarital intercourse. (A large proportion of American girls, however, confine premarital sexual relations to their fiancés.) Since the sample is biased in several ways, this percentage is not very meaningful without qualification. A smaller percentage of the women born before 1900 than of the women born after 1900 have had premarital intercourse by the age of 25; and Kinsey's sample of females includes too few

[2] Murdock's book is based on studies of 250 societies, most of them nonliterate—i.e., lacking a written language.

[3] For a comparative analysis of many societies with respect to premarital sexual activity, see Ford and Beach, 1951, pp. 180-92. For descriptions of patterns quite different from those of the American middle class, see, for example, Ralph Linton's account of the Marquesans, 1939, or the selections on the Muria (of India) by Verrier Elwin, 1947, in Mead and Calas, eds., 1953, pp. 202-13.

women over 50. The sample also includes disproportionately small numbers of Catholic women and devout Jewish women. On the other hand, the categories of women with little education are also underrepresented, and there is reason to believe that more of these women have premarital intercourse (Ehrmann, 1954). As for men, the percentage of those who have had premarital intercourse is higher. In Kinsey's sample, 98 per cent of the men whose education had not gone beyond the eighth grade had had premarital intercourse. Of those with nine to twelve years of education, 85 per cent had had premarital intercourse; and of those with thirteen or more years, 68 per cent (Kinsey *et al.*, 1953, pp. 330-33)

The number of American men and women who have extramarital intercourse is lower. In Kinsey's total samples, 26 per cent of the women and about 50 per cent of the men had had extramarital intercourse by the age of 40 (Kinsey *et al.*, 1953, pp. 436-38).

These statistics tend to confirm what one might expect, that the private views of many people on sexual relations are not quite so strict as their "public" views. The statistics do not mean, however, that the norms against premarital and extramarital sexual relations are without force in American society. One must consider not only the number of persons who have violated the norms but also the proportion of total sexual behavior represented by such violations. Considering the latter point, the Kinsey reports leave no doubt that in the United States by far the greater amount of sexual intercourse takes place within marriage. On the other hand, the Kinsey reports do show that the norm against premarital intercourse is stronger in some social groups than in others. In particular, it is stronger in the middle classes, roughly speaking.

No society leaves marriage unregulated. It is so important that children be cared for and properly trained that there are always norms concerning what persons, under what conditions, and in what manner may establish a marriage relationship; what they will be expected to do once they are married; and how they may dissolve their relationship (if at all), and under what conditions. The total pattern of these norms for a particular society is the institution of marriage.

Forms of Marriage

The two basic forms of marriage are monogamy and polygamy. Monogamy is the form in which an individual is institutionally permitted to have only one spouse at a time. Of 238 societies included in Murdock's sample (1949, p. 28), only forty-three were monogamous.[4] Since there is

[4] Murdock was unable to find the relevant data for twelve of the 250 societies included in his sample. Ford and Beach (1951, pp. 102-08) found twenty-nine monogamous societies in their sample of 185 for which relevant data were available. Their sample includes 122 societies also included in Murdock's. Both samples include societies from all parts of the world. As in the Murdock study, most of the societies in the Ford and Beach study are nonliterate.

TABLE 4

Chinese married men with concubines, according to education, 1936-37 *

	Education of husband		
N =	COLLEGE 430	157 HIGH SCHOOL	TRADITIONAL SCHOOL 453
Richest group	10.4%	18.8%	16.0%
Less prosperous group	9	12.1	11.7

* Adapted from Olga Lang, *Chinese Family and Society*, Yale University Press, 1946, Table VIII, p. 223n.

a strong tendency for large modern societies to be monogamous, however, we shall devote most of our attention to monogamy.

"Polygamy" is a term covering both polygyny (the institution of marriage that permits a man to have two or more wives at the same time) and polyandry (the institution that permits a woman to have more than one husband at the same time). Of the 238 societies in Murdock's sample, 193 were polygynous.[5] In about sixty-one of these 193 polygynous societies, however, fewer than 20 per cent of the married men actually had more than one wife.

> In a numbe of societies which are polygynous according to the above definition, monogamous unions may actually be considerably commoner for men of all ages because economic conditions strongly favor them. Only a few unusually energetic or capable men, perhaps, can successfully support two families. In other cases, polygyny is confined largely to chiefs or men of wealth and status, or is limited in other ways. So long, however, as it enjoys superior prestige and is not the exclusive prerogative of a very small status group, it is assumed to be the cultural norm [Murdock, 1949, p. 28].[6]

Polygyny as an institution is not found only in primitive societies. Mohammedanism, of course, holds up polygyny as the ideal, and concubinage at least (which one might or might not wish to call polygyny) is fairly common in such highly civilized non-Mohammedan societies as China, India, and the countries of Latin America. Table 4 shows how many Chinese married men in a sample of 1040 had concubines in 1936–37. (The number has probably decreased, and will continue to do so, because of the "emancipation" of women attendant upon industrialization and the growth of cities, and the opposition of the Communists to concubinage.)

---

[5] Ford and Beach found 154 polygynous societies in their sample of 185. According to Claude Levi-Strauss (1949, pp. 46-47), there is a universal tendency toward polygyny in the sense that many men in every society form stable relationships with more than one woman at a time, and many more would do so if they could.

[6] Ford and Beach say that in seventy-six of their 154 polygynous societies most of the married men had only one wife (1951, p. 108). Widespread polygyny in a society is often associated with heavy losses of men in warfare.

Probably few American women feel that they could tolerate sharing their husbands with another woman. Yet many anthropologists report that women in polygynous societies often urge their husbands to take another wife. How can we understand this? We must remember that in particular societies the feelings of satisfaction involved in sexual exclusiveness depend, in part, upon its being the cultural ideal. For a woman especially, in our society, self-esteem, security of affection, and the esteem of other people are defined in relation to the cultural pattern all take for granted and regard, often, as sacred. Where this ideal does not prevail, as in Mohammedanism, for example, self-esteem, emotional security, and good reputation are fully compatible with being one of several wives of the same man. Indeed, where polygyny is the ideal, sanctioned even by religion, a woman's self-esteem can be the greater the more wives her husband has; for his prestige, and therefore her prestige, may depend in part on his being rich enough or competent enough or well born enough to have more than one wife. Moreover, the tasks of bringing up children and working in the fields—assigned to women in many societies—may be lighter if they can be performed by several women in cooperation. Finally, it must be remembered that in many polygynous societies women are permitted to have certain sexual relations outside of marriage.

Nevertheless, the possibility of rivalry and jealousy certainly exists in polygyny. These feelings might arise, for example, if the common husband neglected some of his wives sexually or humiliated them by publicly treating one wife with special favor, or if the wives disagreed about household management. Certain rules, however, tend to minimize these dangers or forestall them altogether. For example, commonly one wife, usually the first, is recognized as the primary wife, with some authority over the secondary wives. In some societies a man is expected not to take another wife without first gaining his previous wives' consent to his specific choice. Another common rule is one that we have mentioned earlier, that plural wives must be sisters. Sororal polygyny makes it possible for sisters to prepare long in advance, consciously and unconsciously, for the task of getting along together in a polygynous marriage. Another arrangement that must reduce friction in polygyny is to have each wife live with her children in a separate house or in a distinct part of the same house. This arrangement is particularly common in nonsororal polygyny. Finally, there is often a rule or expectation that the husband will rotate among his wives, spending a certain number of nights with each in turn. This arrangement at least prevents public humiliation of less-favored wives (Murdock, 1949, pp. 30-31).[7]

---

7 Among the Mormons in the United States, polygyny seems to have been unstable, with a good deal of friction, for three reasons: (1) Many of the women (but fewer of the men, apparently) had some doubts about the sanctity of the arrangement; they had come but recently, after all, from a Christian society. (2) Outside of Utah, the stronghold of Mormonism, there was much indignation, based to some extent on

The other form of polygamy—polyandry, in which a woman is permitted to have two or more husbands at the same time—is extremely rare. One of the best-described examples is the marriage system of the Marquesans of Oceania (Linton, 1939, pp. 137-96). Among the Marquesans, the joint husbands are unrelated by blood, whereas among the Todas of India, for example, the joint husbands are often brothers. Polyandry also occurs in western Tibet.

It is probable that early writers often treated as polyandry relationships that were not stable marriages of several men to the same woman and hence were not "genuine" polyandry. Among the Shoshoni Indians, for example, a man's younger brothers have sexual privileges with his wife, but the younger brothers are not full husbands. Among the Jarawa of Africa, old men with young wives permit younger men to visit the wives for sexual relations, but the younger men have none of the responsibilities of husbands. In this case, the older men are indulgent in order to prevent their economically productive wives from running away; moreover, any children the wives may produce belong to the husband. Such quasi-polyandrous patterns remind us that the three forms of marriage are ideal types—concepts that serve as reference points for analysis of the complex patterns of particular societies.

Polyandry seems to be associated with poor economic conditions. In western Tibet, for example, the wealthy nobles are likely to be polygynous, while poor men in the lower strata have to be content with polyandry. In this case it may be that the polygyny of the upper stratum reduces the number of women available to the lower strata. Female infanticide brings about the same result. One of the most effective means of making scant economic resources go around is population control. Although Linton, the most authoritative investigator of the Marquesans, found no direct evidence of female infanticide among them, he reported that men outnumbered women five to two.

So-called group marriage, which earlier writers postulated as the original form, is even more rare than "genuine" polyandry. It occurs infrequently among the Kaingang of Brazil. A statistical analysis of Kaingang genealogies showed that during one hundred years, 8 per cent of the mar-

---

misinformation and misunderstanding, and there was pressure against the Mormon practice. (3) The Mormons did not evolve some of the safeguards of domestic peace that most polygynous societies have. In particular, the first wife did not necessarily have authority over the others, and the husband often tended to neglect his "old" wives in favor of the latest one. See K. Young, 1954.

English anthropologists sometimes distinguish between the *pater* and the *genitor*. The pater is the "social" father, the one with a father's rights and obligations; the genitor is the biological father, who may or may not be the pater. For a good discussion of polygyny, see Opler, 1943, and also the "Comment" by Burgess, 1943. Opler discusses nine societies that have what might be called quasi-polyandrous practices. He also suggests that more careful investigation would probably reveal that some so-called polygynous societies are actually monogamous but recognize extramarital sexual privileges.

riages had involved two or more men jointly married to two or more women. Fourteen per cent of the other marriages had been polyandrous and 18 per cent polygynous. The rest were monogamous (Henry, 1941, p. 45n., as reported in Murdock, 1949, p. 24). Group marriage also occurs, infrequently, among the Marquesans.

As one might expect, marriage in some form is virtually universal in human society. But the Nayar (Nair) caste of southeast India does not have marriage in a strict sense. A wedding ceremony does take place, but the "husband" leaves his bride after three days. Thereafter the "married" woman is free to have liaisons with other men, and any resulting children are regarded as the legitimate children of the original "husband." For the Nayars, even the distinction between pater and genitor (see p. 152, n. 8) hardly suffices. The nonsexual duties ordinarily performed by a husband and father are performed by the woman's brothers (Lévi-Strauss, 1949, p. 150; Hoebel, 1949, esp. pp. 223-24; Opler, 1943, pp. 132-33).

Rules of Residence

As we have seen, the incest taboo, in its primary form, forbids marriage between father and daughter, mother and son, and brother and sister. The primary incest taboo limits choice of marital partner in every society, excepting only certain ancient royal families—for example, the Egyptian, Incan, and Hawaiian. These societies permitted marriage between the heir to the throne and his sister (usually an older sister); but the other families in the same societies were all expected to observe the primary incest taboo in its entirety. The incest taboo, therefore, is one of the most nearly universal norms in human societies. We have pointed out that as a consequence of the incest taboo, at least one of the partners in a marriage must leave the household of the family into which he was born and move into a different household. (The only exception, apparently, is the Nayar system.) For any society, the pattern in accordance with which most married couples decide where to live is known as the "rule of residence."

There are five basic rules of residence, with two or three minor variations:

Patrilocal residence is the rule or pattern by which the married couple establish residence with or quite near the parents of the groom. In other words, the groom does not leave his household or neighborhood; he simply brings his wife (or wives) to it.[9] A minor variation of patrilocal residence is called by Murdock "matri-patrilocal" residence. According to this rule, the couple live for a time with the bride's parents, then go to live permanently with the groom's parents. This pattern is a form of "bride service," in which the groom "pays" for his bride by working for her family for a while. This

[9] Some writers erroneously describe patrilocal marriage as marriage in which the bride goes to live with her husband.

is one of several forms of "marriage with consideration " The marriages of Jacob in the Old Testament are good examples.

Matrilocal residence is the rule by which the married couple typically establish residence with or near the parents of the bride.

In some societies, the couple have a choice: they may live with the parents of either the groom or the bride. This rule is known as *bilocal residence*.

Avunculocal residence (from the Latin word for "uncle") is the rule by which the married couple go to live with a brother of the groom's mother.[10]

Neolocal residence is the rule in our society: the married couple establish their own residence in a "new" place—that is, in a household neither that of the groom's parents nor that of the bride's.[11]

The strictness with which the "rule" of residence is applicable varies for different societies. The rule of residence is at the very least a modal pattern, but it usually tends to be normative. That is, in a particular society a newly married couple is *expected* to follow the usual pattern. Nevertheless, it seems to be true in many societies, as it is in ours, that the "rule" of residence can be violated without any more unpleasant result than a little gossip. Our society must be characterized as neolocal, but if circumstances are unusual, young couples do sometimes go to live with the parents of the bride or of the groom.

> It should be recognized, of course, that not all couples establish a separate home when they marry. In ordinary times, approximately one couple out of every five moves in with relatives or lives in rented rooms as lodgers for a while after marriage. The proportion of couples living in this manner declines sharply until middle age and reaches a low point of about 3 percent for couples in their 50's [Glick, 1947, p. 166]

Matrilocal residence tends to be found in settled agricultural societies in which women own the fields and do most of the agricultural work and men have no important possessions. When conditions change so that men come to own important facilities, such as large herds, then patrilocal residence is more usual. If the male role in hunting is economically important, or if the society is one that is frequently engaged in war or open to attack and in which fighting is a male role, then patrilocal residence is to be expected—partly because hunting and warfare enhance the importance of men. Further, in these activities, an intimate knowledge of the terrain is desirable. Since it would be inefficient for a boy to learn all about his home region and then

---

[10] The Dobuans of Melanesia have the apparently unique rule that the couple must live in alternate years with the bride's parents and with the groom's maternal uncle: a combination of matrilocal and avunculocal residence (see Fortune, 1932a).

[11] The classification of rules of residence is taken from Murdock, 1949, pp. 16ff. Murdock's sample of 250 societies contained "146 patrilocal, 38 matrilocal, 22 matri-patrilocal, 19 bilocal, 17 neolocal, and 8 avunculocal. It is probable, however, that some of the tribes reported as patrilocal actually follow the neolocal rule" (p. 17).

leave it just when his knowledge would be of most use, the patrilocal "rule" generally applies in such societies. The concentration of wealth in the hands of men and success in military campaigns also tend to favor polygyny, and hence patrilocal residence. In fact, except for the sororal type, polygyny is hardly compatible with matrilocal residence. Monogamy, however, by throwing the conjugal family (the married pair and their dependent children) into prominence, tends to favor neolocal residence. Neolocal residence is also favored by a rule of inheritance requiring an equal distribution of property among the children or, especially, among the sons (Murdock, 1949).

Types of Family

The Bureau of the Census defines a family as "a group of two or more persons related by blood, marriage, or adoption and residing together; all such persons are considered as members of one family" (quoted in Winch and McGinnis, 1953, p. 101). In so large and heterogeneous a population as that of the United States, the composition of particular families varies enormously. Yet it does not vary nearly so much as the composition of families in the world as a whole. For every society, the prevailing rule of residence and the prevailing form of marriage necessarily affect the typical composition of families. The fundamental structure of "the" family in any society is, of course, only a basic type that most of the particular families either exemplify perfectly or approximate more or less closely. In this discussion, we shall for the most part ignore random departures: we shall be interested in the structurally or *systemically* significant types themselves.

Just as marriage is found almost universally, so is the conjugal family. Because this unit is sometimes combined with others to form more complex families, it is called the "nuclear family" (Murdock, 1949, Chap. 1). Even in combinations such as polygynous families, the component nuclear families are always treated to some extent as relatively separate units. This is possible because each wife knows which of the children are hers, and she feels somewhat more responsibility for them.

Because of the incest taboo, every person who marries is a member of at least two nuclear families. The one into which he is born is called his "family of orientation," because it is in this family that he is given his basic "orientation" to life in his society. A nuclear family that he starts by marrying is called a "family of procreation." [12] The two families are, of course, similar in structure; the difference between them lies in the fact that a particular person has the position of son or daughter in one and the position of husband or wife in the other.

The rules of residence help to determine whether *composite families* will be formed. Composite families due to a rule of residence are known as "extended" families. The only rule of residence that does not produce

---

[12] These terms were suggested by W. Lloyd Warner. They are now widely used.

extended families is the neolocal. Matrilocal residence, for example, produces matrilocal extended families (see Queen and Adams, 1952, Chap. 2). The daughters in each generation bring their husbands to the ancestral household, compound, or village. Such a family obviously has generational continuity. Nuclear families that form part of an extended family are called "dependent" nuclear families.

The forms of marriage also help to determine whether composite families will be formed. As we have seen, marriages are either monogamous or polygamous, and polygamous marriages are either polygynous or polyandrous or, in the rare cases of group marriage, "mixed." A nuclear family that forms part of a polygamous family is also called a dependent nuclear family. A polygamous family that itself forms part of an *extended* family is called a dependent polygamous family. We can also speak of "independent" polygamous families.

Taking into account both rules of residence and forms of marriage, we can classify families according to a typology. Table 5 so classifies a sample of 187 societies. In this table, all the monogamous extended families and all the polygamous extended families have been grouped together, regardless of the differences between patrilocal, matri-patrilocal, matrilocal, bilocal, and avunculocal subtypes. "Independent" families, of course, result from the neolocal rule of residence.

TABLE 5

Classification of societies according to prevailing type of family *

Prevailing type of family	*Number of societies*
INDEPENDENT NUCLEAR	
With monogamy exclusively	24
With infrequent polygyny	23
COMPOSITE	
Monogamous extended (composed of dependent nuclear families)	
With monogamy exclusively	16
With infrequent polygyny	26
Independent polygamous	
With polygyny	51
With polyandry	2
Polygamous extended (composed of dependent polygamous families)	
With polyandry	0
With polygyny	45
Total	187

* Adapted from George P Murdock, *Social Structure,* Macmillan, 1949, Table 5, p. 32. Data for 63 of the societies in Murdock's sample of 250 were insufficient for classification.

Since extended families are uncommon in the United States, we might briefly describe the Chinese type as an example. For centuries, the ideal type of family in China was the patrilocal extended family, with or without secondary wives. In each generation, the men brought their wives to their father's house, and as the "family" grew larger, new apartments might be added. The strongest social tie in China, at least in theory, was that between father and son. The oldest man was the ruler of the joint household, and he was succeeded by his eldest son. The second strongest tie, hardly less strong in theory, was that between brothers. The oldest living brother was respected especially, but in general the brothers were ranked from the oldest to the youngest. They were more likely to be referred to by birth-order number ("Number Two" son) than by name. If a man had to leave the household to take a position in a distant place, he might leave his wife and children behind. The strong ties in the male line of descent were symbolized in the institution of ancestor worship. A large family had a family tomb, in which rituals had to be performed regularly.[13]

A large family sometimes split up because of personality clashes. According to the ideal, a man's relation with his father and mother was expected to take precedence over his relation with his wife. A man was even expected to divorce his wife if his parents demanded that he do so, and many personal tragedies resulted from this rule. Sometimes, however, a man was so closely bound to his wife that he would take her side and leave the ancestral home to found a new household. Lang tells of an old man who was honored by the emperor for his outstanding success in keeping a large extended family intact. On being asked how he had managed to do it, the man is reported to have taken his brush in hand and painted the Chinese character for "forbearance, patience" a hundred times (Lang, 1946, p. 31).

A more "normal" way for a traditional family to break up is known as "fission." When the extended family became so large that the household could no longer provide room for everybody, a nuclear family would split off. This was likely to happen, also, when a younger son had a good opportunity in government service far from home. A departing nuclear family made an effort to keep in touch with the original family and considered itself a junior branch.

Like polygyny, the large extended family was never the most common arrangement in China. It was the *ideal* for the entire society, but for the most part only wealthy landlords could afford it. For the poor, lack of land and a high death rate made the ideal difficult to achieve. Throughout the history of China, perhaps 80 per cent of the population lived in fairly small families. Of more than a dozen samples of families, rich and poor, rural and urban, studied by various people between 1926 and 1937, the group

---

[13] For descriptions of the traditional Chinese family, see Lee, 1953; Hsu, 1949, 1949a, 1953, pp. 125-34; Fei, 1946; Lang, 1946, Part I; and Levy, 1949. For a vivid but no doubt idealized picture of an extended family in China, see Nora Waln's novel *House of Exile* (1933).

with the largest families consisted of Fukien landlords; for this group, the average size of family was 11.8. For the whole of China, the average family size was closer to 5.[14]

A common modification of the patrilocal extended family is the "stem" family, in which generational continuity is maintained on a farm by having one son in each generation bring his wife to the family residence while the other sons seek their fortune elsewhere. Sometimes the inheriting son is the first-born (the pattern known as primogeniture), sometimes it is the youngest son (ultimogeniture), and sometimes the family head decides according to circumstances. Ultimogeniture is the pattern among the Marquesans, for example, and among the Kachin Hills people of Burma. After all the older sons have been provided for, the youngest inherits the land and household. Primogeniture was the pattern in England and in parts of France during the *ancien régime*. The flexible pattern (father chooses one of the sons) is the pattern in rural Ireland, parts of France, and the Ozark Mountains.[15]

Table 6 shows the distribution of family types in three samples from China, as reported by Lang. Statistics like these can be somewhat misleading, since the various families included may be at different stages of the family cycle. Some of the "stem" families may be broken joint families, and some of the "conjugal" families may become stem families. Further, some of the "joint" families may be only superficially of the traditional type, for their component nuclear families may keep their finances separate; and some of the "stem" families may actually be joint families with one of the sons temporarily absent. Lang's investigations took account of these possibilities.

Even though most Chinese peasant families were (and are) independent nuclear (conjugal) in form, they were different in spirit from the independent nuclear families we know in the United States. The Confucian ideal was alive and operative in the relation between husband and wife and in the relations between parents and children. On account of her classically defined role, the mother was typically loved, whereas the father, as disciplinarian and acknowledged possessor of authority, was seldom loved but often respected. Whenever a poor family became rich enough, it sought to enhance its prestige by founding a patrilocal extended family according to the Confucian ideal. Families rose and fell. Financial difficulties sometimes broke up a large family of the classical type. Once in the grip of usurers, the family might have to sell part or all of its land and disperse. Over the generations, many families lost gentry standing while other families, by buying up lands, following the classical family ideals, and helping their sons to study for the government examinations, rose.[16] But contact with the West and social

---

[14] For a survey of studies, see Lang, 1946, pp. 147-54.

[15] For good descriptions of the stem family, see Arensberg and Kimball, 1940, Chaps. 7, 8; and Zimmerman and Frampton, 1935, Chap. 7, "The Stem Family," and Part III, "American Studies"—case studies of stem families in the Ozark Mountains.

[16] For an excellent presentation of evidence of vertical mobility in China, and references to additional evidence, see Hsu, 1949b.

changes resulting from it are causing a new family ideal to evolve in competition with the ideals of the Confucian classics. The new type of family is based on an ideal of marriage and family life closer to our own. Still more recently, the Communist government of China has forced many families into communal arrangements somewhat similar to those in the Israeli *kibbutzim*.

Since the Nayars of India, as we have seen, have no marriage relationship in a strict sense (husband and wife separate after three days), they

TABLE 6

Family type and social class *

1. Villages in North China (458 families)

	Farm laborers	*Poor peasants*	*Middle peasants*	*Well-to-do peasants*	*Landlords*
NUMBER OF FAMILIES	61	163	125	58	51
FAMILY TYPE					
Conjugal (independent nuclear)	54%	41%	27%	17%	12%
Stem	35	44	44	42	35
Joint (patrilocal extended)	11	15	29	41	53

2. Nonindustrial cities in North China (mainly Peiping) (1,365 families)

	Wage earners	*Lower middle class*	*Middle class*	*Upper class*
NUMBER OF FAMILIES	426	251	496	192
FAMILY TYPE				
Conjugal	58%	51%	50%	52%
Stem	34	36	34	28
Joint	8	13	16	20

3. Shanghai (208 families)

	Industrial workers	*Lower middle class*	*Middle class*	*Upper class*
NUMBER OF FAMILIES	143	42	15	8
FAMILY TYPE				
Conjugal	71%	62%	73%	50%
Stem	24	33	27	50
Joint	5	5	—	—

* Olga Lang, *Chinese Family and Society*, Yale University Press, 1946, Table 1, p. 136-37.

do not have the full nuclear family either. But they do have a kind of extended family, called the *taravad,* consisting of brothers and sisters, with all the children of the women. The men, having left their "wives," support their own sisters' children and carry on sexual relations with the abandoned "wives" of other men. The *taravad,* of course, persists from generation to generation (Hoebel, 1949, pp. 223-24).[17]

Marriage as a Form of Exchange

One of the most variable aspects of different marriage systems is the degree of choice open to the individual. In no system is there absolute freedom of choice. At the very least, the incest taboo limits choice in every society.

Any marriage system may be regarded as a system of exchange between groups. In the United States and most European countries, the groups involved are families, and the "exchange" is indirect. Each family, of course, is bound by the incest taboo. This means that the unmarried men in each family must "renounce" the girls in the family and seek a partner from some other family. In "giving up" its girls, any family has the assurance that other families will do the same, providing chances for its boys to find partners. In this way, the society is bound together by a complicated network of marriages connecting families. This "exchange" is only one kind of exchange, and there is a tendency for marital "exchange" to take place in the same social universe in which the other kinds occur: trade, exchange of gifts, ceremonial exchange of greeting cards, exchange of hospitality (Lévi-Strauss, 1949, Chap. 5).

In detail, the systems of marital exchange that can be found in a survey of many societies vary almost infinitely, but they can be reduced to a few broadly defined types. The most fundamental distinction is that between "closed," or "elementary," systems, on the one hand, and "open," or "complex," systems, on the other.

ELEMENTARY SYSTEMS OF MARRIAGE

All elementary systems are characterized by "preferential marriage"—that is, marriage in which ego's spouse is someone who is already related

[17] The *taravad* should be distinguished from a *susu,* which is a kind of kinship group in Dobuan society. The *susu* is not a household group at all. It is, however, a local group, with its house sites in one village. Like the *taravad,* it consists of brothers and sisters, with all the children of the women. As in the *taravad,* the brothers support their sisters, but in the *susu* the brothers are not allowed to enter their sisters' houses. The Dobuans have extended families with alternating matrilocal and avunculocal residence. The women inherit their house sites and houses from their mothers, and their brothers inherit sites and houses in the same village but from their mother's brothers (Fortune, 1932a, Chap. 1). The rule of alternating residence means that any particular brother-sister pair will be living in the same village (but not in the same household) part of the time, and part of the time not. Among the Nayar, as we have mentioned, husband and wife do not live together very long.

to him in the kinship system. There are two subtypes: "restricted" and "generalized." In restricted exchange, two kin groups other than families supply each other with marriage partners: the men of one group marry women from the other, and vice versa. Such systems occur in all parts of the world, but they are particularly common in Australia. In the Kariera system, for example, every member of the society belongs to one of four so-called sections. If we denote the sections by the letters A, B, C, and D, the marriage rule may be represented by the following diagram:

in which the double lines connect the pairs of sections that supply each other with marriage partners (A and B, C and D). All four sections are connected with one another through the fact that children do not belong to the section of either of their parents. For example, a man of Section A marries a woman of Section B, and their children will belong to C; a man of Section B marries a woman of Section A, and their children will belong to D. Similarly, C and D intermarry and their children are A or B, depending on the particular father-mother combination. A or B never intermarries directly with C or D. Note, further, that a "section" is not a local group in any sense but merely a status group whose members must marry members of a certain other group (Radcliffe-Brown, 1931)

The other subtype of elementary marital exchange, generalized exchange, also involves preferential marriage between groups larger than the conjugal family. Unlike the Kariera sections and other examples of restricted exchange, however, these groups do not exchange with each other directly in pairs: the arrangement is circular:

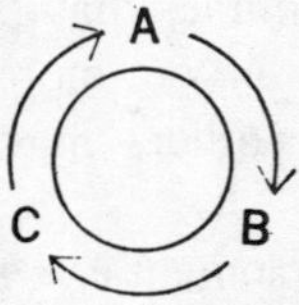

Any number of groups over two may be involved, so that the circle may be "short" or "long." In principle, boys from A marry girls from B, but girls from A never marry boys from B; the girls from A get husbands from the "last" group in the "circle." In particular cases, the system is complicated by the fact that any group in it may give wives to (or take them from) several other groups, but no group ever takes wives from any other group to which it gives wives. Thus any group may be involved in several "circles" at the same time.

This type of system is found among the Kachin Hills people of north-east Burma (Lévi-Strauss, 1949, pp. 293ff.). The preferred marriage takes place between a boy and a daughter of one of his mother's brothers. (As we noted in Chapter 3, this is known as matrilateral cross-cousin marriage. It was once common in China and still occurs in some districts there.) The groups involved in Kachin marriage "rings" or "circles" are known as *htinggaw*. A *htinggaw* may be a conjugal family, a group of related conjugal families living in the same village, or a still larger group of related families living in different places (Leach, 1954, pp. 125-27). In the Kachin Hills area, political or territorial groups may also be involved in marriage circles of the elementary generalized type. But in these cases, the arrangement affects mainly the sons of chiefs and village heads, and any two groups so involved may keep up their relationship with only one or two marriages in a generation (Leach, 1954, pp. 76-77).

An elementary generalized system of marital exchange, like the Kachin, presupposes a rough equality in social rank between the groups participating in any circle. But in the course of time, the participating groups tend to become unequal in wealth, prestige, and sometimes in formal rank. They also become unequal in size; one group may not have enough daughters to supply its partner in the ring, or may have too many. These changes make the system unstable. If two groups that have been partners in the ring become too disparate in rank or size, the relationship tends to break down (Lévi-Strauss, 1949, p. 325). Polygyny also contributes to instability: the wealthier groups want more women. Among the Kachins, two kinds of evasion have developed: (1) A man may marry someone from a distantly related branch of his own large *htinggaw*. (In such an event, the distant branch would be reclassified as a different *htinggaw* and one from which the man's *htinggaw* might henceforth expect to receive other women.) (2) A man may marry outside the circle simply by not having the ordinary marriage ceremony (*num shalai*) performed. Such respectably unmarried married couples are increasingly common. The growing popularity of this kind of "evasion" indicates, of course, that the system of elementary generalized exchange is breaking down—or, more exactly, that particular marriage circles are breaking down (others may be forming) (Leach, 1954, pp. 73-77).

Speaking more broadly of elementary generalized exchange, when a system breaks down, it may change into a system of a different type. Lévi-Strauss lists the following possibilities:

1. "Islands" of elementary restricted exchange may develop. When this happens, the new system tends to spread, for otherwise some groups might be left without partners.

2. Some of the groups might tend toward the pattern of inmarriage, or endogamy (marriage within the group itself). If the inmarrying group is small, this pattern approaches incest. If the group is large, it simply becomes an "endogamous group." The caste system of India is in principle

a system of endogamous groups. More informally, "races," social classes. religious groups, and ethnic groups in the United States (and elsewhere) tend to be endogamous groups. Within a particular endogamous group, additional patterns of marital exchange may of course become institutionalized.

3. A system of *complex* generalized marital exchange may develop. This type of system, which we shall examine below, is distinguished from both types of elementary exchange, restricted (e.g., Kariera) as well as generalized (e.g., Kachin).

All elementary systems of marital exchange, if they are to be stable, presuppose societies with relatively little vertical social mobility and little technological change. We have already noted the instability of the generalized Kachin system. Systems of restricted exchange presuppose an even more static kind of society. It is significant that such systems are most common among the Australian aborigines, whose culture is technologically "primitive." Many Australian tribes are only now beginning to emerge from the Stone Age level.

OPEN SYSTEMS OF MARRIAGE

Complex generalized exchange, such as prevails in the United States. most of Europe and much of Africa, is the most flexible type of system. Here the incest taboo is the only *kinship* rule that determines marital choice; there is no "preferential marriage." In all cases the primary and secondary incest taboos merely prohibit certain marriages; they do not specify either which particular person one must marry or which groups one must choose from. Such a system of marital exchange is compatible, therefore, with a high degree of vertical social mobility and with rapid social change in general.

Complex, or open, systems of marriage choice may be divided into two categories: (1) marriages arranged by parents of the prospective partners, or by agents of the parents, known as "go-betweens"; (2) marriages arranged by the prospective partners themselves. The former has been the common system in China and Japan for centuries and has only lately been challenged. The same pattern exists in rural Ireland (Arensberg and Kimball, 1940, pp. 107ff.). In India, two families sometimes agree that if one gives birth to a boy and the other to a girl, the boy and girl shall marry when they come of age (see K. Davis, 1942; Mandelbaum, 1949). It does not seem possible to give the individual less choice than by arranging his marriage before he and his fiancée are born. In the contemporary United States, of course, we tend to feel strongly that each person who is old enough ought to be allowed to choose his own marriage partner. This norm is at the center so to speak, of a more or less elaborate pattern of competitive dating. It is also expressed in and strengthened by a tremendous cultural emphasis on romantic love. No one in the United States needs to be told that one of the most serious preoccupations of young unmarried men and women is the question "Am I in love?" or "When shall I fall in love and get married?"

Romantic love as a basis for marriage is so much taken for granted in the United States that we lack perspective on it. In the old-fashioned French system, which is rapidly changing, romantic love is not viewed in the same way. The French distinguish between a *mariage d'inclination* and a *mariage de convenance* (or *de raison*). The first is roughly the same as the American love-match. The second, perhaps more common, is defined in the *Nouveau Petit Larousse* as a match "in which relations of birth or of fortune weigh more heavily than love." According to a Spanish observer, "The dominant feature in the French family is perhaps the *mariage de raison*. . . . A marriage . . . is a carefully discussed business, in which, the feelings of the future partners being taken for granted, the positive side of the contemplated concern is attentively examined in consultation with the family solicitor. The *situation* is the main preoccupation of both sides" (de Madariaga, 1929, p. 139). A French writer has remarked that "wise parents fear so-called marriages 'of inclination' " (Duprat, 1924, p. 51). The late French journalist de Roussy de Sales reacted to "love in America" in an ironic, somewhat myopic fashion, which throws into relief the French conception with which he contrasts it. American motion pictures, he says, ". . . indicate that in such matters the popular mind likes to be entertained by the idea (1) that love is the only reason why a man and a woman should get married, (2) that love is always wholesome, genuine, uplifting, and fresh, like a glass of Grade A milk; (3) that when, for some reason or other, it fails to keep you uplifted, wholesome, and fresh, the only thing to do is to begin all over again with another partner" (de Sales, 1938, p. 646).[18]

A French girl's chances of marrying used to depend a great deal on her dowry (*dot*), often explicitly called her "hopes" (*espérances*). The dowry, however, was legally protected and was customarily managed in the interest of the family as a whole.

In contrast to marriage itself, from which they may be a partial escape, *liaisons* in France are based on "inclination." French tolerance for such affairs, provided that they are carried on discreetly and do not jeopardize the dignity of the wife or the interests of the legitimate family, is well known (see Hermant, 1924, p. 70; Carr, 1931, p. 50; Muret, 1936, p. 255). Here it is necessary to guard against thinking on the basis of certain more or less unconscious assumptions of American culture. In the United States, we tend to associate love, marriage, and sexual relations. Consequently, marital infidelity on the part of either spouse tends to be regarded, and quite realistically, as a threat to the *status* of the other. But in France the husband's

---

[18] One of the main themes of *The Little French Girl*, a novel by Anne Douglas Sedgwick (1924), is the conflict between French *raison* and English romance; the English hero refuses to marry the French heroine when her mother makes a very "reasonable" proposal, although the proposal suits his "inclination." He finally marries the girl much later, when she herself chooses him independently.

infidelity does not threaten the wife's status to the same extent. His roving is condemned only if it jeopardizes the welfare and dignity of his family. In Latin America, many wealthy men maintain two households, one for the legal wife and one for the concubine. The relationship of *concubinato* is tolerated in custom, but it may be broken without formality at the will of either party. Kingsley Davis attributes the frequency of *concubinato* in Latin America partly to the indissolubility of marriage required by the Church (1942, pp. 104-06). The same thing may be true to some extent in France, also a predominantly Catholic country.

Strong erotic attachments have, of course, arisen in all times and places. Ancient Chinese and Japanese poems, moving even in translation, often treat the theme. The popular theory of romantic love can itself be traced back to the "courtly love" of the twelfth century, although profound changes have occurred since then in ideas concerning the social relations in which love is appropriate (Goodsell, 1935, pp. 233ff; Beigel, 1951). The distinctive thing about romantic love in the United States is its status as a prerequisite to marriage. Medieval courtly love was ideally a relation between a knight and a lady who was married to someone else, and although the relation was sexually tinged it was supposed to remain unconsummated.

Romantic love has its critics in the United States (see Merrill, 1949, Chaps. 2, 3; Truxal and Merrill, 1947, pp. 121-30; Folsom, 1934, pp. 68-76). They charge that it is unrealistic, leading young people to ignore more prosaic but more solid grounds for choice, such as common interests and common background, and to expect romantic thrills to continue through the everyday, week-in, week-out unromantic circumstances of marriage itself. Therefore, they claim, the entirely normal settling-down process in marriage may be experienced as a letdown; romantic expectations may even lead to divorce.

This aspect of romantic love can easily be overemphasized. Our knowledge is not complete by any means, but it is a fact that, perhaps despite romantic love, most marriages in the United States take place between people who are alike with respect to race, social class, religion, ethnic group, and age (Hollingshead, 1950). Two factors help to explain this. First, one's early training in the family inculcates certain tastes and preferences: most people do not wish to marry someone with whom they would be grossly incompatible culturally. Secondly, there is a strong tendency for young people to be thrown together socially with others of the same race, social class, religion, ethnic group, and age much more frequently than with others of different social status in these respects. It follows automatically, then, that most marriages will occur within these groups, even though the more extreme versions of the romantic-love ideology sound as if love usually hits at random, like lightning. The social structure, it would seem, guides Cupid himself.

A study of 1000 engaged couples indicates that engaged couples, at least, not only tend to be alike with respect to sociability, drinking and smoking habits, and recreational preferences but also tend to have similar conceptions of what is desirable in marriage. For example, the prospective partners tend to agree on the relative authority of husband and wife, the desirability of the wife's working, and the number of children desired (Burgess and Wallin, 1943). This study is significant even though not all engagements end in marriage, though the couples may have arrived at agreement through discussion, and though some of the agreement may not have gone very deep and may have been a temporary effect of romantic love itself. The agreement at least shows that engaged couples are concerned with important aspects of their future relationship.

Also opposed to the negative view of romantic love is the growing tendency among investigators of dating to emphasize its function in helping the participants to make a better informed, less impetuous choice of marriage partner. (See, for example, Winch, 1952, pp. 435-41; Kirkpatrick and Caplow, 1945) It is notable that the term "courtship" is hardly used any more in the United States. In an earlier period, when a man called upon a girl more than once or twice, it was understood that he wished to gain her consent to marriage. This understanding was so well established in the common culture that the man was subjected to social pressure to carry out his implicit declaration of intention. *Dating,* however, is quite different. Even engagements are no longer regarded as absolutely binding, and dating or "going steady" does not necessarily involve any intention to marry. This being so, young people in the dating period have an opportunity to know many persons of the opposite sex without committing themselves to any one until they have learned a good deal about him as a unique personality.[19]

That boy and girl in our society usually take time to know each other fairly well before getting married is shown by data on the length of time between first date and engagement (see Table 7) and on length of engagements. A study of three generations of Ohio women showed that the median length of time between first date and marriage was one to one-and-a-half years. Members of the third generation took less time to reach the point of marriage, but they dated their future spouses more frequently and with less chaperonage (Koller, 1951).[20]

In several ways the "lightning-bolt" ideology of romantic love is a distortion of what actually happens in choosing a marriage partner in the United States, for the American norm of individual choice based on romantic

---

[19] This distinction between courtship and dating, and the obsolescence of the old-fashioned regulative norms of courtship, are noted by Lowrie, 1951.

[20] Koller had 200 cases for each generation. Most studies show that happiness in marriage tends to be associated with long engagement. See, for example, H. J. Locke, 1951, p. 94. Of the happily married men in this study, 63.5 percent had been engaged for six months or more, as against 45.7 per cent of the divorced men. The corresponding percentages for happily married and divorced women were 67.5 and 44.0. Note, however, the high proportion of rather long engagements for *all* cases. (Locke's cases were all from Indiana.)

TABLE 7

Time elapsed between first date and engagement *

	Number	*Percent*	*Cumulative percent*
3 years or more	114	21	
1-2 years	142	26	47
9-11 months	39	7	54
5-8 months	105	19	73
3-4 months	70	13	86
1-2 months	50	9	95
3-4 weeks	15	3	98
1-2 weeks	11	2	100
Total	546	100	

* Adapted from Judson T. Landis and Mary G. Landis, *Building a Successful Marriage*, Prentice-Hall, 1948, Table 15, p. 165.

love only mitigates or softens other influences that must be nearly universal in human society. Above all, most parents are interested in the welfare of their children. We should expect, therefore, that if the decision to marry is an important one, as it is in most societies, parents will not wish or be able to refrain from using their influence. Moreover, children are almost universally attached to their parents and are therefore unable to remain unaffected by their parents' attitudes and opinions. The attachment between parents and children is especially close in the United States, partly because of the very structure and size of most American families. In one important study (A. Bates, 1942), 136 young married persons were interviewed concerning the part their parents had played in their choice of a marriage partner. These interviews were supplemented by documents written by seventy-five unmarried college students concerning their parents' influence on their dating. Most of the parents used indirect influence, such as showing whether or not they liked and approved of their children's dating partners; but all the parents exercised some influence.

The motives of the parents varied. The most obvious, of course, was their love for their children. More subtle was their dependence upon their children. Just as many children in our society find it hard to emancipate themselves from their parents, so many parents experience their children's independence as an emotional crisis in their own lives. The two facts are related: the more dependent are the parents, the harder it is for the children to emancipate themselves.

The most subtle motive parents have for attempting, often successfully, to influence their children's courtship is projection of ambition.

> . . . the life goals which are taught to individuals in this country are heavily weighted in the direction of financial success, social prestige, excitement,

> power, and dominance over others. . . . For millions, discouragement, disillusionment, and frustration are inevitable. . . . The stage is clearly set for the appearance of ambition projection. "I won't let my child suffer what I went through" is a common statement on the lips of American parents [A. Bates, 1942, p. 85].

Since boys are in general given greater freedom than girls, parents tend to put more pressure on their daughters than on their sons. And since mothers have in general more to do with the children than fathers have, we are not surprised to learn that mothers put more pressure on their children in courtship. The parents who exert the most direct and "tyrannical" influence, however, are more often fathers.

Through many specific conversations, gestures, meaningful silences, and comparisons, not to speak of their own example, parents gradually teach their children certain standards by which to judge potential marriage partners. The fact that much of this teaching is done casually and unconsciously does not make it less effective.[21] During the child's early dating experiences, the parents' prohibitions and expressions of approval and disapproval may be regarded as part of socialization. Later, when the "child" is old enough to marry, the parents' influence may be regarded as *sanctioning* the norms they have been teaching implicitly for years. When the parents disapprove now, however subtly, they are exercising *social control,* in the technical sense of checking incipient deviation from norms. This control, however, must very often be subtle or even covert, because the institutionalized right to individual freedom of choice on the basis of romantic love makes it legitimate for the "child" to rebel. The point at which socialization passes over into social control is somewhat arbitrary in our society, and the ill-defined boundary is one of the causes of conflict between parents and children. Conflict is sometimes intensified, of course, by the fact that parent or child, or both, being unconsciously dependent, make "unreasonable" demands.

We shall see in the next section that, regardless of the influence of the romantic-love ideology one way or the other, a high divorce rate is virtually inevitable in the present social structure of the United States. To some extent, the ideology of romantic love counteracts disruptive forces in marriage by putting the subjective emphasis, at the time of the decision to marry, upon the ideal permanence of marriage. It would be hard to say whether the decision is subjectively more difficult to make for men or for women. But however much the ideology may gloss over the more prosaic realities of married life, few men can be unaware of the fact that they are taking on a serious responsibility, and few women can be altogether unmindful of the fact that in marrying a particular man they are choosing, in effect, a standard of living and a social-class position as well as a life companion. These aspects are objectively important since the chances of

---

[21] Such teaching is a virtually continuous aspect of family living. For intimate glimpses of family members interacting, see Bossard, 1954, Chap. 8: "Family Table Talk."

marrying again for a woman whose marriage has failed diminish with increasing age more rapidly than a man's do

There have been many attempts to give a sociopsychological explanation of the romantic-love complex in the United States (see esp. Parsons, 1943). In the vast majority of societies, a married couple live in close relations with other people in the same local area. Even without polygamous or extended families, there are personally known neighbors, among whom will probably be the parents of the couple. The marriage, that is, has to fit into a pre-existing pattern of intimate social relations. Under these circumstances, it is not surprising that parents take an active role in selecting their children's marriage partners; romantic attachments could even appear to be potentially disruptive (see Lee, 1953, p. 276). In the United States today, however, the married couple is relatively isolated. The local community is not so often the lifelong stage of one's intimate relationships. Hence it makes less difference to other people whom one chooses for one's marriage partner. Relatively free scope can be allowed to romantic love since it will not disrupt other people's lives.

At the same time, the married couple are also subject to less pressure from others to conform to traditional patterns of interaction in marriage. They must depend almost exclusively upon their own mutual loyalty. Moreover, in the highly competitive, relatively impersonal world around them, they have few other opportunities to form deep and secure attachments to others. Even their children will eventually leave them and go about their own business. Hence the marriage tie is emotionally strong, or one feels that it should be, and the choice of marriage partner is necessarily one of the most important choices an individual can make. No wonder emphasis is placed upon a strong personal attachment *before* marriage. In this perspective, romantic love seems to be a safeguard of mutual loyalty. It partly compensates for the loss of social pressures and supports that once surrounded married couples.

The median age at first marriage in the United States in 1951 was 22.6 years for men and 20.4 years for women. The median age has been going down steadily since 1890, when it was 26.1 for men and 22 for women (Winch and McGinnis, 1953, p. 97). Since in our occupational system a high value is placed upon ability and objective achievement, the system is highly competitive. Especially in the middle class, people do not regard their position as fixed once and for all; they strive to "better themselves," and many people do in fact rise (or fall) in their occupational spheres. We may speak of vertical mobility wherever there is a social hierarchy of any kind in which people move "up" and "down" through some selective processes. The great competitiveness in the American occupational system, and consequently the rather high degree of vertical mobility in the class structure, mean that a woman marrying a man in his early or even late twenties cannot be sure exactly what her future life will be like. We pointed out that her decision is objectively important to her, on the less romantic side, because she is choosing a standard of living and a social-class position. More precisely, however, especially in the middle class, she is choosing to *take a chance* on the "success" of a particular young man. The romantic-love complex cannot altogether obscure this fact from her view, but it can ease the potential strain.

It is likely that the more industrialized other countries become, the more like the United States they will become in the pattern for entering marriage. In China, for example, the pattern of parental matchmaking is still dominant, but in the cities more and more young people are beginning to demand freedom of choice. Romantic love is becoming fashionable. The break-up of the old system is accompanied by bitter conflict, but sometimes the new way is smoothed by compromise.

> In the cities three deviations from the old pattern appear: (1) parents arrange matches and ask their children's consent; (2) children choose their mates and ask the parents' approval; (3) children marry without asking their parents' approval. The first two deviations are compromises. The third often involves a complete break with the parents and is rather uncommon.
>
> In many cases concessions to modernism are only formal. A Peiping official might show his son a picture of his future bride. The boy remaining silent, the father might assume his approval and then boast that he had arranged his boy's marriage in a modern way. On the other hand, many who choose their own mates ask their parents' consent only for the sake of appearances [Lang, 1946, p. 123].

When the Crown Prince of Japan violated tradition by marrying a commoner, the ministers of state denied that romantic love and free choice were involved. In this way, presumably, everyone's face was saved, and the imperial family could support a conservative pattern even while violating it.

Similar changes are occurring in the cities of France, northern Italy, the Balkans, Brazil, Egypt, Thailand, and India, although most of these countries are still on the whole "old fashioned" from an American point of view. The American type of pattern is already well established, independently, in England, the Scandinavian countries, and Germany.[22]

---

[22] See articles on the individual countries in *Marriage and Family Living*, v. 16, Nov. 1954. The instability of parent-child relations in a transitional period is well illustrated in Jules Romains' multivolume novel *Men of Good Will*, which is an attempt to describe French life from before World War I to World War II. See especially *The Wind Is Rising*, which takes place in 1927. Francoise Maieul, a student at the Sorbonne, has a rather strained conversation with her upper-middle-class mother on the subject of sex and marriage (Bk. 23, Chap. 8). Francoise has a self-consciously "sophisticated" manner. It is clear that for her, on a somewhat confused "intellectual" level, sexual freedom is a symbol of the new emancipation of women. Mme. Maieul, afraid to direct her daughter's life frankly, resorts to rather transparent subtlety. Young men, it seems, are naturally "on the make," and one can't blame them; but a decent girl should keep her purity intact till marriage. See also Bk. 23, Chap. 11, in which at a young people's garden party the uncomfortable older women self-consciously condone the younger generation's conduct. It is interesting to note that Françoise later is shocked to learn that her mother is capable of proposing a rather

Divorce

Between 1867 and 1948, population in the United States increased about 300 per cent, marriages slightly over 400 per cent, and divorces about 4000 per cent (Waller, 1951, p. 502). We cannot infer that marriages are in general less happy in the United States than in other countries. Spain, Italy, and Ireland do not permit divorce, and laws in the countries that do are not equally permissive. We cannot even infer that all Connecticut marriages that end in divorce are unhappier than all Connecticut marriages that do not, for there are, of course, great individual differences in attitude toward divorce. There can be no doubt that many married couples that do not get a divorce live in misery together.[23]

CAUSES OF HIGH DIVORCE RATES

Any particular divorce is almost always the outcome of a long process of mutual alienation between the married pair. Yet we cannot say what the "causes" are in any strict sense, for we may be able to find a "worse" case of mutual alienation that did not end in divorce.[24] We can say, however, that certain aspects of culture and social structure are likely to be associated with a high divorce *rate*.

In general, when conditions make incompatibility between husband and wife more likely, when barriers to divorce are lowered, and when relatively satisfactory alternatives to unhappy marriage are available, then the divorce rate rises. The factors that produce a high divorce rate impinge unequally upon different groups in the population of any particular country. Consequently the divorce rate varies according to religion, occupation, race, social class, and other kinds of status (see Goode, 1956, pp. 30ff).

Among the "causes" of a high divorce rate are the following:

1. *Religious tolerance of divorce or a decline in the influence of "strict" religions.* The high divorce rate of Egypt and Japan is due, in part, to lack of religious barriers. Protestant countries usually have a more tolerant attitude toward divorce than Catholic countries. Further, the decline of Christian influence in some places is in itself the result of complex forces, some of which have independently increased the divorce rate.

---

old-fashioned plan after all: a plan for Francoise to marry a wealthy young man whom the girl hardly knows; a plan, moreover, which seems to have the purpose not only of seeing Francoise settled but also of recouping the family's fortunes (Bk. 24, Chap. 25).

23 Facts can do little against a settled moralistic or religious opposition to divorce, but, as Waller says, anyone who thinks that any two married persons ought to be able to get along, or can be forced to get along if divorce is out of the question, should read a few detailed cases of unhappy marriage. See Waller, 1951, pp. 544-52, esp. cases 2-4.

24 For a brilliant though properly modest analysis of the processes of alienation, see Waller, 1951, pp. 513-29. On the inadequacy of the concept "cause of divorce," see Goode, 1956, pp. 64ff., which presents an "accounting scheme for divorce-rate differentials."

2. *Legal tolerance of divorce.* However unpopular strict divorce laws may be, they do tend to hold down the divorce rate. The experience of England is especially instructive. The cost of divorce used to be £500 or more, and the only ground permitted was adultery. A series of liberal changes in the law was followed by a sharp increase in the number of divorces: In 1914 a new law made it possible for the poor to obtain free legal counsel. In 1923 women as well as men were permitted to sue for divorce. In 1926 another law prohibited the press from reporting the details of divorce cases, thus removing the deterrent of unfavorable publicity. In 1937 Parliament added new grounds for divorce: desertion, cruelty, and insanity. The results were clear evidence that many people had previously been prevented from obtaining divorces that they wished to have. The divorce rate rose from 2 per thousand marriages in 1913 (in England and Wales) to 138 per thousand marriages in 1947. Within five years after women were given equal rights with those of men in suing for divorce, nearly twice as many women as men were plaintiffs (Cavan, 1953, pp. 490-97).[25]

With some qualifications, a divorce case in the United States is regarded legally as a contest: one party is supposed to be seeking the divorce and the other is supposed to be against it. Actual practice bears little resemblance to the theory. Many if not most divorces are agreed upon before they get to court. Evasions of the law and technical perjury are common. In many cases the alleged grounds are not the real grievances of the person seeking a divorce; and, indeed, in many cases the person seeking the divorce, usually the wife, is not the one who wants it (Baber, 1953, pp. 458-61, 517-25).[26]

3. *Increased industrialization.* The factory system of production has reduced the importance of the family as a producing unit and has provided jobs for women, freeing them from economic dependence on men. (Not all these jobs, of course, are in factories; many are clerical positions connected with large-scale business and industrial corporations.) At the same time, commercialization of services has freed both men and women, to some extent, from dependence on the home for meals, clothing, laundering, and recreation. The divorce rate has been going up in all industrialized countries (K. Davis, 1950, p. 333).[27] Stable relationships in general tend to be based on common participation in recurring activities. Industrialization and the commercialization of services have tended to reduce the number of

---

[25] This example shows that the law may lag behind the folkways (or popular sentiment, at least) and still have considerable effect. Sumner (1906) maintained that laws "seek their standing-ground" on the folkways.

[26] As a result of his Detroit study, Goode had the strong impression that more often than not the husband was the partner who first wanted the divorce, but that husbands frequently adopted the strategy of acting in such a way as to get the wife to ask for the divorce (Goode, 1956, p. 135).

[27] Davis shows that the divorce rate cannot go up indefinitely. It is likely to stay at a high level, however.

cooperative activities in the home. The husband and father is probably still the chief executive in most families, but his authority is being exercised in a more and more restricted area and has therefore declined; and because it has declined, it is more resented. It is at least plausible that all these results of industrialization are connected with high divorce rates (Homans, 1950, pp. 276-80).

4. *Urbanization*. This factor is related, of course, to industrialization. Sweden, with a high divorce rate, is industrialized, while Norway, with a low rate, is rural. Comparison of these two countries is particularly interesting since they have about the same general culture (Burgess and Locke, 1953, p. 576). Probably the main reason that city life is associated with a high divorce rate is that urban neighbors exert less social control over one another's conduct.

5. *Birth control*. Industrialization is soon followed by a decline in the birth rate. Since children in urban conditions seldom contribute to the family income, they are much more expensive. Children are not a great barrier to divorce, as we shall see, but couples with children are less likely to get a divorce than couples without children. Only couples that have been married thirty years or more are just as likely to get a divorce whether or not they have children; but very few couples get a divorce after being married that long (see Jacobson, 1950, p. 340). Many writers have pointed ou that the decision not to have children and the decision to get a divorce ar probably both due to some third factor. This is no doubt true, but the fac remains that the decision not to have children is to some extent encouraged by modern urban conditions. Moreover, the relationship between *deliberate* childlessness and divorce is closer than the relationship between divorce and childlessness in general, for childless couples that want children are known to be among the happiest couples (Burgess and Cottrell, 1939, p. 260).

6. *Greater geographical mobility*. Moving from one place to another, which of course is made easier by the transportation facilities developed in industrialized countries, reduces still more the social influence of local groups.

7. *High vertical social mobility*. Vertical mobility increases the divorce rate (Goode, 1956, p. 98) because the partners may not adapt equally well or with equal speed to the new social environment. Often the husband has wider social contacts and is more adaptable.

8. *Heterogeneity of population*. Marriage between culturally and socially incompatible persons is more likely in a religiously or ethnically heterogeneous population (Burgess and Locke, 1953, pp. 576-77; J. T. Landis, 1952).

9. *High demands on the intimate affectional side of marriage*. As we have noted, some critics maintain that romanticism is overemphasized in modern marriage. As we have remarked, these critics at the very least err by ignoring other aspects of the so-called romantic-love complex. In our

type of society, romantic love has some positive functions. It may be true, however, as these critics say, that in some cases the ideal of romantic love causes young people to have excessive expectations of happiness in marriage. Perhaps one of the problems in modern marriage is the difficulty of knowing what expectations *are* excessive. The fact remains that if marriage is no longer a prerequisite to more or less comfortable adult living (see paragraph 3, above), then the relative importance of various motives for entering marriage and remaining in it must have shifted. Affectional and sexual needs are, relatively speaking, even more important now than in the past. No doubt this has something to do with the present emphasis on romantic love. Whether this emphasis produces more stability, on the average, or more instability in marriage is hard to say. The point here is that neither thesis can be taken as self-evident.

It is only for convenience that we have listed the foregoing factors as if they were independent of one another. Of course they are not. For example: Industrialization has had an important part in bringing about urbanization, more effective and more widely available contraceptives as well as a greater demand for them, increased geographical and vertical mobility, and, at least in the short run, greater heterogeneity of population. The decline in the hold of certain religious hopes and scruples has probably helped to make people demand more out of this life, including earthly marriage, and has no doubt contributed to the demand for relaxed divorce laws and for better means of birth control.

CHILDREN OF THE DIVORCED

The divorce rate is highest after two to three years of marriage, declines sharply to the seventh year, and then declines more gradually (Jacobson, 1950). Since divorce is more frequent in the early years of marriage, almost three fifths of divorced couples have no children (p. 523). Nevertheless, the 421,000 divorces and annulments granted in 1948 involved about 313,000 children under the age of 21. About two and a half million children were involved in the divorces granted between 1940 and 1949 (Waller, 1951, p. 542). No one thinks that divorce is good for the children affected, but no one knows whether it is worse for them than continuing to live with unhappy and quarreling parents would be; nor does anyone know whether children suffer more from divorce itself or from the conflict that led to divorce (Waller, 1951, pp. 542-43; Goode, 1956, p. 307).

It seems very likely that divorce has worse effects on children in our society than on children in many others (K. Davis, 1944). As we have seen, many societies have composite families. In such families, the loss of one parent is not so disastrous for the child, partly because there are more adults around and partly because the tie between parents and children is probably not so close as it typically is in our small families. In most societies, the custody of children goes automatically to one of the parents: there is no possibility of custody fights or of divided custody, as with us. The large family with generational continuity also has the advantage that the problem of supporting the children does not arise. This advantage is independent of the wealth of the family, for the larger family will go on regardless of the divorce of one couple. In our system, children are often given to the wife, to whom they are frequently a burden since she usually has to go to work to support them. (Alimony is seldom ample enough for full support, and many divorced husbands are delinquent about paying.)

Probably one of the worst aspects of divorce in our society is the frequency with which the custody of children is divided. The divorced parents are often bitter toward each other, and one often embitters the children against the other. With divided custody, it is difficult to see how a child can avoid feeling some conflict of loyalty.

RECOMMENDED READING

Perhaps the most authoritative general work on kinship systems is G. P. Murdock, *Social Structure,* Macmillan, 1949, which is based on materials on 85 societies from the files of the Cross-Cultural Survey (now called the Human Relations Area File) at Yale, plus data on 165 additional societies. For a technical analysis of the American kinship system, see T. Parsons, "The Kinship System of the Contemporary United States," *Amer. Anthrop.,* Jan.-Mar. 1943. v. 45 (reprinted in T. Parsons, *Essays in Sociological Theory,* rev. ed., Free Press, 1954, Chap. 9). On various aspects of marriage and the family, especially in the United States, see three collections of articles: J. T. Landis and M. G. Landis, eds., *Readings in Marriage and the Family,* Prentice-Hall, 1952; R. F. Winch and R. McGinnis, eds., *Selected Studies in Marriage and the Family,* Holt, 1953; and M. B. Sussman, ed., *Sourcebook in Marriage and the Family,* Houghton Mifflin, 1955.

On the forms of marriage, see, in addition to Murdock, M. K. Opler; "Woman's Social Status and the Forms of Marriage," *Amer. J. Sociol.,* Sept. 1943, v. 49, pp. 125-46. This article is a good study of polyandry and criticizes earlier work. E. W. Burgess in turn analyzes the defects and isolates the contributions of Opler's article in his "Comment," *Amer. J. Sociol.,* Sept. 1943, v. 49. pp. 147-48. For a study of Mormon polygyny, based on interviews and family records, see K. Young, *Isn't One Wife Enough?* Holt, 1954.

Certain studies of marriage and the family in other societies are especially valuable for the light they throw on American culture by contrast. K. Davis. "Changing Modes of Marriage: Contemporary Family Types," in H. Becker and R. Hill, eds., *Marriage and the Family,* Heath, 1942, pp. 92-116, deals briefly with several societies (e.g., India and Latin America) and shows the trend toward the conjugal type of family. C. M. Arensberg and S. T. Kimball, *Family and Community in Ireland,* Harvard University Press, 1940, is a first-rate study of the Irish rural family (an example of a stem-family system) in the setting of work. Perhaps the best study of the Chinese family is Olga Lang, *Chinese Family and Society,* Yale University Press, 1946; drawing upon field research, scholarly reports, and Chinese literature, it is well documented and highly readable, and it presents the kinship system in relation to change in the larger social system. Shu-Ching Lee, "China's Traditional Family, Its Characteristics and Disintegration," *Amer. sociol. Rev.,* June 1953, v. 18, pp. 272-80, is an admirably compact discussion. Fei Hsiao-T'ung. "Peasantry and Gentry: An Interpretation of Chinese Social Structure and Its Changes," *Amer. J. Sociol.*, July 1946, v. 52, pp. 1-16, is an excellent paper showing how the composite family type enabled the gentry to retain political and economic power. A glimpse of the control of marriage arrangements in the old-fashioned Japanese system is given in E. I. Sugimoto, "Old Love and New," in Winch and McGinnis, eds., 1953, pp. 45-47. In the same collection, pp. 56-63, R. F. Winch, in "Some Observations on Personality Structure in Japan," discusses personality structure as related to family life. Brief studies, with brief bibliographies, are given in S. A. Queen and J. B. Adams, *The Family in Various Cultures: A Survey of Eleven Family Systems in Eleven Cultural and Historical Settings Throughout the World*, Lippincott, 1952.

On sexual behavior, see C. S. Ford and F. A. Beach, *Patterns of Sexual Behavior*, Harper and Paul B. Hoeber, 1951, which summarizes data on 190 human societies and on many other species. See especially Chap. 13, "Human Sexual Behavior in Perspective." A. C. Kinsey, W. B. Pomeroy, C. E. Martin, P. H. Gebhard, *et al.*, *Sexual Behavior in the Human Female*, Saunders, 1953, contains comparisons with the results reported in *Sexual Behavior in the Human Male* (1948) and excellent references to other studies.

H. G. Beigel, 'Romantic Love," *Amer. sociol. Rev.*, June 1951, v. 16, pp. 326-34 (reprinted in Winch and McGinnis, eds., 1953; and in Sussman, ed., 1955), is a lively article on changes in the cultural meaning of romantic love. Ai-Li S. Chin, "Some Problems of Chinese Youth in Transition," *Amer. J. Sociol.*, July 1948, v. 54, pp. 1-9, is an analysis of letters sent by young Chinese adults to a popular periodical, which reveal their uncertainty about romantic love and their guilt about breaking with the past.

Probably the best available discussion of divorce as a process and an experience is W. Waller, *The Family: A Dynamic Interpretation*, rev. by R. Hill, Dryden, 1951, Chaps. 23, 24. For data on many countries, see K. Davis, "Statistical Perspective on Divorce," *Annals* of the American Academy of the Political and Social Sciences, 1950, v. 272, pp. 15-21 (reprinted in Landis and Landis, eds., 1952). For detailed statistics, see P. H. Jacobson, *American Marriage and Divorce*, Rinehart, 1959. W. J. Goode, *After Divorce*, Free Press, 1956, based on interviews in Detroit with divorced women with children, attempts to show under what conditions post-divorce adjustment is likely to be good The adjustment of children of divorced parents is discussed in the broad perspective provided by comparing widely differing societies in K. Davis, "Children of Divorce," *Law and Contemporary Problems*, 1944, v. 10, pp. 700-10 (reprinted in Landis and Landis, eds., 1952). Several sociologists have done research on the factors that tend to produce "happiness" in marriage, and have attempted to predict marital adjustment. H. J. Locke, *Predicting Adjustment in Marriage: A Comparison of a Divorced and a Happily Married Group*, Holt, 1951, reports the results of one such research project and summarizes earlier studies.

7. Consanguineal Kin Groups and Clans

Kin groups other than the family are relatively unimportant in modern Western society, but they are more important in some other societies. In any case, our conception of kinship systems would be too narrow if we thought of each type of kinship system as simply a network of families, nuclear or composite. Accordingly, in this chapter we shall briefly describe some kin groups other than families.

Every kinship system distinguishes between blood relatives (biologically related, actually or by social fiction), who are technically called *consanguineal relatives,* and relatives by marriage, technically called *affinal relatives.* Except for married couples without children, all groups of relatives living together include some consanguineal relatives, but few groups of relatives living together consist of consanguineal relatives exclusively. Married couples may in some systems be related by blood, but they are always regarded as affinal relatives since the marriage bond is socially the most important bond between them. The various types of family therefore always include some affinal relatives. The only exception we know of is the Nayar *taravad,* which, as we have pointed out (pp. 153, 160), consists of brothers and sisters, with the children of the sisters and of the women in successive generations. All these consanguineal relatives can live in the same household only because among the Nayars husband and wife do not live together for more than three days.

There are many nonresidential kin groups, however, that consist of consanguineal relatives alone. Such groups are accordingly called *consanguineal kin groups.* The composition of these groups depends upon the prevailing rule of descent (Murdock, 1949, Chap. 3).

Rules of Descent

In our own society, our consanguineal relatives are always related to us biologically; this is what we mean, of course, when we loosely call them "blood" relatives. In all societies, some consanguineal relatives are biologically related in the sense we take for granted, but there are many societies in which ego may have consanguineal relatives who are related to him not by "blood" but by a social fiction. Moreover, in no society does ego recognize as relatives by descent all those who are in fact genetically related to him. If his society is very large, many living "blood relatives" are strangers to him. Ego has four grandparents, eight great-grandparents, and sixteen great-great-grandparents; of all these, many had siblings, and many of them and their siblings may have descendants living in ego's generation. All these persons (and more, if we go further back) are ego's so-called relatives by blood.

Ego's recognized consanguineal relatives—the ones to whom he is bound by the kinship system—are, in general, persons to whom he may normally look for emotional support and various kinds of help in case of need. Their importance depends upon the fact that they are few in number as compared with the whole population of the society. Ego's consanguineal relatives are expected to be helpful to him not so much *vis-à-vis* "foreigners" as *vis-à-vis* his unrelated fellow-countrymen. If the number of ego's consanguineal relatives approached the total number of his actual biological relatives, then mutual aid between relatives would become virtually meaningless, since for most individuals it would be nearly the same thing as mutual aid between members of the society. Hence every society limits the circle of ego's consanguineal relatives. The principle or set of principles by which ego's consanguineal relatives are determined is known technically as the rule of descent.

There are three basic rules of descent: patrilineal, matrilineal, and bilateral. In *patrilineal descent,* each individual automatically becomes a member of any consanguineal kin group to which his father belongs, but not of those to which his mother belongs. In *matrilineal descent,* ego joins the consanguineal kin group or groups of his mother but not those of his father. In either patrilineal or matrilineal descent, therefore, ego is socially "closer" in certain respects to one parent and to one set of grandparents, and so on, than to the other. This is true even in a unilinear society which is fully aware that ego is equally close biologically to his mother and to his father.[1] In *bilateral descent*—the rule in our society—ego "inherits" some but not all of his father's consanguineal relatives, and also the *corresponding* consanguineal relatives of his mother. In this system of descent, ego's four grandparents, for example, are equally related to him. In a general way, the significant relatives in this system are also the close biological relatives; how far in the ever-widening circles of relationship the kin relation is recognized

[1] "Fully aware" is perhaps too strong: the laws of heredity are only now becoming known. Some scholars believe that certain primitive peoples, the Australian aborigines in particular, are ignorant of biological paternity, but this is doubtful. In any case, even these people nevertheless recognize patrilineal descent. Goodsell, 1935, pp. 82-83, mentions that the ancient Greeks, who were strongly patrilineal, "tended to exaggerate the physiological role of the father in conception"; but the evidence adduced—a quotation from Aeschylus' *Eumenides*—should not be taken too seriously in view of its context in the play.

(i.e., involves social obligations) will vary somewhat from one bilateral society to another. We tend to become rather vague about our kinship with relatives beyond first cousins.

Strictly speaking, probably no society is perfectly bilateral. In our own, which perhaps comes as close as any other, we favor the patrilineal side slightly by taking our names from our fathers. On the other hand, no society is perfectly unilinear either, if by that term is implied total neglect of one side in favor of the other (Lévi-Strauss, 1949, pp. 134-36).

In addition to the three basic rules of descent, there are several others which are more complex.

> It is also possible for a particular society to combine two rules of descent. Combinations of matrilineal and patrilineal descent are particularly common. Thus in certain Indonesian societies with *ambil-anak* marriage the usual patrilineal rule is suspended for a generation in the case of a family without sons, and matrilineal descent through a matrilocally residing daughter supervenes to continue the family line.[2] Among the Apinaye of Brazil, matrilineal descent prevails for females and patrilineal descent for males. Among the Mundugumor of New Guinea, on the other hand, a daughter is affiliated with her father, and a son with his mother, in a kin group which zigzags between the sexes from generation to generation like sex-linked characteristics in heredity. Among the Buginese and Macassar of Celebes, the first, third, and other odd-numbered offspring are affiliated with the mother, and even-numbered progeny with their father. In all of these cases, it is important to note, one unilinear rule is applied in particular individual cases, the other in others. Both are not applied at the same time to one individual.
>
> When patrilineal and matrilineal descent are applied together, and not alternatively in combinations like the above, their joint application is known as *double descent* [Murdock, 1949, p. 45].

Double descent, which is found only in primitive societies, obviously has some resemblance to bilateral descent. In bilateral descent, however, ego's relatives on his father's side exactly correspond, in degree and kind of closeness to him, biological and social, to those on his mother's side. In double descent, on the other hand, although ego does have relatives on both sides, the rules by which they are ascribed on the two sides are not symmetrical, and ego's social relations with the two sets of relatives involve different obligations.

In general, whatever the rule of descent may be, ego's consanguineal relatives will always be roughly equal in number to those of either of his parents. Thus in double descent ego "inherits" his father's patrilineal relatives and his mother's matrilineal relatives, but not his father's matrilineal relatives or his mother's patrilineal relatives. Double descent produces bilinear kin groups known as *sections*. We showed how such a system works in Chapter 6, in our description of the Kariera system of restricted exchange.

In every society, the rule of descent is important for at least two reasons: (1) It automatically establishes for every individual a network of social

---

[2] *Ambil-anak* marriage is also found in China and in rural Ireland

positions in which he participates with obligations and rights. Aside from mutual aid of various kinds, the rights and obligations ascribed on the basis of descent always include some regulation of marriage and sexual relations. (2) Descent always prescribes, to some extent, inheritance of property, and it often prescribes succession to titles of rank. No system permits complete testamentary freedom, and some systems permit almost none. By law or well-established custom, the rule of descent automatically defines some rights of inheritance. Perhaps the most important supplements to descent for the disposal of property rights at death are: rights established by birth order, as in primogeniture or ultimogeniture; rights established by marriage; rights established by creditors unpaid before the death of the deceased; inheritance taxes; and the right of testamentary freedom, which is restricted by all or most of the preceding rights.

UNILINEAR CONSANGUINEAL KIN GROUPS

The most important consanguineal kin groups associated with unilinear rules of descent are lineages and sibs. A *lineage* consists of descendants in one line, either patrilineal or matrilineal, who know their exact genealogical relationship and who recognize obligations to one another. Except in the upper class, lineages are not formed in the United States. The Rockefeller "family," for example, is a lineage. A *sib* is a patrilineal or matrilineal kin group whose members are assumed to have a common ancestor but who do not all know their exact genealogical relationship to one another. It is as if all persons named Smith at birth considered themselves bound by ties of kinship. Sibs are often bound together by a common totemic name and by a ritual taboo against eating the flesh of the totem animal. The fiction is solemnly maintained that the sib members are all descended somehow from a common ancestor of the totemic species. This complex of beliefs, taboos, and ceremonies serves to keep alive the sense of mutual obligation between sib members who may be widely scattered in residence.

Sibs are sometimes divided into subsibs or allied in larger groupings to which various technical names have been given. Most lineages and sibs are exogamous. (A group is said to be exogamous if its members are forbidden by established custom or law to choose one another as marriage partners.) In fact, there is a general tendency for consanguineal kin groups to be exogamous. When they are not, the presumption is that they either are not yet fully established or are on their way out. Roughly speaking, the smaller the consanguineal kin group, the greater the likelihood of its being exogamous. In all societies, the extension of the incest taboo to consanguine relatives outside the family has effects similar to those that the primary incest taboo has for the family: it ensures that the consanguineal kin groups will be interconnected through marriages, and it helps to maintain the solidarity of each of the groups.

BILATERAL CONSANGUINEAL KIN GROUPS

In the United States at present, the most important consanguineal kin group is so ill defined in membership and so tenuous in organization that we do not even have a name for it in everyday speech. Technically it is known as the *kindred*. Its membership is rather loosely defined by the bilateral rule of descent. Ego's kindred consists of all those relatives on both sides who would normally be expected to attend his wedding or his funeral. He might or might not exchange Christmas gifts with them. He might feel some obligation to keep in touch with them and to wish them well, but in all probability his connection with them is not very demanding.

Seen in comparative perspective, the kindred has a peculiar feature: its membership and duties are defined strictly in relation to a given ego. Unlike lineages and sibs, therefore, kindreds are not mutually exclusive in membership; they overlap one another. The members have no group activities apart from their several connections with one specific person, and even then their cooperation involves little regard for one another. For example, when ego gets married, his kindred probably will not, as a unified group, plan a joint wedding gift or a harmonious set of gifts; they will send their gifts individually and independently, with unfortunate duplications and omissions. When ego dies, his kindred disintegrates altogether as a group.

The tenuousness or weakness of the kindred as a cooperative group points up a more general fact; namely, that bilateral descent, unlike either kind of unilinear descent, may be best thought of in negative terms: it amounts to a lack of emphasis on either line of descent and hence on descent as such. The expectation that ego will balance his attentions between the two sides of the family means that he is relatively independent of both. This relative independence is enhanced by the fact that his wife's relatives are no more or less important than his own (see Parsons, 1943).

It should be emphasized that the independence of our neolocal nuclear families is only relative. A study made in New Haven (Sussman, 1953) found that out of ninety married sons, eighteen entered their fathers' business firms. In other cases, the help from parents was less far-reaching but still important:

> In 154 of the 195 cases in the sample parents had established a pattern of giving moderate help and service to their married child's family. This included gifts, such as furniture, household and kitchen equipment, to the young couple upon marriage; financial assistance in some of their larger expenditures . . . , such services as gardening, landscaping, house construction, painting and repairing the house; and such personal assistance as care of grandchildren during their parents' vacation or provisions of inexpensive vacations for them or the grandchildren. In return for this assistance parents expected from their children continued affectional response, inclusion in some of their activities, and personal service and attention.

> Under no circumstances did parents feel that the children should be supported by regular weekly or monthly money contributions except for emergency periods [pp. 23-24].

Help is especially lavish at the birth of grandchildren (see Sussman, 1953; Albrecht, 1954).

A study made in London during the floods of 1953 showed that most evacuees took refuge with relatives rather than in official evacuee centers. As one might expect, this tendency was especially strong for evacuees who had relatives within a short distance of the disaster (M. Young, 1954).[3]

Clans

Thus far the only important residential kin group we have considered is the family in its various forms. There is another important kin group, which is based on both a unilocal rule of residence and a unilinear rule of descent. A *clan* consists of families bound to one another by three things: (1) a unilocal rule of residence, patrilocal, matrilocal, or avunculocal; (2) a unilinear rule of descent, either patrilineal or matrilineal; and (3) as with any other group, a sense of solidarity and some common activities.[4] A unilocal rule of residence means, of course, that typically the units of a clan are extended families. The fact that the clan consists of families living in the same village or other local area means that it includes affinal as well as consanguineal relatives. A patrilocal, patrilineal clan, for example, consists of men joined by a recognized unilinear rule of descent, their children, and their wives. When their female children marry, therefore, they will join the clan of their husbands. The men might be called core members, while the women are either temporary members (before marriage) or peripheral members (after marriage to a core member). The consanguineal kinship of the core members, however, is based on the fiction of a common ancestor, not on specific genealogical relationships. A full-fledged clan is also exogamous (Murdock, 1949, Chap. 4).

The unity of a clan may be symbolized in a common name for its members. Possession of a common name helps, no doubt, in the formation of sibs, which probably never arise except as a development from clans already existing. For sibs to develop, it is necessary only for the core clan members to retain some kinship connection with the siblings who leave the clan upon marrying. Thus, with patrilineal, patrilocal clans, the men are the core members and each woman must join her husband's clan; but if the women, even after marriage, feel a special bond with their brothers

---

[3] If Young had followed Murdock's usage, which we are adopting here, his paper, "The Role of the Extended Family in a Disaster," would have been entitled "The Role of Kindreds. . . ." It will be remembered that we have used the term "extended family" in a different sense from Young's.

[4] Like most of the technical terms in sociology, the term "clan" has been used in other senses.

and with other core members of the brothers' clan, then we have sibs. (It is not enough that the women continue to feel close to their own brothers, for this may be expected in any kinship system.) Each clan would be associated with a definite sib, overlapping in membership but not coextensive. Each woman would belong to her brothers' sib but to her husband's clan. A society may have clans for a long time without developing sibs; on the other hand, once sibs have been developed, they may continue to exist even after the clans from which they arose have disappeared.

Among civilized societies, China is one of the most famous for its clans. At the present time, clans are most prevalent in the south of China, less so in the central provinces, and almost nonexistent in the north; but they are presumably moribund everywhere. Nevertheless, for hundreds of years, patrilineal, patrilocal clans have played an important part in Chinese political, economic, and religious life. (Since the sources from which the facts in the present account are taken all date from before the Communist revolution, it is hard to know whether, in making any particular point about the Chinese clans, one may safely use the present tense or should use the past. We shall straddle this question by shifting tenses now and then, but the reader should not take these shifts too seriously.)

Clans in China have been of great importance in maintaining and extending the political and economic power of the rich. This fact has, of course, conditioned the life of the poor as well, mainly by restricting their opportunities. The Chinese village may consist of one or more clans and of families not organized in clans (the "village poor"). The formal clan association is organized and run according to well-established traditional patterns.

Of twenty-six clans investigated in 1937, twenty-four in Kwangtung and two in Fukien, the smallest had four families, the largest 546, "but most had between 40 and 70" (Lang, 1946, p. 174).[5] These clans included poor families as well as wealthy ones. Despite the traditional veneration for age, the rulers of the clan—executives, treasurers, and committee members—were not necessarily the oldest heads of families; they were middle-aged or elderly, but they were above all wealthy. Some had inherited their positions, some had been co-opted, and some were elected by acclamation in annual meetings of male members in the ancestral temple.

> The social composition of 52 clan leaders investigated in Kwangtung is characteristic: 26 landlords, 2 officials, 16 merchants (most of them landowners), 2 rentiers supported by their sons (businessmen overseas), 1 teacher, 1 school principal, 1 geomancer, and 11 peasants. All but 3 of these 11 peasants were well-to-do and employed several laborers. The leadership of the 2 clans investigated in Fukien consisted of 2 merchants, 1 landlord, and 1 owner of a private school [Lang, 1946, pp. 175-76].

---

[5] See also Weber, 1951, esp. pp. 14, 82, 85ff., 96. H. H. Gerth, the translator, uses the term "sib" where we should use "clan."

Each clan owns, typically, from 50 to 70 per cent of the land held by its members; the rest the members own privately. The clan association is a business enterprise: it rents land to members and nonmembers; it may also operate stores and pawnshops; and, in former times at least, it maintained facilities for weaving and for processing rice. The proceeds of business are used to build and maintain strongholds for protection against bandits, to maintain schools and provide scholarships for selected clan members, to pay for the upkeep of the ancestral temple and for the annual rites there, and to pay the funeral expenses of poor members. The clan settles disputes between its members, keeps members in line with the standards of the community by threatening to exclude them from the temple or drive them from the community, and intercedes for them with the local representatives of the government. Clan heads often used to hold government offices at the same time.[6]

There is a tendency for clan heads to manipulate the affairs of the clan in their own interest: they award scholarships to their own sons, sell some of the clan land to themselves, rent to themselves the choicest land, or even appropriate profits outright. Although the clan maintains a united front against outsiders, it is not necessarily all harmony within.

The clans in China are found mostly in rural areas. In the cities, a clan may have a transformed existence as a club of those with the same name whose ancestors came from the same village. Throughout China people of the same name are not supposed to marry each other.

So firmly rooted in Chinese social structure and culture were clan associations that they often survived emigration, or at least were revived in the United States and Canada.

> These family organizations are essential units of Chinatown. Every member of the organization looks to it for protection from injustice done to him by the Chinese or Canadians. . . . Troubles between members of different associations are often settled between their respective heads. They resort to the law courts only when they cannot reach an agreement. . . . These family associations are so powerful that all important undertakings in Chinatown either of a benevolent or patriotic nature have to seek their aid and approval [Hayner and Reynolds, 1937, p. 355].

CLAN-BARRIOS AND CLAN-COMMUNITIES

In a society with clans, each local community (e.g., village) may have one clan or more; in some societies (e.g., China), some villages have one clan and others have several. As a clan expands in number of members, it may come to occupy the whole local community, other clans moving out. In fact, a solitary clan may outgrow its local community and have to split, part remaining and part moving to a different place; the process is known as fission (see p. 157). It is a fact that patrilineal, patrilocal clans often

---

[6] For an account of an episode in which a clan succeeded in having a government official removed, see Burgess and Locke, 1953, pp. 33-34.

live in single-clan communities, but matrilineal and matrilocal clans "never" do; matriclans, as they are called, always live in communities with at least two clans in each (frequently exactly two). (The only exceptions, and they are extremely rare, are found in nomadic societies, in which, obviously, there are "local communities" only in an equivocal sense.) [7] Why this difference between patriclans and matriclans?

The explanation is simple. We noted earlier that the characteristic activities carried on by men often require, or at least make desirable, an intimate knowledge of the physical environment in which they live, its resources and hazards, seasonal changes, natural strongholds, etc., whereas this is seldom true of the activities in which women engage. Consequently, it is often inconvenient for men to leave their home community when they marry, and much less inconvenient for women. If a patriclan occupies a community all by itself, no inconvenience results for the men, for they will not have to move out of the community when they marry. But they *would* have to move out if a single *matri*clan occupied each community. Hence matriclans are "never" distributed one to a community.

If a village is made up of several clans, each located in a fairly definite part of the village, each of the clans is technically known as a "clan-barrio." If the whole village consists of one clan, we call it a "clan-community." But social phenomena do not always fall neatly into a few categories. For example, the reality of clan organization in China is more complex than our description has suggested. In the 1930's the village of Kaihsienkung in Kiangsu Province had four recognized territorial subdivisions (Yu). All fourteen families with the surname Lü lived in the same subdivision of the village; but the families with the surname Chou, for example, were more scattered: of the ninety-eight, forty-nine lived in one subdivision, twenty-four in another, twenty-three in a third, and two in a fourth. This dispersion might be reduced somewhat if we knew the spatial distribution of each of the two sets of Chou families (for there were two unrelated Chou lines in the village), but even so there was undoubtedly considerable dispersion.

The village as a whole was like a clan-community in two respects: (1) there was a strong tendency for the village to be exogamous, and (2) people in the village called one another by kinship terms even when they were not related; for example, biologically unrelated boys of about the same age called one another "brother." The use of kinship terms served as a device for classifying people according to age and sex, but it also suggested some feeling of kinship, especially since it was linked with a virtual rule of village exogamy. To be sure, ego used kinship terms in addressing the people in his mother's village as well, but these terms were the ones that would have been appropriate if the persons in his mother's village had all been relatives of his mother. The whole society was of course strongly patrilineal, and ego was allowed to marry a girl from his mother's village: in fact, the

---

[7] For a more detailed exposition, see Murdock, 1949, pp. 213-15.

preferred match for him was with his mother's brother's daughter—preferably his mother's actual brother's actual daughter. Therefore, the use of kinship terms in both cases—that is, in ego's own village and in his mother's—reinforces the point that the village was similar to an exogamous clan-community. It fell short of the ideal type in that the members of the village were not clearly and unequivocally bound to one another by a rule of descent, and the village otherwise did not have so strong an ingroup spirit, perhaps, as many fully developed clans do (Fei Hsaio-T'ung, 1939).

Thus in Kaihsienkung we find an *approximation* to clan-barrios within the village and an approximation to a clan-community in the village as a whole. Social reality is complex, but we are able to achieve some clarity in describing it by using ideal types as points of reference. In this case, our ideal types are the concepts of clan, clan-barrio, and clan-community.

CLAN SOLIDARITY AND CONFLICT

Although a marriage joins two groups (families or clans) and helps to establish friendly relations between them, it also opens up the possibility of friction or downright conflict. This may be especially true with a unilocal rule of residence. If the women have to leave their extended families or clans upon marrying, they are likely to do so with some misgivings. Probably most persons feel some tension between their attachment to the family of orientation and their attachment to the family of procreation—or, more accurately, between attachment to consanguineal relatives and attachment to affinal relatives. Sometimes this conflict is a rather conspicuous feature of social life, as, for example, among the Dobuans of Melanesia (Fortune, 1932a) or the Ashanti of Africa (Fortes, 1949).

The tension is increased by the fact that the kinsmen of a woman marrying out are likely to retain an interest in her and feel an obligation to protect her. The Murngin tribes of northwestern Australia have patrilocal clans and both patrilineal and matrilineal sibs. Brothers and sisters belong to the same sibs throughout life, but the sisters, when they marry, are lost to the clans into which they were born and are taken into their husbands' clans. This situation produces some strain in the network of obligations. There is a custom of ceremonial spear-throwing, engaged in when a man swears at his wife in the presence of her sib brothers. On such occasions, the brothers call all their sisters *wakinu* ("without relatives": equivalent to "worthless") and throw spears at them, including in the target sib-sisters who were not involved in the incident that gave rise to anger. The spear-throwing is only ceremonial: the brothers have no intention of hitting their sisters. But they throw no spears at all at the husband, who has committed the offense. The custom may be interpreted as follows: (1) the brothers throw spears at their sisters and say they are without relatives in order to affirm the fact that the women are no longer members of their brothers' clan; (2) they throw spears at *all* their sisters, and they deliberately miss, in order to emphasize the generality of the affirmation in (1) but also in order to show their awareness that none of the sisters, not even the one involved in the incident, is really at fault, and thus express a covert anger toward the husband, the real offender; and (3) the brothers do all this as relatives of the woman.

If the clan brothers went off in high dudgeon to punish the offender, what would be the result? The marriage tie between the sister and the offender would be threatened. So would the principle that a woman belongs to her husband's clan. Moreover, the *husband's* fellow clansmen would rally to his side, and there is a possibility that a general row between the two clans would ensue. In short, if there were no conventional and relatively harmless way of meeting such situations, the feelings involved would be quite disruptive; cumulatively, they might threaten the very structure of marriage and clan.

This particular example is complicated by the fact that the out-marrying sisters, although lost to their brothers' clan, are still members of their brothers' sib. In general, however, whether there are sibs or not, the existence of clans does involve the possibility of tension and conflict. Clan solidarity provides a protection for the individual, since his clan will be behind him if anyone in another clan does him an injustice. On the other hand, this very solidarity could, as we have just noted, disrupt the society. On the whole, among the Murngin the balance of power tended to prevent war between clans: no clan was so powerful that it could ignore the possibility of retaliation from other clans. Moreover, since the clans were exogamous, each had given hostages to some of the others, in the form of out-marrying women (Warner, 1937, pp. 109-13).

Some of the phenomena we have described in this chapter probably seem rather strange to American readers. The Murngin of Australia would probably consider our system strange. In the next chapter, we shall attempt to develop a little further one of the themes implicit in Chapters 6 and 7: namely, that kinship systems, although varying widely, do not do so wildly, and that our own system, from a neutral point of view, is neither more nor less "natural" than any other.

RECOMMENDED READING

The basic distinctions in this chapter are taken from G. P. Murdock, *Social Structure*, Macmillan, 1949, Chap. 3: "Consanguineal Kin Groups," and Chap. 4: "The Clan."

8. The Kinship System as a Whole

If a kinship system were simply a development from the universal biological facts of sexual union and descent, all kinship systems would be the same. The comparative analysis of kinship systems, however, might well begin with a clear exposition of the biological relationships that all systems build upon in different ways. We shall discuss this subject under the heading "terms for kinsmen."

Terms for Kinsmen

As we have seen, the villagers of Kaihsienkung use kinship terms in ways different from ours. Thus ego calls women of his mother's generation and from her village by the same term he uses for his mother's sisters, whether or not they are his mother's own sisters. This terminological neglect of differences that we regard as important is extremely common; moreover, we ourselves fail to make certain distinctions that many other societies make. It is not yet possible to explain such variation perfectly, but a great deal of progress has been made. In this brief section, we can only touch upon some of the lines along which an explanation must be sought.

In every society, people *address* their relatives by a wider variety of terms than they use to *refer* to them. In our own society, for example, some people call their male parent "Father," some say "Papa," some say "Pa," some say "Daddy," and some use several terms, depending upon mood and situation; but virtually everyone refers to his "father," especially when speaking with persons outside the circle of intimate friends and relatives. Because of the relative stability of terms of reference, these are the ones we shall discuss.

Some terms of reference are very specific. "Father" in our society is a good example: used by a particular ego, it refers to one person only. The term "brother" is more ambiguous: ego might have several brothers, and the term ignores birth order. The term "uncle" is highly ambiguous: it might refer to mother's brother, father's brother, maternal aunt's husband, or paternal aunt's husband; and it also ignores birth order (mother or father might have several brothers or sisters). Terms such as "uncle" are said to be "classificatory," since they class together relatives of different types. Whether a particular term is called classificatory or not obviously depends upon how elaborately we wish to distinguish among different "types" of relative. For example, if we decide to regard birth order as important (as the Chinese do), then we should have to regard "brother" as a classificatory term.

At this point, we might ask three questions: (1) What distinctions can be made in principle among kinship terms? (2) Why do some kinship systems sometimes ignore some of these possible distinctions, and why do other systems ignore others? (3) Why are these questions important? The rest of this section will give rough answers to these questions.

KIN-TYPES

Some nine or ten distinctions among kin-types are inherently possible, but only six of these are of general importance.

1. *Sex.* The terms "brother" and "sister," for example, specify the sex of the relative referred to. The only term in our system that does not do so is "cousin," which is highly ambiguous in several respects. In some systems there is no simple term for grandfather; one must say "male grandparent" or "father's father" or "mother's father." (In all systems it is possible to specify exact relationships by means of qualifying terms. For example, we can say "mother's brother's daughter" instead of "cousin." That societies differ in the inherent distinctions they consider important is epitomized in the fact that we ordinarily do not use the longer term whereas there are societies that use some such term—not necessarily a "long" one—as a matter of course.)

2. *Generation.* The terms "father" and "son," for example, specify a generational difference, and the terms "brother" and "cousin" specify sameness of generation. All our primary kinship terms—that is, the terms by which kinsmen in the nuclear family are referred to—explicitly indicate the relation between the generation of the speaker and the generation of the relative referred to. In some systems, grandfather and grandson, for example, refer to each other by the same term. This term we should therefore call classificatory.

3. *Affinity.* Most of our kinship terms observe the distinction between affinal and consanguineal relatives, but a few do not. Compare "son-in-law" and "uncle."

4. *Collaterality.* Among consanguineal relatives, some are lineal and some are collateral. Relatives in a direct line of descent are lineal (e.g., grandfather, father, son, grandson). Ego's collateral relatives include his own siblings, all the siblings of his lineal relatives above his own generation, and all the descendants of these two groups. (In this discussion of inherent distinctions, "ego" means the focal person regardless of sex.) "Uncle" may refer to an affinal relative (aunt's husband), but when it refers to a con-

sanguineal relative, that relative is collateral. The basic reason for our vagueness about uncles and aunts is that the consanguineal and affinal relatives to whom we refer by these terms are treated socially in much the same way. Many kinship systems do not specify collaterality in some of their terms. Thus the term for mother might also be used for mother's sister.

5. *Bifurcation.* Failure to recognize the distinction of bifurcation is failure to specify the sex of the relative through whom ego is related to the relative being referred to. Our term "niece," for example, can refer to brother's daughter or sister's daughter. "Uncle" and "aunt" fail with respect to both bifurcation and affinity. Our term "great-grandson" fails twice with respect to bifurcation: a great-grandson might be a son's son's son, a son's daughter's son, a daughter's son's son, or a daughter's daughter's son.

6. *Linkage.* This distinction is important only when the relative being referred to is affinal. Failure to recognize linkage might be defined as failure to specify whether the affinal relative being referred to is linked to ego through another affinal relative or through a consanguineal relative. Our term "brother-in-law," for example, not only fails to specify the sex of the intervening relative (sister, wife, or husband) but does not specify the relationship of the intervening relative to ego.[1]

If a system of kinship terms regularly observed all six of these distinctions whenever possible, it would have to distinguish among more than 180 types of kinsmen ("kin-types"). "A kin-type is a class of relatives defined by all six major criteria—i.e., consisting exclusively of relatives between whom no inherent distinction exists."[2] Apart from seldom-used descriptive elaborations such as "mother's younger sister's second son," most systems of kinship terminology actually use about twenty-five terms. Some systems use a few more, but no system approaches 180. It is clear, therefore, that every system has many classificatory terms. We should note, however, that

---

[1] These distinctions were developed mainly by A. L. Kroeber and R. H. Lowie. Except for linkage, they are defined and discussed by Murdock, 1949, pp. 101-04. G. S. Ghurye, 1955, has more recently proposed that linkage should be substituted for Murdock's distinction of bifurcation. But linkage should probably be distinguished from bifurcation. Ghurye is probably correct, however, in rejecting Murdock's sixth major inherent distinction, which is "polarity." Polarity is recognized when the term ego uses for a particular relative is different from the term the same relative uses when he refers to ego. Thus "grandfather" recognizes polarity, but "brother" does not (when the relationship in question involves two brothers). According to Ghurye, failure to recognize polarity is not an independent matter; it results in all cases from failure to recognize sex or generation or both. Ghurye wishes to substitute "reciprocity" for "polarity," but it is difficult to see what would be gained: reciprocity (use of the same term by ego and by the relative to whom ego refers) results either from failure to recognize sex or generation (if Ghurye is right about polarity) or from the fact that no inherent distinctions exist between ego and the relative to whom he is referring: in either case we cannot speak of a new inherent distinction. For other, true distinctions, see Murdock, 1949, pp. 105-06: to which we might add that "relative age" and "birth order" are not quite the same.

[2] This sentence is quoted verbatim from Murdock, 1949, pp. 133-34, but we have added linkage as one of the six major criteria and omitted Murdock's "polarity."

application of the same term to relatives of different kin-types does not mean that the relatives are treated alike in all respects. For example, sexual intercourse with one's own sister is a much more serious offense than sexual intercourse with a distant clan-sister. The villagers of Kaihsienkung are certainly more intimate with their father's own brothers than with his village "brothers," whose genealogical relationship to him is not known precisely.[3]

The inherent distinctions are not observed in kinship terms of reference with equal frequency. We do not have a statistical test for the frequency with which the distinction of sex is applied, but Murdock finds that if generation has an efficacy of 25, the relative efficacy of affinity is approximately 5 and that of collaterality and bifurcation is 1 each (Murdock, 1949, p. 134).[4] Under what conditions are the inherent distinctions likely to be ignored?

SOCIAL EQUALIZERS AND DIFFERENTIALS

Since the six (or more) kinds of biological relatedness are the same for all societies, we can assume that differences in systems of kinship terms are due to differences in the corresponding systems of social relations. Consanguineal kin groups, forms of marriage, and rules of residence—probably in descending order of relative efficacy—operate as "social equalizers" and "social differentials," sometimes overriding inherent distinctions and sometimes reinforcing them. For example, patrilineal descent operates to bring several persons into the same consanguineal kin group or groups, and their common membership may blur or override one or more inherent distinctions between them. By the same reasoning, participation in different groups will tend to reinforce inherent distinctions. Thus consanguineal kin groups, forms of marriage, and rules of residence are both social equalizers and social differentials, depending upon how they affect relatives of different kin-types. Common participation is a social similarity between certain relatives, and participation in different groups is a dissimilarity between others. Consanguineal kin groups, forms of marriage, and rules of residence produce similarities and dissimilarities—or equalizers and differentials—of the following kinds:

1. *Participation,* or group membership.
2. *Coincidence.* Sororal polygyny, for example, makes it likely that ego's wives will be sisters of one another. Therefore wife and wife's sister

---

3 Anthropologists sometimes refer to "classificatory systems of kinship terminology." As we have seen, every system includes classificatory *terms.* We should speak of a classificatory *system* only when ego in some cases classifies together, with one term, some relatives whose exact genealogical relationship to him is known and others whose exact genealogical relationship to him is not known.

4 For consanguineal relatives, Ghurye says that the order of efficacy of the other inherent distinctions, from greatest to least, is sex, generation, collaterality, and linkage (including bifurcation, which he treats as a special case of linkage). For affinal relatives, the order of efficacy is sex, linkage, generation, and collaterality. (Ghurye, 1955, p. 55.)

will be interchangeable, or, from another point of view, will coincide. If two positions are occupied by the same person, the difference between them will be blurred.

3. *Proximity.* Matrilocal residence, for example, which brings certain relatives together in the same house or local area, might blur other differences between them.

4. *Analogy.* If two relatives are called by the same term, there is a tendency to extend the "equivalence" by analogy throughout the system of terms. Thus if ego calls his mother and his mother's sister by the same term, he will probably also call his mother's daughter and his mother's sister's daughter by the same term.

5. *Immateriality.* If all the relatives of two kin-types are not very important socially to ego, this fact alone may be enough for him to lump them together, ignoring one or more inherent distinctions. The expression "distant cousin" is an example.

The aspects of our own kinship system that probably account for most of our classificatory kin terms are bilateral descent and neolocal residence. As we have noted, bilateral descent produces the kindred—a group so weak and unorganized that some writers refuse to regard it as a group at all and consider bilateral "descent" the negation of the principle of descent. In any case, bilaterality certainly accounts for our consistent ignoring of bifurcation. It also accounts for our ignoring of linkage (a man treats his sister's husband and his wife's brother as equally related to him and calls them both "brother-in-law"; a woman calls both brother's wife and husband's sister "sister-in-law"). Neolocal residence is important because it reinforces the effect of bilaterality.

We are now in a position to answer our second question. (Why do some kinship systems sometimes ignore some inherent distinctions, and why do other kinship systems sometimes ignore others?)

> The relatives of any two kin-types tend to be called by the same kinship terms, rather than by different terms, in inverse proportion to the number and relative efficacy of (a) the inherent distinctions between them and (b) the social differentials affecting them, and in direct proportion to the number and relative efficacy of the social equalizers affecting them [Murdock, 1949, p. 138].[5]

Terms for relatives are an important subject, first, because the inherent distinctions have to do with the underlying biological basis of all kinship systems. Consequently, they afford a good starting point for comparing different systems. Systems of kin terms help to differentiate and classify total kinship systems. Secondly, establishing knowledge about the determinants of kinship terminology is a good way of checking theories about the

[5] This is Murdock's "Postulate 1." For his discussion of social equalizers and social differentials, see pp. 135ff.

way in which kinship systems work. The terms of reference used in any particular kinship system are easy to find out, and the classificatory terms are clues to the structure of the whole system. At the very least, we cannot be said to understand the system until we understand why certain terms ignore one or more of the inherent distinctions. Finally, since kin terms tend to change more slowly than other aspects of kinship systems, they afford a clue to processes of change. Some terms in some systems appear to be "residues" of an earlier state of the kinship system as a whole.

Changes in Kinship Systems

Kinship systems are changing all the time. The changes in important structural parts, such as the form of marriage, the rule of residence, the rule of descent, and the types and composition of kin groups, are usually slow; that is, they usually emerge clearly in the course of generations rather than days or even years. Moreover, the forces behind such changes are of many interrelated kinds—the discovery, development, or depletion of resources and the development and spread of new methods of production; the growth of new patterns in the relationships of men in their productive activities; changes in the internal ordering of societies insofar as the use of force is concerned and in the relation of one society to another in this respect; changes in the size and age-and-sex composition of populations. These various factors do not necessarily move kinship structure in the same direction; some factors reinforce others, some neutralize others. Any change that takes place in kinship structure is therefore necessarily the resultant of many other social changes. It follows, also, that a really adequate theory of change in kinship systems would have to be part of a more general theory of change in social systems as wholes.

The problem of analyzing change in kinship systems, however, is similar to the problem of analyzing change in languages. In its vocabulary, its semantic rules, its syntax, a language also reflects the myriad influences of the whole culture and social life of those who speak it. Yet linguists are able to say significant things about change in the structure of a language without pretending to be authorities on everything in the world. The fundamental reason for this is that a language is a *system;* its various parts or elements are interrelated in such a way that if any element changes very much, for any cause or combination of causes, adjustive changes will take place in other elements. For example, there is a "drift" in English toward dropping flexional endings. Since flexion helps to indicate which words go together (adjectives with nouns, nouns with verbs, etc.), the loss of flexion constantly creates a need for some functional equivalent. Flexion in English has been replaced, to some extent, by increasing rigidity in the order of words in the sentence. The drift toward loss of flexion is a long-range gross trend, made up of many small specific changes and caused, no doubt, by many extralinguistic factors. The drift itself could be observed even if we had no knowledge of the factors causing it, and the structural problems created by the drift can be understood without this knowledge.

So it is with kinship systems. If a drift occurs in one part of the system, for whatever causes, adjustive changes will take place at the same time or soon afterward. Before we could hope to approach the problem of change successfully, therefore, it was necessary to have a clear idea of what a kinship system is, what its elements are, how widely they can vary, and how they go together in the system.[6]

THE BASIC PATTERN OF CHANGE

As we have noted, almost anything can affect the kinship system. A religious movement might introduce new moral principles touching marriage and the family. For example, under religious influence the Mormons practiced polygyny for a time, in the midst of a predominantly monogamous society.

In general, however, the rule of residence is that part of any kinship system which is most vulnerable to change. We have already mentioned some extrakinship factors that strongly affect the decision of newly married couples about where they will establish their residence (see Chap. 6, pp. 154-55). If we begin by assuming that various extrakinship factors have started a drift toward a new pattern of residence, then other steps will follow in a rough sequence:

1. A drift or gradual change in the normativeness of the "rule" of residence.

2. Adjustive changes in existing residential kin groups. Extended families and clans will gradually develop, disappear, or change their form in accordance with the new rule of residence.

3. Partly in conjunction with (2) and partly as a consequence, "the development, disappearance, or change in form of consanguineal kin groups, particularly kindreds, lineages, and sibs," in structural consonance with the new types of residential kin group. This step or stage involves a change in the rule of descent.

4. Gradual adjustment of kinship terminology in accordance with all these changes. Residence has its influence, but the new rule of descent and the associated consanguineal kin groups have more influence on terminology.[7]

This generalized description of change is simplified in certain respects. Events rarely fall in so neat a sequence. The theoretical sequence of change is what occurs *if* the original change in the rule of residence is allowed to work itself out. Before the total sequence is completed, however, new

---

[6] The analogy between kinship systems and languages is used by Murdock, 1949, pp. 198-99.

[7] This admittedly simplified account of change is taken from Murdock, 1949, pp. 221ff. It has been questioned by Ghurye, 1955, and will no doubt continue to be questioned. Nevertheless, it serves as a good hypothesis to be tested by further research.

extrakinship factors may begin to assert themselves and initiate a new sequence, overlapping the first sequence and modifying it in its course.

But however varied and numerous and strong the pressures for change may be, the old kinship system does not permit all conceivable modifications. The great variety of structural principles that are found in a survey of *many* societies are not joined in random configurations in particular societies. Some known structural principles are incompatible with others.

> The various types of [kinship] organization with their subtypes admit of so many combinations of traits, especially when allowance is made for survivals of past structural types and anticipations of future ones, that the reader may have gathered the impression that any combination is possible. This is, however, definitely not the case. A very large number of combinations not expected according to our theory do not occur in fact in any of the 250 societies. For example, matrilocal extended families are never associated with patrilineal . . . descent, . . . nor patrilineal extension of incest taboos with exclusively matrilineal descent, . . . nor matrilocal residence with patrilineal . . . descent. . . [Murdock, 1949, pp. 248-49].
>
> * * *
>
> . . . the evolution of [kinship] organization is always channelized by the characteristics of the existing structure, which regularly limits the possibilities of change and in some instances also predetermines its direction. Sometimes the alternatives are exceedingly few [p. 250].

Enough has been said, perhaps, to show that the structural aspects of kinship tend to combine in definite ways to form kinship *systems*. Taking account of kinship terminology, rules of descent, rules of residence, forms of marriage, family types, and types of other residential and nonresidential kin group, Murdock distinguishes eleven major types of kinship system, each type consisting of three to six subtypes. (There are forty-seven subtypes in all.) The most brilliant thing about Murdock's typology is that it incorporates his theory of change in kinship systems. Of the eleven major types, all but two transitional ones include a "normal" subtype, defined as the subtype from which the other subtypes are usually derived. (The "normal" subtype within each of the two transitional major types is merely the most common subtype.) Furthermore, for each one of the forty-seven subtypes, Murdock states which of the other subtypes it could have been derived from, and the possible paths; and which of the other subtypes it could change into directly—that is, without going through intervening subtypes. Thus the typology is at the same time a table of the limitations and possible directions of change in the structure of kinship systems.

Theoretically, a kinship system of any subtype can be transformed into a system of any other specific subtype of the entire forty-seven. In some cases, as we have said, no intervening steps would be necessary; in other cases, the process of transformation would be long and circuitous, involving passage through a *sequence* of many intermediate subtypes, as if through a maze. The theoretical possibility that any system can be transformed into any other type could be realized in any given instance only if the necessary empirical conditions obtained. In general, however, it is extremely probable that some types of kinship system that have been common will be less common in the future. Extended families, clans, and sibs are certainly not likely to arise in a highly industrialized society. Industrialization tends to push societies in the direction of the type of kinship system exemplified in extreme form in the United States. For this reason, we do not reproduce Murdock's typology of kinship systems. Its theoretical and even practical value, however, should need no emphasis.

Kinship Variation in the United States

The ideals and practices of the urban middle class are probably predominant in the United States. Even segments of the society whose kinship lives differ in some respects from the middle-class pattern nevertheless tend to regard that pattern as better than their own, although perhaps unattainable. For example, poor and poorly educated women in the slums of the "Black Belt" in Chicago, living almost promiscuously in ephemeral, insecure relationships with men, daydream about the kind of family life that is typical of the white and Negro middle classes (see Drake and Cayton, 1945, Chap. 20).

In any society as large and complex as the United States, however, we must expect to find departures from the main patterns. These departures include not only violations but also, in some segments of the population, different normative patterns—that is, different standards of expected behavior and consequently different patterns of actual behavior. We have already noted, for example, that in the remote hills of Arkansas and Kentucky the "stem family" type is common.

The influences of slavery are still visible in many Negro families in the United States. Under slavery, the Negro family was largely at the mercy of the slaveowners. The owner exploited his women slaves sexually, and Negro men could do little about it. The Negro husband and father was not the provider, for wife and children worked too. It was difficult for the Negro man in these conditions to play the role we consider proper for a middle-class husband and father. Negro children often felt much more closely bound to their mothers than to their fathers. After "emancipation," the conditions did not change so radically that all Negro men could now be husbands and fathers of the middle-class type. Some could, for they had had a head start: they had saved enough money to buy their freedom early, or had been freed early for sentimental reasons; or they had worked mainly in their masters' households instead of in the fields and thus had acquired the ideals and skills necessary for middle-class life; or, being favorite illegitimate sons of their masters, they had been educated in special schools. Some had had two or more of these advantages. Many of the uneducated field slaves, on the other hand, had become accustomed to a looser family type. The lower-class Negro man, as compared with the Negro élite or with the white middle class, was not *expected* to feel permanent loyalty to his "wife" and offspring, or responsibility for them. Moreover, after emancipation many Negro men found it hard to get permanent employment, whereas an adult woman could in various ways usually earn a little.

There is considerable variation in kinship patterns, therefore, among Negroes in the United States. There are old mulatto families of "culture" and "tradition," proud of their ability to trace their descent from men freed before general emancipation; there are "new" middle-class families, who know little about their ancestors and care little, but whose family life is as similar to that of middle-class white families as restricted incomes permit; there are Negroes who own their farms and live out a strictly "respectable" pattern in which the husband controls the family and expects fidelity from his wife; there are rural "families" in which the head is an old woman and the other members are her daughter or daughters with their children, who according to an alien white man's law are illegitimate; and there are unstable lower-class urban families, as we have mentioned (Frazier, 1939).

Even if we had space to survey the whole range of variation in kinship patterns within the United States, we should be struck, after reading about the range of variation in the world as a whole, by the fact that the United States is relatively homogeneous. Some American Indian tribes, to be sure, have very different kinship systems, but these tribes are to a considerable extent isolated from the vast non-Indian population; they are like tiny islands off the coast of a vast mainland. There are class and ethnic peculiarities here and there on the mainland, but the tendency in these cases is still to approximate the urban middle-class pattern. The peculiarities are mostly *within* the broad patterns of American kinship as we have described them. No group has matrilineal descent. There are no sibs.

Immigrant families begin almost at once to adjust to the prevailing American patterns. For example, the south Italian peasant family in Italy is a close-knit unit; the father directs its productive activities, has considerable authority over his sons, keeps a stern eye on his unmarried daughters to see that they are chaste, and, when the time comes, arranges their marriages and provides dowries for them. The first-generation south Italian family in America changes in the direction of conformity to American standards. The father is "fictitiously patriarchal"; his sons begin to pursue their own careers; his daughters are harder to chaperon; they choose their own husbands, with parental consent, and receive no dowry. The second-generation south Italian family in America "tends to be democratic"; the sons strive for success in school and then for success in their several occupational roles outside the family; sons and daughters participate in the American dating pattern and choose their marriage partners regardless of parental approval (Campisi, 1948). This is only one example of a process that has gone on in many immigrant groups.

Some Advantages and Disadvantages of Our Kinship System

Every kinship system is, of course, a structural subsystem of a total society. It is therefore hardly worthwhile to attempt to evaluate specific systems as better or worse than others. Nevertheless, each system has its characteristic advantages and disadvantages. It does not seem possible to combine the advantages of all systems in any one. For example, the advantages of polygyny are obviously not compatible with the advantages of monogamy. The following discussion of our system is by no means exhaustive.

DISADVANTAGES

In an openly competitive courtship system such as ours, many people suffer disappointments and consequent emotional injury. We cannot calculate how many people are made temporarily or permanently less effective generally, as well as less happy, by broken romances. The experience is similar to bereavement in some ways, but it is sometimes worse, since breaking up a love affair or an engagement often means giving or receiving a blow to

TABLE 8

Responses of students to broken love affairs *

Behavior	*Male N = 230 (488 responses)*	*Female N = 414 (977 responses)*
Frequenting places with common associations	11.3%	10.0%
Avoiding places with common associations	2.9	3.4
Avoiding meetings	4.7	5.1
Attempting meetings	5.9	4.3
Remembering only unpleasant things	2.3	3.9
Remembering only pleasant things	15.6	15.8
Dreaming about partner	15.5	11.2
Daydreaming	14.3	11.4
Imagining recognition	6.4	7.9
Liking or disliking people because of resemblance	5.5	5.4
Imitating mannerisms	1.8	2.1
Preserving keepsakes	7.0	10.8
Reading over old letters	6.8	8.7
Total	100.0	100.0

* From Clifford Kirkpatrick and Theodore Caplow, "Courtship in a Group of Minnesota Students," *Amer. J. Sociol.*, 1945, v. 51, pp. 114-25; Table 12 as reproduced in in Judson T. Landis and Mary G. Landis, eds., *Readings in Marriage and the Family*, Prentice-Hall, 1952, p. 90.

self-esteem. There is good reason to believe that people cover up, even to themselves, the amount of suffering they endure on this account. The results shown in Table 8 are only crude indications. In the same study (Kirkpatrick and Caplow, 1945), 5 per cent of the men and 6.3 per cent of the women reported that they required a year to get over their suffering; 2.3 per cent of the men and 5.3 per cent of the women said that they required several years. Of the men, 7.1 per cent said that they "often felt trapped" and 23.1 per cent felt so "occasionally"; of the women, 5.4 per cent "often" and 15.2 per cent "occasionally." From one fourth to one half of college engagements are broken (Landis and Landis, 1948, pp. 170-71).

We have noted that divorce is common in our type of system and that our arrangements for the custody of children are (perhaps inevitably) more harmful than those in some other systems. Our emphasis on romantic love and the ideal permanence of marriage probably aggravates the trauma involved in divorce.

The system of independent nuclear families is particularly hard on older people. Their children have usually married and established their own households. In 1948-49, 6 per cent of the men and 3 per cent of the women over 65 in the United States were living without relatives in homes for the aged, rooming houses, or hotels; 9 per cent of the men and 18 per cent of the women were living with their spouses only (Bureau of Census statistics, reported in Havighurst and Albrecht, 1953, p. 148). The number of persons affected is large and growing.

> Since 1900, the population of the United States has doubled, but the number of persons 45 to 64 years has tripled, while the number 65 years and older has quadrupled. There are now (early 1952) 13 million men and women 65 years of age and over. This number is increasing currently at the rate of about 400,000 a year [Winch and McGinnis, eds., 1953, p. 305].

Our form of family and the relative looseness of our consanguineal ties are not, of course, the only sources of difficulty for the aged in our society. Persons over 65 include the richest persons in the United States, but they also include the poorest, and the poor are more numerous. The housing, health, and recreational problems of the aged are acute.[8] Moreover, our occupational system forces people to retire rather suddenly. Retirement leaves many older persons with a sense of uselessness and a fear of being a burden on others. In predominantly rural societies, men and women retire more gradually and often have a legitimate place of honor surrounded by their relatives of the younger generations.[9]

According to Burgess (1952), older persons, although poorer on the average, have a greater feeling of economic security. But he goes on to

---

[8] For details, see Sellin, ed., 1952, and Burgess, ed., 1954.

[9] Parsons, 1942, pp. 230-31, suggests that some of the economic complaints of the aged are the result of displacement—that the deeper complaint, perhaps, is loss of social importance. This is a good point, but there is no doubt that housing and medical care for the aged are serious and real problems.

imply that the feeling of economic security is the result of psychological adjustment to a lowered level of living: "The greatest economic insecurity seems to be in the 60's, when the adjustment to loss of employment is necessary. In each succeeding decade the economic condition of the person becomes further stabilized." Some of the phenomena of aging, such as loss of hearing, sight, or memory, are in part psychosomatic defenses against the insults of old age (Havighurst, 1952, pp. 15-16).

ADVANTAGES

The disadvantages we have mentioned are in part the price we pay for things we value: personal achievement and relative autonomy in directing our lives. These values are directly expressed in our system of mate selection, our independent households, our looseness of consanguineal ties, and the relative ease with which we can get divorced.

The flexible relation between the economic system and class structure is another result of our kinship system. One of the most important features of our occupational system is the relatively open competition for jobs, or, looking at it from another point of view, the pattern of hiring and promoting people to a large extent on the basis of objective achievement and promise. Such an occupational system virtually requires the pattern of establishing and changing household according to the occupational opportunities of the husband (neolocal residence).

Neolocal residence is also compatible with a high degree of mobility in the class structure. Father and son, brother and brother, can fare unequally in the competition for prestige without undue strain on kinship relations. Living as an adult in his own independent nuclear family, each finds his own place in the class structure—his own level of living, his own circle of intimate friends. There would be serious tension if father and adult son were expected to live in the same household, or if adult brothers were expected to share the same roof. Matrilocal residence would be no less incompatible with our occupational system and class structure (Parsons, 1942).

RECOMMENDED READING

For the more technical and theoretical topics of this chapter (kinship terms, change in kinship systems), see G. P. Murdock, *Social Structure,* Macmillan, 1949, Chaps. 6, 7, 8.

For a study of the history of a large minority of the American people as that history relates to varying family types, see E. F. Frazier, *The Negro Family in the United States,* University of Chicago Press, 1939.

The problems of the aging are seen in a much broader setting in a famous article by T. Parsons—"Age and Sex in the Social Structure of the United States," *Amer. sociol. Rev.*, Oct. 1942, v. 7 (reprinted in Parsons, *Essays in Sociological Theory Pure and Applied,* Free Press, 1949, pp. 218-32). Although this article contains few if any statistics, it is nevertheless empirical, since it is the result of seeing well-known facts in a technical and comparative perspective.

part four

THE ECONOMY

9. The Economy as a Subsystem of Society

Every society has a structural subsystem technically called its kinship system. The universal functions of the kinship system, socialization and tension management, place it mainly in the pattern-maintenance subsystem of society; but, as we have seen, particular kinship systems also have other functions —for example, economic and political. In this respect, the kinship system is like all other *structural* subsystems: it cuts across the four functional subsystems of society. There is no structural subsystem whose functions are purely economic. The economy, therefore, must be studied as a *functional* subsystem of society.

In this chapter we try to make this conception clearer by discussing the nature of economic functions and the ways in which they are related to other functions. In particular, we try to show that from the concrete *structure* of any society we can abstract certain aspects which together make up a system of their own, a functional subsystem, focused on the adaptive problem of the society as a whole. In Chapter 10 we shall consider in greater detail the variety of structural patterns—social institutions— whose functions are primarily economic. Finally, in Chapter 11, we shall turn to a somewhat more detailed description of the economy of the United States and attempt to assess its level of performance.

Economic Action

"Economic" action is provision of goods and services for the satisfaction of wants. Provision includes exchange and transportation of goods, since exchange and transportation help to place goods where they are actually "wanted." [1] The term "provision" and the economists' term "production of utilities" emphasize that the goods and services produced are *means* for the

---

[1] There is much confusion among laymen about economic distributors ("middlemen"). See A. P. Lerner, 1949.

satisfaction of wants. Action that directly satisfies wants is therefore noneconomic; preparing a meal is an economic act, but eating it is not.[2]

To the extent that noneconomic action is functional at all, it is part of one or more of the other functional subsystems of society (or of some other group). For example, providing medical care and teaching are activities in the pattern-maintenance and tension-management subsystem of society; military action is in the political subsystem; a judge deciding cases in a court is acting in the integrative subsystem. These distinctions are of more interest to sociologists than to economists. From the economist's point of view, a medical doctor, since he sells his services in a competitive market, is part of the economy. Whereas the economist emphasizes the fact that manufacturing and doctoring and judging and soldiering are all, in different ways, capable of being analyzed in terms of "supply and demand," markets and prices, the sociologist emphasizes functional differences.

SCARCITY

Many of the resources of nature are inherently scarce. Even for those that are abundant, prolonged effort may be necessary to transform them from their original state into immediately useful objects. That is to say, at any particular time many utilities are scarce. The inherent scarcity becomes more obvious the more distant the future for which utilities must be provided; storehouses are never inexhaustible. Hence economic activity always involves allocation of resources, and this of course implies choices—choice between different applications of available resources, choice between different applications of effort, choice between present and future needs. The universality of scarcity does not imply that there are certain universal "natural" wants; specific wants are always cultural to some extent and therefore variable from one society to another. But whatever the wants of individuals and groups within a particular society may be, some of them are satisfied less fully than might be desired, because of the scarcity of resources.

In some societies, wants are adjusted so well to the existing level of technology and to the existing resources and the economic system functions so well that scarcity is almost never felt as a problem. This rare insouciance is possible, however, only because the implicit "problem" of scarcity has been unusually well solved. Frequently, of course, choices are made quite consciously, after consideration of alternative possibilities, but sometimes the choices are implicit, "automatic": the culture "dictates" that such and such goods are to be produced and that they are to be allocated in such and such ways. To some extent, therefore, institutional patterns forestall consciousness of the "problem" of scarcity, choice, and allocation.

"Economic" action should be distinguished from "economizing." Econo-

---

2 "Wants' is ambiguous, for the direct satisfaction of wants *within* the economic system *is* production. For example, the supplier of paper to a printing company is satisfying a "want" that arises in the production of books. This "want" is intermediate: it is the books that can (more or less) satisfy wants outside the economic system itself.

mizing, in the simple sense, is allocating scarce resources among two or more different ends. As we have just seen, all economic action involves at least implicit economizing. But economizing is also involved in noneconomic action; for example, it is involved in the noneconomic consumption of goods. The medical doctor cannot give the best treatment to all his patients, for this would be too expensive; his resources, and the resources of patients, are too limited. The military commander has to decide how to allocate his men and weapons, for he cannot have maximum force everywhere at once. The housewife, too, must budget her resources, implicitly or explicitly. ("Household economy" is household management or, sometimes, skillful household management: different senses of "economizing." "*The* economy" or "*an* economy" refers to a system in which goods and services are produced and provided.)

RATIONALITY

These considerations show that economic action is rational in a double sense. In the first place, production of utilities obviously requires some degree of *technical* rationality: utilities are not utilities unless they will in fact satisfy wants. In the second place, production of utilities requir econo-mizing: the producer must think of *costs.* (The expression "economic rationality," which is often used for this element of economizing, is perhaps confusing, since purely technical rationality in production is also "economic," although not necessarily economical.)

Rationality in both senses is a matter of degree. The analyst of economic systems is always concerned with the problem of efficiency. As we shall see in more detail later on, productive processes may be technically more efficient or less, and they may be more, or less, economical. The problem of assessing economic efficiency, in both senses, is difficult. In certain economic systems, often called "traditionalistic," the very modes of production are fixed so firmly in custom that they are virtually ends in themselves; in such cases, concern for technical efficiency, in the sense of active concern for *improving* the want-satisfying aspects of utilities, may be slight. Traditionalistic economies also give little scope for rationalizing production in the sense of producing utilities with the minimum cost. We cannot say, therefore, that "economic" action as such is always directed toward *maximizing* the amount of production, the want-satisfying properties of utilities, or economy.[3] Nevertheless, economic rationality is and must be a value in every society.

---

[3] Parsons and Smelser, 1956, p. 20, seem to have stated the contrary. In the passage cited, they seem to be thinking of an "ideal" economy: if the actual economy were not tied with other functional subsystems and hence were not to varying degrees "hampered" by them its "goal" would be to maximize utility. This is a useful assumption even though it cannot be proved. (At the same time, of course, the economy is always *dependent upon* the other functional subsystems.) Parsons and Smelser, upon whose important book our text leans heavily, are well aware that actual economies are not organized to maximize production. On economic action, see also Weber, 1947, pp 158-66.

One of the most important sociological questions about any economy, however, is the *degree* to which economic rationality is limited by other values. Another, related question is also important: *In what ways* do other values limit economic rationality? To answer these questions, one must consider in detail the variable ways in which the economic subsystem of a society may be interconnected with the three other functional subsystems of the same society. We shall have more to say about this problem.

THE ROLE OF FORCE

The use of forced labor in production has been and is extremely common. A good example is the so-called blackbirding practiced in remote Pacific islands in the middle of the nineteenth century. The blackbirders "recruited" labor for farmers and stock breeders in Australia.

> It soon became common knowledge that the Pacific blackbirders were as proficient a band of slavers as ever shocked an abolition society. They captured savage chiefs and their families and held them hostages until enough able-bodied followers had signed on. Then not infrequently they would deliver the hostages to the sharks and scatter shot at the village to make the place unhealthy for rival recruiters [Oliver, 1951, p. 94].

Greek and Roman civilization depended, to some extent, on the fact that full citizens had slaves to relieve them of drudgery. The ancient Aztecs conducted war mainly to acquire tribute and slaves. Some of the Indian tribes of the northwest coast of North America also organized slaving expeditions against other tribes. During the seventeenth and eighteenth centuries and in part of the nineteenth century, the leading maritime nations of the Western world, including Holland, Spain, Portugal, England, and the United States, took captives from Africa in crowded slave ships, floating hellholes, to the plantations of the American Deep South and to those of Brazil and the West Indies (see Davie, 1949, Chap. 1; Handlin, 1957, Chap. 1). Slave labor or virtual slave labor has been common wherever there have been large plantations producing a single crop, such as cotton, coffee, sugar, or rubber. Ironically, freed slaves in the United States sometimes bought slaves of their own. And Negroes in Liberia, descendants of American slaves, have to some extent enslaved the original inhabitants of Liberia, although the practice may have been discontinued. These are only a few well-known examples of an institution that has been practiced, in varying forms, on every continent and is still practiced, in Arabia at least (see Ingram and Lugard, 1957).

England, France, Belgium, Holland, and other nations with colonies have more or less ruthlessly exploited the native populations of Africa and the East Indies. The methods of exploitation have often amounted to barely disguised forms of force. For example, subject peoples have been forced to work on public projects, such as road-building. (Before the Revolution in France this kind of labor tax, forced upon the home subjects, was known as the *corvée*.) In Africa, subject peoples whose native culture does not include money have sometimes been required to pay a money tax; in order to do so, they have been forced to work, at low wages, for white men. Another method of forcing natives to work is to threaten to arrest them for "vagrancy." Taxes in kind are also levied; for example, the natives may be required to turn over a certain proportion of the rubber they collect. Peonage, or "debt slavery," is also fairly common; the debtor cannot seem to work himself out of debt to his "master." Again, the system of so-called indirect rule frequently reduces native chiefs to the status of puppets; under threat of removal or loss of pay or prestige, these puppets must stimulate recruitment of labor for the white masters, or they must exact tribute on a quota basis (see Frazier, 1957, Chaps. 5-10).

Despite their recognition of the widespread use of force and threats of force for economic purposes, some students (e.g., Weber, 1947, pp. 158-60) nevertheless have defined "economic action" as *peaceful* provision of goods and services for the satisfaction of wants. The reason is that in all societies the basic institutions by which production is carried on rule out the use of force. The institution of contract, for example, provides for peaceful exchange: a "contract" involving force or the threat of force is commonly regarded as invalid. Most transactions, moreover, involve property rights —and the very concept of property *rights* implies that they are recognized as legitimate (that is, the possessor of property rights does not enjoy them because of his *personal* command of force). Otherwise it would make no sense to speak of the *institution* of property.

The use of force is one of the most characteristic features of government. Indeed, by definition the government is the organization that has a practical monopoly of the use of force within the territory of a society. Any other group within the society that uses force does so either with the consent of the government or in defiance of it. By definition again, if a criminal or revolutionary group is strong enough to defy the government successfully, the government is to that extent purely nominal.

Integrative functions

The government's use of force may have integrative or political functions or both. The integrative subsystem of a society, it will be recalled, is concerned with the relations between units (individuals and groups) within the society, and in particular with the prevention and settlement of conflict. The government's use of force is integrative, therefore, when it counteracts the illegitimate use of force or otherwise upholds the institutional structure of the society. The use of force as a sanction of institutional patterns (including property and contract) is an important mechanism of social control.

Since force is always a potential means of influencing others and can be extremely effective, no society can be regarded as stable unless, on the whole, superior force can be mustered to support at least some of the institutional patterns when these are violated or challenged. Institutional patterns therefore tend to be supported by force as an ultimate sanction. In a stable society, however, force is in the background. In such a society, the main reason force can be mustered, at need, to sanction institutional patterns is that these patterns are widely regarded as morally right; violation of them therefore arouses indignation, which may take the form of forcible suppression of the deviant.

Now we can see why it is possible to characterize action that is primarily economic as peaceful. As Weber says, ". . . the fact that an economic system is . . . dependent on protection by force, does not mean that it is itself an example of the use of force" (1947, p. 160).

One of the striking things about our examples of the use of force for economic purposes is that the people forced stand in some way outside the society and hence beyond the protection of its institutions. They are conquered foreigners, perhaps, as in colonial countries; or they are captives brought home to be slaves, to be *in* the society but not *of* it; or they are criminals or political prisoners, hence "written off" as normal members of society, "lost" to it.[4] Other cases of the use of force for economic purposes within a society are merely criminal, hence deviant, hence presumably not ordinary.

The integrative function of *controlling* the use of force in order to permit economic activity to go on is often achieved by nongovernmental mechanisms. This amounts to saying that the integrative subsystem of society, like the other functional subsystems, is not a concrete group but cuts across concrete groups. Among the highland tribes of Berbers in North West Africa, for example, peace is maintained in the intertribal markets, somewhat precariously, by various means in addition to governmental control.

> . . . the simplest solution in the areas where religious personages played an important role in the Berber parts of Kabylia and Northern Morocco consisted in turning control over to a holy man (*murabit*) or a family of *murabits*. Such markets under murabitic authority, we are told, while exempt of all specific regulations, offer a picture of general harmony
>
> To the same type belong in the tribal areas of the Makhzen the markets of religious teachers (*tolba*). Their origin is ancient; in olden times in these places of reunion young men or students would get together to discuss professional questions. Merchants, attracted by the periodic congregations, put up shops and stalls and started a market. . . .
>
> The *murabits* to whom the market had been entrusted could be long dead. The market place then would continue as a shrine and there remained only the malediction (*tagat*) of the saint venerated in the sanctuary to punish troublemakers. . . .

---

[4] For example, at the port of Whydah, which was controlled by the (Negro) King of Dahomey, the French, English, and Portuguese were allowed to maintain permanent stations for trading. The slaves they bought were provided by agents of the King. These slaves were either enemies of Dahomey, captured in war, or Dahomean criminals, sold for punishment. (See Arnold, 1957, pp. 154-76.) The so-called "slave laborers" of the Soviet Union are either political prisoners or ordinary criminals. (See Schwartz, 1950, Chap. 13; Bauer, Inkeles, and Kluckhohn, 1956, Chap. 7.)

> In the regions where these religious institutions could not insure neutrality, private individuals were entrusted with the policing of the market. . . . [T]he purpose of this method was . . . to hand the police of the market not to a superauthority, but to a nonauthority, so as to make it more palatable to visiting aliens. . . . Nevertheless the person had to be rich and well connected . . . [Benet, 1957, pp. 200-01].

Despite these integrative institutions, the mutual hostility of the warlike Berber tribes is so great that it sometimes erupts in the marketplace (*suq*):

> There is a customary name for the sudden, panicky "snapping" which breaks the peace of the *suq*: the *nefra'a*.
>
> * * *
>
> The very tenseness of the crowd in the market place sometimes acts as a mechanism of control.
>
> * * *
>
> The Berber social structure permits a chain-reaction of ever larger conflicts. In this politically cleft society it is more important to isolate trouble spots than to punish merely because there was breach of the law. . . . To unsheath a yatagan in the *suq* is as bad as to stab someone. And no meddler in a dispute not his own can get away without a fine [Benet, 1957, pp. 203, 204-05].

Political functions

Force used for economic purposes is integrative when the economic aim is secondary and the primary aim is punishment of offenders by forcing them to work. But this is a negligible case. The use of force in slavery, for example, is not integrative; on the contrary, slavery, like many other institutions, usually *depends* in part upon the integrative sanctioning force of government.

In the most important cases, the use of force for economic purposes is political rather than integrative. Hence we call it "economically oriented political action"[5] and distinguish it from "economic action" itself, which is peaceful. The term "political" in this context requires comment. The "polity" has been defined as the *functional* subsystem of society that is concerned with the attainment of societal goals. In complex societies, the government is the *concrete* organization most directly concerned with the goals of the whole society. (The government, therefore, having a part in both goal attainment and maintenance of integration, cuts across the political and integrative subsystems of society.) Sometimes the political character of force is obvious, as when a whole society mobilizes for a war of conquest. In other cases, economically oriented political action is less obviously directed toward the attainment of *societal* goals. Institutionalized slavery, except when practiced by the government itself, depends, in effect, upon a delegation of political power to private individuals and groups. In some cases, political power is not delegated from a central source but is

---

[5] This is Max Weber's term. The characterization of the polity which follows is based on Parsons and Smelser 1956.

merely widely diffused. The Berber tribes, for example, may be regarded as more or less distinct centers of power, and if we consider the interrelations of the tribes as a single system, we must say that political power in this system is so widely diffused and so little integrated that the system as a whole can hardly be regarded as a society. We must remember in general, however, that "society" is a limiting concept, which some systems fit more closely than others. At present in North Africa, the Berber tribes, on account of their common hostility to France, no doubt come closer to the conceptual type of a society.

Societies that have a great deal of economically oriented political action also have a great deal of peaceful economic cooperation. For example, the Cheyenne, the Crow, the Comanche, and other warlike Plains tribes, which were continually raiding one another for horses, provided for most of their wants by highly organized tribal buffalo-hunts. In any society, moreover, the cooperative manufacture of arms and the provision of other supplies for political expeditions are of course examples of economic action (peaceful production of utilities).

Economics and Sociology

Since there already exists a well-developed science called economics, one might ask how it happens that economic action is also treated in sociology. In order to answer this question, we shall have to have at least a rough idea of what economics is. It is a science dealing with systems in which goods and services are produced and allocated. Its primary variables are such that they can be expressed quantitatively, often although not always in terms of money: prices (of goods and services, including labor), amounts of particular goods and services produced, amount or rate of unemployment. Viewing all these quantitative variables as interdependent in a system, economics tries to show how variation in any one will affect variation in the others. Some generalizations of economics, such as the principle of diminishing returns or the principle of marginal utility are widely applicable but are so abstract that they yield no specific predictions by themselves. In dealing with the interdependence of variables such as demand and supply, price, production, and employment, economists build theoretical "models" which are, in effect, purposely simplified assumptions that do not hold true in any actual society. The prediction of economic events in actual societies, therefore, is somewhat hazardous and must allow for the great difference between abstract theory and concrete reality. The scientific models developed by economists can, of course, be made to fit actual conditions more and more closely. Economists have developed models for an economy of perfectly competitive enterprises (without monopoly), for an economy of "imperfect" competition (i.e., an economy containing some monopolistic power), and for socialist economies. No one of these models, however, fits any actual society exactly.

When a sociologist approaches the economy, his focus of attention is a little different. Instead of making various simplifying assumptions about social institutions and the distribution of economic power and then asking how certain variables are interrelated within such a purposely simplified framework, the sociologist focuses attention on the framework itself and asks what the institutional patterns are within which economic action is carried on, in what ways they are alike in all societies, in what ways they differ from one society to another, and how a society comes to change its institutional pattern. Moreover, sociologists, being professionally concerned with functions and dysfunctions, are ultimately interested in the consequences of various sets of institutions for the amount and quality and efficiency of production, as well as in the consequences for allocation of products to the component households of the society.

When economists become expert advisers to governments, they necessarily go beyond their theoretical competence. "In truth, economic analysis has little to say about the delicate problems of timing, public psychology, political obstacle, and social equity which are the very essence of democratic policy" (Lekachman, 1954, p. 263). Nevertheless, there is often widespread agreement among economists for extratheoretical reasons. For example, the measures commonly recommended to combat economic recession —"public works, lower interest rates, reduced taxation, increased unemployment compensation, enlarged farm supports"—are favored for political and humanitarian reasons, not merely for economic reasons. Most economists agree with Lekachman

> that the governments concerned possess enough sophistication in public administration to introduce and control the application of these remedies. [They have] a conviction that our society will not willingly bear a great deal of economic privation and unemployment for more than a brief period. . . . Economists would rather relieve human need than preserve fiscal orthodoxy [1954, p. 264].

Since the variables with which economists are concerned are concretely affected by the particular values, social institutions, and subgroups of actual societies, it is of course possible that the sociology of economic activities will aid economists in their role of technical adviser. There are already promising beginnings, but they lie outside the scope of this book (see Parsons and Smelser, 1956, Chap. 4).

Fusion and Differentiation

Our earlier discussion of the fusion of economic and political action can be extended. Every economic system is to some extent fused with the noneconomic subsystems of society. This fusion is a matter of degree, and there are economies, such as our own in the United States, in which *primarily* economic organizations are quite prominent. Even in these economies, as we shall see, there is some fusion; yet the striking thing is the degree to which the economy is structurally differentiated from the rest of the social system.

In discussing fusion between economic and political systems, we have thus far emphasized the role of force. However, fusion of the economic and the political, even to the degree characteristic of socialism, need not rest on force to any greater extent than any other institutional pattern does.

> In Chile, there are some forty or fifty "Fomento" corporations all devoted to the promotion of economic development. These corporations were set the task of output of goods and services in response to the general feeling that these were inadequate, and that the government could best take on the task of improvement. In all, these corporations, directly and indirectly, are responsible for some 50 per cent to 60 per cent of the total national income [P. D. Bradley, 1949].

This quotation brings out the peaceful character of the Fomento corporations and also the fact that production is a societal goal. Even in the Soviet Union, which is far more socialist than Chile, only a small part of production is carried out by so-called slave labor. In the United States, one of the most remarkable examples of democratic socialist planning is the Tennessee Valley Authority (TVA). This huge government project was planned in detail only after many consultations with the people in the region to be affected.[6] The following quotation may give some idea of its scope:

> Power development, reforestation, flood control, improvement of navigation and betterment of the standard of living in an area reaching into Mississippi, Alabama, Georgia, Tennessee, Kentucky, North Carolina, and Virginia were objectives. As of June 30, 1951, TVA had added about 2,000,000 kw. in hydro capacity and 700,000 kw. in steam capacity to the power resources of the valley, bringing its total to about 3,200,000 kw. By 1951 TVA had contracts in effect for interchange, sale, or purchase of surplus power with 27 other utilities and was selling power to 150 municipalities and co-operatives for resale at TVA retail rates. It was also selling to many industries which had been attracted to the valley by the availability of the large power and water supplies [Dibble, 1957].

We have already had occasion to notice the widespread fusion of economic activities in roles that are also involved in the pattern-maintenance and tension-management subsystem of society. The most common examples are family farms all over the world. The spread of socialism and large-scale private enterprise has gradually reduced the importance of family farms, but they are still predominant in many "backward" countries. In the "putting-out" system (an earlier stage of capitalism), production of textiles (especially) was also carried on by families; an enterprising "middleman" would supply materials to family heads and agree to buy the finished products.

---

6 See the excerpts from D. E. Lilienthal, 1944, in Freedman, Hawley, Landecker, and Miner, 1952, pp. 639-45.

As the pressure for more and cheaper production became more acute, very nearly the whole family might engage in getting out the quota demanded by the merchant or necessary to support the family. . . . [I]n the development of the textile industry and trade in England, hand looms were essential. These looms were rather more costly "tools" than most workers could well afford to buy, and were customarily rented or leased by the merchant to the family [W. E. Moore, 1951, pp. 22-23].

"Domestic" production was of course a step toward factory production. In the eighteenth century in Russia the opposite development took place.

. . . [F]actories proved to be most important for the dissemination of all sorts of skills in the countryside. . . . [A]n important home industry developed under the direct influence of the factories, especially around Moscow. Textiles, metal and leather goods were produced cheaply and in large quantities.

. . . The estate owners found it advantageous to forego the compulsory services and payments in kind from those peasants who worked in the home-industry, and to substitute for these obligations a steep monetary assessment. . . .

Thus, the Russian factory which was based on forced labor had created a dangerous competition for itself at the end of the 18th century [Brutzkus, 1953, p. 534].

Some primarily religious organizations also engage in production. "For example, the Trappist Monastery at Fort Garry produces and sells some of the best honey in Canada" (Easterbrook, 1949).

This concrete fusion of the economic system with the other subsystems of society has been called the "embeddedness" of the economy (Polanyi, Arensberg, and Pearson, eds., 1957, pp. 71 *et passim*). It goes so far in some societies that the economy may be said to be "imprisoned" in a primarily noneconomic social structure: "imprisoned" in the sense that the values of economic rationality are severely restricted. The highest level of rational production has probably been achieved in modern capitalist countries, in which the economy is to a remarkable extent differentiated concretely from the rest of the social system. But it is quite possible that a certain kind of socialist fusion of economy and polity, especially when economic production is one of the main goals of the society, might give even greater scope to rationality. We shall consider this difficult question briefly when we discuss the performance of the American economy (Chap. 11). In Chapter 10 also we shall have more to say about social institutions that give wide scope to economic rationality. Among others, freedom of contract, a highly self-consistent and impersonal system of law, a rational money system, and production in groups specially organized for the purpose are important. Forced labor, for example, which is one kind of limitation of freedom of contract, is relatively inefficient except under special conditions. One of the reasons for its inefficiency is obvious: the low morale of forced labor reduces its productivity. This was one of the basic reasons that home production was able to compete successfully with the forced labor in Russian factories under Catherine II. The peasants in their homes were working for themselves to a greater extent. When the workers in factories are formally free to make their own contracts of employment, factory production is more efficient than home production, in large part because the management is less restricted (or perhaps not at all) by economically irrelevant family ties in hiring, disciplining, or replacing workers. Management can also change more easily to new forms of production.

The embeddedness of the economy in pre-industrial societies is of course disturbed when factory organization and the use of money become more important. One of the most common effects of industrialization is the gradual weakening of kin groups and kin relationships beyond the immediate family. For example, in southern and eastern Africa, the marriage arrangement typically includes payment of a bride price in the form of cattle; for this payment the young bridegroom has traditionally depended upon the help of his father and other kinsmen. Marriage is thus a focus of economic obligations. But with the increase in factory work, many young men pay for the cattle out of their own earnings; the next step is to give the bride's family money instead of cattle. These developments of course weaken the old kinship ties (see W. E. Moore, 1951a, pp. 81-82).

Industrialization tends to substitute universalism for particularism; the individual is to some extent cast adrift from the close interpersonal relations of the traditional village community. In Asia, for example:

> This crumbling and shrinking of village life is of the utmost importance: all the village festivals and ceremonies gave color and bloom to the peasants' life, took the place of the numerous material comforts of the city dwellers, prevented the villager from feeling poor, kept strong his social ties with his fellow villagers, filled his life, strengthened his sense of social standing, and gave him a fixed place in the world. With the weakening and falling off of all this, the village becomes poorer, emptier. . . . Thus it has come about that the economic elements in the farmer's experience have been laid bare and brought into consciousness [Boeke, 1948, p. 542].

Considering this disruption, one might ask why peasants ever go into the impersonal factories. There are, of course, several reasons. For some individuals the modern factory provides an escape from kinship ties and other ties of the old local community. In some colonial countries, as we have noted, the subject natives are virtually forced into the factories (or mines) in order to get money to pay taxes imposed by the alien authorities. In many "backward" countries, poverty drives many people into the factories, despite the low rates of pay and the attendant loss of community standing. This was brought out in W. E. Moore's study of two Mexican villages (1951a), which showed that the poorer villagers were more likely to be attracted to factory work. The same thing is true in China and India. After the process of industrialization has reached a certain point, other motives come into play. People become more and more conscious of what money can buy; their *standard of living*—their "wants"—changes. Thus they become dependent upon modern industry. To some extent, the new skills and the new standard of living associated with modern industry are new sources of prestige. The hierarchy in the peasant or primitive community changes, to the disadvantage of the traditional rural leaders (see Broom and Selznick, 1955, pp. 517-18). Along with factory organization, there comes a commercialization of agriculture itself. "Westernized" middlemen induce the farmers to change their crops, agree to buy the new produce, then force the farmers to pay charges of processing the crops; finally they transform the independent, more or less self-sufficient proprietors into a rural semi-proletariat, dependent upon greedy middlemen and vulnerable to fluctuations of price and demand in a wider market. Thus, in the Far East especially, the factory managers have available a mass of impoverished or exploited peasants as a source of labor (see Boeke, 1948, pp. 543-46).

The Analytical View of the Economy

The economy, it will be remembered, is conceived as one of four functional subsystems of society—specifically, the subsystem that fulfills, more or less adequately, the *adaptive* function of society. All four functions must be performed in every social system, whatever its scope and level of concreteness. We can distinguish at least six *system levels:* (1) the society itself, (2) a functional subsystem of society (e.g., the economy), (3) a functional sub-subsystem (e.g., the investment-capitalization system—the adaptive subsystem of the economy), (4) a functional subsystem at the next lower level (e.g., the adaptive subsystem of the investment-capitalization subsystem, concerned with the procurement of facilities), (5) an industry (e.g., the steel industry), and (6) a particular concrete organization (e.g., a firm or a plant). These six system levels are, of course, not the only ones that might be distinguished.

We must keep in mind two general principles of functional analysis. The first is that any system tends toward *structural* specialization with respect to the four *functional* problems. The *general meaning* of these problems is the same for all system levels: the pattern-maintenance and tension-management problem is to furnish, maintain, and renew the motivational and cultural patterns integral to the interaction of the system as a whole; the goal-attainment problem is to mobilize and coordinate human and non-human resources for the attainment of the goals of the system as a whole; the adaptive problem is to meet situational exigencies, either by adjusting demands to inflexible reality or by actively transforming the environment; the integrative problem is to mitigate the distinctness of each of the other three subsystems, to regulate their interrelationships, and in general to promote harmonious interaction. Yet the *exact content* of the partially differentiated substructures that meet these problems does differ from one level to another, and from one system to another at the same level. For example, the "investment-capitalization" subsystem within the economy is different in content from the total economy, even though both the economy and the investment-capitalization subsystem fulfill adaptive functions. The economy fulfills the adaptive function for the society; the investment-capitalization subsystem fulfills the adaptive function for the economy. For each functional problem, therefore, there is both a *general* meaning and a *particular* meaning at each particular system level.

A second general principle is one we have met before: no one of the functions is performed by any one concrete structure alone. The actual groups, roles, or other patterns that fulfill a particular function differ from time to time and from place to place, and any particular group, role, or pattern may fulfill more than one function. Any particular functional subsystem, therefore, as opposed to a group or to any aggregate of groups, is a complex *abstraction* from the concrete structure of a social system. The more fused the four functional subsystems are in any particular case, the more drastic will be the mental abstraction required to distinguish and describe the economy as a separate functional subsystem. But the analysis in terms of four system problems, although difficult, will still be possible and probably worth the trouble.[7]

The analytical view of the economy has sometimes been criticized, however, for the very thing that most gives it merit: its abstractness. We must emphasize, therefore, that in this section we are not attempting to describe any specific economy. Rather, we are specifying the problems to which *every* economy must somehow provide more or less patterned solutions. Concerning the institutionalized patterns themselves, we assume nothing more than has already been implied: (1) whatever these institutions are in detail, they must meet these inherent problems: and (2), these institutions (like all other institutions) will be sanctioned to some extent. We must remember, of course, that the essence of sanctions is reciprocity: A does things for B because he expects some reward from B (or from someone else) and because if A does not do what B legitimately expects, then B will withhold what A has hitherto expected from him. Many of the details of the analytical view of the economy are based on this broad assumption about sanctions.

THE FACTORS OF PRODUCTION [8]

Whatever the degree of fusion or differentiation in the economy, the process of production requires four factors, which have been named, respectively, "land," capital, labor, and entrepreneurship. Just as the total society is composed of four functional subsystems, of which the economy is one,

[7] The last three paragraphs are virtually a quotation from Parsons and Smelser, 1956, p. 197. The slight paraphrases, omissions, and additions are not supposed to be improvements; they are merely intended to fit the original into our more elementary text. Serious students should of course read the Parsons and Smelser text itself.

[8] The following exposition is based on Parsons and Smelser, 1956, pp. 25-28. Their treatment, in turn, is based on a long tradition in economics.

so the economy itself has four functional subsystems (sub-subsystems) of its own.[9]

"Land"

"Land" as a factor of production is to be distinguished from physical land (hence the quotation marks); yet we shall see that this factor is not inaptly named. It includes three kinds of resource, all of which are regarded as being committed to production in general, relatively regardless of the more specific questions: what resources, in what amounts, to what production in particular? First, there are *physical resources* committed to production; these include land in the narrow sense, such as the land used for agriculture, but they also include many other resources, both those given in "nature" and those already modified by human effort. Secondly, there are *skills*, based partly on knowledge (technology, intuitive knowledge of market conditions, and "business experience") and partly on ability, of which there are various kinds and degrees. Finally, there are certain *attitudes* or motives that to some degree are necessary to production as a continuous, orderly social process; these include willingness and eagerness to work and willingness to reserve some physical resources for production rather than consumption. All these components of "land" underlie the whole process of production. They are relatively stable or constant in the sense that, regardless of fluctuations in particular opportunities for production and particular rates of remuneration, they are always present to some extent. In this respect they are all like physical land itself, which, though only one of the components, gives its name to the whole complex.

"Land" is most closely associated with the pattern-maintenance subsystem of the economy, which is called the "economic-commitments" subsystem. The term "commitments" is of course intended to suggest the relative permanence and stability of the knowledge and motives involved. All the components of "land"—even, to some extent, physical resources—depend upon culture. The cognitive components (technology and the rest) are obviously cultural in the main. As for the attitudinal or motivational components, they obviously rest on certain cultural values: the value of work as a good in itself, independently of its being necessary for production; the values of economic rationality; the values of saving and investment. Indeed, willingness to work and willingness to reserve some resources for production are these same values internalized in human personalities, just as technical skills are the internalization of cultural knowledge which in turn is partly the result of committing ability to the task of learning. It should hardly be necessary to say that the prominence or intensity of these

[9] For a more thorough discussion, see Parsons and Smelser, 1956, pp. 196-205: "The Internal Structure of the Economy." For a discussion of the "interchanges" of the subsystems of the economy with one another, see Parsons and Smelser, pp. 205-18: "The Internal Boundary Relations of the Economy."

values varies from one society to another; nevertheless, they are in some degree necessary to all production.

Moreover, these values and patterns of knowledge are not given in man's inborn nature; they depend upon socialization in the first place, and in the second place upon management of psychic tensions that threaten to sap their strength—for example, failure, worry, loss of friends, gross injustice. Any one of these or a thousand other slings and arrows can make work seem futile and skill vain Economic "commitments," therefore, require a functional subsystem in the economy. This functional subsystem is a more specialized sector of the pattern-maintenance and tension-management subsystem of the whole society

Capital

The second factor consists of the resources available for production. This factor differs from "land" in that it is more fluid and more changeable in quantity, and it is made available for consideration of some more or less specific return. The consideration of return is in many cases implicit; that is, it is not necessarily agreed upon in a formal contract. Every economic system involves capital in the sense specified (in this sense, then, capital is not peculiar to so-called capitalist systems). Moreover, every institutional patterning of production, regardless of variations in detail, involves the general expectation that capital will be transformed into utilities.[10] These utilities may or may not "return" directly to the source of the capital, however; the direct return to the source of capital may take the form of "interest."

Since it is the "means" of production, capital is the special concern of the adaptive subsystem of the economy, which is called the "investment-capitalization" subsystem.

Labor

The third factor of production is parallel to capital in the sense that it stands in a similar relation to components in the "land" complex. Like capital, labor is relatively fluid and is given to particular productive projects in response to particular opportunities for remuneration. In this respect "labor" contrasts with the skills and motivational commitments of the "land" complex, which are more general in focus, less tied to specific projects and specific expectations of *quid pro quo*.

Labor is the particular concern of the goal-attainment subsystem of the economy, called the production system.

---

[10] This point has been misunderstood. We are dealing here with the factors of production in all economic systems. Of course some systems, such as our own, do permit speculators and manipulators to advance "capital" merely to "make" money, regardless of whether or not goods are made. This cannot be the prevailing practice for long in any system, however, nor can it be the pattern that is given the greatest moral approval.

Entrepreneurship

The fourth factor of production is the function of combining the other factors of production in new ways, to adjust to changing conditions, to introduce new technical methods, new products, or new forms of organization, or to open new markets. The entrepreneur is an innovator, and although in particular cases he may also be engaged in routine administration, the entrepreneurial function is not routine in itself.

> [T]his function would be an exceedingly simple matter and essentially a matter of administration if the combinations that have been carried into effect in the past had to be simply repeated or even if they had to be repeated subject to those adaptations which common business experience suggests in the face of conditions that change under the influence of external factors. Administrative or managerial activity of this kind, however necessary, need not be distinguished from other kinds of nonmanual labor . . . [Schumpeter, 1949, p. 68].

Again, an entrepreneur may be an inventor in the popular sense, as typified by Edison or Steinmetz, but he need not be. The test is whether factors of production are actually combined in some new way, regardless of whose ideas are used. The entrepreneur may also be a capitalist, but, again, he need not be. The capital necessary for entrepreneurial activity often comes from someone else—e.g., "temporal and spiritual lords," banks, insurance companies, individuals who have saved. Sometimes entrepreneurs, to free themselves from the conservatism of bankers, go into banking themselves. Finally, entrepreneurship is a *function* and hence need not be performed by a single person acting alone; the entrepreneurial function is often performed by a committee of executives and may be performed by a manufacturing concern or an agency of government. For example, progress in agriculture in the United States depends for the most part upon nonfarmers. The corporations that produce fertilizers and farm tools carry out a good deal of research and development; the State Agricultural Experiment Stations are also important innovators; and especially important is the federal Department of Agriculture, which not only makes discoveries but teaches them to farmers (Schumpeter, 1949, pp. 71-72; Galbraith, 1956, pp. 90-91; Robertson, 1955, p. 412).

The factor of entrepreneurship is the concern of the entrepreneurial subsystem of the economy, which of course is the integrative subsystem.

INTERCHANGES BETWEEN THE ECONOMY AND OTHER SUBSYSTEMS[11]

The economy, we have said, is a complex subsystem "embedded," to some extent, in the social system or society as a whole. The factors of production are of course involved in the economy, but they do not come from the economy; with the exception of "land," which we shall comment on presently, the factors of production are contributed to the economy

[11] This section is based on Parsons and Smelser, 1956, pp. 51-84

other subsystems of the society. Briefly: labor is supplied by the pattern-maintenance system, capital by the polity, and entrepreneurship by the integrative system.

Concretely, labor may be thought of as a contribution of families. In our own society, the head of a family is expected to work to support his family. The family in its capacity as supplier of labor may be regarded as part of the pattern-maintenance system. "Labor" is here being treated, we must remember, in a somewhat abstract way: as brains and brawn actually given to work. It could conceivably be withheld, and sometimes is, as when the jobs available are not attractive enough. The abstractness of this "labor" is seen when we reflect that in concrete reality labor is inseparable from various skills and attitudes that we have regarded as part of "land." In order to contribute labor power that will be of some use in production, a man must have learned many things, and he must in general have the attitude that work is worthwhile. These aspects of the family's contribution—these skills and values—are part of "land." "Land" is not a contribution in the same sense that labor is. "Land" is *part of* the pattern-maintenance system of the *society,* of which the pattern-maintenance system of the *economy* is only a special part.

The peculiar status of "land" may be a little difficult to grasp. "Land" is different from the three other factors of production in that it is relatively stable. It underlies the whole economy in the sense that without it there would be no "movement" of the other factors of production. Labor, for example, varies in the quantity available and in the specific fields of activity to which it is applied, but it always presupposes "land"—for example, a recognition of the value of working in general. Since "land" is relatively permanent and unchanging, economists tend to take it for granted and to give more attention to labor, capital, and entrepreneurship, which are more directly variable according to short-run market conditions. In the long run, however, "land" itself—that is, the values and knowledge relevant to production—changes. For example, in the Near East there are no longer any followers of St. Simeon Stylites, who spent most of his life sitting in contemplation atop a series of pillars, each higher than the preceding. Cults not dissimilar once existed in the Western world, but the values expressed in them are hardly given even lip-service today. Long-run changes in science and technology are of course equally striking. In the short run, however, "land" is not a variable contribution, as labor is; it is continuously present, as the "ground" on which ever-changing social interaction occurs.

Turning from "land" and labor to capital: concretely capital is provided by banks, insurance companies, individual investors, and many other sources. In a more primitive society the old men might get together and decide to have a fishing boat built, or a huge corral to trap animals in: they are providing capital, encouraging production. If we regard the creation of credit as a form of power and productivity as a societal goal, then we may regard capital as a contribution of the polity to the economy.

This way of thinking of capital may seem strange at first, but a moment's reflection will show that encouragement of production, in various ways, has always been one of the main activities of government. In any case, the conception of capital as a contribution of the polity to the economy shows, once again, the abstract nature of the functional subsystems of society. In our own economy, many business firms provide their own capital, at least in part (this means, in practice, that they expand their plant with money that might otherwise have gone to shareholders, to employees, or perhaps to customers in the form of lower prices); these self-financing business firms, although primarily economic organizations, are here regarded as performing a "political" function. In this analytical view, therefore, the difference between socialism and capitalism is not that in the former there is more political control over the economy; the difference is that in capitalism political control over the economy is shared by many relatively uncoordinated agencies, whereas in (extreme) socialism political control is concentrated in one organization, the government alone. This difference of course has far-reaching consequences.

The integrative system contributes the fourth factor of production, entrepreneurship. This way of thinking about entrepreneurship is by no means self-evident, for innovation is frequently disruptive rather than integrative. We must keep in mind, however, that we are dealing here with generalized problems of social systems. Any particular social system has institutional patterns *within which* most entrepreneurial activity will be carried on: to this extent the disruptive effects of entrepreneurial innovations are necessarily held, for the most part, within tolerable bounds.

Further, as time goes on, the conditions to which a social system must adjust change: certain raw materials may give out or become more scarce; trade relations with other social systems may be cut off. Some innovation, therefore, is necessary to keep the social system functioning. It is in the nature of innovation that it involves risk of failure: one can never predict all the consequences of customary acts, much less of methods hitherto untried. To the extent that functional innovation arises in the economy, entrepreneurship provides it. Concerning any particular entrepreneurial innovation, however, we must, as always, be alert to its possible dysfunctions as well as to its possible functions. The failures of entrepreneurial activity are part of the cost of its successes. (No research laboratory expects all its projects to work out.)

As for the social institutions within which entrepreneurship is for the most part carried on, one of the most important questions to ask about them, in a comparative perspective, is: How favorable are they to innovation, as compared with other possible institutions? This is one of the issues in the continuing controversy about the comparative merits of socialism and capitalism. "Favorableness" to innovation in turn breaks down into two questions: (1) Do the social institutions put unnecessary barriers in the way of innovators? and (2) Are the institutions such that, compared with conceivable functional alternatives, they tend to make the cost of innovation too high? (These are aspects of the more general problem of efficiency versus "waste.")

Each of the systems that contribute a factor of production to the economy receives something in return. In return for labor, the pattern-maintenance and tension-management system receives consumer goods and services; these of course are necessary to all households if they are to carry out their functions. In return for capital, the polity receives the means by which system goals may be attained. (The polity, remember, is the goal-attainment system of the society.) In return for entrepreneurship, the integrative system receives new products; these are important, from the integrative point of view, as symbols of values and of status. Part of the satisfaction derived from a new automobile, for example, is that it symbolizes one's ability to pay for it, which in turn presumably depends upon one's having done something that was valued. Such symbols are integrative only to the extent that they are regarded as deserved and legitimate "rewards" for good performances. New products, like entrepreneurship, may also be disruptive to some extent. Again, however, new products, like entrepreneurship, will be less likely to be disruptive the more firmly the patterns of interaction are institutionalized. If institutions are unstable, then necessarily every action and every object connected with action will tend to have different values for different groups and individuals in the social system.[12]

When we say that the pattern-maintenance system contributes labor to the economy and receives consumer goods and services in return we do not imply that there are necessarily explicitly recognized transactions in the form of contractual exchanges. So with the other contributions and counter-contributions. The economy and the three other subsystems of society are, as we have repeatedly noted, abstract systems. The exact forms by which contributions and counter-contributions are made vary from one society to another according to the types of group involved and the institutionalized patterns of interaction. The range of variation is great. When a business firm, for example, finances plant expansion out of its own funds, there is no contract between groups; there is no *exchange*, properly speaking, at all. Yet this action on the part of the firm, one group, involves a contribution of capital from the political system of the society to the economic system; and this "contribution" is ordinarily made in the expectation that the economy will make a counter-contribution of increased production or productivity In other cases, of course, both in our own society and in others, exchange in the ordinary sense *is* involved. In so-called gift ex-

---

[12] Parsons and Smelser treat the interchange between the economy and each of the other subsystems of society as a *double* interchange. For example, in return for labor the family receives wages, and then in return for consumer spending it receives consumer goods and services. The double interchange between the polity and the economy, and that between the economy and the integrative system, are too subtle to be treated here.

change, found in many primitive societies, an individual may give some valuable object or service to another with the purely tacit understanding on both sides that the other will at some future time give something of equal or greater value in return. This is true exchange, although it may lack the formality of a contract.[13]

The transactions between the abstract functional systems had best be called "interchanges." This purposely ambiguous (i.e., general) term is intended to cover all the "contributions" and "counter-contributions" we have been discussing, whatever form they may take in particular cases, whether it be a budgetary arrangement as in self-financing, an implicit contract as in gift exchange, or a formal contract. A particular interchange may involve more than one transaction. In our own economy, for example, an employee contributing labor receives wages, but when he spends as a consumer, his money goes for the most part to firms other than the one from which he receives wages; he contributes labor to one firm but receives his ultimate economic compensation, consumer goods and services, from many others. The same situation, under different forms, exists in many primitive societies.[14]

RECOMMENDED READING

This chapter has depended to a great extent on T. Parsons and N. J. Smelser, *Economy and Society: A Study in the Integration of Economic and Social Theory*, Free Press, 1956, which is probably the boldest and most successful attempt to provide a systematic framework for the sociological analysis of economies. One of the most important sources of Parsons and Smelser is M. Weber, *The Theory of Social and Economic Organization*, trans. by A. M. Henderson and T. Parsons and with an introduction by T. Parsons, Oxford University Press, 1947. Part II, "Sociological Categories of Economic Action," is a systematic and subtle treatment of many of the topics dealt with in the present chapter. For a view of economics somewhat different from the one given in our chapter, see K. Polanyi, C. M. Arensberg, and H. W. Pearson, eds., *Trade and Market in the Early Empires: Economics in History and Theory*, Free Press and Falcon's Wing Press, 1957, Chaps. 12-15. Chap. 12, by Polanyi, Arensberg, and Pearson, deals with "The Place of Economics in Societies"; Chap. 13, by Polanyi, with "The Economy as Instituted Process." Chap. 14, by T. K. Hopkins, "Sociology and the Substantive View of the Economy," and Chap. 15, by Pearson, "Parsons and Smelser on the Economy," are largely criticisms of Talcott Parsons.

---

13 In such cases, nevertheless, we may speak of an "implicit contract," since custom has established within fairly well-defined limits what shall be regarded as equivalent objects in fair exchange. Moreover, such transactions are sanctioned: if the receiver of a "gift" fails to reciprocate properly, he will at the very least suffer a loss of prestige.

14 In this discussion we have deliberately omitted reference to the classic "returns" to the factors of production: rent, interest, wages, and profit. Parsons and Smelser use these terms but they necessarily give to some of them meanings that are slightly different from those understood by economists. This results from the high level of abstraction of Parsons and Smelser's analysis. Of course, in economics itself the meaning of some of these terms (notably "profit") is not the same for all writers.

10. Economic Institutions

Although no society has a purely economic structural subsystem, every society does have certain normative patterns whose functions are mainly economic. To these we now turn. We have three tasks:

1. To analyze the institutional patterns commonly referred to as property, occupation, contract, and money. Property rights are universally institutionalized; production is universally organized in productive roles; and, in a broad sense, contract always organizes productive roles and property in concrete economic activities. Money is not found everywhere, but its importance in "advanced" economies is so great that we cannot afford to omit considering it.

2. To give a fairly systematic account of the variation from place to place, and from time to time, in all these primarily economic institutions.

3. Finally, to bring together many of the ideas in this chapter and the preceding one and show their bearing on the motivation of economic activities.

Property

The institution of property in any society delimits rights in scarce valuable things. (As we mentioned in Chapter 3, the term "property" in popular speech often refers to the things themselves as well as to property rights.) Since the assertion of rights always implies the possibility of denial or abrogation, the objects of property rights are scarce and valuable as a matter of definition, for there would be no point in denying or abrogating "rights" in things that are either as free as air or as worthless as a bad reputation.

Scarce valuable things," as we have seen, may be either tangible or intangible. Among the tangible objects of property rights are land, mines, houses and other buildings, roads, waterways, furniture, tools, clothes, conveyances of all kinds, jewels, and raw materials. Among the intangible objects of property rights are names, trade marks, good will (of a company), jobs, access to markets, and intellectual and artistic products such as books, symphonies, and technical processes.

Slaves have often been treated much as "things" and objects of property rights. They have been bought and sold, bred like cattle, maintained as one would maintain valuable equipment. The status of slave has varied from the extreme condition of having no rights at all to a status hardly distinguishable from that of a member of the household; moreover, whatever the slave's legal rights have or have not been, there has always been great variation in practice in the relationship between the slave and his master. Inevitably the social interaction between master and slave makes the relationship so different from that between an individual and his ordinary "property" that, somewhat arbitrarily, we shall not consider slaves as objects of property rights. Voluntary servitude may be regarded as a social relationship of contract for services. Involuntary servitude is essentially a political relationship, although of course the master often has economic purposes.

Concretely, the objects of property rights are not always distinguishable from what have been called "rewards." The good reputation of a business firm, for example, is essentially a reward for its good faith in the past, and the name of the firm is, in one aspect, a "reward symbol" of its good reputation. Here is a reward symbol that is at the same time an object of property rights; thus the firm may sell its name (and its good reputation) as an object of utility. Some rewards, such as the love a wife has for her husband, are not transferable to another through gift, sale, lease, or bequest. The husband who possesses this reward may lose it by alienating his wife, but he cannot transfer it; only the wife can do that or something like it. Strictly speaking, however, property rights are inherently capable of being transferred from one possessor to another. To be sure, some property rights, said to be "inalienable," are not *institutionally* transferable, but an inalienable right in a plot of land, for example, is always *inherently* capable of being transferred: that is why an institutionalized pattern is necessary to prevent alienation. From these considerations, we may say that some rewards and reward symbols are at the same time objects of property rights while others shade off gradually until they cannot be objects of property rights. In general, a reward or reward symbol is less and less likely to be an object of property rights the more clearly it is nontransferable and the more its "utility" depends upon particular personal attachments.

The existence of rights implies the existence of obligations. Those who do not possess a particular property right are under the general obligation not to infringe upon the possessor's right. The institution of property is thus, like all other institutions, a normative patterning of the relations between individuals and or groups. Again like other institutions, property is sometimes violated. The stability of a system of economic transactions, however, depends in part upon the institutionalization of rights in scarce valuable "things." Without this, economic action, in the sense of peaceful production of utilities, would obviously not be possible.

KINDS OF PROPERTY RIGHT

The many kinds of right in "things" may perhaps be summarized as possession, use, alteration, using up, usufruct, income, and disposition. A tenant, for example, has the right of possession or occupation. The right of possession shades over into various rights of use, depending on the nature of the object. The borrower of a book from a public library may of course use the book for research or pastime. Most forms of use of physical objects involve some deterioration of the object (for example, reading a book tends to wear it out gradually), but rights of use do not include all rights of alteration; for example, the book-borrower may not make marginal notes, and the house tenant may not without permission knock down a partition. Restrictions on alterations may include the prohibition of alterations that might be considered improvements.

The right to use up, which is sometimes called the right of "abuse," is illustrated by the right of an oil company to take the oil from ground belonging to another. In return, of course, the owner may have some right to income or some other recompense. For example, the government of Venezuela owns all subsoil rights and leases them to private companies in return for royalties, which amount to a large proportion of the government's income. "The estimated national income for Venezuela, in 1945, amounted to something like $1.5 billion or $1.8 billion. In 1946, petroleum royalties in the sum of $233 million were paid in to the national treasury" (P. D. Bradley, 1949, pp. 39-40).

The right to the produce of land or animals may be distinguished from ownership itself, and also from rights of use. For example, the owner of a thoroughbred male animal may turn the animal over for breeding in return for a certain part of the resulting litter; or one may simply buy the produce of a plot of ground without having bought the ground itself or cultivated it. Such rights may be called rights of usufruct.

The term "royalties" often refers to the financial return for the use of essentially intangible goods; thus a playwright may receive royalties from a theatrical company that produces his play for profit. In this case the object in being used is neither used up nor necessarily altered in any way, although putting on a play may of course reduce the subsequent ability of the same play to attract an audience in the same market.

Rights of disposition include the right to destroy as well as the right to alienate. Food, for example, is "destroyed" in the eating. The right of alienation, by gift, sale, or lease, is essentially a right to dispose of other kinds of property right. That is to say, in "alienating" land, for example, one transfers certain rights in connection with the land: one turns over to another, altogether or in part, one's rights of possession, use, using up, or enjoyment of produce. It is evident, therefore, that rights of disposition also define rights of acquisition. Certain rights of inheritance, for example, prevent a present possessor from alienating his rights to any except the proper heir or heirs. Actual opportunities to dispose of rights, or to acquire them, depend, of course, not only upon the institution of property but also upon the state of the market—that is, upon the existing supply of disposable rights of the relevant kind and upon the effective "demand" for such rights. Note also, however, that fluctuations of supply and demand occur *within* the relatively stable limits set by the institution of property.

Any kind of property right may be vested in either an individual or a group. Since both individual property and group property are common in our society, we need not give examples, but the reader is probably less familiar with rights vested in both a group and an individual. Such, for example, were the rights to land in the Russian *mir* before the revolution. A *mir* was a peasant community. Each family head had a right to a part of the land, but exactly *what* part was decided by the community as a whole, and there were occasional redivisions of all the land belonging to the *mir*. Here rights were neither exclusively of an individual nor exclusively of a group. No one could sell his share of land; "ultimately" it belonged to the whole *mir*. This institution provides us, incidentally, with a good illustration of the interplay of institutionalized property rights and economic power used illegitimately:

> The law contemplated a twelve-year interval of redivision but in fact it usually took place oftener, every one, three, or six years. The right to the land (*nadyel*) . . . was perpetual; even the factory worker whose forefathers had emigrated from the mir generations before might come back and assert the right. Conversely, no one could leave the community without its consent. The nadyel found expression in the right to a periodical redivision. However, the equality of all members of the village usually existed on paper only, as the majority required for a redistribution was almost never obtainable. In favor of redivision was every family which had increased in a large ratio; but there were other interests arrayed against them. The decision of the mir was only nominally democratic; in reality it was often capitalistically determined. In consequence of the need for provisions the single households were usually to a varying extent in debt to the village bourgeoisie or "kulaks," who held the mass of the propertyless in their power through money lending. According to whether they were interested in keeping their debtors poor or allowing them to acquire more land, they determined the decision of the village when redivision was in question [Weber, 1950, pp. 17-18].

Apart from this inequality, the *mir* could hardly be regarded as a great success from a functional point of view. Since the land might be redivided, the peasants were discouraged from introducing technical improvements in farming, and since they all had a right to village land, however illusory this right was in some ways, they were encouraged to have more children than the land could well support (Brutzkus, 1953, p. 525). Yet the reforms of Stolypin in 1906-07, which abolished the *mir* as an institution, had the effect of increasing inequality among the peasants (see Weber, 1950, pp. 18-19).

As we have mentioned, the tenure of property rights is highly variable

In our system many property rights are held, according to contract, for a definite period of time; for example, a tenant may have a lease that extends for a year or some other period; certain machines can be leased by the day or even by the hour. In the early period of European feudalism, the vassal's right to a fief extended only until either the vassal or the lord died, but in most cases the rights in the fief became hereditary. The "forces" that brought about this transformation are interesting; they illustrate once again the interdependence of an economic system and the noneconomic institutions and interests of a society.

In the first place, there was strong pressure from the vassals themselves to gain the right to pass their fiefs down to their sons. In a society such as France under the Merovingians and later after the decline of the Carolingians—a society in which the central government was extremely weak and political power was scattered and insecure—the ties of kinship were especially strong. It was partly on account of the need for greater security against the force of others that many of the vassals had originally turned over their estates to more powerful men, on the understanding that the estates would immediately be returned to them as fiefs with tenure for life. In these formerly "alodial" estates (French: *alleüx*), the vassals had previously enjoyed hereditary rights, for the alodia were essentially family estates built up over generations. Therefore the vassals, despite their feudal contracts with the lords, continued to think of their fiefs as hereditary; they had a kind of moral presumptive right to expect that their sons would succeed them as vassals.

There were also factors that made the principle of hereditary succession advantageous to the lords as well as to the vassals. For one thing, most of the lords (French: *seigneurs*) were also vassals to other lords, and as such they were eager to establish the right of hereditary succession for their own sons. Moreover, although in a particular case a lord might prefer to choose someone other than a vassal's son as successor to the vassal, the lord had to weigh this preference against the danger of weakening the loyalty of his other vassals, who of course were also solicitous for their sons. Moreover, every lord needed new "men" (that is, new armed and loyal vassals), and on the whole the most readily available were the sons of his present vassals. Indeed, in some cases a son would take over his father's duties before the latter's death and thus strengthen his hope and moral right. Finally, the lords had a source of revenue in the fees that the inheriting sons had to pay when they were formally invested with their fathers' fiefs; the inheritance fee or tax was known as a "relief."

Lords and vassals alike had an interest in establishing the belief that they were "natural" rulers, rulers by "blood," as distinguished from the numerous serfs, whose lot in life was to do the menial work on the land in return for protection and the hereditary right to a modest living; the principle of hereditary serfdom virtually necessitated the principle of hereditary rule and vassalage.

As for those fiefs that in principle were revocable even before the death of the incumbent, they soon became hereditary too, for similar reasons. These were the fiefs granted to administrative officers of the crown. A *comté* in France was originally a government position, and the *comte* (English: *count*) could be removed at the pleasure of the king; for example, the *comte* might be given a more responsible position. The fief in land given to a count was in principle given only for his maintenance for as long as he held his position. In practice, however, the counts soon made both the position and the associated fief hereditary. Having a following of assistants tied to them by personal loyalty, and using their positions to enlarge their personal following, they became both difficult to remove and virtually indispensable. This process was almost inevitable since the kings had neither strength to prevent it nor the universities and military academies from which to draw trained administrators to supplant the counts (see M. Bloch, 1949, v. 1, Chap. 4).

We cannot fully appreciate the difference between property rights under French feudalism and modern property rights unless we realize that "hereditary rights" have a double aspect. The lord could not prevent his vassal from bequeathing the fief to a son, but neither could the vassal bequeath it to anyone else. As a matter of fact, the feudal contract, with hereditary right, in principle tied the hands of all concerned. We have to say "in principle" because in the feudal system, as in any other, power was sometimes used illegitimately (that is, rights were sometimes ignored with impunity). The weight of the system as a whole was such, however, that property rights tended to be relatively frozen. In a hypothetical extreme case, property rights could not be alienated at all as the result of anyone's decision; they could only be inherited. This extreme state of affairs was never reached in France, first because the ceremony of *hommage* and investiture (making a man a vassal) constantly created new rights, and secondly because the institutionalization of rights was never strong enough to prevent all violations of hereditary right. As we have noted, however, the forces supporting hereditary right were very strong. As for the practice of becoming a vassal, it merely created new hereditary rights. Our own system, of course, permits testamentary freedom.[1] Moreover, the "owner" of something is free to lend, give, sell, or lease any of his rights.

The prominence of hereditary right in the feudal system had another consequence. Consider the use of land. No one could be said to "own" land under the feudal system. Instead, various persons—lords, vassals, serfs, and others—had different rights, called *seisins,* in the same piece of land. This meant that no one of the property holders was free to change the use

[1] Paradoxically, the right of testamentary freedom sometimes creates as much rigidity in the use of wealth as the feudal system did, for a person is thereby free to impose narrow restrictions on the use of wealth he leaves to another. Thus many colleges must use certain donations for specific purposes even when other uses would be more advisable in view of needs unforeseen by the donors.

of the land as a whole; each property holder was severely restricted by the rights of all the others. In our own system, by contrast, it is possible for "all" the rights in a particular object to be held by the same person. This fact, combined with the freedom with respect to alienation, makes possible a much greater degree of flexibility in the use of wealth generally.

The Roman *dominium* was different from both modern "ownership" and medieval *seisins*. *Dominium* was similar to modern ownership in the sense that all the rights in an object could be held by the same person; but *dominium* was unlike ownership in that the rights in a particular object—say, a piece of land—tended to constitute an indivisible bundle of rights.[2] The indivisibility of property rights (relatively speaking) was of course another kind of restriction on the use of wealth. The possessor of *dominium* was more like a trustee than an owner.

This comparison with Roman *dominium* and feudal *seisin* brings out the fact that one of the most important characteristics of modern property in capitalistic countries is flexibility. Whether this flexibility is on the whole greater than that under socialism may be doubted. In some ways the great number of capitalistic owners makes for great flexibility in the use of wealth; at the same time, the very multiplicity of owners obviously makes it difficult to use the resources of the community according to a single plan.

MODERN CORPORATE PROPERTY

Our concept of ownership in the United States is somewhat complex, almost ambiguous, on account of the property aspects of the modern business corporation. A corporation, as a legal "person," owns buildings, grounds, raw materials, tools, and other assets; yet the stockholders are said to own the corporation. Before examining the meaning of ownership in these two cases, let us note the tremendous importance of corporate property in our economy. We have no direct comparison of corporations, business partnerships, and sole proprietorships with respect to the total assets of each category of business firms, but several related statistics show that corporations are probably more important than partnerships and proprietorships combined. In 1947, 6.9 per cent of the business firms in the United States were corporations, but corporations accounted for 69 per cent of the total receipts. By 1953 the number of business firms had risen 16 per cent and the total receipts 48 per cent; the corresponding increases for corporations were 26 per cent and 52 per cent. The net working capital of all United States corporations excluding banks and insurance companies was $108.2 billion in 1956.[3]

Few of the stockholder-"owners" of corporations have the rights that we ordinarily associate with ownership. Typically a stockholder has prac-

---

[2] For a detailed comparison of Roman, feudal, and modern property, see Noyes, 1936.
[3] See Bureau of the Census, *Statistical Abstract of the United States, 1957*, Table 592, p. 486. On corporate income and the income of unincorporated enterprises, see Tables 595 and 596, p. 489

tically no voice in the management of the assets of the corporation he "owns." What the stockholder actually owns, in the full sense, is a certain number of shares of stock, which entitle him to dividends, almost always in the form of money. He has no voice in deciding when dividends are to be declared and what their amount is to be. On the other hand, he can freely sell, give away, bequeath, or use as security the shares of stock he owns. To understand this typical situation, it will be necessary to see how corporations are run.

The executive officers of a corporation, who make most of the decisions we ordinarily associate with ownership, are elected by the stockholders according to the principle "one share, one vote." Any stockholder who owns more than 50 per cent of the shares can therefore appoint or remove the executive officers of the corporation. Actually, however, it is very rare for one person to own more than 50 per cent of the shares. Indeed, in the largest corporations, the ownership of shares is so widely scattered that no single stockholder has any voice. It is more and more common for the top management of a corporation to be a small group that in effect replaces its own members by co-optation. When officers are to be elected, the existing management nominates certain persons, and all the stockholders have a chance to vote; their votes do not count equally, of course, since the ruling principle is "one *share,* one vote," not "one vote per stockholder." Yet in the typical situation—how "typical" it is we shall consider in a moment—the stockholders who are not part of management *are* just about equally uninfluential, regardless of differences in the number of shares they hold. Since the stockholders are not organized as a group and have no communication with one another, they can do nothing but accept the candidates proposed by the management. If a stockholder writes in some unexpected name, his choice will be an isolated one; if he simply does not vote, the management, which controls a large number of votes by proxy, will of course have its way. The scattered stockholders are in effect in the same position as the voters in the Soviet Union: they can vote for the nominees of the "management" or they can abstain from voting. The task of organizing an effective opposition to the entrenched management would involve enormous expense, enormous skill, and an enormous amount of time. As we shall see, this does not mean that the management has nothing to worry about. If the business fails, they will of course lose their positions; if they lose the confidence of stockholders, the latter can always withdraw support by selling their shares. We shall consider some other "controls" over management below.[4]

The situation just described is complicated by the fact that many corporations are also complete or part owners of other corporations. By pyramiding corporations with a so-called holding company at the top, it

---

[4] It is of course by no means certain or probable that the average stockholder or the society at large would be better off if corporations were run democratically.

is possible for a small group to control several corporations effectively, even though the combined shareholdings of the members of the group may be only a small fraction of the total shares of stock in any one of the corporations. The holding company is simply a legal device for concentrating the control of several corporations; that is to say, the holding company itself is not a directly productive organization but only a managerial device.

With respect to the relation between stockholding and the management of a corporation's affairs, there are three types of corporation. In corporations with "ownership control" the management owns nearly all the shares of stock of the corporation. Corporations of the second type have "financial control."

> The financial control of a corporation usually rests upon ownership of certificates of stock, whether a majority, substantial minority, or small minority. . . . [T]he proportion of stock necessary to control the corporation is smaller the more widely dispersed the general ownership and therefore, to a certain degree, the larger the capitalization. It is not unknown, however, for bondholders without vote to control the policies of a corporation by their position as powerful creditors [W. E. Moore, 1951, p. 56].

The third type of corporation is characterized by "managerial control."

> It is possible . . . to carry the separation of ownership and management (or rather the division of various property rights) to such an extreme through very wide dispersion of security ownership that no actual financial control centers do or can exist. Stock ownership in such a situation carries with it no control rights for any investors, making their position similar to that of dispersed majority or minority shareholders in corporations under financial control. Thus control is in fact vested in a self-perpetuating management, acting in the dual capacity of salaried employees of the corporation and "trustees" of the investors' funds. . . .
>
> The classic case of this separation between an investing public and the management of the corporation is that of the largest American corporation, the American Telephone and Telegraph Company. Only two of the twenty largest stockholders are individuals, and those two together own less than one-third of one per cent of the total stock. The other leading shareholders are insurance companies, investment trusts, banks, and brokers. The leading twenty shareholdings account for less than four per cent of the outstanding stock [W. E. Moore, 1951, pp. 56, 59].

Of the two hundred largest nonfinancial corporations in the United States in 1937-39, two or three were under "complete ownership," about sixty were under "managerial control," and the rest were under "financial control" (W. E. Moore, 1951, p. 55).[5]

Since the managers of a large corporation almost always own some shares of its stock, the separation of ownership and management is not complete. Nevertheless, it is clear that as far as the *average* American shareholder is concerned there is all but complete separation between owner-

---

[5] The pioneering work on the modern corporation was A. A. Berle, Jr., and G. C. Means, *The Modern Corporation and Private Property*, 1933.

ship and management of the corporation. In a system of private enterprise (as opposed to socialism), this separation has at least two distinct advantages. The corporate form of enterprise permits the concentration of vast resources for production. This is due to the principle of limited liability, according to which the shareholders risk in the enterprise, not their whole private fortune as does the sole proprietor or a partner, but only the money they have paid for their shares; thus the enterprise may go into bankruptcy without ruining most of the shareholders. To this advantage we must add another; namely, that the vast resources available to a large corporation, despite their dispersed ownership, can be managed according to a rational plan. This is particularly important as far as long-range planning is concerned. If the plans of a large corporation were constantly subject to the agreement, by vote, of thousands of shareholders, many of whom are ignorant of the total business situation, it is doubtful whether a rational long-range plan could be carried out.

Socialism has the advantage of even more comprehensive planning, but a question that has always disturbed many students of socialism is whether or not a truly rational, comprehensive, long-range plan for an economy can be carried out democratically. Whether this question *should* be disturbing and, if so, how it should be answered depend upon political theory. For the moment, let us note that although the modern capitalist corporation is in itself fundamentally undemocratic, it is nevertheless subject to a kind of regulation that is decided by largely democratic political institutions. This regulation is to a large extent "negative": the distinct corporations are free within the "rules of the game." The productive process is thus both democratic and undemocratic. Since in a socialist economy, on the other hand, regulation and the actual details of a comprehensive plan are merged, *both* aspects, regulation *and* goal-deciding, must be either democratic or undemocratic. In less abstract terms, since governmental control in a socialist economy is more extensive than in a capitalist economy, the nature of that governmental control is more important. Our capitalist economy has some of the advantages and some of the disadvantages of democracy; a socialist economy, broadly speaking, has either all the advantages and disadvantages of democracy or all the advantages and disadvantages of some nondemocratic regime.

LIMITATIONS ON PROPERTY RIGHTS

In Chapter 9 we noted that economic institutions, including property, are partly supported by force. Usually this force is in the background, but if the institutional pattern is not fully approved, the relative importance of force in supporting it may be greater. For example, the peasants in France, Russia, and China, before the great revolutions in those countries, almost certainly did not think that their absentee landlords deserved to own the land. The peasants in Russia, at least, often revolted when they could get the support of the mounted Cossacks. In all three countries the peasants supported the great revolutions, and the strength of their anger was shown by the ferocious "guillotine justice" they dealt their former landlords when the revolutions were successful. It seems doubtful whether the prerevolutionary ownership of land could have prevailed if the peasants had had the political strength to change it.

Opposed to the broad tendency for property rights, once established, to become "sacred," there is sometimes a tendency for those who are using the land and making it productive to feel that it ought to be theirs, regardless of legal patterns.

> . . . whenever property rights in productive instruments come to be exercised by individuals who are too far removed from the instruments to operate them efficiently, the rights tend to get transferred to users and possessors. What rights the absentee owners retain (for property rights are highly divisible) depend upon a variety of factors, of which two are of special significance: (1) the social functions performed by absentee owners apart from any specific connection with their property and (2) the intensity of the society's struggle for survival either against other societies or against nature [K. Davis, 1949, p. 466].

Both in France and in czarist Russia, the moral position of the absentee landowners was weakened by the fact that they had long since lost their important feudal functions. In Russia the nobles were finally released from their services to the state (or to the czar as suzerain) by the Manifesto of 1762; and while the nobles were developing in their own minds a more nearly absolute right both to the land and to the serfs, the latter were developing the *mir*, based on the idea that every peasant family has a hereditary right to some part of the village land (see Brutzkus, 1953, pp. 520-21, 522-23).

Feudalism itself provides an especially clear-cut illustration of the general fact that property and political institutions are closely interdependent. European feudalism arose because, in the absence of a powerful central government, every man who had anything worth having, including his life, had to worry about whether he had strength enough to keep it; the powerless submitted to the powerful in return for protection, and the powerful submitted themselves and their followings to those who were still more powerful. Fiefs in land were the economic means by which fighting men were paid, so that they could keep themselves in a style becoming their status. This means of payment was necessary because the sluggishness of trade, due to poor communication and political unrest, made payment in money impossible, and the local resources of the lords made it difficult for them to support a large following at their own tables. Indeed, in return for his land, one of the services a vassal was often expected to perform was hospitality to the lord and his retinue when they were traveling. Thus the whole property system depended in part upon the political situation.

One of the most important factors to which we should look for an explanation of the differences between the feudal regimes of various countries is the strength or weakness of the supreme political authority. In France the feudal regime grew up because the political authority at the top was weak. In England the feudal regime was imposed by a strong conqueror, who rewarded his soldiers and administrators with fiefs. Whereas in France the lord was seldom strong enough to prevent a vassal from vowing loyalty to several other lords, in England the authority of the king went down the pyramid of ranks with more schematic neatness, and every vassal was allowed to have only one lord. The same thing was true in the seven or more centuries of Japanese feudalism; the emperor, although he was long kept without active control of the state, never lost the tremendous prestige of his divine origin, and it was always in his name that the actual ruler, the *shogun,* was able to impose his will on the feudal lords. In every feudal system, of course, the lords tried to establish the principle that if a vassal broke his agreement, *his* vassals should support the superior lord and refuse to defend the malefactor against punishment. This principle depended, of course, upon widespread recognition of what the rights and obligations of a feudal contract were.[6]

The interdependence of property and political institutions is not peculiar to times past. The connection is intrinsic. Even where there is no formal government, there is always force, more or less institutionalized. Property rights are always limited by the other interests for which force can be mobilized. The property holder is never absolutely free to use his wealth for any purpose he may conceive. When the command of force is institutionalized, its use to restrict or even to abrogate property rights is always exercised in the name of the broader interests of the group. In the United States today, private property is rather closely regulated by all the governments, municipal, state, and federal; and under broad conditions specified in the law, political authorities can and do effect numerous reallocations of rights. "The legal grounds upon which this creeping abrogation of private rights of property are founded are the doctrines of police power, public necessity, taxing power, and the right of eminent domain" (Noyes, 1936, p. 302). This quotation, which may sound slightly biased, by implication points out that the limitation of any particular property right may or may not serve the "general interest of the community." Broadly speaking, institutionalized political regulation of property does help to attain goals of the whole society; but of course a detailed empirical investigation would be required to show whether, how, and for whom any particular case of regulation is functional.

[6] On feudalism, see M. Bloch, 1949; Weber, 1947, pp. 373-82; also see articles by Asakawa, Bloch, Franke, and Lybyer in the *Encyclopaedia of the Social Sciences,* v. 6, 1931, under the general heading "Feudalism." We shall have more to say about this subject in our discussion of political institutions (Chap. 13)

The Division of Labor

Every society has a certain amount of specialization in its productive system. The basic reasons for this are easy to see. First, variations in human endowments of intelligence, strength, and talent are always recognized and, to some extent, taken advantage of. Secondly, the economy is the adaptive subsystem of society, and what it adapts to, in part, is the physical environment, which is often highly variable from place to place; these variations give rise to some division of labor. For example, people living near a sea coast can engage in fishing and ocean trade, whereas people living inland must find other pursuits. Thirdly, as the cultural store of knowledge increases, it eventually becomes so vast that no one person can master it all and use it for production; consequently specialization becomes necessary. And finally, up to a point, specialization permits greater efficiency by making it possible for the individual to develop a high degree of skill in what he does. We say "up to a point" because specialization also raises problems that would not otherwise exist, and these problems can become acute enough to counterbalance the gains of specialization.

Two such problems deserve particular mention: (1) If the tasks of production are broken down until many of them are utterly routine, many workers will suffer from boredom and their morale will be impaired. As we shall see, to some extent this is a problem in our own economy. (2) The more specialization there is, the more complex becomes the task of coordinating the work of different persons in the same organization. In large organizations with a high degree of specialization of roles, a great deal of attention has to be devoted to problems of communication; on the one hand, information of a highly technical and diversified nature has to flow in to the executives so that they can make rational decisions; and on the other hand, these decisions, in the form of orders, have to pass down a series of levels, with possibilities of misunderstanding at every level. The very existence of a high degree of specialization means that to some extent the different specialists live in different "worlds," each with its own daily concerns and specialized vocabulary, insulating it to some extent from intimate acquaintance with the other specialized "worlds"; thus information and orders have to be interpreted and reinterpreted at every level. Nevertheless, a high degree of specialization is possible before these counterbalancing problems become so acute as to reduce over-all efficiency.

The term "role" is somewhat ambiguous. The Balinese, we are told, are fond of "mass production" methods. In "preparing offerings for a ceremony (*metjaroe*) to purify the houseyard," for example:

> First a large number of little leaf trays are folded and stitched; then the trays are laid out; then each tray is filled . . . from mass stores of each appropriate object. One woman puts a special kind of cake in each tray; another distributes little puddings; another betel; and another flowers, etc. [Bateson and Mead, 1942, p. 67].

Each of these women, we might say, has a distinct role, but not in the same sense in which an electrician and a garage mechanic have distinct roles. The Balinese women can all perform all these differentiated tasks and no doubt do so on different occasions; and no doubt every adult Balinese woman is expected to be able to take any one of these "roles." In our society, on the other hand, a garage mechanic is not expected to be able to exchange places with an electrician; each has a distinct role in the sense of a "permanent," socially recognized, technically specialized complex of skills, with corresponding obligations and a distinctive status. It is in this second sense that we shall speak of division of labor. There are, of course, transitions from the first sense to the second. We saw, for example, that wiremen and solderers in the bank-wiring observation room sometimes exchanged roles to relieve the monotony (p. 7). Many of the jobs in modern industry require so little training that almost anyone in the shop can master several of them.

KINDS AND DEGREES OF SPECIALIZATION

In most primitive societies productive roles are differentiated largely by sex. Among the Plains Indian tribes—the Crow or the Cheyenne, for example—men's work was hunting and fighting; the drudgery was performed by women for the most part, although the men also helped in the heavy work of skinning the buffalo and bearing the meat back to camp. The clash of two cultures is shown in the ethnocentric remarks of a white visitor to a Cheyenne camp in 1846:

> After a ride of two hours, we stopped, and the chiefs, fastening their horses, collected in circles, to smoke the pipe and talk, letting their squaws unpack the animals, pitch the lodges, build fires, arrange the robes, and when all was ready, these "lords of creation" dispersed to their several homes, to wait until their patient and enduring spouses prepared some food. I was provoked, nay angry, to see the lazy, overgrown men, do nothing to help their wives; and, when the young women pulled off their bracelets and finery, to chop wood, the cup of my wrath was full to overflowing, and, in a fit of honest indignation, I pronounced them ungallant, and indeed savage in the true sense of the word [Garrard, 1938, pp. 106-07; see also Lowie, 1956, pp. 72-76, 84-88].

The inevitable result of division of labor mainly by sex is that every adult is expected to have a wide variety of skills. Thus an Eskimo man is a jack-of-all-trades. The scope of detailed knowledge is often astonishing. Every boy among the Lovedu of South Africa has to herd cattle, and in the long association with the older boys the younger ones acquire a vast store of knowledge as a matter of course: "A herdboy walking along with you will give you the names and uses of almost every tree or shrub you pass in that rich veld environment, and once a boy of fifteen astonished us by being able to name over 200 specimens of plants from that area" (Krige and Krige, 1943, p. 108). This kind of knowledge would be regarded as technical in our society, but it is hardly technical among the Lovedu since all the men have it.

The division of labor by sex is not so firmly institutionalized in the United States today as it is in most primitive societies. The *Statistical Abstract* for 1957 contains a table headed "Detailed Occupation of Employed Persons, by Sex: 1950" (pp. 214-18), which lists over five hundred occupational categories; in every one of them women are to be found as well as men. Of course it also indicates that close to 41 million men were employed in 1950 as compared with only 16 million women, and that certain occupations tend to be provinces of one sex or the other. Under the heading "Engineers, technical," subheading "Mining," there are 10,656 men and only 109 women; but 130,304 women, and only 5,598 men, were practical nurses. More informally, there are certain skills that a woman is definitely expected to possess to some degree, and others that a man is expected to possess. Few women can swing an axe properly, and few cannot sew on a button.

Presumably, skill is a compound of talent, training, and experience. Along this dimension, our economy has a wide range of variation, from highly technical engineers to "unskilled" laborers. The technical expert in general is characterized by long training in relatively generalized knowledge, as opposed to the "unskilled" laborer, who may be trained in a matter of hours and whose skill consists of a routine operation or two, barely understood. Generalized knowledge of basic sciences and the related technology confers a kind of "authority" upon the technical expert, for his opinion in his field is acknowledged to be worth more than a layman's, and he is called upon to apply abstract principles to concrete problems in a far from routine manner. At the highest level of responsibility, the technical expert has a creative role. By contrast, the unskilled laborer has no "authority" in this sense and repeats the same operations over and over again.

Indeed, in more than one way the roles that might be classified together as unskilled labor are unenviable. They are, in Parsons' term, "residual roles"—what are left over, so to speak, after the more desirable roles have been taken by more able, better trained, or more ambitious persons. Broadly speaking, unskilled or "semiskilled" laborers have roles of which the following description is true:

1. The training necessary is easily acquired, sometimes on the job.

2. The operations are so simple that the workers at this level are regarded much as the interchangeable parts of a machine. Indeed, they often work on an assembly line, to whose mechanically controlled speed their own motions, prescribed by time-and-motion analysts, have to be geared. Here is one worker's description of his job in a mass-production automobile plant:

> I work on a small conveyor which goes around in a circle. We call it the "merry-go-round." I make up zigzag springs for front seats. . . . The only operation I do is work the clip gun. It takes just a couple of seconds to shoot

six or eight clips onto the spring, and I do it as I walk a few steps. Then I start over again [Walker and Guest, 1952, p. 46].

3. Since the work is so easy (in one sense) and the workers are so easily replaced, these roles have little prestige and relatively low pay.

4. The workers being ignorant, and presumably lacking in devotion to the company, they must work under supervision, partly human and partly not. This reduces, perhaps, the dignity of their work. Here is one reaction, not unusual, to the pace of the moving belt in the automobile plant referred to above:

> The work isn't hard, it's the never-ending pace. . . . The guys yell "hurrah" whenever the line breaks down . . . [Walker and Guest, 1952, pp. 51-52].

5. The assembly line is often so arranged that the workers cannot talk with more than two or three other persons, sometimes with none. The management sometimes prohibits talking, but this rule is universally violated.

6. The monotony of the work, plus the fact that the worker often finds it hard to take a great deal of pride in his own contribution, tends to produce boredom. Both these characteristics, monotony and lack of pride in one's own contribution, are of course subjective and rather variable from worker to worker, and they can easily be exaggerated. Nevertheless, in the Walker and Guest study of 180 automobile-plant workers:

> Workers were asked to list the most important reasons for liking or disliking their present jobs. They listed pay as the most favorable factor and the following factors as the most undesirable: "(1) cannot set my own pace; (2) physically tiring; (3) do not have interesting work; (4) cannot do different things; and (5) cannot use my brains" [p. 62].

Note that the last three complaints, and possibly the last four, amount to saying that the work is monotonous and boring. As one worker put it:

> The job gets so sickening—day in and day out plugging in ignition wires. I get through with one motor, turn around, and there's another motor staring me in the face. It's sickening [p. 55].

7. The unskilled-labor role is a virtual dead-end. Only a few workers can hope to become foremen, and almost none can go higher. For all these reasons, the emotional focus of an unskilled laborer's life is presumably not his work but his leisure; he works so that he can enjoy himself afterward.[7]

We must remember, of course, that not all unskilled workers are on

---

[7] See, on this point, D. Riesman *et al., The Lonely Crowd* (1955), esp. Chap. 7. These authors think that people in the United States now work mainly in order to have leisure. The emphasis has shifted, they think, from achievement and production to taste in consumption. We need careful empirical studies (as well as perceptive impressions) of the attitudes of workers at all levels toward their work. Whether the interest in consumption patterns is greater today than earlier is hard to know. It seems probable that it is mainly unskilled workers who lack interest in achievement at work.

conveyor belts. One of the defects of the conveyor belt, from the workers' point of view, is that it makes informal relations on the job difficult or almost impossible. More typical in industry, however, is the kind of work group that does permit informal social relations. As we saw in our brief description of the bank-wiring observation room, the workers form cliques, with a kind of unofficial subculture of their own. The fact that horseplay, candy-buying, gambling, and conversation about sports and sex are not looked upon with favor by management does not prevent these activities from providing satisfaction and relieving monotony. Indeed, we can surmise that the deviant character of these activities, from the point of view of management, is itself one of their sources of satisfaction to the workers. In the same way, the normative restriction of output ("Don't be a rate-buster") also gives the workers a sense of controlling their own work which the formal regulations of the management would deny to them. At the same time, of course, the restriction of output expresses and counteracts the workers' fear that if they produced more, the rate of pay might be lowered or some of them might become unnecessary, since presumably the management retains only enough men to accomplish the total output presently being accomplished. In light of the fact that the informal organization of the workers helps to keep their morale up, we cannot safely regard it as dysfunctional, even from the point of view of management, despite the fact that superficially the informal organization causes a "waste" of time. By reducing competition among the workers, the informal organization also contributes to the integration of the work group.

Even the conveyor-belt system, which narrowly restricts the workers' autonomy, can be made somewhat more tolerable. The foreman has a strategic role. A few studies show that both the workers' morale and their efficiency tend to be better when the foreman regards himself primarily as a protector and friend of his men rather than an "eyeball" for the management. Among other things, the "good" foreman (1) introduces new workers to their prospective associates on the job, (2) shows a new worker how his task fits in with other tasks to create the final product, (3) permits workers on routine jobs to relieve the monotony by swapping tasks occasionally, and (4) takes a permissive, understanding attitude toward infractions of those company rules, such as the rule against talking and "wasting time," which if rigorously enforced would threaten to make the work intolerable (see M. Weinberg and Shabat, 1956, pp. 437-38; Mayo and Lombard, 1944, pp. 152-54).

Thus far in our treatment of specialization we have focused mainly on differences of skill and knowledge. We have only touched upon another line of variation; namely, differences in authority. This topic will be discussed later at several points, particularly in Chapter 12, on bureaucracy, and in Chapter 13, on political organization. In the present context we can afford to be brief. Obviously the uneven distribution of authority in the modern corporation is one of its outstanding characteristics. As we have noted, one reason for the low prestige of the labor role is that it possesses no authority; it is, on the contrary, subject to detailed supervision. At the other extreme is the executive, whose work consists in making decisions and giving orders, with a more or less heavy burden of responsibility. In business it is customary to distinguish between "top management" and "middle management"; foremen and supervisors are at the bottom of the managerial hierarchy but still above clerical workers and so-called shop-and-bench workers.

As far as authority is concerned, technical experts fall between executives and laborers. Strictly speaking, the expert's "authority," as such, is not authority *over* others but authority *in* a field of knowledge or practice, and this authority makes his advice sought after and respected. Many technical experts, however, also have authority over others, partly on the basis of their superior technical knowledge. This is notably true, for example, of directors of research. The highest officers are always line officers, even though some top executives began as staff officers and thus have some degree of expertness in a technical field.

Every productive organization, like any other social system, can be analyzed into four functional subsystems. As we have noted, there is a tendency for structural differentiation to arise as a response to the four functional problems. Sometimes, of course, there is no role-differentiation at all, as in the "one-man organization" of an old-fashioned artisan, a carpenter perhaps, who fulfilled all the functional requirements by himself; and structural differentiation never separates the four functions rigorously. But the "divisions" and "departments" into which the typical modern corporation is divided provide another basis for classifying productive roles. The Standard Oil Company of New Jersey, for example, has the following departments, among others, classified here roughly according to functional problems:

Adaptation: Treasurer's Department, Law Department, Tax Department

Goal attainment: Producing Coordination, Refining Coordination, Transportation Coordination, Marketing Coordination

Integration: General Economics Department, Coordination and Petroleum Economics

Pattern maintenance and tension management: Employee Relations Department, Medical Department

This company, which has many subsidiary companies in various parts of the world, has other departments as well as those named. The classification above is extremely rough and may be misleading: actually every department is multifunctional. Every department also has, of course, its own wide range of skill and its own hierarchy of authority.

When we realize that such diversity is repeated in many other industries, we can begin to appreciate the extent of specialization of roles in our economy. The *Dictionary of Occupational Titles,* prepared by the Department of Labor, lists and briefly describes 17,452 distinct jobs, and the editors say that the list is far from complete (see W. E. Moore, 1951, pp. 441-46).

MODERN OCCUPATIONS

We should notice at once, however, that while the vast majority of occupations are indeed economic roles in our sense, some occupations—among them some very important ones—are primarily roles in one or more of the other functional subsystems of society. The roles of politician and soldier are not economic but political; that is, they are involved mainly in the goal-attainment subsystem. Although many politicians have passed the bar, lawyers as such have primarily integrative functions. There are many occupational roles mainly in the pattern-maintenance and tension-management subsystem: minister, priest, and rabbi, teacher, physician, scientist, professional athlete. These roles of course cut across the functional subsystems to some extent.

Despite the fact that some occupations are primarily noneconomic, it will be appropriate here to summarize briefly the main characteristics of modern occupations as a class of roles, for in doing so we shall be describing the institutionalization of economic services in our society. Occupational roles are "primarily" economic institutions in the same sense that property is: after all, the institution of property is also important to schools, churches, and hospitals. The following, then, are perhaps the main characteristics of modern occupations:

1. Occupations tend to be highly specialized. This needs no further emphasis.

2. Occupations in our society, since they are "achieved" roles rather than "ascribed," are in principle open to anyone who wishes to qualify for them and who has the necessary means to do so.[8] The institutionalization of "achievement," in this technical sense, is in marked contrast with the productive roles of India, for example. While the Indian castes have a religious basis in part, they are in effect hereditary groups that monopolize particular crafts and other productive services. One is born into a particular

[8] For simplicity, we have treated "occupations" as institutionally based on achievement, as opposed to ascription. Strictly speaking, two variables are involved. In the terms used by Talcott Parsons (and briefly discussed in our Chap. 5), modern occupations are based on "performance" as opposed to "qualities," and they are "universalistic" as opposed to "particularistic." These variables are not easy to keep distinct. All economic roles must stress performance rather than qualities, yet hereditary roles are based on "qualities," since group membership—for example, membership in a caste or clan—is treated as a quality. The difference lies in this, that particularism stresses social relationships and group memberships from the point of view of a particular actor and in relation to *his* social relationships and group memberships, while qualities, as opposed to performance, are independent of the particular network of social relations the actor or judge is himself involved in. Thus discrimination against Negroes is particularistic, but choosing an M.D. for one's doctor is not, even though possession of an M.D. degree is a "quality" or "attribute" and involves, moreover, membership in a status group. See Parsons and Shils, 1951, pp. 81-83; and Parsons and Bales, 1953, p. 66.

caste, and frequently one's productive role is thus narrowly ascribed. In this sense (and others as well), the productive roles of traditional India are not, strictly speaking, "occupations." Neither are the productive roles of East Africa.

> In certain kingdoms of East Africa, especially the Bakitara and the Banyankole, birth determines occupation [i.e., economic role]. . .
>
> The nobility are stock-breeders exclusively; they raise no crops and engage in no industries. The peasants control agriculture and all industries. Among them are clans of iron-workers, salt-workers, potters, wood-workers, clothmakers. All skills tend to be hereditary in certain clans. Iron- and salt-working are definitely so. The peasants supply the cattle people with grain, manufactured articles, and services in house-building and public works, in return for feasts, gifts of butter, and protection of their land from predatory beasts [Bunzel, 1938, pp. 373-74].

Here, in addition to castes, we find in the peasantry economically specialized clans, which of course are still more narrowly restricted hereditary groups. Our system, based on "achievement," perhaps has the advantage of greater flexibility, for the principle of hereditary succession tends to be associated with traditionalistic methods of production. The degree of skill attained by Indian craftsmen, however, is often astonishing; their technical virtuosity, in alliance with an exuberant spirit which has religious roots, has produced, among other things, temples carved out of rock and decorated with the orderly profusion of a garden.

We said above that occupations in our society are "in principle" open to anyone with objective qualifications. No reasonably alert person in the United States needs to be told that the principle is frequently violated; on the one hand, there is considerable discrimination against women and against certain ethnic minorities; and on the other hand, positive ties, of kinship, friendship, college, or fraternity, frequently work in favor of candidates who may not be the best qualified. In appraising such facts, however, we should notice two things, which for lack of comparative perspective we tend to take for granted. First, in practice the principle *is* effective in a wide area. Who can doubt that women in our society have more opportunities than in most societies of the past? Even our discrimination against Negroes is less restrictive than a caste system. Secondly, and more important, most of us regard all these restrictions as forms of "discrimination," which word, in this context, definitely connotes disapproval, a sense of injustice. It will be a long time before such feelings become common in the thousands of villages of India.

3. The third characteristic of modern occupations is that the role-incumbent works on the basis of a more or less formal contract with an employer or client. He is employed "with ceremony" (as lawyers say); he is paid according to the specific services he performs for a specific employer or client. The emphasis in our occupational system, as opposed to the organization of work roles in many primitive societies and in India, for

example, is on the formality and explicitness of the contract and on the specificity of its terms. The contract, moreover, is entered into by specific decision, perhaps by bargaining; it is not merely implicit in the quasi-permanent relations between status groups.

This aspect of modern occupations is considerably modified for certain professional roles. The medical doctor, for example, is institutionally expected to give his services on a relatively disinterested basis, having regard more for the patient's objective need than for the patient's ability to pay the socially recognized monetary value of the medical service. In general, the professions, in comparison with other occupations, lay great stress on the welfare of the client and on the maintenance of ultimate values; hence there is more emphasis on the ethical code of doctors, lawyers, and scientists than on the ethics of plumbing. This difference, however, is by no means absolute.[9]

4. For the most part, modern occupations are carried on in specialized organizations, in work premises located apart from private homes. The relative importance of factories, offices, and "industrialized" farms is of course related to the much greater degree of specialization in our economy.

5. For the most part, the incumbent of a modern occupational role works with tools he does not personally own. Most facilities are owned by corporations. This of course is somewhat less true of the disappearing old-fashioned crafts. Even in medicine, the most efficient practice requires a variety of expensive equipment such as only hospitals and clinics can possess, and in this sense the "free" professional, exclusively relying on his own office equipment, is technologically outmoded and rapidly becoming socially outmoded also.

6. For a variety of reasons, modern occupations are highly competitive. The degree of competition is especially high in those occupations in which there is a career pattern—a progress of the individual through a series of fairly typical stages, each of which involves more pay, more responsibility, and more prestige than the last. In the residual "dead-end" jobs, of course, the element of competition is much less prominent from the point of view of individuals; here the most individuals can do is to support their unions

---

[9] Since the professions are somewhat peripheral to the present chapter, we do not treat them so fully as we might. The following references will guide the interested student. On the medical profession, see Parsons, "The Professions and Social Structure," 1939. On lawyers, see Parsons, 1954, pp. 370-85: "A Sociologist Looks at the Legal Profession." On scientists, see Merton, 1957, Chaps. 15, 16; Merton, "Priorities in Scientific Discovery: A Chapter in the Sociology of Science," 1957b; and B. Barber, *Science and the Social Order,* 1952, esp. Chaps. 3-8.

The professional's concern for the client or employer and his concern for ultimate values are not necessarily the same. "By virtue of a commitment to his profession, the engineer . . . is responsible for the maintenance of technical engineering standards even if this at times is not fully in accord with his business employer's interest" (Parsons and Smelser, 1956, pp. 151-52). Similar remarks obviously apply to lawyers. For an extremely interesting discussion of the economic and noneconomic aspects of professional roles, see Parsons and Smelser, 1956, pp. 151-56.

in the fight against the competition implicit in impersonal technological progress. The monopolistic aspects of unions are matched by the monopolistic aspects of professional associations; but the ethical codes of the professions, and the legal protection they enjoy in the name of public welfare, severely embarrass attempts to withhold purely technological advances from application. As for monopoly in industry, about which we shall have more to say in the next chapter, it does not prevent a high degree of competitiveness between the individual managers and the individual technical experts within a firm and between firms.

These common characteristics of modern occupations are of course compatible with great differences among them in other respects. Great differences are implied in the very fact of specialization. An individual's occupation is ordinarily such an engrossing part of his life that it affects his family and friendships, and widely separated occupations amount sometimes to different social worlds. In railroading, for example, time is of greater importance than it is in most occupations.

> Delays at crossovers may mean a reversal in the order in which trains use the intersection, possible increased delay while clearance is secured. . . . Silk trains, valued in millions, speeding from Pacific Coast ports to silk centers the width of a continent away, were heavily insured. The insurance was high and calculations not in days but hours. . . . For instance, lettuce can be picked only during two or three hours of the day if it is to remain fresh and firm, and a delay of an hour or two in delivery to a commission house means that morning auctions are over, buyers surfeited and huge losses must be sustained. . . . Assemblage of an automobile on the Pacific Coast from parts manufactured at a half hundred or more widely scattered plants all over the United States makes the railroad *part of the assembly line.* [W. F. Cottrell, 1939, pp. 190-98].

No wonder the railroader is conscious of time.

> It becomes a marked irritant in his relationship with other less time-conscious groups. "Dinner at eight" means *eight*, not eight-ten or eight-twenty. . . .

Ironically, some railroaders, "men on the extra-board, or trainmen and enginemen working on a 'chain gang,' in which crews take their turns on whatever business is handled . . . and many others," cannot make definite plans for anything, because they are liable to be called at any time to work. Their wives and children have to be ready to have meals whenever the railroad work makes it convenient; neither the workers nor their wives nor even their children dare to commit themselves to any definite time schedule, whether for community work, practice for a play, or mere sociability; consequently they are cut off from others to some extent.

OCCUPATION AND FAMILY

Although different occupations have different effects on family life. it is more important to see the way in which all occupations, as characterized above, are structurally related to our family system as a whole. The institutional emphasis on achievement rather than ascription, the competitiveness of the occupational system, the separation of home and work, and the existence of fairly well-marked career patterns all make for a considerable amount of moving about from one place to another. All these factors are compatible only with the type of family we have—the independent nuclear. It is hardly conceivable that extended families could have the flexibility necessary for modern industry.

The separation of home and work has tended to bring about a sharper differentiation of sex roles than existed in a predominantly rural society. As we have noted, women participate to some extent in all the occupations men engage in, but a far higher proportion of married men than of married women are employed (have an "occupation"). It would be manifestly impossible for women to be involved equally with men in the occupational system unless we developed some other arrangements for taking care of children and for managing households. New arrangements are of course conceivable. It has been suggested, however, that the present tendency toward differentiated sex roles helps to forestall a possible source of competition and conflict within the family; that middle-class women who work tend to have jobs with less prestige than their husbands' and hence are not competing; and that the greater instability of lower-class marriages, as indicated by a higher divorce rate, may be due in part to the fact that, when lower-class women work, their jobs are more nearly equal in prestige to their husbands' (Parsons, 1942, p. 94).

At the same time, the present importance of "occupational" roles, in our technical sense, is a source of strain for *all* marriages. The basic reason for this is that the occupational organization of work, as opposed to the older family organization of work, "deprives the wife of her role as a partner in a common enterprise. The common enterprise is reduced to the life of the family itself and to the informal social activities in which husband and wife participate together" (Parsons. 1942, p. 95). Perhaps this relative lack of a common enterprise is a cause of our high divorce rate, as we have noted, for there is good evidence for the generalization that positive sentiments and the strength of an organization (even a marriage) depend upon common activities (Homans, 1950, esp. pp. 276-80).

Indirectly women, as mothers, do of course contribute to the occupational system by the important part they play in socialization. As we have emphasized earlier, a boy learns the attitudes appropriate to men not only from his father but also from his mother.

Types of Exchange

The division of labor and the possession, by different individuals and groups, of different scarce goods, tangible and intangible, make exchange necessary for higher levels of efficiency in production. It is equally true that exchange makes division of labor possible. In any case, exchange is found in every economy, even the most primitive. There are six possible kinds of exchange, according to the items exchanged: goods for goods, services for services, goods for services, money for goods, money for services, and money for money. The use of money occurs only in relatively advanced economies. There is a wide variety of ways in which exchange is effected, but in no society is it purely haphazard; institutions regulating exchange are just as important a part of an economy as are the institutions of property and the division of labor.

DIRECT EXCHANGE

It is convenient to distinguish between indirect and direct exchange. There are several forms of each. Let us consider, first, four fairly clear-cut forms of direct exchange: barter, administered trade, exchange with the use of money without fixed prices, and money barter. These forms are discussed here in a merely convenient order, not in the order in which they have appeared historically.

Barter

The essential characteristics of barter are these: (1) Goods for goods, goods for services, or services for services are exchanged without the medium of money. (2) Every transaction involves two parties—i.e., individuals or groups. More complex transactions can always be broken down into a series of these simple transactions. And (3) in each transaction the parties are explicitly concerned with the problem of "proper" or "just" equivalence in that particular transaction. Sometimes the "equivalence" between two kinds of good or service, with due attention to quality and quantity, is established in custom; sometimes a more or less protracted process of bargaining or haggling may be involved; and of course both types of barter (with and without *ad hoc* bargaining) are often found in the same economy. Herskovits (1940, pp. 159-60) describes a crude form of barter as follows:

> In the so-called "silent trade" . . . goods are exchanged without any meeting of the two parties to the transaction. The procedure is for one of the principals to deposit in a customary spot whatever commodities are to be disposed of, while the other, the receiver of these goods, leaves in their place some other commodity or commodities. . . . Ibn Batuta, the Arabic traveler, gave some attention to the silent trade in the far northern "Land of Darkness." . . . Whenever the merchants were not satisfied with the payment left for them, they refused to take the skins away, and on returning the next day discovered, either that more skins had been added to the number previously deposited or that their goods had been returned. Similar means of effectuating "silent" exchanges occur today, or did occur until recent times, between the Chuckchee of Siberia and the inhabitants of Alaska . . .

This form of barter presumably occurs only between different tribes or peoples.

Administered trade

Trade is said to be "administered" when prices, whether in kind or in money, are fixed by political authority. Strictly speaking, a modern system of "frozen" wages and prices, such as the United States had during World War II to some extent, is administered trade. At the port of Whydah, when it was controlled by the native king of Dahomey, the king fixed by law the prices for the slaves his agents exchanged for European goods. These prices, however, were changed by negotiation from time to time (see Arnold, 1957).

Use of money without fixed prices

This of course is the type of exchange with which we are most familiar. Prices are determined, in principle, by competition among sellers on the one hand and among buyers on the other. We have to say "in principle" because in almost all actual markets there are monopolistic elements which restrict, more or less, the play of competition. Moreover, as we shall see, monopolistic elements are not the only ones that prevent or preclude a purely competitive determination of prices.

Money barter

In this form of direct exchange, some commodity—that is, some intrinsically valuable good—also serves as a medium of exchange, with fairly well-recognized equivalence, by number or weight or quality, to many other commodities. One of the best examples is the use of rice as "money" by the Ifugao of the Philippines. Money barter is commonly practiced along with ordinary barter; it merely facilitates exchanges between persons with different wants. One of the great advantages of "true" money is that it widens the possible market for a commodity one wishes to dispose of. One does not have to encounter someone else who happens to have exactly the thing one wants in exchange; one sells for money and then buys from someone else the thing one wants. Exchange with "true" money shares one advantage with "gift" exchange (see pp. 248-49), and that is that one may buy without selling *anything* at the moment, or *vice versa*. In a sense, exchanges for money are indirect, but they are far more convenient than barter. So-called money barter is a transitional step between crude barter and exchange with "true" money; indeed, the peoples that use money barter seem to have had contact with peoples that use money (see Herskovits, 1940, pp. 184-90).

The definition of "true" money is of course arbitrary. There are many transitions. In functional terms, money is anything that is widely used in the following ways:

1. As a medium of exchange. This is one of the most important uses of money.

2. As a standard of value. There are cases in which accounts are kept in terms of some recognized unit even though there is no tangible medium of exchange.

3. As a means of payment. Payment is involved not only in exchange but also in fines.

4. As a store of value. One of the advantages of "true" money is that it does not have to be consumed within a certain time, as does rice, for example; nor does it have to be exchanged within a certain time lest it deteriorate physically.

It is in the physical properties of the medium of exchange that kinds of "money" have most widely differed. In a narrow definition ("true" money), the thing used as money has little or no intrinsic value; its value is based entirely on convention and the prestige of the governments that guarantee it. Our engraved paper and bank checks are good examples. Paper money, as opposed to cattle or even gold, has the further advantage of being easy to handle and transport. It can also be printed in many degrees of value, which facilitates all kinds of exchange. Finally, it can be made difficult to counterfeit. In most of these respects, commodities, such as cattle or ornaments, are less convenient.

INDIRECT EXCHANGE

All the forms of exchange we have described thus far are "direct" in the sense that two parties in one transaction each give something in return for something else in an explicitly reciprocal fashion. In contrast, there are several forms of "indirect" exchange. We shall distinguish only two, which are probably the most important historically; they are so-called gift exchange and "redistribution."

Gift exchange

Gift exchange is probably the most common form of exchange among primitive people. As with all exchange, reciprocity underlies gift exchange, but its distinctive characteristic, perhaps, is that the calculation of *quid pro quo* is played down. One party to the exchange ostensibly makes a pure gift, of goods or services, to the other, without any explicit bargaining or agreement concerning a return benefit. Many writers have stressed, however, that in the long run reciprocity operates and, according to implicit customary equivalences, a gift will be repaid, perhaps with "interest," at some future time (see Mauss, 1954).

To the casual observer the element of reciprocity may be hard to see. Among the Lovedu of South Africa, for example, various kinds of work are done in large companies. Word gets around that so-and-so is clearing a field; relatives and neighbors go to the place and work away without haste; and afterward the host serves beer—a much-appreciated refreshment among the Lovedu. Everything goes so casually and cheerily that one might think that the whole affair is a party, something like an old-fashioned husking bee. Some participants are there from the beginning, others join the work later on, and some show up just before the beer is served: but all share equally in the beer and friendly conversation at the end. Superficially one might say that the work to be done is almost an excuse for a beer party, that the party is more important than the work. Certainly one does not get the impression that the beer is payment for work contributed. There is no doubt that institutionally the whole affair is in spirit unlike a commercial exchange; open calculation of self-interest is frowned upon. Yet underneath the genuinely smooth surface there is indeed a rough reciprocity. Relatives and neighbors are expected to help one another with certain tasks, and if anyone is egregiously on hand whenever beer is served but never works, he is ridiculed and finally rejected (see Krige and Krige, 1943, Chap. 4).

Reading ethnographic descriptions, one sometimes gets the impression that gift exchanges are evened out, in the long run, between any two individuals who participate, and that, informally and half-consciously at least, everyone keeps his reckoning straight with everyone else. Sometimes, however, as with the Lovedu, one gets the impression that the tacit reckoning is much more easygoing, that the important thing is not to balance this against that but at the same time not to acquire a reputation as a sponge. In any case, a widespread characteristic of gift exchange is that it is less clearly than barter a matter of transactions between two parties; one can "repay" one's "debt" to A just as well by doing something for B. This seems to be one of the principles of the caste system as it operates in the villages of India.

> Every member of each caste contributed his services and skills to the support of every member of the other castes. . . . Rather than a simple dual symmetry, a multiple symmetry underlay the caste system. . . . The members of the society could survive only if each caste did its job for the others . . . [Neale, 1957, p. 227].

Exchange is most genuinely economic when each party to a transaction acquires something he wants and cannot easily provide otherwise for himself. If "economic exchange" is to be defined in this narrow way, then many gift exchanges are noneconomic. Ceremonial gift exchanges are of this kind. For example, when the Lovedu visit a son-in-law, they take twelve calabashes (35-40 gallons) of beer with them; the son-in-law gives them two goats in return, one of which is killed and eaten on the spot; some of the beer is also drunk by the whole party. This exchange is hardly economic since the son-in-law probably has plenty of beer anyway (he has to take beer to his own sons-in-law), and the visiting party already have goats at home. The function of the exchange is primarily integrative; it symbolizes friendly attitudes and cements a social relationship. In this respect, it is quite similar to our exchange of Christmas and birthday presents or cards.[10] Indirectly, however, ceremonial gift exchange does have an economic function: it provides additional motives for production.

---

10 There is a subtle and perceptive discussion of gift exchanges in Levi-Strauss, 1949, Chap. 5. One of the basic ideas is that gifts reaffirm friendship when there is an underlying possibility of mutual hostility. Gifts also reinforce prestige (another aspect of status).

Redistribution

Redistribution, the second form of indirect exchange, "means that the produce of the group is brought together, either physically or by appropriation, and then parcelled out again among the members. Again [just as in gift exchange] there is no implication of equality of treatment, fair shares, or payment for value. The social pattern is characterized by centricity—peripheral points all connected with the central point" (Neale, 1957, p. 223).

Neale gives a striking example from the Indian villages before British influence. Although the caste system also involved gift exchange, as we have seen, agricultural products were "redistributed." The following description applies to the district of Gonda, but a similar method existed in other parts of India.

> Distribution in Gonda took place in three stages: From the standing crop; from the individual grain heap of each cultivator; and from the heaps after the cultivator had contributed to the Raja's heap.
>
> From the standing crop of each cultivator the watchman, the blacksmith, the carpenter, the herdsman, the priest, and often the cultivator himself cut a twentieth of a *bigha*. Next, the crop was harvested and threshed by the whole community, the grain from the fields of each cultivator being heaped in a separate pile on the community threshing floor. The "slave-ploughman" took a share varying from a fifth to a seventh of the heap of the cultivating family to which he was attached. To this share he added a *panseri*. From each pile each person who had cut or threshed the crop (and this meant everyone) took a sixteenth of the rice and the "fattest sheaf in thirty" of the other crops. Then the carpenter, blacksmith, barber, washerman, and watchman each took twelve *panseris* of threshed grain from each cultivator for each four-bullock plough he owned, and six *panseris* for each two-bullock plough. When these shares had been passed out the grain heaps were divided in half, the cultivator retaining one half and the other going to the Raja, subject however to further distributions. One *sir* in every *maund* of the Raja's heap was returned to the cultivator, another *sir* was given to the scribe, a "double handful" to the priest, and a tenth of the remainder was given to the village headman. From the cultivator's remaining heap the blacksmith and the carbenter each received three more *panseris*, the herdsman one more, and a *sir* or two went to the scribe [pp. 224-25].

Some steps in this procedure no doubt symbolize reciprocities within the community, but Neale makes no mention of this possibility.

There are many other examples of redistribution, often connected with kings or chiefs. A somewhat disguised form of the same thing occurs among the Lovedu. The queen receives "wives" from district heads and others and pays the "bride price" of cattle; then she gives some of these "wives" to other district heads, in return for cattle; these exchanges initiate the usual sequence of exchanges in connection with marriages, a sequence which in principle goes on for generations; but in the case of the queen the exchanges are always weighted in her favor, so that in effect she is taxing her people as well as cementing relations with them (see Krige and Krige, 1943, Chap. 10). Indeed, all forms of taxation exemplify, in part, exchange by redistribution.

Is redistribution a form of exchange at all? Although reciprocity is obviously involved in the examples we have mentioned, the lack of concern for "equivalence" is so extreme that some of the beneficiaries seem to have given nothing at all in return for their shares. Everyone benefits, to some extent, from the "redistribution" of taxes, yet some people pay no tax, and certainly in most cases there is no effort to make what each taxpayer receives equivalent to what he pays. Another example: In a patriarchal family such as the old-country Polish peasant families, the contributions of all adults are "pooled," so to speak, and then redistributed by the family head, and among those benefiting are children too young to have contributed anything (see W. I. Thomas and Znaniecki, 1927). In this case we might say that the principle of reciprocity is broadly involved, in the sense that the children, when grown, will contribute to *their* children "without recompense"; and of course this balancing-out over generations is often explicitly recognized. But to argue in the same way concerning all the beneficiaries of taxation would be stretching the concept of reciprocity too far.

In general, any system of redistribution does involve some economic exchange, but redistribution is at the same time political. Systems of taxation, such as the gathering of wealth in the hands of a Trobriand or Maori chief or of the Lovedu queen, obviously serve goals of the group as a whole. Thus the head of a tribe represents his people in meeting foreign ambassadors, and some of the wealth of the community has in effect been allocated for the necessary entertainment. Another common purpose (as well as function) of taxation is to control the economic system as a whole (e.g., to combat inflation), or to maintain stores in reserve against bad harvests. These political functions of redistribution were common in the ancient world (Egypt, China) as well. Nevertheless, a considerable amount of economic exchange is also involved.

From our whole discussion it should be clear that the institutionalized system of exchange, in conjunction with property, productive roles, and political authority, determines the distribution of utilities in society ("who gets what").

Contract[11]

Exchange is a social process, a certain kind of transaction; "contract," in the sense we wish to give it here, is the institutionalized pattern to which exchanges are subject. Since there are many types of exchange, the pattern of contract is rather complex in any society. Moreover, like other social

---

[11] The sections on contract and markets are heavily indebted to Parsons and Smelser, 1956, Chap. 3.

institutions (for example, property and the normative definition of productive roles), contract is variable from one society to another and from time to time. For example, in strictly economic exchanges, force is prohibited as a means of inducement, and fraud of various kinds is also prohibited; but the definition of fraud and the consequent restrictions upon the parties to an exchange are continually being modified by legislation.

A contract is a particular agreement involving an exchange, an agreement whose terms, both in content and in the process by which they are reached, are subject to the sanctioned pattern we call the institution of contract. In every contract there is at least a latent conflict of interests between the two parties directly involved. Sometimes the conflict of interests is so far from latent that we might ignore the other elements involved. For example, perhaps the most obvious aspect of labor-management bargaining in our economy—that is, of bargaining leading to the terms of contracts of employment—is the fact that the representatives of labor would like to obtain higher wages whereas the representatives of management would like to keep the wages lower. Nevertheless, there are always important factors that counteract the conflict of interests. Of these, probably the most obvious is the sheer fact that the process of bargaining could not have started in the first place unless *each* side had at least the prospect of gaining something desirable from the other. Another factor mitigating the conflict of interests is more often neglected in our thinking, because we tend to take it for granted. This factor is the *institution* of contract—the whole complex of values and norms which, being more or less understood and accepted by both parties, is the common ground on which bargaining proceeds. Like all other institutional patterns, contract defines the limits and modes within which the pursuit of self-interest is legitimate. It does not determine particular terms automatically; it is merely a framework, but without it organized economic activity would hardly be possible.

A contractual relationship, a particular agreement for exchange, is usually a bond between two social systems. Each of the contracting parties, that is to say, may be regarded as having a representative role in a distinct social system. For example, in the contract of employment the "employer," in the sense of the *person* who negotiates, ordinarily represents an organization—say, a business firm—and the prospective employee represents, ordinarily, a family or household. Each negotiating party has his own goal or interest to pursue: the prospective employer wishes to engage economic services that will fit into the organization he represents, and the prospective employee wishes to earn enough money to support his family according to a standard appropriate to his social class and training. The "primary exchange" involved in the contract, then, is the exchange of services for wages. This exchange is of course subject to institutional regulation: for example, neither side may use force or fraud; the employee may not sell himself into slavery; the services engaged for must be legally permissible.

At the same time that the contracting parties are representatives of distinct social systems, they also compose a social system together; and this system, like any other, has four subsystems.

The *goal* of the contractual relationhip is to reach and maintain agreement with respect to the "primary exchange"—the exchange of labor services for wages, fee, or salary.

The relationship is also *adaptive* to both the productive organization and the employee's household. As for the productive organization, the contract commits the employee to a role and status in the organization, thus specifying the organizational context in which the employee is to give his labor services. As for adaptation to the household, certain features of the contract recognize the employee's responsibilities outside the firm; for example, the hours of work specified in the contract limit the demands the firm can make on the employee's time. This adaptive subsystem of the contractual relationship involves a kind of exchange in addition to the "primary exchange" of labor services for remuneration. Since the contract of employment ordinarily extends over a period of time, the employer in effect extends to the employee and his household a certain credit-standing in the community; this is obviously important to the employee's household for such things as installment buying and obtaining loans. In return for this credit creation, the employee accepts the authority of his superiors in the productive organization. Each of these elements in the secondary exchange is the sanction of the other. If the firm is too weak or unfaithful to meet the adaptive requirements of the employee's household, he will withdraw his acceptance of its authority. On the other hand, if the employee fails to show proper acceptance of the firm's authority over him, the firm will withdraw the credit-standing it has "created."

The contractual relationship of employment also has an *integrative* subsystem. This subsystem is another secondary exchange. The firm gives the employee a kind of diffuse support on the job and for his household a certain degree of job security, sometimes also "fringe benefits." In return, the employee gives to the firm an attitude of loyalty more diffuse than the specific terms of the contract. For example, the employee has the power to enhance or reduce the reputation of the firm as a "good" employer. Certain employees might be expected to show their loyalty by using the products of the firm if these are conspicuous. (Imagine an official of General Motors driving to work in a Dodge.)

Finally, the contractual relationship has a *pattern-maintenance* subsystem which is also part of the pattern-maintenance system of the society as a whole. This consists of values that are shared by employer and employee, although some of these values are more immediately important to the employer and some to the employee. They are all values that are held independently of the particular contract but that enter into it, affecting its terms and its general spirit. For example, the firm relies to some extent on the fact that the employee has been socialized in such a way that he values efficient production of useful commodities in general. Both the firm and the household appreciate the value of being a "good" worker, with pride in one's skill and accomplishments. Of particular importance to the household is the fact that the employer, as well as the employee and his family, recognizes and values the employee's desire to be a "good provider"—that is, to be able to maintain a certain level of living in the household. All these values are inculcated in practically all the members of society in the course of socialization. Their particular meaning, as they affect particular contracts of employment, will vary depending upon the nature of the firm, its position in its field, the social position of the particular household involved, and the degree to which the employee's particular services are valued. These "background" aspects of the contract also involve a kind of secondary exchange. In return for entrusting the security of his household to the economy in general and to the specific employer in particular, the employee receives from the firm moral approval for his performances. The exchange involved is an exchange of confidence for moral approval.

From the foregoing analysis we see that a contract of employment is by no means merely an *ad hoc* agreement peculiar to the contracting parties; its specific terms are always conditioned by an institutionalized pattern.[12] One might quarrel with this analysis on the ground that it applies only to contracts in a modern capitalist economy. This objection, however, would be short-sighted. To be sure, contracts in our economy are to a high degree explicit, and the productive roles are to a large extent structurally differentiated from household roles. Nevertheless, even in "primitive" economies the same basic *interchanges* take place and are to some extent institutionalized. As we have noted, the system of gift exchange, for example, is a system of *implicit contracts*. The same is true of a redistributive system.

Markets

In our economy contracts are always made in a "market." There are markets for labor, for entrepreneurial services, for consumers' goods, for professional services, for capital, for investment funds. Each of these types of market in turn may be broken down into many smaller, more specialized markets. For example, the market for labor consists of submarkets for each kind and grade of labor—labor in the steel industry, in the rubber industry, and so on.

A market exists when there are many suppliers of a particular good or service and many persons or organizations seeking that particular good or service. In the most clear-cut cases, the suppliers are competing with one another and so are the seekers. Although markets are usually *regulated* to some extent by law, they are not usually *organized* formally. Nevertheless,

---

[12] This analysis of the contract of employment follows closely, even in its language, the analysis given by Parsons and Smelser, 1956, pp. 114-19. These authors show that other types of contract—for example, the contract of investment—are also capable of being analyzed as systems, each with four subsystems.

a market can be analyzed as a social system with four subsystems (see Parsons and Smelser, 1956, pp. 143ff.). The continuing competition of "buyers" and of "sellers" tends to establish a kind of equilibrium with respect to prices, quality, and other terms of particular contracts in the market in question.

Does every economy have markets? The answer to this question depends, of course, on how narrowly or broadly one defines "market." In the narrowest sense, there would have to be explicit bargaining about the terms of exchange, and there would have to be explicit competition on *both* sides of the exchange process—competition among "sellers" and competition among "buyers." This narrow definition, however, does not fit every exchange, even in our own economy. For example, take the exchange between patient and private medical doctor (see Parsons and Smelser, 1956, pp. 152-53). Bargaining about terms is virtually excluded by the institutional pattern; it is understood that the patient pays, not what the services would be "worth" in a competitive market, but what he can afford in view of his other household requirements; the "sliding scale" is institutionalized. Moreover, competition is also virtually excluded: doctors are not supposed to advertise in a commercial fashion, and the patient is expected to trust his doctor and not to "shop around" for medical service.

Now consider the administered trade for slaves in the port of Whydah (see p. 247). Superficially viewed, there was no market: the Europeans came to the one seller, the king of Dahomey, and they did not compete with one another but simply paid the price established by law. Yet closer inspection shows that this account is not quite realistic. There were in fact other sources of slaves, and the price established at Whydah certainly was determined in part by this fact; indeed, the Europeans, through negotiation, were able to get the king to alter the terms of exchange from time to time. If the king's prices had been "too high," the Europeans would not have been able to buy the slaves, for they would not have been able to resell them in the New World and still make a profit. We see, therefore, that although the slave trade at Whydah was "administered," it was nonetheless involved in a market. Consider another case referred to earlier (p. 242). As we have seen, gift exchange prevails in the East African kingdoms of the Bakitara and the Banyankole. The nobility breed cattle, and the peasants are engaged in all other industries, especially agriculture. Despite the institutionalization of gift exchange, we can see from the following quotation that, though the system of exchange may be highly stabilized as to terms, there is in fact a good deal of implicit competition.

> The peasants are bound to no place and no master. Since the cattle people depend on them for the necessities of life and for services for themselves and the king, the power and influence of a chief at court depend on his ability to attract large numbers of peasants to his domain. When the king needs cattle he sends out his tax collector to take them; when he needs services from the peasants, he requests them with gifts. Although the peasants own

> no cattle, they keep sheep and goats, and altogether form an economically self-sufficient group, which the cattle people most decidedly do not. The one important commodity which they lack is butter, for which they depend on the chiefs [Bunzel, 1938, p. 374].

From this description it is safe to infer that the traditionalistic exchanges, apparently "fixed" in the custom of exchanging "gifts," actually involve a good deal of implicit bargaining and competition; more intensive investigation might well reveal that the "fixed" exchanges are less stable than they at first appear to be. Just as there are implicit contracts, so there are implicit or "concealed" markets.

Further examination of the doctor-patient relationship in our society will drive the point home. Although bargaining and competition are "played down," nevertheless any patient who feels that his doctor is exploiting him or is incompetent is of course at liberty to go to another doctor—in short, to a competitor. Some writers regard an auction as a nonmarket form of exchange, since there is only one seller. Reflection shows, however, that the buyers make their bids with competing sources of supply in mind. The auction itself is not a market, but it is definitely involved in a market (or in several markets).

MARKET "IMPERFECTIONS"

Although, as we have just seen, the existence of markets is more common than one might at first think, perhaps not all exchanges take place in markets, even implicit ones. Economists have in effect recognized that the existence of markets is a matter of degree; they speak of "perfect" and "imperfect" markets. As we shall see, there are different kinds, as well as different degrees, of imperfection.

Market perfection is a technical, not a moral, matter. There are two criteria. The one most stressed by economists is perfect competitiveness: a situation in which no "buyer" (or "seller") is strong enough, in relation to his competitors, to affect the price. This first criterion has been expressed by two sociologists as follows: There is "either sufficient regulation or sufficient competition so that the settlement of terms is not skewed toward the advantage of either side of the market as a whole or toward any unit or units on either side. This assumption includes an equality of power on both sides of the market" (Parsons and Smelser, 1956, p. 146). Equality of power, then, not competition, is the first criterion; and regulation can protect such equality just as well as competition can. Nevertheless, economists are of course correct, given our type of economy, to stress the market factors that impair competitiveness—i.e., that tend toward monopoly. Accordingly, the variables most often discussed by economists are the strength (size and financial power) of individual buyers and sellers, the number of buyers and sellers, the amount of product differentiation in the field of competition, and the elasticity of demand for the particular product or service in question. All these variables have to do with the nature, not with the exercise, of monopoly power. Since for various reasons a possessor of monopoly power may refrain from using it to the full extent possible, a list of factors determining the exercise of monopoly power is a little different from a list of factors that create (or constitute) monopoly power. With this note of caution, let us turn briefly to the list just given.

Obviously a seller who is financially strong enough can afford to undersell his competitors till they are driven from the market, and a relatively strong buyer can force down the price by threatening to produce for himself or to give large orders to a more cooperative seller. This factor of financial power is obviously related to the number of buyers and sellers in the market; at one extreme, for example, a single seller has a great advantage over buyers, whereas one seller among many has little control over price. Both financial power and number of competitors are in turn affected by the amount of product differentiation in the relevant field. A single seller has less monopoly power if there are other sellers offering products that may readily be substituted for the monopolized product. If the producers of glass containers put the price too high, their customers may switch to metal or paper containers. Closely related to product differentiation is the relative elasticity of demand for a particular product. "Elasticity" refers to the variable extent to which demand for different products changes with changes in price. For example, the demand for tobacco is not very elastic; within broad limits of price, smokers will continue to smoke about the same amount; but the demand for phonograph records might be more elastic.

The second criterion of market perfection is perhaps more difficult to grasp. Some market exchanges take place strictly *within* the economy, whereas other market exchanges may be regarded as interchange *between* the economy and some other subsystem of society. For example, a labor contract is an interchange between the economy and the pattern-maintenance system. If one firm buys a product from another firm, the exchange is within the economy. Exchanges within the economy are far more rigorously subject to economic values than are exchanges between the economy and some other subsystem. Perhaps the best illustration of this point is the market for "control of productivity" (see Parsons and Smelser, 1956, 169-73). This market has to do with some of the interchange between the economy and the polity (for purposes of our present illustration, the government). Many industries would of course like to have government support in the form of tariffs or subsidies. There is a kind of market for such support. It is clear, however, that such support is not given or withheld for economic considerations alone. In principle at least, an industry is protected in the national interest and, frequently, despite the fact that protection may be *against* economic values. In other words, in the market for control of productivity, political values have primacy over economic values. For example, the president of the United States (it happened to be President Eisenhower) favored protection of the relatively uneconomic American watch and clock industry on the ground that in time of war the supply of foreign watches and clocks might be cut off. Here we have a case in which economic weakness is a better claim to success in the market than economic strength. Such markets are by definition "imperfect." The second criterion of market "perfection" is that the exchanges involved take place *within* the economy (Parsons and Smelser, 1956, p. 146).

The watch-and-clock example points up the technical nature of market perfection. Many imperfect markets would not be improved, from a moral or a functional point of view, if they were made more nearly perfect. This is especially true of markets that involve interchange between the economy and some other subsystem. It is also true of markets that involve exchanges largely within some subsystem other than the economy. The doctor-patient exchange takes place largely within the pattern-maintenance system. Better social arrangements for providing medical services are certainly conceivable; but changes in the direction of greater economic competitiveness would not be functional in relation to the values of our society. Commercial advertising would have the effect of reducing the quality of service and increasing the distrust of patients for their doctors; distrust in turn would make the doctor's task much more difficult. Moreover, if medical services were "sold" for what they would be worth in a competitive market—that is, if the "sliding scale" were abandoned—then the rich would be the only ones who could afford many kinds of medical service; yet we regard good health as something everyone should have, as far as possible.

This functional defense of the imperfection of the market for medical services must not be construed as complacency. There is little doubt that social arrangements somewhat different from those we have at present would ensure an even greater degree of equality of opportunity. As we have noted before, the functional value of any particular structure is a relative matter. To show that a particular structure—e.g., the "sliding scale"—is functional is not to prejudice evaluation of alternative structures in the same field.

A complete analysis of the kinds and degrees of market imperfection would have to take account of the following variables in addition to degrees of economic power:

1. Inequality of sides in the market due to differential evaluation of different *societal subsystems.* As we have seen, some exchanges (or interchanges) occur within the economy whereas others occur between the economy and other subsystems of society. For a particular type of interchange, the value system of society may give greater weight to the values of one of the societal subsystems between which interchange takes place. In the market for control of productivity, for example, political values have primacy over economic values.

2. Inequality of sides in the market due to differential evaluation of different *subsystems of the contract.* The value system may also give different weights to the four subsystems *within* any type of contractual relation-

ship, and the relative weights may differ for different types of contract. For example, in the doctor-patient relationship the integrative subsystem is predominant, whereas in the contract for the purchase and sale of consumers' goods the goal subsystem is predominant. Moreover, the value system may tip one or more of the subsystem exchanges, within the contractual relationships, in favor of one side of the market. For example, in the labor market the goal subsystem probably is skewed in favor of employers. If this is true, it means that production is more highly valued in our society than a high level of living for the household. (These variables have to do with the *value* hierarchy, not with the relative economic power of the two sides in exchange. Like all questions having to do with the relative position of cultural values in a particular society, this one needs a great deal more empirical study.)

The Motivation of Economic Activities

In its narrow meaning, "motivation" consists of the purposes of action plus the emotions or sentiments that are the "springs" of action. This meaning is familiar to readers of detective stories: the detective first establishes what has been done, then asks himself what the motivation might have been and who among the suspects might have had the requisite motives. If we consider such cases more closely, however, we become aware that all motivated action involves at least implicit ideas, on the actor's part, about the situation in which he is acting. For example, if a criminal commits a crime for money (his purpose or motive in a narrow sense), he must of course have the idea that his particular victim *has* enough money to make this particular crime "worthwhile." In a broad sense, therefore, his motivation includes his *cognitive* definition of the situation, which of course may be correct or incorrect or partly correct and partly incorrect. Moreover, among the "sentiments" that lie behind action are various feelings about the moral rightness of different possible courses; even criminals will stop at some means to their ends. In the broad sense, then, motivation includes values, norms, and cognitive assumptions, as well as feelings and purposes.[13]

Motivation is complex in another way: there are different levels. We might ask the question: Why do people work at all? At this abstract level, we should focus on broad motives such as the internalized values of economic rationality. Useful work as a value is often supported by religious beliefs, political loyalty (when production is explicitly an important goal of the group), or both. At a "lower" level of abstraction, we might ask why people of a particular culture tend to prefer one kind of work rather than another. At this level, we should have to consider the hierarchy of values in the culture and the cultural definition of sex roles, as well as institutionalized patterns such as occupational castes and other patterns whereby occupa-

---

[13] For a systematic exposition of the elements of motivation, see Parsons and Shils, 1951.

tional roles are inherited. A very general element in motivation is the striving for prestige. Whereas many tasks are approved, some are given more prestige than others. Such Plains Indian tribes as the Cheyenne and the Crow, who once depended on hunting and fighting, are now miserably trying to make a living farming on their reservations; their misery is due not only to their ignorance of farming and to the fact that the reservation land is poor but, perhaps more, to the fact that in the "classical" Plains culture farming was despised.

At a still lower level of abstraction, we might ask why men in a particular work-role typically act in a certain way. Most people to some extent, but those in high positions especially, fear the loss of prestige and authority. For example, many of the decisions of business executives are made with this motive:

> The desire for distinction and esteem is effective not only as a positive drive in its own right; it has a negative aspect as well. The fear of failure, not simply the desire to maximize profits, is an expression of this motive. The speaker emphasized that he did not mean financial failure alone. He meant also the kind of failure that results in a loss of status and authority [Barnard, 1949, p. 7].

Finally, at the "lowest" level of abstraction, there are the "concrete" motives of particular persons, with all their freight of unconscious elements deriving from their personal history. At this level, which is the least interesting from a sociological point of view, a particular executive, for example, may have a repressed "dependency drive," masked by a "reaction formation," a somewhat defensive drive to activity and dominance; and this complex may give a slightly pathological quality to this particular executive's culturally normal fear of failure and desire for distinction.

Leaving aside the quirks of individual personalities and the motives peculiar to particular roles, we may say that the following elements are quite common in the motivation of economic activities:

1. *Internalized cultural values and norms.* Closely associated with these values and norms are the wish for self-respect and the desire for recognition from others. Living up to the standards prescribed for one's role, whatever it is, is a condition of self-respect and the approval of one's fellow group-members.

2. *The wish for remuneration* (ultimately, goods and services). This is perhaps the most obvious element in economic motivation, especially to people living in the United States, where many ideologists treat "the profit motive" as if it were, like sex, an innate drive. Actually the businessman's goal of profit is virtually forced upon him by the institutional framework within which he must act. In the capitalistic system a business firm must make a profit, in the long run, or fail. In our system much unprofitable but highly productive activity is carried on by the government; but people are so deeply convinced that the profit motive is part of human nature that

it does not occur to them to ask what motivates the directors of the postal service.

Among some nonliterate peoples, the idea of profit-making is virtually unknown. A famous example is the so-called *Kula* ring of New Guinea. The natives of a wide ring of islands carry on productive trade with one another, but in their own minds their exchanges of economic goods are incidental to the maintenance of correct relations with their *ceremonial* partners in the *Kula* ring. Each participant has a lifelong partner in each of the other tribes with which his own tribe is trading. The ceremonial or quasi-religious exchange, which, as we have mentioned, is the aspect of the relationship most stressed by the natives themselves, involves nonutilitarian objects—white-shell bracelets and red-shell necklaces. If a man gives a bracelet to his partner, the partner gives him a necklace; in turn, the receiver of the necklace will give it to another partner in the ring, on another island, who will give him a bracelet for it. While these elaborate ceremonial exchanges are going on, the participants are also exchanging economic goods. The function of the shell exchange, no doubt, is to symbolize and maintain attitudes of mutual trust between distant peoples whose contacts are so infrequent that mutual trust could not otherwise be taken for granted.[14]

So far is the profit motive from the minds of the native women of Haiti that they refuse opportunities to sell their wares profitably on the way to the marketplace; they could lighten their burden and make their sales more quickly thus, but the desire for prestige is stronger in them: they take pride in having a fine big display of their produce in the market (Herskovits, 1940, p. 178). For a similar reason Plains Indian warriors would risk their lives raiding enemy tribes for horses, then come home and often give away all the horses they had captured.

The importance of institutional variation in shaping individuals' motives has been well expressed by Bunzel:

> Attitudes toward wealth and property institutions constantly interact in a powerfully dynamic relationship. The existence of acute anxiety stimulates individuals to accumulate property and use it to control others; the existence of private control of the necessities of life produces anxiety in those who are shut out and also in those who have, but fear to lose. This in turn produces a tension between groups and individuals which serves to increase the rigidity of institutions. This is the dynamic character of Chukchee or Ifugao civilization, where it is based on a real inadequacy in the environment, and of our own.

---

[14] The classic description of the *Kula* ring is Malinowski, *Argonauts of the Western Pacific*, 1932: ". . . this simple action—this passing from hand to hand of two meaningless and quite useless objects—has somehow succeeded in becoming the foundation of a big intertribal institution. . . . Myth, magic and tradition have built up around it definite ritual and ceremonial forms, have given it a halo of romance and value in the minds of the natives, have indeed created a passion in their hearts for this simple exchange" (p. 86).

> The dynamic trend may also be in the opposite direction; institutions which permit free access to the necessities of life to all promote a sense of security. People with no worries about the future see no need to accumulate to the exclusion of others. This is the Zuni or Samoan picture. How these tendencies get started we do not know, although we can see how, under cultural pressure, they are built up individually in children. Once started the process pursues its course, sometimes with increasing intensity, or with diminishing vigor, until some new element is introduced. In Zuni the introduction of strict property rights and profit in sheep-herding has altered the direction of economic development. It will be interesting to see whether the socialization of wealth under [a] Soviet régime will diminish the Chukchee manifestations of anxiety [1938, pp. 350-51].

Although the "profit motive" is not universal, everywhere people who engage in economic activity do expect that they will somehow be rewarded with a share of economic goods and services. This share, which they may of course redistribute according to some accepted pattern, may be regarded as their "remuneration" in a narrow sense.

3. *The desire to maintain social attachments within the work group.* This element in "economic" motivation has often been stressed by those who have studied work teams in industry. The cliques we discussed in Chapter 1 are a good example. The maintenance of friendships on the job depends to some extent on one's doing one's part in the work itself. (See Bakke, 1940, Chap. 1.)

4. *The desire to maintain social attachments apart from the job.* In an economy such as ours, in which one's work is ordinarily carried on apart from the family, the desire to support the family is nevertheless a powerful motive for working. Many other social attachments, however, also depend upon one's working. For example, unemployed workers tend to stop going to church: they cannot afford to make the necessary financial contributions, to pay carfare, to keep up the appropriate standard of dress. Friendships also suffer in a prolonged period of unemployment. The unemployed worker begins to avoid his friends for fear that they will suggest having a friendly, and expensive, drink in a tavern. An unemployed ironworker had this to say:

> It's all right to talk about being friends, but, you know, there are certain things that go with having people to your house. For instance, you can't even have a card game without serving sandwiches and coffee, or pretzels and beer or something, but that all costs something. We had some people with whom we kept our contacts, and by common agreement we decided that we wouldn't serve refreshments. Somehow it wasn't much fun any longer and very soon we broke up [Bakke, 1940a, pp. 10-11].

5. *The pleasure of exercising skill.* There can be no doubt that many people work for the sheer pleasure of it. It is probably true that slaves develop a kind of pride in their proficiency. The work of coal-miners seems dirty, dark, and hazardous to most people.

> Yet the miners like their work. The older ones, and especially those who labor in mines that have not yet yielded to mechanical loaders and other

> brain children of the efficiency experts, take particular pride in their craftsmanship. They feel in digging coal a stirring challenge from nature—a pitting of human skills against the resistance of the earth ["The Coal Miner . . . ," 1947, p. 2].

This may sound a trifle too rhapsodical, but men do develop a sense of craftsmanship about any repeated activity that distinguishes them. At the same time, certain routine or heavy or otherwise "unpleasant" tasks are commonly held to be less desirable than others. Studies have shown, to be sure, that individuals vary in what they consider pleasant or unpleasant, and this variation is of course fortunate, since people cannot all specialize in the same thing.[15] To some extent, however, some men and women in our own economy must do things for a living that they would rather not be doing. This is presumably true especially of unskilled and semiskilled workers. Other factors therefore play a part in workers' motives for preferring one job to another, even though neither job is intrinsically absorbing. A summary of sixteen studies covering in all more than 11,000 workers reveals the order of importance workers attach to various aspects of their jobs. From most frequently mentioned to least frequently mentioned, the attractive features of "good" jobs are as follows: security, opportunity to use acquired skills, opportunity for advancement, recognition on the part of superordinates for one's work well done, fairness of management and good reputation of the company, intrinsic aspects of the job apart from how easy the work is, wages, intrinsic nature of the whole job (not particular aspects), good supervision on the job, social aspects of the job, specific working conditions apart from hours, good communication in the cooperative system, working conditions on the job as a whole, hours of work, ease of work, and benefits connected with the job (Herzberg *et al.*, 1955). These same features, where relevant, are of course important to those in managerial positions also. Many of these variable aspects of "jobs" and "positions" *can* be factors considered in the choice of work only in an economy that permits considerable freedom of choice and freedom of movement. In the caste system of India, for example, the caste of sweepers hardly considers whether sweeping the streets free of garbage and excrement is a "pleasant" task; since the occupation is hereditary, it is presumably taken for granted, much as one takes one's sex role or one's ethnic-group membership for granted.

Any careful analysis of the motivation of economic activities shows once again the interdependence of the economy and the other subsystems of society. It also shows once again that some degree of fusion is quite common.

---

[15] "Strange as it may seem to others, coal miners find a satisfaction in working their man-made caverns. Underground the temperature is equable. . . . The darkness bothers them not, and they seem to enjoy their relative freedom from the distractions and furies of the upper world" (*A Medical Survey of the Bituminous-Coal Industry*, 1947).

RECOMMENDED READING

The best theoretical treatment of the subject of the present chapter is T. Parsons and N. J. Smelser, *Economy and Society: A Study in the Integration of Economic and Social Theory*, Free Press, 1956, Chap. 3: "The Institutional Structure of the Economy." This chapter is probably easier to read than the rest of the book. For a systematic treatment of money, the division of labor, and some other topics, see M. Weber, *The Theory of Social and Economic Organization*, trans. by A. M. Henderson and T. Parsons, Oxford University Press, 1947, Part II. The introduction by Parsons, especially Sections III and V, is well worth reading for its own sake. For a well-organized presentation of a wealth of facts about many important topics which we lack the space to discuss here, see W. E. Moore, *Industrial Relations and the Social Order*, rev. ed., Macmillan, 1951. On feudalism, see four excellent articles in *Encyclopaedia of the Social Sciences*, 1931, v. 6: K. Asakawa, "Feudalism: Japanese"; M. Bloch, "Feudalism: European"; O. Franke, "Feudalism: Chinese"; and A. H. Lybyer, "Feudalism: Saracen and Ottoman." For primitive economic systems, see M. J. Herskovits, *The Economic Life of Primitive Peoples*, Knopf, 1940; there is a second edition, called *Economic Anthropology* (1952). See also R. Bunzel, "The Economic Organization of Primitive Peoples," in F. Boas, ed., *General Anthropology*, Heath, 1938.

In K. Davis, *Human Society*, Macmillan, 1949, the section on property in Chap. 17, though brief, is especially good. For a good example of traditionalistic redistribution, see W. C. Neale, "Reciprocity and Redistribution in the Indian Village: Sequel to Some Notable Discussions," in K. Polanyi, C. M. Arensberg, and H. W. Pearson, eds., *Trade and Market in the Early Empires*, Free Press and Falcon's Wing Press, 1957, pp. 218-36. This essay shows how early English administrators failed to understand the system and applied their own ethnocentric concepts. B. Malinowski, *Argonauts of the Western Pacific, An Account of Native Enterprise and Adventure in the Archipelagoes of Melanesian New Guinea*, London: Routledge, 1932, Chap. 3, is the classic account of the famous *Kula* ring. E. J. Krige and J. D. Krige, *The Realm of a Rain-Queen: A Study of the Pattern of Lovedu Society*, Oxford University Press, 1943, Chap. 4, is a good description of economic "gift" exchange; without ethnocentrism, it well conveys the relatively easygoing attitude of some primitive societies. The Lovedu are a South African, Bantu-speaking tribe.

Although it has been superseded by his later work, T. Parsons' "The Motivation of Economic Activities," *Canad. J. Econ. polit. Sci.*, 1940, v. 6, pp. 187-203 (reprinted in Parsons, *Essays in Sociological Theory*, rev. ed., Free Press, 1954, Chap. 3), is still worth reading for particular points.

11. The Performance of the American Economy

To the many questions raised in the present chapter, all the answers will be tentative. Before attempting a rough assessment of functions and dysfunctions, we must have a few descriptive facts.

The Tendency Toward Concentration

All economists agree that there are many monopolistic or quasi-monopolistic elements in the present economy of the United States. We shall see below that these elements are not necessarily "bad" in all respects, although the American tradition of "trustbusting" and the ideological praise of competition make "monopoly" a harsh-sounding word. First, however, let us consider briefly the various forms economic concentration has assumed

SHAREHOLDINGS

> It has become the fashion to classify the economy of the United States as a new form, "People's Capitalism." The expression was developed by the Advertising Council, which prepared a "People's Capitalism" exhibit, shown internationally under the auspices of the United States Information Agency [Perlo, 1958, p. 333].

In 1959, one adult in eight in the United States was a shareowner (New York Stock Exchange, 1959). We may assume that the number of share-owning *families* was somewhat smaller. The median household income of shareowners was $7,000. Of the total number of shareowners, 16.4 per cent were "proprietors, managers, and officials"; toward the other end of the occupational scale, 0.6 per cent of the shareowners were farmers and farm laborers, and 3.4 per cent were "operatives and laborers."

For estimating the degree of concentration of shareownership, the number of shareowners is a much less significant datum than the distribution of shares among shareowners. The following extract combines several quotations from Perlo's careful survey of the available data on shareownership in the United States:

> Assuming a mean stockholding of $1,000 [known to be higher than the actual figure], the total value of stocks held by all wage earners' families in the country . . . was equal to 0.3 per cent of the marketable supply of stock in the United States. . . . Indeed, the market value of Rockefeller holdings in a single corporation, Standard Oil of New Jersey, was twice the market value of all the holdings of all American wage earners. . . . The staff of the Senate Committee on Banking and Currency deduced from the 1952 Survey Research Center report that 8 per cent of all stock-owners, comprising: "less than one per cent of all American families owned over four-fifths of all publicly held stocks owned by individuals." . . . [T]he effect of the main form of institutional stockholding is to *increase* the concentration of stock-ownership. . . . In 1937-39, the 20 largest stockholders of record in each of the 200 largest nonfinancial corporations owned altogether 31.6 per cent of the common stock and 30.47 per cent of the preferred stock. In practical terms, these 20 very large holders, voting typically about one-third of the stock, exercise full effective voting control of the corporation. . . . Concentration of control is furthered by the role of institutional stockholders, particularly the large trustee banks [Perlo, 1958, pp. 338, 339, 345, 346].

GIANT CORPORATIONS

In 1954 there were more than four million corporations in the United States.

> If, however, it be supposed that the largest corporations employ indirectly only one person for every individual they employ directly, it seems likely that at least one-half of the nonfarm, nongovernmental working force is tied directly or indirectly to the 200 largest corporations. This estimate tallies with a consensus of estimates on the proportion of business assets held by the 200 companies—one-half. Since, moreover, these 200 companies affect the business of an indeterminable number of independent retailers, it is not too much to say that the 200 largest corporations strongly influence, at the very least, more than half and perhaps as much as three-quarters of U. S. business life [Maurer, 1955, p. 8].[1]

LINKS BETWEEN CORPORATIONS

Not only are certain individual corporations enormous in themselves, but there are numerous links between them, some links of little importance no doubt, and others strong enough to warrant our speaking of groups or groupings of corporations. The most important organizational and contractual links are the following: (1) intercorporate stockholding, (2) interlocking directorates, (3) interlocking through large stockholders, (4) interlocking through common servicing firms (financial, legal, accounting, advertising, engineering, public-relations counseling, and labor-espionage firms) (National Resources Committee, 1939, pp. 136-38; Lynch, 1946, pp. 232-34).

The National Resources Committee found in 1935 that there were eight especially powerful groupings of corporations, each with millions or billions of dollars' worth of assets in two or three or all of the major

---

[1] See also Galbraith, 1956, Chaps. 3, 4; Samuelson, 1951, pp. 125-32. According to *Life* Magazine, May 13, 1957. the fifty biggest corporations in the United States got 27 per cent of all sales.

categories (industrials, rails, banks, and utilities). The eight groupings were also to some extent linked to one another. There is no reason to suppose that the interconnections between corporations are less numerous today than they were in 1935.

These interconnections are effective in two ways. They help to create a general climate of business opinion, and they are, to varying degrees, effective in controlling or determining specific business transactions. The activities of "trade organizations" are intermediate. They do not control particular business transactions, but on the other hand they go beyond creation of public opinion. They help to control the economy by providing standards and rules of behavior for their members. They also seek to influence governmental legislation, either directly or, through propaganda, indirectly; that is, they act as pressure groups. Roughly speaking, the associations we have in mind are of three types. First, there are specialized trade associations, whose members are firms in a particular industry. There are perhaps 12,000 specialized trade associations in the United States. Secondly, there is a "peak association," the National Association of Manufacturers (N.A.M.), whose 17,000 or so member firms, in a wide variety of industries, employ "about half of the industrial workers and [produce] more than half of the total manufacturing output" (Kreps, 1957, p. 362). Finally, there are the chambers of commerce, whose members include not only business firms but also public officials and interested private citizens. The Chamber of Commerce of the United States has about 20,000 member groups, including the local organizations, many trade associations, and many employers' associations (Kreps, 1957, pp. 360-61).[2]

OLIGOPOLY

Another index of concentration in the American economy is the extent of oligopoly. An industry, or a certain line of production, is said to be "oligopolistic" if it is effectively controlled by a small number of companies. A study of 113 companies in twenty-six manufacturing industries in 1947 showed the following results. In each of thirteen industries, three companies owned 64-100 per cent of the net capital assets of the whole industry. In each of six industries, six companies owned 60.4-69.9 per cent of net capital assets. In each of three industries, fourteen companies owned 53.8-60.1 per cent of net capital assets. And in each of two industries, fifteen companies owned 57.5-59.2 per cent of net capital assets. Twenty-four of the twenty-six industries, then, were oligopolies or near-oligopolies (Robertson, 1955, pp. 492-93).

---

[2] On the U. S. Chamber of Commerce and the N.A.M., see Key, 1958, pp. 97-100. Key shows that the N.A.M. is dominated by a few large companies and that it spends large sums of money on disguised propaganda in support of extremely conservative policies; the Chamber of Commerce, having a broader membership, is not always so conservative.

CONCENTRATION IN AGRICULTURE

The number of farms of all sizes decreased by 11.1 per cent from 1950 to 1954, yet the number of large farms increased: the number of farms in the size-category of 260 to 499 acres increased by 0.9 per cent; in the category of 500 to 999 acres, by 5.2 per cent; and in the category of 1000 acres and over, by 7.5 per cent. The growing importance of large-scale commercial farms by no means amounts to oligopoly, however: in 1954 there were 130,481 farms with 1000 or more acres each.[3]

Two factors largely account for the growing concentration in agriculture. The first is technological change; new farm machinery and new methods of irrigation and protection against pests make large-scale operations more efficient. The second is government policy, which has benefited large-scale producers more than small producers. The relatively large-scale farmers have been the chief beneficiaries of government buying of farm products to support prices. Payments to farmers for keeping part of their land out of cultivation of certain crops have benefited the farmers with the most land; and the same is true of payments for keeping land unproductive altogether (the so-called "soil bank" policy).

In 1910 the farm population was 34.9 per cent of the total population; in 1950, 16.6 per cent; and in 1956, 13.3 per cent.[4] For many years, we have had tremendous agricultural surpluses, and although increase in consumption of agricultural products offers some hope of relief for small-scale commercial farmers, most of them will have to give up farming eventually. The prospect of increased concentration in agriculture and relative decline in the farm population need not affect the "farms that are really rural residences."[5] These tiny farms, of which there are approximately 1,700,000, produce only about 7 per cent of total farm output; and the number of such "farms" is growing.

Labor Unions

There is little doubt that without unions the hours and working conditions in factories would be much worse than they are (Millis and Montgomery, 1945, pp. 364-66). With respect to wages and, more generally, the share of goods and services that goes to "the working class," the success of unions is more controversial.

Many union demands, both "good" and "bad"—demands for safety devices as well as demands for disguised "featherbedding"—are of course costly. Sometimes increased costs are compensated for; improvement in

[3] Bureau of the Census, *Statistical Abstract of the United States, 1957*, p. 622, Table 787.
[4] Bureau of the Census, *Statistical Abstract of the United States, 1957*, p. 615, Table 779.
[5] This term comes from *Business Week*, Dec. 10, 1955, and is quoted by Huberman and Sweezy, 1956, p. 2.

the morale of workers, for example, may reduce turnover and hence the cost of training workers; the cost of supervision may also be reduced. In these cases, there need be no rise in prices. In some cases, moreover, the cost of labor is a small proportion of the total cost of production. But in most cases the net cost of production is appreciably increased by a union success (Millis and Montgomery, 1945, p. 375). Usually increased costs are "passed on" to consumers in the form of higher prices, and higher prices of course reduce real wages (wages in terms of purchasing power). Although some of the increase is obviously borne by managers, professional workers, and pensioners as well as by union members and nonunion workers, nevertheless the relation between higher wages and higher prices does weaken the argument of union ideologists that union pressure for higher wages supports the economy by raising purchasing power. To some extent, moreover, consumers may shift to competing products, thus reducing employment both for union members and for nonunion workers in the original industry.

Economists are not sure whether the over-all effect of unions on wages has been beneficial to workers or not (Samuelson, 1951, pp. 606-08; Millis and Montgomery, 1945, pp. 366-88). In general, the long-run rise in real wages is due above all to increasing productivity (production per man-hour). Whether pressure from labor unions has greatly helped to increase productivity is a question. Managers have undoubtedly tried to offset increased costs by improving techniques of production—an economic benefit from unionization. But against this indirect benefit must be set union demands for featherbedding, monopolistic control of the supply of labor, and opposition to technical improvements. In any case, productivity might have increased just about as much whether or not unions had been active. Managers try to increase profits for many reasons.

Millis and Montgomery, close students of unions, are of the opinion that strikes and collective bargaining are much less effective in redistributing the total national product in favor of workers than political action would be; they stress in particular the importance of government-financed social welfare, combined with less-regressive taxation (1945, pp. 385-88).

THE FUNCTIONS OF UNIONS

Although unions exist to fight against management, the chief function of unions for the economy is integrative. It would be difficult to say what "equality" of bargaining power between employer and employee would mean exactly. Nevertheless, it is fairly clear that, without unions, workers, as individuals, would be at a considerable disadvantage. This disadvantage would be, and was, a source of poor morale. The first aspect of the integrative function of unions, therefore, is to counterbalance the greater bargaining power of employers. The second aspect is closely related: the union acts as the bargaining agent for its members in detailed negotiations with management. "Union statesmanship," to some people, means action on the part of union leaders in the objective long-range interests of union members, of workers as a category, and even of the public at large. Other writers, less demanding, say that union leaders cannot know about, let alone control, all the factors that determines whether workers' real wages rise or fall, and that union statesmanship, realistically viewed, displays itself in the ability to allay mutual suspicion and bitterness, to bring about short-term agreements (see Ross, 1948, p. 95; Kerr, 1954).

An integrative function is sometimes hard to distinguish from a tension-management function. Tension management, it will be remembered, has to do with the internal state of individuals in their capacity as role-and-status occupants, whereas integration has to do with the relations between social units (individual and individual, group and group, individual and group). But the two kinds of function are obviously related and occasionally blend. The worker's anxiety about his job, or indeed about his occupation, does not derive solely from his distrust of management. Technological progress, from whatever source, might make his contribution obsolete, and this might happen whether his own particular employer has good intentions toward him or not. Seen in this light, union insistence upon "featherbedding," which in one aspect is obviously dysfunctional for the system of production, is also functional. It helps to relieve the worker's anxiety about technological progress in general, viewed as an aspect of the situation to which both management and workers must adjust; it slows down the pace of *social* change under the impact of *cultural* change, and thus gives individual workers more time to accommodate themselves to the unpleasant facts. This is a tension-management function. This function could be performed equally well or better, in theory, in a "planned" economy; but in a "free enterprise" economy, unions to some extent fill the gap.

Unions have another tension-management function. They provide a channel of social mobility for holders of the "residual" jobs in the economy. A study of a representative sample of labor leaders in 1940 showed that six out of ten were sons of "working-class" men (Mills, 1948, p. 88). The labor role in production, as we have said before, is to a large extent a "dead-end" role. Yet there are of course many workers of great native ability, and some with considerable ambition. Labor unions, once established and accepted, provide opportunities for able and disgruntled men to express their resentment without disrupting the productive process too greatly; indeed, as we have noted, labor leaders, whatever their initial discontent may have been, are in a position to make an important integrative contribution to the economy.

As a channel of mobility, however, the union is attractive to relatively few, although these may be unusually important workers. Unions have a hard time getting their members to assume positions of responsibility (Chinoy, 1950, p. 159). Though less striking than the provision of opportunities for great careers, a more important tension-management function of unions is to provide a sense of dignity to the ordinary worker, the rank-

and-file member, whose job has little prestige and whose position in the union is not pre-eminent either. He nevertheless can derive self-esteem from his identification with a powerful organization.

The functions of unions do not consist in specific accomplishments only. By its very existence, the union symbolizes the worker's anxiety, and some union activity is "semi-ritualistic" (anxiety-allaying).[6] Some students of union-management relations emphasize the exaggerated extent of workers' anxiety and attribute it in part to poor communication between workers and managers. A study of the shoe industry in a small New England town contrasts the early days of the industry with the present. In the early days, the owners of the shoe plant were known personally to the men. They had all gone to local schools together. The owners lived in the local community, belonged to numerous local civic organizations, saw their men almost daily, took pride and responsibility in the prosperity of the community as a whole and in the welfare of their employees. Nowadays the owners live in New York, are never seen in the local community, and have no interest in it except as a source of profit; their hired managers are also outsiders and send their children away to school (Warner and Low, 1947).[7]

The way of life of managers and owners is now far removed from that of the workers. It is quite likely, therefore, that unions have arisen to negotiate between parties that were once intimate and are now estranged. We need not inquire whether the estrangement is important chiefly because it has made communication more difficult and therefore has created exaggerated anxiety, or because it has indeed caused owners and managers to neglect the welfare of workers unless they are forced to consider it. Both results have undoubtedly occurred, and both help to explain the rise of unions.

The High Level of Production

According to estimates made by the United Nations, the industrial output of the United States in 1937 was 34.41 per cent of world industrial output (see Woytinsky and Woytinsky, 1953, p. 1000). Since that time production has of course increased a good deal. Since World War I, moreover, the average working time has gone down from forty-eight hours a week to about forty or thirty-five (Robertson, 1955, p. 534). Purchasing power has steadily risen. Whereas in 1914 a pound of bread cost seventeen minutes of factory work, it cost the equivalent of six minutes' work in 1951.[8]

Among the reasons for our high level of production are the following:

1. Abundant natural resources.
2. A large, well-trained population.

---

[6] This point is made, for example, by Parsons and Smelser, 1956, p. 148.

[7] A similar development took place in the rubber industry in Akron, Ohio. See A. W. Jones, 1941. For a study of changes in the textile industry, see Ellsworth, 1952; neatly summarized by Graham, 1957, pp. 263-68.

[8] *Tide*, Dec. 12, 1952, p. 46; see the table reproduced in Graham, 1957, p. 237.

3. Use of mass-production techniques.

4. Universalistic standards. Imagine the level of efficiency that must have been obtained in Chinese business before the Communist revolution. An employer was expected to offer jobs to his relatives first. He was even expected to make jobs for them. Sometimes two employers, desirous of escaping, to some extent, the inefficiency inherent in such a system, agreed to employ each other's relatives (Lang, 1946, Chap. 16).

5. The high value placed on innovation.

> Nearly one-third of the employees of the General Electric Company are working on products not manufactured by the company in 1939. The Corning Glass Company received three-fourths of its income in 1955 from products it had developed since 1940. The DuPont Company estimates that half of its current sales are in products developed during the past twenty years . . . [Keezer, 1957, p. 25; see also Robertson, 1955, pp. 475ff., 484ff.].

6. The competitive system of private enterprise. To some extent, competition and the famous "lure of profits" undoubtedly merit the praise of American ideologists. (This does not mean, of course, that the motives that would operate in a socialist economy might not be equally or more effective.)

7. Government regulation. To say that our prosperity depends on government regulation is not inconsistent with recognizing the creative role of private enterprise. The word "regulation" is here used in a broad sense, for government not only makes the "rules of the game" but also plays a leading part.

Some "Defects" of Our Economy

For several reasons, functional assessment of any system of economic arrangements is difficult First, it requires a large amount of factual knowledge about social processes and their results. Secondly, the arrangements for allocating scarce resources affect not only the kinds, amounts, and efficiency of production in a narrow sense but also other interests and values—e.g., consumer choice, education, medical care, leisure, political freedom, and national security. Thirdly, all social institutions benefit different segments of the population in different ways and degrees. And finally, institutional patterns are always valued, to some extent, for their own sake. For example, many people extol socialism for *moral* reasons, to some extent regardless of its relative "efficiency" or "inefficiency." For other people capitalism is something like an absolute value.

Nevertheless, if we regard any system as in effect a "choice" from among alternatives, and if we recognize that any choice involves certain "costs"—at least renunciation of the merits of the alternatives not "chosen" —then we can acknowledge that our system does have some dysfunctional aspects. Among them we might include the following:

1. *Great economic fluctuations.* Whatever their opinions about socialism in other respects, most economists would probably agree that socialist economies can avert inflation. deflation, and unemployment more easily than capitalism can. The control of depression is somewhat easier under capitalism than the control of inflation is (Galbraith, 1956, Chaps. 13, 14). During a period of full employment, prices tend to be driven up by an excess of demand over supply. Labor unions demand higher wages, and management then raises prices, usually by more than enough to cover the higher cost of labor. The boom encourages unsound speculation, which eventually must result in recession. The chief measures theoretically available to government for combating inflation are difficult to apply. Two such measures are reduction in government spending and increase in taxes. Because these measures inevitably produce some unemployment, they are politically unpopular even in peacetime. In time of war or threat of war, the government cannot reduce expenditures very much and cannot afford to have idle workers. A third way of combating inflation—government control of wages and prices—is sure to work if vigorously applied, but, since it is a big departure from the system of free markets, it is politically hard to adopt.

2. *A tendency to neglect "social revenues" and ignore "social costs."* "Social revenues are greater than private revenues whenever there are benefits accruing to third parties who make no payment for them" (Weiler, 1952, p. 717). Health care and education, for example, benefit not only those who pay for them but, to some extent, the whole society. On the other hand, "Social costs and private costs are different . . . whenever there are losses suffered by third persons or by the general public as a result of the private economic activity" (Weiler, 1952, pp. 717-18). The list of "social costs" under capitalism is long: loss of life and injury to health through failure to provide safety measures in industry, air and water pollution, soil erosion, deforestation, "unnecessary" duplication of services, waste due to "unnecessary" advertising, inefficiency in scientific research and technology due to duplication of effort and commercial secrecy (see Kapp, 1950). It is true that a wealthy society such as ours can afford waste much better than a poor one can, and that our neglect of social costs is in part a measure of our affluence (see Galbraith, 1956, Chaps. 9-11). But a rich island of inefficiency is increasingly hard to defend in an ocean of need. It is true that tax exemption for socially valuable activities, and high taxes on activities with high social costs, can to some extent mitigate the "evils" of the system. Government support of health and education, however, is considerably hampered in our system by the need to stabilize the economy as a whole. For example, in a time of rising prices government expenditure for schools, on top of defense spending, tends to make inflation worse; and in time of recession, local governments tend (wisely or not) to cut expenditure. Perhaps the main point, however, is that a system of private enterprise

tends almost inevitably to stress private benefits and to ignore social costs. A crude but common version of the "official" ideology states that competition automatically results in the most "efficient" allocation of resources.

The economist J. K. Galbraith has recently stated very forcefully and persuasively the same point we have just made. He thinks that one ot the chief faults of American society is the "social imbalance" between privately produced goods and services and publicly produced goods and services (1958, esp. Chaps. 18, 19).

> In the years following World War II, the papers of any major city—those of New York were an excellent example—told daily of the shortages and shortcomings in the elementary municipal and metropolitan services. The schools were old and overcrowded. The police force was under strength and underpaid. The parks and playgrounds were insufficient. Streets and empty lots were filthy, and the sanitation staff was under-equipped and in need of men. Access to the city by those who work there was uncertain and painful and becoming more so. Internal transportation was overcrowded, unhealthful, and dirty. So was the air. Parking on the streets had to be prohibited, and there was no space elsewhere [p. 252]

The contrast between a modern supermarket and the services Galbraith mentions is striking. A conservative economist might answer that in an economy with "consumer sovereignty" (or, he might say, in a democratic society) the "voters" by their purchases decide what they want. They prefer beautifully packaged soap chips and "TV dinners" to public safety and adequate schools. To this hoary argument Galbraith replies that the consumers have no effective choice. By what he calls "the dependence effect," they do not buy what they want so much as what a multimillion-dollar advertising industry persuades them to want. As a result they go on stuffing themselves and paying for "slenderizing" while they grumble about the taxes that pay for schools. They think it a great investment for the future to pour millions into research on synthetic fibres, but, for lack of the same kind of advertising, they begrudge a few dollars as an investment in human beings. Perhaps Galbraith has a point.

3. *The bad effects of oligopoly*. Price competition in oligopolistic industries has almost become a thing of the past (Galbraith, 1956, Chap. 4). The "forces" working against imperfect competition, though considerable, are not enough to prevent it. What are these forces?

First we must mention competition *between* industries.

> Before World War II the Aluminum Company of America was the classroom example of monopoly in a nationwide market. Since World War II this industry has been the best example of an oligopoly, with only three major firms and a newcomer from the copper industry.
>
> It is possible to speak of a demand for "primary aluminum," but primary aluminum includes some 106 wrought and casting alloys in many different shapes of innumerable lengths and thicknesses. In comparing the demand for these alloys with that for the other metals we must first specify

> uses. To be specific about the competition of aluminum with other metals in categories of uses, let us consider first the category of electrical cable and conductors. It is well known that aluminum and copper compete in this use, but it is not enough to remark the fact and pass on. The essence of the competition is in the "bundle of properties" of the two metals, the two bundles having marked likenesses and differences. Both copper and aluminum have high electrical conductivity, but the specific gravity of aluminum is slightly less than one-third that of copper so that the mass conductivity of aluminum is twice that of copper. Thus, a steel-reinforced aluminum cable, both stronger and lighter than an electrically equivalent copper cable, can be used in longer spans with fewer supporting structures. . . . Given aluminum and copper prices prevalent in the last few years, copper has lost or is losing the high-voltage transmission line business. At the other extreme, copper with its higher electrical conductivity still has a decided advantage over aluminum where wire of fine sizes is used and the space factor is important. Between the two extremes there is a vigorous, persistent competition on a pure cost basis, where costs included are those of product design, investment in tools and dies, etc. Large motor windings, power and feeder cable, and bus [a kind of electrical conductor] in central power stations are today alternatively made from either material. In this use four firms in the copper industry and their copper and brass fabricating subsidiaries are direct rivals of the three aluminum companies [Robertson, 1955, p. 494].

For other uses, aluminum competes with many other products: zinc, brass, magnesium, iron, steel, lead, plastics, wood, rubber, Fiberglas, brick, and stone. Between industries, therefore, there is plenty of competition, although there is practically none within the aluminum industry itself.

Recently much attention has been given to a second factor mitigating the "evil" effects of oligopoly. There is a tendency for "countervailing power" to arise whenever any economic group gains "monopoly" power (Galbraith, 1956, Chaps. 9-11). For example, powerful corporations are to some extent counterbalanced by powerful labor unions. Large producers are counterbalanced by large distributors; Sears, Roebuck and Co. and the A & P can force manufacturers to sell at lower prices, and in turn these distributors pass on the savings, to some extent, to consumers. Countervailing power, however, has its limitations. For example, in the struggle between management and the countervailing power of labor unions the general public may be the "victim."

Big-business ideologists, typified in *Fortune* Magazine, stress that the potentially harmful effects of "monopoly" power are not realized to any great extent because business leaders are increasingly imbued with a sense of professional responsibility toward the public as a whole (see, e.g., Maurer, 1955, esp. Chap. 10; Allen, 1952). It is freely admitted that prices are not competitive, but the argument runs that competitive prices would be ruinous and that oligopolistic prices are set, not for maximum profits, but in the interest of long-run company stability, high employment, and high, widely diffused purchasing power. There is little doubt that there is some truth in these propositions. To some extent, however, this new ideology is an exaggeration of the actual motives of business leaders; there are many degrees of "enlightenment." [9]

We must remember, of course, that the evils of oligopoly, such as they are, are associated to some extent with the benefits of large size. Big companies, for example, finance the development of new methods and new products; the most competitive industries are also the most "backward." Our business corporations, moreover, trying to forestall more government intervention, have become our greatest philanthropists, supporting education, medical research, community improvement, and many other worthwhile projects (see Prentis, 1957; Zurcher, 1957). Finally, the very control of economic change made possible by oligopoly to some extent smooths out the disturbing effects of competition: e.g., failure of business firms, with attendant unemployment.

Nevertheless, oligopoly does have negative aspects (Galbraith, 1956, pp. 44-47, 103-04). To some extent, "monopoly" power is used to keep production down and prices up. The "administered prices" of big business protect small, inefficient companies as well as the more efficient. To the extent that monopoly keeps employment "artificially" low in the affected industry, it keeps workers in, or drives them to, the competitive, already distressed industries, such as agriculture. Finally, monopoly tends to create some "maldistribution" of wealth. The distribution of income is steadily evening out, but there remain pockets of poverty in the midst of affluence (see Galbraith, 1956; Grampp, 1951; Weiler, 1952, pp. 790-801; Dewhurst *et al.,* 1955, pp. 88-95). We have a housing problem and a problem of medical need.

4. *Hostility to planning.* Perhaps the "defect" of capitalism that is broadest in scope is a tendency to underestimate the advantages of planning. Not planning for the individual company—there is no hostility to that. What is underestimated is the value of over-all planning for the whole economy. Many of the "defects" already mentioned are perhaps reducible to this. It is doubtful whether existing links between corporations, combined with the most dedicated professional management, could be enough to prevent a tremendous amount of inefficiency. Even the federal government, acting presumably in the interest of the whole society, is severely hampered. As one indication among many that might be mentioned, take the following characterization of the transportation industry, a characterization by a "conservative" economist:

> The logical inconsistencies of many of the developments just recounted are readily apparent. There must be something the matter with a transportation system in which all the major agencies except the railroads and pipelines are subsidized by the government. Furthermore, it is illogical to pour public funds into all forms of transportation facilities without attempting to coordinate expenditures by some accepted principle [Robertson, 1955, p. 435].

[9] See, for example, the report of a conference of business leaders in *Life* Magazine, June 24, 1957, pp. 161-62.

The Capacity of Our Mixed Economy to Improve

The very definition of "capitalism" is not agreed upon (see Schumpeter 1957). Students are agreed, however, that fairly rapid change is inherent in our economic system. Although "basically" a private-enterprise system, it has already been modified so much by the expansion of governmental services that many economists call it a "mixed" economy.

Most of the changes have improved the functioning of the system. When the federal income tax was first proposed, a lawyer addressing the Supreme Court said that such a tax is "socialistic." and the Court declared it unconstitutional; but Congress passed the Sixteenth Amendment to the Constitution (Curtis, 1947, pp. 41-42). The American Bankers Association condemned the Federal Reserve System as "socialistic," but that System is now operating smoothly. Along with the Securities and Exchange Commission, it is now one of the interdependent structures that together make unlikely a speculative boom such as the one that preceded the stockmarket crash of 1929; these structures would also operate to forestall a great depression if a crash did occur (Galbraith, 1954, Chap. 11).[10] The Federal Deposit Insurance Corporation protects banks, and therefore individual depositors, against failure; no insured bank has failed since 1944, although it had previously not been uncommon, even in years of prosperity, for 600 banks to fail. Leaving the field of change by legislation, we can mention "the big change" from the owner-managers of the past, one of whom expressed a common attitude in the words "The public be damned!" to the professional managers of today, whose ownership is almost negligible (see Allen, 1952; Parsons and Smelser, 1956, pp. 249ff.).

Many functionally desirable changes are still possible in our system without anything resembling a violent revolution. Economists have shown that the antitrust policy of the federal government could be modified to advantage. The tax structure could and will be gradually changed. More social-welfare legislation is "inevitable." It is even possible that in time such lack of coordination as exists in the transportation industry will be corrected.

RECOMMENDED READING

For a learned, provocative book on the topics indicated in the title, see J. A. Schumpeter, *Capitalism, Socialism, and Democracy*, 2nd ed., Harper, 1947. A succinct statement of Schumpeter's views on the history, dynamics, and prospects of capitalism is given in his article "Capitalism," *Encyclopaedia Britannica*, 1957 printing, v. 4 pp. 801-07. For a less controversial presentation of much descriptive material as well as theoretical analysis, see the excellent textbook by P. A. Samuel-

[10] On the remarkable changes in the American banking system, see Robertson, 1955, pp. 440-61.

son, *Economics: An Introductory Analysis,* McGraw-Hill; the present writer used the 2nd ed., 1951, but the later editions are no doubt even better. A compact, highly readable, but somewhat more controversial discussion of important aspects of our economy as a whole is given in J. K. Galbraith, *American Capitalism: The Concept of Countervailing Power,* rev. ed., Houghton Mifflin, 1956. Galbraith adds to his analysis in his equally readable and equally controversial *The Affluent Society,* Houghton Mifflin, 1958.

For a rather detailed and critical history, see R. M. Robertson, *History of the American Economy,* Harcourt, Brace, 1955, esp. Part 4: "1921 to the Present." The author is financial economist for the Federal Reserve Bank of St. Louis. In *The Big Change: America Transforms Itself, 1900-1950,* Harper, 1952, F. L. Allen gives a vivid factual account of the change in living standards and the change from the relatively irresponsible owner-managers of an earlier period to the relatively professional salaried managers of today. For a good implicit contrast between the "universalism" of the American economy and a particularistic system, see O. Lang, *Chinese Family and Society,* Yale University Press, 1946, Chap. 16: "Nepotism."

For factual, well-balanced discussions of labor unions, see H. A. Millis and R. E. Montgomery, *Organized Labor,* v. 3 of their work *The Economics of Labor,* McGraw-Hill, 1945, Chap. 8: "The Union in Industry: The Theory of Collective Bargaining"; and W. E. Moore, *Industrial Relations and the Social Order,* rev. ed., Macmillan, 1951, esp. pp. 311-17, "Aims and Functions of Unions," and pp. 401-07, on the scope of collective bargaining.

K. W. Kapp, *The Social Costs of Private Enterprise,* Harvard University Press, 1950, is the most extensive factual survey of its subject. A shorter, well-balanced treatment covering the same subject in part is given in E. T. Weiler, *The Economic System: An Analysis of the Flow of Economic Life,* Macmillan, 1952, Part V: "Political Economy." The same problems are put in a wider perspective in Galbraith, 1958, esp. Chaps. 9-11, 18-19. We urge the student to read Galbraith, then either Kapp or Weiler.

Three primarily statistical works deserve special mention. The broadest in scope is W. S. Woytinsky and E. S. Woytinsky, *World Population and Production: Trends and Outlook,* Twentieth Century Fund, 1953, an enormous compendium of facts, with considerable analysis. For the United States in particular, see J. F. Dewhurst and Associates, *America's Needs and Resources: A New Survey,* Twentieth Century Fund, 1955, which contains 352 tables and a good discussion and projects needs and resources for the near future. Finally, for authoritative and detailed statistics, see the annual volumes of Bureau of the Census, *Statistical Abstract of the United States,* Washington, D.C., Government Printing Office, which also give many references to other publications.

part five

THE POLITY

12. Formal Organizations

Large-scale formal organizations, often called "bureaucracies," are prominent in economic, political, and religious activities, among others. A large business corporation, for example, is a "bureaucracy." The so-called executive branch of the United States government is also "bureaucratic."

"Organization" refers to an aspect of interaction systems: namely, their structure insofar as this may be regarded as having a bearing on the attainment of system goals. Every interaction system has some goal or goals that require the coordination of the participants' activities to some extent. In all cases, this coordination implies specialization and some mode or modes of communication; in most cases, it requires some differentiation of participants according to power, although of course this need not be "authority" in the sense of the recognized *right* to command.[1]

Note that organization is an *aspect* of interaction systems. Every interaction system has this aspect, but it has other aspects as well. For example, although the members of a modern urban family sometimes cooperate for the attainment of goals, as in washing dishes or getting ready for a trip, the organization aspect of most urban families is not prominent: for the most part, we tend to think of a family, not as an organization, but as a social system valuable to its members regardless of their joint accomplishments or "products." Nevertheless, even a family does have goals, of which at least one—the socialization of children—is at the same time an important function for society. If the goal-directedness of a group's activities is the basic reason for its existence, we are likely to call the group "an organization"—thus naming the "concrete" interaction system after its most important aspect.

Most organizations are to a large extent *formal*—that is, many norms of interaction in them are issued and enforced by persons in specially designated roles. Prominent examples of formal organizations are armies, government bureaus, political parties, business corporations, schools, universi-

[1] For a more or less systematic treatment of these aspects of *formal* organization, see Barnard, 1938; Simon, 1945.

ties, hospitals, and libraries. As we shall see, not only is the organization aspect of such groups an abstraction from the total action system, but the formality of organization is also an abstraction, for every formal organization also develops informal relations among its participants.

Organization Goals and Individual Motives

Some writers deny that there is any such thing as an organization goal (purpose, objective). Goals, they say, are always individuals' goals, and to speak of organization goals smacks of an untenable "group mind" theory. It is true that the participants in an organization have a variety of personal goals; it is also true that their conceptions of the *group* goals may not be exactly alike (for the communication system is never perfect, and no group, perhaps, is perfectly integrated). Yet the concept of organization is meaningless unless there is a significant amount of agreement about the *common* objectives of cooperation. "Organization," as we have seen, implies some coordination of activities, and "coordination" implies orientation to common goals, specialization of contributions to the common effort, and some form of command or leadership. To the extent that individuals have a place in a "table of organization" and are geared into a *plan* of the organization's activities, the organization may be said to have goals. It is not by chance that the varied activities, variously motivated, of perhaps thousands of managers and workers in a shoe factory, let us say, end up by producing shoes. One of the advantages of specialization-and-coordination, indeed, is that it is not necessary for all participants in the plan of cooperation to have an exact idea of the common goal. For example, it is seldom possible and never necessary for an army private to have an exact conception of the grand strategy of a campaign. *His* conception of the complex goal may be simply "winning" something—a hill, a battle, "victory." In the heat of battle, his personal goal of survival may override even this simple conception, may drive it from his mind. Yet the army does have a grand strategy with goals, and the average private does contribute to goal attainment, provided that the strategy is successful. We must remember, of course, that attainment of group goals is almost always a matter of degree.

INDUCEMENTS TO PARTICIPATE OR CONTRIBUTE

Although organization goals should be distinguished from individual motives, the latter are of great importance to the functioning of an organization. In general, the members of an organization must be induced, coerced, or forced to participate in it. Many of the motives for participating in an organization are similar to the motives for economic activity (Chap. 9). Among them are desire for remuneration in money or in kind, the prestige derived from membership in the organization, the desire to exercise acquired skills, the attraction of good working conditions, the maintenance of social connections incidental to membership, and concern for the goals of the organization. If participation is not strictly voluntary, as often in armies, then an important motive is the desire to avoid negative sanctions, including social disapproval and loss of social prestige.

The motives for participating in an organization are closely related to the factors that make for strong (or weak) identification with the organization. We may, however, distinguish between the motives for joining the organization and the motives for staying in it.

As for the factors that make for strong (or weak) identification with an organization, there is evidence that the following are important (March and Simon, 1958, pp. 65-75):

> The greater the number of individual needs satisfied in the organization, the stronger the identification with it.
>
> The greater the extent to which organization goals are perceived as shared, the stronger the identification.
>
> The greater the perceived prestige of the organization, the stronger the identification.
>
> The greater the frequency of interaction in the organization, the stronger the identification.
>
> The less the competition within the organization, the stronger the identification.

Each of these major factors in turn is capable of further analysis; for example, we might ask what factors determine the perceived prestige of the organization. Moreover, there is a reciprocal relationship between any one of the major factors and the strength of identification with the organization. For example, if the individual perceives the prestige of the organization as high, his identification with it will be strong; but the stronger his identification, the greater will be his tendency to perceive the prestige of the organization as high. The chairmen of 157 departments in nine universities were asked to rate their departments in comparison with the corresponding departments in other universities: "Among the first five" in the field, "Better than average," "Average," or "Poorer than average." The chairmen of eighty of the 157 departments rated their own department "Among the first five" (Caplow and McGee, 1958, p. 104).

In keeping with the tendency to overestimate the prestige of an organization with which one identifies oneself is the tendency to "overestimate" the importance of organization goals. Up to a point, this tendency is functional. For example, if the head of a fire department thinks that preventing losses from fire is a very important goal, then he is likely to devote himself to the task. Fortunately, he is not expected to consider the relative importance of that goal and others, such as improving schools; if he were, he would tend, as the fire chief, to regard fire-fighting as more important than it perhaps is. For this reason, it is desirable that the task of weighing the relative importance of heterogeneous goals should be given to a higher body, such as the city council.

As a result of his tendency to "exaggerate" the importance of fire-fighting, however, the fire chief is likely to complain that the city council is stingy about providing him with the "necessary" facilities. If such feelings become excessive (so that they lower the morale of subordinate organizations), then we might say that the tendency toward strong identification with one's own (subordinate) organization is to that extent dysfunctional. At any rate, this tendency does pose a problem for higher executives and policy-making bodies. The common focus of the dissatisfaction with which they must cope is the budget (Simon, 1945, Chap. 10).

The success of an organization depends upon the cooperation of many people in addition to its members. Other individuals, and also other organizations, must therefore be induced to make the necessary "contributions" Among important contributors other than members are suppliers of money and materials and "clients" of the organization—e.g., customers of a firm. Patients of a hospital, students of a university, and the people served by libraries may usefully be regarded as members as well as clients of the respective organizations. Mindful of the great importance to a business firm of its customers, some writers treat them as members of the firm. Here, however, we regard as members only those persons who to some extent share in, or are subject to, organizational authority. We must recognize that members of various categories participate unequally in the organization. For example, the ordinary stockholders of a business firm participate far less than do its salaried managers, although the "contributions" of stockholders are of course important.

A future science of formal organization will certainly take into account systematically the varying possible relations between an organization and its "clients." A small neighborhood store often depends upon its customers' loyalty in a way that a large department store does not. Since the turnover of customers is likely to be small in a small area, any loss of regular customers is likely to be a net loss. Customer loyalty, however, tends to stabilize the clientele of all organizations of the same class, whether small or large, local or more extended. This kind of particularistic tie is said to be common in France. Large American business organizations seek to establish "permanent" ties with their customers, but on a more universalistic basis. One device is to issue credit cards. Another device, used especially by manufacturers of durable goods, is to establish servicing agencies for the repair and replacement of parts (see Parsons and Smelser, 1956, pp. 157-60) But these ties are not nearly so close as that between a school and its "clients." The nature of a school's "production" is such that the clients must be bound into the organization itself for a period of time. The "product" is a transformation, more or less great, of the client's personality. The functional requirements of a school are therefore rather different from those of a manufacturing concern (see Parsons, 1958).[2]

---

[2] Among the important ranges of variation that a typology of formal organizations would have to take into account are the kind of product, in terms of its functional significance to society; relation to clients (several ranges of variation, not just one);

An organization may be said to have attained "equilibrium" when the various kinds of inducement are adequate to maintain the continued contributions of all necessary categories of participants—members and others. Equilibrium, in this sense, may be achieved at various levels, and the state of equilibrium may change over time. In particular, the scope of an organization's activities may remain roughly constant or may grow or diminish and settle for a time at another level. Relatively few organizations survive for generations.

> In our western civilization only one formal organization, the Roman Catholic Church, claims a substantial age. A few universities, a very few national governments or formally organized nations, are more than two hundred years old. Many municipalities are somewhat older, but few other corporate organizations have existed more than one hundred years [Barnard, 1938, p. 5].

> Even during the postwar boom of 1945-48 almost 30 per cent of the businesses in the United States were discontinued, while in the same period every year with the exception of 1948 [there opened] new businesses equal to about twice the number . . . closed [Lipset and Bendix, 1952, p. 500]

Most of these businesses were very small (three employees or fewer).

CHANGES IN ORGANIZATION GOALS

Not only organization size but organization goals as well change over time. This is true even though the organization remains a "school" or a "hospital," for in societies in which formal organizations are numerous the *specific* goals of "education" and "medical care" change with changes in knowledge, in age and sex composition of the population, and in patterns of economic activity in the social environment of the organization. The survival of organizations depends in part on their having enough flexibility to adapt their goals to changes in the environment. "Adaptation," strictly speaking, is thus a two-way process as far as social systems are concerned: a social system must adapt the environment to its goals and must adapt its goals to the environment. Now that polio has largely come under control, owing to the successful development of the Salk vaccine, the National Foundation for Infantile Paralysis would have to go out of existence if its managers were not willing to shift its goals to some extent (Sills, 1957, Chap. 9). Many organizations go out of existence once their goals have been achieved, or when circumstances change radically. After World War II the

---

the social sources of personnel and the kinds of inducement to participate; the sources of financial support; the degrees of possible decentralization; the possible tests of efficiency. The article by Parsons ("Some Ingredients of a General Theory of Formal Organization") touches upon some of these topics in the framework of a discussion of variation with respect to the nature of subsystem problems (goal attainment, adaptation, pattern maintenance and tension management, and integration) and three levels of organization (technical, managerial, and "institutional"). The "institutional" level is so named because any particular organization—say, a college—is geared into the wider society through its being subject to society-wide institutions ranging in formality from custom to formal state law.

American Red Cross, which during the war had built up a large organization, was faced with an organizational crisis. The Red Cross proved to be flexible, for it turned its organizational resources to the nationwide blood-donor program. At an earlier time the Young Men's Christian Association (Y.M.C.A.) had adjusted to the secularization of society without abandoning its original goal altogether. Founded for the spiritual guidance of young men, the Y.M.C.A. shifted to a program of sports and other wholesome recreation. There are good reasons to believe that the National Foundation for Infantile Paralysis will also make a successful transition to new activities. As Sills shows, it has a record of innovation (despite its focus on infantile paralysis); it has a large and unusually enthusiastic group of volunteer workers; its chief fund-raising activity, the annual March of Dimes, is capable of being used for other goals that could inspire enthusiasm; and its present goals are obviously members of a close family of possible goals.

> It has supported fundamental research in virology—to such an extent that William L. Laurence, Science Editor of the New York *Times*, has recently suggested that "its next goal should be to develop, with March of Dimes funds, an all-embracing multiple vaccine against all viruses attacking the nervous system" [Sills, 1957, p. 270].

Presumably business firms are more flexible with respect to subsidiary goals than are organizations of other types. The reason is that a business firm in a largely free-enterprise economy is oriented toward making a profit, and businessmen, although by no means indifferent to the kind of product or service they provide to the community, are probably less interested in this than are educators or hospital administrators. It is quite possible that even in business, however, some participants identify with an organization more or less regardless of what it produces, while others can maintain their identification only so long as the organization continues to produce a certain kind of good or service.

It would be sociologically inconvenient to treat profit-making as the only organization goal of business firms, for the analysis of organization must take into account the "product" of the organization, a product that may of course be intangible. Moreover, the functional significance of business firms to society must be assessed not in terms of their profits but in terms of the goods and services they provide and in terms of the effects they have on their members (Barnard, 1938; Parsons, 1956).

Nevertheless, profit is of course of tremendous concern to business organizations. As we shall see, in considering the effectiveness of organizations one must have some indicator or index of effectiveness (i.e., of degree of success in attaining goals).[3] One of the difficulties in the objective study

---

[3] Paul F. Lazarsfeld and Morris Rosenberg (1955, p. 166) have made a useful distinction between indicator" and "index" ("we use the word 'indicator' when we refer to one specific observation, we use the word 'index' when we are confronted with a combination of several indicators into one measurement"), but in doing so they have left us with no good general term; therefore, the distinction is sometimes ignored here.

of nonbusiness organizations such as government bureaus, hospitals, and universities is that there are few ready-made indicators of effectiveness, such as profit for a business firm. Profit cannot be taken as an indicator of effectiveness; the best examples of such organizations do not support themselves mainly by the sale of products or services; moreover, they could not so well perform their functions for society if they did. On the other hand, one of the difficulties in the objective study of business organizations is the fact that profit is likely to be viewed as the *only* indicator of success, and "social costs" are ignored (see Chap. 11). A government bureau cannot ignore the "social costs" of its operation. For example, the federal government is expecte to take into account the effects of its operations on the general state of the economy—e.g., effects on employment and price levels.

The main point of the foregoing is not that profit *should* be taken as the indicator of the degree of effectiveness of business firms but that profit *can be* and conventionally *is* so regarded. High salaries and bonuses of business executives are often regarded as a result of stiff competition for rare talent, but this view is probably not altogether sound. High salaries for business executives are also regarded as *symbolically appropriate* since a high rate of profit is the main recognized measure of the success of business firms. Needless to say, an important reason for the high salaries and other financial rewards of business executives is that corporations have high profits and executives are in a position to assure themselves high remuneration. At the same time, executives in nonbusiness organizations are "paid" (in part) in the satisfaction they are supposed to feel as a result of making a rather direct contribution to the welfare of the community (Parsons, 1958).

The foregoing paragraphs perhaps justify the tentative conclusion that business firms are more flexible with respect to organization goals than are nonbusiness firms, because opportunism in the interest of organization survival is more approved in business. We can probably conclude, further, that in all types of organization there are probably two kinds of participant, those who identify with the organization more or less regardless of its goals, and those whose identification would be weakened if organization goals were to change very much.

EFFICIENCY

Formal organizations are usually planned to some extent as a means for attaining certain objectives. Whether the objectives are *worth* attaining is ultimately not a question of rationality. Once values and objectives have been decided upon, we can always ask to what extent the means used to attain them are effective and efficient.

Effectiveness is a question of the extent to which the organization's activities attain specific goals. *Efficiency* is more complex. The most rigorous (but unattainable) measure of efficiency would involve taking into account *all* the effects, "good" and "bad," of organizational activity, and all the effects of all possible alternative expenditures of the same energy, time, and money. Obviously such a measure would require a system of weighting heterogeneous effects—e.g., workers' productivity and impairment of workers' health. Considering these difficult matters, "the criterion of efficiency dictates that choice of alternatives which produces the largest result for the given application of resources" (Simon, 1945, p. 179). Given the tremendous difficulties of measuring efficiency in this comprehensive sense, we cannot be surprised to learn that organization policy-makers seldom seek optimal solutions.

> The fact of the matter is that momentous decisions are made every day as to the allocation of resources to one or another competing purpose, and that, particularly in noncommercial organizations, the decisions are made in almost complete absence of the evidence which would be necessary to validate them. The principal reason for this, of course, is the difficulty, except in enterprises that have a relatively tangible product, of determining the actual production functions.
>
> To recognize how far actual decisions fall short of rationality is no criticism of the administrator, who must act whether or not he possesses the information that would be necessary for the complete rationality of his decisions. It is, however, a criticism of apologies that would make his ignorance a virtue, and would question the need for extensive programs of research in this direction [Simon, 1945, pp. 189-90; see also March and Simon, 1958, pp. 140-41 *et passim*].

Nevertheless, many—or perhaps most—formal organizations do use various indicators and indices of their efficiency, and few problems are worth more careful attention than the devising of such indicators for continuing organizations. Even organizations with nonempirical goals make use of indicators of efficiency. The basic goal of the Roman Catholic Church —the salvation of souls—is of course not capable of being measured or counted or observed empirically. Yet the Church no doubt makes use of many indicators of the efficiency of its parishes. For example, keeping in mind such statistics as size of the Catholic and non-Catholic population of a particular parish, average income and wealth of the Catholic population, and facilities and official personnel of the parish, a bishop could interpret, as indicators of its efficiency average attendance at regular Mass, frequency of confession, financial contributions of parishioners, the proportion of Church vs. secular marriages involving Catholics, the rate of conversions, and many other observations and statistics.

According to one view, "organizational effectiveness" has three components:

> . . . (1) organizational productivity; (2) organizational flexibility in the form of successful adjustment to internal organizational changes and successful adaptation to externally induced change; and (3) absence of intraorganizational strain, or tension, and of conflict between organizational subgroups [Georgopoulos and Tannenbaum, 1957, p. 536]

These investigators devised a composite index of organizational effectiveness and rated thirty-two "stations," identically organized subdivisions, of a company that specializes in delivering retail merchandise for department stores; they then compared the index ratings with independent ratings of the same thirty-two stations by high company officials who were familiar with the stations but who were not personally involved in any one of them.

Station productivity was measured with the help of company records. The indicator of intraorganizational strain was the "average" answer that nonsupervisory station personnel gave to the question: "On the whole, would you say that in your station there is any tension or conflict between employees and supervisors?" There were five possible answers to choose from, and they were given a value of 1 to 5; the average value of the workers' choices was the indicator of intraorganizational strain for the station being asked about. Organizational flexibility was measured similarly with the help of two questions: "From time to time changes in methods, equipment, procedures, practices, and layout are introduced by the management. In general, do you think these changes lead to better ways of doing things?" and "In general, how well do you think your station handles sharp changes in volume during peak periods?"

The correlation between the index ratings of "station" effectiveness and the independent ratings of experts was .77, which of course is very high. Georgopoulos and Tannenbaum also made sure that each component of the index contributed something to the total predictive or rating power of the index. They point out that their task of devising a satisfactory index was made easier by the fact that they did not have to consider the quality of station productivity but could confine themselves to quantity. Their work was also made easier by the fact that the company chosen for study was simple in other respects as well. The absence of strain or tension is not necessarily a good indicator of effectiveness for all organizations, since the clash of opposing views and interests up to a point contributes to keeping an organization alert and flexible and to preventing the subterranean growth of potentially more disruptive conflict (see L. A. Coser, 1957). The work of Georgopoulos and Tannenbaum helps to direct attention to the important task of finding objective indices of effectiveness and efficiency. Eventually, of course, we shall have indices that do much better than correlate highly with "expert opinion," which, as Simon reminds us in the passage quoted earlier, leaves much to be desired. It is a question, of course, whether any simple index can be devised that will serve equally well for organizations of all types.

One of the reasons that formal organizations are rational is that they are deliberately planned to be so. Rules are devised, communication systems are set up, and personnel are trained, all in the interest of attaining certain goals with as little cost (undesirable expenses and side-effects) as possible. Nevertheless, we cannot assume without specific inquiry that carefully laid plans have the effects intended and no others. Indeed, there are always hidden costs and probably hidden benefits. A state employment agency provides us with a good example. Before statistical records of performance were instituted, the officials of the agency were likely to discriminate against nonwhites in making placements, but when the system of keeping performance records came into operation the officials were too busy to discriminate: they were eager to place as many unemployed people as they could. The policy-makers of the employment agency regarded nondiscrimination of whites and Negroes as a basic rule of the agency, but when they instituted the system of keeping performance statistics they had no idea that their new system would affect the treatment of Negroes. Nondiscrimination was a latent function of the system of keeping performance records (Blau, 1955, Chap. 5).

Any structural feature of an organization has multiple consequences for efficiency, some of them functional, some dysfunctional. Consequently, any change in organization also has multiple consequences. Since the change is a new feature, the probability is greater that some of its consequences will be unanticipated and may go for a time unnoticed. In the state employment agency referred to above, the introduction of statistical records as a basis for measuring the performance of individual officials had the unanticipated function of reducing discrimination against nonwhite clients. But this was not the only effect of the structural change. Another effect was to reduce the tension between officials and their supervisors. Before the statistical records were kept, officials had been reluctant to consult their superiors for fear of giving the impression of incompetence, and when supervisors commented on the work of subordinates, their comments were likely to be perceived as criticism. After the statistical records were introduced, the relations between supervisor and subordinate became more relaxed, for now the supervisor was making judgments about competence on the basis of objective records, not on the basis of impressions. The subordinates had less reason to fear approaching the supervisor for help, and if the latter approached his subordinates his comments were perceived as helpful advice that might lead to a better performance record. This of course was another (latent) function of the performance records, for now there was better cooperation.

The new records also had a dysfunction, however. Now that individual performance was objectively measured, officials of the same rank tended to feel more competitive toward one another, and in some ways this new feeling reduced the efficiency of operations. In particular, the officials in the "regular" sections became uncooperative toward the officials in a special section for placing physically handicapped persons. The officials who interviewed handicapped applicants had to rely on the "regular" interviewers for knowledge of job openings. Now that the pressure was on for the "regular" interviewers to make as many placements as they could, these interviewers tended to withhold information from the special interviewers.

This dysfunctional effect was in turn counteracted by a new adjustment. With the sanction of supervisors, the two types of interviewer made an exchange of services. The special interviewers, who were already used to longer, more difficult interviews, agreed to take over the excitable, less cooperative clients ordinarily handled by the regular interviewers, and the latter in return were more cooperative about helping to find jobs for the physically handicapped. This particular sequence of changes and effects illustrates a process that presumably goes on in all formal organizations: a structural change solves one or more problems but gives rise to some other problem or problems; these in turn give rise to new structural changes; and so on (Blau, 1955, pp. 40, 44-46; see also Blau, 1957).[4]

Some Characteristics of Formal Organization

Modern sociological analysis of formal organizations began with the work of Max Weber.[5] His propositions about the characteristics of "bureaucracy" are largely based on historical data, some of which he presents, but at the same time he sought to describe a so-called pure type of bureaucracy, the characteristics of which, he asserted, are functionally connected with the rationality or efficiency of organization. That is to say, his "pure" type of bureaucracy seems to be a complex hypothesis or set of hypotheses concerning the institutional characteristics of the most efficient possible kind of organization. No critic has rejected the bulk of Weber's propositions, especially as they apply to government bureaus, but several critics have questioned particular points, some of them important.[6] Broadly speaking, these criticisms maintain —successfully—(1) that Weber failed to distinguish significantly different types and subtypes of highly rationalized bureaucracy, (2) that even those of his hypotheses that are most plausible for particular types and within particular social environments of bureaucracy need much more empirical verification and specification before they can be accepted as scientifically established, and (3) that Weber tended to neglect the dysfunctional aspects of certain features both of his "pure" or "ideal" type and of actual modern organizations. We shall take account of these criticisms, but first we shall set forth the essential features of bureaucracy very much as Weber described it.

---

[4] It is possible, of course, that some organizations, after "shaking down," achieve a more stable equilibrium.

[5] The present account depends on two translations of Weber's works: *The Theory of Social and Economic Organization*, trans. by A. M. Henderson and Talcott Parsons, Oxford University Press, 1947, pp. 329-41; and *From Max Weber: Essays in Sociology*, trans. by H. H. Gerth and C. Wright Mills, Oxford University Press, 1946, pp. 196-244.

[6] See, in particular, R. K. Merton, "Bureaucratic Structure and Personality" (1940); T. Parsons' Introduction to Weber, 1947, pp. 58-60, n. 4; C. J. Friedrich, "Some Observations on Weber's Analysis of Bureaucracy," in Merton *et al.*, eds., 1952, pp. 27-33, Blau, 1955, pp. 202-06 *et passim;* and Helen Constas, "Max Weber's Two Conceptions of Bureaucracy," 1958.

THE PREDOMINANCE OF FORMAL RULES

The structural importance of explicit rules is the defining characteristic of "formal" organization. The participants' orientation to common rules is a source of predictability of behavior, hence of rationality, for any one person's rationality in action is severely limited unless he can count on what others will do in particular circumstances (Simon, 1945, Chap. 4). The *regularity* of official behavior is also important for the rationality of action of all those who interact with the bureaucracy or are affected by it. Moreover, the rule of law helps to ensure universalistic standards, for these are typically embodied in the formal regulations governing official behavior. Finally, explicit rules make it possible, under certain conditions, to maintain discipline, since superordinate officials can apply definite and well-known sanctions to violators. Much of the training that takes place in formal organizations is inculcation of the formal rules, which are often quite complex.

Weber has little to say about the origin of bureaucratic rules, but one can infer, partly from his emphasis on discipline, that he had in mind rules imposed from above. One of the questions that interest present-day students of bureaucracy is this: Under what conditions is it possible to attain better morale and more willing compliance with rules if they are democratically decided upon—devised and imposed by those who will be subject to them? In a gypsum plant, for example, the workers complained bitterly about the company rules concerning absenteeism, but they accepted the safety regulations of the plant; yet the latter were rather complicated whereas the rules on absenteeism were simple. The important difference between the two sets of rules, apparently, was that the safety rules were established after discussion with the workers, during which the workers could make suggestions and come to see for themselves the desirability of preventing accidents, however bothersome the necessary restrictions, whereas the rules on absenteeism were simply imposed by management without any discussion or educational campaign to make them acceptable (Gouldner, 1954).

To this example one might object that the situations were rather simple, involving interaction in a face-to-face group, and that many problems with which formal organizations have to deal are much too complex to permit discussion in a "democratic" fashion. For example, the regulations to which a disbursing officer in the Navy are subject are so complicated that weeks of study are necessary to master them, and then never completely; they are intended to provide for many contingencies that an individual officer might not foresee. There would hardly be time or place to explain in detail, let alone discuss and choose democratically, rules that must for efficiency apply uniformly throughout a vast impersonal organization. This example is no doubt extreme, yet such cases are perhaps not rare. At the same time, there are other situations in which some degree of democratic rule-making would be possible but is not thought of on account of the unexamined and untested assumption that "management" always knows best. It is also possible that morale, hence discipline, would be improved in many parts of an organization if the rationale for rules were at least explained when the rules cannot be democratically determined. These questions are raised by modern students not only from a preference for democracy but from the broad hypothesis that democratically established rules will be more cheerfully obeyed, therefore that the functions of the rules will be more fully served.

Rules are in effect broad decisions that set conditions within which more specific decisions, at lower levels, are to be made. Just as participation in the making of rules may improve morale, so may participation in the making of lower-level decisions. With some qualifications, this conclusion is justified by empirical studies. In general, perhaps it is more important for subordinates to *feel* that they are participating in decision-making than for them actually to do so to any great extent. For example, in "conferences" between superordinates and subordinates the former are likely to prevail, but because the differences of power are less visible in conference than in the simple issuing of orders, subordinates are more likely to prefer conferences and to have better morale as a result of them.[7] However, since it is possible for managers to provide the appearance of joint decision-making without the substance, members of the organization who are aware of this are likely to resent being manipulated.

The best way of distributing and exercising authority depends upon many circumstances. Close supervision of subordinates is sometimes good for morale and sometimes bad. If subordinates have knowledge and skill equal to the tasks they must perform, they are likely to resent very much supervision, but if they are less well trained they will resent not having enough supervision (March and Simon, 1958, p. 55).

Military organizations tend to emphasize a strict hierarchy of authority. Officers are trained to make decisions quickly and firmly, as they often must in battle conditions, and subordinates are trained to obey without hesitation. This kind of organization seems to arise from functional requirements. In the planning phase of military operations, however, the staff officers consult with one another on a more "democratic" basis. Staff work usually goes on well behind the combat area. Rapidly changing military technology is affecting the exercise of authority further down the line as well. More individual initiative is required in combat situations, and to some extent the old ideal of crisp officers and unquestioning subordinates is giving way to an arrangement more functional under present-day conditions. It is increasingly felt that, wherever possible, officers should explain the reasoning behind their orders and should genuinely try to profit from the knowledge of their subordinates. Although most military organizations are already more like civilian bureaucracies than the public stereotype recognizes, most armies still do and will probably continue to emphasize the hierarchy of formal

---

[7] For summaries of research, see March and Simon, 1958, p. 54.

authority to a greater extent than civilian bureaucracies do. The Israeli Army, however, comes close to representing what Morris Janowitz calls "the fraternal type of authority."

In a training hospital, a striking difference can be observed between the behavior of medical doctors and the behavior of surgeons. The medical doctors consult one another quietly and rather formally when dealing with a patient. Although all, including internes, are allowed to express opinions, there is a recognized hierarchy of authority, and a physician of higher rank delegates authority to one lower in rank, who in turn delegates authority to one still lower. In the surgical ward, on the other hand, the surgeon in charge of a case issues orders without consulting anyone, and he is so firmly in charge that assistant-resident surgeons, internes, and nurses are all reduced to relative equality. The functional requirements of surgery are somewhat like those of combat: the head surgeon, like the line officer in command, must be able to make decisions quickly and firmly. Internal medicine, by contrast, permits more leisurely reflection and analysis. The medical doctor is more like a staff officer in the army. (It goes without saying that surgeons plan their operations in advance, but like line officers they often encounter unexpected "complications" and must make on-the-spot decisions [see Feld, 1959; R. L. Coser, 1958].)

THE ROLE OF KNOWLEDGE

The rationality of formal organizations has two sources. The first, which we have just considered, is the predominance of rules that have been devised to help achieve definite results in "production" of goods or services. The second is the systematic reliance on knowledge in the operation of the organization. "Knowledge" here means more than knowledge of the bureaucratic rules themselves, although, as we have mentioned, this kind of knowledge is in some cases impressive in scope.

Most bureaucracies require the services of technical experts. Business firms, for example, depend to a large extent upon lawyers, scientists, and engineers. Hospitals depend upon medical doctors, nurses, pharmacists, and many technicians (and, behind them, upon physicists, biologists, and biochemists). Armies depend upon chemists, physicists, engineers, medical doctors, and a wide variety of other specialists.

In addition to "professional" knowledge—systematic and more or less generalized—bureaucracies also depend upon knowledge of "concrete" facts. For example, the Department of State has detailed knowledge of the economic conditions, treaty arrangements, internal politics, and political sympathies of many countries, friendly and unfriendly. Business firms study the products of competitors and the characteristics of the market. Among concrete facts of great importance to a bureaucracy are the records of its own operations. Hence every bureaucracy keeps more or less detailed and systematic files, and, until recently, the larger the organization the larger the clerical staff.

Finally, the rationality of an organization depends upon the knowledge gained through systematic checks on its own efficiency. To some extent, these checks enable the organization to correct its operational errors as it goes along. For example, a business firm not only keeps track of production and sales but also analyzes the statistics to see on which items it is making the greatest profit. In recent years some business executives have employed social scientists as consultants to analyze the operation of firms in order to improve production levels or morale or both.

Since knowledge is important, the recruiting officials of a formal organization often make appointments on the basis of special competitive tests, or on the basis of educational certificates (diplomas, degrees, records of grades). Few bureaucracies, however, depend exclusively on the training their recruits have received before entering the organization. Most bureaucracies have training programs of their own. Modern military organizations are especially noteworthy in this respect.

The dependency of organizations on knowledge makes it difficult to make any general statement about their optimal size. Presumably, at any given time the limitations of communication systems impose some limits on the size of an organization if it is to maintain a high level of efficiency; and beyond a certain point record-keeping becomes cumbersome. But as knowledge becomes greater, the limits of organization size are extended. Improving technology makes accurate and rapid communication easier and easier. Automation is rapidly making obsolete even the efficient mass-production methods that have made large-scale factories possible. Automation is also transforming the methods of record-keeping. Electronic equipment now makes it possible (and economically desirable) for a government bureau or a private insurance company, for example, to handle millions of records rather than thousands. Information can now be stored and at need recovered, with amazing speed. Finally, the growth of scientific knowledge about organization itself will presumably affect the optimal size of organizations of different types.

As we have noted, universities, hospitals, many government agencies, libraries, and large business firms are increasingly dependent upon the services of professional experts (see, e.g., Goss, 1959). These organizations, however, are seldom *managed* by people whose competence is primarily in a field of abstract knowledge. The efficiency of service organizations, including business firms, depends in part upon the fact that most professional men belong to professional groups (medical and bar associations, engineers' societies, the American Association of University Professors, and many more). Professional associations are important for the maintenance of high technical standards (see Merton, 1958). The professional expert is concerned about his standing in his profession as well as his standing in the organization that employs him. Moreover, he can call upon the support of his organized colleagues if nonprofessional administrators impose restrictions or make demands upon him that are incompatible with professional standards. At the same time, administrators have an additional sanction that they can apply to professionals, for they can threaten to expose incompetent professionals to their colleagues. This reciprocal social control is an example of the operation of "role-sets" (Parsons, 1958).[8]

Official secrecy is another characteristic of bureaucracy. What knowledge is withheld from general circulation varies from one type of organization to another. A university, for example, does not open its academic records to any casual inquirer, but it ordinarily tries to share the results of research with as many people as possible. A business firm, on the other hand, may try to keep its production processes secret.

The first reason for secrecy is that the efficiency of an organization may depend upon it. The extreme example of this is an army: surprise being one of the most important principles of strategy, an army takes precautions to keep its strategic plans out of the hands of potential enemies. Another manifest function of official secrecy is the maintenance of morale within the organization. For example, American presidents have always denied the right of Congress to inspect the official files of government agencies; senators and representatives are not always so discreet and responsible as they might be in their accusations against bureaucratic personnel.[9] (On the other hand, bureaucrats may protect their secrets in part in order to enhance their power, for of course knowledge is a kind of power.)

A latent function of secrecy *within* an organization is the maintenance of the authority of superordinate officials. If authority is real (as opposed to nominal, or "paper," authority), it consists in the readiness of those subject to it to obey without much question. Although we ordinarily distinguish between "line" authority and "staff" authority—the first being the authority to issue orders, the second the kind of authority that resides in recognized superiority in knowledge—actually this distinction is not absolute. Part of the authority of "line" officials rests on their subordinates' presumption that the superior *knows* more about the concrete situation of action and the probable outcome of alternative plans. This presumption is usually sound; for one thing, the higher the line official, the greater the likelihood that he has had the benefit of expert opinion as well as access to relevant facts. One might think that authority in the army rests on rank and fear of

[8] On the importance of professional standing to university professors, see Caplow and McGee, 1958. On role-sets, see Chap. 2, *supra,* and R. K. Merton, "The Role-Set: Problems in Sociological Theory" (1957a). A role-set, it will be recalled, is "that complement of role-relationships in which persons are involved by virtue of occupying a particular social status" (Merton, 1957a, p. 110).

[9] The irresponsibility of some representatives in this regard is so gross that it is hard to believe. For several examples, see M. Lehman, "The Watchful Congressmen and the Wasteful Army" (1953). The cases mentioned won valuable headlines for the representatives and unjustly undermined public respect for the Army. These cases, however, were less notorious than Senator McCarthy's gross charges against the State Department.

punishment alone, but these would matter little in the heat of battle (after all, the enemy can "punish" too) if it were not that subordinates presume the officer in command to be in possession of more facts. In all organizations, but especially in armies, there is a tendency for information to go up and commands to come down (see Feld, 1959, esp. pp. 18-19).

One cannot take it for granted that official secrecy is always functional for an organization. For example, secrecy in research organizations not only is contrary to the ethos of science but hampers scientists in their cooperation *within* the organization. Some scientists believe, for this reason, that the United States government should relax (not abandon) "security" regulations for military research, and depend on alertness and "massive cooperation" more than on secrecy.

> It was recently pointed out that if security provisions such as now exist in the United States had existed in Germany early in the present century the discovery of nuclear energy might not have occurred. Professor Einstein's postulation of the equivalence of mass and energy through the concept of relativity was possible only on the basis of Max Planck's work on high temperature radiation. If present security relations existed at that time, Einstein might never have known of Planck's work since it would have been classified as relevant to military security [Shils, 1956, pp. 188-89].

Despite the importance of knowledge to organizations, they also depend to a large extent upon executive authority, and, as we have noted, managers (or executives) are not primarily technical experts in a field of learning.

THE ROLE AND STATUS OF OFFICIALS

In the typical bureaucracy today, officials are appointed rather than elected or installed through hereditary succession. It has been maintained, but it would be difficult to prove, that appointed officials are in general more competent than elected ones (see Chap. 3, n. 13). Much depends, presumably, upon who does the appointing or the electing. Appointment by superiors does have one indubitable effect, however. It assures, much more than election would, that subordinate officials, being dependent upon the judgment of superiors, will be inclined to recognize the authority of superiors. Appointment, then, helps to ensure that discipline which is one of the bases of the predictability of organizational behavior.

An exception to the pattern of appointment occurs frequently at the top of a bureaucracy. For example, the president of the United States, who is the official head of the bureaucratic part of the American government, is of course an elected official. The head of a university is often elected by a board of trustees or some similar, relatively small body. The smaller the body of electors, the closer the pattern of election is to appointment. As we have seen, the president and other high officials of a business corporation are elected by the stockholders. In some corporations, especially the largest, however, the pattern of election is hardly more than nominal. In effect, the top officials, having control of proxy votes, co-opt new top officials as need arises. They may elect one of their own number to replace a retiring president and co-opt a third person to take the place of the one promoted. According to *Webster's New Collegiate Dictionary,* to "co-opt" is "to choose or elect (a person) as a fellow member or a colleague," and this is the sense we intend. A sociologist (Selznick, 1949) has included in his definition of "co-optation" an enlightening statement of its usual purpose: co-optation is "the process of absorbing new elements into the leadership of an organization as a means of averting threats to its stability or existence."

Officials are appointed (or promoted) by way of entering into a free contract. Except when the law requires that the appointee be selected from a list of successful candidates in an examination, the appointing officials are free to offer the open position to anyone they wish; but, in what Weber would call the "fully developed" type of bureaucracy, the appointing officials are expected to select according to universalistic standards of competence for the position.

The role of official

Perhaps the most important feature of an official's role is that it consists of definite and formally defined duties and a definite and formally defined sphere or scope of authority. Authority is also an aspect of the official's *status,* but we are here calling attention to the fact that the official is *expected* to exercise his authority; this obligation is a role aspect.

We often think of authority as an attribute of persons, but closer analysis shows that it is not. In order to contrast bureaucracies with less formal organizations, we sometimes say that the authority of a bureaucratic official resides in his office, not in his personality. Even this way of speaking is elliptical. Actually, authority is always an emergent in the *relations* between people. The concept of an office, or of any other social position, is meaningless apart from a system of interdependent positions. Orders have no "authority" unless the person to whom they are directed submits to or recognizes the relevant degree of superiority in the position of the one issuing the orders. This recognition depends partly on the whole structure of the organization. The subordinate must presume, for example, that if he disobeys a superior, not only will the superior punish him, but other persons in the organization will effectively support the superior. The idea that authority resides in a person is an illusion. In formal organizations, this illusion arises from the fact that duties are allocated explicitly and clearly throughout the organization, so that the multiple consequences of blatant disobedience will usually be easy to imagine (see Barnard, 1938, Chap. 12).

Wherever authority is divided, as it is almost always, there must be a final authority. Whoever has the last word in case of conflict is simply the person whose decision will be supported and carried out in the necessary ways by all persons involved.

Relatively speaking, a person recognizes the authority of another when he acts upon that other's orders without an independent investigation of their wisdom (Simon, 1945, p. 126). This is a limiting case, however, and is perhaps seldom desirable for the efficiency of organizations. For example, if a superior (unwittingly, perhaps) gives contradictory orders, the subordinate is usually expected to point out the contradiction. Ultimately, a person recognizes the authority of another when, after all discussion and whether or not he regards them as wise, he obeys orders.

A bureaucracy as a whole is a hierarchy of various levels, with a varying number of officials at each level, all the way up to the managing executive or the board of directors at the top. In a very large organization, there may be several coordinated hierarchies, so that any particular subordinate official is subject to the authority of those above him in his particular hierarchy but not to the authority of *all* higher-ranking officials in the total organization. Although higher officials issue orders to their subordinates, they typically do not interfere directly in the spheres of authority formally allocated to their subordinates. In the most formal bureaucracies, such as the typical army or navy, regulations require that orders go through the chain of command without skipping any link in the chain. A colonel does not issue orders to a captain except through a major. At the same time, information is also passed upward through all the links that may be involved. A captain reports to a major, not to a colonel.

This characteristic of bureaucracies may seem, at first glance, to be wasteful of time and therefore inefficient. It may seem to be the focus of the numerous complaints about bureaucratic red tape. As we shall see, many of these complaints are based on a limited perspective and are in this sense unjustified. Even when such complaints are justified in terms of organizational efficiency, however, the focus of complaint is not the requirement that orders and information should in general pass through a chain of command; it is, rather, the location of discretion. Thus one might complain, in some cases, that an official at a certain level "ought," rationally, to have the authority to decide an issue himself, without having to pass the relevant information upward and then wait for a decision to come down. Such complaints are no doubt often legitimate, but they are no argument against the general organizational rule that a superior official should deal with his immediate subordinate and a subordinate official with his immediate superior. (Needless to say, we are considering the question in relation to the objective efficiency of organization, not out of a generalized preference for hierarchy.)

The functional justification of the chain principle is that it helps to maintain the organizational authority allocated to each official. If a colonel, for example, issued orders directly to captains, ignoring the intervening majors, it might seem that he distrusted his majors and he would thereby undermine their status dignity and authority in the eyes of *their* subordinates. Moreover, the majors would thereby be denied some of the information on which, as we have noted, their authority partly depends. Finally, the colonel would be causing resentment in his majors and thus undermining his own authority in their eyes.[10]

Typically an office in a bureaucracy is a full-time position; it is at least the primary occupation of its incumbent. Presumably the official's role is therefore the focus of a basic subsystem of his personality. The preoccupation of long days, day after day, makes for close identification with the bureaucracy, detailed knowledge of its affairs, and routine (habitual) efficiency.

The status of official

Let us turn now to the status aspects of bureaucratic office. The contract of employment, which may be renegotiated from time to time, gives the official a fixed salary, usually in money, although in some cases (e.g., the "living" of a clergyman) money income is supplemented by other kinds of income. In modern bureaucracies, the incumbent of office is expected to distinguish sharply between his private resources, including his salary, and the funds that may be made available to him for the conduct of official business. Typically he does not personally own the nonmonetary facilities he uses in his office. In particular his place of work, often called his "office" just as his position is, is separate from his private household and is owned not by him but by the organization. We have already noted the tendency in modern occupations for work facilities to be owned by the employing company. This tendency reflects the large scale of modern organizations. The buildings and equipment necessary for high levels of "production," whether in a factory or a hospital, are well beyond the private means of most individuals. The fact that the official does not own his "tools" undoubtedly increases the control the organization has over him.

The bureaucratic position itself is not "owned" by its incumbent. He has a right to it only within the terms of his contract. In many nonbusiness organizations, however, the incumbents of high positions have life tenure, subject to their maintaining a minimum level of performance and hewing to a minimum standard of personal conduct. In some cases, "life" tenure means tenure up to a certain retirement age; in other cases, the age of retirement is to a large extent left to the discretion of the incumbent himself. Life tenure is not regarded as "appropriation" of the office; it is regarded, rather, as a safeguard of official authority and integrity. In universities, for example, life tenure (for faculty members above a certain rank) is a safeguard of academic freedom. The life tenure of judges protects them from the political vagaries of popular prejudices. (For a discussion of the dysfunctions as well as the functions of life tenure, see Chap. 3.)

Although officials do not own their positions—for example, no official can give or sell his position to another person—they do in general have the moral right to expect to be able to make a career within the bureaucracy

---

[10] There are many treatments of the chain principle of command; for a good [illegible]le, see Homans, 1950, pp. 429-31

if they wish. This "right" is subject, of course, to their good performance and also to the continued prosperity of the organization as a whole. Promotion in a bureaucracy is based partly on merit (as judged by superiors or tested in examinations) and partly on length of service. The criteria are supposed to be universalistic, but of course interpersonal relations bend practice to some extent away from the universalistic ideal. The seniority rule, which is common in bureaucracies, may seem to be irrational (i.e., against organization efficiency), but we cannot definitely say that it is. We have already noted that employees identify more closely with the organization, other things being equal, the *less* competition there is within it. We may assume, also, that much competition within the organization would militate against a spirit of friendly cooperation between fellow officials. This seems to be virtually a tautological statement. A problem for management, therefore, is to arrange for enough competition to encourage initiative but not so much that cooperation and loyalty suffer. It does not seem possible to say *in general* what the optimal amount of competition is.

The "right" to a career does imply reasonably steady advancement within the organization. It certainly implies *some* advancement. But at the lower levels of large organizations the opportunities for advancement are usually few, and the ceiling is low. Unskilled workers and clerical workers are usually doomed to remain what they are. For this reason, one might be tempted to reserve the word "bureaucratic" for the upper part of large organizations—the part that includes managerial, semiprofessional, and professional personnel. The possibility of a career, however, is a relative matter. Not every official can expect to reach the top of the organization, and in some organizations many officials are permanently stuck in fairly low ranks.

Bureaucratic organizations always make some distinction between the private affairs of officials and their official obligations. This is implied in the fact that even the highest officials have limited spheres of authority over their subordinates. Where the line between private affairs and organization affairs is drawn varies a good deal from one type of organization to another, and no doubt from one society to another. An officer in the army or navy may have to get permission to marry. Bank employees are expected to be more circumspect in their private lives than the employees of a library. Such cases of unusual surveillance by the organization may be functionally justified, perhaps, as being in the interest of the general prestige of the organization and its officials, and sometimes, as in a bank, in the interest of maintaining the confidence of clients in the trustworthiness of officials. It is for organizational prestige, internal harmony, and morale that some business firms, according to W. H. Whyte, Jr. (1956), choose their personnel to some extent on the basis of the ability of the candidates' wives or prospective wives to fit into the increasingly self-contained social life of the great corporation. Moreover, some corporations put pressure on salesmen through their wives; they inform the women that their husbands will receive such and such a bonus if they sell a certain number of units

These are some of the ways in which, according to Whyte, some corporations try to make wives unofficial members of the firm and to some extent break down the line between official and private matters.

As for differences from one society to another, department stores in Germany forbid their employees to call one another by the familiar form "du" (instead of the more impersonal "Sie"), and the same writer who mentions this (Dreyfuss, 1938, v. 1, pp. 1-18) also quotes the following section from the rules of an Austrian provincial bank: "The management looks unfavorably upon personal social relations of its employees outside the Bank." It is probably safe to say that such rules, which are apparently intended to discourage "too much" solidarity among employees, or perhaps only to maintain crisp formal relations while on the job, would not be tolerated by employees in the United States. On the other hand, it would probably be ethnocentric to regard these rules as "authoritarian," for there is probably a greater degree of formality in German society generally.

One more status aspect of a bureaucratic office should be mentioned. Formal organizations usually have arrangements by which officials who feel mistreated can appeal the decisions of their immediate superiors.

Informal Organization

It is unthinkable that the members of a bureaucracy, some of whom interact with one another day after day, should confine their behavior to what is required by the formal organization. Informal relations inevitably develop. These are sometimes functional, sometimes dysfunctional, as far as they affect attainment of the goals of the formal organization.

A common basis for the growth of informal relationships of the clique type is the fact that the members of any organization are also members of a variety of other groups. If these other groups each have a fairly strong in-group feeling, their members are likely to carry over their prepossessions and antipathies into the formal organization. Sometimes these attitudes prevailing in the wider society are formally recognized in a bureaucracy, in discriminatory practices with respect to recruitment and promotion. More often perhaps, discrimination is quasi-official or *sub rosa*. In any case, a wide variety of social differences often do divide the members of the organization. Cliques may form on the basis of ethnic groups, religions, castes, regional origins, colleges from which the officials have been graduated, or fraternities to which they belong.[11] Such cliques may or may not be dysfunctional for the formal organization. Despite the empirical importance of such cliques, we shall devote our attention here to aspects of informal organization that arise independently of the outside affiliations of officials.

[11] For a good example of informal promotion patterns based on ethnic-group affiliation, see O. Collins, "Ethnic Behavior in Industry: Sponsorship and Rejection in a New England Factory" (1946). For a good analysis of informal relations based on regional origins, see Shih Kuo-Heng, *China Enters the Machine Age* (1944).

Social interaction systems with a fairly continuous existence always develop normative patterns. This is true of the informal relations in primarily formal organizations. We saw an example in Chapter 1, where we examined the bank-wiring group, which of course was part of a large formal organization. In that group, one of the *informal* norms was the rule against rate-busting. This rule illustrates something that is true of a good deal of informal organization: it is deviant from the formal organization of the same group. Although requiring deviant behavior, the informal organization is not necessarily dysfunctional for the formal. By eliminating the anxiety that competition in productivity might have engendered among the workers, the rule against rate-busting might well have reduced mistakes and turnover in personnel. As we have noted, individual members tend to identify more closely with groups within which there is less competition.

A good example of functional "deviance" required by informal norms is provided in a study of a federal enforcement agency. The officials of the agency had to inspect the books of business firms to find out whether the firms were complying with certain federal laws. According to official rules, the inspectors were to report to their superiors any attempt made by a business firm to bribe them. The inspectors, however, not only did not usually do so but disapproved of any fellow inspector who did, and the informal disapproval was strong enough to enforce the informal rule against reporting offers of bribes. This "deviant" informal rule was functional for the formal organization. If a representative of a business firm attempted to bribe an inspector from the agency, the inspector could threaten to expose the attempt unless the firm cooperated in the future in making adjustments to comply with the law. It would have been much more difficult to "close" a case if the inspector had promptly reported the offer of a bribe without giving the firm a chance to mend its ways (Blau, 1955, pp. 148-53).

Much "deviant" informal organization is in fact well known to the formal authorities and tolerated by them. There is no doubt fairly widespread recognition at all levels that the informal rules are functional for the formal organization and that, in any case, it would often be foolhardy for higher officials to attempt to suppress them. Chester I. Barnard, who has had much experience as an executive in formal organizations, has this to say:

> It is surprising how much that in theory is authoritative, in the best of organizations in practice lacks authority—or, in plain language, how generally orders are disobeyed. For many years the writer has been interested to observe this fact, not only in organizations with which he was directly connected, but in many others. In all of them, armies, navies, universities, penal institutions, hospitals, relief organizations, corporations, the same conditions prevail—dead laws, regulations, rules, which no one dares bury but which are not obeyed; obvious disobedience carefully disregarded; vital practices and major institutions for which there is no authority, like the Democratic and Republican parties, not known to the Constitution [1938, pp. 162-63].

The point can perhaps best be driven home by a brief description of certain widespread, functionally vital, and illegal practices in the centralized economy of a "totalitarian" society, the Soviet Union (Berliner, 1957). When the hard-pressed managers of Soviet enterprises submit production estimates to the top planners, as a help to the latter in planning annual production for the Soviet Union as a whole, the bolder, more successful managers deliberately underestimate the production capacity of their plants. They also deliberately overestimate the amount of materials they will need. They sometimes produce goods with a quality of workmanship or materials below what the official plan calls for. They regularly employ illegal *tolkachi* ("pushers"), a kind of resourceful middleman, who range far and wide obtaining spare parts, odd pieces of equipment, and materials in short supply, and who expedite shipments by adroit personal intervention, making use of the principle of *quid pro quo*.

It is impossible to make any definitive functional assessment of these illegal but common practices. One might suppose that they aggravate the very "disorder" they are intended to alleviate, for how can the central authorities plan intelligently if they do not have accurate information about production facilities and supplies of materials? Yet there is reason to believe that within limits the informal system *is* functional for the economy. The system has to be appraised in light of the fact that the top leaders are continuously pressing for higher and higher levels of production. Their pressure does result in higher production, but at the same time their zeal, if not counteracted in some way, would cause them to make excessive demands on the plant managers "in the field." Indeed, a high proportion of plants are not able to fulfill the goals set for them. The practices of submitting underestimates of capacity and overestimates of needs help to create a "safety factor" for the individual plant manager—a margin for those unforeseen emergencies that the top leaders, in their overoptimism, do not adequately provide for. Although these safety devices create some confusion, and provide work for the *tolkachi* to do, the pushers would be functionally necessary in the system anyway; the reason is that it is impossible to plan for a vast economy without making some mistakes, and if the economy is not to break down, at least locally here and there, there must be a generous provision for flexible troubleshooters—men such as the *tolkachi*. Given the goals of the top leaders, even the production of shoddy goods is not entirely dysfunctional; for the plant managers, cutting corners in the production of the "less essential" consumers' goods, save scarce materials and time for the production of goods in which the leaders are more interested.

If the informal practices ran riot, without control, they could hardly be functional. In fact, however, they do not. The larger system of which they are part has mechanisms that keep informal practices within bounds. In particular, the production goals set for any year are based on the actual production of the preceding year, and the new goals are always higher. Secondly, the government employs many enforcement agents or inspectors, who, although they often connive at the informal practices, cannot permit too much deviance without jeopardizing their own safety. Finally, the system of incentives (apart from ideological zeal) is such that plant managers as a status group are eager to produce as much as they can. In general, one gets the impression that the fast-rising level of production in the Soviet Union probably depends upon the mutually complementary interplay of formal and informal practices.[12]

The line between formal and informal organization is not always clear. In the state employment agency to which we have referred (pp. 289-90), two days of the formal training of new officials were spent on the code numbers of occupations and on the method of describing the requirements for available jobs; yet in one of the divisions, which was devoted to the clothing industry alone, the code numbers and job descriptions were not used; they would have been a waste of time. The decision to dispense with them was made by the director of the division, not by the head of the agency (Blau, 1955, pp. 22-24). Were the simplified practices formal or informal?

If the formal organization breaks down at some point, it may be replaced by informal organization. In an electrical equipment company, the president, who was gradually retiring, paid less and less attention to company affairs; informally his duties were increasingly taken over by the treasurer. To some extent this new arrangement, one of several changes in organization, was not only informal but latent, in the sense that the new allocation of authority and responsibilities in the company was not fully recognized by all personnel. Just as there may be latent functions, so there may be latent structure. In small informal groups, latent structure is common and probably works well enough, but in predominantly formal organizations there is usually some advantage in having the lines of authority fairly well recognized, whether they are formal or informal. In the electrical equipment company, failure to make the new lines of authority explicit caused a certain amount of bad feeling, or low morale (see Homans, 1950, Chaps. 14, 15).[13]

Dysfunctional Aspects of Bureaucracy[14]

In popular speech, the word "bureaucracy" often means a "bad" kind of organization: too big, too impersonal, and ridiculously, or irritatingly,

---

[12] This extremely tentative conclusion is in no way affected by the fact that the *tolkachi* continue to be attacked in the Soviet press. For an account with some statistics, see the New York *Times*, April 19, 1959, p. 7, cols. 1, 2.

[13] As Homans' analysis shows, the "latency" of the new structure was not the only cause of low morale. The term "latent structure" was introduced by Marion J. Levy, Jr., in *The Structure of Society* (1952). *Emerging* structure is perhaps always latent to some extent. As Homans puts it there is a tendency for norms to change more slowly than actual behavior.

[14] The ensuing discussion of the dysfunctional aspects of bureaucracies is based mainly on Merton, 1940; and A. K. Davis, "Bureaucratic Patterns in the Navy Officer Corps" (1948). Both articles are reprinted in Merton *et al.*, 1952.

inefficient. The popular complaints cannot be accepted at face value—indeed, as we shall see, terms such as "red tape" and "bureaucratic bungling" are often highly ambiguous. The aspects of bureaucracy that are objectively dysfunctional are not quite the same as those that arouse popular disapproval. But popular disapproval, whether "misguided" or not, does exist, and we shall therefore examine some of its causes, as well as causes of true dysfunctions. In neither case is the present treatment intended to be exhaustive.

To a certain extent, the criticism that some bureaucracies are wasteful and otherwise inefficient is true. As we have noted, the predictability of behavior which is characteristic of bureaucracies arises in large part from the system of formal rules and roles. The bureaucrat is encouraged to stick to the rules because promotion is often virtually automatic, provided that he does not show himself to be definitely incompetent. He can get into trouble by violating those rules that are actually enforced. The pervasive emphasis on standardized procedures may, however, become excessive. The rules were presumably framed in order to facilitate the achievement of organization goals; in this sense, the rules are a *means*. But undue attention to the rules may result in their being treated as ends in themselves, and the bureaucrat may at times lose sight of the practical purposes for which they were intended. The effect of this transformation of means into ends can be extremely irritating to the unsophisticated public being served by the bureaucracy. To the bureaucrat, a client is a routine "case"; but to the client himself his problem is unique, and to him the routine treatment may seem Procrustean.

Moreover, the bureaucrat may resist a change in procedures even when change would be functional. Having become adept in the established intricacies, he may have a kind of misplaced sense of craftsmanship, a pride in his superior knowledge. One can imagine that having mastered the system of writing in Chinese characters (no small feat), the Chinese scholar might be reluctant to see any merit in a simplified writing system, even if a good one were presented for consideration.

Some bureaucracies apparently suffer from overcentralization. Centralization is a matter of degree. An organization may be said to be centralized to the extent that decisions are made by higher officials, leaving little room for discretion to the bureaucrat who deals directly with clients. The effect of overcentralization is that lower officials merely record what they consider to be relevant facts, then pass the information to a superior, who in turn comments on it and passes it on to a still higher official; eventually someone with enough responsibility makes a decision and passes it down the hierarchy to the first official, whose client, in extreme cases, has by this time died or lost hope. The remedy for overcentralization is to train lower officials in the basic policies and purposes of the organization and then to trust them with authority and responsibility for a wider range of decision-making.[15]

A second criticism of some bureaucracies is that they discourage initiative by encouraging a tendency to "pass the buck" or to do nothing, even when the official has the technical authority to act. Closely connected with this reluctance to innovate or to assume responsibility is the tendency to restrict output. In extreme cases, the prevailing spirit is manifested in relaxed paper-shuffling, active inactivity. Of the many possible sources of such a lack of initiative we shall mention only two. Although lack of initiative is distinguishable from overcentralization, nevertheless overcentralization can lead to a fear of acting even when authority exists, for centralization creates a fear that one will be accused of overstepping the bounds of discretion. It may seem safer to do nothing or to send the matter up the hierarchy. Secondly, fear of superiors in the bureaucracy may be reinforced by fear of one's equals. Both the formal and the informal rules may discourage anything that might look like competitiveness. The too energetic or too imaginative bureaucrat may be accused of "polishing the apple" or "brown-nosing."

Strictly speaking, to call such tendencies dysfunctional is to imply that they can be eliminated or reduced. No doubt this is sometimes possible, but we must also recognize that the most efficient system has to strike some sort of balance between competitiveness and routine cooperation.

Inadequate filing systems may result in waste of time. Another kind of inadequate systematization may tend to discourage initiative. A study of the government bureaucracy of modern Egypt shows how this can happen

> The lack of job-descriptions and codes . . . discourages the government official from using his initiative even if he is able to overcome other powerful deterrents. Since he is not certain where his authority and functions begin and end, the civil servant has one more reason to play everything safely by assuming that the responsibility lies elsewhere than upon himself [Berger, 1957, p. 36].

A third criticism of some bureaucracies is that officials are "overbearing" or "arrogant" in their dealings with clients. This charge is one of those popular complaints that might not always mean what they seem to mean. The very fact that a bureaucrat's activities are to a large extent routine may foster an impersonal attitude. The worried or insecure client can easily mistake impersonality for arrogance. It is true, however, that some bureaucracies (for example, police departments) are conscious of possessing a good deal of corporate power in relation to a large part of the public. There is also an inherent tension between career bureaucrats and elected representatives that may lead to a certain amount of arrogance on both sides. The career bureaucrat, being an expert in his field, may regard

---

15 For a good discussion of centralization *versus* decentralization, see Simon, 1945, pp. 234-40. A famous example of overcentralization is the French government bureaucracy under the Third Republic; see Sharp, 1931.

legislators as ignorant bunglers. On the other hand, elected representatives are conscious of their general power of surveillance and their control over appropriations. As we have noted, many senators and representatives do not hesitate to attack "bureaucrats" openly and bitterly. Students from Max Weber to Herbert Simon have noted that bureaucrats may or may not carry out programs in the way in which the legislators intended.

It is sometimes thought that competition between business firms protects the public from bureaucratic arrogance, but this point can perhaps be overstressed. Public servants are also vulnerable to public criticism and employees of private monopolies (e.g., telephone and power companies) may be trained to be routinely polite since public dissatisfaction could lead to a movement for public ownership.

The last dysfunction we shall mention (though not the only one remaining) is the loss of morale in some bureaucracies due to a sense of injustice in the treatment of subordinates. It goes without saying that "injustice" is always possible in any organization; we are referring to injustice (or the sense of injustice: not always the same) that arises in certain bureaucracies, notably military groups in peacetime, owing to the peculiar nature of their organization and to the circumstances in which they operate. Superordinate officers in an army have much more drastic sanctions at their disposal than have superordinate officials in most civilian bureaucracies. The subordinate cannot quit the service at will; he can be confined to quarters, given extremely unpleasant work assignments, imprisoned, dishonorably discharged, or, in extreme cases, put to death. In battle conditions, the possibility of disobedience due to loss of morale is so great, and its consequences are so grave, that an army spends much time creating discipline, inculcating swift and unquestioning obedience to superiors. The formal hierarchy of authority is "exercised" in peacetime, to keep it trim for the occasions when it must be ready for serious action. The great authority of officers, however, can easily be abused. To the subordinate, demands for machine-like obedience may seem petty and arbitrary, especially if many of the subordinates are nonprofessional soldiers drafted for service. During World War II, a sample of 2377 enlisted men and 5000 officers, all stationed in the United States, were asked to say which common complaints enlisted men "usually have good reason to gripe" about. Of the enlisted men, 71 per cent thought there was "too much 'chicken' to put up with," but only 49 per cent of the officers agreed. Fifty-one per cent of the enlisted men and 23 per cent of the officers agreed that "discipline [was] too strict about petty things" (Stouffer *et al.*, 1949, v. 1, Table 3). The great temptation to abuse authority is not diminished by the fact that the army is reluctant to punish officers. The reason for this reluctance is that the army wishes to do nothing that might undermine officers' authority.

Article 96 of *Navy Regulations* shows the organization's concern for this functional prerequisite: "No officer shall use language which may tend to diminish the confidence in or respect due to a superior in command; and it is the duty of every officer who hears such language to endeavor to check it. . . ." [A. K. Davis, 1948].[16]

While thinking about the dysfunctions of bureaucracy, we must not lose our sense of proportion. Large formal organizations are able to accomplish things that probably could not be accomplished without them. Whoever doubts the relative efficiency of modern bureaucracies should read, for comparison, Lewis' description of the French army in Louis XIV's time, before the "modern" reforms of Louvois (1954, Chap. 5). The inefficiency of older armies as compared with some of the armies developed during the nineteenth century was due in part to the fact that the officers were usually aristocrats who fought for personal glory or adventurers who fought for money. Bureaucratization of armies, which was necessary to their increased efficiency, depended upon transforming the feudal officer-gentleman into a professional man and an official. Here is a scholar's description of European officers before the great reforms instituted in Prussia after 1808:

> The eighteenth-century officer corps was designed for the needs of the aristocracy rather than for the efficient performance of the military function. Wealth, birth, personal and political influence dictated the appointment and advancement of officers. Children and incompetents frequently held high military rank. No body of professional knowledge existed. Consequently, no institutions, except for a few technical schools, were available to impart military knowledge, and there was no system for applying that knowledge in practice. Officers behaved and believed like aristocrats rather than like officers. The backward state of the military profession may be contrasted with the condition of the legal, medical, and clerical professions at that time. The rudimentary independent existence of each of these made unthinkable the sort of prostitution to which the military vocation was subject. In brief, the military profession was simply nonexistent [S. P. Huntington, 1957, p. 28].

Before leaving the subject of dysfunctions, let us consider briefly some of the factors that make people complain about "defects" that may not be present at all. Most of the "unreasonable" complaints arise from a somewhat inappropriate frame of reference.[17]

1. The layman often lacks understanding of the functional requirements of a large formal organization. What is called "red tape" is often necessary if the organization is to maintain adequate communication and adequate records.

2. In dealing with clients, who are often not known personally, an organization cannot rely on their word or opinion without question. It is always necessary to check whether clients are entitled to the treatment they think they deserve. To the client, however, investigation of details may seem like an attack on his personal integrity or an unjustified invasion of his privacy.

---

[16] On organizational safeguards of authority, see also Barnard, 1946, pp. 207-43. We drew on this article in Chap. 3, "Structure and Function."

[17] The rest of this section is based, with slight changes of emphasis, on Gouldner, "Red Tape as a Social Problem" (1952). Gouldner's study is based on interviews

3. Many clients of large nonprofit bureaucracies seem to be unconsciously contrasting its methods with those of a small organization, such as a "friendly" neighborhood business, or else they are annoyed because they cannot get what they want simply by offering money, as they often can when dealing with commercial enterprises. The resulting frustration often leads clients of a hospital or a university or a government agency to charge that the bureaucrats are time-serving or arrogant, that they play favorites, or even that they deliberately try to frustrate the poor but honest applicant for simple justice. Such charges are sometimes true, but sometimes they are merely symptoms of an inappropriate frame of reference, a set of expectations that are foredoomed to be disappointed.

4. Some persons complain of "red tape" when their "real" objection is to the purposes for which the organization exists. For example, a landlord may displace his ideological objection to rent control onto the methods of the rent-control agency.

5. On the other hand, some persons complain because a bureaucracy does not do easily something it is not organized to do. For example, students of bureaucracy sometimes forget that bureaucratic officials are not trained to facilitate research conducted by unauthorized outsiders.

Formal Organizations and Society

Our discussion of common complaints against bureaucracy may have suggested that public reaction to impersonal organization must depend to some extent upon the values prevailing in the wider society of which any particular bureaucracy is a subsystem. For example, one would expect that bureaucratic procedures would be better understood and accepted in countries with an established system of government under law, and with a high rate of literacy. Technically speaking, "universalistic" values are established in broader areas of social interaction in the United States than, say, in Egypt or the Near East generally.

> Much more than in the West, people in the Near East seem to feel there is always a way to get around a regulation or to find one that helps instead of hurts your case. Such a situation, of course, adds to the power and prestige of the civil servant—and increases the temptation to act arbitrarily or upon the basis of irrelevant loyalties.
>
> This vague structuring of relations between citizen and government exemplifies the fact that Egypt has not yet become a rational, secular state of the Western type, in spite of its efforts to do so [Berger, 1957, pp. 16-17].

Although Egypt is making rapid progress in education, it has a long way to go. The estimated rate of illiteracy in 1937 was 88 per cent of the population. Despite progress in education, the gap between the general public and the bureaucracy remains great, since a relatively large proportion of the educated enter the expanding civil service. Between 1942 and 1949 from 32 to 45 per cent of secondary-school graduates entered government service, as did 85 per cent of university graduates in 1948-49 and 72 per cent in 1949-50. Directly comparable figures are not easy to obtain for the United States, but we know that only 2 to 4 per cent of those who acquired the bachelor's or a higher degree in 1952 entered the federal government service (Berger, 1957, pp. 80-81).

Even when the goals and methods of a bureaucracy are widely accepted, continuing support cannot be taken for granted. Every organization has to keep on justifying its existence in terms of values that are either widely accepted or, perhaps, not widely enough accepted. An important part of the activity of a university president, for example, is to remind the public of the value of universities to society and to persuade legislatures or philanthropists that the university deserves more financial support. The members of boards of trustees are chosen, in part, because they are men (or women) so placed in the social system that they can presumably represent the needs and the deserts of the organization to varied influential sections of the society. Even in a totalitarian country such as the Soviet Union, the government, which allocates resources among organizations of varying kinds, takes pains to create, through propaganda and agitation, a kind of legitimacy for its decisions.

We have already observed that bureaucracies manifest a tendency to routine, a resistance to new ways of doing things. This resistance is not absolute and it may be that critics usually exaggerate it, but the evidence seems fairly good that when new goals are assigned to a bureaucracy by "outsiders" the regular bureaucrats will tend to sabotage these new goals more or less deliberately unless they are prevented from doing so. The only effective way of preventing sabotage is to put new men who accept the new goals into key positions in the bureaucracy. When a socialist party came into power in Saskatchewan, Canada, in the 1940's, its leaders, being inexperienced in the details of government, felt obliged to retain some of the old civil servants in key posts. The "radical" program of the party was carried out in various departments to the extent, roughly speaking, that it was supervised by convinced socialist experts—that is, by new men. The old civil servants did their best to sabotage the program.

> A number of civil servants were able to convince their ministers that certain changes were not administratively feasible or that they would incur too much opposition. Some deputy ministers exchanged information with other deputies on their techniques of controlling their ministers. It is difficult to demonstrate concretely—without certain breaches of confidence—which policies were drastically affected by civil-service action, but it is a fact that some key officials boasted of "running my department completely," and of "stopping harebrained radical schemes" [Lipset, 1950].

The Nazi "Party" under Adolf Hitler was able to "nazify" the German state bureaucracy, which had been famous for its high standards of universalistic service. In some respects, "nazification" meant radical changes in the ideals, goals, and methods of the bureaucracy. The methods by which the transformation was achieved have been identified as follows: (1) transfer of some state functions to Nazi "bureaucracies," such as the Party itself, (2) "personal union" (appointment of Party officials to state positions), (3) "parallelism" (establishment in the Party of positions that were similar in field of activity to positions in the state bureaucracy), (4) nazification at the top of the state bureaucracy, (5) "permeation" (putting Nazis in other key positions, promoting Nazis, recruiting personnel from Nazi indoctrination centers such as the law schools), (6) conversion to National Socialism, (7) dismissal of "undesirable" personnel, (8) transfer of "unreliable" personnel to less strategic positions, (9) enforced compliance, (10) replacement of law by discretion. Some of these methods could take effect only over time, but all together did "transform" the bureaucracy (Burin, 1952).

RECOMMENDED READING

The classical treatment of bureacracy is found in the works of Max Weber. See *From Max Weber: Essays in Sociology,* trans. by H. H. Gerth and C. Wright Mills, Oxford University Press, 1946, pp. 196-244, 416-44. In addition to Weber's analysis of the so-called pure type of bureaucracy, these selections contain brief characterizations of some of the great formal organizations of the past (e.g., ancient Chinese and Egyptian bureaucracy). For a brief treatment of the bureaucratic aspects of one type of political system, see Max Weber, *The Theory of Social and Economic Organization,* trans. by A. M. Henderson and Talcott Parsons, Oxford University Press, 1947, pp. 329-41.

Perhaps the best recent introduction to the study of formal organizations is H. A. Simon, *Administrative Behavior: A Study of Decision-Making Processes in Administrative Organization,* Macmillan, 1945. Another classic in the field, a beautifully written work, is C. I. Barnard, *The Functions of the Executive,* Harvard University Press, 1938. Its contents are broader than the title might suggest. See also C. I. Barnard, "Functions and Pathology of Status Systems in Formal Organizations," in W. F. Whyte, ed., *Industry and Society,* McGraw-Hill, 1946, pp. 207-43. In *Organizations* (Wiley, 1958), J G. March and H. A. Simon, in collaboration with Harold Guetzkow, have attempted to set forth systematically the results of a large number of previous studies. Their book also has a good bibliography.

For an excellent collection of articles and excerpts from other books, see R. K. Merton, A. P. Gray, Barbara Hockey, and H. C. Selvin, eds., *Reader in Bureaucracy,* Free Press, 1952. Three of the articles were prepared specially for the volume, and there is a good classified bibliography.

We recommend two very broad essays by Talcott Parsons, although they might be a little difficult for readers not familiar with his previous work. See "Suggestions for a Sociological Approach to the Theory of Organizations." *Admin. Sci. Q.,* June and Sept. 1956, v. 1, nos. 1, 2, pp. 63-85, 225-39. This article analyzes some of the functional problems of business organizations, military organizations, and universities. The analysis is meant to suggest the value of a systematic theoretical approach. The other essay by Parsons is "Some Ingredients of a General Theory of Formal Organization," in A. H. Halpin, ed., *Administrative Theory in Education,* Midwest Education Center, University of Chicago, 1958, Chap. 3. This is a suggestive analysis of selected problems which takes account of different types of organization and three levels within each type.

For a functional analysis based on field studies of two formal organizations, a state employment agency and a federal enforcement agency, see P. M. Blau, *The Dynamics of Bureaucracy,* University of Chicago, 1955.

E. A. Shils, *The Torment of Secrecy: The Background and Consequences of American Security Policies,* Free Press, 1956, although frankly evaluative and even polemical, contains a valuable analysis of some aspects of the relation between the bureaucratic and elective parts of the American government. These more general observations spring from Shils's attempt to analyze the causes of disequilibrium in the "proper" mutual adjustment of privacy, publicity, and secrecy.

Another topic of far-reaching importance is brilliantly treated in S. P. Huntington, *The Soldier and the State: The Theory and Politics of Civil-Military Relations,* Harvard University Press, 1957. Huntington's analysis is sharpened by the fact that he develops "ideal types" of civil-military relations, taking account of four ideal types of ideology, and then compares systematically the civil-military relations of several countries at various periods of their history. The analysis of some historical periods, particularly of American civil-military relations during World War II, seems rather sweeping, and at times Huntington overreacts against the ignorant and shortsighted stereotype of the so-called military mind that is widely held in American society; but his book is an excellent example of theory-building in a field of great practical importance. On the broader education of military leaders, see J. W. Masland and L. I. Radway, *Soldiers and Scholars: Military Education and National Policy,* Princeton University Press, 1957. Masland and Radway, writing independently of Huntington, regard as possible what he regards as certain; namely, that military leaders can best fulfill their professional functions of estimating the requirements of military security and training and commanding combat forces if they remain out of politics. However, all these writers agree that professional military men, like other professionals, need a broad liberal education as well as professional training.

13. Political Systems

What, if any, are the universal functions of government? What are some of the ways in which governments differ from one another? What specific meaning should we give to the word "democracy"? What are the factors in society that may limit the extent to which governments can "abuse" their power? In what ways do these "controlling" factors vary from one society to another? These are some of the questions to which we shall attempt to give at least tentative answers in this and the following chapter.

Government, State, and Nation

A government exercises imperative control within a definite territory, and within that territory it successfully claims a monopoly of the use of force. "Imperative" control is simply control by the issuing of commands, including laws. "Monopoly" of the use of force has to be interpreted somewhat loosely. There are some governments that successfully claim a monopoly of force only with respect to certain rules, while other governments enforce other rules within the same territory. The government of Massachusetts, for example, is no less a government because the federal government also exercises imperative control, by means of force if necessary, within the territory of that state. Further, a government may within limits permit or tolerate the use of force by persons who are not members of the government itself—for example, by parents. Finally, there are almost always crimes involving the use of force by unauthorized persons or groups. The government may be said to exist, nevertheless, as long as its rules are stil important determinants of the vast majority of the acts covered by those rules. If violent criminals and resisters are relatively few and the government successfully "contains" their activities, then we may for practical purposes continue to speak of a successful monopoly of the use of force.

Virtually all governments claim to be legitimate and strive to some extent to achieve or maintain legitimacy. Legitimacy in a sociological sense is not quite the same thing as legitimacy in law. The two kinds of legitimacy tend, however, to be associated in fact. In law, a government is legitimate if it holds power according to some cultural rule or tradition, especially a rule of succession. In this sense, Farouk was the legitimate King of Egypt. In sociological usage, a legitimate government is one that has the support of those who are subject to it. In this sense, Colonel Nasser of Egypt may well be a legitimate ruler even though he came to power without benefit of any law of succession; and King Farouk, whom he ousted, may well have been illegitimate. Legitimacy in the sociological sense is a kind of authority, and like all authority it is a matter of degree. Few governments enjoy the wholehearted support of all those governed, and probably few have the support of none. Obviously, if a rule of succession is institutionalized, then those who hold power according to the rule are more likely to be "legitimate" in both senses.

A government may be legitimate, legally or sociologically speaking, and yet may employ illegitimate force, either in the sense that it violates some institutionalized rule or in the sense that this particular use of force is unpopular. In general, however, there is obviously a close connection, in the long run, between a government's sociological legitimacy and the "legitimacy" of its use of force.

A government does not include all the persons within its territory. A *state* includes the governed as well as the government; more specifically, a state consists of all persons within a definite territory in their social positions as members of a sovereign government or as citizens or subjects. All subjects and citizens are members of the state and may enjoy rights not enjoyed by nonmembers, such as aliens living within the territory. On the other hand, certain aliens—for example, diplomatic representatives of other states—may have some rights or immunities not given to citizens or subjects. But in certain respects the actions of all—citizens, subjects, and aliens—are in principle controlled by the government, insofar as these actions take place within the territory. Moreover, a government usually has considerable control over its citizens or subjects even when they are abroad, for the government can withdraw their citizenship, confiscate their property, imprison their relatives, or refuse them permission to re-enter its territory.

"Sovereignty," in the sense intended here, is roughly the same thing as political autonomy. Sovereignty is perhaps never absolute. All governments must, of course, take into account the wishes and aims of other governments. Sometimes this "taking account" goes so far, however, that a state, while not exactly a satellite of another, tacitly yields, in particular disputes, to more or less veiled threats of force. In extreme cases, a nominally sovereign state may in fact be ruled by another.

The governmental organization of the United States is a good illustration of the facts that sovereignty is divisible and that it is also a matter of degree. The Constitution gives the fifty states certain rights of control within their several territories; in these respects the states are all sovereign. Even these rights, however, are subject to revision or abrogation at the hands of the federal government, for the Constitution itself can be amended with the approval of fewer than all the states; to this extent, the fifty states are not severally sovereign, even in the legal spheres of control reserved to them by the Constitution.

One thing should be stressed. However extensive and secure sovereignty may be, the state is an abstraction from the total lives of its members. That is to say, the members of a state always belong to a variety of other groups at the same time. Some governments, of course, leave relatively little to private discretion.

Some primitive societies do not have a government in the sense of a group, smaller than the society as a whole, that by recognized right or by self-imposition exercises imperative control within a definite territory. On the other hand, there are probably few societies in which all adults, or even all adult males, have an equal part in making decisions binding upon the group as a whole or in using force to uphold a traditional order. These activities are culturally assigned to certain roles or groups, if only the informal council of family heads. The very existence of government in a society, therefore, is a matter of degree. We know enough about the organization of quite small continuously functioning groups, however, to say that such groups always have at least informal leadership.

What is the difference between a state and a nation? A nation is a group of people who, normally living in a particular territory, wish to form their own state; if they already have it, then they wish to keep it as the most important social bond that expresses their sentiment of belonging together and sharing a common destiny (see Weber, 1946, pp. 171-79).[1]

Although a common language, a common religion, or a common "racial" origin undoubtedly helps to produce and cement the sentiment of nationhood, these things, individually or together, are not sufficient or necessary. Many a group whose national sentiment is strong is diverse in language, religion, and "race." Switzerland and Belgium are good examples. The existence of a nation does, however, presuppose some common historical experience or, in later times, the cherished tradition of common experiences. Often diverse peoples are fused into a nation through being subjected to oppression at the hands of common enemies. Such was the experience of the thirteen colonies that waged the American War of Independence. Such has been the experience of India. The Arab countries of today, in which nationalism is quite strong, are to some extent united by religion, but they are also united by what they regard as common oppression from Western imperialists. Most of the people of Alsace speak German, yet they belong by sentiment to the French nation.

> The reason for the Alsatians' not feeling themselves as belonging to the German nation has to be sought in their memories. Their political destiny has taken its course outside the German sphere for too long; their heroes are the heroes of French history. If the custodian of the Kolmar museum

---

[1] Our treatment of government and the state is largely based on Weber, 1947, pp. 152-57.

wants to show you which among his treasures he cherishes most, he takes you away from Grünewald's altar to a room filled with tricolors, *pompier*, and other helmets and souvenirs of a seemingly most insignificant nature; they are from a time that to him is a heroic age [i.e., the French Revolution and the Napoleonic era; Weber, 1946, pp. 176-77].

We see, then, that a nation and a state are not necessarily the same, for a state often includes people of different nations. Once a national state has been formed, the national sentiment offers strong resistance to loss of independence. If independence is lost nevertheless, the national sentiment is a powerful force for restoration of the national state. Modern examples are the Irish and the Poles. On the other hand, incorporation in an alien state may in the long run bring about a new sentiment of nationhood. Strictly speaking, Wales and Scotland, as such, are no longer nations. They once chafed under English rule, but now, although they are proud of their separate national histories—proud, that is, of the past—they share in the transcending nationhood of the United Kingdom. The English won this loyalty by making important concessions. Even so, there exist today Scottish diehard patriots who resent the tie with England. There may also be reservations in the affection of other Scotsmen for England

There is another reason for distinguishing between state and nation. It will be remembered that a state includes a government (as well as the people in their roles as citizens or subjects). One of the strongest bonds that may unite the people of a nation is common allegiance to the *form* of their government—that is, to the prevailing political institutions. Sometimes, however, although the people of a nation are united in their wish to have a common independent government, they are divided in their ideas about the form that government should have. For this reason, it was necessary to distinguish sharply, after the 1918 revolution in Germany, between the German state and the German nation. One of the most prominent themes of Hitler's propaganda to the German people was that the Weimar Republic, which had signed the Treaty of Versailles in behalf of Germany, had "betrayed" the German nation.

A similar situation existed in France before World War II. Although most Frenchmen were loyal to the Third Republic, there was a rather vociferous minority of royalists. One of their spokesmen, Charles Maurras, became the official ideologist of the Vichy regime after the defeat of France in 1940. The kind of government the royalists wanted is suggested in the following comment:

the Vichy regime almost immediately took on nostalgic forms. Relics of the dead France of Louis XIV and Richelieu, or indeed from any epoch anterior to the authentic French Revolution, began to turn up in Vichy terminology and even on its money. A portrait of Henri IV appeared on a treasury bond-selling poster; Jacques Coeur, fiscal servant to Charles VII, was commemorated on the new bank notes. The Ministers were renamed Secretaries of State, as they had been known under the monarchies, and they functioned among such dusty nomenclature as *commanderies*, *intendants*, a... even *compagnonnages,* straight out of the good old *moyen âge.* Vichy was marked by leftovers from everything except France's three republics [Flanner, 1944, pp. 39-40].[2]

The United States is fortunate in that the national tradition stemming from the American Revolution is directly expressed in the basic political institutions. Even in the United States, however, a somewhat different national tradition, that of the Southern Confederacy, still has a certain amount of vitality, although the threat of secession is no longer present. England is more fortunate still in this respect, for although English history has included bitter struggles over the form of government, those old struggles no longer awaken divisive sentiments, and the present form of government appears to be firmly associated with the sentiment of nationhood.

Power and Influence

We have already defined "power" in general as the ability to get one's wishes carried out despite opposition, if any. In any process of interaction, some participants usually have more power than others. When we assert that someone has more (or less) power than someone else, we usually imply the existence of a more or less extended field of potential conflict; we often have to specify what the field of potential conflict is, however, for frequently it is true that A has more power than B in some situations while B has more than A in others. If a man tries to lift a certain weight and fails, he is not therefore judged to have no strength at all; he simply does not have enough strength for that task. So with power. Power is a relative matter. Until someone's power is actually tested in a particular situation, there is only a certain probability that he will be able to carry out his will against opposition. In a different situation, the probability will be different. The same remarks apply, of course, to the power of groups.

One exercises power largely by influencing the actions of others, but these others need not be the persons against whom one is pitting one's power. In an electoral campaign, for example, the successful candidate shows his greater power not mainly by influencing the opposing candidate but by influencing the voters. Thus A may have more power than B even though he has little or no influence over B.

It remains true, however, that power largely consists in the ability to influence the actions of other people. There are two general ways in which people can be influenced. One is to work on their ideas, sentiments, or goals, without changing the objective situation in which they act; the other is to work on the situation and let that have its calculated effect on goals, ideas, and sentiments: these approaches are often combined.

The *mode of influence* used may be one or more of the following:

[2] The split in France over the form of government is clarified in Vignaux, 1943.

Conveying new information (enlightenment or clarification).

Conveying misinformation (distortion or invention).

Advice (effective according to the prestige of the source: his presumed experience, knowledge, judgment, and good will).

Commands having authority.

Appeal to values and sentiments (apart from those involved in authority).

Inducement (sometimes called exchange: offering something valued in return for compliance).

Coercion (threat of harm: the opposite of inducement, in one sense; in another, a subtype of inducement [If you do as I wish, then I won't do what you'd rather I'd not do]).

Use of force, with or without authority (the *threat* of force is coercion)

Nonverbal symbolic acts (these can be equivalent to commands or requests, indeed to any one of the preceding modes: consequently this is not strictly a distinctive mode).

Unwitting prototypes for imitation (since there is no intention on the part of the influential person, unwitting prototypes that may be imitated are not symbolic in the context of influence. This mode calls attention to the fact that influence may be unconscious; the person influenced may also be unaware of the source or fact of influence).

All these modes of influence may be used directly or indirectly. By exercising direct influence on B, A may exercise indirect influence on C. Two or more modes of influence are often combined. Propaganda, for example may contain information, misinformation, and appeal to values and sentiments. Persons exercising influence may or may not let those influenced know what is desired of them, or why. Influence exercised without candor is sometimes called "manipulation." [3]

The bases of influence are numerous. Among the most important are position in a formal organization (e.g., a command post in an army), money, social connections, prestige due to past performances, knowledge, skill, and physical characteristics (e.g., strength, height, sex appeal). To some extent, of course, these and other bases of influence can be converted into one another.

To return to the *modes* of influence, every government makes some use of force and coercion. In 1950 all governments in the United States—federal, state, and local—spent approximately $725 million for police and crime control (Dewhurst *et al.*, 1955, p. 626). Expenditures on military forces were much greater, but in the United States, at least, military forces

[3] This brief discussion of power and modes of influence draws from the following works, all reprinted in part in L. A. Coser and Rosenberg, eds., 1957, Chap. 5; Simmel, 1950; Weber, 1946; Goldhamer and Shils, 1939; Barnard, 1938; Bierstedt, 1950; and Gerth and Mills, 1953. See also Merton, 1957, pp. 419-20.

are not used mainly against citizens. In many countries with governments less well established, military force is important for the maintenance of internal order. Even in the United States, not so long ago, a civil war had to be fought to prevent the secession of the South; and a short time ago, when a Southern governor, acting as a demagogue, inflamed citizens to the use of violence and commanded state troops to prevent "integration" of a public high school, the federal government had to use force to enable nine Negroes to attend in safety a school with hundreds of white students. This example shows that if people feel strongly enough about a particular issue, they will resist the government with violence, even when their cause seems to be hopeless in the long run. We can only guess how many people, how often, submit to other government orders only because they do not object strongly enough to be willing to fight against superior force.

Force and coercion, then, are probably essential instruments of government in large states. Nevertheless, every government strives to win legitimacy. Even dictatorships, which depend to an unusual extent upon force and terror, make use of all the other modes of influence as well, from publishing information to appealing to loyalty to Home and Fatherland. The Ministry of Propaganda in Nazi Germany was not solely occupied with influencing people outside the country. "Propaganda" and "agitation"—both directed at people's attitudes, partly in order to gain their willing assent to government control—are among the most important instruments of the Soviet government. This was so even under Stalin.

> Thus, at a special plenary session of the Central Committee in 1937 devoted largely to ideological questions, Stalin set the party on a new direction in its propaganda efforts. . . .
>
> As a result of the decisions thus reached by the Central Committee, a new history of the party was prepared. . . . from that time forward the chief goal of party propaganda was to be the inculcation of the intelligentsia with the principles of Marxism–Leninism as interpreted by the party leaders [Inkeles, 1950, p. 50].[4]

It is easy to see why governments try to establish their legitimacy. The use of force and coercion is inefficient as compared with the exercise of authority (imperative control recognized as rightful by those subject to it) If a government is illegitimate, many of its resources have to be "wasted' on the task of forestalling and suppressing resistance. People may obey, but if their morale is low (from the point of view of the government), they will drag their feet as much as they dare. Finally, if the government leaders are unpopular enough, their very lives are in constant danger from the population.

---

[4] Inkeles adds (p. 39): "The basic Bolshevik position on propaganda and agitation derives from the classic definition of Plekhanov, who stated: 'A propagandist presents many ideas to one or a few persons; an agitator presents only one or a few ideas, but he presents them to a mass of people.'" As Inkeles is well aware, propaganda and "agitation" are not intended merely to win acceptance for the rulers (i.e. legitimacy); yet, although this may not be the main intention, it is one.

No great astuteness is required to see that legitimacy and force are to some extent substitutes for each other. The more a government depends on armed guards, secret police, and an army to maintain internal order, the less "legitimate" that government is.

Political Systems

Among the important activities in which the federal government of the United States participates are the conduct of foreign policy; national defense; the encouragement of private economic production; government economic production; regulation of the economy as a whole; education; scientific research; the provision of welfare services, including a large amount of medical care; enforcement of the criminal law; and settlement of civil disputes between "private" individuals and organizations. In a sense, the goals of all these diverse activities must be regarded as goals of the society as a whole. When we speak of societal goals, however, we do not mean to imply that all members of society agree. It is probably rare for all the members of any large organization to know about, let alone agree on, all its aims. In particular, the leaders may have different aims from those of some or all of the other members. It can happen that the resources of the organization, including the efforts of its members, are mobilized for purposes that would be rejected if they were made public. The leaders of a labor union, for example, sometimes engineer strikes not for the ostensible purpose—getting higher wages, say—but in order to keep up the general fighting spirit and unity of the union; to convince the rank and file that the leaders are vigilantly and aggressively representing the union members; or, in rare cases, to set up a situation in which the leaders may, at the expense of the workers, make a profitable deal with management.

What is true of a labor union is all the more true of a group as large and complex as a society. The very concept of politics implies the existence of conflicting ideas about how the facilities and personnel of government should be used. When we say that the goals of governmental activities are goals of the society, therefore, we are merely referring to the fact that the government acts to some extent in behalf of all the people, decides on policies that at least *affect* all the people, and even, to some extent, mobilizes all the people and coordinates their action. The people do not benefit equally from governmental activities; but, regardless of who benefits, virtually all the people are forced (if necessary) to make contributions of money and effort to attain the goals set by government. (Needless to say, we are not contending that it makes no difference whether or not the public understands and approves of those goals.)

If the "polity" is defined as the goal-attainment subsystem of society, then obviously the government is an important part of the polity. As we have pointed out, however, the polity is not an explicitly coordinated structural subsystem of society; like the economy, it is a *functional* subsystem.

The government, as a "concrete" group, participates in all four functional subsystems; at the same time, other groups in addition to the government participate in the polity.

Among "political" groups other than the government, perhaps the most important are parties and pressure groups. We shall have more to say about them in the next chapter. For the moment it is enough to point out that both parties and pressure groups have a great deal to do with determining the personnel and policies of government.

We have already noted that governments, being concrete groups, have political, integrative, and frequently economic functions. They may also have pattern-maintenance functions; for example, governments often run the school system and support an "established" church.

Forms of Government

SIMILARITIES AMONG GOVERNMENTS

Before attempting to set forth some of the ways in which governments are unlike one another, let us list some important ways in which all governments are similar.

1. The effective government of every society consists of a small proportion of the population. Rule is always the rule of a few. This is true even in "pure" democracies such as the New England small town and the democratic type of city-state in ancient Greece. In the New England town many questions, to be sure, are settled in the town meeting, in which all citizens have the right to vote. But perhaps the main business of the meeting is to elect a small number of officials who, for definite terms of office, will represent the whole citizenry. In any case, only those above a certain age have the right to vote; in an earlier time, only adult men; in a still earlier time, only male property holders. As for the famous "pure" democracy of Athens (see Bryce, 1921, v. 1, Chap. 16), the "free" citizens had below them as many slaves as there were citizens, or even more, and the slaves of course could not vote. Although many important civil offices were filled by lot and the chief military posts were elective, there always was a small group, even from among the citizens, which in effect ran the *polis*. These were the popular orators and the outstanding generals. The remarkable feature of these "pure" democracies, a feature made possible by their small size, is the unusual extent to which political questions and the conduct of officials were (or are) subject to the check or control of the ordinary citizens. It was as if officials in modern democracies were continually being guided by referenda.

2. Every government consists of a chief and an administrative staff under the chief. This statement asserts (a) that no society can be run by one person without assistance and (b) that the members of every government are always unequal in actual power and authority, whatever the nominal situation may be. We are mainly concerned, in any case, with those societies

in which a government has been "differentiated out" and is explicitly recognized in the culture. If there be any primitive society that *is* ruled by one man without assistants, we shall say that that society has a political system but no "government": to this extent, the statement that a government is always composed of a chief and an administrative staff may be regarded as a partial definition of "government."

The "chief" need not be a single person. In some cases the "chief" executive authority is shared by two or three men—but if the number at the top is much larger than that, we can be sure that their equality is only nominal. One of the most important ways in which governments differ is in the relation between the chief and the administrative staff; we shall later consider some common types distinguished from one another in this respect.

3. Every government claims to be legitimate; that is, it regards obedience to it as a matter of duty. The *extent* to which a government emphasizes legitimacy is of course highly variable, Some governments (for example, most conquerors in their colonies) depend much more on force and coercion. But at the very least the element of legitimacy is involved in the chief's claim to authority over his administrative staff. In our subsequent discussion of the forms of government, we shall devote particular attention to differences in the nature of governments' claims to legitimacy.

4. Though legitimacy is important, it is never the sole basis of the government's power. Both the administrative staff in relation to the chief and the governed in relation to the government as a whole are motivated to obey, not only by their variable and possibly tenuous sense that they *ought* to obey, as a matter of duty, but by various combinations of other motives: personal affection or admiration for those above; an interest in protecting property rights or other advantages; the motive of gain; fear, whether of secular power or of supernatural sanctions; the desire to further some "ideal" goal or cause to which the government happens to be committed. Those who disobey are also motivated in a variety of ways, and not merely by a feeling that the government has no right to expect obedience. In almost all cases, the motives for obedience or disobedience are mixed, and the "real" motives are often rationalized to some extent.

5. Whether a government acknowledges the fact or not, every government is and must be concerned to some extent with the welfare of *all* segments of the population. In the United Kingdom (British), wide and deep concern is ensured by the *institutional* structure: all classes and ethnic groups are enfranchised. In the United States of America, although many Negroes are illegally deprived of the right to vote, the government must consider their welfare anyway, partly because many other Negroes and many white sympathizers do have the right to vote, and partly because any segment of the population, if pushed too far, can express its dissatisfaction by troublesome uprisings or by passive resistance. One factor in the stability of Athenian democracy was that the citizens feared slave uprisings and were thus kept from forming too-divisive factions These examples show that

there is wide variation in the extent to which concern for the governed is a recognized obligation of government, and in the extent to which the obligation, when institutionalized, is enforced by formal procedures whereby the governed may remove the government from power. History gives ample evidence, moreover, that when concern for the governed is not clearly institutionalized, there is wide variation in the benevolence of governments and in the astuteness with which they judge what they can "get away with."

One of the problems in the sociology of revolt and revolution is this: Under what conditions will an oppressed group rise up in aggressive protest? That the answer to this problem is not obvious is shown by the hundreds of historical examples of oppression carried on for long periods; moreover, the oppressed often far outnumber the oppressors. Historians would certainly agree with the following statements, even when they take into account the cultural relativity of "injustice":

> It is an amazing fact, but one amply attested, that some human beings have an infinite capacity to endure injustice without retaliation, and apparently without resentment against their oppressors Instances of this phenomenon are numerous, and they come from every part of the world where one group dominates another. Militant leaders of protest movements have been driven to despair by the apathy they have encountered among those they would lead to freedom; and members of dominant groups have often commented on the cheerfulness and loyalty they observe among those who would seem to have no reason for such sentiments [B. Berry, 1958, p. 479].

For obvious reasons, the chief, however constituted, is more likely to be concerned about the welfare of the administrative staff than about the welfare of the population at large. Again, whatever the form of government may be, the chief and his staff are never *equally* concerned with all segments of the population under them. Legitimacy is unequally recognized; and every institutional pattern of government—even more, every particular government holding power under the pattern—depends upon a particular constellation of interests within the population governed. An oligarchy is a state in which the government obviously owes its power to, and feels largely responsible to, one segment, to the relative neglect of the rest of the population. The favored segment may be the free citizens (over against slaves), a caste, a combination of castes, an ethnic group, or a social class based to a large extent on specific property interests, such as land ownership. Even a modern democracy is not equally supported by all segments of the population; nor is the government of a democracy in practice equally devoted to all the people. Let us repeat, however, that no government is totally lacking in concern for the mass of people under it.

DIFFERENCES AMONG GOVERNMENTS

Any classification is somewhat arbitrary. In our treatment of the forms of government, we shall ignore many bases of classification that have been used by other writers. Indeed, what we shall give most attention to is not a classification at all, strictly speaking, but a typology.[5] Perhaps no actual government is a pure example of any one of the three types we shall describe, although some governments come close to being "pure" examples. We shall describe what a pure example would be like, at least roughly; but we recognize that all governments are mixed in terms of this typology.

The basis of the typology is the variable nature of the government's claim to legitimacy. The three types of authority are rational-legal, traditionalistic, and charismatic. In the *rational-legal* type, the members of government (the chief and the administrative staff) claim obedience on the ground that their commands fall within the impersonal, legally defined scope of their office: authority is felt to inhere, so to speak, in the legal order itself, and not, except by derivation, in the personalities of office-holders. This notion is familiar to us from our study of bureaucracy.

As the term implies, *traditionalistic* authority rests, theoretically, on the sanctity of tradition alone. The wielders of power point to the immemorial past, to precedent, as the "reason" for obeying their commands. There are two differences between the rational-legal system and the traditionalistic.

First, part of the "rationality" of the rational-legal type lies in the fact that particular laws are thought of as more or less effective means to achieve certain goals, whereas in the traditionalistic type laws or precedents are more likely to be thought of as sacred in themselves. The consequence is that the rational-legal type allows explicitly for the possibility and necessity of new legislation, whereas the traditionalistic is likely to maintain the fiction that traditional prerogatives and obligations have always existed and never change. We use the term "traditionalistic" rather than "traditional" to emphasize this theoretically exclusive reliance on the wisdom and sanctity of the past. The rational-legal type is also traditional, of course, but it is not traditionalistic; it does not assume that tradition cannot be improved upon. The framers of the American Constitution, for example, provided rules for amending the basic law itself.

The second difference between the two types is related to the first. The rational-legal type is "rational" also in the sense that the body of laws is thought of, ideally, as a perfect system of abstract rules, logically consistent and comprehensive enough to provide for any situations that might arise. The emphasis, again, is on law. In the traditionalistic type, on the other hand, laws are thought of as discrete precedents, not necessarily related to one another in any systematic fashion. The laws, consequently, are relatively concrete and may or may not provide adequate guides for new situations. Partly for this reason, traditionalistic systems allow an unspecified sphere of whim or "grace" or discretion to the holders of authoritative positions. In this sense, the traditionalistic type, even in pure form, puts a

[5] What follows, unless we specify otherwise, is indebted above all to Weber, 1947, Part III: "The Types of Authority and Imperative Co-ordination."

greater emphasis on the particular persons who hold positions in the government. Their traditional sphere of discretion is the source of new legislation, or at least of new precedents; but, being more or less opportunistic or even whimsical in exercising their discretion, they are less likely, of course, to build up a *system* of law. There is always room for relatively arbitrary exercise of authority

The *charismatic* type of authority puts the main emphasis on the supposedly unique or at least unusual qualities of the persons who claim authority. The word "charisma" means "gift of grace" and comes from a religious context. The charismatic leader may not always claim to have supernatural power, but he does claim to have some qualities, as a person, that distinguish him from ordinary people and justify his expectation of obedience. The pure type of charismatic authority must be revolutionary. As we shall see, charismatic elements of various kinds can be mixed with rational-legal or traditionalistic elements, but the *purely* charismatic leader necessarily claims authority *against* tradition or against a rational-legal order. He stresses a new dispensation. In their pure forms, the three types of authority are conceptually distinct.

Rational-legal systems

"Not under men but under laws": this motto, which in its Latin form is incised over the portals of the Harvard Law School library, is not an exact description of either practice or institutional pattern in American government, but it does express the rational-legal ideal, and every American will understand its spirit. The ideal is never fully realized. In England, for example, the monarchy is a traditionalistic element. The powers of the king (or queen) are so strictly limited by the constitution, however, that the government of England remains fundamentally both democratic and rational-legal. As everyone knows, the "chief" is the prime minister, not the monarch; the Speech from the Throne, delivered at the opening of Parliament, is written by the prime minister and his staff.[6]

In the courts of both England and the United States, earlier decisions—that is, precedents—play a greater role, perhaps, than they would in a strictly

[6] It must not be thought that the traditionalistic elements in the English government are necessarily defects; we are not attempting to exalt one type of legitimacy above another. The Italian sociologist Vilfredo Pareto (1935, v. 1, pp. 146-68) attributed the success of the British government in no small part to the tendency of the English to adhere to certain forms even when the substance is radically changed. This tendency he compared to the Roman piety (*religio:* a strict feeling of the duty of doing things in a certain way). He thought that in both cases the continuity thus preserved, through ingenious legal fictions and heroic efforts to rationalize departures from tradition, helped in the development of what we are here calling a rational-legal system. The Athenians, on the contrary, were too much interested in substantive justice—that is to say, in satisfying all their sentiments in each concrete case that arose before the assembly or before a court. As a result, the Athenians never developed a complex system of law. In the next chapter, we shall point out another advantage of the British system.

rational-legal system. Yet unofficial codifications also play a great part, both in the law schools and in the courts; moreover, it is hard to see how the influence of previous decisions could be entirely eliminated (if this were desirable) from any judicial system in practice.

Rational-legal systems also commonly have charismatic admixtures. In particular, officials at the top are often elected rather than appointed. In modern democracies an election is a mixture of the rational-legal and the charismatic. It is conducted according to strict rules, and the elective offices, including the highest, all have circumscribed spheres of authority: these are the rational-legal elements. Election, however, being based partly on the personalities of the candidates, is a kind of charisma (though not necessarily revolutionary). A president elected by a landslide, for example, is said to have a "mandate." This means that his election is taken as a sign that he has the moral support of "the people"—if necessary, against the opposition of bureaucracy and legislature. In other words, his authority rests upon the charisma of election as well as upon the legally defined scope of his office. At the same time, every other elected representative also feels the charismatic afflatus. Although the president has the advantage of having been elected by "all" the people, the independent charisma of all the other elected officials further prevents the government as a whole from being a pure rational-legal system. Even in the bureaucracy, moreover, not all appointments are rational-legal. Patronage (the "spoils system") means that at least some appointments are made to strengthen the party in power: in other words, past or potential service to the *party* is considered, as well as technical qualification for office in the *government*.

In the courts, the jury is essentially a charismatic institution. Jurymen are selected not for their expert knowledge of the law or of psychology but for the presumed ability of the ordinary citizen to weigh evidence fairly and wisely. The unanimous verdict is similar to the charisma of popular election. Sociologists as well as others have pointed out that in fact juries often give verdicts on the basis of their sentiments or prejudices, more or less in disregard of the law. It is well known that in the South, for example, juries have often freed a guilty white defendant when the crime he was charged with had been committed against a Negro. Insurance companies try to settle claims cases out of court, because juries have a tendency to favor the "needy" plaintiff and to think that the impersonal company, being "rich," can well afford to pay handsome damages. All this is of course quite contrary to the rational-legal ideal.[7]

[7] Legal experts are men too, of course, and may be just as "weak" as juries. In France, the judges are given a great deal of discretion in asking questions and making comments. For an absorbing case of judicial bias, see Peter Matthiessen, "Annals of Crime: Peut-etre un peu excessif," *The New Yorker,* Nov. 1, 1958, pp. 110ff. For a famous satire on French justice, see Anatole France's story *Crainquebille*: this satire, though perhaps a little excessive, could as easily have been directed against courts anywhere else. Rational-legal justice remains an *ideal*—as such, influential, but never realized fully.

Despite the charismatic aspect of democracy, it is in democracies that the rational-legal type of government has been most closely approximated. The basic reason for this is easy to see: democracy puts the governors more directly at the mercy of the governed than any other system. Other systems have "subjects"; democracies have "citizens." The citizens' power has been used, as one might expect, to set limits to the arbitrary exercise of power by the government—in other words, to define the scope of office by law. The rights of citizens are of course obligations of government and restrictions on it.

The rational-legal type of government manifests itself, then, not only in relations within the bureaucracy but also in relations between the bureaucracy and private organizations and individuals. In the judicial system, there is an emphasis on the technicality of law. Thus in criminal cases the prosecution must keep within certain rules of evidence. The question is not "Is the defendant guilty?" but "Can we show, *in the approved way,* that the defendant is guilty?" The rational-legal spirit is also revealed in the attitude of individuals in preparing income-tax returns. There is no objection to looking for "loopholes" in the law, in order to make the amount of the tax as low as possible.

One result of rational-legalism is that many "guilty" persons are freed without punishment. This kind of result may be expressed by saying that there is frequently a difference between rational-legal justice and "substantive" justice.[8] The same gap is found in income-tax returns. If the intent of the income-tax law is (roughly speaking) to make those with the highest incomes pay the most in taxes, this result is by no means perfectly attained. For example, businessmen do not have to pay taxes on "expense accounts," although such accounts often conceal a great deal of actual income. Corporations legally defeat the intent of the law by devising ingenious pension and bonus schemes whereby highly paid executives can pay a lower tax on part of their income.

There is another reason for the gap between rational-legal justice and "substantive" justice. The technicality of the law puts a high premium on legal talent. This means, inevitably, that people who can afford the ablest lawyers have a great advantage in the courts.

Although democracy is favorable to rational-legalism, democracy also contains the inherent possibility of destroying a rational-legal system. Millions of voters in some European countries vote for Communist candidates who, if they got control of the government, would certainly take it further away from the rational-legal type. Although the Nazi party in Germany was never able to win a majority of the votes in any reasonably free election, it

8 The distinction between rational-legal and substantive justice is made by Max Weber in his work on the sociology of law. The University of Chicago Press has published a translation by Max Reinhardt (1954). For a glimpse of a rather different spirit in a legal system, see Hazard, 1957, pp. 52-53.

did win enough votes to obtain for Hitler the chancellorship, from which vantage point he proceeded to destroy the Weimar Republic.

Perhaps because of their size, the democratic Greek city-states did not develop a notable rational-legal system. The group of citizens was small enough to permit a fairly good approximation to direct democracy. The citizens had absolute power in the great popular assembly. They had a constitution and made some attempt to safeguard it, but the sovereign assembly would not have tolerated the restraints that modern democracies put on mere representatives of the people. The assembly was so large that the orators often appealed to the passions of the moment and did not worry much about logic. The result was an extension, into virtually the whole business of government, of that nonrational-legal spirit which we have noted in "juries of peers." Another nonrational feature of the Greek democracies was their reliance upon the charismatic device of drawing lots to fill offices and committees. Selection by lot is not purely charismatic, however, since the method itself is traditional and the office-holder is expected to act within the legal system.

The narrowing of the sphere within which government can be arbitrary, under a well-developed rational-legal system, makes possible that predictability of conduct which we mentioned as an advantage of bureaucracy. This has been important for the development of large-scale economic enterprise. Entrepreneurs and private investors dare to risk large sums on large plans only when they can be reasonably sure what the courts, and the government generally, will and will not do under specified conditions. The thing to stress here is the predictability of government, not the scope of its functions.

Traditionalistic systems

> In the pure type of traditional authority, the following features of a bureaucratic administrative staff are absent: (a) a clearly defined sphere of competence subject to impersonal rules, (b) a rational ordering of relations of superiority and inferiority, (c) a regular system of appointment and promotion on the basis of free contract, (d) technical training as a regular requirement, (e) fixed salaries, in the type case paid in money [Weber, 1947, p. 343].

The most common way for the chief of a traditionalistic government to come into his position is through the operation of a law or custom of hereditary succession. Sometimes, however, the chief designates his successor, usually from among his sons. Other principles are also found. When the Dalai Lama dies, he is supposed to be reincarnated in a newborn infant, and a search is made to discover the proper successor, who theoretically could be found in any stratum of society. The successor will be known by certain charismatic signs. These signs being traditionally fixed, however, the system is essentially traditionalistic. In any case, Tibet has for much of her history been under the control of the rulers of China, as she is today. The following quotation provides us with one of many instances that might be given of the need to distinguish between an institutionalized facade and the reality behind it.

> Manchu control over the Tibetan church and state was more definitely established in 1751 by the emperor Ch'ien Lung. An imperial decree of that year placed both spiritual and temporal authority in the hands of the Dalai Lama as supreme pontiff, but it also provided that the two resident Chinese advisers—*ambans*—should exercise control over all his political acts. Ch'ien Lung decreed, moreover, that the two ambans should have a controlling influence in the important question of establishing the identity of the successor to the post of Dalai Lama when that office became vacant . . . [Steiger, 1936, pp. 506-07].[9]

The subjects of a traditionalistic chief are expected to obey him within a range of action that can never be specified exactly. True, many of his powers are defined in tradition, but he always has a traditional sphere of arbitrary grace also. His personal prestige, moreover, is almost always enhanced by the accepted idea that he is more or less sacred. Royal blood is somehow different from the blood of commoners. This belief—or, rather, the prestige it gives the hereditary ruler—is "hereditary charisma." The great frequency with which it is found in history illustrates once again the fact that the three types of authority are seldom found in pure form.

Among the ways in which traditionalistic regimes differ from one another, the following are perhaps the most important: (1) the social origins of the chief's personal administrative staff, (2) the methods by which the administrative staff is paid, (3) the extent of the chief's sphere of grace (i.e., arbitrary power), and (4) the degree of centralization of the government.

For his administrative staff, the chief often makes use of persons who are already bound to him by personal ties of loyalty. Kinsmen and slaves have been especially important. Slaves had the highest posts in the Ottoman Empire and in certain periods of the history of Egypt. Other persons of this general sort who have been given government posts are serfs, freedmen, and men who already have positions in the chief's household. From all the foregoing we can distinguish members of the administrative staff who have no other bond of personal loyalty to the chief: such are favorites, vassals, and men who have entered his service of their free will, for pay.

The members of the traditionalistic administrative staff do not distinguish sharply between their pay, their personal resources, and the means of administration: this fusion is of course not found in the rational-legal type except as a form of crime. Among the types of income that have supported traditionalistic administrative staffs are maintenance in the household of the chief, allowances in money or in kind from the chief's storehouses, tax farming, income from land, and rights to other income—for example, fees and fines. Each of these types of income admits of considerable variation, ac-

---

[9] For another "curious" way of determining succession in a traditionalistic government, see Krige and Krige. 1943, Chap. 10.

cording to the terms of the grant: whether it is for the duration of the chief's pleasure, for life, or is to be hereditary; whether the recipient may alienate his rights freely or not; whether the rights are granted for services or not; whether or not the rights to income are accompanied by judicial or other kinds of authority over some of the chief's subjects. Some of these differences will be discussed below in connection with variation in the degree of centralization.

The traditionalistic chief with a personal administrative staff claims his right to govern as a kind of personal property right. "He is . . . entitled to exploit it, in principle, like any economic advantage—to sell it, to pledge it as security, or to divide it by inheritance" (Weber, 1947, p. 347).[10] When this claim is successfully upheld, we may speak of "patrimonial" authority. In a feudal system, however, the chief does not have the full right of patrimonialism.

The patrimonial chief also claims to have absolute authority, but this claim can never be upheld. The sphere of arbitrary grace ranges from that of a weak monarch in a decentralized feudal system to "sultanism." A good example of almost absolute authority was given by the Ottoman sultan Selim I (1512-20), known as Selim the Grim.

> During his reign of eight years the empire nearly doubled its extent. Although he uprooted corruption and the people enjoyed a severe but just administration, his cruelty in executing eight grand viziers is alluded to in the popular saying: "May you be vizier to Sultan Selim." . . . Although among his subordinates he punished small offenses with death, his sheikh ul-Islam, Ali-Jemali Efendi, who was fearless and outspoken, was able to make him desist from his plan of converting the Greeks to Islam by the sword if necessary, by reminding him of the conqueror's (Selim's grandfather's) firman, which gave religious freedom to the Greeks. At one time Selim tried to make Arabic the official language, to further his Pan-Islamic policy [Adnan and Lewis, 1957].

The question of the chief's sphere of arbitrary discretion is obviously related to the degree of centralization of his realm.

The chief of a large centralized state has to have an administrative staff that approximates the bureaucratic type, at least to the extent that he can appoint and remove his subordinates partly according to their ability. In a feudal system, however, which is a decentralized traditionalistic system, the chief's administrative staff consists in part of vassals, who of course inherit their fiefs and with them certain kinds of traditional authority. In other words, the chief's sphere of grace may be rather severely restricted

[10] In primitive societies without governments in our sense—that is, without recognized administrative staffs—the chief, however constituted, is expected to make decisions in the interest of the whole group. Primitive political systems are traditionalistic. Weber calls them "gerontocratic" or "patriarchal," but these terms are too narrow. They fit the aboriginal tribes of Australia, for example, but not, let us say, the Plains tribes of North America. Though basically traditionalistic, primitive political systems often have charismatic elements—for example, election, visions conferring supernatural power, and, sometimes, hereditary charisma. See Lips, 1938; and Hoebel, 1954.

by the traditional prerogatives of many of his subordinates, some of whom may be great lords whose power he must respect. Short of feudalism, there is a tendency in all patrimonial systems for the administrative staff to acquire, over time, considerable power more or less beyond the chief's control. The chief's authority is often limited also by the traditional rights of various elements in the population who are not part of the government, such as peasants

In a narrow sense, feudalism is based on fiefs. The relation between lord and vassal is determined by the feudal contract, which binds the vassal to give certain services but also binds the lord to respect the honor and hereditary rights of the vassal. The lords and vassals all belong to a definitely recognized status group, with a sharply distinguished way of life and code of honor. Not only is the fief a certain piece of land, from which the vassal can derive an income, but it includes rights over the occupants of the land—rights to services and fees, rights of deciding cases in the courts. The vassal holding a particular fief may also have vassals of his own.

In a broader sense, "feudalism" may be based on benefices (also called prebends). A benefice is any bundle of rights to income, granted freely by a lord in return for services. A benefice differs from a fief in that it is not hereditary, does not necessarily involve political powers, and is not based on a contract binding the lord to loyalty to the benefice-holder. In principle, the lord may revoke a benefice; on the other hand, he may promote a benefice-holder. The benefice may or may not involve land. The "beneficiary" may or may not be a member of a prestige-bearing status group of knights, whereas the feudal "vassal" always is. A fief is desirable in part for the status honor that goes with it; a benefice is desirable mainly for the income it yields. However, it is possible for benefices to become similar to fiefs: for example, during periods when the sultans were weak, military commanders in the Ottoman Empire were able to make their benefices hereditary and to a considerable extent autonomous. In general, a tendency of feudal systems of either type is to combine property rights and political rights.

All traditionalistic governments suffer from one or more inherent weaknesses which are sources of change. The principle of hereditary succession provides continuity and permits the early training of the chief, but there is a good chance that some of the heirs will be men of little native ability. Moreover, hereditary monarchies often have a good deal of bloodshed at the top. The possibility of inheriting the throne has been a temptation for sons to kill their fathers. In order to forestall disloyalty, fathers have sometimes killed sons. For a long period in the Ottoman Empire a sultan on accession to the throne murdered some of his brothers. Ahmed I (1603-17), who was of a mild and religious disposition, broke this custom and had his brothers confined to a walled area. In at least one African Negro kingdom. the brothers of a new king were put in a stockade and allowed to die of starvation.

Traditionalistic governments are also plagued by intrigues and factions involving court favorites, male and female, harem eunuchs, scheming wives, and household servants.

The prestige and traditional sphere of grace of the chief sometimes tempt him to neglect his realm for personal pleasure or to abuse his power over his subjects. But perhaps the most important tension-point and source of change is the relation between the chief and his administrative staff. Feudalism may be a stage in the building up of centralized authority or a stage in its decline. In any case, the traditionalistic chief typically tries to increase his control over his administrative staff, by using spies or setting personal agents over them, by requiring hostages, by arranging marriages, or by granting subjects and minor subordinates a right of appeal to him. In a feudal system, the vassals try to extend their autonomy, and to do so they may form combinations against the supreme chief. We may catch a glimpse of the forces at work, and of the attempts made to cope with them, from the following account of Tokugawa Iyeyasu's policy after his suppression of a revolt in 1600 in Sekigahara (Japan).

> The lands which thus came into his possession were allotted by the Tokugawa dictator to two groups of feudatories: the *fudai* daimyo, or "hereditary" vassals, and the *tozama* daimyo, or "outside" nobles. The former groups, which included the members of the Tokugawa family and those who, before Sekigahara, had been reckoned among its loyal supporters, received as fiefs lands located in the Kwanto, in the home provinces, and in the region lying between these two important areas. The tozama daimyo, being those who accepted Tokugawa overlordship after Sekigahara, received fiefs in Kyushu, Shikoku, the western and extreme northern provinces of Honshu, and the island of Yezo. By this arrangement the less dependable "outside" nobles were relegated to the outlying portions of the empire, while the central provinces constituted a solid block held by the Tokugawas and their most trusted supporters [Steiger, 1936, pp. 407-08].

Almost everywhere in the world, the struggle between the chief and his feudal staff has resulted in victory for the chief and for bureaucratic administration.

Patrimonial systems, including feudalism, are usually unfavorable for private enterprise and for a high degree of rationality in economic activity. Taxation and the imposition of fees tend to be erratic. Entrepreneurs are discouraged by the struggles for power, by the unpredictability of arbitrary authority, and also of course by the weight of tradition. Under some circumstances, however, the government itself has organized monopolies in a fairly rational manner and has given "systematic attention to the prosperity of its sources of taxation" (Weber, 1947, p. 355).

Charismatic systems

As we have said, the pure type of charismatic authority is revolutionary in purpose. The term "revolution," however, is somewhat vague. The great revolutions of modern history—the French, the Russian, the Nazi—have all been alike in certain respects. In each case the revolutionary movement resulted in profound changes in the social structure of the society involved; the kinship system, the economy, religious organization, the class structure, and of course the political system were all affected. Secondly, these changes were accompanied by much social mobility: many persons previously low in rank rose to great power and prestige, and many others once among the social élite were humbled. Thirdly, these changes did not take place without considerable violence, amounting to civil war. Finally, though the process could always be traced to causes in the more remote past (any historical "event," after all, is the arbitrarily isolated "end" of many interrelated chains of events, going back as far as one wishes to go), nevertheless the revolutionary period at its height was marked by great changes taking place within a short span of time—a year or two.

With respect to each of these points, however, there were of course quantitative and qualitative differences between those big revolutions; and many relatively minor revolutions have not displayed such marked changes. Only two things are true of all the social upheavals, from mere *coups d'état* to "total" transformations, to which the term "revolution" is ordinarily applied: (1) the institutionalized pattern for acquiring or exercising governmental power has been ignored to some extent; and (2) the irregular course has been successful in the sense that the leader or leaders have actually been able to entrench themselves and, at least for a time, wield supreme power. An unsuccessful attempt to carry through a revolution is known as a "rebellion." A "revolt" may or may not succeed.

Since all revolutions are carried through with a certain amount of violence, and with even more threatened violence to those who might resist, the question might be asked whether charismatic authority need be involved at all.[11] There is a great range of variation, certainly, in the extent to which the new government seeks to justify its seizure of power by basing it on some legitimizing theory. All three of the great revolutions mentioned above have been notable for the elaboration of ideology; but many of the "palace revolutions" in traditionalistic systems, and many of the *coups d'état* in Latin American countries (for example), seem to have made little claim to any kind of "legitimacy" other than preponderant force. No revolutionary leader, however, can hope to succeed without the support of more or less dedicated followers. They, at least, must acknowledge his right to obedience.

With few exceptions, the Latin American revolutions have not made far-reaching changes in the social structure. The *coup d'état* has merely changed the personnel at the apex of the government and diverted the booty of power from one small group to another. The propertied classes have remained in the enjoyment of their traditional privileges, provided that they

---

11 Perhaps it is to leave this question open that some writers, though familiar with Max Weber's work, use the term "dictatorial" rather than "charismatic." See, for example, MacIver, 1947, pp. 151ff.; and Timasheff, 1954.

were willing to share some of the gains with the revolutionary *junta*. The masses of the population have been affected only to the extent that the new government might be a little more, or a little less, oppressive than the old. Indeed, government at the local level often goes on in the old traditionalistic way.

The Latin American form of traditionalism, moreover, stresses the relatively unrestrained will of those in power. This is a heritage from the days of the *conquistadores*. The supreme chief and the sub-chiefs have had a broad sphere of grace. The long tradition of relatively arbitrary power has habituated the population to dictatorship. A more subtle point is that a daring, flamboyant, even cruel show of great personal power, provided that it is successful, is almost self-legitimizing. The force of character displayed is widely understood, admired, and envied. Gomez of Venezuela was a typical Latin American charismatic dictator.

> . . . I do know at first hand that the relationship which I have assumed to have existed between aboriginal and Spaniard existed in Gomez' day in Venezuela on the part of the exploited population towards its political masters. One has actually to hear a disinherited Venezuelan say of one of the political *jefes, Ese es un chivato* ("That one is a big shot"—but the psychological connotations are not carried of course by the American phrasing) to appreciate how deeply grounded is that admiration. Gomez and his clique were intensely hated but even in those who hated him most intensely it was not difficult to perceive a certain measure of unmistakable respect because Gomez was a real *macho*. a male, *todo un hombre*, in the utterly untranslatable sense in which the Venezuelan uses that word "man." In English of course when the word "man" is used eulogistically it conveys the sense of courage as it does in Spanish. But when a Venezuelan uses it, it refers to more than courage. It refers to a quality of aggressiveness as well as of defensive courage [Vivas, 1945, pp. 188-89; see also Tax, 1945; and Bryce, 1921, v. 1, Chap. 17]

The very word "leadership" implies possession of certain personal qualities; it also implies that these qualities are manifested in action and are recognized by a following. Whatever other basis authority may have, successful decision-making confers a kind of charisma. The charisma of success was implicitly recognized in the traditionalistic ideology of the Chinese empire. If the emperor was disastrously unsuccessful in war, or even if his realm suffered from a great famine, he was said to have lost "the mandate of Heaven." On the other hand, if he was successful, his success confirmed his hereditary charisma. A successful Latin American dictator is more often purely charismatic; moreover, his "success" is merely his demonstrated ability to gain and keep power against whatever opposition offers itself.

Adolf Hitler was a pure charismatic leader, complete with legitimizing ideology, a zealous following of millions, and astounding success, at least for a time (long enough to convulse the world).

> Hitler himself, in many of his addresses, justifies his being endowed with absolute and supreme powers by the fact of his "mission" for the German people, and the achievements—such as destroying the decadent "system" of

> the Weimar Republic, wiping out the Versailles Treaty, creating "Greater Germany"–he has contributed to German history and to the welfare of the nation. His followers . . . attribute his achievements as much to supernatural gifts as to the undefinable though omnipresent qualities of leadership. His book *"Mein Kampf"* [is] the Bible of the Third Reich. . . . It is impossible for the non-believer to argue within the limits of reason with the faithful who believe in these facts with the strength, devotion, and fanaticism of a religious creed [Loewenstein, 1940, pp. 34-35].

Hitler came into power by ruthlessly perverting the democratic electoral process; and once installed as chancellor he gave up all but the pretense of parliamentary government. Although officially the chancellor, he soon dropped this title and decreed that he should be officially given the title he had acquired early in his revolutionary career; like Mussolini in Italy, he emphasized his contempt for the institutions he had overthrown, and his pure charisma, by calling himself "the Leader" (*il Duce, der Fuehrer*).

Hitler was deified during his lifetime. The leader of the Russian Revolution, Lenin, was not deified until after his death. Although a pure charismatic leader, Lenin was of a slightly different type from Hitler. They were different in the relative emphasis placed upon the *personal* charisma of the leader himself and the "divine" truth of the ideology on which, to some extent, each based his claim to authority. Both were leaders of great personal force of character, and both were of necessity flexible in taking action; but Lenin stood upon the higher authority of the works of Karl Marx, he was an interpreter, whereas Hitler and his followers to a much greater extent emphasized the unique vision of the leader himself. Lenin demanded obedience on the ground that he understood the revealed canon better than others; Hitler demanded obedience on the ground that he was the incarnation of the spirit of the "true" Germany and that whatever he said was true. The relatively impersonal basis of Communist authority was re-emphasized after the death of Stalin when the personal idolization of that dictator was condemned as "the cult of personality." It is doubtful that the worship of Stalin ever reached the intensity of the worship of Hitler.

Needless to say, not all the supporters of a charismatic leader are genuine worshipers. Many are opportunistic careerists. Many have allowed themselves to be "bought off." Many are simply afraid not to hail the leader as they are told. Even the genuine worship is to a large extent produced by propaganda. Nevertheless, personal qualities and success are indispensable.

We should make explicit the relative sense in which the charismatic dispensation is "new." Every "new" ideology is a combination of ideas that have been present in the culture for a long time. Historians have written books about the long prehistory of the French Revolutionary ideology, of the Communist ideology, and of National Socialism. What is new in each revolution is the forcefully asserted "no nonsense" demand that the ideology be taken as the basis of legitimacy of the actual government; the ideology is "new" merely in the sense that it displaces the old official ideology

Wherever the concept of revolutionary charisma is applicable, it raises a sociological problem: it merely identifies a phenomenon; it does not explain why certain personal qualities and certain "new" ideas should be so attractive and why the revolutionary movement succeeds. A revolutionary movement never attracts all segments of the population, and it attracts different segments for different reasons. There are certain common characteristics of all prerevolutionary situations, but they are necessarily of a rather general nature. In order to "explain" a particular revolutionary transformation, one must make an analysis of the structure and dynamic processes of the particular society in which it occurs. We shall return to this problem later in the book.

The leader of a revolutionary movement chooses his lieutenants on the basis of their presumed loyalty to him, their enthusiasm for the cause, and their own charismatic qualities. He has absolute authority over them, assigning tasks, changing his mind, commanding and countermanding at will. He delegates authority, but everyone in the movement is in principle responsible to him. He may have a policy or a strategy, but he does not organize his administrative staff in a rational-legal way. No one has a sphere of authority into which the leader may not intrude.

Such a system, however, is necessarily transitional. Especially after the movement has successfully seized governmental power, its pure charismatic nature must be transformed, more or less gradually, into something else. The "routinization of charisma" can move toward a traditionalistic system, toward a rational-legal system, or toward some mixed type. With regard to these developments, there are two questions to answer. First, why is routinization of some kind inevitable if the movement remains in power? And secondly, what factors tend to drive the process of routinization in a traditionalistic direction, and what factors drive it in a rational-legal direction? The first question is easier to answer than the second.

Among the factors making for routinization are the following:

1. Upon seizing governmental power, the movement is confronted with much greater tasks of administration. For these it needs a more assured and a larger flow of income than it has enjoyed in the rise to power. Hitherto it has depended upon gifts from supporters and upon more or less haphazard plundering. Now it proceeds to confiscation, more systematic "solicitation" of funds, and taxation. The collection of taxes especially will tend toward some kind of system or routine. The problem of maintaining continuity will in general assert itself.

The more important lieutenants must be entrusted with great governmental tasks. Controlling the army, the police force, the civilian bureaucracy (if there is one), looking after taxation and economic affairs generally, directing foreign policy—all these pressing matters require some sort of system. The chief cannot do everything, decide everything, himself. The lieutenants tend to become entrenched to some extent. They build up their own staffs, their own organizations. While the chief may still have "absolute" authority, he cannot exercise it so freely, for he is more dependent than ever upon his lieutenants.

2. In the early months or years of the movement, the leader, his charismatic lieutenants, and all the more active supporters have had to dedicate themselves ascetically to the cause. They have had to be constantly vigilant lest they betray the movement or be crushed by the authorities they were struggling to overthrow. They have not been able to lead a "normal" family life. Such a pitch of enthusiasm and dedication cannot be maintained forever. Once their self-abnegation and tremendous sustained effort have been crowned with success, many of the lieutenants and underlings want to relax a little, enjoy their new prosperity, settle down to a less hectic, more secure way of life. In short, they *want* routine.

3. One of the most important problems the movement will face, if it lasts long enough, is the problem of succession to the leader's position. It is partly in preparation for the crisis that the lieutenants have built up their own followings. A struggle goes on, not always in the open. We need not assume, however, that this struggle is necessarily a mere dogfight for power. If the movement has been united and vivified by a great cause, a vision, a mission, expressed in an ideology, then some at least of the lieutenants will be concerned that the successor to the leader be "worthy" of the position. Among the possible ways of deciding upon a successor are the following:

a. An open struggle, possibly an appeal to arms, with rival claimants mobilizing their forces behind them.

b. A choice on the basis of the conception of hereditary charisma. Sometimes a precedent in favor of primogeniture is established. Sometimes the leader's close kinsmen are thought to share his charisma, and the choice among them is made by a personal contest of some kind to determine which one is most worthy.

c. A search for a person manifesting the qualities of the leader. The selection of the Dalai Lama is an example. Since the successor in this case is an infant, the search is for *signs* of charisma, not for the manifest qualities. This course, like course b, leads in a traditionalistic direction.

d. Selection by oracles, drawing of lots, or some other magical procedure thought to reveal divine will.

e. Designation of his successor by the leader himself. This method may confirm hereditary charisma if the leader names his son. Whether he designates his son or someone unrelated to him, his decision may or may not be accepted by the administrative staff. In other words, designation by the leader will not necessarily prevent an open struggle and seizure of the supreme power by force.

f. "Designation of a successor by the charismatically qualified administrative staff and his recognition by the community."

> In its typical form this process should quite definitely not be interpreted as "election" or "nomination" or anything of the sort. It is not a matter of free selection, but of one which is strictly bound to objective duty. It is not to be

determined merely by majority vote, but is a question of arriving at the correct designation, the designation of the right person who is truly endowed with charisma. It is quite possible that the minority and not the majority should be right in such a case. Unanimity is often required. It is obligatory to acknowledge a mistake and persistence in error is a serious offense. Making a wrong choice is a genuine wrong requiring expiation. Originally it was a magical offence [Weber, 1947, p. 365].[12]

Our question about the factors that drive the pure charismatic government toward a rational-legal form and the factors that drive it toward a traditionalistic kind of "routine" is similar to the question why the revolutionary movement was successful in the first place: it cannot be answered without an analysis of the balance of forces within the society as a whole. Nevertheless, we can perhaps indicate, in a broad way, what some of the relevant factors are.

As we have mentioned in passing, the particular mode of succession to the top leadership is an important factor. This suggestion is no solution to our problem, however, since we should have to ask why one mode of selection is adopted rather than another. Moreover, the mode of selection by itself does not tell us very much about the sphere of authority the successor will have, nor about the relation between the new chief and his administrative staff. We are nearly back where we started. Since our knowledge is so unsatisfactory, let us be content to list four further questions, the answers to which would help us with the main question:

1. Did the original charismatic leader seek to legitimize his position, in part, by holding plebiscites? However much a plebiscite may be "rigged," it helps to establish the presumption that democratic values are given some weight. If the government tends nevertheless toward traditionalism, at least the chief's sphere of arbitrary power will be somewhat restricted in principle. Moreover, election for "offices" means that there *are* more or less clearly defined positions in the government. This fact, along with the plebiscite itself, works in the rational-legal direction.

2. What was the nature of the system the revolutionary movement overthrew? In particular, was there any sort of bureaucracy, and was the population accustomed to democracy or to autocracy? If bureaucratic norms have been firmly established, they are difficult to displace altogether. The example of Nazi Germany shows, to be sure, that a rational-legal bureaucracy can be perverted almost beyond recognition, but the sheer efficiency of bureaucracy, once known, will remain as a model. The pressures that produced the bureaucracy in the first place may reassert themselves and restore impersonal rules, perhaps within narrower limits. As for the nature of the

[12] These comments of Weber may throw some light on the process of selection in the Soviet Union. Theoretically the supreme authority is vested in the Central Committee; but one man has always been at the apex. Obviously the possibility of having to expiate a "wrong" choice must lead to guessing and calculating the distribution of support within the top group.

general population, if it was poorly educated and accustomed to the rule of tradition and arbitrary authority, we cannot expect that any new government will quickly develop a rational-legal system.

3. What is the international situation confronted by the charismatic government? If the government is menaced by external enemies, the chance of developing a rational-legal system of the democratic type is much reduced. Great emergencies, especially if prolonged, will tend to favor a purely traditionalistic development or a charismatic succession based on traditionalistic criteria.

4. The preceding factors are interrelated in the sense that they will modify one another. They are all related also to the next factor: What is the nature of the ideology of the charismatic movement? This is a complex question. We can only suggest its relevance. It seems, for example, that Communism has an inherently greater chance of developing eventually in a rational-legal direction than National Socialism had, despite the fact that the Nazi movement arose in a country with a much more highly developed rational-legal system. The Nazi ideology was explicitly antirationalistic. Two of its most emphasized elements were racism and the so-called leadership principle. The "race" doctrine included not only anti-Semitism but the idea that all non-Germans are inferior to "Aryan" Germans. This means that the rational-legal aspect of bureaucracy would have been severely restricted indeed, not only within the bureaucracy but in the relation between the government and the governed. This restriction is especially important if we remember that, had the Nazi movement succeeded in its aim of "world domination," many "inferior" peoples would have come permanently under Nazi rule. The "leadership principle" stressed the right of an elite to rule and the duty of the masses (even of Germans) to obey without question. Such an ideology pointed away from a rational-legal development.[13] In thinking of Communism, by comparison, we are focusing attention, in the present context, on ideology. Whereas the Nazi movement was ideologically particularistic, Communism is universalistic: mankind is one; racism and even nationhood are to be decried. Ideologically, the dictatorship is temporary. According to its lights, it is dedicated to raising the level of all the people—indeed, of all peoples. Although, as always, ideology and practice do not perfectly coincide, there are pressures, stemming partly from ideology, toward widening participation in decision-making. These pressures are partly the result of ideological emphasis on the spread of education. A regime that calls itself democratic is inevitably under some pressure to make good its claim. Moreover, there are degrees of democracy, and we shall see in the next chapter that even at present the Soviet system is far from being at the bottom of a hypothetical scale.

---

[13] In the present chapter, the exact meaning of "ideology" is left implicit. For a more formal treatment, see Chap. 21.

RECOMMENDED READING

In his introduction to M. Weber, *The Theory of Social and Economic Organization*, trans. by A. M. Henderson and T. Parsons, Oxford University Press, 1947, Parsons asserts that Weber's theory of the types of political authority is the greatest achievement of social science thus far, not excepting the theory of classical economics. At any rate, it is the chief source of the present chapter. See Part III: "The Types of Authority and Imperative Co-ordination," and do not overlook the introduction by Parsons, especially pp. 56-77, which not only explains but adds some original points. Two somewhat different schemes of analysis may also be suggested. The first is R. M. MacIver, *The Web of Government*, Macmillan, 1947, especially Part III: "The Forms of Government," which is extremely well written, learned, and thoughtful. The second is N. S. Timasheff, "Totalitarianism, Despotism, Dictatorship," in C. J. Friedrich, ed., *Totalitarianism*, Harvard University Press, 1954, pp. 39-47. This concise paper presents quantitative indices for the classification of particular governments. It draws to some extent upon work done for P. A. Sorokin, *Social and Cultural Dynamics*, American Book, 1937, v. 2. An excellent short treatment of political institutions is given in K. Davis, *Human Society*, Macmillan, 1949, Chap. 18.

For a fascinating account of a charismatic movement, see K. Heiden, *Der Fuehrer: Hitler's Rise to Power*, trans. by R. Manheim, Houghton Mifflin, 1944. Three papers by T. Parsons show how a sociological mode of analysis helps us to understand the Nazi movement. In some ways the broadest perspective is given in "Some Sociological Aspects of the Fascist Movements," *Social Forces*, 1942, v. 21, pp. 138-47 (reprinted in T. Parsons, *Essays in Sociological Theory*, rev. ed., Free Press, 1954, Chap. 7). "Democracy and Social Structure in Pre-Nazi Germany," *J. Legal Polit. Sociol.*, 1942, v. 1, pp. 96-114 (reprinted in *Essays*, Chap. 6), explains the Nazi movement, in part, by references to peculiarities in the social structure of pre-Nazi Germany. "Max Weber and the Contemporary Political Crisis," *Rev. Politics*, 1942, v. 4, pp. 61-76, 155-72, shows how Weber's theory of types of authority illuminates the Nazi movement.

14. Structure and Functioning of Political Democracy

Several of the most important governments in the world today are democratic; and it is a striking indication of the prestige of democracy that many of the other governments, somewhat ambiguously, *call* themselves democratic. In this chapter we shall be interested mainly in the federal government of the United States, but our analysis will be couched in terms broad enough to warrant many comparisons with other political systems.

Institutional Criteria of Political Democracy

Democracy is a mixture of the rational-legal and charismatic types, with a touch of traditionalism in some instances. Its defining characteristic, at least for the purpose of this discussion, is that the members of the government are directly accountable to the citizens in periodic free elections. Several points in this definition require elaboration and modification, but let us note at once that the emphasis is placed on the mode by which the members of government acquire and keep authority "Checks and balances," apart from elections, are secondary, and democratic government is not necessarily "limited" government in the sense of government with few responsibilities. Democracy is not the same thing as distrust of government in general. In most democratic countries it would be unnecessary to make this remark, but in the United States there is still, though it is rapidly changing, an ideological tendency to favor government limited in scope. This preference is a peculiarity of American democracy, not a defining characteristic of the type.

It is not necessary for all the positions in a democratic government to be elective. It is necessary, however, for the appointive members to be responsible to and hence removable by the elective members.[1] The British

[1] One might think, at first glance, that appointive judges with life tenure do not come within the democratic pattern. They do, however, for their offices as such are ultimately defined by the elective legislature, which could change the Constitution if it wished to do so. This possibility, although important, is not the most important control over the conduct of judges. The most important controls are, first, the rational-legal definition of the scope of their offices and, secondly, the glaring publicity attending their official acts.

monarch of course has a hereditary position, but that fact does not prevent England from being democratic, for the governmental authority of the monarch is strictly limited. More important, even this limited authority, and the institution of the monarchy itself, could by existing democratic procedures be eliminated altogether. Since there is good reason to believe that the monarchy enjoys widespread popular support, there is little chance that it will be voted out of existence.[2]

Another question that inevitably arises in connection with our brief definition of democracy is this: How many of the citizens must be entitled to vote? Merely asking the question shows that "democracy" is a matter of degree. A regime that denies the vote to women is to that extent undemocratic. So is the system in some parts of the South, which on paper grants Negroes the right to vote but denies it in practice. Many whites as well as Negroes in the United States are effectively disfranchised by the poll tax. We shall find other aspects of the political arrangements in the United States that are substantively, if not formally, undemocratic. In considering any political system, it is necessary to distinguish between paper form and underlying reality. No one has yet proposed social arrangements that would ensure perfect democracy. At the same time, if democracy is the ideal, we shall find that at several points the American system is quite realistically capable of improvement.

Another point in our definition requires clarification. We spoke of "periodic" elections. In England, a general election is held only when the cabinet in power (the "government" in a narrow sense) cannot win a majority in Parliament on some important question. The "government" itself may declare a question to be "a question of confidence." The "periods" between elections, therefore, are of unequal length, whereas in the United States, of course, elections are held at regular intervals. Neither system is more "democratic" than the other. The main point is that in both systems the ultimate appeal is to the electorate.

Finally, we must say a word about "free" elections. As everyone knows, elections are held in the Soviet Union, which is not, according to our conception, a democratic country. The elections in the Soviet Union are not "free" for two reasons. First, only one political party, the Communist, is allowed. This means that, practically speaking, the voters have no choice. The most they can do is cross out the one name for each office that is presented on the ballot. The election alone cannot possibly unseat the existing government. Secondly, the ballots are not necessarily cast secretly. This is more important than might appear at first glance. One *may* vote secretly, but the "patriotic" thing to do is to stand in the middle of the room and ostentatiously vote for all the nominees with one gesture. Communists are present to see

---

[2] It could almost be argued, in any case, that the British monarch is not mainly a part of the government. The main function of the monarch is to serve as a symbolic focus of the nation as a whole, and in that function the monarch "stands above" the political arena of conflicting interests.

which voters are "patriotic." This system means that a certain amount of courage is necessary to avail oneself of the possibility of voting secretly.[3] In a democratic system, one *must* enter a curtained booth to mark one's ballot or to use the voting machine. This requirement is a safeguard of freedom.[4]

It should be noted that there are other meanings for the word "democracy." Loosely, the word may mean no more than government that enjoys popular support. We have already noted, however, that any form of government may, under certain circumstances, be popular; the distinguishing mark of democracy is that the popularity of the government personnel—and implicitly of the form of government—is regularly tested by an institutionalized means. This testing, moreover, which involves free elections in which parties compete for votes, also involves the right to criticize the government's policies and acts at all times, for without this right the free elections could not mean very much.

Another meaning of "democracy" is self-government. It may well be that in a society in which democratic government is firmly rooted there is a tendency toward self-government in small informal groups, especially when the matters to be decided are well known and understood by all the members. This tendency is recognizably democratic in spirit. Nevertheless, self-government in this radical sense is not possible for a total society of any great size. It is safe to say that most of the issues that come up for decision in a modern legislature are issues about which the average citizen does not and could not have a clear opinion. In a modern democracy, therefore, the voters delegate the responsibility of making decisions to their representatives.

As a matter of fact, the very concept of "representation" is not absolutely clear-cut. Some people think that it is the representative's duty to

---

[3] The rulers of Russia are not satisfied with these controls. "The elections of 1954 seated 1,347 deputies in the Supreme Soviet of the U.S.S.R." Note the number of deputies. "That there are no such public dissenters—at least in the Supreme Soviet, to which foreign diplomats and correspondents are invited as observers—is proved by the fact that there has never yet been a vote, on any subject, which has not been unanimous" (Hazard, 1957, pp. 42, 49).

[4] Here is a good place to emphasize the fact that democracy is a matter of degree. In 1956 the population of the Soviet Union was approximately 200 million. The Communist Party had about 7 million members (about 3.5 per cent of the population); even allowing for the relatively wide base of the Soviet population pyramid—the large proportion of children—we can say that the Party was and is a small, exclusive group. Moreover, as we shall see later in this chapter, the internal organization of the Party itself is far from perfectly democratic, although it has certain democratic features. Yet the Soviet system comes closer to being democratic than dictatorships based on the narrow support of an army. The Communist Party of the U.S.S.R., although small and exclusive, does at least consist of seven million persons from all levels of society, representing all interests except those fundamentally opposed to the basic social institutions; and the top leaders are extremely concerned about keeping the "understanding" and support of the Party and, through it, of "the people." See Duverger, 1954, pp. 425-26.

act as he thinks his constituents would act if they could decide for themselves. This view is of course relevant (but not necessarily correct) when the issue to be decided is one on which many citizens do have a fairly clear opinion. Even in this case, however, some people maintain that it is the duty of the representative to decide according to *his* opinion of the best interests of the electorate—an opinion that might be unpopular. This is the view expressed by Edmund Burke in his famous Letter to the Electors of Bristol.[5] In practice, of course, there is some compromise between these views. In general, the institutionalized accountability of the representatives, through elections, ensures that politicians will be sensitive to the opinions of that part (at least) of their constituency that actually takes advantage of the right to vote.[6]

The Soviet Russian conception of democracy is that the government should represent the people in the sense of making decisions in their interest, *regardless of how the people feel about it* (see Weinberg and Shabat, 1956, pp. 209-15). As we have just seen, this conception is not different from one that is held quite seriously by intelligent persons in the Western world. What *is* different is the Western conception that the government should nevertheless be voted in—and voted out, if the electorate so wishes. With this institutionalized provision, there is of course less chance that there will be a difference of opinion between the representative and his constituents on any important matter. Nevertheless, our government is a compromise between government by mechanical reflectors of "the popular will" and government by those who "know best."

The great gulf between Western democratic and Soviet conceptions is revealed in Stalin's statement: "The Party [which rules Russia] is no true Party if it limits its activities to a mere registration of the suffering and thoughts of the proletarian masses . . . if it cannot rise superior to the *transient* interests of the proletariat" (quoted by Inkeles, 1954, pp. 96-97).[7] The austere ideal expressed in this statement is to ignore the present aspirations of the "masses" in favor of a more distant, higher goal. Undue pity for the present generation is made to appear as a temptation, a weakness of character, and a falling from grace.

Finally, "democracy" often means easy, egalitarian manners, with no expectation that anyone will show marked deference to another. In a state

---

[5] In *Capitalism, Socialism, and Democracy* (1947), Joseph A. Schumpeter goes so far as to maintain that voters should not write letters to their representatives. Few people would agree with him. In any form of government, it is obviously desirable for those in power to know what the governed are thinking. A moment's reflection, however, will show that the advantages of role specialization would be lost if representatives always tried to reflect public opinion as faithfully as possible. The presumption is that to some extent the professionals know more of the relevant facts on which to base an intelligent decision.

[6] For an able exposition of the conflicting moral demands to which the elected representative is subject, see J. F. Kennedy, *Profiles in Courage* (1956), Chap. 1.

[7] We have removed Inkeles' italics and added others in order to bring out a different [illegible] of the statement.

in which ordinary persons have the right to vote and in which the vote counts for something, the dignity of citizens does perhaps make for an egalitarian spirit; but we should note that considerable elaboration of formal distinctions of rank (as in England) is quite compatible with political democracy in the sense of our definition.

In addition to the institutions we have already mentioned, there are at least three others that are necessary if democracy is to be more than a name or a pious hope. First, the positions in government should be *offices* in the technical bureaucratic sense. We usually distinguish between "political" and "bureaucratic" offices, but all are alike, in the United States, in the respect that the scope of responsibility and authority of each position is defined by law. The reason such an institutional pattern is necessary to a modern democratic system is that it makes it possible to "take for granted" the rational-legal hierarchy of offices in the struggle for votes. The field of political controversy is large enough as it is, but it would be prohibitively large if political candidates had to present promises covering the whole range now covered by the law The voters would be utterly confused and there could be no order in government. As it is, a *particular* law may become a campaign issue, but for the most part all the candidates implicitly agree to act within the established legal pattern, even if some of them propose to work toward modifying the pattern here and there.[8]

The second requirement for substantive democracy is that the citizens should have the right to organize parties and pressure groups. An electoral system is not democratic if only one party is allowed. It is necessary, note, that there be more than the right to offer oneself as a candidate for office; one must be able to build up an organization for making one's program known and persuading the voters to support it. The reason, of course, is that lone individuals would have little chance of electoral success against the one permitted electoral organization.[9] On the other hand, theoretically it is not necessary that there actually *be* two or more parties; what is necessary is that the citizens have the right to form a new party if they wish to. It is doubtful, however, whether any democracy has ever had only one party. India is sometimes mentioned as an example, but it certainly is not. Although the Congress Party is by far the strongest, other parties do campaign for electoral support.

A political party is an organization the purpose of which is to get its candidates elected (or re-elected) to government office; it is one of an

8 Communist and fascist parties in democratic countries do not, of course, promise to act within the established legal pattern once they are able to control the government. These are parties, however, only in an ambiguous sense. When not in power, they must keep more or less within the law; but they are fundamentally revolutionary movements, not parties, as is shown when they acquire power.

9 In the Soviet Union, which permits only the Communist Party, non-Communists are sometimes elected to office, but this happens only when the Communists wish it to. A "one-party system" is a contradiction in terms if the one "party" is the only one *permitted*.

indefinite number of such organizations in a political system, all of which are expected to compete within an institutional framework of law.[10] Since the whole process of government affects the population in multitudinous ways, and since the population in turn tries to influence the process of government, it is necessary in a democracy to have the right to form pressure groups as well as parties. A pressure group is different from a party in that its main purpose is not to elect candidates but to influence the government (however the latter may be composed) in behalf of some interest or goal. A pressure group may work for certain candidates, to be sure; but since its main purpose is to mobilize the power of government behind specific, and usually somewhat limited, projects (e.g., tariff protection for a certain industry, better schooling for Indians, a revision of the calendar, a federal law prohibiting capital punishment) a pressure group will ordinarily support particular candidates regardless of the party they belong to, and will shift its support from one party to another if such a shift seems to be favorable to its specific projects. The right to form pressure groups is necessary to democracy precisely because of the fact that a *party*, in order to be successful, must appeal to diverse people on many issues; voting, while terribly important, may not in itself give many citizens sufficient opportunity to pinpoint their wishes concerning the operation of government.[11]

The third additional institutional requirement for democracy is "freedom" for all the media of communication: newspapers, books, radio, television, movies, speech-making in public assemblies. Undue restrictions in communication obviously make democracy a sham, for the voters can then have only a distorted view of what they are voting for.[12]

One of the main criticisms leveled against Western democracy by Communists is that great concentrations of wealth are used to twist the machinery of elections and governing. According to this view, the right to vote is a fraud. Private wealth, it is maintained, perverts the system in the interests of a relatively small part of the population: rich corporations and individuals, the doctrine explains, own and control the media of communication, and they largely finance political campaigns, in return for which they demand

---

[10] This definition of "party" is obviously somewhat narrow. Every political system has legal and illegal, formal and informal, secret and open organizations the purpose of which is to affect the composition of government. Every courtier has supporters and enemies. But it does not promote clarity in our thinking about democracy to call all political factions, cabals, revolutionary movements, and other combinations "political parties." Terms are of course arbitrary to some extent, and there is good precedent for using the term "party" in a wider sense than we give it here. See, for example, Weber, 1946, pp. 194-95.

[11] Any group may at times, or in one phase of its activity, be a pressure group. For example, the American Medical Association is a pressure group as well as an organization for setting and maintaining professional standards.

[12] We cannot go into the complex question of defining "undue" restrictions. Some cases are clear enough. Another desideratum for democracy is widespread education. Without it, a democracy is not likely to be very efficient, but democracy is *possible* without it. Most voters in India are illiterate.

a preponderant voice in framing party platforms. This criticism is not wholly without foundation. No workable proposal has yet been advanced for making the political influence of all citizens exactly equal. It is extremely doubtful, we should note, whether this end, if such a proposal were advanced, would be a good thing. On the other hand, if the Communist charge were literally true, one would have to admit that Western democracy is substantially a fraud.

The charge, however, is greatly exaggerated.[13] When we examine the American system in more detail, we shall see that its operation is more complex than the Communist ideology makes it appear. For the moment, let us note the following points:

1. Even the rich accept certain social institutions and values that benefit the poor. For example, there is at present little criticism of public education as an institution (although there is, of course, criticism of its detailed operation).

2. There are many sources of information besides those controlled by the rich. For example, labor unions issue news and propaganda.

3. The rich need to be informed just as much as the poor, and they expect a high standard of accuracy in news reporting.

4. Journalism has to a certain extent become a profession, with high standards of competence and faithfulness to truth. Many journalists take pride in being able to dig out and publish facts that powerful persons and groups might like to suppress. The high ideals that, in Anglo-Saxon countries especially, have been developed for free, honest, intelligent, and complete coverage, interpretation, and dissemination of news are so difficult to attain perfectly that most students of our mass media are critical of them, and no doubt this is a good sign.[14] Without wishing to decry those ideals in the least (on the contrary, they need the greatest attention in a society that wishes to remain a democracy), we might suggest that a realistic appraisal of our mass media might better be made in a historical and a comparative perspective. In these perspectives, the performance of the present-day American press as a whole is one of the great achievements of the United States. The improvement in the average performance, as well as in the journalistic ideals, of the American press since the early days of the country has been enormous (Brucker, 1949, esp. Chap. 18). A single historical comparison will serve to indicate what it would take much more space to document adequately:

> It is often argued . . . that in 1936 and 1940 and 1944 most of our newspapers were defeated at the polls by Franklin Roosevelt. So they were, in so

[13] It was much more nearly true in the nineteenth century, when Marx wrote. However, the Communists, in their criticism of Western democracies, do not always take account of the changes since the time of Marx.

[14] For a good idea of what those ideals are with respect to the press, see Commission on Freedom of the Press, 1947, esp. pp. 107-33; with respect to censorship, see McKeon, Merton, and Gellhorn, 1957.

far as their editorial pages were concerned. *But they elected him by means of the objectivity of their news pages.* For, no matter what bias in reporting may remain, our anti-Roosevelt and pro-Roosevelt papers hardly differed in that for a dozen years they covered their front pages with substantially accurate accounts of everything the President said and did. This, and not the fulminations on their editorial pages, is what they really told their readers; and this is what elected him, as he used to say, again and again and again.

We can appreciate the extraordinary achievement that such honest reporting represents if we . . . look back upon a standard of comparison. If the press of our day sinned in reporting, what of the account of the inauguration of Thomas Jefferson on March 4, 1801, in the *Columbian Centinel*, of which this heading is typical:

YESTERDAY EXPIRED
Deeply regretted by MILLIONS of grateful Americans
And by *all* GOOD MEN
The FEDERAL ADMINISTRATION
Of the
GOVERNMENT of the UNITED STATES
Its death was occasioned by the
Secret Arts, and Open Violence;
Of Foreign and Domestic Demagogues.

Surely the *Baltimore Sun*'s coverage of the 1940 rallies that so aroused Mr. Ickes [a prominent member of President Roosevelt's three administrations] was more objective than that [Brucker, 1949, p. 272].

Brucker gives other examples of early American journalism that would startle any reader of today. We might note in passing, however, that while the *news* suffered then, there were no more shackles on the *critics* of the government than there are now.

In considering our press from a different comparative perspective, the following comment by the Commission on the Freedom of the Press is particularly impressive in view of the fact that the Commission had many very critical things to say about the American press:

> Outside the United States the coverage of mass communications is much less complete than it is in this country. Whole populations are cut off from the interchange of news and discussion by poverty, by censorship, and by poor physical facilities for intercommunication [Commission on Freedom of the Press, 1947, p. 67].

5. There is considerable competition within any medium of communication and between different media. One reason that relatively few people read the Communist *Daily Worker* is that it does not contain very much news.

6. There are laws regulating the media of communication, and these laws, while no doubt capable of improvement, ensure a certain amount of fair play.

7. Most important of all: the relatively poor have far more votes than the relatively rich, and they vote partly on the basis of their personal experience. If a man is out of a job, for example, he is more likely to be

influenced by this fact than by propaganda to the effect that everything is just fine. This influence of personal experience is of enormous importance when we remember that political parties *compete* for votes.[15]

The Constitution and the Supreme Court

We have already noted the great importance of law in American government. It is partly on this account that lawyers are so prominent in politics. (Another reason is that running for office is risky, and lawyers, if they fail, can always go back to private practice. Other occupations are less flexible.) In 1949–51, 57 per cent of the United States senators gave law as their principal occupation, and 68 per cent had had legal training. These percentages are more striking when we remember that lawyers constitute about 0.1 per cent of the population (see Matthews, 1954).

Probably nothing in American culture is more "sacred" than the Constitution, and no group of men has more prestige than the Supreme Court.[16] Yet the role of the Constitution in American political life is not exactly what its "sacredness" might lead one to suppose.

> A stranger to our institutions would, in fact, obtain only an incorrect and artificial conception of our government if he confined his attention to the Constitution itself. He would have to be told that certain features of the Constitution are never carried out in practice, while some of the most fundamental powers of our government are exercised without any definite constitutional authorization. He would have to learn that the President is not in reality chosen by the electoral college; that his power to adjourn Congress has never been exercised; that taxes have rarely been apportioned according to population; and that certain reconstruction amendments have not been enforced [Randall, 1926, pp. 6-7].

We should recognize, however, that the relatively brief document known as the Constitution is different from constitutional law, which includes, in addition, amendments and hundreds of pages of judicial decisions, especially decisions made by the Supreme Court over the years.

The Supreme Court has an important position in our government, not only because every legal system requires an ultimate authority to interpret the law, but because our federal system makes necessary an arbiter between

---

15 Campaign expenditures are also regulated by law, but, except for some important parts of the Hatch Act, most of this regulation is so easily evaded as to be virtually useless. Regulation is much more successful in England See Penniman, 1952, Chap. 24. The reader should note carefully that we are considering the question of variable approximations to an "ideal type" of democracy. We are *not* considering the comparative advantages and disadvantages of democracy and some other system, such as the Soviet. On democracy, see Bryce, 1921, esp. Part I; Weber, 1947, pp. 412-23; MacIver, 1947, Chap. 8; Dahl, 1956; and Burns and Peltason, 1957.

16 In 1947 a survey by the National Opinion Research Center found that, of eighty-eight occupations, U. S. Supreme Court justice was ranked at the top For various reasons, the results of the survey cannot be taken seriously in detail, but at least we can assume that most people had a rough idea of what a Supreme Court justice is.

the fifty states and between each of them and the central government. Moreover, the Supreme Court also has a latent law-*making* function, since Congress sometimes passes ambiguous laws, leaving it to the Supreme Court to define their exact application.

The "sacredness" of the Constitution has led to the popular misconception that the Supreme Court does nothing but interpret the provisions of that ancient document. The justices are thought of as supremely wise men who see to it that the sacred tradition is never violated. As a matter of fact, the Court is almost always called upon to use its discretion and to decide cases not only on the basis of its knowledge of the Framers' intentions but also on the basis of present-day social conditions. The Constitution is highly ambiguous. The Framers themselves were probably to some extent aware of this, for, like any other committee of men with diverse interests and opinions, they took refuge in ambiguity. They left it to future generations to supply more exact meanings in some places (Curtis, 1947). Moreover, the Framers were of course unable to foresee the legal "requirements" of the future. Finally, in many cases the Court must somehow reconcile, or choose between, different constitutional principles that might apply. Every decision changes "the" meaning of the Constitution at least slightly.

If we bear in mind the foregoing facts, we should not be surprised that the Court sometimes reverses itself. For example, in 1936 the Court decided, 5 to 4 (in Morehead, Warden *v.* New York ex rel. Tipaldo), that a New York state law regulating wages of women workers was unconstitutional, on the ground that to regulate the wages of women workers would interfere with the freedom of contract between employee and employer; but in 1937 (in West Coast Hotel Co. *v.* Parrish) the same Court, with the same members, decided, 5 to 4, that a State of Washington law fixing minimum wages for women and minors was constitutional, on the ground that a state has the right to regulate wages of women workers because of their weak bargaining position (see Weinberg and Shabat, 1956, pp. 600-01). Justice Roberts had changed his mind.

Self-reversals by the Supreme Court do not mean that the law is like shifting sand, or that the justices act only on whim or personal prejudice. In many of these cases there is room for genuine difference of opinion. If we considered dissenting as well as majority opinions,[17] we should find a good deal of continuity in the thinking of the Court as a whole. Further, reversals are of course striking, and they may draw our attention away from the infinitely more numerous cases, in all our courts, in which the application of law is routine and predictable. In most court cases (but not in those before the Supreme Court), the question at issue is not so much what the law means as what the facts are. Taking the body of law as a whole, it changes with majestic, almost imperceptible slowness.

---

[17] It is instructive that the word used for the written statements of the majority and the minority is "opinion."

The great prestige of the Supreme Court was shown in 1937, when President Franklin D. Roosevelt, exasperated by the fact that the Court had declared several New Deal measures unconstitutional, proposed a measure to increase the number of justices from nine to fifteen. Most people (including Mrs. Roosevelt, as she said in a candid radio interview about twenty years later) were against this so-called Court-packing plan. Many people were shocked, or professed to be. The widespread objection to changing the number of justices was remarkable in view of the following facts: (1) the legislation that had been overturned by the Court had been passed by great congressional majorities, under perhaps the most popular president in American history just after his greatest electoral landslide, and had been passed with obvious public approval; (2) the offending Court decisions were always close (5 to 4), and there was a widespread feeling (even among people who opposed the Court-packing plan) that the majority in the Court were rather stubbornly obstructing the popular will and that, unless someone changed his mind or died or retired, the President and the Congress would have a hard time doing anything constructive to solve the tremendous problems brought by the depression; and (3) the Court-packing plan was perfectly constitutional, for the Constitution leaves it to Congress to decide how many members the Supreme Court should have. Yet President Roosevelt probably never proposed a more distasteful measure. It would probably be fair to say that the majority of voters disagreed with the "obstructive" majority in the Court but somehow perceived the President's proposal as an attack on the *institution* of the Supreme Court. This perception, of course, was fostered by the President's opponents, who cleverly labeled the proposal "the Court-*packing* plan." [18]

Despite its great power and prestige, the Supreme Court is dependent

---

[18] The "old men" in the Court were creating a temporary impasse in government, and Roosevelt was trying to get them to resign. The intensity of feeling aroused by his plan was not due to reverence for the Court alone. Something like a class struggle was going on; and in relation to our earlier discussion of the Communist charge that a so-called capitalist democratic government is "the executive committee of the bourgeoisie," it is interesting to note, in passing, that the "bourgeoisie" did not get what it wanted. The following comment is sound as well as ironical: "The storm that developed around the 1937 proposal revealed the intensity of the interests affected by the New Deal program. The central feature of the proposal, to permit the president to appoint an additional judge in any Federal court where a judge failed to retire within six months after reaching the age of seventy, was not new. The identical suggestion had been made in 1913 by Wilson's Attorney General, James C. McReynolds, one of the 'old men' at whom the Roosevelt attack was aimed" (Truman, 1951, p. 497). On the Supreme Court and the Roosevelt plan, see Curtis, *Lions Under the Throne* (1947), and Brogan, *Politics in America* (1954), Chap. 9. For a list of the major events in the controversy, and a study of Congressional reaction and general public reaction to them, see Cantwell, "Public Opinion and the Legislative Process," 1946, which shows how timid most legislators are in declaring their opinion before finding out what "the public" thinks. Their fear of not *following* the public correctly amounts to cowardice. We must remember, however, that in the Supreme Court case many members of Congress were probably just as ambivalent as the general public.

on Congress for its jurisdiction, for its terms of court, for enforcement of its judgments, and for the number of its justices. When the Court declares a congressional act to be unconstitutional, the majority in the Court must give a written opinion supporting their decision. This written opinion is an appeal to the legal profession and to the enlightened public in general. For in reality the members of the Court do not necessarily know more either about the needs of the times or about the Constitution than the president and Congress do. There is a struggle, and the Court must make out a "good case," for if Congress wishes to, it can always win by passing an amendment to the Constitution. This is partly what is meant by saying that the Court is dependent on Congress for its jurisdiction.[19]

The Presidency and Its Structural Context

The power and prestige of the president's office are enormous. As head of the executive branch, he has vast constitutional authority For example, he is commander in chief of the armed forces; he is chiefly responsible for foreign policy; he is head of all the executive departments and agencies (the more strictly "bureaucratic" part of the government); he can veto congressional bills. As head of his political party, he is mainly responsible for the party's legislative program. His control of party patronage, combined with his official powers of appointment and removal, gives him more political leverage than the holder of any other office. Apart from its specific powers, the office has become symbolic of the nation. Part of this symbolic position derives from the fact that the president is one of two representatives elected by the country as a whole, and the other, the vice-president, has far less constitutional authority. The president's charisma of election is particularly great in a federal system. All the senators and members of the House are, in comparison. local figures. Moreover, Congress is divided within itself. Being nationally elected, the president can afford to ignore local pressures to a far greater extent than the members of Congress can, for he knows that these local pressures cancel one another out to some extent. With the increasing importance of national and international affairs, all these advantages of course become more important too. Finally, the president has incomparable opportunities for mobilizing public opinion. He can hold a press conference, or make a nationwide radio and television broadcast. Anything he says is given great publicity.[20]

On the other hand, the president is also limited in certain ways. Al-

---

[19] This paragraph is based on Curtis. *Lions Under the Throne* (1947). The "for" phrases in the first sentence are headings in his Chapter 5.

[20] A common criticism of the American presidency is that it is too difficult a job for one man. In a sense this is true, but the criticism is based partly on a misunderstanding of the nature of executive roles in general and partly on ignorance of the fact that the Executive Office of the President is actually a rather large group. One advantage of the British system, however, is the fact that the royal family frees the prime minister from many of the ceremonial duties the American president has.

though he can veto congressional bills, Congress can override his veto with a two-thirds vote. Moreover, in the struggle that sometimes takes place between the president and Congress, Congress can attach distasteful amendments or clauses to bills that the president otherwise approves of, and since the president can accept or veto the whole bill only (he has no "item veto"), he often finds it expedient to swallow his opposition to the offending clauses. He is dependent on Congress for legislative support and for funds for all the executive departments and agencies. He is checked by the Supreme Court also. Although he is officially head of the government bureaucracy, his relatively limited experience and span of office put him to some extent at the mercy of the professional bureaucrats. Finally, the publicity given his utterances is a disadvantage as well as an advantage, especially in view of the fact that freedom of the press is freely used to attack him.

Political scientists frequently criticize the system by which the president is elected. The gist of their criticism is that the system is imperfectly responsive to the wishes of the people and in that sense is undemocratic. The reasons they give are as follows:

1. All the electoral-college votes for a state must go to the candidate who wins a plurality in that state, regardless of the size of his plurality. This means, of course, that the voters for the minority party in a state that is securely controlled by the majority party are almost disfranchised. In an extreme case, as in the Hayes-Tilden contest (1876), it is possible for a candidate to lose the election despite having won a majority of the votes actually cast in the country as a whole.

2. Each state is given a number of votes in the electoral college equal to the number of its representatives in Congress. Since each state, regardless of size, has two senators, this rule tends to cause the smaller states to be "overrepresented."

3. Each of the major political parties has the power to decide how many votes to give to each state delegation to the national convention which nominates the party's candidate for the presidency. Although in recent years each national committee has given some weight to the electoral strength shown by the state party in previous elections, in general the size of a state's population is a more important factor than the effective size of the party in the state (see Penniman, 1952, Chap. 20). This means, inevitably, that the nominee may not be the actual choice of the party in the sense of the rank-and-file members and supporters across the country. This fact is particularly important for the Republican Party, which gives a grossly disproportionate weight to the delegations from the South, where the Republican Party actually has little electoral strength. The Democratic Party is more nearly a nationwide party, but here again the South is "overrepresented," since many Negroes, who of course are counted in the population of the states, are not actually permitted to vote.

4. The influence of the electoral-college system is felt in another way at the nominating conventions of the two great parties. There are several

criteria of "availability" for the nomination. For example, a candidate for the nomination is hardly "available" if there is any great scandal in his record of public service. A candidate's "availability" is greater if he has not alienated any great bloc of voters, such as labor or the farmers. These criteria and certain others are essentially negative. But one of the chief positive criteria, important on account of the electoral-college rules, is in itself almost irrelevant if the goal is to select a "good man for the job." Because all the electoral-college votes for a particular state have to be given to the presidential candidate who wins a plurality of the popular votes in that state, each of the nominating conventions is prone to nominate a man from a large "doubtful" state—that is, from a state that might go either way in the election. The hope, of course, is that the "favorite son" vote will be large enough to carry the doubtful state, with its large bloc of electoral-college votes. It is partly for this reason that so many candidates have come from New York state (17 out of 46 from 1868 to 1956). This criterion of "availability" does not mean, of course, that an incompetent man will be nominated. The chief effect of the criterion is that it restricts the field of choice open to the convention; a man from a small and "safe" state, however "good" he is, has little chance of being nominated.

5. The convention method of selecting nominees is imperfectly democratic in that the delegates to the convention are not chosen in the "best" possible way, *from a democratic point of view*. In 1956, only nineteen states had presidential primaries, and these were of at least six significantly different types (see Key, 1958, pp. 447-51). In most states, delegates to the national conventions are chosen in state conventions, which are largely controlled by professional politicians. Even in states that hold primaries, delegates are usually not closely bound by the results.

The convention system of nominating candidates for the presidency and vice-presidency is one of the most frequently attacked of American political institutions. Television has helped to reveal to a larger audience certain features that political scientists have been criticizing for years. There are too many people in attendance; the weather is often uncomfortably hot; the time for deliberation is too short, yet much of it is "wasted" on windy speeches for "favorite sons" known to have no chance or on long, noisy, obviously synthetic demonstrations for the many candidates (see, e.g., Brogan, 1954, Chap. 6; and Penniman, 1952, pp. 434-35).

Given the values implicit in them, all these criticisms of the national conventions are well founded. Nevertheless, the convention system does have some democratic merit and even some functional flexibility, as Brogan has pointed out. The delegates are not chosen in the most democratic way possible, but they are a fairly large cross-section of the voters—men and women of all ages and all social classes except possibly the highest and the lowest. As for flexibility, the Republican convention of 1940 showed one of the advantages of the convention system:

> . . . since the delegates had been chosen, since Senator Taft and Mr. Dewey had taken their stand, Hitler had swept over Denmark, Norway, the Low Countries, France. A great crisis was at hand, and the doctrines and dogmas of a few weeks before seemed irrelevant. An amateur, like Willkie, could meet the crisis in a way the professional could not or, at any rate, did not. And the Convention could meet the crisis, too, in a way a body tied to primary instructions would have been unable to do [Brogan, 1954, p. 214].

Above all, in appraising the electoral-college rules and the convention system, we must remember that no society has institutions that are perfect from a highly abstract point of view. To a considerable extent, the "imperfections" of our system arise from federalism. The states have somewhat different traditions; they have entered the Union at different times; they had developed their own state loyalty; they might not have been able to participate in the Union at all if a considerable amount of autonomy had not been reserved to them and if the smaller states had not, "undemocratically," been given disproportionate representation "against" the larger states. In more than one sense, the Union is still in the making. As everyone knows, the "states' rights" issue is still alive.

The Social and Political Structure of Congress

"The number of bills and resolutions introduced in the 79th Congress (1945–46) was 11,656. In the 81st Congress (1949–50), this figure had jumped to 16,670" (Bailey and Samuel, 1952, p. 8). It is, of course, impossible for every senator and member of the House to make a thorough study of the merits of so many bills and resolutions. It would be impossible even if he could devote all his working time to the task. As things are, he can spend only a fraction of his time in studying current bills. He must keep his constituents informed of his activities, answer their questions, follow out the individual requests for help with which he is besieged. If he is sponsoring some particular bill, he must spend time attending committee hearings, lining up support among his colleagues, keeping alert so as not to be caught off guard by the strategy of the opposition. As a member of one or more congressional committees, he must spend a good deal of time investigating complex facts to see whether new legislation is advisable: legislation, that is, in addition to the mountain of bills already framed and presently being considered. And periodically he must drop all this business and go back home to campaign for re-election.

This list of activities is by no means complete. For example, we have not mentioned the representative's continuous obligations to his political party, which in some cases are quite time-consuming. Nor have we mentioned the more or less onerous and hardly avoidable social life of the capital. In face of all these demands, it is a wonder that the senator or representative ever arrives at rational decisions in voting on the endless complex bills.

In this task, of course, he has help. Perhaps the most important arrangement permitting the task to be accomplished at all is the existence of specialized committees in both houses of Congress. To a considerable extent, every senator and representative must neglect many problems, relatively speaking, and concentrate on "small" areas in which he may hope to become something like an expert. Thus he may be particularly concerned with labor legislation, national defense, taxation, or conservation of natural resources. When he has to vote on bills in other areas, he inevitably pays a good deal of attention to the opinions of other members whom he presumes to be better informed and whose general political orientation, "conservative" or "liberal," he shares. Many members of Congress on many issues simply accept the guidance of their party leaders.

Specialization helps to make the legislative task more manageable. In addition, of course, the representative has a personal staff of assistants, he has the informed opinions presented by bureaucratic experts in the government departments and agencies, he has the cooperation of the Library of Congress, and he perforce relies heavily on the facts and opinions marshaled for him by pressure groups. Pressure groups, which often present the interests of one segment of the population as if they were the interests of all, are of course suspect as objective sources of information, but in our political system they are virtually indispensable as well as inevitable. They do at least help to inform the legislators about the views of organized groups in the country.

In most parliamentary systems, there are two houses, one of which can be called the "upper" and the other the "lower" house. The upper house is conservative, for it tends to represent vested interests. Like the British House of Lords, it is generally not an elective body. The United States Senate was once an "upper" house in that its members were not directly elected by the voters but were elected by the state legislatures, which tended to be conservative. Now that senators are directly elected, it is a question whether the term "upper house" is appropriate to the Senate.[21]

As we have already noted, however, the Senate is a less "democratic" body than the House of Representatives. The fact that every state, regardless of size, has two senators means that the conservative, rural parts of the population are overrepresented, from a democratic point of view. In this sense, the Senate is at least similar to the upper house in a parliamentary system. But there is a big difference also. In modern parliamentary systems, the upper house has much less power than the lower house. Relatively speaking, however, the whole cast of American government is "conserva-

---

21 The United States, strictly speaking, does not have a parliamentary system. As we have noted, the president is (more or less) directly elected to his position, whereas in a parliamentary system the prime minister, whose office corresponds roughly to that of president, is himself a member of the legislature and owes his position as chief executive to the fact that he is the recognized leader of the majority party or coalition in parliament.

tive," in part because the "upper" house, the Senate, has decidedly more power and prestige than the House of Representatives.

The greater *power* of the Senate rests on the fact that the House can do nothing without the agreement of the Senate, whereas the latter has special powers of patronage and impeachment. The difference in *prestige* is greater still, and of course prestige is a source of power. The greater prestige of the Senate rests partly on the fact that a senator is elected by an entire state, whereas a member of the House is elected by a district, which is only part of a state. In our federal system the states have tremendous prestige and power. A member of the House of Representatives is identified with a district that bears an impersonal number, is subject to redefinition with population changes, and thus has no particular tradition or glamor. Further, a senator has a six-year term of office, whereas a member of the House has only a two-year term. A representative is hardly in office before he has to begin worrying about his next campaign. The short term keeps him tied more closely to his purely local supporters, to local interests. A senator, on the other hand, having more time and a wider base of support, has a little more leeway and can afford to concern himself to a greater extent with national issues. Moreover, he has a longer time in which to become competent. (An incumbent from a "safe" congressional district may, however, keep his position for many terms—provided that he does not alienate his relatively small constituency.) Finally, the small size of the Senate permits greater scope for individual personalities and makes it possible for debate to be carried on with more dignity and freedom. The much larger number of representatives has made it necessary for the House to adopt rigid rules for debate.[22]

ROLE CONFLICT AND LOCALISM

A senator or a representative has obligations to several different groups, and these obligations are not always mutually compatible. The resulting complexity of motivation should not be viewed as personal corruption or as primarily a matter of personality at all; it is an example of role conflict. The conflict, always possible, is more acute in some situations than in others. Another way of putting the same thing is to say that when voting on bills in Congress, the officeholder must sometimes choose between different reference groups. He is or may be influenced, to varying degrees, by at least the following motives, all deriving primarily from the social structure:

1. Conscientious concern for the over-all, long-run interests of geographical units larger than his own constituency. If he is elected by a district, he may feel that the interests of the state, the region, or the nation deserve

[22] We should note, however, that the relative size of the two houses of Congress is an important factor only because our political parties are weakly organized. The English House of Commons can permit long debates because the speakers are almost always speaking as representatives of their parties, not merely as individuals trying to impress their constituents back home.

prior consideration in cases in which the interests of different units seem to conflict.

2. Loyalty to his party and concern for its program. Certain parts of the party's program may not be popular with the majority of his constituents.

3. Concern for the views and interests of the majority of his constituents, as expressed, for example, by their votes in the last election.

4. Concern for the views and interests of particular supporters, especially large contributors to his campaign funds. Some of these supporters may come, of course, from outside the geographical area he represents. It would be a great error to assume that campaign unds are always contributed for "selfish" interests, but it would be naive to imagine that businessmen and labor unions expect no special consideration in return for their contributions. (Apart from his interest in being re-elected, a member of Congress might be influenced by personal interests; for example, he might have a business of his own that might be affected by a pending bill.[23] In general, however, at least two interrelated aspects of social structure make this kind of motivation relatively unimportant. The votes a member casts on many issues are a matter of public record [roll-call votes], and in election campaigns rival candidates attack each other's voting record, if any, and also point out private interests that might conflict with the public interest. In other cases, a candidate may be elected partly *because* he is known to have certain private interests—"As a businessman [or a farmer], I know the problems of business [or farming] at first hand." In these cases, the private interests are presumed to coincide with those of constituents, or at least of su rters.)

It would be extremely difficult to determine exactly the relative strength, statistically, of these various motives. There is good reason to believe, however, that the American political system is so constituted that local interests are given great weight as compared with national interests. The importance of localism in our system can be judged, to some extent, if we take a comparative perspective. In such a perspective, certain structural features of the system which we ordinarily take for granted are seen to favor local and short-run as against national and long-run interests. Indeed, this tendency of our system has long been a standard object of criticism on the part of political scientists.

What structural features of our political system tend to make legislators acutely conscious of local interests—those of their constituents and of their

---

[23] For an example, see Bailey and Samuel, *Congress at Work* (1952), p. 119. For a good discussion of the conflicting loyalties to which representatives are subject, see Kennedy, 1956, Chap. 1. Motives, like anything else, can be classified in many ways. We might consider the influence on representatives of their social class, religion, ethnic group. These and similar sources of influence *cut across* the list given in the text above; they are not concretely different motives, they are the same motives classified in a different way.

particular financial supporters? First, there is the never-to-be-forgotten fact that ours is a federal system. Each of the states has its own proud tradition. Although the Senate is less parochial than the House of Representatives, the difference is only relative. The senators from Georgia can never forget their allegiance to that state.

Secondly, as compared with parties in some other systems, our political parties are poorly organized and poorly disciplined. The local candidate for office is little obliged to his party. He depends on his own organization to get him elected. If his party were strong and unified, he would be obliged to support values and opinions held by an important part of the whole country. As matters stand, he crusades under a party label, but his opinions reflect the prejudices and parochial interests of his own geographical unit. The party platform, ambiguous by design, is not binding upon the individual candidates.

Thirdly, according to unwritten rule—unwritten, but never violated—a candidate for elective office must reside in the geographical unit he wishes to represent. For both candidate and voters, this rule focuses attention on the duty of the representative to concern himself with local interests. To some extent, the rule must also favor candidates with relatively parochial experience and outlook.

Fourthly, as we have noted, the short term of office in the House of Representatives makes the politician more dependent on his constituents.

Finally, the great power of committee chairmen in both houses of Congress, combined with the seniority rule (according to which the chairmanship goes automatically to that member of the committee who has been in the house for the longest time), tends to favor conservative local interests. Districts and states that return the same man to office term after term are of course "safe" areas, and they are safe because relatively stable interests have become established in them. When the Democrats are in power, conservative Southerners are likely to have a disproportionate number of committee chairmanships. But Republicans from Vermont, which is a relatively "safe" state for the Republicans, are no less unrepresentative of the party as a whole, or of the country. (In all these cases, of course, the committee chairman may be conservative on some issues and liberal on others.)[24]

We have emphasized the fact that there is a kind of role conflict inherent in the office of United States senator or representative. At various times, probably every incumbent feels pulled in opposite directions by local interests and national interests. We must not assume, however, that when local interests win out it is always because the representative deliberately chooses to support these rather than national interests. No doubt many

---

[24] Localism in American politics is probably strongest in the South. See the selection on voting behavior in Alabama reprinted from Key, 1949, in Lazarsfeld and Rosenberg, eds., 1955, pp. 194-97.

representatives rationalize their decisions.[25] But perhaps more important in the long run is the fact that the social institutions listed above have a tendency to direct the legislators' attention toward local matters and away from possible projects of national scope. The social structure conditions *knowledge* (and ignorance) as well as interests. Moreover, the same institutions condition the voters in the same way, and we may assume that voters and legislators reinforce each other's local preoccupations.

Social change is gradually shaking legislators out of their localism. Business interests, as we have seen, increasingly cut across local and state boundaries. So do the pressure groups that foster business and labor interests. At the same time, changes in the international situation are making more and more people aware of national interests. The hostility and growing power of the Soviet Union and China, and the growth of nationalism in Africa, whose ultimate ideology is still uncertain, worry American citizens all over the country. What makes these changes so frightening, of course, is the unprecedented destructiveness of modern weapons. By 1960, most of the leading aspirants to the presidency were senators.

Moreover, the organization of Congress, although slow to change, is not fixed for all time. Changes have taken place to reduce the influence of local prejudices and, incidentally, to make Congress somewhat more democratic. For example, the Rules Committee of the House of Representatives used to exercise autocratic power. Although it was originally formed to evaluate bills sent to it from other committees and to schedule these bills for presentation to the full House, its members, who were among the representatives with the longest tenure, gradually assumed the right to pigeonhole bills they did not approve of, and they even dictated to the chairmen of other committees changes that would have to be made in particular bills if these bills were to be allowed out of the Rules Committee. In 1948, however, a representative from a Pennsylvania district made a careful plan of action and succeeded, after a bitter fight, in reducing the power of the Rules Committee.

> With the help of a technician from the House Legislative Counsel and an expert from the Legislative Reference Service of the Library of Congress, he drew up a new rule which would allow a committee chairman to ask the House, by direct vote, to place on the calendar any bill approved by his committee and held up in the Rules group for more than twenty-one days. The second and fourth Mondays of each month were reserved for such motions [Bailey and Samuel, 1952, p. 77].

---

[25] In regard to the complex questions Congress must deal with, rationalization is frighteningly easy. A rather detailed study of hearings conducted in 1946 by the Senate Committee on Banking and Currency (Huitt, 1954) shows that one of the easiest paths for rationalization to take is the unconscious manipulation of "facts and figures." On question after question the Committee, which was investigating the OPA price-control and stabilization program, could not agree on the facts. Sample questions: What causes inflation? How has labor fared in the postwar economy? The same paper also shows quite convincingly the tremendous importance of local (here, state) interests to legislators

Party Systems and Electoral Systems

In a democratic regime, the party system is of great importance: it is more important, for example, than the question whether the regime is parliamentary or presidential. On the other hand, the electoral system is also important, for it is perhaps the prime factor in determining the nature of the party system: in particular, the electoral system affects the number of parties. According to a distinguished French political scientist (Duverger,. 1954), the number of parties is the most important basis for classifying all modern political systems (not only democracies). This thesis, for which a good argument can be advanced, depends, of course, upon considering the Communists in Russia, the Fascists in Italy under Mussolini, and the Nazis in Germany under Hitler as political parties. In that case, there are three basic types of party system: the one-party, two-party, and multiparty types.

The term "electoral system" refers to the legal and customary rules governing political candidacy, voting rights, and the counting of votes. For example, proportional representation differs from the so-called simple-majority system and from the plurality system; the so-called list vote differs from the single-member constituency; universal suffrage differs from limited suffrage; and so forth. As we have mentioned, the electoral system and the type of party system are closely connected. Both have a profound effect on the molding and registering of public opinion. According to an old-fashioned and naive view, opinions on public questions simply exist, and it is the business of the democratic process to record these opinions—to make them visible, so to speak—so that the representatives of the people will know how to act. Actually, of course, without party activity there might not, probably would not, *be* a majority (or a plurality, if the electoral system requires only that) cohesive enough, homogeneous enough, to form a government at all. Assuming that a technical majority is necessary, it is the function of parties to *create* a majority. Each of the main competing parties tries, of course, to create a majority behind a certain program or general "philosophy" of government. The function of party campaigns is, first, to make people aware of certain issues and, second, to mold a sufficient degree of consensus to permit the formation of a government. Which issues are presented to the voting public for consideration, and in what light they are presented, will depend upon the nature and number of the competing parties.

Obviously a one-party system will mold public opinion very differently from a two-party or a multiparty system. In a system with two or more parties, each party selects and "handles" issues not only with reference to its ideals and interests, its conception of the objective needs and possibilities for political action, but also with reference to the campaigns of the other parties. Thus the number and range of different views presented depends somewhat on the party *system* as well as the particular character of each party taken by itself.

In the creation of public opinion the electoral system also comes into play by affecting the campaigns of all the parties in the system. For example, in the United States the Republicans do not campaign vigorously in the South, and the reason is not that the South is "solidly" Democratic. As a matter of fact, the South is not solidly Democratic. The reason for the relative neglect of the South is that the electoral system, which gives the victory to the majority candidate in each single-member constituency, virtually guarantees that the Republican votes in the South will count for nothing.[26] If we had larger constituencies and proportional representation, and if each party had to present, in each constituency, a *list* of candidates, of whom some might win and some might lose *in the same constituency*, the so-called solid South would soon dissolve and the Republicans would not neglect it.[27] (This probable result, however, is not necessarily enough to recommend proportional representation and list-voting.) It is easy to see that the electoral system also affects the campaigns of Democratic candidates in the South, since they have a weak or nonexistent party to campaign against.

Now let us suppose that the parties have all finished their appeals to the voters, and the voters go to the polls. They record their opinions in the form of votes for the various candidates. (In this context, we shall use the term "opinion" to cover not only beliefs but also feelings, wishes, and concern for personal and group interests.) We may say that at this point some sort of more or less coherent public opinion exists, having been created, in part, by the election campaign. We must observe, however, that the procedure of voting does not simply register existing opinion, even at this late stage. For if the voters are going to make their opinion felt at all, they are forced to choose between the alternatives presented to them at the polls, even though none of these alternatives may reflect exactly what they think. Thus the party system not only creates public opinion of a certain kind, it also *distorts* whatever opinion has been created.

---

[26] In the election for the presidency, as we have said, *all* the electoral-college votes for each state are awarded to the majority candidate in that state. The Republican minorities in the whole South, if they could be added together, would be substantial, but the electoral-college system (which treats each state as if the presidency were a state office) scatters the Republican vote in such a way as to nullify it. The effect is the same as if the entire South were gerrymandered in favor of the Democratic Party. The importance of this fact cannot be gauged simply by noting the actual size of the Republican vote. If the electoral system were different, it is probable that many people would vote who now do not bother, and others would vote Republican who now vote Democratic.

[27] The chief effect of this change would be to encourage the rise of third parties. But if the present party system persisted, it is possible that the relative strength of the two main parties would remain substantially unchanged. The reason is that as soon as voting in the South became "meaningful," more Democrats, as well as more Republicans, would vote.

There is no existing combination of party system and electoral system that does not create and distort public opinion in some way and degree. Different combinations are different ways of creating and distorting. (We should note, however, that voting is not the only way in which the public "registers" opinion.)

In the following sections, we shall focus on American parties and the American party system, but we shall keep a comparative perspective in mind.

PARTY STRUCTURE

Many variables could be considered in an attempt to classify political parties according to their structure. We shall confine our attention here to a brief consideration of five ranges of variation (see Duverger, 1954).

Direct and indirect membership

The members of the socialist parties of Europe join the party directly and participate as individuals. The members of the labor parties, on the other hand, are first of all members of trade unions or cooperatives; as a member of a trade union, a man is indirectly a member of the labor party with which the union is affiliated. We may speak of this difference as a difference between "direct" and "indirect" membership, although from another point of view we might speak of "indirect" membership as "double membership." Socialist parties and labor parties are similar in ideology, but the double membership of labor parties seems to make them much stronger; participation in the union seems to strengthen participation in the party, and vice versa. American political parties have direct membership and are therefore weaker than they might otherwise be.

Component subgroups

Each party participating in a nationwide political system is made up of smaller groups, which differ in nature from one party to another. The unit in the oldest parties is technically called the *caucus*. (The term used by particular parties varies.) There is a great range of variation in the way in which members of a caucus are chosen, but all caucuses are alike in that they are small groups and tend to be exclusive. To a large extent, they co-opt their members. The caucus system is characteristic of parties whose program appeals to middle classes predominantly. A caucus tries to confine its membership to influential people, sometimes called "notables."

The socialist parties and the so-called Christian democratic (Catholic) parties of Europe are made up of local *branches*. The branches try to recruit as many members as possible from all classes, but especially from the working class. Whereas a caucus is not very active between election campaigns, a branch is continuously active; it holds regular meetings and has a program of ideological indoctrination for its members. It is likely to shape the purely "social" life of its members to a large extent, very much as some union locals do.

Communist parties and some fascist parties are organized in *cells*. A cell is a small group of highly selected persons, of proved devotion to the cause. The communist cells are typically organized not on a local basis but according to place of work. There may or may not be regular meetings, but the members are expected to give whatever time may be necessary to the tasks of propaganda and agitation assigned to them, and communication between cell members is fairly continuous and easy since they all work in the same place. There are (in principle) cells at all levels of society.

With the exception of the negligible Communist Party of the United States, American parties are based on caucuses. The exact composition, method of recruitment, and coherence of these caucuses vary from place to place. In all types of party it is necessary, of course, to distinguish between the professional or full-time politicians and the ordinary members. This distinction is especially important in parties based on caucuses. As we have noted, the members of a branch or a cell often have nonpolitical occupations by which they earn their living. This is also true of some members of caucuses, but a larger proportion of these are professional politicians. A particularly important difference between parties based on branches or cells and parties based on caucuses is in the method of financing. Caucus-based parties depend on fairly large contributions from relatively few persons and groups. Parties based on cells or branches depend mainly on dues regularly collected from rank-and-file members, although of course few parties will refuse to accept large contributions. The average "Democrat" or "Republican" in the United States does little more than vote for the candidates of his party; even if he is registered as a party member, he often votes across party lines, and he rarely makes a financial contribution. For their voting strength, therefore, caucus parties must appeal to relatively unorganized members.

Articulation of components

Parties may also differ in the articulation of the units just described. The articulation of communist, socialist, and labor parties is usually fairly strong. The smallest units elect representatives to higher bodies, and these representatives communicate with one another a good deal.

American parties are weakly articulated. Notables from different caucuses get together on an informal basis. The most important general party meeting is the nominating convention, which of course meets only once every four years. American parties are so weakly articulated that one of the chief functions of the national convention is to introduce various presidential possibilities to a large gathering of comparative strangers. Long before the convention, of course, and all during the convention, the more or less private and separate organizations of the leading aspirants are working quietly behind the scenes, making promises and arranging for exchanges of support. The state delegations are to a large extent controlled by professional politicians. It is worth noting, however, that these professionals are relatively uncoordinated. The outcome of the convention is never a foregone conclusion except when an incumbent president desires a second term. In that case, his party would not dare to repudiate him in its convention, for fear of seeming to depreciate his performance in office; the party in office will have to defend that performance during the approaching campaign, no matter who its candidate will be.

Since millions of votes will be necessary to get the nominee elected, the professionals must try to drum up enthusiasm for him among the rank and file. Part of this task is to send all the delegates home filled with fervor and hope; they will presumably leaven the thousands of relatively uncoordinated local organizations. A second part of the task is to get as much publicity as possible for the convention. This is the official "kick-off" for the campaign, during which all the local and state caucuses, ordinarily isolated from one another to a large extent, will try to cooperate and will establish temporary campaign headquarters in every local community. After the campaign, each party will tend to fall apart again.

Degree of centralization

Party structure may also vary in degree of centralization. Poorly articulated parties are always decentralized, but highly articulated parties are sometimes decentralized also. This is true of many socialist parties.

The chief examples of highly centralized parties are the communist parties in various countries. Their great centralization is made possible by the peculiar nature of the articulation of cells, which is relatively (but not wholly) undemocratic. There are several levels of organization, beginning with the cell. Each group at each level elects a representative to the next higher level. This representative, however, is mainly responsible not to the persons who elected him but to the higher-level organization to which he is sent. He has two tasks: first, to transmit the higher-level orders to the lower level and try to explain them; second, to transmit lower-level problems and reactions to the higher level. In principle, the orders from above are not to be questioned, but at each higher level the authorities presumably take into account the reports they receive concerning the specific reactions and general state of morale of the lower levels. This system is known as "democratic centralism." The elements of democracy that it contains are not so strong as the centralism. Any representative may be replaced *from above;* it is virtually impossible for the rank and file to remove authorities at the higher levels. At the top level, co-optation is the rule (that is, the highest body chooses its fellow members). The technical perfection of this system explains how a relatively small party is able to exert such disproportionate power.

This example of extreme centralization puts in relief the extreme decentralization of American political parties.

Oligarchy in political parties

A political party is of course a voluntary organization (the members are not compelled to belong). Sociologists have long been familiar with the fact that in most large voluntary organizations, whatever their formal structure or ideology, a relatively small number of persons—a so-called oligarchy—tends to entrench itself in power and stay there for a long time.[28] More generally, this tendency toward oligarchic rule is extremely common in all large organizations in which it is possible for most of the participants to be relatively inactive. Thus oligarchy is not only common in "service" organizations, such as Rotary, the American Legion, and the Red Cross, but it is virtually universal in labor unions, which are not always "voluntary" organizations except in an equivocal sense.

The term "oligarchy" is slightly ambiguous. It could mean that the top leaders always come from a relatively small category within the total membership of the organization. There would of course be nothing remarkable about oligarchy if it meant nothing more than a tendency, in large organizations with complex problems requiring difficult decisions, to place in power only members from the category of the trained and experienced. "Oligarchy" could also mean that a small group of the very same men keep themselves in power. Finally, it could mean that, although the actual composition of leadership changes, nevertheless a small clique tends to *co-opt* new leaders according to principles of selection that to some extent ignore the ostensible purposes of the organization and frustrate the ambitions of able persons who might be more loyal to those purposes. The theorists of oligarchy are interested mainly in the last two senses.

It is of course no problem to account for oligarchy in organizations whose official ideology is explicitly antidemocratic, such as the fascist parties, or in organizations such as the communist parties, whose "centralism" is an imperfectly democratic structural principle. But oligarchy is also found in the socialist parties, which are formally and actually more democratic than any other parties we know of. The top leadership of socialist parties is remarkable for its stability over time.

---

[28] The classic treatment of this subject is Robert Michels, *Political Parties: A Sociological Study of the Oligarchical Tendencies of Modern Democracy,* 1915. Much of Michels' analysis is still valid, and his pioneering work remains a reference point for research on oligarchy. As we shall see, however, Michels underestimated the significant variability of structure in voluntary organizations. To paraphrase a well-known French maxim, he seems to have thought that the more such organizations change, the more they remain the same. But his so-called iron law of oligarchy, that, regardless of its form, every large group is run by an oligarchy (see Part 6, Chap. 2), is actually only an empirical generalization, a first approximation which must now be qualified. He was prematurely pessimistic, and he occasionally pushed his thesis to absurd lengths. For example, he seems to imply that even social revolutions are "tragicomedies" in which people madly exert themselves only to end up where they began.

There is not necessarily anything sinister about the oligarchic tendency in socialist parties or in other democratic organizations. To a large extent, four facts account for it:

1. If there is no rule *requiring* short terms of office, the members of an organization may see no reason to change their leaders. Their present leaders may seem to have devoted themselves loyally to the goals of the organization, and in any case they have already acquired valuable experience.

2. There is a tendency for the leaders of an organization to become identified in the minds of ordinary members with the goals and ideals of the organization. That is to say, the leaders become symbols and as such are venerated.

3. Most members of any organization are reluctant to assume heavy responsibilities.

4. Most members of large voluntary organizations are relatively inactive. Their so-called apathy has many causes, but in large part it arises from the fact that participation in the organization is only one of their interests and is secondary as compared with job, family, and recreation. We must remember that in large voluntary organizations the leaders are full-time members (ordinarily), whereas most of the members are part-time contributors at best, and some are only nominal members (see B. Barber, 1950).[29] This is true even in parties with the "branch" type of unit.

In some voluntary organizations, however, there are additional factors making for oligarchy; factors, moreover, that are less favorable to efficiency and to democracy. A position at the top of a large organization ordinarily confers high income and prestige upon its holder. If stepping down will mean a great reduction in prestige and income, the leaders will of course be reluctant to give up their positions. Labor leaders and party bosses would often suffer a good deal if they were forced to find some other employment. Under these circumstances, it is easy for leaders to rationalize their sense of insecurity by telling themselves that their experience and ability are indispensable to the organization. Then they are likely to use the power of their positions to entrench themselves. Their detailed knowledge of the affairs of the organization, combined with their skill in parliamentary procedure and their command of organs of communication, enables them to order things in their own interest. They take advantage of their opportunities to promote members known to be favorable to them, to make friends of other members strategically located, to spike in advance the guns of potential rivals. All this can happen unconsciously, and it is possible even if the leaders are consciously devoted to the organization in good faith. "Corrupt" party bosses and union officials may, of course, serve the ideal purposes of the organization only to the extent that action in this direction does not

---

[29] The unpublished doctoral dissertation on which this article is based (B. Barber, 1948) is ably summarized, with some additional material, in Weinberg and Shabat, *Society and Man* (1956), pp. 29-42. Barber shows that it is unrealistic to hope for intensive participation on the part of most members in large-scale voluntary organizations.

interfere with their personal racket and may be necessary to hoodwink the rank and file.

All these factors that tend to create oligarchies in formally democratic organizations vary in importance from one organization to another. Some of them may not be present at all. Some may be counteracted. A detailed study of a democratic labor union (Lipset, Trow, and Coleman, 1956) has helped us to specify some of the conditions favorable to democracy in general. This union, the International Typographical Union (ITU), of the United States and Canada, whose members set type in printing establishments, is perhaps the only labor union in the world that has an institutionalized two-party system of government. (The two "parties" have no relation to the Republican and Democratic parties in American politics.) The ITU parties have for many years ensured rotation of office in the top leadership. From one point of view, of course, the existence of two functioning parties within the union *is* democracy, not an explanation of it; but the institutionalization of the two-party system also shows the strength of democratic values and discourages oligarchic tendencies from manifesting themselves. How the two-party system arose is partly a question of specific historical events, but the following facts help to explain how events could have had such a result and how it is possible for the system to be maintained.[30]

1. The ITU has strong locals, which are centers of relatively independent power.

2. Many members of the union work nights. Night work is rarely as strenuous as day work, and there is plenty of time for informal conversation among the men. The conditions of work in other respects foster conversation; for example, there is often an idle period between successive editions of a newspaper. The unusual working conditions of the typesetters separate them from other workers, develop a spirit of camaraderie on the job, and foster social relations off the job. There are many social clubs and newspapers for printers and typesetters, and these organizations are not controlled by the union. Like the union, they are a "spilling over" of work solidarity. These social clubs and newspapers, however, obviously provide independent channels of communication and opportunities to develop leadership skills—for example, ease in public speaking. Needless to say, such institutions also tend to reduce the "mass apathy" usually characteristic of labor unions. All these conditions strengthen democracy.

3. The printing industry is not organized in a few vast bureaucracies. Therefore it has not been necessary for the ITU to develop a vast bureaucracy to countervail the power of management. (One of the factors making

---

[30] When the Federalists in the United States first lost an election, some of them advocated seeking to keep office by force. A two- or multiparty system cannot be taken for granted. See Dauer, 1953.

for oligarchy in labor unions is the demand for "responsible unionism," which means that management wants union officials to accept responsibility for wildcat strikes and for unofficial breaches of contract. If union leaders are to have such responsibility, they must also have great power.)

4. The typesetters have high pay and high prestige in the ranks of labor. They are intermediate between the lower class and the middle class. Therefore there is a relatively small social gap, or none at all, between ordinary typesetters and their union leaders. Leaving office, a leader does not suffer a shattering drop in status.[31]

Few if any political parties have so democratic an internal structure as the International Typographical Union. On the local and state levels, American parties have a considerable tendency to oligarchic control, especially if we take into account the fact that actual party leaders are not necessarily officeholders in the government; some party bosses prefer to rule from behind the scenes. On the other hand, strongly entrenched control in some states and in many large cities and suburbs helps to prevent oligarchy on the national level. These local bosses do constitute a kind of loose national oligarchy in the sense that they have some control over the delegations to the national conventions, but on the national level the various delegations, to the extent that they are severally organized, are as likely to be factions within the national party as they are to be harmonized parts of the whole. As we remarked earlier, the outcome of the convention can rarely be predicted in advance. Nevertheless, the party candidate, whoever he may be, must be acceptable to at least a coalition of the "professional" leaders.

The presidential candidate of a party automatically becomes the national leader of the party; for example, he names the national chairman, who has a large part in planning the strategy of the presidential campaign and lining up support for it. When George Washington refused a third term in office, he established a precedent which remained unbroken till 1940. For various reasons, including widespread reluctance to change national leaders in the international crisis, Franklin Delano Roosevelt was elected to a third term; and once the tradition had been broken, there was little surprise when he was elected to a fourth term in 1944. Nevertheless, the two-term tradition was strong enough (coupled, some believe, with a kind of symbolic aggression toward Roosevelt on the part of his old political enemies) to reassert itself in the form of a constitutional amendment limiting subsequent presidents to two successive terms in office. The old tradition, now a law, has made it difficult for the main parties to build up permanent internal leader-

[31] In most unions and professional organizations of the semibureaucratic type, the longer a leader stays in office, the harder it will be on him if he is forced to step down, for he will have lost even the lower-ranking skill of the ordinary member. But once the two-party system with its short terms of office is established, officials will not lose heir old skills and hence will not be inclined so much to oligarchy. With respect to any system, it is inherently impossible to distinguish sharply between cause and effect.

ship on the national level. The Socialist Party has had more stable leadership partly because it has never even hoped to win a national election.

From our analysis of party structure, we are justified in concluding that in some sense American political parties are "weak" organizations. Their members have a "direct" tie to the party, and, as we have noted, this kind of tie is weaker than the "indirect" or double tie of the European labor parties. Each of the major American parties, moreover, is composed of weakly articulated (therefore, decentralized) caucuses, little modified by the system of direct primaries operating in some states. Finally, the national leadership is comparatively unstable. Some political theorists think that stronger parties would improve our political system; others see in our "weak" parties a sign, even a source, of political stability.

Why do American parties have the characteristics we have mentioned? Among the causes, no doubt, are the federal system of government; the unwritten rule requiring candidates to come from the district or other constituency they seek to represent; the fact that we have single-member constituencies (the list-vote tends to encourage greater party coordination, if not centralization); the ease with which the electoral system permits the voter to split his vote between parties ("cross-voting"); and the relatively fluid class structure, fairly general satisfaction with the two-party system, and ideological agreement, within fairly narrow limits, in our society. These factors are so closely connected as virtually to constitute different aspects of the same thing. The general significance of these factors for the question we are considering is that they have stabilized the "old-fashioned" type of party based on caucuses. It has been observed that the parties with the "strongest" internal structure are parties of either the extreme left or the extreme right. To the extent that our total social structure has been relatively stable and satisfactory to the majority of voters, there has been relatively little incentive to form (or at least to join) extremist parties. The reluctance to join parties of the left, which tend to be identified with the lower classes, may be explained in part by the more general reluctance of Americans to identify themselves with the lower class permanently; but this reluctance, in turn, depends upon the existence of a certain amount of actual social mobility. It is hardly likely that the hope of mobility would be sustained forever if there were not some lower-class persons in every generation who rise to the middle class (see Chap. 19).

Another probable reason for continued satisfaction with our parties of the "old-fashioned" type is that our political system as a whole gives fairly easy access, at several points, to pressure groups of all kinds. That is to say, important political groups other than parties can influence the existing parties, the president, and both houses of Congress. This freedom for pressure groups (which is directly institutionalized and encouraged in the form of congressional committee hearings) obviously reduces the incentive to join extremist parties.[32]

In attempting to account for the characteristics of the main American parties, we have implicitly taken for granted the fact that there *are* two of them. There are fewer adjectives more ambiguous than "weak." Our political parties are indeed weak in the structural sense we have specified, but they are "strong" because of their considerable flexibility, and this characteristic of each of the parties taken separately depends upon the nature of the *system* of parties.

THE SYSTEM OF PARTIES: STRUCTURE AND FUNCTIONING

Although we always have "third" parties, ours is essentially a two-party system.[33] Key (1958, Chap. 10) divides American third parties into three groups, and his classification, though inadequate, will serve as a starting point for discussion. The three are doctrinal parties, parties of economic protest, and secessionist parties.

Third parties

The so-called doctrinal parties, as the term suggests, place great emphasis on the importance of some particular doctrine as a path to political salvation for the country. The best examples are the various Marxist parties, but there are others, such as the Prohibition Party, which presents a slate of candidates every year. The rough nature of Key's classification is shown in the fact that this category includes parties as diverse as the Communist and the Socialist. The Communist Party is of a special type in that it ultimately challenges the very nature of the party system; for Communists, the *idea* of competing parties is wrong. If a "party" of this type gained power, therefore, we can only assume that a one-party system would supervene almost immediately. Thus far, however, parties of this type have had no electoral success to speak of in this country; not a single avowed Communist has ever been elected to Congress. The Socialist Party, if it were in power, would also institute rather far-reaching changes in the relations between government and the economy; but this party is profoundly different from the Communist in that it genuinely accepts the party system and democratic institutions generally. This type of doctrinal party has also had negligible success in the United States.

In a sense, the Marxist parties are "parties of economic protest," but Key uses this term to refer to the type of third party that arises in response

---

[32] We might note explicitly that we have conceived of the problem as one of accounting for the failure of "strong" parties to displace the older parties, whose "weak" structure was partly set in an historical epoch when the middle class dominated politics more surely than it does now.

[33] The term "third parties" is indicative. Although there may be a half dozen or so of these parties at any time, they are all known as "third" parties.

to a wave of economic discontent. Such parties have had far more influence in American politics than the parties of the doctrinal type. Good examples are the Populists of 1892 and the Progressives of 1924. One in six votes cast in 1924 went to Robert M. La Follette, the Progressive candidate for the presidency. When we speak of the functions of third parties in our political system, it will be chiefly the parties of the second type, and to a lesser extent parties of the third type, that we have in mind, for these two types of party have had enough influence to have notable functions for the system.

The third type of third party is the secessionist. A party of this type arises to protest against some policy in one of the existing parties. For example, the Southern "Dixiecrats" in 1948 hoped to weaken the Democratic stand on civil rights by threatening to form a third party. Failing to achieve their purpose, the Dixiecrats carried out their threat. As they were well aware, their splitting-off weakened the Democratic Party only and therefore strengthened the Republican Party (although, as it turned out, not enough to affect the outcome of the election). The Dixiecrat strategy presumably was to ensure, if possible, that the civil-rights policy of the Democrats would not succeed. If the Democratic Party had lost the election as a result of the Dixiecrats' "taking a walk," that party would presumably have had to weaken its civil-rights program in the next campaign in order to win back the necessary Dixiecrat support in the South. In short, the Dixiecrat "third party" was actually a faction in the Democratic Party, and its purpose was to *control* that party with respect to one issue. Another secessionist third party, the Progressive Party of 1912, led by Theodore Roosevelt (not to be confused with the La Follette Progressives of 1924), split off from the Republican Party

The newborn Republican Party of 1854 is hard to fit into any one of Key's types. It was not a secessionist party except in the sense that any new party must draw supporters from older parties. The Republicans drew their support from the Whigs, the Free Soil Democrats, and the Independent or Free Democrats (Moos, 1956, Chap. 1). (The two main parties at the time were the Democrats and the Whigs.) Nor was the new Republican Party a party of economic protest—at least, not exclusively. The occasion for the rise of the party was the Kansas-Nebraska Act of 1854, which would permit Kansas and Nebraska to enter the Union as slave states (i.e., as states in which slaveholding would be legal). The fervor behind the Republican Party of 1854 was to a large extent moral indignation over the extension of slavery. (The "high moral tone" of Lincoln's famous Springfield speech of October 3, 1854, caused his hearers to applaud vigorously again and again [Moos, 1956, pp. 20-21].) Yet the new party was not a doctrinal party in the sense that it regarded the abolition—much less, the nonextension—of slavery as a panacea for the nation.

The precise classification of third parties is not very important, for to the extent that they have any influence they tend to have the same functions in the political system. As we have said, there are normally two main parties in the American system. An influential third party either modifies the program of one or both of the existing main parties or replaces one of the main parties, as the Republicans replaced the Whigs. Normally, electoral victory goes to one or the other of the two main parties at irregular intervals, owing to an orderly, more or less gradual shift of more of the less deeply committed voters to one party than to the other. These shifting voters are "less deeply committed" only in the sense that their allegiance to one of the two main parties is less unquestioning; their commitment to a particular stand on one or more *issues* may be deeper than that of most voters.

Each of the main parties must try to keep most of its regular supporters and at the same time win over some of the so-called independent voters and some of the opposition. But if neither of the main parties offers a program attractive enough to a fairly large number of the relatively independent voters, then there is a danger (from the point of view of the main parties) that these voters will bolt the "standard" parties altogether and vote for one of the existing third parties or even form a new one. The ordinary term for these third-party votes, "protest votes," indicates the typical motive behind them and also points to their functions for the system as a whole. If the number of protest votes reduces the electoral strength of *one* of the main parties only, then that party will have to modify its program, either in office or in the next campaign or both, if it wishes to regain its strength. If most of the protest votes cut into the strength of *both* main parties significantly, then obviously both parties will have to modify their programs.

It is important to see that, in the American party system, the main parties are "deviant" if they depart so far from their potential supporters that third-party votes become significant. Third parties perform a social-control function for the system as a whole. The *threat* of a third party, which will appear great or small depending upon all the signs indicative of public opinion, may be enough to cause one or both of the main parties to modify their programs before the voting takes place. If the threat is insufficient, then the protest voters show that they mean business by voting; if they are a significant political force, there is an even greater chance that one or both of the parties will be brought into line with the change in public sentiment.

The fluctuating fortunes of third parties, as well as the specific content of their programs, serve as fairly sensitive barometers to the main parties. Whether the voters merely threaten to form a third party or actually do so

[34] This does not mean, of course, that all voters who shift from one party to the other have deep convictions about issues. Some voters merely follow shifts in the climate of opinion in the groups with which they are most closely connected (family, work group, church). But this reaction, either for an individual or for the aggregate of voters, is necessarily secondary, for before there can be a "bandwagon effect," there must be a bandwagon.

and vote, they give warning in time to forestall serious "damage" to the system. For we must recognize that unusual third-party voting is also deviant behavior. (Note, however, that deviant behavior is not necessarily morally reprehensible; it is simply behavior that violates a norm.) In the first place, those who cast the *unusual* third-party votes have obviously been "disloyal" to their usual parties. In the second place, if more and more voters turned away from *either* or both of the two main parties, then obviously the two-party system would be in danger and there would be a serious threat to the stability and continuity of the government, unless a third party could succeed in replacing one of the main parties. The danger would take the form of a paralysis of policy-making, an inability to form a stable majority in Congress—the kind of situation so common in France under the Third Republic. This danger would be the greater precisely because the growth of a strong third party in an ordinarily stable two-party system could occur only as a result of serious conflicts over programs. From this point of view, not only third-party voters in our system but also the main parties exercise social control. The third parties exercise social control by checking the deviant behavior of the main parties; the main parties, in modifying their programs, exercise social control by winning back the deviant voters to the two-party system.

The social-control function of third parties is clearly integrative since it catches conflict and deviance before these can go "too" far. Third parties also have a tension-management function. They provide the disgruntled voter with an outlet for his dissatisfaction. In fact, his "motive" for bolting his usual party may be to express aggression against it. That is, for any particular third-party voter, the integrative function of third parties may be latent.

It is important to see that both the social-control and the tension-management functions of third parties are *auxiliary* functions for the party system as a whole. They come into play only when the ordinary social-control and tension-management mechanisms of the system prove insufficient. Ordinarily the two main parties are sufficiently different from each other to enable a voter to protest against his own party "satisfactorily" (from his point of view) either by voting for the other party or by not voting at all. If these reactions, in the aggregate, do not affect the two main parties equally, then their relative electoral strength will obviously shift, and each will draw its own inferences. In short, the ordinary means by which voters "control" their parties, and parties "control" their supporters, are significant shifts of votes from one party to the other and the party reactions to these shifts. The possibility of forming third parties and voting for them is an additional mechanism, a kind of insurance.[35]

---

[35] For illustrations of the functioning of third parties in the American system, see Key, 1958, Chap. 10.

The two-party system

The question of why there are two main parties in our system could be answered in different ways. We might begin by answering the question of why there were two parties in the time of Hamilton and Jefferson; this would require an analysis of the social structure of the United States at that time. Then the problem would be to explain why no third party has succeeded in permanently breaking through the two-party system. To generalize: any problem of explaining the state of a social system can be broken down into two parts. First, one can analyze the process by which the system reached the state to be explained—how that state developed out of some previous state. Secondly, one can analyze the mechanisms or processes by which the new state tends to be maintained. Neither of these analyses of process would be sufficient in itself to account for the particular state of the social system that we are interested in explaining. An explanation of how social structure is maintained is, of course, not a satisfactory explanation of how it arose in the first place (see Lipset, Lazarsfeld, Barton, and Linz, 1954, pp. 1165-66).

We shall not attempt to explain the origin of the American two-party system. Instead, we shall "explain" the system in the same way we "explained" the so-called weakness of the American parties themselves. Indeed, the two problems are related. The "weakness" of each party, combined with the fact that there are two parties competing for votes, helps to account for the flexibility of each party and of the system as a whole. The relative fluidity of the class structure; the high degree of ideological agreement in the country as a whole; the freedom for pressure groups; the freedom to form third parties, which perform a control function for the main parties—all these interrelated factors help to account both for the retention of old-fashioned "weak" parties and for the stability of the two-party system.

There is another structural fact about our political system, however, that encourages the rise and persistence of two main parties. This is the electoral system. As we have noted, we use the simple-majority system for declaring victory in an election. Up to a point, this tends to force politicians to resolve their differences. In any constituency it is possible for a candidate to win a majority if he is backed by one of *two* major parties, but victory becomes more and more difficult the more roughly equal parties there are

We also have the single-ballot system. The force of this system can be appreciated if we compare it with the two-ballot system of France. On the first ballot the voters indicate which party among those presented they "really" favor. They take little chance of throwing away their vote because, there being several parties, a majority is rarely won on the first ballot. This ballot, however, although incapable of establishing a government, does reflect fairly sensitively the relative strength of different currents of public opinion. A week later, a second ballot is cast, but this time the competitors in each constituency are the two parties that have won the most votes on the first ballot in that constituency. Now those who voted for parties that were eliminated have a chance to vote for whichever of the two first parties they dislike the less. The two-ballot system obviously encourages the growth and persistence of several parties, most of which have to be even more flexible than the parties in a two-party system. Duverger has summarized the effects of different electoral systems as follows:

> The general influence of the system of balloting may be set down in the following three formulae: (1) proportional representation encourages a system of parties that are multiple, rigid, independent, and stable (except in the case of waves of popular emotion); (2) the majority system with two ballots encourages a system of parties that are multiple, flexible, dependent, and relatively stable (in all cases); (3) the simple-majority single-ballot system encourages a two-party system with alternation of power between major independent parties [1954, pp. 204-05].

In any political system with more than two parties, there is a tendency for each party to campaign most vigorously against whichever other party in the system is closest to it ideologically. It is easy to see why this tendency exists. Parties A and B, close to each other ideologically, have little chance of winning votes away from Party Z, but they have a fair chance of enticing some votes away from each other. In order for Party A to cut into Party B's following, however, Party A must make some promises of a sort that apparently have led voters to support B in the past.

From this simple analysis, it is easy to see why the main parties in a stable two-party system tend to be very much alike. Each opposes the other with a program a little different, but not so different as to alienate irretrievably either its own normal supporters or the normal supporters of the other party.

In the United States, both the Republican and the Democratic parties appeal to all social classes; both include "liberal" and "conservative" politicians; and both are supported, to a large extent, by funds contributed by big-business interests. Of the two, the Democratic Party since 1936, if not before, has tended more than the Republican to favor measures for greater economic equality. Among the reasonably objective and well-established indicators of this difference are the facts that much more money is contributed to the Republican Party than to the Democratic, that far more newspapers are Republican than Democratic, that voters from the well-to-do areas tend to vote for the Republicans, and that the labor unions clearly favor the Democratic Party.[36] We must stress, however, that these differences are relative.[37] The stability of American political life depends upon the fact

[36] For evidence, see Penniman, 1952, Chap. 23; Brogan, 1954, pp. 73-74; Keefe, 1956; and Eulau, 1955.

[37] After the election of 1936, a partisan newspaper editor exaggerated the relative difference between the parties when he announced the Democratic electoral-college victory as follows: "Country 46; Country Club 2" (Brogan, 1954, p. 73n.).

that the two main parties to a large extent cut across all the important class, religious, sectional, and ethnic divisions of the society. Both the overlapping of the two main parties and the relative difference between them were shown in a study by Eulau (1955). His study found that 69 per cent of middle-class people in 1952 voted for the Republican Party and 54 per cent of working-class people for the Democratic Party, that people tend to identify the Republican Party with the middle class and the Democratic Party with the so-called working class, but that 67 per cent of middle-class Democrats thought that the middle class as a whole would tend to vote Democratic and 51 per cent of working-class people who "didn't know" how the working class as a whole would vote themselves voted Republican.

Whether two parties seem to be similar or different obviously depends upon one's frame of reference. In 1948 the Progressive Party, a small "third" party commonly regarded at the time as "left," campaigned against the two main parties with the charge that they were "Tweedledum" and "Tweedledee." The composition of the million or so votes cast for the Progressive Party showed, however, that whatever strength it had was gained at the expense of the Democrats almost exclusively.

Even if the two main parties were exactly alike ideologically, the two-party system would still be functional, for as long as the party in office has to fear that the party out of office might win the next election, the elected officials of government are to some extent kept honest and sensitive to public opinion.

PARTIES, CONGRESS, AND THE PRESIDENCY

The power of the president varies a good deal according to the strength of his party in Congress. If his party has a large majority in both houses of Congress, the president is roughly as powerful as the British prime minister. But the president's party might control either or both houses by a big or a small margin; the other party might control either or both houses by a big or a small margin.

The margin of control is important because of the lack of centralization in each party. The president can almost never be sure that all the members of his party will vote as he wishes them to.

On the other hand, the "weakness" of both parties and their extensive ideological overlapping prevent a complete stalemate in the relation between president and Congress. Even if the opposite party controls both houses, the president can win some support for his ideas from both parties. Clearly, however, the so-called separation of powers is greater when the president is of one party and Congress of the other.

Voting

Social scientists have devoted so much attention to the social and psychological determinants of "voting behavior" (see Lipset *et al.,* 1954) that in the brief space available to us here we must focus attention on a few selected problems. In particular, we shall give tentative answers to these questions: (1) Why is the voting rate higher for some groups and social categories than for others? (2) Why is it that lower-income groups do not always vote for the more liberal party or parties? (3) Why do some states and regions continue to vote for the same party even though the total party system includes other parties? (4) How can we account for the alternation in power, at irregular intervals, between the two main parties in the United States (or in other two-party systems)?

SOCIAL DIFFERENCES IN VOTING TURNOUT

Our knowledge concerning high and low voting rates has been summarized by Lipset, Lazarsfeld, Barton, and Linz (1954), and the generalizations below are virtually quoted from their account (see pp. 1126-34, esp. Table 2).

1. A group will have a higher rate of voting if its interests are more strongly affected by government policies—for example, through
   a. Dependence on the government as employer. (Thus government employees, both in the United States and in Europe, have a higher turnout than any other occupational group.)
   b. Exposure to economic pressures requiring government action. (Thus wheat farmers, long subject to periodic collapses in the price of their product and to the monopolistic power of banks, railroads, processors, and dealers, have a high voting turnout.
   c. Exposure to government economic restrictions (e.g., businessmen).
   d. Possession of moral or religious values affected by government policies (e.g., Jews' fear of anti-Semitism, women's interest in such issues as prohibition and corruption).
   e. Availability of relevant policy alternatives in the programs of competing parties. (Thus the lower turnout of American workers, especially before the New Deal period, has been attributed to the basic conservatism of both parties in America's two-party system.)
   f. General crisis situations. (Depression and international crises increase the turnout of virtually all groups.)
2. A group will have a higher rate of voting if it has more access to information about the relevance of government policies to its interests—for example, through
   a. Direct visibility of the effects of government policies (e.g., direct taxes *versus* indirect taxes)
   b. Occupational training and experience making for general insight (e.g., the better-educated, executives, and business owners)
   c. Contact and communication within the group. (Thus miners, who live in isolated communities and whose social interaction is largely with one another, have a high turnout.)
   d. Relatively large amount of leisure. (Thus rentiers—people who live on pensions, dividends, and rents—have a high turnout.)
3. A group will have a higher rate of voting if it is exposed to social pressures demanding voting—if it has, for example
   a. A relatively high class position. (Thus some groups, for example the

"lower-lower class" of people who have "given up trying," have a *low* turnout.)

b. Strong class political organization. (Thus European working-class districts, organized by centralized, class-conscious parties, have a high turnout; compare American workers.)
c. Broad social contacts within the group. (Contacts within the group not only spread information, they also tend to create pressure to vote. Compare high-turnout miners and businessmen with low-turnout domestic servants.)
d. Absence of group norms opposing voting. (Thus Negroes in the South and women in some places have low turnouts.)

4 A group will have a higher rate of voting if the pressures to vote are not directed in different political directions so as to create conflict over which way to vote. (Conflict due to "cross-pressures" tends to produce "apathy," withdrawal, hence nonvoting.) Sources of conflict include:

a. Conflicting interests.
b. Conflicting information.
c. Conflicting group pressures.

(These three types of conflict tend to occur together. The lower-income groups in most stratified societies are exposed to strong upper-class influences through the press, radio, schools, and churches. Yet the lower classes are also exposed to influences from their class organizations and from their own life experience.)

For the purpose of analysis, these "forces" are listed individually, but as they impinge on any particular group some of them may, of course, reinforce others, and some may counteract others. For example, many mutually reinforcing factors (1c, 1e, 2b, and 3c, at least) all influence businessmen in the direction of a high voting rate. And miners, although they have little leisure (2d), have a good deal of social interaction (2c, 3c) and are relatively well organized (3b); they are also relatively isolated from upper-class pressures (4a, 4b, 4c).

Nonvoting may in particular cases be explained by failures of democratic government: e.g., threats of harm against Negro would-be voters in the South; lack of relevant alternatives offered by the main parties. But political scientists have also pointed out the important fact that a moderate-to-low general turnout is to some extent an indication of general satisfaction with things as they are. The integration of American society would not be well served—in a sense, would not exist—if opposed groups of voters, full of animosity toward each other, went to the polls to the last man, all in the hot conviction that the outcome of the election might decide between happiness and misery. A high voting turnout, as in Germany at the time of the rise of the Communist and Nazi "parties," may be a symptom of deep social conflict (see Lipset, 1956, p. 85)

THE "CONSERVATISM" OF LOWER SOCIAL STRATA

If a group votes as one would expect it to vote on the assumption that it is seeking to advance its economic interests, we demand no recondite explanation; for voting studies show that, on the whole, the desire to promote (or protect) economic interests is the main motive for voting one way rather than another. To this general rule, however, there are numerous exceptions, or apparent exceptions, and these do invite analysis. In particular, some low-income groups vote for "conservative" parties although more "liberal" parties exist and woo them. (In this discussion, we shall treat as relatively "conservative" any party that seeks to maintain existing inequalities in the distribution of economic benefits and as "liberal" any party that seeks to change social arrangements toward economic equality.)

As we saw in an earlier chapter, "economic" motives are various. The wish for a higher income is common, but so is the wish for *security* of income and for better working conditions, including freedom from arbitrary authority. Closely related to these sources of discontent, which often lead to voting for "liberal" parties, is the wish for greater social recognition of the value of one's work. Certain groups have the special grievance that their opportunities are restricted arbitrarily, by "discrimination." Under certain conditions, any one or all of these sources of discontent lead to what might be called rational "liberalism" in voting; for discontented groups, if they have the vote, have objective power (see Lipset *et al.*, 1954, pp. 1137-40).

They may not be aware of this power, however, or they may not wish to use it. Why?

> The main conditions influencing the extent to which deprivations will lead to leftist voting are the following:
>
> 1. *Channels of communication* are required through which the deprived group can become aware of its common problem and develop collective political action.
> 2. *Individualistic solutions,* as through social or geographical mobility, must be relatively unavailable, so that discontent will be channeled into collective action.
> 3. *Traditionalistic attitudes* and relationships which limit people's aspirations and inhibit attacks on existing social institutions must be weak [Lipset *et al.*, 1954, p. 1137]

As we have seen, when a group has a high degree of social interaction within itself and has developed self-conscious organizations facilitating communication and awareness of common problems, then its rate of voting is high. If such a group also feels deprived in a relative sense, it will tend to vote to the left. On the other hand, if a lower-income group has poor intragroup communication (e.g., domestic servants and other service workers), it not only will have a low turnout but will tend to vote conservative.

Up to a point, the *belief* that individuals can get ahead legitimately by their own efforts—the belief in social mobility—seems to be more important than the actual state of affairs. We must admit, however, that this statement is intolerably vague. There is some evidence that actual rates of social mobility are not very different in Europe from the rates in the United States;

yet European workers, because they believe that there is little chance of mobility, vote to the left, whereas American workers, who are confident that their children, if not they themselves, can rise in the existing class structure, are more conservative in voting (Lipset *et al.*, 1954, p. 1141).

As for traditionalistic (and conservative) voting, there is a saying that "every country has a South." [38]

> The most powerful deterrent to leftist political action by the impoverished workers and peasants of backward areas . . . is the extent to which their minds are dominated by "traditionalistic" values—resignation to a traditional standard of living and loyalty to the "powers that be." In these areas the social structure remains much as it was before the age of capitalism and the free-market economy. The positions of rich and poor are defined as the natural order of things, supported by personal, family, and local loyalties, rather than being a product of impersonal economic forces, subject to change without notice. At the same time the poor peasant or worker performs a role which has an obvious meaning and value and he derives gratification from stable personal relationships and ceremonial activities embracing the whole community. Religious belief tends to be strong and to support the status quo [Lipset *et al.*, 1954, p. 1142a].[39]

SOCIAL BASES OF ONE-PARTY AREAS

"Backward" traditionalistic areas not only are conservative in voting but are often attached to a particular party. As in the so-called solid South, there are always historical reasons for such an attachment. The traditionalism of both the South and northern New England stems from the struggle over slavery. The northern New England states were violently abolitionist and became fervent supporters of the Republican Party. These New England states are hardly a one-party area today, however, and they are hardly even "safe" for the Republicans any more. Even the South, which is much closer to representing the type of one-party area in a two- or multiparty country, is breaking up under the impact of industrialization and the gradual economic and cultural emancipation of the Negroes. As a one-party area becomes less "backward," it becomes more like the rest of the country. Nevertheless, the South in particular and northern New England to a lesser extent have remained remarkably loyal to one party, the first to the Democratic Party and the second to the Republican. The question is how such an attachment can be maintained in the face of new circumstances. To some extent, of course, the attachment to a particular party is due to the factors we have just reviewed to account for liberalism and conservatism.

[38] Lipset *et al.* (1954, p. 1141b) mentions the West of Norway, the Scottish Highlands, southern Italy, Bavaria (Germany), and Quebec (Canada).

[39] This statement applies more closely to certain areas of Europe than to the American South, although it applies to the old South too. The authors cite a famous work by André Siegfried: *Tableau politique de la France de l'Ouest sous la Troisième République* (Paris, Armand Colin, 1913). For discussion of all three factors helping or hindering the leftism of "deprived" groups, see Lipset *et al.*, 1954, pp 1140-43; Table 5, p. 1143, brings out the fact that various types of deprivation and various conditions facilitating liberalism or conservatism may be combined in particular cases.

If one party in the party system is consistently conservative, then of course conservative voters will tend to remain loyal to it.

Loyalty to one party may persist, however, even despite a shift in the liberalism or conservatism of that party. One reason is that traditionalism in voting is to some extent "normal." There is a strong tendency, for example for people to vote as their parents did (see Maccoby, Matthews, and Morton. 1954, p. 300). Once identified with a particular party, a voter may to some extent become blind to its defects, even from his own point of view. There may be a lag in his recognition that a shift has occurred in the party system, a shift such that his own interests would be better served by voting for a different party. Such "faults" in perception may be regarded as a normal aspect of loyalty to any group one belongs to. They can be reinforced, in a one-party area, by a similar lag in other people's perceptions. Moreover, opposition-party leaders also fail to grasp some of the opportunities open to them; they identify a particular area with a particular party. For example, although New Hampshire had already become a heavily industrialized state and had a large Catholic population—two factors generally associated with a Democratic vote—the Democratic Party, thinking of New Hampshire as safely Republican, had not sent a single major party figure to campaign there in 1948 (Lipset *et al.*, 1954, p. 1166a). Such lags in perception, however, cannot account for loyalty to one party in the long run.

Another cause of the stability of one-party areas is that the party may be so strongly identified, traditionally, with loyalty to the area *vis-à-vis* other areas that persons who run for office under another party label are subject to severe sanctions. A similar situation exists if the opposition party is identified with another area or ideal. In the South, the Republican Party is associated with the emancipation of the Negroes and with the North. In some countries, Catholic parties as such command great loyalty in particular areas because other areas are anticlerical; the issue becomes involved with sectional loyalty.

One-party stability in some areas is also caused by the flexibility of the single party under certain conditions. Factions arise representing different interests and presenting alternatives to the voters. At its best, a two-faction system is much the same as a two-party system. Candidates with a new program are listened to, provided that they declare themselves in favor of the socially correct party.

However, a careful analysis of the politics of the eleven Southern states, taken severally and together, compels the conclusion that a one-party system tends to favor vested-interest groups and leave the poor largely unrepresented in politics. Three Southern states in which Democratic factions do provide significant alternatives to the voters have a small but significant Republican opposition; these states are North Carolina, Tennessee, and Virginia (to less extent). For other reasons, cohesive factions have developed around personalities in Georgia and Louisiana. The other Southern states—South Carolina, Alabama, Mississippi, Arkansas, Texas, and Florida

—all have many fluid, nameless, faceless factions, and the voters are seldom presented with issues of any importance. The beneficiaries of this system are the relatively rich; the losers are the poor. There is no faction with enough continuity to be punished for its record or to be supported as a reform organization. A long-range program is impossible. Demagogues further confuse the voters by hammering on old regional issues, under cloud of which more pressing needs of deprived groups are ignored (see Key, 1949).

If there is actually a shift from conservatism to liberalism in a one-party area, it seems unlikely that the factors so far mentioned could prevent the rise of support for opposition parties. "Normal" party loyalty and lags in perception; sanctions against deviations; factionalism, offering real or spurious alternatives—it seems unlikely that these alone could maintain loyalty to one party. It may be suggested that *to some extent* a *small* region —and these "backward" areas are always small relative to the whole country —can both have its cake and eat it. That is to say, such a region can enjoy its conservative loyalty while still enjoying some of the fruits of reform brought about by the political action of the rest of the country. To put the same point in another way: a small relatively "backward" region is not allowed to suffer the *full* effects of its "backwardness." In this way, the conservatives of the region are protected to some extent against opposition from within the region itself.

Thus a small one-party area, althougn somewhat isolated, is inevitably part of the country as a whole. The favorite issue of its single party—race or religion—can be kept alive only because the rest of the country has a different view, which must be opposed. At the same time, the relative economic liberalism of the rest of the country protects the one party against some of the repercussions of its conservatism.

THE ALTERNATION OF PARTY POWER

To return to a consideration of the two-party system as a whole, it is normal, of course, for the two main parties to succeed each other in power, at irregular intervals. We usually take this fact for granted, but it is perhaps worth our attention. To some extent, alternation between the two main parties is also alternation between the relative left and right.[40]

Many changes occur between elections. Population shifts take place, affecting the social composition of constituencies and the relative support for the major parties. New pressure groups arise, and the old ones change in relative strength. The international situation changes. All these changes interact to create new political "needs," or at least some realignment of political forces; they create uncertainty for all political parties. The outcome of the next election will presumably depend upon the changed attitudes of the voters toward the parties, upon the sensitivity of party leaders to the new

[40] In a multiparty system, the alternation is between left and right coalitions. "Left" and "right" are always relative.

political "needs," and upon the ability of the leaders to do anything about the "needs."

It seems reasonable to assume that the rise of new political issues will almost always affect one party more favorably than the other. Although the Republican and Democratic parties are similar in many ways, at any particular time each is identified with certain policies. Above all, one is generally thought to be relatively conservative and the other relatively ready to institute certain kinds of change. For these reasons and others, each of the parties has its basic support in fairly well-defined segments of the population. If new issues call for economic "liberalism," for example, the leaders of the Democratic Party can more easily react in a liberal direction without running the risk of alienating the regular supporters of the party.

It is probably true for total social systems as it is for small groups that periods of relatively intense activity are followed by periods of relative passivity. As we pointed out in Chapter 3, intense concentration on goal achievement tends to generate conflict within the group. If the conflict does not go too far, it will create a felt need for group integration, to the relative neglect of achieving new goals involving social change. If this is so, then liberal or left periods in power will tend to generate strains that can be relieved only by periods of conservative power. On the other hand, during periods of conservative power, new needs for liberal action will arise.

It also seems reasonable to assume that the successful party in one election will tend to raise the same issues and in general use the same methods in the next campaign, whether these are still appropriate or not. In other words, success will tend to make a party's leaders relatively insensitive to new issues. On the other hand, the unsuccessful party will be abnormally sensitive to new possibilities of regaining power.

When the left is in power, it tends to build up a new conservatism in the very groups it helps. These groups, having achieved their goals, now wish to protect them and are less eager for new changes (see Lipset *et al.*, 1954, p. 1169b.). The combination of an increased "need" for integration (relative "passivity"), the insensitivity of a party in power to changes that have taken place since the last election, and the presence of new "conservative" groups will tend eventually to favor the more conservative party again.

Great troubles, such as depression or defeat in war, tend to be blamed on whichever party is in power and thus favor the electoral chances of the other party. Continuing crises should perhaps be distinguished from new crises. It is the latter in particular that favor the party out of power.

The Stability of the American Political System

In a society as heterogeneous as the United States, with many groups striving vigorously to achieve goals not always compatible with one another, the fairly stable—comparatively speaking, remarkably stable—functioning of the national government deserves some analysis. What has already been said provides us with some materials for understanding, and some further points can be made. Focusing on the problem of stability, we might emphasize the following facts about the American political system:

1. There are very few citizens who have no means by which to express their wishes effectively enough to influence the government. The right to vote is virtually universal, and almost everywhere there are competing parties or factions trying to garner votes. Even such groups as the Negroes in the South, whose legal right to vote is often denied in practice, have pressure groups, such as the National Association for the Advancement of Colored People, that have demonstrated their not inconsiderable political effectiveness. Moreover, there is no large segment of the population that is everywhere deprived of the vote. The votes of Northern Negroes can and do benefit Southern Negroes to some extent.

2. Not only are there broadly based political organizations for influencing the government but there are many points at which organized citizens have access to the government. Pressure groups can influence parties, can appear before legislative committees, can by mail and other means affect the president. Thus an extremely large proportion of the population can not only express their general wishes and reactions by voting but can pinpoint their wishes and their reactions to decisions taken.

3. The organized groups that compete and conflict in politics are not, strictly speaking, distinct segments of the population pitted against one another. In one sense, Democrats do not overlap with Republicans, nor members of the National Association of Manufacturers with members of the AFL-CIO. But the two great parties do overlap in membership in the sense that they both contain many businessmen and many members of labor unions; and the NAM and CIO-AFL also overlap in many ways (for example, both contain many Democrats, Republicans, Catholics, Protestants, Jews, Irish-Americans, Italian-Americans, American Legionnaires, Masons, and so forth, through a potentionally long list).[41] Truman specifies the important consequences of this overlapping of membership as follows:

> Organized interest groups are never solid and monolithic, though the consequences of their overlapping memberships may be handled with sufficient skill to give the organizations a maximum of cohesion. It is the competing claims of other groups *within* a given interest group that threaten its cohesion and force it to reconcile its claims with those of other groups active on the political scene. The claims within the American Medical Association of specialists and teaching doctors who support group practice, compulsory health insurance, and preventive medicine offer an illustration.

---

[41] Strictly speaking, the members of the NAM are organizations, not individuals. The officers of the NAM, however, ultimately have to take into account the attitudes and opinions of people (the leaders of the member organizations).

The presence within the American Legion of public-housing enthusiasts and labor unionists as well as private homebuilders and labor opponents provides another example. Potential conflicts within the Farm Bureau between farmers who must buy supplementary feed and those who produce excess feed grains for the market, between soybean growers and dairymen, even between traditional Republicans and loyal Democrats, create serious political problems for the interest group. Instances of the way in which such cleavages impose restraints upon an organized group's activities are infinitely numerous, almost as numerous as cases of multiple membership. Given the problems of cohesion and internal group politics that result from overlapping membership, the emergence of a multiplicity of interest groups in itself contains no dangers for the political system, especially since such overlapping affects not only private but also governmental "members" of the organized group [Truman, 1951, p. 510].[42]

4. Another important source of stability in government is the institutionalization of role responsibility in office, especially at the highest levels. Whatever his party or personal background may be, a president of the United States can hardly fail to feel a heavy burden of responsibility toward the country as a whole. Even if the "public interest" is not easy to identify, the institutionalized expectations of public office are such that a crude image of officeholders always using their power to further the interests of their social class or of the Standard Oil Company is certainly a gross oversimplification.[43] A good illustration of the influence of office was provided by Senator Homer Capehart, Republican of Indiana. Senator Capehart had been interested in helping the cheese industry (for example), and as a member of the Senate Committee on Banking and Currency he had been extremely sympathetic toward the businessmen who appeared before the Committee to attack price control. (He was a businessman himself.)

But in 1953 Capehart assumed the new status of Chairman of the Banking and Currency Committee, and with it a new role requiring him to accept primary responsibility for the legislation reported by the Committee. In his new role he advocated stand-by controls for prices, wages, and rent. He found it hard to understand the intransigence of groups which were "unalterably

[42] Truman's point is well illustrated in a 1951 study of the Associated Industries of Vermont, an association with about 450 member concerns in a variety of fields; this study shows how conflicts of interest within the AIV prevented its legislative agent (lobbyist) from pushing AIV claims too far in the Vermont legislature. The attentive reader will note another point also illustrated in this study: two groups are seldom opposed to each other on *all* issues, and in opposing the other on any particular issue each is mindful of the fact that on a later occasion it may be seeking the support of the other. See Garceau and Silverman, "A Pressure Group and the Pressured: A Case Report" (1954), esp. p. 258a.

For a more realistic conception of power, see Parsons, "The Distribution of Power in American Society" (1957). Lipset points out (1959, p. 107) that many studies of the social origins of legislators and officeholders implicitly assume that social power is always used on one or the other side of a conflict, and that the wielder of power uses it to favor the groups he belongs to personally. This assumption, of course, neglects the importance of group pressures ("access" to the wielders of power), the institutionalization of social roles, and values common to all or most groups in society.

opposed" to any concession to the principle of controls, and understandably shocked to hear himself accused by a business lobbyist of espousing a philosophy of the "left." It would be hard to find a more striking example of the effect of a change of status [Huitt, 1954, p. 300].

As we have noted, senators and representatives are subject to role conflict, so that it is relatively easy for them to neglect "the public welfare" in favor of local interests that, after all, they were elected, in part, to promote. There is, however, an important part of government that is relatively free from local pressures and whose task it is to know the facts as they are, affect whom they will in whatever way they will. This, of course, is the bureaucracy, properly speaking. Special interests have to face the relatively impersonal experts of all the government departments and agencies. With respect to any particular issue, especially as it affects *many* groups ("the country as a whole"), these bureaucratic officials, backed by full-time staffs, are at least as competent and strategy-wise as lobbyists and partisan legislators. In a relative sense at least, the bureaucracy constitutes a kind of pressure group representing the general interest as against special interests.[44]

5. Probably the most important source of stability in our system is the all-but-complete consensus regarding constitutional law, the party system, and the electoral system. The basic rules of the political game are institutionalized. We mention this vital fact only after reviewing the preceding facts in order to suggest *why* the rules of the game are themselves stable. They are stable partly because they work out fairly well (points 1–4 above). The additional significance of the institutionalization of rules is that it stabilizes interaction in the system, giving legitimacy to particular decisions even when these are not, in all cases, completely in harmony with everyone's conception of substantive justice. The virtually common interest in maintaining the rules themselves to a large extent overrides and harmonizes all the more divisive special interests.

6. Finally, the system is stable because of "potential groups" (see Truman, 1951). At any given time, there are people who, though not organized for a common purpose at the moment, *could* be mobilized if an occasion demanded it. Under special circumstances some interest that they share will bring them together, not necessarily physically, but together in the sense that they perceive the situation in the same way and add, each his mite, to the collective action. For this discussion, the term "group" can be understood in the broadest sense, to mean any concert of people, whether they form a definite organization with a charter or merely interact in such a way as to reinforce one another's attitudes and push one another's separate actions in the same direction.

Potential groups are a great source of flexibility and stability. They exert influence at all times because actual groups fear them. It is especially

---

[44] Government employees, of course, have a special interest of their own, namely, the security of their jobs; but this interest hardly affects the point we are making.

important that they can be activated in support of the rules of fair play. The National Association for the Advancement of Colored People was once a potential group. And that group included many influential whites as well as Negroes.[45]

We shall not appreciate the full importance of potential groups unless we realize that their influence is felt within every actual group. Then we must realize that they cut across many actual groups, thus being great latent sources of power.

> Violation of the "rules of the game" normally will weaken a group's cohesion, reduce its status in the community, and expose it to the claims of other groups. The latter may be competing organized groups that more adequately incorporate the "rules," or they may be groups organized on the basis of these broad interests and in response to the violations [Truman, 1951, p. 513].[46]

In short, "potential groups" are a form of social control latent in every group and in the society as a whole. They remind us of the great importance of the press and other channels by which publicity is given to people's actions.

A fairly good indicator of social cohesion and the stability of our political system is the fact that a political drift toward the right or toward the left tends to include *all* groups, although not equally (Lipset, 1959, p. 96).[47]

At least once in our history, two sections of the country drifted *apart* politically and, of course, eventually went to war against each other. It would be presumptuous for a nonspecialist to attempt to explain so complex

---

[45] Whether a potential group, even if aroused, will be successful is of course a separate question in each case. Studies of attitudes and opinions can give us a rough idea of the strength of potential groups; see, for example, Stouffer, *Communism, Conformity, and Civil Liberties: A Cross-Section of the Nation Speaks Its Mind* (1955); this is a careful study of a sample of 6433 people—4933 "ordinary" people and 1500 local leaders (personages such as the mayor, the president of the Chamber of Commerce, etc.). We might keep in mind potential members of existing groups as well as potential groups. Latent interests, when aroused, can often express themselves through existing organizations. A poll conducted by the American Institute of Public Opinion in 1940 suggests that perhaps as many as four million people voted for Roosevelt although they thought Willkie might be better for one or another of their private interests; they voted for Roosevelt in the belief that he was a better leader for the war situation. See Key, 1947, p. 613.

[46] We should point out that the concept of potential groups "interested" in the rules of the game adds nothing to the concept of institutionalization, for the latter implies that social rules are sanctioned (i.e., that known violations will set off more or less organized social disapproval). The concept of potential groups is not only a useful reminder of this fact, however; it also reminds us of the fact that untoward events, including overweening action on the part of existing groups, may create a new common interest uniting people formerly united not at all or not in just that way.

[47] Lipset cites two works by Louis Bean which present the statistical evidence of *general* drift in American elections: *Ballot Behavior: A Study of Presidential Elections* (1940), and *How to Predict Elections* (1948). Bean's own summary (short version): "As your state goes, so goes the nation."

an event in a sentence or two, but we may relate it to the foregoing discussion of the factors making for stability. One striking fact is that the divided groups were divided by at least three important factors: ideology, economic interests, and sectional loyalty based in part on intensive interaction within each group and relatively little interaction cutting across the two groups. At the same time, the main interest shared by both groups—national union—was not so strong then as it is now. For one thing, the international situation presented no threat in those days of relative American isolation; therefore, the two sections were not drawn together to face a common potential danger.

The integration and stability of American society depend only in part upon its fairly sensitive and flexible political system. In particular, the class structure is not so full of conflict as the class structure of certain other countries—for example, France or Italy. We shall study class in more detail in Chapters 18 and 19. In the very next chapters, however, we turn to religion, which, in the United States, is also for the most part a source of unity and stability. Although we have some religious conflict, it seems mild as compared with the conflict between Moslems and Hindus in India, to take one example.

RECOMMENDED READING

For a good general treatment of democracy, see R. M. MacIver, *The Web of Government,* Macmillan, 1947, Chap. 8. For a thoughtful and modest statement, see Talcott Parsons, "The Distribution of Power in American Society," *World Politics,* Oct. 1957, v. 10, pp. 123-43. Although this is a careful and critical review of C. W. Mills, *The Power Elite* (Oxford University Press, 1956), it can be read as an essay on power, without regard to Mills's book. A quite different study of power is R. K. Merton, "Patterns of Influence: Local and Cosmopolitan Influentials," Chap. 10 of *Social Theory and Social Structure,* rev. and enlarged ed., Free Press, 1957. Among other things, this paper identifies and describes two different social types of influential person, shows clearly that social influence is to some extent independent of social class and education, and gives an unusual glimpse of the research process. For a study bearing on a general theory of oligarchy and democracy, see S. M. Lipset, M. A. Trow, and J. S. Coleman, *Union Democracy: The Internal Politics of the International Typographical Union,* Free Press, 1956, esp. Chaps. 1, 18.

For a systematic comparative study of political parties, see Maurice Duverger, *Political Parties: Their Organization and Activity in the Modern State,* trans. by Barbara North and Robert North, with a foreword by D. W. Brogan, Wiley, 1954. This edition incorporates revisions of the French edition of 1951. If the student has time to read only one book in this whole list, he should read Duverger. For a valuable collection of papers and selections from books, see Heinz Eulau, S. J. Eldersveld, and Morris Janowitz, eds., *Political Behavior: A Reader in Theory and Research,* Free Press, 1956. On parties, see pp. 308-17 in this collection, W. J. Keefe, "A Comparative Study of the Role of Political Parties in State Legislatures," reprinted from *Western polit. Quart.,* Sept. 1956, v. 9, no. 3. Although this paper compares Illinois and Pennsylvania in particular, Keefe also reviews and classifies other studies. In general the evidence at present supports the idea that each of the major parties pursues fairly similar policies in different state legislatures, and that there is a fairly consistent difference between the two parties. In the same collection, pp. 317-24, Duncan MacRae, Jr., "The Relation Between Roll Call Votes and Constituencies in the Massachusetts House of Representatives," reprinted from *Amer. polit. Sci. Rev.*, Dec. 1952, v. 46, pp. 1046-55, is a study of the relationship between "party loyalty" on roll calls and certain characteristics of the representative's constituency. Party loyalty is strongest in those who represent fairly "safe" districts.

On Congress, see S. K. Bailey and H. D. Samuel, *Congress at Work*, Holt, 1952, which presents well-written case studies of many aspects of campaigning for and working in Congress. See also J. F. Kennedy, *Profiles in Courage*, Harper, 1956 (Pocket Books edition, 1957), Chap. 1, "Courage and Politics," a sensitive essay on role conflict in the role of senator or representative. The case studies are highly readable. Senator Kennedy's book is relevant to reference-group theory and the theory of nonconformity (see the comments by Merton in his *Social Theory and Social Structure*, 1957, p. 367, n. 111).

A first-rate book on the role of "private" groups in influencing government is D. B. Truman, *The Governmental Process: Political Interests and Public Opinion*, Knopf, 1951. Oliver Garceau and Corinne Silverman, "A Pressure Group and the Pressured: A Case Report," *Amer. polit. Sci. Rev.*, Sept. 1954, v. 48, pp. 672-91 (reprinted in Eulau, Eldersveld, and Janowitz, eds., 1956, pp. 253-64), reports the results of interviewing a sample of members of the Vermont legislature concerning the 1951 session; the paper specifies the social characteristics of the members who were, and of those who were not, sensitive to the role of pressure groups in the session. (For a statement of the technique and advantages of the focused interview, exemplified in the Garceau-Silverman study, see R. K. Merton and P. L. Kendall, "The Focused Interview," *Amer. J. Sociol.*, 1946, v. 51, pp. 541-57.)

A highly readable book on the Supreme Court, spiced with controversy but scholarly, is C. P. Curtis, Jr., *Lions Under the Throne: A Study of the Supreme Court of the United States Addressed Particularly to Those Laymen Who Know More Constitutional Law than They Think They Do, and to Those Lawyers Who Know Less*, Houghton Mifflin, 1947. Mr. Curtis, a lawyer himself, refers to many other good books by scholars and judges.

Of the many textbooks on American government, one of the best is V. O. Key, Jr., *Politics, Parties, and Pressure Groups*, 4th ed., Crowell, 1958. A little more elementary and confined to the federal government is J. M. Burns and J. W. Peltason, *Government by the People: The Dynamics of American National Government*, 3rd ed., Prentice-Hall, 1957; this is an unusually readable and thoughtful textbook. A remarkably impartial and informative book, strong on the historical background of the topics it treats, is H. R. Penniman, *Sait's American Parties and Elections*, 5th ed., Appleton-Century-Crofts, 1952.

part six

RELIGION

15. Religious Beliefs and Ritual

A religion is a more or less coherent system of beliefs and practices concerning a supernatural order of beings, forces, places, or other entities: a system that for its adherents has implications for their behavior and welfare: implications that the adherents in varying degrees and ways take seriously in their private and collective life.

Religions vary so widely in doctrine, practice, and organization and religious feelings are so personal and difficult to describe objectively that any definition of religion will necessarily seem inadequate. Nevertheless, some definition is desirable as a starting point for analysis. Our definition is of course designed to be serviceable for sociological analysis; a theologian or a psychologist might begin with a somewhat different emphasis.

There are supernatural beings (gods and goddesses, angels); supernatural places (heaven and hell and purgatory); supernatural forces (for example, the Holy Spirit; *karma,* the Hindu "law" of cause and effect, by which men's deeds have inevitable consequences not only in this life but in the next life; and *mana,* the magical power that in Polynesia is thought to be controllable by certain gifted individuals); and other supernatural entities (for example, souls). Anything is "supernatural" if its existence is believed in on some basis other than the kind of evidence acceptable in science. In this sense, supernatural entities are nonempirical. Science cannot show either that they "really" exist or that they "really" do not exist. The believer may point to evidence of some kind (for example, revelation or miracles), but the evidence, whatever it is, would not be regarded as cogent in support of a scientific theory. Religious ideas are not usually *un*scientific, as we shall see; they are *non*scientific—incapable of being confirmed or disproved empirically.

Supernatural things or beings are not necessarily thought of as being located above or outside the world; they may be aspects of things and persons that in other aspects are part of the world. A familiar instance is Jesus in orthodox Christianity: Jesus was in the world, but he is nonetheless a supernatural being in so far as people think of him as the Son of God, for that belief about him is a nonempirical belief.

The believer takes religious beliefs seriously. He is committed to them (to some extent): he is interested in the implications they have for his conduct, and he regards it as his duty to take these implications into account when he acts. This *commitment* is what distinguishes religious from philosophical ideas. The line between religion and philosophy is sometimes hard to draw, but in general philosophy is closer to science in that philosophical ideas are supposed to be examined critically, even skeptically; at the least, they are held more tentatively than religious ideas (Parsons, 1951, pp. 367ff.)

When religious beliefs are institutionalized, they are supported, like other institutions, by sanctions. Sometimes the punishment for heresy is severe; it may even be death. More commonly, the heretic is formally excommunicated from the religious group or informally shunned. Religious beliefs that are officially regarded as orthodox in a religious group are often called dogmas. Of course, not all religious beliefs are dogmas.

The very nature of religious beliefs is such that one might wonder how it is possible for a scientist to say anything about them. Sociologists do not attempt to pass judgment on the truth or relative merit of religious beliefs; whether Jesus was born of a virgin, whether there is an afterlife, whether God is one or many or three in one—these theological questions cannot be given sociological answers. What sociologists can do is note the *empirical fact* that people to some extent behave differently according to their religious beliefs, and this is so whether their religious beliefs are "true" or not. Among the questions this chapter and the next two chapters will answer tentatively are the following:

1. Why do groups create and accept nonempirical beliefs? (Regardless of one's own theological position, some religious beliefs are in some sense created by men, since different beliefs are often mutually incompatible and cannot all have been divinely revealed.)

2. What effects, if any, does religion have on other aspects of society—kinship, the economy, the political system, stratification? Do different religions have different effects? In what ways are the effects of religion functional or dysfunctional?

3. In what ways, if any, do these other aspects of society affect religion?

4. How and why do new religious movements get started?

Religion and the Problem of Evil

As the economy is "focused" on the "problem" of scarcity, religion may be said to be focused on the problem of evil: no evil, no religion. But what is "evil"? Evil is the difference between the "Heart's Desire" and the "sorry scheme of things." Evil is any and all aspects of man's experience to which emotional adjustment is difficult.[1] Why did the righteous Job suffer more than many of the unrighteous do? Why did he suffer at all? Why does anyone suffer? Why does a beloved man suddenly die, perhaps at the height of his vigor, when his wife and child, who have themselves lived what is ordinarily called a good life, most need him and least expected to lose him? Scientific answers that might be suggested to such questions would only seem perversely irrelevant: they would not be answers at all

Religions do not necessarily attempt to justify the existence of evil in our sense. They always do attempt to "explain" evil in a way that meets some of man's emotional difficulties, and they provide something to do about these difficulties. The "unknown" that religion defines and charts is not the scientifically unknown—not essentially. It is the part of experience that would seem meaningless or arbitrary even if our scientific understanding of it were complete.

KINDS OF EVIL

Evil of all kinds amounts to physical and emotional suffering, which are difficult to separate from each other. Emotional suffering arises from frustration and the anticipation of frustration: thwarted ambition, unrequited love, disappointment of all kinds, grief, jealousy, envy, and hate. Since these forms of suffering are common, we also suffer from fear; and fear is the more acute since we cannot always be certain just when, how, and to what extent evil will fall on us: that is, uncertainty itself is an occasion and a form of suffering. To some extent, these forms of suffering would exist even if everyone were morally perfect, but of course suffering arises in part from violation of moral norms—not only impersonal violations, such as organized crime, but also disloyalty and breaches of implicit trust.

The very existence of moral norms is due to the evil inherent in human life: if everything automatically turned out for us all as we could wish, then there would be no need to inculcate moral norms; there is no reason to think men would have any. By supporting such norms as the Ten Commandments and the (Confucianist) Standards for the Five Relationships (between husband and wife, parent and child, older and younger, ruler and subject, friend and friend), religion to some extent forestalls evil and reduces the total amount that would otherwise exist.

The social order, however, may produce frustrations that are due, not to violation of its norms, but to the fact that its norms are widely respected. The institution of property, for example, inevitably sanctifies inequalities of

[1] Some religions appear to deny the existence of "evil," but no religion does or could deny the existence of what we are talking about. There may be verbal differences. "I conceive it to be no comfort at all, to a man suffering agonies of frostbite, to be told by science that cold is merely negative and does not exist. So far as the statement is true it is irrelevant; so far as it pretends to be relevant it is false" (Murray, 1955, p. 184).

wealth. Political institutions often sanctify inequalities in the use of the power of the state; some people benefit from it more than others. Such inequalities are not always perceived as unjust, but the poor in goods and power might well wish that they were richer in both; they might regard their lot as relatively evil and experience some emotional difficulty in adjusting to it.

Most religious groups are somewhat critical of the social order, seeing some degree of injustice in it. For example, in 1945 the Congregational Christian Church reported expenditures of $50,000 a year on "social action"; the Presbyterian Church of the United States of America, $40,000; and the Protestant Episcopal Church, $25,000. These and other churches publish materials for youth groups, conduct special conferences, prepare films, and try in other ways to influence federal and state legislatures. The large denominations were most interested in reform in labor relations, race relations, and urban conditions (J. T. Landis, 1947).[2] As is well known, the Roman Catholic Church has also been critical of some aspects of the social order. The papal encyclicals *Rerum Novarum* (1891) and *Quadragesimo Anno* (1931), for example, were both critical of excessive selfishness on the part of some capitalists.

Some small religious groups, as we shall see in Chapter 16, go much further than the Catholic Church and the large Protestant denominations in attacking the evils of the social order; some go so far as to repudiate the secular order altogether, on the ground that it is wholly evil. Some other religious groups are indifferent to the secular order of the larger society. The most widely accepted religious orientations of any society, however, tend on the whole to support the existing institutional structure and hence to legitimize the positions of those whose power and wealth are held in accordance with the political, economic, and other institutions. It would be wrong to say that the social action of the dominant religious groups has no effect, but even its avowed purpose is not revolutionary. *Quadragesimo Anno,* for example, rejects class warfare and supports the idea of class harmony; but this class harmony is not to be achieved by dispossessing the capitalists—Marxist socialism is expressly condemned. The discussion of the place of labor organization could easily be interpreted to mean that unions were in practice to be curbed by employers—and in France it was so interpreted freely. Catholic employers in France, where the "class struggle" is acute, did in fact tend to favor mixed syndicates before World War II. (Mixed syndicates are organizations of which both workers and

---

[2] As we shall see, this "social action" is for the most part far from "radical," and many of the churches spend very little. The sums named in the text were the largest expenditures for Protestant groups. "One of the largest Protestant denominations, with 4,000,000 members, reports that they believe the church should initiate social action in all areas of life, yet their national organization to develop this program consists of two people working one-fourth time on a budget of $1,000" (Landis, 1947, p. 522).

employers are members—"company unions" on a national scale. Some organizations of this type in effect emasculate labor.)[3] From a sociological point of view, the social action of the big churches does more to strengthen the existing social order than to change it. It enables the well-placed for the most part to think that their good fortune is deserved and ought to be respected. At the same time, as we shall see, the poor and powerless are also able to get satisfaction from religion.

In general, one of the most important forms of evil in any society is the disparity between desert, or merit, and reward, or destiny. No social system is so well integrated and functions so well that social rewards are distributed in perfect accordance with people's moral sentiments. Men who are deserving in the sense that they fulfill all their obligations do not necessarily have happy lives, and men who violate institutionalized patterns outrageously sometimes seem to fare pretty well in this life. In one of his most famous poems, the Jesuit priest Gerard Manley Hopkins complains that

> . . . the sots and thralls of lust
> Do in spare hours more thrive than I that spend,
> Sir, life upon Thy cause

This problem of the disparity between merit and destiny is the aspect of evil that religious systems seem to be most concerned about. It is not merely suffering that must be explained but apparently undeserved suffering. Relative good fortune, if it seems undeserved, must also be explained.

Religious explanations of evil

There have been three self-consistent religious explanations of the existence of "undeserved" good and bad fortune (Weber, 1946, p. 275). Of these, dualism is the most common; indeed, if "dualism" is interpreted broadly, every religion is dualistic. According to this conception, there are supernatural beings or forces which work for "good" and supernatural entities opposed to them which work for "evil." In Christianity itself, despite its proclaimed monotheism, there used to be more emphasis than there is now on the struggle between God and the Devil. Witches, for example, were supposed to have made a pact with the Devil, like Faust. The most thoroughgoing example of dualism, however, is Zoroastrianism, which originated in Persia (see G. L. Berry, 1947, Chaps. 6, 10, 12). In the seventh century B.C., this religion had doctrines similar to some of those of Christianity; indeed, it influenced Christianity through Judaism and Mithraism. Among these doctrines were belief in a divine savior born of a virgin and belief in the end of the world, to be followed by the resurrection of those who had taken the side of Ahura Mazda, who had created everything good, in his great struggle with Aingra Mainyu, or Ahriman, who had created everything bad. Ahura Mazda would eventually conquer the world and reward the righteous.

---

[3] For a balanced discussion, by a sympathetic Catholic, of the conflicting interpretations made by French Catholics, see Vignaux, 1943.

Another explanation of evil is the doctrine of *karma*, the Hindu "law' of cause and effect and the transmigration of souls. As developed by Brahman thinkers, these ideas became an explanation of the caste system of India, which to non-Hindus has often seemed the most unjust social system in the world. If a man's caste position is poor now, the explanation is that he has behaved badly in his previous incarnation; if he performs his caste duties (*dharma*) faithfully now, he will be rewarded by a better caste position in his next incarnation. It follows, of course, that if he does not follow his caste *dharma* now, he will have a worse position in his next life; he might even be reborn as a parasite in the intestine of a pig. These religious ideas provide a kind of ideological support or justification for aspects of the caste system that might seem bizarre or repugnant to a non-Hindu. A person's caste *dharma* is not only his duty but his fate in this incarnation. It has been shown (Stevenson, 1957, esp. p. 980) that "the Hindu pollution concept," which justifies the ranking of the castes, is carried through with remarkable consistency. The six most important principles are as follows: (1) the Life Principle is sacred (thus oilseed-crushing is a polluting occupation, but selling oil is not); (2) "death and decay are polluting" (even Brahmans who officiate at funerals have a low status); (3) "all human emissions are polluting"; (4) the cow is sacred; (5) the drinking of alcohol is polluting; and (6) the remarriage of widows is polluting. If a caste way of life permits anything polluting, that caste will have a low status. Low status means, in practice, that one is shunned in various ways by those of higher status. The rules for eating and drinking are very elaborate. Anyone may safely take food from a person of higher caste, so that persons of unequal castes may eat together ("interdine" is the word in India) if the food is cooked and served by a Brahman of high caste, except that certain castes are so low in status that the very shadow of a member of them may be polluting to a high-caste person.

A third explanation of evil is the belief in predestination, which has had varying degrees of prominence in religion. Early Calvinism is usually regarded as the classic example. "Predestination," in Calvin, refers to the doctrine that each person's soul is irrevocably destined, before its incarnation, to go after death to Heaven or to Hell, regardless of the person's conduct in life. Predestination is arbitrary from a human point of view; yet it is perhaps the most logical form of the doctrine of grace (salvation as pure gift rather than as the reward of merit). In reality the doctrine does not so much explain evil as affirm that the meaning of evil is and must be unknown to us. *Why* God predestines a particular soul to Heaven and another to Hell man cannot presume to say, any more than he can explain why God created for His own glorification men whose lives were destined to be full of suffering. Theologians speak of "the hidden God" (*Deus absconditus*).

One of the inherent sources of instability in Christianity as a cultural system is the difficulty of explaining evil without embarrassment. It is difficult to stress God's love without attributing to Him less than omnipotence, and it is difficult to stress His omnipotence without casting some doubt upon His love. For if He is all-powerful, why does He permit evil to exist? If He cannot prevent evil, then He cannot be all-powerful. If He created men who are capable of sinning, and if there is some explanation for this that is compatible with His love, there remains the question whether all evil that befalls every man is due to that man's sin. If so, where is love, and if not, where is justice? These puzzles have led to various attempts at solution within Christianity. It seems that the problem of evil is less difficult for religions that believe in an impersonal supernatural order, or for religions that are more frankly dualistic.

Death as a form of evil

The death of another affects us in varying degree, depending upon the closeness of our attachment to the deceased, the strength of other attachments, and the effect of the death on our general situation in life. In extreme cases of bereavement, a mourner has to cope with grief, financial problems, and the necessity of painful readjustment to persons still living. Among the feelings involved, besides frustrated love, there are likely to be guilt and fear. Guilt arises from all the negative feelings the survivor had for the deceased while he was alive, for in all close attachments there is of course ambivalence. There is another source of guilt: in conflict with th impulses *toward* the deceased is an impulse to shrink *away* from him, a repugnance for the corpse itself, so horribly different from the remembered form of the living person. Sometimes an heir has a special reason for feeling guilty. He cannot help feeling pleasure at coming into some money, but he feels that he ought not to derive pleasure from the death of one he loved—and loves. If this feeling is strong, the sufferer is likely to make himself more miserable by imagining that other people are condemning him for his selfishness; this of course is an example of the mechanism of projection. The death of an intimate friend or relative also arouses fear. One is reminded of one's own approaching death; and this reminder, grim enough in itself, may be worse if it brings thoughts of the grief of those who may be left behind. If the lost friend died prematurely, the mourner may well have a feeling of injustice and rage: *why* did it have to happen? Finally, there may be a feeling that effort is futile and meaningless—a yielding to grief and rage, a revulsion from the "normal" course of living.

The symptoms of bereavement vary of course with the meaning of the loss. If the loss was great, the bereaved struggles, at first, against the realiza-

---

[4] This catalog of the feelings produced by the death of a close friend or relative owes a great deal to Malinowski, 1954; and to Waller, 1951, Chap. 22. What follows, on the process of mourning, is taken largely from Waller. Of his sources, besides literary works, which he quotes to the enrichment of his discussion, two sociological studies may be recommended especially: H. Becker, "The Sorrow of Bereavement," 1933; and Eliot, "Bereavement: Inevitable but Not Insurmountable," 1948. The latter has an especially good bibliography.

tion of death. This struggle may take the form of numbness, then possibly of flight from reality—increased use of alcohol is one mode. The mourner typically has a waking dream in which the deceased is still alive, and his dreams at night also reveal the struggle between wish and reality.

> Sometimes the person is going about his daily business in the usual way; he is dead but does not know it and the dreamer feels that he will remain alive if the dreamer can keep him from noticing his condition. Sometimes he is alive and seems pitifully weak and ill. Sometimes he seems perfectly normal, but when one touches him he is cold as ice. Sometimes he is alive and somehow inaccessible. The dream has endless variations [Waller, 1951, pp. 476-77].

Throughout the mourning process, the mourner's memory is highly selective and even distorted; he tends to idealize the deceased. In one aspect, this idealization is an effort to keep the dead person alive, part of the effort to resist facing reality. Another symptom of mourning is self-absorption, which results from the struggle to adjust. There is a characteristic devaluation of everything except memories of the deceased; the mourner's self and his usual activities lose significance; he may have an impulse to die, a sincere wish that he had died instead of the person actually dead. If remorse and guilt are important components, mourning may be prolonged in melancholia.

The healing process would go [illegible] course, with or without religion. The mourner gains some relief by expressing his feelings and by comforting other mourners. He feels his burden lightened by sharing it with sympathetic friends. Nature itself has provided a gradual healing process, by permitting the full realization of loss to come gradually, in flashes of insight and stabs of memory that can be handled one at a time. Nevertheless, religion is almost always called upon to help. There are supernatural consolations, which are perhaps more convincing since, being part of culture, they are often repeated, and one feels perhaps that they must be true. The belief that the dead person has gone to Heaven, for example, must be strongly supported also by the wish of the mourner to keep the dead person alive somehow.[5]

Religion provides no escape from death in a strict sense. Religious people die, as others do, and they know this and expect it. But their beliefs make the problem of adjustment easier. Moreover, even apart from beliefs, religion can be a great help. The funeral ritual provides the mourner with a well-marked path of action, gives him something meaningful to do, a means of acceptably expressing some of his strong emotions. The occasion is one in which many people must be attended to, many people have to be comforted, and many are there to comfort. The idealization of the dead, which is itself a comforting process, is aided by the fact that the mourners

---

[5] Waller notes that grief supports religion as religion supports the grief-stricken: "The need for rationalizing death often causes the individual to turn to religion, and the affects released by death often find a permanent repository in religious values" (1951, p. 487).

get together as a group and, acting on the cultural rule to speak well of the dead, reinforce one another's private tendencies to idealize. The people gathered are paying a tribute, and their tribute is a source of pride. On a cruder level, the funeral service itself is an occasion for displaying the status of the family, and those most directly concerned in the preparation can even get some satisfaction from praise for good taste and their unsparing expense to honor the dead. On a still cruder level, perhaps, public mourning is a means of attracting attention to oneself, a desirable thing to some people even in their sorrow. Yet the most important thing about a funeral, perhaps, is the fact that it helps the mourners to face the simple reality against which they have been struggling and are still struggling, the reality of death. Here with a ceremony arranged to be impressive the fact is proclaimed and made "official" that the dead really is dead. The religious words common in such ceremonies may or may not be believed literally; but their association with death having long since been established, a harsh and unique private event is assimilated to a continuous rhythm in which all humanity shares.

Types of Religious Belief

Like other institutions, institutionalized religious beliefs tend to be taken for granted; they tend to exclude from consciousness other possibilities of orientation. For example, it is a Christian doctrine that every human being has a soul, but unless we are familiar with other religious orientations we may be unaware of the further Christian doctrine that *only* human beings have souls. In the religions of India and many other parts of Asia, animals and insects, if not plants, also have souls. In Christian belief, every soul lives only once on earth and is thereafter immortal. In Hinduism, a soul may have many incarnations on earth, and it not only *will* live forever but *has* lived forever.

An "official" creed, where there is one, is a rather crude indication of the actual religion of those who accept it: "The rules of metre are not the same thing as poetry" (Murray, 1955, p. 166). There are several reasons for approaching religious beliefs cautiously. In the first place, many important beliefs are so much taken for granted that people do not make them explicit in their creeds. Secondly, the meaning of the verbal formulas may change even though the words remain the same. From one point of view, it is a tragedy of history that many heretics of the Middle Ages were probably closer, in their deep religious views, to the orthodox thinkers of the time than those orthodox thinkers would be to faithful enlightened Catholics of today. Thirdly, the actual bearing of religious beliefs on people's lives depends very much upon their whole life situation. To some extent also, as we shall see in the next chapter, social position helps to determine what kind of religious belief people are attracted to. Fourthly, there is a certain amount of conscious disagreement among those who accept the same creed. A study published in 1929 reported that 28 per cent of the 500 Christian *ministers* who were questioned did not believe "that heaven exists as an actual place or location," and 34 per cent of the same ministers did not believe "that hell exists as an actual place or location." Yet only one per cent did not believe "that there is a continuance of life after death" (Betts, 1929). These findings might be a little startling to those who think that "Christianity" is a fixed doctrine. The answers of 500 theological students were markedly different from those of the ministers, showing change in belief from one generation to the next. Sixty-nine percent of the students did not believe "that heaven exists as an actual place or location," and 76 per cent did not believe "that hell exists as an actual place or location"; 4 per cent did not believe in the continuance of life after death.

Finally, the very meaning of "belief" is obscure as applied to religion. Certainly religious "belief" is different from "belief" that the world is roughly round. Indeed, people often do not define their religious beliefs too closely: ". . . men could and can adopt a position in which they never allow themselves to ask just what they mean by what they are doing" (Nock, 1933, p. 97). Nevertheless, verbalized religious beliefs are an important indication of the subjective meaning of people's religious behavior, and they often help us to understand how religion influences behavior in general. Table 9 (pp. 402-03) gives some examples of religious beliefs of three types. (The characterization of each of the religions included in the table is of course incomplete.)

To people familiar with the Christian tradition, "salvation" means an afterlife in Heaven. We shall speak of salvation, however, in a more inclusive sense. Men are striving for salvation, for themselves or for a group, to the extent that they are trying to escape from "evil" by supernatural means. Exactly what evil men try by supernatural means to escape *from* and exactly what goal of salvation they try to escape *to* vary over quite a wide range. Salvation may be temporary or permanent, partial or complete. Praying for rain is a form of salvation-seeking in our sense, no less than is the goal of seeing God in Heaven. The various goals are not all mutually exclusive. An individual might strive for worldly prosperity or good health or long life by supernatural means and also be interested in attaining a temporary supernatural state of bliss or union with God. In some sense, however, religious persons are always seeking salvation *here and now*. They wish to feel that they are on good terms with the supernatural order, personal or impersonal. Even the early Calvinists, who believed in predestination and therefore feared that they might be damned regardless of their "merit," sought and cherished "the certainty of grace" (*certitudo salutis*)—that is, the subjective assurance here and now, however irrational, that God had elected them for eternal salvation.

A common term in religious discourse is "the world," used in a special sense. The precise reference varies, but the core meaning seems to be concern for this life and for such empirical values as wealth and social prestige, as opposed to concern for the afterlife or the state of one's soul. In a religious

TABLE 9

Some examples of religious beliefs

Religion	*Cosmic beliefs*
HINDUISM (Includes cults and sects of Vishnu and Shiva, as well as orthodox Brahmanism.)	*Karma* and *samsara* (transmigration). Gods are essentially different symbols of impersonal pantheism. Endless wheel of incarnations, even for gods.
BUDDHISM (Originally a revolt from Hinduism and a "purification" of Brahman doctrine. Caste *dharma* is meaningless. Many subsequent developments.)	Reincarnation. Evil is the result of unrealistic desires. The world is guided by Buddhas ("Enlightened Ones").
CONFUCIANISM ("Official" religion of precommunist China. Largely a social ethic, with much tolerance for popular magic.)	Shadowy gods; virtual pantheism. *Tao* is the harmony that pervades all things unless it is disturbed by wrong conduct. The cosmos is essentially unchanging.
JUDAISM (The characterization is of the main stream and ignores certain sects; e.g., Hassidism.)	One supramundane god of power, justice, and mercy. The world does not pass through cycles but is passing through a history that will eventually come to an end.
CATHOLICISM (Largest Christian church. Proclaims itself to be the only true church as an organized body.)	One perfect God "in Trinity, and Trinity in Unity": Father, Son (Christ), and Holy Spirit.
PROTESTANTISM (Great variation in belief; therefore, present characterization mentions tendencies.)	Most churches accept Trinity. Some are unitarian.
ISLAM (Mohammedanism. Partly grew out of Judaism and Christianity, partly had a common source with them.)	One supramundane god, called Allah. Mohammed is his prophet. A Day of Judgment is to come.

Beliefs about salvation	*Myths* (see pp. 405-06)
Fulfilling one's *dharma* will lead to a better incarnation, perhaps as a god The especially devout may hope to merge with the "All-One" (thus losing personal identity forever). Asceticism and mysticism common.	Krishna was a reincarnation of the god Vishnu. Stories of the achievements of the Brahmans by magical power.
Escape from the eternal wheel of *karma* and *samsara* by following the "Noble Eightfold Path." Monastic mysticism. Much popular (uncanonical) magic.	After hundreds of lives of effort, Gautama, while sitting in the lotus posture under a fig tree, became the fourth historical Buddha.
Happiness through following ethics of Confucius. Gods need sacrifices in order to keep the world in harmony. Ancestor worship. "Worldly" religion; no asceticism; no mysticism.	In 1832 the emperor brought rain by making a public confession of his faults. This sort of thing had happened many times before.
Salvation of mankind at the end of the world, after the coming of the Messiah. Stress on ethics and (in Orthodox Judaism) on ritual acts, pervading life Nonascetic; little mysticism.	God created Heaven and earth out of nothing. He gave the Ten Commandments to Moses. Moses made the Red Sea roll back so that the Hebrews could pass across it to safety.
Salvation achieved by the Spirit and sacrifice of Christ, especially with the help of the seven sacraments of the Church. Prayer. Little concern for this world except as theatre for creating saints and saving souls. Ascetic monasticism. Little mysticism.	Jesus born of a virgin free of sin. After being crucified, Jesus rose from the dead. He gave the power of redemption to Peter and his successors. Many miracles performed by Christ and the saints.
More emphasis on the love of God and on the saving power of faith, less emphasis on sacraments. Most churches now nonmystical and nonascetic, but some exceptions.	Some groups accept all the stories in the Bible as literally true; others leave exact beliefs to the individual member.
By following Mohammed and taking a pilgrimage to Mecca if possible, men attain Paradise after death. Hell for the wicked. Some asceticism (fasting), but little mysticism in the main tradition.	Mohammed received his revelation from Allah through the angel Gabriel.

context, "the world" is usually looked upon as secondary or unimportant or even evil. It is possible, however, to pursue religious interests or goals while at the same time participating in the everyday affairs of men—family activities, work, politics—just as it is possible to pursue quite worldly interests by supernatural means, e.g., magic. We shall use the term "innerworldly" to refer to any means to salvation that permits or requires participation in secular life, and the term "otherworldly" to refer to any means to salvation that tends to remove the religious actor from secular life.[6] An extreme example of otherworldly salvation-seeking is the life of a Trappist monk, who is sworn to silence, devoted to prayer and ritual, withdrawn from the everyday concerns of other men. Mysticism, which is found in virtually all religions but is especially prominent in certain religions of the Far East (e.g., Hinduism, Buddhism, and Taoism), tends especially toward the otherworldly. The mystic is seeking union with God. To achieve this he may use music and dancing, prayer, contemplation, drugs, fasting and exposure, social isolation, special postures and bodily exercises, alcohol, or sexual orgies. The physiological and introspective peculiarities of mystical states are empirical enough: what is nonempirical is the interpretation given to them by the religious zealot. We should note, however, that mysticism may be (but rarely is) associated with innerworldly (not "worldly") activity. For example, the Quakers seek mystical experience of the "Inner Light," yet their concern for social issues and their participation in the affairs of the world have always been great; they are innerworldly mystics. Moreover, the example of the Trappists shows that one may be otherworldly without necessarily being a mystic.

Mysticism, as with the Quakers, tends to be associated with the impersonal, pantheistic conception of God: God is *in* all men. The conception of a personal supramundane God, more usual in Christianity than pantheism and common to Judaism and Islam, tends to be associated with the conception of man, not as the vessel of God, but as His agent or subject. The word "Islam," for example, means surrender or submission (to the will of Allah, as revealed to Mohammed). However, there have been Christian, Jewish, and Moslem mystics too; the conception of God seems to affect the relative emphasis on man as "agent" and man as "vessel." [7]

---

[6] All religions, of course, are "otherworldly" in the sense that they use a supernatural frame of reference. Note the distinction made in the text.

[7] Technically, the Catholic Eucharist is mystical in that the communicant receives the blood and body of Christ (a man-god) in the bread and wine. The Catholic emphasis, however, is on the objective presence of Christ, not on the communicant's subjective mystical feeling; and there is a big difference between the mystic St. Teresa and the average Catholic. The connection between pantheism and mysticism is shown in a story told by Konow, a Danish scholar: ". . . in 1925, a . . . Mahârâjâ, who ruled over about half a million subjects in Central India . . . had conceived the idea that I could work wonders, and he wanted me to put him into communion with a deceased friend, . . . a lad he had 'loved,' and who had acted Krishna's role at the cultic plays at his court.

Innerworldly and otherworldly means to salvation are not mutually exclusive. They are often combined in various degrees. Moreover, either course can be pursued with unremitting thoroughness or with less demanding rigor. "Asceticism" is discipline and renunciation of immediate satisfactions in the interest of attaining the religious goal. The Trappist monks are otherworldly ascetics; the Calvinist Puritans were extreme innerworldly ascetics (with of course some individual variation).[8]

From religious beliefs about the relatively permanent aspects of the supernatural order and about salvation, we may distinguish "myths," which are beliefs about supernatural *events* that are supposed to have occurred at some definite point in time. Such beliefs have the general functions of completing the system of ideas about the supernatural order and of reinforcing belief in it. Most myths have to do with origins—the origin of the gods, of the world, of culture, of certain features of nature. Other myths are stories of exploits of the gods or exploits or miraculous events in the lives of religious leaders. An example of a myth in Christianity is the belief that Jesus, a man-god, was born of a virgin.

Note that "myth" is a technical term. It implies nothing whatsoever about the truth or moral value of the belief in question. Of course, the myth of Christ does contain the empirical proposition that one Jesus of Nazareth did in fact live, and there is some evidence to support this proposition; but even if this proposition were established beyond reasonable dispute, the evidence would not *scientifically* justify the religious significance attached to the myth by believing Christians, for Jesus might have lived whether or not he was the son of God. (Of course the reverse is not true: if grave doubt were cast on the mere contention that Jesus lived at all, then the whole myth would certainly be undermined.)

A special class of myth has to do with the element of revelation in religion. Being nonempirical, religious beliefs cannot claim acceptance on the basis of evidence in the ordinary sense. Religious "truths" are therefore authoritatively "revealed" to someone. The story of when, where, to whom, and under what circumstances the revelation or series of revelations took

---

"I told him that I could not, and that I would not have done it if I could . . . that I presumed that his friend was now above all mundane imperfections, and that any attempt at coming into touch with him might diminish his happiness and even do him harm.

"He whispered something to his secretary, who went out and returned with a tray of roses, which His Highness began to throw over my head. I asked him what he was doing, and he answered: 'I worship you.' I said that I would accept this worship presuming that his reason was that he felt that he had heard from my mouth what struck him as divine truth. 'So it is,' he said, and he wanted me to make a long stay. He would build a temple for me!" (Konow and Tuxen, 1949, p. 10).

[8] This section on paths to salvation is much indebted to Max Weber but is not a perfectly faithful account of his views. See Weber, 1946, pp. 267-301, 323-59. He tends to oppose mysticism and asceticism to each other. For us the main contrast is that between innerworldly and otherworldly means to salvation, and mysticism and asceticism cut across each other.

place is, technically speaking, a myth. The person to whom the revelation is made is technically known as a prophet if he feels that the mission is supernaturally laid upon him of spreading the news of the revelation among men for their salvation. Mohammed is supposed to have received his divine call to "recite" while he was meditating in a cave just outside Mecca. It is for this reason, among others, that Mecca is a holy city to Moslems.

The Sacred and the Profane

Supernatural entities are always sacred—that is, worthy of being treated with respect—whether they are good or evil. The Devil, evil spirits, and the destroyer gods of various religions are "bad," but in any religion the supernatural order as a whole is "good," in the sense that one can always bring its powers to one's side, or at least neutralize them, if one acts in the right way. On the other hand, these supernatural entities can be dangerous if they are not treated correctly or in the proper spirit.

Supernatural beings and forces are holy (or unholy if they are "bad"): this means that one must use special precaution in dealing with them. Supernatural beings and forces are of course invisible and intangible, but there are also sacred objects that are quite tangible and visible. Such, for example, is the Ark of the Covenant in a synagogue, or the altar in a Christian church. Catholics genuflect and bow the head when passing before the church altar: this is typical of the respect shown to tangible sacred objects. Some of these objects are sacred because they are symbols of the invisible supernatural beings—this is true of images, for example. Other objects are sacred and therefore treated with special respect because of their close association with the supernatural. Thus everything in a church shares to some extent in the sacredness of the more specifically sacred objects. It is sometimes said that the sacred is "contagious," and this word is not altogether inappropriate when one remembers the power of sacred objects to do harm if they are not treated carefully. Some sacredness is enjoyed by the priests or ministers or other specialists who are more closely associated with the sacred than are ordinary people; even their robes are not ordinary garments but share in the contagion. Among peoples, such as the Chinese, who worship the spirits of their ancestors, it is not too much to say that a man acquires a certain sacredness as he becomes old and approaches death.

Everything that is not holy or unholy is profane—every place, being, thing, or act. Prescriptions and taboos surround the sacred: to violate the rules is profanation. "Profanity" is using sacred names without the proper respect. (Sometimes the name of a god is not supposed to be pronounced at all.)

Some theorists once held that certain objects are sacred because of their intrinsic qualities. Thus, they thought, the sun is often worshiped because it is bright and hot and helps the crops to grow; the Ganges is sacred because it is a mighty river; Mount Fuji, Mount Sinai, Mount Olympus, and other sacred mountains are worshiped because they are lofty and awe-inspiring. That this theory is erroneous is strongly suggested by the fact that sacred objects are not always very awe-inspiring in themselves, nor are all high mountains and great rivers sacred. ". . . [I]n the mysteries of Demeter and Persephone at Eleusis, we regularly find the most lovely of all goddesses, Demeter and Persephone, habitually—I will not say represented by, but dangerously associated with, a sacred Sow. A Pig is the one animal in Greek religion that actually had sacrifice made to it." The Greek ritual of the Diasia was dominated by a sacred snake (Murray, 1955, p. 15). There is a tendency to think that ancient or primitive (i.e., nonliterate) religions were crude and "superstitious" because of ignorance. Lest anyone think that ignorance explains the sacred pig and the sacred snake, we should recall that in India, which is not primitive, the cow is venerated by all Hindus. Cow dung is used to purify a dwelling that has been profaned in some way, and the devout dip their hands in cow urine and sprinkle their garments with it. In fact, almost anything can be treated as sacred. Sacredness is not a quality inherent in objects; it is, rather, inherent in the attitudes of the devout. Anything toward which the devout feel a nonrational attitude of respect and caution is thereby sacred. By "nonrational" we mean that the attitude and the actions manifesting it cannot be explained by the intrinsic properties of the object. The Ganges may be filthy, yet bathing in it is believed by Hindus to be purifying; moreover, a Hindu does not have to be ignorant of the germ theory of disease in order to feel respect for the sacred river.

The key to an understanding of tangible sacred objects is the realization that they are tangible, visible symbols of the intangible, invisible supernatural order. Handling sacred objects helps to bring the supernatural order more vividly to our imagination and presumably reinforces our belief in it. God and the saints are far away, invisible, and perhaps in themselves ineffable; but one can see an ikon and burn a candle to it. The form of a symbol bears some relationship to the form of the thing symbolized. Thus the pig is an appropriate symbol to use in a fertility ritual. The Diasia was a ritual to appease "the dead and the lords of death"; the snake, which figures prominently in the ritual, lives underground and is often dangerous—like the spirits of the dead (Murray, 1955, p. 18).[9] The symbolism of the Holy Mass and the Holy Communion for laymen has been more consciously elaborated. In the sacrament of the Mass, Christ is present under the appearances of bread and wine, but these homely substances are symbolically appropriate for numerous reasons. The bread symbolizes the Flesh of Christ and the wine His Blood. As bread and wine are common sources of nourishment, so the sacrament is performed for the spiritual nourishment of the

---

[9] It is not necessary to assume that the religious person always thinks consciously of the tangible sacred object as a symbol. Confusion of symbol and concept symbolized is quite common. The analysis of symbols is a rather recent form of sophistication.

communicants. The bread is unleavened to symbolize the purity of Christ's body, without corruption; but the wine is mixed with a little water, to symbolize both the fact that blood and water flowed from Christ's side during His suffering on the Cross and the fact that in the communion the Blood of Christ is mixed with the water of the people. As the grain was ground and the grapes crushed, after enduring all the trials of the weather, so Christ suffered for man; and as the bread was made of many grains and the wine of many grapes, so the body of Christ is made of many people in the Church.[10]

In another sense, a "church," like any other building, is not merely an artifact for serving utilitarian purposes; it is also an elaborate symbol, a "virtual space," a domain symbolic of culturally patterned activities and values. The symbolic aspects of a church or temple are of course more prominent and obvious than those of most secular buildings.[11]

These examples are perhaps sufficient to show that sacred objects are sacred because of their symbolic value and not because of their intrinsic properties. As we have noted, they are in a sense manageable, as the non-empirical entities they represent are not. They facilitate worship and strengthen faith. Moreover, being tangible, they serve better than beliefs alone to unite the faithful. The verbal formulas of belief may mean somewhat different things to different people, but the visible sacred objects are perhaps more nearly the same for all; and whereas sharing beliefs is not a very direct evidence of unity, performing certain acts in relation to sacred objects makes unity manifest.[12] This point leads us directly to ritual.

Ritual

For many people, a great many actions indeed have significance in terms of ideas about supernatural beings or forces. "Religious" action is not necessarily something concretely different from "economic" or "political" or some other kind of action: it may be an aspect of almost any action. To the extent that a businessman or a politician acts on the basis of religious scruples, his action is religious, even though it is action in the marketplace or a senate cloakroom. On the other hand, people often go to church for

---

[10] This incomplete interpretation of the symbolism of the Holy Eucharist is taken from a pamphlet published by St. Benedict's Home Missionary Society, Benet Lake, Wisconsin: *Why?* ed. Abbot Richard Felix, O.S.B., issue of May 1956, v. 12, no. 7, Section 4, Catechism Lesson No. 105: "What Is the Matter of the Sacrament of the Holy Eucharist?"

[11] For a discussion of architecture as the art of creating "virtual spaces," see Langer, 1953, pp. 92-102. For an excellent illustrative analysis of the Gothic cathedral as a complex symbol of medieval theology, see Summerson, 1949, Chap. 1 (and cf. Chap. 6, on Viollet-le-Duc's rationalistic approach to Gothic, which missed its symbolic character). See also the analysis of the plan and symbolic meaning of the temple of Barabudur (Java), perhaps the greatest example of Buddhist art, in Rowland, 1953, pp. 260-67. More plates are to be found in Grousset. 1931

[12] For a sociological analysis of the significance of sacred objects, see Durkheim, 1947.

other reasons besides religious ones; for example, they may wish to promote their business or political interests.

Religious action more narrowly defined is action in which the supernatural order is appealed to or manipulated or worshiped. Such action may be simply an expression of reverent attitudes—worship in a narrow sense—or it may be directed toward some goal—for example, the goal of healing the sick or the goal of assuring the repose of the soul of some dead person.

GENERAL CHARACTERISTICS

Ritual is a particularly important form of religious action. We can identify at least six general characteristics:

1. Ritual often involves the manipulation of tangible sacred objects, and the action is meaningful within the frame of reference of the supernatural order.

2. The performance is part of the religious system for attaining salvation in some form. Sometimes its effectiveness is presumed to depend upon the "will" of a supernatural being; thus, when people speak of prayer or supplication, they imply that the supernatural being who is addressed may or may not fulfill the wishes of the petitioner. In some rituals, however, the performance is automatically effective provided that it is carried out according to certain prescriptions. "A sacrament is not fulfilled by the fact that one believes in it, but by the fact that it is performed" (Adam, 1954, p. 197).[13]

3. The ritual may be happy, even joyous, but it is not regarded by the faithful as primarily a form of entertainment; it is, as Durkheim says, "part of serious life itself."

4. Being goal-directed, ritual is a kind of instrumental action; but it is also expressional—that is, it is charged with symbolic content expressing, among other things, the *attitudes* of the participants and possibly of onlookers (passive participants) who may be regarded as co-beneficiaries. This aspect of ritual distinguishes it from those purely technical exercises which mystics sometimes use in order to facilitate contemplation or blissful apathy.

In rational action, such as putting together the parts of an airplane, the operations are constrained to a considerable extent by "the nature of things": certain acts must be performed if success is to be achieved at all. Operations may be modified in the course of time for various reasons, including developments in physics and engineering; but there is always bondage to the brute facts of empirical reality. In ritual, on the other hand there is no such bondage, for the relation between means and goal is not of the same kind; it is not an intrinsic relation but a supernatural or symbolic

13 The sacraments, of course, depend upon the will of God in that He is presumed to have instituted them and promised that they would be efficacious: but they do not depend upon the will of God in the sense that on a particular occasion they might not be efficacious: in this sense, fulfillment is "automatic."

one. There can be no empirical test of whether or not the means are adequate for attaining the goal sought. Consequently, ritual action admits of virtually infinite variety; attitudes may be expressed symbolically in many ways, and the supernatural world is not bound by the same laws as the world of nature.

5. Nevertheless, any given ritual tends to be bound to a particular form over long periods of time. Just *because* symbols are arbitrary within broad limits, ritual action must be stereotyped if it is to retain its meaning. (Formal rigidity is thus a secondary aspect of ritual, but it is so prominent that in popular usage the term "ritual" often refers to any action that is frequently repeated in the same pattern and that seems to have no "practical" result.) In the Mass, for example, the wafer of bread must be circular in shape and must be larger than the wafers used by lay communicants; the bread must be fresh and unleavened; the wine must have no preservative in it; the amount of water added must not exceed a third of the total liquid.

6. Ritual must be distinguished from "moral action"—that is, from action in conformity with social norms valued for their own sake. The performance of a ritual often does involve the cooperation of several actors in more or less differentiated roles, but the role pattern as a whole, instead of being intrinsically valued, is valued because it is regarded as a necessary means to the attainment of good relations with the supernatural. Moral action, on the other hand, is at least in part valued intrinsically. Thus obeying the commandment not to steal is a religious duty, but it is not a ritual; and, in general, ritual is to be distinguished from all religiously sanctioned moral duties, even though fulfillment of the latter may be thought to have (nonempirical) consequences for one's soul.

Relatively speaking, Protestant sects and denominations have always had a distaste for ritual, even a distrust of it. Luther's doctrine of justification by faith rather than by "works" was not meant as a denial of the importance of morally good deeds for attaining salvation. He meant to stress the *general* sinfulness or "health" of the soul, as opposed to particular sins; and above all he meant to stress God's love and grace for men's repentance and their faith in Him, as opposed to the then-prevalent "bookkeeping," which mechanically balanced particular sinful acts against ritual "works." Needless to say, a mechanical spirit is not inherent in ritualism, although it is, from a certain religious point of view, a prevalent and potent danger. This is one source of the Protestant distrust of ritual. Luther's emphasis was a reaction to the religious tone of his historical period (McNeill, 1951, Chap. 8).

"RITES DE PASSAGE"

Some rituals, called rites of transition (*rites de passage*), supernaturally mark the transition from one social status to another. Of the seven sacraments of the Catholic Church, five are *rites de passage;* these are Baptism, Confirmation, Extreme Unction, Ordination, and Matrimony. Ordination, for example, confers upon a man the status of a priest—that is, the supernatural power of administering all seven sacraments and thus giving grace. *Rites de passage* have the sociological function of impressing upon the recipient and those who will henceforth interact with him the rights and obligations of his new status-role.

MYTH AND RITUAL

Many rituals are symbolic representations of myths, in our technical sense. The Holy Eucharist, for example, represents the Last Supper— the communion meal that Christ shared with his disciples. The Mass, in Catholic dogma, is a re-enactment of the Crucifixion. In the "threefold form" of the Eastern Orthodox Churches, the Mass "represents symbolically the life of Christ from the beginning of his preaching until the ascension into heaven" (Fedotov, 1948). Somewhat similar is the Roman Catholic ritual known as the Stations of the Cross, in which the believer passes before a series of pictures or bas-reliefs, each surmounted by a cross, and meditates upon the scene depicted (for example, Pilate's condemnation of Jesus or Jesus carrying His cross). Pilgrims to the Holy Land make the Stations of the Cross upon the scene of the original events.

Especially in some so-called primitive tribes, where often only one religion and one structure of society are known, religious rituals may symbolize not only myths and the supernatural order and man's attitude toward it but also aspects of the natural order and the social order. Among the Murngin tribes of Australia, for example, there is an annual ritual cycle called *Wawilak*. The Wawilak cycle dramatically represents a series of myths about the snake-god *Yurlunggur* and two prehistoric (mythical) women, the Wawilak sisters. Yurlunggur represents the rainy season, which in this part of Australia is in fact accompanied by a great many snakes. The Wawilak cycle is at the same time a *rite de passage*—the boys in the tribe who have reached a certain age are admitted, through circumcision and other symbolic ceremonies, into manhood and the sacred presence of Yurlunggur. Besides the social-structural principles of male superiority and age-grading, other aspects of the social order are also represented—for example, the division of the society into kinship moieties and the division of the tribal territory into totemic-clan territories. Many aspects of the natural order, associated with the life-dominating cycle of dry and rainy seasons, are represented. In the rituals (as in the Mass) the *same* symbols have multiple meanings, or levels of meaning, at the same time. Thus myth and ritual embody a "total" conception of ultimate order, a legitimation of the social system, an explanation of the existence of evil, and a way of bringing supernatural powers into the service of men (W. L. Warner, 1937, Chap. 9).

INTEGRATIVE FUNCTIONS

Many people besides sociologists and anthropologists have observed that the performance of rituals has an effect on the attitude of the performer (or other beneficiary). Ritual not only affirms certain attitudes, it also confirms them. Sophisticated Confucianists do not believe in ancestral spirits, but they approve of ancestor worship because it tends to strengthen the socially important attitudes of respect of son for father, and of younger brother for older brother (Chan, 1948). The effects of ritual tend to be heightened when the ritual is performed in public. The worshiper *sees* that his attitudes are held in common with other people. Concerning the pilgrimage (*hajj*), Salma Bishlawy notes: "This ceremony is the most unifying influence in Islam. Hundreds of thousands of Muslims, rich and poor, Arabs, Turks, Persians . . . meet on common ground and are impressed with their equality before God" (1948, p. 163).

Magic

The goal of assuring the repose of the soul of a dead person is nonempirical: that is, an impartial observer will have no *empirical* evidence available to him that would enable him to tell whether the soul is in repose or not—or, indeed, whether there is a soul or not. Healing the sick, on the other hand, is an empirical goal, in the sense that when the action is completed an impartial observer will be able to determine whether the patient is visibly well or still visibly sick. The *goal* here is empirical, whether or not the means used to attain it were effective. When the goal of action is empirical and the means are supernatural, we call the action *magic*.

This usage is admittedly somewhat arbitrary. Max Weber used the term "magic" to refer to religious action believed to be automatically effective, whether the goal is empirical or nonempirical. Bronislaw Malinowski defined "magic" as the use of supernatural means to try to obtain empirical ends; but he distinguished "magic" from "religion." [14] This usage has the disadvantage that many prayers become difficult to classify, for many prayers (which are certainly directed to the supernatural and are commonly regarded as "religious") are directed toward empirical ends—prayers for the recovery of the sick, for example. Almost any technical distinction one might like to make between "religion" and "magic" has this disadvantage of running counter to everyday usage. To regard magic as part of religion, as we do here, is technically justified on the ground that in magic, as in other religious activity, there is concern with the supernatural order and with the problem of salvation (escape from evil by supernatural means). [15]

It is useful to distinguish between "white" and "black" magic. All

---

[14] Malinowski's theory is neatly stated by Parsons, 1954, Chap. 10: "The Theoretical Development of the Sociology of Religion." See also the discussion in Homans, 1950, pp. 321-30.

[15] For an attempt to distinguish between religion and magic as ideal types, see Goode, 1951, pp. 50-55. Goode's distinction turns upon several variable factors, but the trouble is that they do not vary together. This is not a decisive objection, however, and Goode's discussion is well worth attention.

magic is used for the benefit of an individual or a group. The distinctive thing about "white" magic is that it is never used to do harm within the magician's own society. Magic to restore health is "white"; so also is magic to ensure victory in war (even though this presumably harms the enemy). "Black" magic, on the other hand, always does harm (in theory) and is often directed against persons in the magician's own society. Thus, magic to inflict disease is "black."

The distinction between "white" and "black" does not coincide perfectly with the distinction between "approved" and "disapproved" or between "legitimate" and "illegitimate." White magic is always approved of; black magic is sometimes approved of, sometimes disapproved of, depending upon circumstances.

WHITE MAGIC

Agriculture, hunting, warfare, and health are the fields in which white magic is perhaps most common. The magic rite and spell may be used for an individual's benefit or for the benefit of some larger group, up to the whole society (as in a cooperative hunt or a ceremony before a war party sets out). The Navaho "singer," by various supernatural means, such as chanting and making sand paintings, tries to restore people to health. He is a specialist, supported by fees. The Sun Dance performed in one version or another by some sixteen Plains Indian tribes always involved several participants, none of whom had to be a specialist in magic, although for (symbolic) supernatural reasons the performers might have to meet certain qualifications, such as proved bravery or virginity.

Why is white magic widely practiced in agriculture, hunting, warfare, and health problems? These activities and occasions typically have in common two characteristics: (1) they are extremely important for the maintenance of the social system, and the outcome of action is a matter of deep concern; and (2) a successful outcome cannot be assured by the use of rational techniques alone. Do what you may most conscientiously to produce a good crop or prepare your forces for battle: still you may be disappointed; drought or hail or a blight of pests or a superior enemy may surprise and ruin you.

When these two conditions are present—emotional involvement in the outcome of action and inadequate rational control—we may expect to find magic. Magical ritual is not used *instead of* known rational techniques; magic is a *supplement*. By performing magic, men assure themselves that they are doing everything possible to produce a favorable outcome. They are expressing their strong wishes symbolically and renewing their confidence. Malinowski describes what happened in a Melanesian lagoon village built on piles when a monsoon hurricane roared in. At first the people were "all in panic."

> When the wind was at its worst a loud chant suddenly arose from . . . the hereditary wind magician of the community. . . . The words of the

> spell were simple: he ordered the wind to abate, to avaunt, to lie still. . . . He asserted that no harm could be done to the village.
>
> What was the effect of his imprecations on the wind does not matter to us skeptics, but the effect of his voice on the human beings was truly magical. . . . It was evident that the villagers now felt safe. . . . And immediately after he had finished his spell the magician took the practical situation in hand: he gave orders what to do, orders which were immediately obeyed in a disciplined, organized manner [Malinowski, 1937, pp. 157-58].

The Trobriand Islanders regarded magic as indispensable for their deep-sea fishing, which was risky both in the sense that lives might be lost and in the sense that the costly fishing expedition might not return with many fish; but the islanders did not use magic in their fresh-water fishing, which involved no risk.

Most magic in modern American life is of course not known as such. People call it astrology or numerology and may even think of it as science; they may have good-luck charms and observe magical taboos in which they half believe. Among the most important fields in which magic is common in America are war, agriculture, health, sports, and the professional theatre, but no serious activity in which the element of uncertainty is great is without it. Combat troops in World War II "might carry protective amulets or good-luck charms . . . a cross, a Bible, a rabbit's foot, a medal. They might carry out prebattle preparations in a fixed, 'ritual' order. They might jealously keep articles of clothing or equipment which were associated with some past experience of escape from danger" (M. B. Smith, 1949, p. 189). Much everyday religion is magic. In a French-Canadian parish, the mass of St. Marc's Day is followed by a special ritual: ". . . the priest blesses a large china bowl full of assorted seeds. The ceremonies finished, a man from each family goes forward and secures a handful of the seeds to take home. The blessed seeds are . . . the first to be planted . . ." (Miner, 1939, p. 295). In a large city with many Catholics, one may see small statues of Mary or Jesus set on the narrow ledge just over the dashboard of automobiles. A priest in Boston has organized a sort of safety club for reducing traffic accidents: by signing a form, one can have one's name read every morning in the prayers at Mass.

Faith healing, as in Christian Science, has always been a flourishing form of magic.[16] Not all forms of nonmedical healing, however, are properly called magic. Many "useless" patent medicines and practices, such as osteopathy, have no reference to a supernatural order but seem to be based on

---

[16] There is no intention here to attack faith healing; some psychosomatic complaints yield more readily to faith healing than to ordinary methods. Some of the technical terms current in the sociology of religion are perhaps infelicitous since they have pejorative overtones in much popular speech. This is true of "myth" and "magic." We repeat that these terms are used here in a perfectly neutral sense—we neither recommend nor depreciate the beliefs and practices referred to.

ignorance and error; they do, however, feed on the same hopes and fears that health magic ministers to (Haggard, 1929, Chaps. 12-14).[17]

As we have noted, many superstitions are followed with a somewhat shamefaced credulity—but they are nevertheless followed. Some college students, for example, feel more confident of success when taking an examination if they wear a particular garment, write with a certain "lucky" pen, or sit in a particular "lucky" place in the examination room.[18]

In societies where science and sanitation are relatively undeveloped, magic tends to be far more prominent than it is in our society (although, as we have seen, magic is by no means unknown in the United States). Science and technology tend to increase rational control over events and thus reduce the need for nonrational techniques. When a cholera epidemic struck "West Town" in Yunnan Province, China, the people held expensive prayer meetings and a ritual parade through every corner of the town. The Taoist priests had the most elaborate explanation of the epidemic, lay participants in the ceremonies the next most elaborate, and "the general public" the least. A fairly elaborate explanation is the following: "The epidemic is caused by sin, the ghosts of those who died without descendants, fate, and sometimes by infection and contamination. The chief agents carrying it are the Wen spirits disseminated by Wen God (god of epidemics) at the command of higher gods" (Hsu, 1952, p. 95).

A few people in "West Town" took advantage of the opportunity to get inoculations at the missionary hospital, but most were afraid to, and those who did were careful to take part in the religio-magical rituals as well. Some of the latter participated in the rituals even though they had no faith, because they wished to keep up their prestige in the community; but others did so on the principle that the more measures they took against the epidemic, the safer they would be. People sometimes make a distinction between rational techniques and magic and sometimes do not. An observer equipped with scientific knowledge, however, can at least make the distinction between rational and nonrational techniques. In most things we must all follow the culture that comes down to us; if the culture provides religio-magical techniques for certain situations, these are the techniques we use, with or without understanding them, but if the culture includes a great deal of science, we are more likely to use science. Many people employ rational techniques without understanding the scientific foundation for them, and sometimes without being aware that anyone else knows it—just as many

---

[17] Dr. Haggard makes no distinction between magic and erroneous practices, although he recognizes the psychological efficacy of some uses of faith healing. He also recognizes that the highly profitable business in dubious methods arises in part from the inadequacy of rational techniques in some cases and from the proscription of magic in orthodox medical practice. Business and quackery step in to supply a widely felt need.

[18] For a rich collection of students' magical and quasi-magical devices, see Tozzer, 1925, pp. 242-66.

people, indeed, engage in religious practices the theological basis of which is vague or unknown to them.

BLACK MAGIC

Under black magic are subsumed sorcery and witchcraft. Sorcery consists of rites and spells that, according to cultural belief, do not depend for their efficacy upon any supernatural power in the magician himself. Thus sorcery can be learned and practiced with efficacy by anyone, provided that the ritual is correctly performed and that the victim or some protector does not use countermagic of greater potency. Witchcraft, on the other hand, is black magic that is thought to depend upon the supernatural power of the magician. Thus it cannot be transmitted, except possibly by heredity (M. H. Wilson, 1951).[19]

Among the Dobuans of the Western Pacific, black magic is used to protect property rights and hence to punish theft.

> Every disease is held to be caused by a *tabu*. *Tabu* denotes an incantation, expressing black hatred in an extremely ugly form, which has the power of inflicting disease. Each disease has its own *tabu* or incantation. Every man and woman knows from one to five *tabus*—I made a census of *tabus* and their possessors in Tewara—how they are distributed and held is common knowledge [Fortune, 1932a, p. 138].

The authority of Maori chieftains in New Zealand is reinforced by their control over black magic. Similar phenomena are common in Africa.

The use, or imputed use, of black magic on a large scale, as among the Dobuans, is an indication of strains or tensions in the social structure of a society. Among the Pondo of South Africa, mothers-in-law and daughters-in-law most frequently accuse each other of being witches, and the most frequent charge is that the witch has sexual relations with a familiar of the opposite sex, who is of lighter color. The social matrix of these accusations consists of the following facts: (1) The Pondo have a system of clan exogamy, which means that sexual relations are prohibited between any given person and a large number of other persons who live with him (or her) in the same village. (2) A Pondo woman lives in her husband's village, under the domination of her mother-in-law, with whom she often has strained relations. (3) The Pondo have some social contact with whites, but sexual relations between white and black are strongly prohibited. The "light-colored" familiar of the witch may be regarded as a symbol of forbidden sexual attraction.

Among the Nyakyusa of Tanganyika, on the other hand, the persons most frequently accused of witchcraft and the charges most frequently made are different; and here again analysis of the social structure illuminates the relation between "structured strains" and witchcraft. It is perhaps significant

[19] Mrs. Wilson's usage in this article (further drawn from in this text) is not standardized among anthropologists; Fortune, for example, uses "sorcerer" for a male and "witch" for a female "black" magician (1932a, p. 150).

that some of the accusers of "witches" in the famous trials that took place in Salem, Massachusetts, at the end of the seventeenth century were slightly deranged little girls: for children in seventeenth-century New England were strictly disciplined, and it is probable that the little girls were unconsciously drawing gratifying attention to themselves at the same time that they were "taking it out" on some of the adults around them (Starkey, 1949)

The religious climate of opinion has changed so much since the seventeenth century that we no longer find social tensions expressed in accusations of witchcraft. We do have similar phenomena, however, in different guises. Modern anti-Semitism in its virulent forms is equally fantastic from a rational point of view, and it is equally capable of analysis in terms of strains in the social structure (see Chap. 21). Moreover, the comparison implied in labeling as "witch-hunting" the more fanatical charges of "red" made against mild liberals is not without considerable justification (Parsons, 1955c).

RECOMMENDED READING

For an easy and good introduction to the sociology of religion, see Kingsley Davis, *Human Society,* Macmillan, 1949, Chap. 19. Another introduction, somewhat more difficult but in some respects more comprehensive, is Talcott Parsons, *Religious Perspectives of College Teaching in Sociology and Social Psychology,* Edward W. Hazen Foundation, 1951. Parsons also treats the functions of religion in *The Social System,* Free Press, 1951, pp. 163-67, 359-84. For a clear statement of the history of the sociological treatment of religion, a statement which is also enlightening about the theory itself, see Parsons, "The Theoretical Development of the Sociology of Religion," in his *Essays in Sociological Theory,* rev. ed., Free Press, 1954 Chap. 10.

One of the most influential contributions to the sociology of religion was Émile Durkheim, *The Elementary Forms of the Religious Life,* originally published in French in 1912; see the translation by J. W. Swain, Free Press, 1947. For a more recent treatment of similar material—a treatment that would not have been possible without Durkheim's work—see W. Lloyd Warner, *A Black Civilization,* Harper, 1937. This book is not light reading, but it presents, among other things, a detailed analysis of the multiple symbolism of the rituals of the Murngin tribes of Australia. The symbolism of religion can also be approached through a study of religious architecture. For an excellent general treatment, see S. K. Langer, *Feeling and Form: A Theory of Art developed from* PHILOSOPHY IN A NEW KEY, Scribner's, 1953, pp. 92-102. For good analyses of architectural symbolism, see John Summerson, *Heavenly Mansions and Other Essays on Architecture,* London: Cresset, 1949, Chaps. 1, 6, which deal with Gothic buildings; and Benjamin Rowland, *The Art and Architecture of India: Buddhist, Hindu, Jain,* Penguin, 1953. Rowland's book has excellent photographs and diagrams. S. K. Langer's *Philosophy in A New Key: A Study in the Symbolism of Reason, Rite, and Art,* Harvard University Press, 1942 (Mentor Book edition, 1948), Chaps. 6, 7, although a little difficult, are a sympathetic and subtle treatment of symbolism in myth and ritual; they contain a few points not usually found in the writings of sociologists. (Mrs. Langer is a philosopher.)

For a sociological treatment of variation in the great religions of the world, see Max Weber, *From Max Weber: Essays in Sociology,* trans. and ed. by H. H.

Gerth and C. Wright Mills, Oxford University Press, 1946, pp. 267-301, 323-59. These essays are not easy reading, but they are a good introduction to the work of one of the two greatest sociologists of religion (the other was Durkheim mentioned above).

On magic, see Bronislaw Malinowski, *Magic, Science and Religion,* Doubleday Anchor Books, 1954. The title essay is a classic of anthropology and sociology. George C. Homans, in *The Human Group,* Harcourt, Brace, 1950, pp. 321-30, discusses the apparent but not real contradictions between Malinowski's theory and that of Radcliffe-Brown (a famous English anthropologist), and in doing so illuminates both theories. For an excellent field study of the use of magic in a civilized society during an epidemic, see F. L. K. Hsu, *Religion, Science and Human Crisis: A Study of China in Transition and Its Implications for the West,* London: Routledge and Kegan Paul, 1952.

16. Religious Groups

Four basic types of religious group are widely recognized in sociology: these are the ecclesia, the sect, the denomination, and the cult.[1] For the purpose of exposition, it will be convenient to adopt this typology, although it was developed for the theoretical treatment of Western religious groups and is somewhat awkward for discussing Oriental religions. Even Western groups, as we shall see, often defy rigid classification in terms of it; they do tend to approach one or another of the types, however, in their dominant characteristics.

It will first be helpful to specify some of the variable aspects of religious groups; we shall then be able to consider all four types systematically in relation to the same questions:

1. Is membership in the group compulsory or voluntary?

2. If membership is voluntary, are the requirements for new members difficult or easy to meet (is the group "exclusive" or relatively open to new members)?

3. What is the group's attitude toward other religious groups? (Many non-Western religions, such as Confucianism and Buddhism, permit adherents to belong to other groups at the same time; but virtually all religious groups prominent in the West require converts to renounce their old beliefs. Given this common tendency, however, there are important differences between one Western religious group and another with respect to attitude toward other groups.)

4. Does the group proselytize or not? (Membership may be compulsory within a particular territory, and the group may have missionary enterprise in other lands. And even though a group is relatively "exclusive," it may work to convince outsiders to try to meet the "high" requirements for membership.)

---

[1] The typology of religious groups is derived from various sources. Max Weber and Ernst Troeltsch were among the pioneers. For a classic treatment of ecclesiae and sects, see Troeltsch, 1931, particularly the selections reprinted in Merton *et al.*, eds., 1952, pp. 79-85. For valuable discussions of all four types, see Von Wiese and Becker, 1932, Chap. 44; and Nottingham, 1954, Chap. 6.

5. Is the internal organization of the group autocratic or democratic? Are decisions about doctrinal disputes and cooperative action passed down from above, or are they subject to discussion throughout the group? (Variation in this respect is necessarily a matter of degree.)

6. Is the clergy, if any, regarded as necessary to the salvation of the lay members?

7. What is the attitude of the group toward the secular affairs of the society as a whole?

These questions make it plain that just as the architecture and rituals of a religious group are intimately connected with its beliefs, so is the form of its organization.

Ecclesia

The model for the concept of ecclesia was undoubtedly the Roman Catholic Church of the Middle Ages. Membership was compulsory, in the sense that heretics were punished by the state if necessary. The only non-Catholics permitted to live on Christian territory were the Jews, and even they were often persecuted.

Most members of the Church were born into it or at least baptized as infants. However, the Church from the beginning proselytized vigorously. Since populations in the Middle Ages were sometimes "converted" and baptized *en masse*—that is, by "fire and sword"—we must assume that the standards for admission were not high. From a Catholic point of view, the sacraments are valid whatever may be the attitude of those who receive them (or even of those who administer them); [2] therefore, even to force people into the Church was a favor to them, as well as a protection to the faithful against infection from paganism and heresy. Today, of course, the Church is not in a position to force people to belong to it, and present-day Catholics often deplore some of the actions of earlier popes and bishops, who, like laymen, are by no means regarded in dogma as always perfect. By peaceful methods, however, the Church still pursues the goal of converting all men. This is also the goal of every other ecclesia.

The Roman Catholic Church is a world-wide hierarchy with the pope at its head; its ramified affairs are conducted by several bureaucratic organs or agencies; and, as in any other bureaucracy, almost all offices are appointive and the individual can pursue a life career within the hierarchy.

---

[2] The impersonality of the sacraments is shown by an incident in Venice. "In 1606, under Pope Paul V's interdict (the sixth and last), a priest who declined to say Mass found a gibbet in front of his church—a piece of sign language he promptly heeded" (McCarthy, 1956, p. 30). For the position of the Roman Catholic Church on salvation, see Karl Adam, *The Spirit of Catholicism,* 1954, Chaps. 10, 11. The Council of Florence in 1439 emphatically declared that there is no salvation outside the Catholic Church; however, by 1713 (Pope Clement XI), the strict interpretation of this dogma had been considerably softened. The objective validity of the sacraments, of course, remains

Historians have made the sociological observation that the bureaucratic organization of the Roman Catholic Church was furthered a good deal by the rule of celibacy for the clergy. This rule made it possible for the Church to participate as a unit in the feudal system; powerful positions in the hierarchy could not be hereditary, and consequently the Roman pontiff and his administrative staff retained the power of appointment. The chief purely religious office (as opposed to executive or administrative office) is that of the priest. Doctrine is rather rigorously defined and heresy rather rigorously controlled. The priest has supernatural powers by virtue of ordination (the sacrament of Holy Orders), and these powers are essential to the faithful laity in their pursuit of salvation. Sociologically speaking, the power of the priest, residing not in his personal character but in his *office,* is of the greatest importance. It has helped in the expansion of the Church, for the layman could be assured of supernatural help without having to worry about the personal worth of the priest in the eyes of God.

The Roman Catholic Church is of course international, but there are national ecclesiae also. For example, the Protestant Episcopal communion as a whole is part of a (theoretically) universal church, but it is now made up of fourteen autonomous national organizations. Similarly, the thirteen or more national churches within the Eastern Orthodox Church have considerable administrative autonomy. The several Lutheran ecclesiae (of Germany, Denmark, Norway, Sweden) are not organized so tightly as the Roman Catholic ecclesia, nor is the position of the clergy so powerful in relation to the laity; but the clergy do administer the sacraments for the eternal salvation of members, despite the Lutheran doctrine of salvation by faith. The national ecclesiae within each of these international communions cooperate with one another by various means (e.g., conferences, joint projects).

An ecclesia (or "church," in one sense of that term) necessarily accommodates itself to secular life, since it ideally includes within it all members of a society. Essentially, there are two ways of life provided, one for the clergy and one for the laity. The clergy are expected to devote themselves to the spiritual welfare of themselves and others; the laity, although of course they are encouraged to set a good spiritual example, are primarily recipients of the grace controlled by the clergy. The vested interests of a church, however—its power, privileges, and possessions, held and legitimized by the established social system—inevitably involve the clergy, and particularly the higher officials, in the secular life of society. Moreover, these interests tend to make the clergy conservative economically and politically. The church actively fights political authority only when the secular government threatens to reduce or rival the political powers the church already has, or when the government actually menaces the very existence of the church. If compromise proves to be impossible, the church may become the chief opponent of the government. Occasionally, of course, it virtually succumbs, as in Hungary today. The interests of a church are primarily spiritual, at least in principle, but history shows that whatever the motivation may be—and church officials being human, their motives of course vary over a wide range—the pursuit of these spiritual interests almost inevitably leads to wealth and temporal power. In this sense, the church as an institution is relatively "worldly."

From a sociological point of view, one of the basic facts about all religious groups, of whatever type, is the tendency for success in meeting spiritual needs to lead to worldly power, freely given by a grateful laity, and the corresponding tendency for the spirituality of the clergy to be transformed into worldliness and greed. This "dilemma of the church" has of course been widely recognized, not only by bitter opponents but by the most sympathetic reformers within the clergy itself, anxious to restore the religious organization to its original mission. The dilemma leads in part to cyclical swings from religious zeal to "backsliding" and around again to renewed zeal; in part to ever-present compromise, especially in established religious groups of the ecclesia type; and in part, as we shall to see, to schism. If this dilemma is particularly acute for the ecclesia, the reason is that the ecclesia must be deeply engaged in the affairs of secular society if it is to fulfill its mission; a religious organization of the withdrawing type is obviously protected to some extent from worldly temptations. As we shall see, however, no type of religious organization can escape "the dilemma of the church."

In the "ideal type" of ecclesia—the concept, which certain particular religious organizations fit more or less closely—the church has control of the state and of the whole of secular life. In the Roman Catholic Church of the Middle Ages, the model for this concept, the ideal of church supremacy came close to realization. It has since had to be modified in the face of schism and secular opposition. Whether it has been abandoned as an ideal is a question. The doctrine that the Emperor (the state) is subordinate to the Pope (the Church) was not unchallenged even in the thirteenth century; the Catholic scholar Etienne Gilson has shown (1948) that the idea of the mutual independence of church and state, each supreme under God in its own sphere, was one of Dante's basic themes and rooted convictions and was expressed in *The Divine Comedy* itself. On the other hand, it is quite clear from officially sanctioned pronouncements that the Roman Catholic Church even today does not regard as ideal the separation of church and state and the toleration by the state of schism and heresy (see *The Course of Religious Instruction*).

The Lutheran churches tend much more to regard the state as a separate institution, not subject to the authority or even the morality of the church. Confucianism in China, Hinduism in India, Judaism in the ancient kingdoms of Israel and Judah, and Islam under the caliphate all had some of the features of the ecclesia, but all departed in various respects also. The emperor of China was not only a temporal ruler but a spiritual or religio-magical ruler at the same time. Once a year, in the spring, he made offerings at the altar of prayer for grain, and, at dawn on the winter solstice, at the great altar of heaven (*T'ien T'an*), the most sacred place in China. An observer has written: "The emperor, prostrate before heaven on the altar, . . . seems to be in the centre of the universe, as he acknowledges himself inferior to heaven, and to heaven alone." The emperor also expounded the Confucian classics in the Hall of the Classics (*Pi Yung Kung*), where the complete text of the nine classics is inscribed on stone steles.[3] Every Chinese is "born" a Confucianist, although he may also be or become a Buddhist or a Taoist, or both. No attempt was made to win the whole world over to Confucius, but within China itself the "state church" was protected against any rival that might have challenged the religio-political order. Above all, secret religious associations were banned, and Taoist and Buddhist monks had to be registered. Taoism and Buddhism were tolerated as popular cults and were even regarded as desirable because of their lack of concern for secular affairs. The churchlike character of Confucianism, however, is shown in the following quotation:

> The imperial edicts on religion, and even a writer such as Mencius, made persecution of heresy a duty. The means and intensity varied, as did the definition and extent of "heresy." Just as the Catholic Church fought against the denial of objective sacramental grace, and the Roman Empire against the rejection of the emperor cult, so by the same means did the Chinese government fight heresies that in its view were inimical to the state: sometimes by precept (as late as the nineteenth century, by means of an officially distributed edifying poem by a monarch), but sometimes by persecution with fire and sword [Weber, 1922, v. 1, pp. 499-500].

The imperial sacrifices to the gods were burned to maintain the order of nature and the stability of the Empire. In a different and more direct way, therefore, the Chinese "church"-state was quite as worldly as the medieval Roman Catholic Church. Confucianism also had a hierarchy, but its hierarchy was the bureaucracy of the state, and its officials were not priests but scholars steeped in the Confucian classics. The officials did not profess to control sacraments that brought grace to individuals, and their superiority over ordinary men was due, not to ordination, but to their having mastered the classics well enough to pass difficult competitive examinations.

Orthodox Hinduism (Brahmanism) also has some of the characteristics of the ecclesia, although the departures are perhaps more striking. Theoretically one is born a Hindu and can become a Hindu in no other way; but in fact the caste system, with Hinduism as its religio-ideological basis, has gradually assimilated most non-Hindu peoples and spread throughout India. "Heretics" are not persecuted as such, since there is the greatest possible tolerance for religious doctrines; but woe to the non-Hindu who wantonly mistreats a cow: he will arouse fury.

---

[3] For pictures of the sacred buildings and descriptions of the rituals, see Bushell, 1909, v. 1, Chap. 3. On the religious role of the emperor and Confucianism generally, see Weber, 1951.

Once the Brahmans had fully developed their theology of *karma* and reincarnation, Hinduization proceeded in at least three ways:

1. Because of their ritual impurity from a Hindu, and especially a Brahman, point of view, non-Hindu tribes coming in contact with Hindus were at first given a low social rank. As a means of adjusting to the system and making a better place for themselves, these tribes gradually adopted some of the social practices and taboos of the Hindus and finally called upon Brahmans for ritual services. In this way, they became essentially Hindu castes.

2. Tribal priests studied the lore of the Brahmans, began practicing as Brahmans, and finally fabricated Brahman family credentials. They sometimes did this with the aid or connivance of established Brahmans, who had a keen respect for the value of money. Non-Hindu territorial princes in the same way established themselves as Kshatriyas (members of the warrior and ruling caste, just under the Brahmans). They legitimized their positions with the help of Brahman priests, whom they repaid with lands and positions as household chaplains. In the course of time, judicious marriages with established members of the caste to which they aspired enabled the newcomers to gain more assured recognition as Hindus.

3. The caste system included considerable occupational specialization by caste. Certain occupations were caste monopolies. Consequently, the members of a non-Hindu group wishing to make a place for themselves in a Hindu community had either to perform services not already performed by some Hindu caste or to compete with Hindus. If they competed, they had to adopt the ritual prescriptions and proscriptions of the caste to which they were in effect seeking entry. Only by so doing could they hope to gain acceptance by the orthodox castes; for not only did they have to find a market for their goods or services but, being specialized, they had to depend upon the orthodox castes for the goods and services they did not produce themselves. This was another reason to conform to Hindu custom. Becoming more and more involved in the system of interdependence, they inevitably acquired a certain position in the rank order of castes, thought and acted more and more like Hindus, and more and more called upon Brahmans for religious services.

All these processes went on concurrently.

The position of the Brahmans at the top of the caste rank-order was securely enough established—widely enough recognized—to force even the few anti-Brahman castes to stay in line if they did not wish to be demoted in the hierarchy. Even partially non-Hindu groups—e.g., Sikhs and Jains—therefore had to submit to the distinctions made by the Brahmans. Even the Moslems were religiously affected by Hinduism (Weber, 1950a, pp. 35-43).

Thus, with no direct proselytizing or compulsion, and despite great freedom for the elaboration of diverse religious beliefs, Hinduism spread like an ecclesia. There was no hierarchy of priest-officials—only a hierarchy of castes and quasi-castes, which is quite different. Although various favorable conditions made it possible, the system may be regarded as an achievement of the Brahmans. By legitimating non-Hindu rajahs as Kshatriyas, they made themselves valuable, if not indispensable, to the rulers. Their income from rents and fees enabled them to preserve their distinctively religious way of life. Unlike the medieval Roman Catholic Church, they claimed no direct political authority; but for that reason they were able to keep their religious prestige intact and to wield indirect political power. Their achievement was the more remarkable in that they established a churchlike orthodoxy without an ecclesiastical organization. Moreover, although their ritual powers were helpful for "salvation," these powers were much less important to Hindu laymen than is the sacramental dispensation of the Roman Catholic clergy to Catholic laymen. The power of the Brahmans was due to their success in defining the standards of ritual purity and to the fact that they enjoyed the prestige of being supreme by those standards. They also "inherited" the prestige of their ancestors. (In religious terms, their birth as Brahmans proved that they themselves had acquired religious merit in previous incarnations.) In the Roman Catholic Church, of course, theological dogma, the celibacy of the clergy, and the principle of bureaucratic appointment all prevented high birth from having any strictly religious significance: all souls are equal at birth.

Hinduism is similar to an ecclesia in another respect—namely, in its acceptance of "the world." Hinduism in this respect goes further than Catholicism. This is clearly shown in the *dharma* of the warrior caste:

> Warfare is the *dharma* of the Kshatriyas in classical sources and medieval times. Except for the intermissions brought by the universal monarchies, war was as ever-present in India as between the ancient city-states [of Greece]. Only when a king had conquered all others was he entitled to the great horse sacrifice. . . . That a king should ever fail to consider how to subject his neighbors by force or fraud remained inconceivable to Hinduistic secular and religious literature [Weber, 1950a, p. 78].[4]

For the ordinary Hindu, following the special *dharma* of his caste was enough. For the man who wished to excel religiously, or perhaps to prepare the way for his ultimate loss of personal identity and immersion in the "All-One," there were quite "otherworldly" courses, such as extreme asceticism and mysticism. But these courses disturbed the "church"-state of the Brahmans even less than the monastic orders disturb the ordinary life of the Catholic Church or the institutional order of secular society.

Sect

In many respects, the pure form or "ideal type" of the sect is sharply distinguishable from the "ideal type" of the ecclesia, or church. Whereas

[4] For a description of the "great horse sacrifice," see Konow and Tuxen, 1949, pp. 71-73 (by Tuxen).

membership in the church is compulsory, membership in the sect is voluntary. Whereas the church is generous in its estimate of personal fitness for membership, the sect is relatively exclusive. Thus some Christian sects (e.g., the Mennonites, the Jehovah's Witnesses) reject the practice of infant baptism partly because they reject the Catholic dogma that the sacraments confer grace objectively, and partly because the aspirant to membership must first prove himself worthy. The exclusiveness of the sect is a fundamental characteristic. Its members welcome genuine converts, but they do not think it possible to convert everyone. Moreover, people who are not earnest in faith and do not desire to excel religiously are, from the point of view of the sect, potentially dangerous to the already devout members. In order to understand this attitude, which might seem inconsistent with the sect ideal of unselfishness, one must understand the implications of the rejection of sacramental grace. With some exceptions, sects believe that grace is won by the individual's personal faith and ethical rectitude; those sects which believe that grace is a pure gift and cannot be deserved believe that it is at least manifested in a visibly "good" life.[5] Consequently, the sect has no grace to bestow automatically, and if it received any and every applicant into its fellowship, the adulterated group would not be able to help its members live the pure Christian life.

For the pure sect, the ideal of fellowship is exacting. It is an ideal of brotherly love and sometimes of communism or near-communism in goods. For example, the Molokan brotherhood, a sect that broke away from the Russian Orthodox Church, takes care of its needy members as a matter of course, and the elders who administer the community funds for this purpose do so without making public the names of those who receive charity. The members symbolize their closeness to one another by eating out of the same dish. Their most valued religious experience, "feeling the spirit," which leads to ecstatic jumping, is induced during their meetings in the *sobranie,* or religious meetingplace; thus, the mystical experience is associated with the group as a whole in their moments of greatest mutual closeness (P. V. Young, 1932).[6]

As for the ideal of communism in goods, the sect may not follow it radically, but often it does to a remarkable extent, as many monasteries do. In any case, the sect characteristically extols poverty or at least frugality as far as worldly goods are concerned. The Quakers, for example, despite their wealth, still largely practice simplicity in dress and pleasures and everything else. In the United States today, another well-known sect is the Amish

[5] "No one can 'work his way' into the kingdom of God. No degree of obedience, no works of penance, no amount of money entitles anyone to any divine favor. Nevertheless, 'faith without works is dead' " (A. S. Maxwell, "What Is a Seventh-Day Adventist?" 1955, p. 136).

[6] Many of the Molokans migrated to the United States. For another sect that emphasizes mystical experience, see Boisen, "Religion and Hard Times: A Study of the Holy Rollers" (1939).

of Pennsylvania, an offshoot of the Mennonites. The Amish forbid the use of buttons, automobiles, telephones, and cameras; the bearing of arms; the taking of oaths; and participation in litigation in the courts. As in all such Christian sects, the Bible is the chief source of values and is known in detail to the elders (see Gillin, 1948, pp. 209-20; and Lundberg *et al.*, 1954, pp. 170-83).

The sect, as one might expect, is intolerant toward other religious groups. The church from which the members may have broken off is in their eyes a perversion of truth, a secularized mockery, a worldly evil. Some sects, such as the Molokans and the Amish, do not proselytize; their concern is chiefly to ward off the outside world. For new members they depend upon their own children. The Shakers, who forbade marriage and sexual relations, eventually died out because too few outsiders applied for membership. Other sects proselytize vigorously; the Jehovah's Witnesses of modern times are perhaps the best example. Every Witness who is not prevented by other grave responsibilities or by physical weakness is expected to be a missionary, to sell pamphlets and books and by other means attempt to attract new members. Their mission is to prepare as many as possible for the approaching advent of Jehovah, who, they believe, will sit in judgment after a great battle in which he will defeat Satan (Stroup, 1945; H. Barber, 1947; and Knorr, 1948).[7] The Seventh-day Adventists have a somewhat similar belief.

One of the chief characteristics of the sect is the obliteration of the distinction between the clergy and the laity. In World War II the Jehovah's Witnesses were granted exemption from military service on the ground that they are *all* ministers. Among the Molokans any respected older man may be elected religious leader; and among the Amish leadership is decided by lot, and every house is constructed with folding partitions so that it may be quickly converted into a "church." The Quakers have no ministers—or, rather, every Quaker, man or woman, is a "lay minister" (see R. P. Miller, 1955). The sect tends to believe that the Bible can be read and understood well enough by anyone who takes the trouble. If the sect stresses mysticism, especially of the noncontemplative type, it may have a tendency toward anti-intellectualism—that is, in the religious sphere, impatience with or even contempt for the refined verbal spinnings of ecclesiastical theologians. This tendency will be more likely to appear if the sect is reacting against an orthodox church.

The sect is, therefore, usually "democratic" in its organization. There are some exceptions. The Jehovah's Witnesses, for example, vie with one another in ability to quote Scripture and try to keep up with the latest publications of the leaders, but at the local level, they accept as authoritative the answers sent down from headquarters. "When heresy is reported to the

---

[7] The Jehovah's Witnesses are perhaps not a typical sect. They do not emphasize "religious experience" so much as points of doctrine, often minor ones.

central organization the heretic is brought before a Company council and is usually immediately isolated from other Witnesses. In the case of Salter [a high official], the organization sent out word by letter and later through the official magazines that Salter was dismissed and that all true believers who valued their connection with the organization should have nothing to do with him" (Stroup, 1945, pp. 125-26).[8]

As the sect repudiates the church, it tends also to repudiate some aspects of the society with which the church is so deeply involved. Christian sects, for example, are often pacifistic. Moreover, since their members are recruited for the most part from socially subordinate strata (see E. T. Clark, 1949; and Niebuhr, 1929, Chaps. 2, 3), they distrust wealth, as we have noted; consequently they do not acknowledge the moral superiority of the upper classes.[9] In fact, for the sectarian the main test of worth is membership in good standing in the sect itself. Sometimes, as in primitive Christianity, even family ties are secondary to work for the sect.

Repudiation of the social order, however, is not necessarily the same thing as "otherworldliness." Many sects are ascetically innerworldly. This springs from their repudiation of what they consider to be empty ritual. The more mystical sects are by definition somewhat otherworldly, yet the Quakers were and are both mystical and innerworldly-ascetic. The active or passive repudiation of some aspects of the prevailing social order will become more understandable if we consider some of the causes of sectarianism.

CAUSES OF SECTARIANISM

Although the causes of sectarianism are not so well understood that we can predict the rise of a new sect in advance, still we do know some of the predisposing factors.

In Christianity, one of the basic "causes" of sectarianism is the Christian tradition itself.[10] The first Christians were a sect, whether one considers Christianity to have been established by Jesus, whose immediate followers were Jews, or by St. Paul, who first began proselytizing among gentiles and who was nearly killed for preaching among the Jews of Antioch that observ-

---

8 The Jehovah's Witnesses show clearly that the concepts of ecclesia, sect, and denomination are "ideal types": many groups have mixed traits.

9 "Intellectual naïvete and practical need combine to create a marked propensity toward millenarianism, with its promise of tangible goods and of the reversal of all present social systems of rank" (Niebuhr, 1929, pp. 30-31). The church type is not in itself unattractive to the lower classes; on the contrary, its splendid rituals and promise of bliss have always had a wide appeal.

10 Although most religions have produced sects, we shall confine our discussion here to Christian sects, for otherwise we should get lost in many confusing theological questions. We should bear in mind, however, that Hinduism, Buddhism, Confucianism, Judaism, Islam—to name only some of the more important religions from a numerical point of view—have all produced sects with formal characteristics similar to those of Christian sects: e.g., exclusiveness, emphasis on faithfulness to the "original" doctrine, and emphasis on personal religious experience as opposed to the mediation of priests.

ance of the ritual law was not necessary to Christians. It would be misleading to assert that the Christian sect represents a more authentic kind of Christianity than the church. Primitive Christianity was complex. Indeed, the first Christians were otherworldly as many sects are not, for they believed that Christ would come again in their own lifetime. Thus the innerworldly Christian sects, while they undoubtedly keep alive *some* of the elements of primitive Christianity more consistently than the churches do, in other respects are departures from early Christianity. In the words of Troeltsch:

> In reality, the Church does not represent a mere deterioration of the Gospel. . . . For wherever the Gospel is conceived as primarily a free gift, as pure grace, and wherever it is offered to us in the picture which faith creates of Christ as a divine institution . . . there the institution of the Church may be regarded as a natural continuation and transformation of the Gospel. . . . On the other hand, the essence of the sect does not consist merely in a one-sided emphasis upon certain vital elements of the Church-type, but it is itself a direct continuation of the idea of the Gospel. Only within it is there a full recognition of the value of radical individualism and of the idea of love; it is the sect alone which instinctively builds up its ideal of fellowship from this point of view, and this is the very reason why it attains such a strong subjective and inward unity, instead of merely external membership in an institution [1931, as quoted in Merton *et al.*, eds., 1952, pp. 84-85].

Although it is wrong to regard the sect as merely a departure from the church type (since both are in different ways "authentic"), still it is true that many Christian sects have broken off from the Roman Catholic, Eastern Orthodox, Lutheran, or Anglican churches. All these churches involve a compromise, as we have seen, with the otherworldliness and the radical idealism of primitive Christianity. A second factor in the rise of sects, therefore, has undoubtedly been the "excess" of worldliness, at times, in the churches—"worldliness" not in the sense of innerworldly asceticism (which is devoted to God and salvation) but in the sense of overconcern for the secular world. Although a few sects, like the early Mormons, claim to have a new revelation, it is more usual for the sect to claim that it is merely purifying Christianity of acquired trappings and returning to its primitive meaning. As we have mentioned, the very success of the early Catholic Church involved increasing accumulation of wealth and participation in worldly affairs, especially politics. "Through gifts made in return for prayer and Mass after death, the Church by 800 A.D. was the greatest single landowner in Europe. At that time it was said that the Church owned one-third of France and similar huge holdings in other countries" (G. Berry, 1947, p. 83). The incongruity between the otherworldly emphasis of theology and the worldly position of the lords of the Church inevitably alienated some of its members. Throughout the Middle Ages, long before the Reformation, heretical sects tended to emphasize the simple moral life in contrast to official Christendom. Monsignor Knox, who has written brilliantly and learnedly about the tendencies toward "rigorism" and "enthusiasm" in most of the defection from Catholicism, remarks:

> It was not so much, perhaps, the private lives of the clergy that gave scandal, though complaints of this kind are frequent even in the best period of the Middle Ages. It was rather the aggressively prominent figure which Churchmen cut in the secular world, the terrific powers they wielded, not always wisely, in defence of their secular rights, the magnificent style they often adopted, that gave the impetus to revolt. . . . Because the age, compared with those which had gone before it, seemed an artificial one, the medieval heretics struck, everywhere, the note of simplicity [Knox, 1950, pp. 104-05; see Chap. 6, as a whole].[11]

Some of the laity were impatient with clerical worldliness for another reason. Even from the beginning, the concept of *official* sacramental authority was not unchallenged, and although this concept came to prevail in the Church, a very different concept had a tenacious "subterranean" life and rose to prominence again during the Reformation. This was the idea that religious authority does not inhere in an office but resides in the individual soul, depending upon the profound inner experience of the individual himself and not upon an external ritual act of ordination.[12]

In addition to purely religious objections to the church, there may be dissatisfaction with the social institutions that the church supports. That is, sectarianism may express to some extent a sense of social injustice. During the Middle Ages, sectarian heresy arose among the discontented weavers of Languedoc and the Low Countries. In the seventeenth century, the English revolutionary armies under Cromwell were composed largely of Puritans.

Sometimes, however, the sect merely expresses its discontent without any real hope of changing the social order. Eighteenth-century Methodism was a sectarian movement, and as such it had a predominantly lower-class membership; its leaders, however, were educated middle-class men and "were impressed not so much by the social evils from which the poor suffered as by the vices to which they had succumbed" (Niebuhr, 1929, p. 67). Methodism stressed good personal character and advocated philanthropy rather than revolution. Later the Salvation Army was similar in these respects (S. D. Clark, 1948). The Jehovah's Witnesses and the Seventh-Day Adventists feel that the growing "evil" of the times is one of the very signs that the end of the world is at hand; they are not seeking to change the social order but are waiting for divine intervention.

Discontent with the social order is of course often discontent, more specifically, with one's own place in it: the sect at least gives its members a chance to feel more self-esteem than the orthodox churches would give

---

[11] There have also, of course, been reform movements *within* the Church.

[12] For a characteristic attack upon the Danish Lutheran ecclesia for its alleged worldliness, see Kierkegaard, 1946, e.g., "What Christ's Judgment Is About Official Christianity," pp. 117-24.

them. The rich in goods and prestige are more likely to stress the world of the here and now (which the churches permit in fact if not in theory), whereas those who are relatively poor and have no particular prestige in the world as it is constituted either must make a virtue of necessity and derive their self-esteem from their poverty or must look to some future status as a source of self-esteem. Frequently they do both. Looking to the future, they may stress a reformation of organized religion or the rewards they are sure they deserve in the afterlife. In any case, they have the consciousness of belonging to the "real" church, which is not the church of wealth and pomp and power but the "invisible" church of those who truly have grace. The compensatory character of the sect must not be overemphasized. The values the sect stresses have deep roots in tradition. Moreover, once a sect is established, it *forms* the personality of its members (that is, its character cannot be explained entirely on the basis of the personality traits of those who join it). Motives for joining are variable (see Faris, 1937, pp. 45-60).

For obvious reasons, the more rebellious sects are often persecuted. Sectarian revolutionary sentiments are usually doomed to disappointment, as were those of the sixteenth-century Anabaptists:

> Honestly and naively the peasants of Germany had believed that Luther's appeal to the New Testament was an appeal not to Pauline theology alone but to the ethics of the Sermon on the Mount as well. All too soon they discovered that the new Protestantism . . . protested less against their masters than against their masters' enemies. . . . From Luther they learned that they could not look to Protestantism for salvation from the dual standard which bade rulers rule in accordance with . . . Old Testament precepts of reward and punishment while it required subjects to obey their political and economic masters in the spirit of a Christian and self-sacrificing meekness [Niebuhr, 1929, p. 35].

From a "realistic" point of view, the social aims of sects often seem naive. A sect seems to provide meaning to the lives of the poor and ignorant who are its members, but by putting their faith in a return to primitive Christian principles the sect members sometimes underestimate the social forces lined up against them. Persecution succeeds in showing many members the error of their ways, drives others to hide or emigrate, and makes martyrs of the rest. It seems that persecution usually succeeds in causing the sect to retreat. In some cases it becomes a secret society, but this mode of adjustment has inherent weaknesses for survival (see Hawthorn, 1956).

The steadfast members are no doubt strengthened in faith by the sacrifices they make for the sect. The older generation of Molokans in Los Angeles kept alive the stories of cruel treatment at the hands of church, government, and people in Russia under the tsar. Up to a point, persecution gives a sect a strong sense of unity. One reason second-generation Molokans in Los Angeles lose their zeal is that the surrounding people do not persecute them. One may surmise that being the object of persecution enhances the feeling of self-esteem and indignation among the sect members by making it appear that the sect is important to a merciless world outside. "Judge" Rutherford, the leader of the Jehovah's Witnesses, seems to have understood this.

> The fervor of the Witnesses was doubtless increased by the various "props" employed during the meetings. The defensive canes which Mr. Rutherford, his assistants, and the ushers have generally carried caused a certain tenseness . . . [O]nce when the convention was held in New Jersey the stage from which Mr. Rutherford spoke was lined with machine guns, purportedly for his protection from the Roman Catholic Hierarchy. The Witnesses at this meeting were brought to a frenzy. . . . Several Witnesses told me that guards were stationed by Rutherford on the roof of the meeting hall in Detroit to report any airplane which came over it . . . [Stroup, 1945, p. 29].

As we have noted, sectlike groups arise in other religions besides Christianity, and for similar reasons. Buddhism, for example, was in part a revolt against the social and spiritual pretensions of the Brahmans in India. Gautama rejected the idea that caste position had any connection with spiritual worth, and in the Buddhist order (*sangha*) people of all castes were welcome. Another sectlike characteristic of Buddhism was its rejection of concern for worldly affairs. This emphasis was at least an implied criticism of the Brahmans. Sects also appeared in Judaism and Islam.

TYPES OF CHRISTIAN SECT

B. R. Wilson (1959) has presented a classification of Christian sects which is rather rough but useful in that it reduces a large number and variety of sects to four types.

The first is the *conversionist* type, represented by the Salvation Army and the Pentecostal sects. Sects of this type tend to be fundamentalist, but they place much more emphasis upon emotional religious experience than upon doctrinal elaboration. In this respect they are unlike the other three types.

The second type is the *adventist* sect, represented by the Jehovah's Witnesses and the Christadelphians. The very early Christians believed that Christ would come again soon after the crucifixion and bring the world as it had been known to an end. This so-called eschatological doctrine was one of the main factors underlying the otherworldliness of primitive Christianity: if the world was coming to an end very soon and men were to be finally judged, there seemed to be no sense in worrying much about worldly goods and honors. As time went on, most Christians adjusted to the nonreappearance of Christ (in the expected form, at least) and either allowed the doctrine to lapse or assumed vaguely that Christ would reappear at some future time, presumably remote. The chief characteristic of the adventist sects is their emphasis on the eschatological doctrine. They see, in certain "evil" events of the present, signs of the imminent end of the world, signs foretold in

Scripture. Some short-lived adventist sects have been bold enough to name the very day of the end of the world.

The third type of sect, the *introversionist,* is represented by the Quakers and the Society of the Truly Inspired (the Amana Community). Sects of this type tend to be mystical, but unlike the conversionist sects they do not seek extreme emotional states. These sects withdraw from the world to some extent, but not to live an otherworldly life. The Quakers, for example, are innerworldly mystics; they not only permit but encourage "concern" (à favorite Quaker word) for the betterment of human society in specific ways. There is an emphasis on Biblical doctrine, but it is not literalist and inflexible.

Wilson's fourth type of sect, the *gnostic,* is represented by the Christian Scientists, New Thought, Koreshanity, and the Order of the Cross.[13] As the examples indicate, the chief characteristic of the gnostic sects is their emphasis upon holding the correct intellectual views, some of which usually seem rather bizarre to the uninitiated.

Denomination

The concepts of ecclesia and sect, as suggested by Max Weber and worked out by Ernst Troeltsch, have been given more attention by sociologists than the concepts of denomination and cult, which may have been introduced to take account of certain historically prominent religious groups that could not easily be forced into the original two types. As we shall see, the line between ecclesia and denomination is not always clear-cut; nor is the line between sect and cult. Partly for this reason, we shall be relatively brief in our treatment of denominations and cults. Table 10 indicates some points not elaborated in the text.

A denomination is what usually results when a sect becomes "respectable" in the eyes of middle-class society and relaxes its moral rigor and religious fervor. Most of its members are somewhat secularized. Some take their religion very seriously, of course, but for many, church-going is merely one of the duties an upstanding member of the community, conscious of his status and dignity, imposes upon himself and upon his wife and children. But religion is now only one of his interests, almost one of his recreations; it no longer binds him to a fellowship of love and a life of religious service. The clergymen are ministers and counselors, sometimes trained in psychology as well as in theology, but they are not thought to have any

[13] Some of these groups would be called cults by other writers, but Wilson has abandoned the concept "cult." We shall keep this concept, although we recognize that the line between cult and sect is not always easy to draw. In general, a cult is easier to get into, although the initiate may have to study hard in order to penetrate the inner meaning of the esoteric doctrine; and cults are not so closely organized, except at the center.

TABLE 10

Ideal types of religious group *

Variables	*Ecclesia*	*Sect*	*Denomination*	*Cult*
1. Compulsoriness of membership	Compulsory	Voluntary	Voluntary	Voluntary
2. Exclusiveness of membership	Relatively open	Exclusive	Relatively open	Open
3. Attitude toward other religious groups	Intolerant	Intolerant	Tolerant	Tolerant
4. Proselytizing	Proselytizes actively	Sometimes proselytizes, sometimes not	Proselytizes, sometimes actively, sometimes not	Sometimes proselytizes
5. Internal organization	Autocratic; hierarchical	Usually democratic, rarely autocratic; little hierarchy	Democratic; sometimes hierarchical, but less so than ecclesia	Variable organization; a dominant leader common
6. Position of clergy	Distinction between clergy and laity important; clergy necessary to salvation	Distinction between clergy and laity slight, sometimes nonexistent	Intermediate between ecclesia and sect, but clergy not necessary to salvation	Distinction slight; clergy not always necessary to salvation; variable
7. Attitude toward secular affairs	Accommodation, except when ecclesia is attacked	Intolerance of, indifference to, or withdrawal from secular affairs	Accommodation; relatively "worldly"	Highly variable

* These "ideal types" are theoretical constructs and do not necessarily describe perfectly any particular concrete groups. This table should be interpreted only with the aid of the text.

special supernatural powers. The present-day Presbyterian, Congregationalist, Methodist, and Unitarian churches, as well as most Baptist groups, are regarded as denominations.

A study of religious groups in Caston County, North Carolina, shows the typical process by which a sect becomes a denomination. In that rural setting, most members of the sects (Free-Will Baptist Holiness, Pentecostal Holiness, Church of God, independent tabernacles) are poor millhands. When a congregation gets started, often on a precarious financial basis, it exhibits the typical characteristics of a sect: religious enthusiasm, spontaneous participation, blurring of the line between minister and laymen. Then two things happen: (1) the success of the group attracts new members, some of whom are more prosperous than the original members; and (2) a few of the old members become more prosperous. These changes bring pressures toward improving the social prestige of the congregation in the community. The more well-to-do members gain control by putting up money for a new church or for better equipment. The order of religious worship is regularized, becomes less spontaneous. The early strict religious and moral requirements for admission are relaxed: all "respectable" people are welcome. During this process, many of the original members of the sect drop out and either form a new sect or seek some more congenial group already in existence. The sect has become a denomination. The middle- and upper-class people now in control give more attention to the formal training of their children, and for this they want formally trained and paid teachers in the Sunday school, just as they now want a formally trained minister for themselves (Pope, 1942).[14]

The same process was revealed in a study of a town in the San Joaquin Valley, in California, in 1944. Unskilled farm laborers, who were predominantly Mexicans and Negroes, belonged to the Catholic Church or, more often, to Protestant sects (Pentecostal, Church of God). The Nazarene Church was hardly a sect any more; in ten years it had "grown from meetings in private homes . . . to a plant which, with the parsonage, is valued at $20,000," and from enthusiastic farmer-preachers to a minister "given to the sane, intelligent presentation of the Gospel Truths." Many of the unskilled workers had dropped out. The Pentecostal group, which was the most sectlike, had split off from the Assembly of God because the latter now had "educated ministers and college students who were stiff shirts . . ." (Goldschmidt, 1944).[15]

In his paper on sects, Wilson (1959) points out that the conversionist type of sect is more likely to undergo the transformation to a denomination than are the other types, whose greater emphasis on intellectual doctrines, combined in many cases with more rigorous control from the center of organization, protects their original character sometimes for generations.

Both church and sect must face the "dilemma of the church," but not so acutely as the denomination. The sect, at least while it remains a sect, solves the dilemma by not seeking to appeal to more than a few. The church

---

[14] Pope uses the term "church" where we should use "denomination." A sect may of course develop into a church, as the history of Christianity shows. However, the church contains all social classes, whereas the denomination tends to be middle and upper class.

[15] The last two quotations are from statements by ministers.

solves it by emphasizing its objective sacramental grace and compromising with the world in order to save it. But the denomination, or its members, lives in the everyday world and has the conscience of a sect underneath. In Methodism, for example, there is a constant tension between "backsliding" and revivalism.

The dilemma is acute because the denominations must face the question of where they should stand on specific social issues. The question, for example, is not whether it is right for a parishioner to cheat his employees at his company store: presumably no church, sect, denomination, or cult would declare itself in favor of cheating. But suppose that it is the custom for steel workers to work twelve hours a day, seven days a week, and suppose that you are a minister and some of the pillars of your church are employers of these steelworkers. The duty of the minister, of course, is to "discover, define, and defend the spiritual and ethical development of the people of [the] community," including the steelworkers (Holt, 1936).[16]

A study of the official action of religious bodies in the United States concerning the labor movement (reported by Yinger, 1946, Chaps. 5, 6) shows that while the movement was weak, the churches and denominations did little or nothing to strengthen it. There were, of course, individual clergymen who were sympathetic toward labor, but the weight of organized religion, although not opposed to labor, was by silence lined up on the side of capital and management; in other words, organized religion tended to support certain powerful segments of the existing social order. When the labor movement, however, had already shown that it was "here to stay" as a legitimate organized power in our society, then the churches and denominations, somewhat cautiously and ambiguously, began to recognize it and support it. Church commissions passed resolutions in favor of mild reforms.

The clergymen were in advance of their parishioners on the average. They became aware of the changed power situation sooner than conservative laymen did, and they helped to get the reforms more widely and quickly accepted. It would be a mistake to think of organized religion as uniformly either a diehard conservative force or the vanguard of social change. It is the task of denominational statesmanship to exert intelligent pressure in the direction of translating religious values into actual social practice. In the nature of the case, this pressure has to be rather cautious. From the point of view of liberal zealots, it may seem to be almost invisible, but it often seems dangerous and radical to the more conservative parishioners.

Here we see the "dilemma of the church" from the point of view of the conscientious denominational minister. If he courageously points out the implications of Christian doctrine for *specific* injustices in the social order, he runs the risk of losing his power to influence events at all. "Radical" clergymen may lose their pulpits; their more conservative parishioners

---

[16] Holt, who is a pastor, was himself faced with such a labor situation.

either protest against them or stay away from church. On the other hand, if clergymen turn their eyes away from social "injustice," or even resist secular attempts to correct it, then they are giving up part of their religious influence; in effect, they are allowing secular interests alone to determine the course of events, and their position as religious "leaders" has become somewhat hollow. (At the same time, the ecclesia in particular must worry lest it lose the respect and support of the victims of social injustice, for if the victims cease to go to church, then the ecclesia loses its religious function of giving sacramental grace.)

Cult

So heterogeneous are the groups that we shall call cults that this type might seem to be a catch-all for religious groups that do not fit any one of the other types. Yet groups such as the Spiritualists, Bahai, I Am, the Theosophical Society, the Buchmanites, the Moorish Science Temple of America, the Father Divine Peace Mission Movement, and the Christian Science movement (especially in its earlier days) do have certain formal characteristics in common. The most obvious, perhaps, is their extreme openness to all who wish to join or participate to any extent. There are a few exceptions, due to some peculiarity of doctrine. For example, the Church of God, which believes that God is black, that Jesus was a black man, that the Negroes are the Jews of the Bible, and that "the world will not get right until the Black Jews go into high places," restricts its membership to Negroes; but any Negro who wishes to join may do so (Fauset, 1944, Chap. 4). The cult, unlike the "ideal type" of church, is a voluntary organization. For a short time, the Roman Empire required people to sacrifice to the emperor, but this requirement was not due to strictness; it was due to the very superficiality of the emperor cult. Apart from the Jews, who had never seemed to be a threat to the Empire, the Romans had never encountered a group so exclusive, and to their mind so disloyal, as to be unwilling to give this purely formal evidence of loyalty to the emperor. The requirement was therefore a political device aimed at the Christians alone; if they had not seemed disloyal, they would have been as free as other sects were to worship as they pleased.

No group can get along without some regulation of its members, and a cult is no exception. At cult meetings, for example, one must not disrupt the proceedings. But a cult shows its looseness of organization by permitting its members to come and go, and to participate in other religious groups at the same time if they wish. The coherence of the group depends upon the emotional hold of a leader over the members, or upon the fascination of the beliefs or rituals. Father Divine, for example, is God, and the followers, especially the women, feel thrills go through them if they are lucky enough to touch him. When he is present at one of the "heavens" of the cult, every dish of potatoes or chicken or ice cream passes through his hands at least once; every member thus communes with God. Anyone who wishes to submit himself entirely to the will of Father Divine may do so (then he must give everything he has to the Father and obey any command the Father might give him); but members of the cult are not required to go so far. When Fauset was studying the organization as an outsider, he found himself granted all the privileges of a member, except that he had to pay a small amount for his board and lodging. In general, cults are not strict except in financial matters.

There is a tendency for cults to emphasize one doctrine above all others, or to focus upon a god or goddess with certain definite characteristics. For example, Father Divine stresses the doctrine that there is no such thing as race; the Christian Scientists stress the "unreality" of evil, especially of physical suffering, and emphasize spiritual healing; Buchmanism stresses the power of "moral rearmament"; Bahai stresses the essential unity of all religions and the need to recognize this unity.

Cults seem to flourish in metropolitan centers—that is, in places where vast populations live close together physically, yet have heterogeneous cultures and many diverse problems of adjustment. It is not so much that cults flourish in a time of transition, for probably every time is a time of transition; but they do flourish in those places where change is most rapid and obvious and impinges upon many people. Rome and Alexandria in the ancient world, London, New York, Los Angeles in the modern, have the following characteristics in common, all favorable to the growth of cults:

1. People from various parts of the world have a chance to influence one another. A relatively high proportion of the population is likely to hear and read ideas unknown to their fathers. Many of the scientific, pseudoscientific, and religious ideas are old, but new people, with other perspectives, are learning them and having to fit them in with what they already know.

2. Many people are removed from the social and cultural contexts in which the traditional religions were formed, and in the new context the traditional religions might seem less relevant to life problems. At the same time, many people are freed from the social controls that might have kept them bound to older religious groups. There is therefore a gap to be filled, a problem of adjustment to be solved.

3. The very presence of different traditional religious orientations tends to weaken faith in any one of them; each religious orientation is implicitly a criticism or questioning of the others. In this sense, secularization takes place. At the same time, many people are no more critical than they were before; the fact that their old beliefs are less meaningful makes them not less but more susceptible to new ones. Moreover, there are plenty of materials at hand to combine in new ways. A Negro in Newark, New Jersey, for example, not long since arrived from the rural South, heard about Mohammedanism and its racial tolerance. "He became obsessed with the idea that salvation for the Negro people lay in the discovery by them of their na-

tional origin. . . . They must henceforth call themselves Asiatics [*sic*], to use the generic term, or, more specifically, Moors or Moorish Americans" (Fauset, 1944, p. 41). From this simple insight grew the Moorish Science Temple of America, with branches in Pittsburgh, Detroit, Philadelphia, Chicago, and many Southern cities.

4. Many people in a metropolis were not born there; they constitute a floating, rootless population, eager for personal attachments. Their personal problems are pressing, and at the same time they are more aware of world problems without being less bewildered by them. Cults tend to ignore or deny world problems, or to provide rather simple solutions. During World War II. members of the "I Am" cult, whose center is in Los Angeles, could feel that the United States was quite safe, since they believed it to be protected by invisible bands of friendly angels. The prophet of the cult, "St. Jerome," had made known many truths of this kind.

Many prophets arise to meet or exploit the diverse special needs of the metropolitan population. People shop around and drift from one cult to another before they find just what suits them. Since change is going on all the time in the social composition of the city and in the personal problems people face, one may suppose that many cults have short lives. Some develop into sects and denominations.

RECOMMENDED READING

The classical discussion of ecclesia and sect, as far as Christianity is concerned, is Ernst Troeltsch, *The Social Teachings of the Christian Churches,* 2 vols., trans. by Olive Wyon, Macmillan, 1931. This work will be too detailed for most readers. An excellent selection from it, which summarizes the basic conceptual distinction between church (ecclesia) and sect, is reprinted in R. K. Merton, A. P. Gray, Barbara Hockey, and H. C. Selvin, eds., *Reader in Bureaucracy*, Free Press, 1952, pp. 79-85. The four types of religious group distinguished in this chapter are discussed in Leopold von Wiese and Howard Becker, *Systematic Sociology on the Basis of the* Beziehungslehre *and* Gebildelehre *of Leopold von Wiese*, adapted and simplified by Howard Becker, Wiley, 1932, Chap. 44. An excellent short treatment, more recent, of the same four types is E. K. Nottingham, *Religion and Society*, Doubleday, 1954, Chap. 6.

For a famous study of an Eastern religion (Confucianism) that is in some respects similar to an ecclesia and in others rather different, as well as a study of what may be regarded as its chief sect (Taoism), see Max Weber, *The Religion of China: Confucianism and Taoism*, trans. and ed. by H. W. Gerth, Free Press, 1951.

In recent years there has probably been more sociological study of sects than of any other type of religious group. For an interesting attempt to classify Christian sects, see B. R. Wilson, "An Analysis of Sect Development," *Amer. sociol. Rev.,* Feb. 1959, v. 24, no 1, pp. 3-15. For a treatment of heretical movements in Christianity as sects, from the earliest times up to the twentieth century, see R. A. Knox, *Enthusiasm*, Oxford, 1950; although it is written from a Roman Catholic point of view, this book is quite objective, and it is certainly one of the best-written works in sociology. For a particularly fine study of a sect of the "ideal community" type see P. V. Young, *The Pilgrims of Russian-Town: The*

Community of Spiritual Christian Jumpers in America: The Struggle of a Primitive Religious Society to Maintain Itself in an Urban Environment, University of Chicago Press, 1932. For a sociologically enlightening study of the problems of a sect driven by persecution into secrecy, see H. B. Hawthorn, "A Test of Simmel on the Secret Society: The Doukhobors of British Columbia," *Amer. J. Sociol.*, July 1956, v. 62, pp. 1-7.

For a secondary study of historical episodes showing the social conservatism of churches and denominations—a study of the "dilemma of the church" —see J. M. Yinger, *Religion in the Struggle for Power: A Study in the Sociology of Religion*, Duke University Press, 1946. One of the best studies of the influence of political and economic interests on religious groups is H. Richard Niebuhr, *The Social Sources of Denominationalism*, Holt, 1929. Niebuhr uses the word "denominationalism" to mean division into separate religious groups, and he deals with Christianity only.

17. Religion and Other Social Subsystems

It should be obvious by now that religion is interwoven with all other aspects of human life. We must now consider in more detail the interrelations of religion with kinship systems, economic and political institutions, and science. After this brief survey, we shall be in a position to summarize the social functions of religion

Kinship and Religion

Sex has always been an important concern of religion. On the one hand, sexual passion is treated as one of the most dangerous allurements of "the world"; on the other hand, because sexual passion is so intense, it has often been connected with religious ecstasy. A sect derived from the Russian Orthodox Church is known as the Castrators, because at one time its members sought to eliminate the sexual aspect of their religious ecstasy by means of castration. Sometimes, however, sexual rites have served as an accepted religious symbol of the creative power and divine possession of the worshipers.

On the whole, religion has sought to regulate sexual expression rather than to eliminate it or exalt it. In Hinduism, for example, it is a religious duty to provide husbands for one's daughters. So difficult is this task sometimes, but so important, that it has led to some of the practices that outsiders have regarded as evil. Parents have sought to ensure the marriage of their daughters by making arrangements even before the children are born; by marrying off their daughters, often at great expense, before the girls are nubile; by paying "absentee husbands" to marry their daughters; and by forming "marriage cartels" (systems of direct marital exchange, which, as we noted in Chaps. 6 and 7, are prominent in India). In despair, many Hindus have avoided the problem by female infanticide: "Despite the severe English laws of 1829, as late as 1869, in 22 villages of Rajputana there were 23 girls and 284 boys." The explanation of these facts is that the men of the upper castes may marry down somewhat, whereas the women may not. Consequently, it is often hard to find husbands for upper-caste girls, even though upper-caste men are sometimes polygynous. Child marriage and female infanticide (before the British occupation) were upper-caste practices. Such desperate measures, however, were taken only because being married and having descendants were religious necessities. Religion in India, therefore, is a powerful support of the kinship system (Weber, 1950a, pp. 57-58).

Chinese ancestor worship is a ritual system that has had a unifying function for extended families and clans.

> The cohesion of the [clan] undoubtedly rested wholly upon the ancestor cult. . . . [I]n historical times the most fundamental belief of the Chinese people has been to ascribe power to ancestral spirits, not exclusively but predominantly to the spirits of one's own ancestors. . . . Furthermore, it was believed absolutely necessary to satisfy the spirits and to win their favor by sacrifices [Weber, 1951, p. 87].

The ancestor cult no doubt helped to maintain strong ties between village clan members and members who had emigrated to the Chinese cities. The latter often continued to depend on the clan. For example, the clan association might grant them funds to finance their study or to support them while learning a craft. The mutual concern and trust involved in such undertakings was expressed and reinforced by the periodic worship in the ancestral temple and by the underlying attitudes solemnly binding the kinship cult together.

Judaism, Christianity, and Islam, in all of which man's duty is to live according to ethical standards revealed by a personal God, have all attempted to regulate kinship relations, especially marriage and the family. In Islam, the personal example of the prophet Mohammed helped to legitimize polygyny. Christianity at first hardly countenanced marriage at all, but eventually the Church made matrimony one of the sacraments. From the point of view of the early Christians, who were expecting the end of the world within their lifetime, marriage and all family ties were quite secondary to their religious interests. In a well-known statement, St. Paul gave but grudging approval of marriage. In the course of time, the new religious group had to adjust itself to the prospect of the indefinite continuation of society, and the emphasis therefore shifted to regulation of marriage rather than relative indifference to it.[1] Nevertheless, the ideal of celibacy was institutionalized in the monasteries and among most of the "secular" (nonmonastic) clergy. Moreover, the ideal keeps being revived in Christian sects

[1] This statement does not mean that the attitude toward marriage became more and more accepting. The height of condemnation came perhaps in the third and fourth centuries A.D. Examples of the asceticism of these centuries are Tertullian's *Exhortation to Chastity* and some of the letters of St. Jerome. St. Jerome wrote, "To show that virginity is natural while wedlock only follows guilt, what is born of wedlock is virgin flesh . . ." (quoted in Goodsell, 1935, p. 163).

such as the Castrators and the Shakers. The Catholic attitude toward sex is still somewhat ambivalent. In 1930, for example, Pope Pius XI declared "artificial" means of birth control to be wrong absolutely. Christian marriage has of course been monogamous, except for a brief period in Mormon history, when a special revelation sanctioned polygyny.

Since religion tends to regulate marriage, the adoption of a new religion sometimes requires modification of existing marriage forms. Christian missionaries have introduced the monogamous ideal among polygynous peoples. Another example: The preferred marital alliance for Moslems is between ego and father's sister's daughter (Fa Si Da). When the Kababish of Africa and the Kurd of Asia adopted Islam, they adopted the preferred form of marriage with it. In doing so, they had to modify another part of their kinship systems. They both had patrilineal sibs, but they had to discard them, because sibs are exogamous, and ego and Fa Si Da, being members of the same patrilineal sib, would not have been able to marry each other (Murdock, 1949, p. 201).

There is some evidence that religious commitment may help to keep down the rate of divorce.

> Studies covering approximately 25,000 marriages showed that there were three times as many marital failures among those with no religious affiliation as among those within given religions. In marriages between persons of different religions, religion is frequently a disruptive factor, yet the failure rate of marriages of mixed religions is generally lower than that among marriages where there is no religion [Landis and Landis, 1953].

Protestants in the United States have a higher divorce rate than Catholics, but the Catholic divorce rate is growing, and Catholics have a much higher rate of "desertion" than Protestants.[2] Jews have lower divorce and desertion rates than either Catholics or Protestants (Monahan and Kephart, 1954).

As the discrepancy between divorce rates and desertion rates shows, the divorce rate is not a safe index of the contribution of religion to marital *happiness*. Other studies, however, have found that a higher percentage of happily married couples than of unhappily married couples are religious. Indices of being "religious" include having a church wedding, being a church member, having attended Sunday school, and attending church during married life. Indices of "marital happiness" are too complex to go into here, but several of them are fairly objective (see Terman *et al.*, 1938; Burgess and Cottrell, 1939; and H. J. Locke, 1951).[3]

---

[2] It is safe to say that the relatively low Catholic divorce rate is due primarily to religious scruples. The relatively high Catholic desertion rate may be due to factors associated with social class.

[3] As Locke and others have suggested, church attendance may be an indication of conventionality and sociability, both of which are associated with marital happiness. In order to assess the influence of religion as a distinct factor, we should have to have more complex studies.

The Economy and Religion

The interaction between religion and the forms and goals of economic life has been most often studied in attempts to account for the rise of "modern" capitalism in the Western world. "Modern" capitalism, which gradually developed during the seventeenth century, differed from "traditional" capitalism in that the new capitalists were more rational in their methods, more impatient of traditional restraints on technological innovation and on the scope of markets, and motivated in part by a new ethical spirit, which gave their enterprise, to their mind, the dignity of being service to God and a fulfillment of His wishes for man. This new ethical spirit was most conspicuously shown by Protestants, especially by Calvinists (Weber, 1930). As opposed to the Catholics, who were either otherworldly (as doctrine required) or merely "worldly" (hence subject to guilt-feelings for their deviation from the teachings of the Church), the Calvinists were innerworldly-ascetic.

As we noted in Chapter 15, Calvin put forward the doctrine of predestination in its most extreme form. An immediate implication of this doctrine is that neither the sacraments nor "good works" can possibly help men to achieve salvation. Yet Calvinists remained intensely interested in the question of whether or not they were among the "elect." Logically, according to the doctrine of predestination, they could do nothing to ensure their own salvation, but ministers offered some relief from anxiety by arguing more and more coherently that if God intended a man to be saved in the world to come, He would see to it that His chosen one would be virtuous in this world. Sobriety, industriousness, and innerworldly asceticism could be taken as *signs* of grace. Calvinists easily passed from this idea to the attempt to prove to themselves that they were saved. The result in their conduct was as if they had believed that innerworldly asceticism is a *means* to salvation:

> Christian asceticism, at first fleeing from the world into solitude, had already ruled the world which it renounced from the monastery and through the Church. But it had, on the whole, left the naturally spontaneous character of daily life in the world untouched. Now it strode into the market-place of life, slammed the door of the monastery behind it, and undertook to penetrate just that daily routine of life with its methodicalness, to fashion it into a rational life in the world, but neither of nor for this world [Weber, 1930, p. 154].[4]

The economic influence of Calvinism would not have been possible, of course, if circumstances had not been favorable for the emergence of mod-

---

[4] Luther had also sanctioned secular callings, but Lutheranism, stressing salvation by faith, was more interested in the inner spiritual life and also did not pose so difficult a problem for those desiring salvation.

ern capitalism.[5] Favorable circumstances were the resultant of many inventions, discoveries, and political events extending back for four hundred or more years: the attack on Constantinople by Venice, the Crusades, the discoveries in the New World, the influx of precious metals resulting from the discoveries, the gradual development of new methods of business calculation and exchange—double-entry bookkeeping, the bill of exchange, bills of lading, banking and the use of checks—the invention and widespread use of printing, the development of science and law, and the secularizing effects of all the new contacts and ideas. The trade of Catholics outside the area in which Catholic ideals held sway no doubt helped to weaken the influence on those ideals. The feudal landlord class had helped to build up an urban bourgeoisie by providing a market for goods and services; at the same time, by weakening itself in wars at home and abroad, it had prepared the way for the rise of the bourgeoisie to political power. Finally, the enclosure movement had released many peasants for urban work and enlarged the potential market for urban products.

The hold of Catholicism over secular life was much weakened by the rise of nationalism, which in turn strengthened Protestantism. Writers who regard the decline of Catholic influence as favorable to the rise of capitalism do not necessarily think that the rise of Protestantism was more favorable; some of them argue, as did Fanfani (1935), that the rise of Protestantism eventually led to religious tolerance and hence to the decline of *all* religious influence on secular activity. Implicit in this view is the idea that the motives necessary to modern capitalism were present under Catholicism but were held in restraint. As we have seen, however, this idea is only partly true. Protestantism provided *new* motives for business activity; and Protestants, provided with these new motives, did in fact take more advantage of objective business opportunities than did Catholics.[6]

To Weber's thesis that "the Protestant ethic" was partly responsible for the rise of modern capitalism, some scholars (e.g., Fanfani, 1935) have

---

5 That the religious development had independent and perhaps decisive influence is made more probable by a nineteenth-century case, in which a religious movement similar to Calvinism arose and in a short time transformed the economy of a nation. See Jonassen, "The Protestant Ethic and the Spirit of Capitalism in Norway," 1947. This case, which was not considered by Weber, seems to strengthen his thesis and weaken the objections of his critics.

6 In this respect, Fanfani's thesis suffers from the same defect as does Marx's thesis: "Marx acknowledged the lack of adaptability of the older interests but did not explain it—except by telling us that theirs was an unprogressive role (which constitutes no explanation but a description after the fact)" (Birnbaum, 1953, p. 136). The question of the lack of adaptability of the older mercantile and financial interests is no doubt a complex one. It seems reasonable to suppose that the methods by which success has been achieved in the past are psychologically difficult to give up, even when conditions have changed. For an illustration of this idea, see Redlich, "The Business Leader as a 'Daimonic' Figure," 1953. In any case, Weber has successfully explained the greater success of Protestants in religious terms. Marx was right (and not in conflict with Weber) to attribute considerable importance to the class struggles that had helped to produce new objective opportunities for the bourgeoisie.

objected that Calvin imposed ethical restraints upon business activity just as great as those imposed by the Catholic Church, and that Calvin's ethics, if not his theology, were in fact largely derived from Catholicism. This objection is not cogent for at least three reasons.

1. We must distinguish between religious ethics and religious interests. Fanfani to the contrary, Calvin's ethical ideas—for example, concerning interest-taking ("usury")—*were* somewhat more favorable than Catholicism to the growth of capitalism; [7] nevertheless, the influence of Calvinism depended much more on the fact that its *ministers* came to define innerworldly asceticism as (virtually) a means to salvation and, perhaps equally important, on the fact that Calvin himself had removed other means (including the sacraments, still available to the Catholics).

2. Calvin was addressing a largely urban audience and took it for granted that they were engaged in urban occupations. The relative conservatism of the Catholic Church at the time arose, in part, from its "universal" character. Embracing as it did rural as well as urban people, all social classes, and men in various stages of economic development, the Church could not come out unequivocally in support of interest-taking. Seeking to maintain a standard of decency in human relations, it opposed usury during the Middle Ages, when interest-taking was often a means of exploiting the poverty and bad fortunes of peasants. When in urban conditions, however, credit was extended for business ventures, and the debtor stood to make a profit from his borrowed money, then it seemed unreasonable to condemn "usury," and the Church was not harsh in such cases. But at best the Church could only wink at certain practices while continuing to maintain its official position against usury. The position of Jews in medieval Europe was due in part to the fact that they, unlike Catholics, had no religious objections to lending money at interest and to devoting themselves in general to worldly pursuits. (On the other hand, Judaism was not ascetic and did not make business a means of salvation.) The relative conservatism of the Catholic Church in this case is an example of the inhibiting influence of religious beliefs under certain circumstances, but the point should not be lost that religious beliefs did indeed have some influence (see Yinger, 1946, pp. 91-92, 104-07).

3. It would be a mistake to suppose that Calvin intended to change the spirit or intensity of economic activity. He did not invent or espouse the idea of predestination in order to justify business profits. The early Calvinists were financially successful precisely because they were not "worldly"; religiously opposed to sloth and pleasure-seeking, they worked hard and lived soberly and saved their money. Calvin, after all, was a religious leader. He specifically condemned the pursuit of wealth for its own sake and gave

---

[7] On Calvin's ethical innovations, see Tawney, 1922; as reprinted by Pelican Books, 1947, pp. 91-115.

to the poor the usual consolations he found in the Christian religion. If Calvinism played a part in creating "modern" capitalism, the creation was quite unintended and no doubt would have been regarded as a monster.[8] Protestant clergymen continued to try to moderate the more rapacious aspects of business activity. But the habits of unremitting hard work, thrift, and ascetic renunciation of worldly pleasure made some of the Calvinists rich, of course, and the usual process of development, from sectarian virtues to denominationalism, took place. When Calvinists became rich, they found it hard to believe that riches are bad, and some of them, coming to regard Calvinism as too repressive, left it for Arminianism. At the same time, some Calvinist ministers were forced to become more tolerant of their worldly parishioners.

Another objection to Weber's thesis (e.g., by T. C. Hall, 1930) is that Calvinists did not always become rich. Calvinism today is strongest in the Highlands of Scotland and the mountains of the southern United States—that is, among poor people. But one must remember that no religious beliefs are sufficient by themselves to make people rich, unless circumstances are favorable. In fact, it is only in the unprofitable highlands that we could expect to find Calvinism still surviving in its original austerity. Amid hardship, the highlanders can still enjoy the consolations of moral and religious superiority.

The final objection to Weber's thesis would be the most crushing if it were true. This is the argument, advanced by Fanfani, among others, that capitalism was flourishing before Calvin. There is little difference of opinion about the facts; the difference comes in the definition of terms. "Capitalism" in some sense has existed from very early times, but "modern" capitalism, which received its characteristic stamp from the Calvinists, differed from the forms of capitalism that preceded it. "Adventurers' capitalism," a pre-Calvinist form, was often unscrupulous and highly risky; it was exemplified in piracy and in the exploitation of opportunities guaranteed by the state. Another pre-Calvinist form, "traditional" capitalism, lacked the drive of "modern" capitalism. Under Catholicism, the finance and trade of earlier times, although often considerable in extent, were at best tolerated; Calvinism made innerworldly asceticism a moral and religious duty.

Not only did the early Protestants soon outstrip the Catholics, but to a considerable extent the Catholics have not yet caught up. The leading capitalistic countries are predominantly Protestant. More striking is the relative success of Protestants even within Catholic countries. There is general agreement among historians that the persecution of French Protestants under Louis XIV, which led to their emigration by the thousands,

---

[8] The consequences have of course not necessarily all unfolded. The emphasis on rational economic planning has already been extended in some places toward socialism.

drained France of her best productive ability.[9] The unusual success of the French Protestants is particularly remarkable because, of all Catholic countries, France is perhaps the least strict. The historical reasons for this are too complex to go into here, but we may note that during the eighteenth century (when the Huguenots were being persecuted), a process of secularization took place in French Catholicism. The activities of the newly powerful bourgeoisie came to be religiously legitimized to some extent. To this gradual reformulation both the Jesuits and their opponents, the Jansenists, contributed; perhaps even more important, the very fact of opposition between these groups weakened the older religiosity of Bossuet's time (Groethuysen, 1927, v. 1). However, even the "new" Catholicism merely released the bourgeois for business activity in behalf of himself and his family; it did not go so far as to make innerworldly asceticism a test of grace itself. Moreover, unlike the Protestant, the French Catholic could still rely on the sacraments of the Church for salvation.

Writing as late as 1936, a French Marxist, despite his concern to show that Catholics were dominating the French economy, estimated that of the leading captains of industry and finance 20 per cent were Protestants and 10 per cent were Jews; further, he claimed, Protestants and Jews had once been even more prominent (Hamon and "X.Y.Z.," 1936, v. 1, pp. 16-17). These proportions are very high in relation to the small number of Protestants and Jews; there were about 900,000 "nominal" Protestants and about 160,000 Jews in a total population of over forty million.

The transformation of secular life to which Calvinism contributed has gone so far that, in the United States at least, religion itself has to a considerable extent been secularized. One of the most popular Protestant clergymen, Dr. Norman Vincent Peale, has formulated "Ten Rules for Getting Self-Confidence," the first of which reads: "Hold in your mind a picture of yourself succeeding. Your mind will seek to actualize this image" (quoted by A. W. Green, 1956, p. 444). There is some evidence that in the United States today Catholics as well as Protestants have adopted the "Protestant ethic." A careful study of a large sample of Protestants and Catholics showed no significant statistical difference between them either in actual social mobility (rise or fall in the class structure) or in aspirations (Mack, Murphy, and Yellin, 1956). The study is not conclusive, however, because the sample was confined to three occupational categories, salesmen, engineers, and bankers. As the investigators note, few of those engaged in these three occupations are likely to be without the typical middle-class orientation to "success." Moreover, since Protestants have on the average higher occupational positions than Catholics in the United States

---

[9] W. H. Lewis writes, "It is not clear why it should have been so but the fact remains that, broadly speaking, the Huguenot was more intelligent, harder working, soberer, and a better man of business than his Roman Catholic neighbor; wherever Huguenots were to be found in any numbers, there the commerce of the town would be found mainly in their hands" (1954, p. 105

(Kane, 1955), there are fewer chances, in such a restricted sample, for Protestants to have moved upward. An adequate test of the hypothesis that Catholics and Protestants in the United States share equally in the secularized "Protestant ethic" would require a sample representative of the entire occupational range.

Medieval Catholicism was by no means so unfavorable for the development of modern capitalism as certain other religions have been. Despite many objective conditions that might have made capitalism possible, such as an abundance of natural resources, many technological developments (more than in Europe until recent times), good communications, accumulated wealth, and long periods of political stability, China has remained economically "backward" from a Western point of view. This is the more remarkable since Confucianism, the dominant religion, is mainly concerned with salvation in this world. Its practical effect, however, was very different from that of Calvinism. As we have noted, the ideal Confucianist is a "gentleman" imbued with the classics and oriented to positions in the state bureaucracy. Business activity would have been regarded as beneath him.

The Confucian ideal of "harmony" of the natural order, the social order, and the supernatural order is fundamentally static. The basic goal is the preservation, by right conduct and ritual means, of a harmony conceived to be already perfect. This harmony could be disturbed temporarily, in the Imperial Chinese conception, but then it was the duty of the emperor and the Confucian bureaucracy to restore it by returning to the correct ritual.

Confucianism, unlike Calvinism, made no attempt to eliminate magical practices. As a matter of fact, Confucianism itself involves a fundamentally magical view of the world, which severely restricts the scope for economic rationality. The other chief religions of China, Taoism and Buddhism, were also either "stuck in magic" or otherworldly-mystical—hence, of course, no ground on which to build up rational mastery of worldly activities.[10]

The influence of Hinduism on the economic life of India has been even more depressing, from a Western point of view. The Hindus are probably no less greedy and hard-working than other people, but the formation of the caste system prevented the development of the economic potentialities inherent in rich natural resources and in social forms such as the guild system, which had made a start in India. The caste system has not prevented factory work in India, *once Westerners had introduced it;* but the spirit of the caste system, which divides society into highly traditionalistic groups ritually segre-

---

[10] In their long history, however, the Chinese have developed an astonishing number of ingenious inventions. See Needham, 1954, v. 1. The very existence of this technological richness underscores the "failure" to develop a highly rationalized economy.

In order to test his thesis concerning Calvinism, Max Weber made several detailed comparative studies. For his study of China, see *The Religion of China* (1951). See also Fei Hsiao-T'ung, "Peasantry and Gentry: An Interpretation of Chinese Social Structure and Its Changes" (1946). On magic in China, see, besides Weber, Francis L. K. Hsu, *Religion, Science and Human Crisis* (1952).

gated from one another, would have made the *origination* of modern capitalism extremely unlikely, if not impossible (see Weber, 1950). Jainism and Buddhism, which were the chief religious reactions against Hinduism, were nevertheless profoundly affected by it. Gautama Buddha and his followers took reincarnation for granted: their whole purpose was to find ultimate salvation from the suffering of endless rebirth. The contemplative mysticism that resulted provided no incentive to an active life in the world. Wherever Buddhism has spread (China, Japan, Ceylon, Burma, Tibet), its forms have tended to strengthen traditionalism in worldly affairs. The dedicated Buddhist retreats to a quiet monastery; the pious layman stores up religious merit by giving alms to the monks (see Konow and Tuxen, 1949, pp. 113-49; and Conze, 1951).

Science and Religion

For the same reasons that Hinduism and Buddhism, and Confucianism and Taoism, have not encouraged extension of the sphere of economic rationality, they have not, on the whole, fostered scientific rationality either. There are exceptions, of course. For example, the interest of Hindu scholars in understanding ancient religious texts was partly responsible for the development in India of the science of comparative linguistics. Until the nineteenth century the Hindus were more advanced in this subject than the Europeans. The interest of the Taoists in alchemy, which is on the borderline between magic and science, undoubtedly led to some empirical (scientific) discoveries. Moreover, with or against religious influence, the intense practical interests of men everywhere—in agriculture and warfare, for example—have led them to observe some empirical phenomena carefully and to formulate theories about them.

Broadly speaking, where religion is strong, and especially where it is supported by the state, its effect on science has probably been negative. Science flourishes best where investigators are not obliged to work within dogmatic preconceptions. In the Western world, we have been heavily indebted to the Greeks, whose religious freedom to speculate was nearly complete.[11] The Renaissance took hold and was most fruitful scientifically where Catholicism had been most weakened by foreign contacts. The hostility of medieval Catholicism to science is well known. St. Bonaventure seems to have expressed in extreme form an attitude widely held in the thirteenth century when he said, "the tree of science cheats many of the tree of life or exposes them to the severest pains of purgatory" (quoted by Merton, 1938, p. 433).[12]

---

[11] *Nearly* complete: as Parsons says, "*Even* in Greece, Socrates was condemned to death" (1951, p. 363n.).

[12] "Science" probably meant knowledge in general. As Merton points out, Catholicism was not completely detrimental to science. For example, scholastic philosophy placed great emphasis on logic (but not enough on empirical evidence).

Religion has not always been hostile to science. The "golden age" of science, the seventeenth century in England, was brought about partly by the influence of the Calvinist Puritans. Numerous writings of Puritan divines reveal ideas and attitudes that were favorable for the advancement of science. The idea of predestination extended beyond the election of souls for salvation or for damnation: nothing that happens in the universe happens without God's knowledge and planning; the universe was rationally designed to begin with, and God does not intervene arbitrarily in the course of events. (Calvin also repudiated the doctrine of "freedom of will.") God Himself is far beyond man's direct comprehension, but man can know Him indirectly, to some extent, by studying His works, great and small. Moreover, such study is a way of fulfilling man's religious duty, which is first to glorify God and secondly (an aspect of the same) to work without sloth for the creation of the kingdom of God on earth. This work is to be done in the world itself, not in a monastery, for neither sacraments nor prayers will change anything. Man's reason is a good thing in that it helps to control the emotions, which might lead away from God, but one must not waste time in mere speculation and logic-chopping (scholasticism): one must study God's creation itself. Dispassionate diligence in such a calling is a sign of grace. (See Merton, 1938, Chaps. 4, 5; and 1949, Chap. 14.)

It would be hard to think of a more favorable complex of ideas and motives for scientific and technological work. Rationalism and empiricism were happily combined, as were personal and social goals. The Puritans in England and America and their European counterparts helped to reform education in a more empirical and utilitarian direction. Among the original members of the Royal Society (which included the greatest English scientists of the time),

> . . . forty-two of the sixty-eight concerning whom the information is available were clearly Puritan. Considering that the Puritans constituted a relatively small minority in the English population, the fact that they constituted 62 per cent of the initial membership of the Society becomes even more striking [Merton, 1949, p. 338].[13]

There is plenty of evidence that the Puritans who devoted themselves to science were not using their religion as a mere "cover" or rationalization to justify what they would have done anyway. They were scientists partly

[13] In his longer work (*Science, Technology and Society in Seventeenth Century England*, 1938), Chap. 6, Merton gives much more evidence, drawn from Havelock Ellis, Alfred Odin, and Alphonse de Candolle, that Protestants were preponderant in science, in England and on the Continent, during the seventeenth century and later. In earlier chapters, Merton gives details of an elaborate statistical study showing that science increasingly occupied English men of genius during the seventeenth century. Concerning Catholic scientists in the United States, Father J. M. Cooper said in 1945 that he "would be loath to have to defend the thesis that 5 per cent or even 3 per cent of the leadership in American science and scholarship is Catholic. Yet we Catholics constitute something like 20 per cent of the total population" (*Commonweal*, v. 42, pp. 147-49; quoted by B. Barber, 1952, p. 136).

because they were Puritans. Some of the greatest scientists and mathematicians were also clergymen (for example, Oughtred, Barrow, Wilkins, Ward, Ray, Grew). The chemist Boyle gave large sums to have the Bible translated, established a lectureship in theology, and took the trouble to learn Greek, Hebrew, Syriac, and Chaldee so that he could read the Scriptures in the original. The botanist Grew also studied Hebrew. The mathematician Napier studied theology. The great Newton wrote a book on the Apocalypse (Merton, 1938, pp. 464-65).[14]

Note, however, that to Calvin himself the advancement of science was no more a goal than was the advancement of capitalism. The transformation of his original doctrine had practical consequences in both fields. Moreover, the two fields were of course interconnected, for business advance helped science and science helped industry.

Still less did Calvin foresee or desire the undermining of religion to which the advance of science undoubtedly contributed. As we noted in Chapter 15, the advance of science inevitably reduces the "need" for that part of religion technically called magic. But the advance of science has more far-reaching consequences for religion (see Parsons, 1951, pp. 516-17, Chap. 8). The line between the empirical and the nonempirical is a shifting one. Some religious beliefs about the origin of man and the earth that in primitive societies or in the Middle Ages were safely in the realm of the nonempirical have been put in doubt or disconfirmed by modern science. In this sense, there is an inherent conflict, at times keen, at other times only latent, between science and religion. It was once "obvious" that this planet Earth is the center of the universe and that man was created to dominate the earth. But modern astronomy presents a very different picture, *on the basis of empirical evidence*. This picture will be modified in detail, but we can be quite sure that the comfortable old conception is gone forever. Similarly, the science of biology has made an evolutionary theory more than plausible, if not demonstrated in detail. Alfred North Whitehead used to say that man, who had thought of himself as but little lower than the angels, suddenly had to adjust to the idea of being little higher than the apes. It is not that older religious conceptions have been disconfirmed, they have only become less plausible to the informed imagination. In a brilliant passage in his *Heavenly City of the Eighteenth Century Philosophers* (1932), Carl Becker says that it would hardly be possible to *refute* Thomas Aquinas' theory of the relations between God, the pope, and the emperor; but the changes in political organization and political thought that have taken place

[14] Such evidence also helps to support Weber's thesis that Calvinism was a spur to business: if religion could influence one "worldly" activity, it could also influence another. Merton makes the important additional point that there are indirect as well as direct influences. For example, an advance in pure science that might have been discovered as a result of zeal for learning about God's rational plan for the universe might have been useful later, when scientists were trying to solve some practical problem in industry.

since Aquinas' time have brought about a "climate of opinion" so different that the problems Aquinas was concerned with now seem largely irrelevant; few serious theorists are now sufficiently involved with them at all to be interested in trying to refute his theory. This conception of the "climate of opinion" is perhaps vague, but it points to a complex phenomenon that is real enough.

In general, empirical knowledge is so important to every society that any advance will be accepted unless there are specific motives for resisting it. The tangible achievements of science impress all who come to be aware of them. Even the sociological and psychological study of religion, although the results are less spectacular, by providing a new perspective, will probably have some effect on religious beliefs. Science, being empirically grounded, *cannot* give way to religion and still be science; but religion can give way and still be religion.

Politics and Religion

It is inevitable that religion and politics should affect each other. Even a religion so otherworldly that its adherents turn away from politics is still affecting political interests, for its adherents are politically neutralized; they are leaving a clear field for those who are actually pursuing political goals. Moreover, those who are politically engaged often make it difficult for the otherworldly to be neutral. For example, in time of war religious pacifists are likely to be subjected to some pressure to gain their cooperation. Usually, however, there is a more direct interaction between religion and political institutions or interests.

As we have seen, political institutions are often sanctioned by religion. The emperor of China was sacred, and his officials had the prestige due to their religious learning. The ruling caste of India was sanctioned by Brahmanism. In Japan, until 1945, State or Shrine Shinto was a religious cult directly supporting the government; the emperor was worshiped as a god, and among the spirits ritually honored were the spirits of men who had given their lives in war for Japan. The kings of France were supposed to rule by divine right. Even today the monarch of England enjoys some of the sacredness conferred by the divine-right theory. The prayer of the Archbishop of Canterbury at the coronation of George VI interwove royal and sacred symbols: "O God, the crown of the faithful; bless . . . and sanctify this thy servant George our King . . . through the King eternal Jesus Christ our Lord. Amen."

It is clear, then, that in the cases mentioned people who believed in the religion were thereby to some extent committed to support their government. But it is also true that the same religions to some extent required that the government should support the people. The emperor of China was responsible for flood and famine control and for protection of the boundaries; if he failed conspicuously in his duties, he was thought to have lost the "mandate of heaven"; under certain circumstances, religion justified revolution. In India, the Kshatriyas were religiously entitled to their positions, but the same religion supported the caste system as a whole; therefore, religion also restricted somewhat the freedom of action of the ruling caste. As we have seen, the Brahmans had a key position. For Louis XIV of France, religion could never justify revolution, no matter how badly a king of France might treat his subjects; but religion did impose upon the king some duties toward God, and these duties affected the king's subjects. "Holding such maxims as he did, Louis' conception of his duties towards his subjects was a perfectly logical one. He had inherited France, just as any other French gentleman might inherit an estate; it was his property, always under God, and it was his duty to conduct himself as a virtuous and enlightened *seigneur*" (W. H. Lewis, 1954, p. 30). In other words, just as religion sanctified the king, so in a measure it sanctified the rights of his subjects, or some of his subjects. Though an "absolute" monarch, Louis was actually committed to supporting an institutional *system*. Needless to say, this system was more favorable to some of his subjects than to others.

The cases we have considered are examples of a relatively stable relationship between religion and political institutions. In the long run, however, social relationships are of course never static. A particularly striking example of how religion and politics may interact to produce a change in the religion itself is provided in the history of prerabbinical Judaism. According to myth, the Hebrew god Yahweh had made a covenant or agreement (*berith*) with Abraham, in which Yahweh promised prosperity to Abraham's descendants in Palestine if they worshiped him alone and followed his commandments. But in 722 B.C. Assyria conquered Israel and sent thousands into exile; in 609 the Egyptian pharaoh conquered the forces of the other Hebrew kingdom, Judah, at Megiddo; in 605 Judah came under the rule of Babylonia; and in 586 the Babylonians destroyed Jerusalem, with its temple.

These events were not unforeseen: the little kingdoms hardly could survive against these mighty empires. But the impending events created a religious problem, for they had to be reconciled with the great covenant. The Prophets (Amos, Hosea, Isaiah, Micah, Jeremiah, Ezekiel, the second Isaiah, and others), who were active between roughly 750 and 550, were concerned with a religious interpretation of the political situation. The prophetic movement in effect transformed Yahweh from the god of the Hebrews, one god among many gods in the universe, to the one universal God; for the Prophets took the line that the plight of the two Hebrew kingdoms was due to the failure of the kings (especially) to live up to the *berith* with Yahweh: instead of keeping to Yahweh, some of the kings had married foreigners with foreign gods, and depended on treaties to keep the kingdoms free. According to the Prophets, Yahweh was in effect making use of mighty empires in order to punish the Hebrews for their failure to live up to the covenant; Yahweh had become the "universal" God. This religious change was due, then, partly to the religious tradition itself (the covenant) and partly to the impact of international politics.

It was also due to the internal political situation in the Israelite kingdoms. The Prophets felt inspired by God; but they were not occupants of institutionalized status-roles, and they were attacking the royal power. Moreover, they frequently prophesied doom. Therefore, they were often physically attacked and prevented from addressing the people. To a certain extent, however, the political authorities feared the Prophets because of their alleged magical powers. The "common" people listened to them with some sympathy (though not always), because the Prophets usually held out some hope for the time after Yahweh's punishment, and also because the Prophets inveighed particularly against the kings, some of whom were resented on account of the magnificence and license of their courts, especially since the luxury was made possible by heavy taxes and forced labor. Above all, the Prophets were legitimated by their fanatical upholding of the Covenant and the Law (Torah). For this reason, they were not opposed by the Levites, the established interpreters of the Law. They were also supported by a few pious families of prominence.

Thus the Prophets were influenced by the political situation inside and outside the kingdoms. But it would not be correct to say that politics was therefore responsible for the rise of monotheism. Being religiously motivated, the Prophets often made demands that were quite unrealistic and inexpedient from a political point of view. Political events were important, however, in making monotheism into something more than the conception of a few intellectuals, as it was, for example, in Greece. The disastrous political situation of the Israelites gave them all a deep *interest* in prophecy, just as it had created a religious problem for the Prophets themselves. Therefore the Prophets were able to influence Judaism profoundly, and, through Judaism, Christianity and Islam (Weber, 1952, Chaps. 11, 12).

Another example of interaction between religion and politics is the spread of the Protestant Reformation. As the name implies, the Reformation arose partly from dissatisfaction with the worldliness of the Catholic Church of the time, but it was also supported by territorial princes who wished to shake off the political power of the papacy. Religious interests, political ambition, and nationalism combined to make the Reformation possible. Numerous national churches and other religious groups testify to the influence of politics on religion. In fact, some of the creeds, such as the Westminster Confession (Anglican) and the Augsburg Confession (Lutheran), were composed partly with the "help" of political leaders (Niebuhr, 1929, Chap. 5).

The relation between religion and politics illustrates the "dilemma of the church," to which we have previously referred. This dilemma can become most severe for a state ecclesia—particularly, perhaps, for one in which priests play a prominent role in the secular affairs of government. If a political regime becomes unpopular and it is associated in people's minds with the state church—an association that must be all but inevitable—then opposition to the regime may be expressed in anticlericalism, with or without the formation of sects or new religious movements. The Catholic Church in France was so closely associated with the *ancien régime* that the French Revolution was almost as much opposed to the Church as it was to the monarchy. Voltaire used to end his letters with the words "Crush the infamous thing!"—by which he meant the Church. By the time a revolutionary situation has developed in a country with a state church, the church is so much involved with the *status quo*—as property owner, as controller of the educational system, as possessor of special privileges in the courts and special immunities such as tax exemption and exemption from military service—that the revolution would be meaningless if the church were to be untouched. Knowing this, the upper clergy, at least, are certain to be among the chief supporters of the existing regime. To attack the regime, the revolutionaries must attack the clergy

French Revolutionaries invented a new religion of sorts—Deism—dedicated to the goddess of "Reason" and "Nature." At the same time, they were not scrupulous and discriminating in their attacks on the clergy; they were sweeping. The Russian Revolutionaries also had an ideology with quasi-religious features (for example, a certain conception of the inevitability of history), and they of course not only dispossessed the Orthodox Church but continued to issue propaganda against all religion except their own quasi-religion. The T'ai P'ing Rebellion (1850-64), in which millions of Chinese were killed and which was put down only with British help, was also inspired in part by a new religion. The leader, a mystic influenced by Protestant missionaries, called his conquered territory the Heavenly Kingdom of Great Peace.

All these revolutions or attempted revolutions involve two striking features: attack on the established religion, and adherence to a new religion or quasi-religion. The essential reason for the attack on the old religion we have noted: the old religion (or its institutionalized organization) has become a bulwark of the vested interests of the political regime. The *functions* of the new religion or quasi-religion are, first, to help reduce the element of guilt involved in attacking the old religion and, second, to provide a system of symbols and goals—a subculture—for the coherence of the revolutionary movement. We speak of the functions of the new religion rather than of the reasons for it in order to stress the objective consequences of action rather than its motivation. At the same time, the term "functions" does underline the fact that the motivation of the revolutionaries, in formulating or accepting the new religion, is not necessarily conscious, whereas a substantial part at least of the opposition to the old religion arises from consciously perceived facts.

The religious or quasi-religious aspect of a revolutionary movement thus is connected with one of the main functions of an established ecclesia:

namely, to sanctify and thus stabilize the institutional order, including of course the political order. This in turn means that the ecclesia, despite its "universalism," necessarily protects the vested interests of *part* of the population. So strong is the nonrational (emotional) hold of the religiously sanctioned institutional order that those who might have something to gain by attacking it feel some guilt about doing so. They are ambivalent toward it: "alienated" from it but also attached to it—however irrationally, considering their own status in life and their total welfare. The very savageness with which the revolutionaries attack the institutional order, its symbolic religious support, and its upholders, including the clergy, may be taken psychologically as evidence of the revolutionaries' ambivalence; in order to attack at all, they must first overcome their own resistance: hence in psychological terms they "overreact." Psychologically, the religious or quasi-religious aspect of the revolutionary movement provides a substitute for the quasi-religious aspect of the institutional order and also a justification for attacking it. The psychological functions (for the *personalities* of the revolutionaries) in turn permit the new religion or quasi-religion to have a *social* function: namely, to contribute to the integration and morale of the revolutionary movement.[15]

"Separation of church and state," such as we have (imperfectly) in the United States, frees religious groups to some extent from the onus as well as the help of government. "Separation" does not, of course, mean that religion and politics do not interact. We have only to think of the "dilemma of the church" as it is faced by denominations.

Where "separation of church and state" is institutionalized, as in the United States, the growth of the Roman Catholic Church tends to be regarded as a threat to the institutional order. In France, for example, where separation of church and state was achieved only in 1905, anticlericalism was still one of the active attitudes of the Radical Socialist Party all during the existence of the Third Republic. This ingrained attitude of distrust was due to the fact that most of the Church hierarchy in France had for a long time been royalist and had refused to accept the republican form of government. After World War II, anticlericalism arose again when the Catholic party tried to re-establish Church control of the schools.

In the United States, anti-Catholicism was not at first the same thing as anticlericalism. It was partly the prejudice of a predominantly Protestant country, and it was reinforced by the supposed cultural inferiority of the Catholic immigrants from Ireland, Italy, Poland, and other places. With the passing of time, however, these late Catholic immigrants have of course been Americanized, and with their Americanization they have acquired more skill in the political system and a more secure position economically and religiously.

---

[15] One of Durkheim's insights (1947) is that social institutions have a quasi-religious aspect. The analysis in the text of the ambivalence of revolutionary movements is largely based on Parsons, 1951, Chaps. 7, 9.

Perhaps the most important religious issue, or series of issues, that has arisen in American politics has to do with the relation between the government and religious schools. In 1930 the Supreme Court ruled that the State of Louisiana had not violated the Constitution when it passed a law "directing the State Board of Education to provide 'school books for school children free of cost to such children'" whether they were in public schools or in private religious schools. In 1947 the Supreme Court (5 to 4) ruled that the State of New Jersey had not violated the Constitution when it passed a law "authorizing local school districts to provide children with free transportation to and from all nonprofit schools" (McSorley, 1947, p. 509). The Court was probably no more divided on this issue than the American people. The issue is so controversial that one can say hardly anything without seeming to be partisan; it is so important that one can hardly be anything but partisan. Although there is certainly still prejudice in the United States, of Protestant against Catholic and Catholic against Protestant, one's stand on the school issue does not necessarily rest on prejudice in the usual sense: "prejudice" usually implies an underlying distortion of facts so great that without it the attitude involved would be substantially different; but one might endorse the Louisiana or New Jersey law—or deplore it—without necessarily distorting facts very much.

Without going into all the questions involved, we venture four comments:

1. The controversial constitutional amendment ("Congress shall make no law respecting an establishment of religion, or prohibiting the free exercise thereof") is so ambiguous that one can with little difficulty make arguments on either side of the school issue seem strained, irrelevant, or ridiculous.

2. What the framers of the amendment meant by it is not the most important question from a sociological point of view. The Supreme Court has reversed itself on less ambiguous parts of the Constitution. Moreover, it is possible, within the law, to change the Constitution.

3. It is unlikely that proponents of state aid to religious schools will stop with the Louisiana and New Jersey laws, or that those laws will be confined to those states.

4. If a trend is established, it could result in a profound change in our society. In 1952 there were 8358 Roman Catholic elementary parochial schools in the United States, as against about 3000 Protestant church-affiliated nursery, kindergarten, and elementary schools. The Catholic elementary schools had 2,692,706 pupils; the Protestant, about 187,000 (B. Y. Landis, ed., 1954, p. 297). Except for higher education, most of the Jewish religious schools are supplementary to the public schools; these afternoon classes are growing in number and importance. (See the article on "Religious Education" in the latest *Britannica Book of the Year*.) If the trend toward more religious schools continues, the society will inevitably be more divided. Perhaps the greatest danger is that the non-Catholic part of the popu-

lation might out of fear overreact to the expansion of Catholic education and the tendency to depart even further from the ideal of separation of church and state.

Social Functions of Religion

The social functions of religion, both for the religious group itself and for the wider society, can be classified as contributions to pattern maintenance, tension management, and integration.

INTEGRATION THROUGH VALUES

The integration of a society seems to depend upon several things: common, or nearly common, values; widespread acceptance of norms, prescriptive and proscriptive; mutual compatibility of these institutionalized norms; a near-monopoly of the means of force in the government, or, at least, a potential concentration of force behind recognized authorities in the society. Religion is never the only integrative power, but it makes contributions to integration. All but universally, it has an important part in crystallizing, symbolizing, and reinforcing common values and norms.

The Ten Commandments in Judaism and Christianity, for example, are religious duties some of which are at the same time moral. The commandment to worship one God is religious only, having no *direct* bearing on patterns of interaction between human beings; but the commandment not to steal is moral as well as religious, since it defines a social pattern, at least in negative terms. This commandment will probably be interpreted to mean "Respect the property rights recognized in the society"; thus it will ultimately reinforce the social *institution* of property, however that may be socially defined. Often, however, religion supports institutional patterns more explicitly, as we have seen in our discussion of kinship and politics in relation to religion. The following statement about religion in rural Japan brings out very well its integrative functions:

> It consists fundamentally of a body of ritual and belief which may be classified under two broad heads: (1) the series of seasonal festivals associated with agricultural and other deities and celebrated on a neighborhood basis; (2) ancestor worship, performed on a kinship basis.
>
> These two aspects of the religious life serve the following functions: (1) to give ritual recognition to things of social value to the society, e.g., rice, silk, wind, water, human life; (2) to strengthen the social relations of the groups involved, especially the local group and the kin group (there are sometimes special deities connected with occupational groups also, such as carpenters or waggoners); (3) to give the individual (a) a sense of dependence on the group through emphasizing his duties toward it, and (b) a sense of security as a member of the group, thus emphasizing his rights as a member of the group. A man of few kin, or a man who lives isolated from the local group, is a poor man, a beggar, a nobody [Embree, 1941, p. 189].

Religious *differences* within a society often—perhaps always—produce tension or conflict; that is, they are disruptive rather than integrative for the society as a whole. Strictly speaking, this statement is oversimplified. Two religions often stress the same or similar values as well as some that are different and perhaps incompatible. Thus in some respects a religion may be integrative for the society while in others it is disruptive.

Moreover, even when there is only one religion, there may be some areas of tension, or even chronic struggle, between the organized religion and the political authorities. In such cases, as for example in medieval Western Europe, detailed analysis would be required to reach any conclusion about the balance of integrative and disruptive aspects of religion. It is hard to believe, however, that medieval "Christendom" would have had as much unity as it had without Christianity. Religion is most unequivocally integrative when political and religious authority are fused.

As we have had other occasions to emphasize, functions are relative to particular groups or subgroups. Moreover, it is necessary to specify the aspects of group structure to which a particular pattern (norm or practice) contributes stability. Finally, it is necessary to keep in mind that the particular aspects of social structure for which a particular pattern is functional may or may not be "good" from everyone's point of view. To repeat, functions are certain *objective* consequences for a social system, regardless of *evaluation*. The creed and ritual of a "crusading" sect following a newly risen prophet may be functional in certain ways for the sect itself but dysfunctional in certain ways for the total society. By providing satisfactions to its members, however, many a quiet sect of the self-isolating kind may change potentially disruptive feelings (a sense of secular injustice, for example) into forms relatively harmless to the established social structure of the wider society.

At the risk of being unduly repetitious, we must emphasize the non-evaluative nature of the concepts of function and dysfunction. To say that Confucianism helped to integrate China, or Brahmanism India, is not to approve (or disapprove) of the particular form of integration, or even of integration *per se*. It is merely a way of stating a complex *fact*.

A functional analysis of a revolutionary religious movement (e.g., Cromwell's revolutionary army, the T'ai P'ing Rebellion, some of the early Protestant movements) requires particularly close attention to the exact social system we are analyzing at a given moment. The culture of such a movement obviously contributes to the unity or integration of the movement itself. Obviously, also, the movement, to the extent that it is successful, is going to be "dysfunctional" to the traditional order of society—that is, to some aspects of it. But at the same time, the very existence of a revolutionary movement may be regarded as a symptom *in* the traditional order. It is not simply a visitation from Mars, disrupting a previously placid utopia; it is the culmination of mounting disagreement, disaffection, tension, and conflict generated in the course of time by and within particular social arrangements in the traditional social order itself. This statement is a truism, but it points up the relativity of functional analysis: for a revolutionary movement further disrupts a society already malintegrated, and yet it may result in a state of society more securely though differently integrated. In other words, in a sufficiently long time perspective, a particular revolutionary movement may have the function of reintegrating a society. For the society regarded as a concrete social system, the revolutionary movement, then, is simultaneously dysfunctional and functional, depending upon which social structure the analyst has in mind, the traditional one or the new one.[16]

To some extent there are nonreligious functional equivalents of religion, which may also help to integrate a society. Nationalism and other ideologies are or may be integrative. Indeed, some writers treat nationalism as a religion, with its "demi-gods," "myths," and "rituals" (see C. J. H. Hayes, 1926, Chap. 4). There *are* nationalistic religions, such as Shinto in Japan, but not all nationalism is religious in the technical sense. A national flag is a "sacred" object only in a figurative sense: it does not really stand for a supernatural entity. So also for national heroes and patriotic ceremonies. The symbolic aspects of nationalism are often nonreligious equivalents of some aspects of religion. A moment's thought will reveal that any group whatsoever, provided that it exists long enough, develops symbols of its integrity: but the group and its integrity exist in the empirical world.

It is certainly true, however, that nationalism and other ideologies may have quasi-religious aspects. Moreover, as Table 11 suggests, there may be historical continuity between religion proper and ideology. Ideology may sometimes be regarded as a secularized form of religion. Needless to say, such a statement is not meant to imply any value judgment about either religion or ideology. Table 11 brings out the fact that secular ideologies may have some roots in religion. This is true of conservative as well as of radical ideologies. In the United States, the appeal (such as it is) of Communism, which is of course a revolutionary and therefore deviant ideology, probably owes something to the fact that the Communists have a bridge, as Parsons puts it (1951, Chap. 7), to the "official" conservative ideology. They claim that Communism would fulfill values that are already accepted (e.g., economic abundance and equality of opportunity) better than the existing social order has. (See Chap. 21.)

MORALE, OR TENSION MANAGEMENT

Morale may be defined as the level of positive motivation to attain group goals.

---

[16] The double aspect of a revolution is sometimes expressed by comparison with a fever in the human body. See, for example, Crane Brinton, *The Anatomy of Revolution* (1938). The idea is that a revolution, like a fever, may be very painful but also may be necessary, in some conditions, to restore the social "body" to health. Moreover, a revolution at its height makes far-reaching changes, some of which are later rescinded as the "fever" cools down.

TABLE 11

*Some Secularized Forms of Christianity **
(Underlying idea: human life has ultimate meaning in the drama of history,

	Source of evil	*God*
MEDIEVAL CHRISTIANITY (the unsecularized "starting point")	Original sin, predestination	Personal God of love and power
DEISM (18th century)	Christian "superstition," especially as represented by the Church and its royal supporters	"Reason," "Nature," "Humanity," "the People," the (remote) Author of all things
COMMUNISM	Exploitation by the ruling class (at present, capitalists); religious and liberal-democratic error	The "dialectic" of history, the inevitable class struggles leading eventually to communism

* Suggested by Carl Becker, *The Heavenly City of the Eighteenth-Century Philosophers,*

Good morale is not possible if goals are ill defined or conflicting, or if they seem impossible to attain. Our discussion of white magic (pp. 413-16) shows that the magician is often able to maintain or restore morale. The magical ritual in the first place emphasizes the importance of group goals. In the second place, it increases confidence that action will be successful. The reducing or forestalling of anxiety that the actor might otherwise feel frees him for whatever rational action may be open to him.

But the use of magic, while it has positive functions for some social systems, also involves a "disadvantage." Since magic relieves emotional tension, it prevents or hinders the development of better rational techniques. Magic is never used when adequate rational techniques are known, of course, and ordinarily it is used in addition to whatever rational techniques may be available; but its very merits reduce the motivation to research and invention. The virtual elimination of magic from modern medicine was probably a necessary step to rapid medical advance (see Merton, 1949. pp. 36-37). This does not necessarily mean, however, that magic is dysfunctional. Its use is

which has a happy ending.)

Path to salvation	*Saints*	*Days of worship*	*Nature of salvation*
The sacraments; resignation	Many heroes of the faith	Christmas, Easter, and many saints' days	Heaven (for the "good"), Hell (for unrepentent sinners); the eventual coming of the Kingdom of God
Fight against the sources of evil; discovery and establishment of the "laws" of Nature	Martyrs of Liberty and Reason, in all ages	The fêtes of the French Revolution (e.g., Bastille Day, the fête of Liberty and Humanity)	The respect of Posterity (a kind of immortality), the perfection of human life on earth
Propaganda, agitation, and revolution for the proletariat, the Communist Party, and the Soviet State	Marx, Lenin, and many lesser ideologists, revolutionary leaders, and martyrs	Fêtes celebrating the great days of the Russian Revolution	The purgatory of the dictatorship of the proletariat, followed by true communism (classless society, no government)

1932, Yale University Press.

geared to the social organization at a particular level of culture. In fact, the introduction of new rational techniques may be dysfunctional for that particular form of social organization. The dysfunctions of rational techniques may be regarded as good or bad or mixed depending upon one's sentiments concerning various aspects of the "original" social structure.

Magic is not by any means the only strengthener of morale in social groups. During World War II, the War Department asked enlisted men five questions designed to find out what helped them "when the going was tough" (that is to say, when morale was perhaps threatened). Four divisions in the Pacific were surveyed and four in Italy. To the question "When the going was tough, how much did prayer help you?" 70 per cent in the Pacific theater and 83 per cent in the Mediterranean theater said it helped a lot; 17 per cent and 8 per cent, respectively, said it did not help at all. But proportions varying from 28 per cent to 61 per cent were also helped by thoughts that they "couldn't let the other men down," that they "had to finish the job in order to get home again," by "thoughts of hatred for the enemy," and by thoughts "of what we are fighting for" or, in Italy, "of the meaning of what we are fighting for" (M. B. Smith, 1949, p. 174).[17]

INTEGRATION THROUGH SOCIAL CONTROL

Social-control functions are the obverse of morale-maintaining functions. Whereas morale has to do with positive motivation to attain goals, social control has to do with the restriction or reduction or elimination of *negative* motivation—that is, tendencies to deviate from institutionalized patterns. Maintaining morale and controlling "alienation" and deviant tendencies shade into each other. To control tendencies to deviate means either to check them in their incipient stage and replace them by acceptable tendencies, or to keep deviation within limits and prevent it from spreading to other individuals or subgroups.

Any social organization requires mechanisms of social control. Religious organizations are no exception. Religion not only defines moral expectations for members of the religious group but usually enforces them. As we noted earlier, specifically religious sanctions are added to purely social ones. In addition to supernatural sanctions in the afterlife, there are frequently supernatural sanctions in this life, such as the threat of disease for violators of magical property taboos. To the extent that moral norms supported within the religious group are at the same time norms of the society, social control within the religious group has functional importance for the wider society as well.

It will be remembered that religion is focused on the "problem" of evil, and that one form of this problem is the disparity between merit and reward. The motivation to conform to role patterns depends upon sanctions, including of course social rewards. If these rewards are not forthcoming, there is danger to the structure of the system: disgruntled people may attempt to change it or to withdraw from it to some extent. This, of course, happens frequently. But it might happen more frequently if people did not have available to them a way of thinking that treats "worldly" injustice as

[17] "Out of these data from two theaters and two widely differing campaigns, a fairly coherent picture emerges in regard to the sort of person who said prayer helped a lot when the going was tough. Such persons, first, appear on the average to have been subjected to a relatively stronger degree of stress than the minority who did not report finding prayer very helpful. Thus, men in the Infantry were more likely to say they found prayer helpful than were men in other branches, and, among infantrymen, men who said they were helped a lot by prayer were more likely than others to say that they had seen close friends become casualties and that they had taken air or artillery attack from their own side several times—situations that would be particularly hard to endure. Secondly, those who say they were helped a lot by prayer appear to have had somewhat less resources for coping with the stresses which they underwent. The replacement, as compared with the original members of a unit, could draw on less support from his ties to other members of the group, and . . . men who said they were helped a lot by prayer were more likely to have been replacements" (pp. 184-85).

only apparent: all deserts will be rewarded properly in an afterlife. In Calvinism the existing social order is not wholeheartedly approved of, since it is obviously not the Kingdom of God on earth, which is to come. But, if anything, this idea makes the problem of explaining evil more acute, for if the social order itself is partly evil, then there is more evil to explain. Calvinism declares that there is plenty of evil in this life and then, by the doctrine of predestination, asserts, in effect, that the evil of this life is continued, not compensated, in the life to come. It is not surprising that Calvin's doctrine was soon modified in practice. In its original form, it failed to meet one of the functional requirements of any religion.

Sometimes misfortune in this world is treated as a manifestation of the supernatural order itself: the victim has sinned secretly or even unconsciously, and he is being punished. All such religious explanations have in common the feature that they cannot be checked empirically, and they tend to divert attention away from possible empirical explanations and hence from criticism of the social order.

It is this control aspect of religion, as well as its tendency to sanctify the existing social structure, that caused Marxist thinkers to call religion "the opiate of the people." Once again, however, we should remind ourselves that functional analysis is in itself nonevaluative. Whether or not something has a certain function is a question of fact; how we evaluate the function goes beyond matter of fact.

In nothing is the control function of religion clearer than in the reaction to death. In Chapter 15, we may seem to have stressed what religion does for the grieving individual personality. But we are primarily interested now in the control functions of religion for *social* systems. The mourner has various statuses in the society. That means he ordinarily has obligations which other people expect and depend upon him to fulfill. He has a family and a job, he is a citizen, and so on. The emotions aroused by the death of an affectively important person are, in Malinowski's term, "centrifugal." That is, they bear the mourner away from the centers of his ordinary life—his role obligations in groups. A person suffering from grief is likely to feel that effort is useless, that nothing is worthwhile, that life is senseless. Such feelings are centrifugal—they are incipient motivation to deviation. Religious consolation to some extent forestalls, to some extent checks, such deviant tendencies. The temporary *status* of mourner provides social tolerance—up to a point. Then the mourner is gently pressed to take up his normal responsibilities again, possibly with some additional ones. This is the important thing, of course, for the maintenance of social systems. In relation to this, the period of permissive withdrawal is only a stage or step in the therapeutic and control process. In this respect, customary mourning is comparable to medical care—in both, the society makes it clear that deviation is permitted on the understanding that it should be temporary if possible and that the patient will do his best to recover. Religion helps to provide the necessary motivation as well as an appropriate reaction pattern in the crisis itself.[18]

Ministering to the grief-stricken is part of the more general religious task sometimes called the "cure of souls." "Cure," from the Latin *cura,* means both "cure" and "care." "Confessor," "chaplain," "minister," "*directeur de l'âme*"—all these terms imply, among other things, the function of seeing to the spiritual health of laymen. Ordinarily the role of "curate," as the literature of pastoral care shows, is thought of as important for integrating and controlling *personalities* (to use a secular term): but with respect to the social system the cure of souls is essentially a control function. This is brought out in the use of sanctions, from admonition and occasional refusal of communion to excommunication. Indeed, the question whether or not to excommunicate always involves some balance between consideration for the spiritual welfare of the individual member and consideration for the integrity of the religious organization. Like most of the social functions of religion, the control function of the cure of souls is "latent" for the most part; that is, the participants are largely unaware of it. The conceptual scheme of sociology helps us to uncover the latent functions of social structure.

RECOMMENDED READING

The introduction to Max Weber's comparative study of religions is one of the great classics of sociology; it has been translated by Talcott Parsons as *The Protestant Ethic and the Spirit of Capitalism*, Scribner's, 1930. The comparative studies themselves have also been translated. These studies are *The Religion of China: Confucianism and Taoism*, trans. by H. H. Gerth, Free Press, 1951; *Ancient Judaism*, trans. by H. H. Gerth and Don Martindale, Free Press, 1952; and *The Religion of India: The Sociology of Hinduism and Buddhism*, trans. by H. H. Gerth and Don Martindale, Free Press, 1958. For a good secondary treatment of Weber's ideas, see Talcott Parsons, *The Structure of Social Action*, McGraw-Hill, 1937, Part III (now published by Free Press, 1949). A work by an Italian scholar, Amintore Fanfani, *Catholicism, Protestantism and Capitalism*, Sheed & Ward, 1935, contains some mistaken criticism of Weber but is good on Catholicism and on the "premodern" forms of capitalism. C. T. Jonassen, "The Protestant Ethic and the Spirit of Capitalism in Norway," *Amer. sociol. Rev*., Dec. 1947, v. 12, pp. 676-86, analyzes a nineteenth-century case of religious influence on economic development in the light of Weber's theory. For a good introduction to the differences between Marx and Weber, see Norman Birnbaum, "Conflicting Interpretations of the Rise of Capitalism: Marx and Weber," *Brit. J. Sociol.*, June 1953, v. 4, pp. 125-41.

---

[18] For an analysis that brings out the processual similarities between mourning, sickness, and other kinds of deviation, see Parsons, 1951, Chap. 7. Mourning has integrative functions also. Sometimes religion—or simply custom—requires a show of mourning even when there is no grief. The prescribed mourning period, which is often quite specific, varies according to the culturally defined "closeness" of the mourner and the deceased. The mourning-scale thus symbolizes and presumably reinforces the social structure.

part seven

STRATIFICATION

18. Social Ranking and Social Classes

Norms and values differ considerably from one social system to another, but everywhere *some* norms and values guide interaction and also furnish standards for making evaluations. According to what is valued, it is always possible to rank people in some order from greater to less or from high to low. The specific bases of ranking are multitudinous: height, weight, physical strength, "intelligence," ability to swim, ability to speak French, physical "beauty," wealth, courage, loyalty to a cause, moral rectitude: it would be futile to try to list them all. In general, the members of a social system are implicitly or explicitly ranked along several continua, according to the degree to which they possess certain *qualities* and according to the relative merits of their *performances* of various kinds. We should note that a person's qualities and performances are usually judged in relation to his age and with reference to a particular social role. Not only persons but also groups are ranked according to the merit of their imputed qualities and performances.

The terms "quality" and "performance" must be interpreted broadly (see pp. 140-41). Thus one's height is a "quality," but so is one's ability to perform an appendectomy, or, in general, any other performance ability. These qualities are intrinsic to their possessors at any particular time and cannot be given over to another (although some of them can be taught). By extension, we may also regard as qualities group memberships and other social positions; aspects of social positions, such as authority; and, finally, possessions. All these "qualities" are not intrinsic but in the last analysis depend upon more or less clearly established relations with other people in social systems; for example, possessions depend upon property rights or upon the extra-institutional power to fend off potential dispossessors. These "qualities" have therefore been called "relational," in contrast to such intrinsic qualities as intelligence and age, which are "classificatory" (Parsons, 1953).

As for the evaluation of performances, we may note that performances are always judged first according to their products or results, valued or disvalued, and secondly according to the manner and style of the performing. Thus performances are always subject to regulatory norms; when these are violated, performances are often disvalued, regardless of their results. Sometimes the manner of a performance (apart from its adherence to or violation of regulatory norms) is of little importance; but sometimes it is the focus of as much attention as the results of the performance. Cricket players, for example, are supposed to pay a good deal of attention to "form," whereas (apart from its relation to results) form is less important in baseball.

Since qualities and performances are closely associated with persons and groups, it is inevitable that persons and groups are evaluated and ranked. Sometimes a person is ranked on a relatively narrow basis and in fairly limited context, such as the shop in which he works; but it is also possible to rank persons in a more general way, according to some combination or "total" complex of qualities and achievements (past performances well done, with valued results). We shall use the word "prestige" to refer to the approval, respect, admiration, or deference a person or group is able to command by virtue of his or its imputed qualities or performances, whether these are of one type only or are heterogeneous. Two persons or groups may be about equal in prestige as a result of measuring up about equally to the same standards, or having different but equally valued combinations of qualities and performances. Nevertheless, it is obvious that the widely varying capacities and attainments of persons and groups in social systems normally result in some sort of hierarchy of prestige. We shall use "ranking" as the most general term referring to degrees of prestige and the term "stratification" for the process or condition in which layers (strata) of persons or groups are ranked differentially so that any one stratum contains many persons or groups of roughly the same rank. Standards of evaluation vary from one social system to another, and from one situation to another within the same social system; thus the fighting ability so much admired in some boys' gangs wins little prestige in a chess club. Whenever we speak of prestige and degrees of prestige, therefore, we should always make clear the specific social system and situation we have in mind.

The Nature of Social Classes

The term "social class" is used in different ways by different writers. It would be difficult to incorporate in a single sentence all the qualifications that should be made in any short definition. Our procedure therefore will be to present a definition and then qualify it in the rest of this section.

A social class, then, is a more or less endogamous stratum consisting of families of about equal prestige who are or would be acceptable to one another for "social" interaction that is culturally regarded as more or less symbolic of equality; as the term "stratum" suggests, a social class is one of two or more such groupings, all of which can be ranked relative to one another in a more or less integrated system of prestige stratification.

THE FAMILY AS THE UNIT OF CLASS

Although there are differences of prestige within a family—differences based on age and sex—these differences are ignored in the stratification of social classes; members of the same family are considered class equals. (Note, however, that by the term "family" we mean a group of relatives who are actually living in the same household. Adult members of the same family of orientation who are living in separate households no longer constitute a family in our present sense.) The members of a family are class equals for the best possible reason: they treat one another in many ways that are commonly regarded as symbolic of broad social equality. Thus they often eat together at the same table, on many informal occasions as well as formal ones; they have many friends in common; they often appear in public as a social unit, and their close connection with one another is symbolized in their common family name; in many ways they share the same style of life—indeed, living in the same household, surrounded by the same household equipment, they could hardly avoid doing so. The tendency on the part of family members to identify with one another and the tendency on the part of others to link the members of a particular family together in their thoughts often result in a lasting imprint on personality, especially on manners, taste, and general way of life. Especially in a small community, family members will continue to affect one another's social prestige even after the family has been divided by marriages and the formation of new households. A boy who wishes to rise in social rank above his family of orientation must ordinarily leave the community in which his family resides, especially if that community is small. The class standing of an adult in a metropolitan community is less affected by the reputation of his family of origin unless that reputation was either very high or very low. Nevertheless, the prestige of a man's family of orientation may remain an element in his class standing for the rest of his life, even though he may later move from the class of his birth to some other class. If his family had no great reputation, that very fact will continue to play a small part in the estimates other people make of his social standing.

The family, then, is the unit of a social class. Ordinarily the family's class rank is mainly determined by the husband's occupation—a fact to which we shall return. Since social classes are to some (varying) extent endogamous, the wife's social origin does not ordinarily affect the class rank of the family unless her class origin is markedly different from her husband's. A marriage between two people of sharply different class origins would equalize the class rank of husband and wife (one would rise and the other fall somewhat). Children, until they grow up at least, have the class standing of their parents.

CLASS ENDOGAMY

Men tend to marry women not too different from themselves in family background and education. Apart from certain occupations for women that, for a particular social class, may be degrading or "disqualifying," there may be, and often is in our own society, a considerable difference between the prestige of the husband's occupation and the prestige of his wife's before or after marriage. This is possible in all classes and likely in the middle and upper classes (if the wife works at all) because the woman's class position before marriage is ordinarily the same as her parents', regardless of her occupation; after marriage, the husband's occupation usually has far more importance than the wife's in determining the class position of the family. Therefore, within broad limits, the wife may have an occupation much inferior to her husband's without endangering the class position of her family of procreation.

The most decisive mark of class equality between families is the fact that they will accept one another's children in marriage without feeling, on either side, that the match is socially inappropriate. (A family may of course oppose a particular marriage for many reasons, some of which are irrelevant to social class.)

The importance for social class of both occupation and eligibility for marriage is brought out in the following quotation, which deals with a particular social stratum in France just before World War II. The author calls this stratum the *peuple.*

> . . . in our contemporary France—in the country, in towns or large villages—one often sees a peasant's son become an artisan, while his wife keeps a small shop; and, aided by their children, they cultivate, in their spare time, one or more pieces of land. If there are several children, some (among the girls especially) will in many cases become domestics in the city.
>
> Let us take a concrete example—not at all imaginary, for we have observed, in rural areas, many similar cases.
>
> Paternal grandparents, tenant farmers.
>
> Maternal grandparents, small proprietors tilling their own land.
>
> Uncles and aunts, farmers.
>
> One of the aunts learned a trade: she's a dressmaker, established in her own shop, with paid assistants.
>
> One of the uncles is a postman, his wife a laundress.
>
> The father: wheelwright and small peasant proprietor.
>
> The mother: grocer.
>
> There are four children.
>
> The eldest son works with his father, whom he will succeed.
>
> The second son is a mechanic in a large city. He marries a worker and forms a new family of urban type. The young couple, however, spend some time in the country every year and are thinking of living there after their retirement.
>
> The two daughters are maids-of-all-work in Paris.
>
> The younger one, who is intelligent, becomes in succession a store clerk, then an employee in a minor office.

> . . . All these persons, despite differences in their occupations and certain shades of difference in their mode of life, definitely belong to the same stratum [Ferré, 1934, pp. 195-96].[1]

INTERACTION SYMBOLIC OF CLASS EQUALITY

Although mutual eligibility for marriage is the principal sign that any two families belong to the same social class, it is not the only sign. However, the forms of interaction that are sensitive to social class are almost all intimate enough to lead to marriage if the participants are otherwise eligible (that is, unmarried and of suitable age). In the United States, dating does not necessarily imply courtship and hence is not a sure sign of class equality; but dating obviously has some implication that marriage is possible, especially if the participants are old enough to marry. (In general, the interaction of children provides less clear indications of their relative class standing than the interaction of adults.)

Another fairly good and widely applicable sign of class equality is frequent visiting between families, especially informal, more or less casual visiting. This is perhaps especially important toward the upper end of the class hierarchy. According to a study made in a section of Boston, Massachusetts, the family as a unit is perhaps less important in the lower class than is the clique of friends of the same sex and roughly the same age. As compared with the middle class, this lower-class population attached less importance to interaction in the house and more importance to interaction outside. Adult men met for their social relaxation on a street corner or in a certain tavern. Although cliques of women often congregated in one of their homes, they also spent a good deal of time, in clement weather, leaning out of windows, watching the life in the street, and chatting in yards and doorways (Miller, 1959a, and no date; see also Warner and Lunt, 1941, p. 119).

Intimate social and recreational clubs also tend to accept only persons of the same social class. Hollingshead and Redlich, writing of the upper class ("class I") of New Haven, Connecticut, use the term "core group" to refer to families whose ancestors have been in class I for several generations and the term *"arrivistes"* to refer to families whose male heads have made their way to the fringe of class I through their own efforts (so-called "self-made men" whose success has been outstanding).

> Three distinct types of clubs characterize this stratum: the one-sex club, the family club, and the special interest club. "Gentlemen's" and "ladies'" clubs represent the first type. The family club is designed to meet the social and recreational needs for all family members. The special interest club is for persons with particular tastes and hobbies. Three "gentlemen's" clubs main-

---

1 Quoted passage translated by the present writer. According to Ferré (Chap. 14), the *peuple* shades off into the *bas-peuple* (streetcleaners, ragpickers, etc.) and finally into the *hors-classes* (prostitutes, tramps, certain street venders). Ferré's study was based to s[illegible] on marriage records, although she does not give us her statistical evidence.

tain club houses where the members may meet, relax, read, have a drink at the private bar, or eat with their equals. Two of these clubs are "exclusive"; the acknowledged members of the core group, the Gentile professional and business elites, are divided between them. No exclusive "ladies'" club maintains a club house. Their members meet in private homes, parish houses, or other clubs. The most exclusive one meets in the home of some member. It has no name other than the one its members have traditionally accorded themselves, namely, Our Society. This is truly a core group of equals where memberships are passed down from mothers to daughters and daughters-in-law with few exceptions. There are a half-dozen acceptable family clubs in the community, but Gentile members of the core group are concentrated in one, the *arrivistes* are clustered in another, professional families in two others, and Jewish *arrivistes* and professionals in another. Several yacht, fishing, hunting, and beach clubs are maintained by Gentile families; in like manner groups of Jewish families maintain beach and country clubs.

Some 97 per cent of the class I families have at least one club membership and 75 per cent belong to two or more clubs. The husband belongs to a men's club, the wife to a ladies' club, and the family to a family club. A relatively small number of leisure time interests are represented in the special interest clubs–tennis, golf, polo, sailing, fishing, and hunting among the men and the raising of flowers and purebred livestock or thoroughbred horses among both sexes [Hollingshead and Redlich, 1958, p. 82].[2]

Other social classes also have clubs, although in the lower class, as Miller points out, the one-sex clique of age peers tends to take the place of formal clubs.

The description of upper-class clubs in New Haven shows that even within a social class there are different degrees of prestige. Fairly intimate social circles in which one person is the center of attraction—the first among equals, regularly the host or hostess at a kind of constantly renewed reception in a kind of "court"—may be found at every level of society.[3] The novelist Evelyn Waugh, referring to British upper-class circles of an earlier day, says:

My memory is that the grandees avoided one another unless they were closely related. They met on state occasions and on the racecourse. They did not frequent one another's houses. You might find almost anyone in a ducal castle–convalescent, penurious cousins, advisory experts, sycophants, gigolos and plain blackmailers. The one thing you could be sure of not finding was a concourse of other dukes [Waugh, 1956, p. 78].

The attendants at such courts are not all of equal social rank, however, and indeed they are not necessarily of the same social class. The king may be fond of his court jester, but he would not be amused if the jester wanted to marry the king's daughter.

---

2 For descriptions of the Harvard College clubs for men from upper-class families, see Amory, 1947. For descriptions of social clubs at various class levels in the Negro community of Chicago, see Drake and Cayton, 1945, pp. 531-36, 687-710.

3 This extension of the ordinary meaning of "court" is taken from Goffman, 1959, pp. 100-01. For good fictional descriptions of nonroyal courts, see Balzac's description of Mlle. Cormon's receptions in *The Old Maid* and Proust's description of the Verdurin dinner parties in *Swann's Way*.

Every form of social interaction short of outright conflict signifies a certain degree of social acceptance. But the fact that A will accept B as an approximate equal in one situation does not guarantee that A will not draw the line against B at some other point. A may invite B to a formal dinner but politely discourage B from dropping in uninvited. A may invite B to his house but may never visit B. Eating, drinking, or smoking together is a mark of mutual acceptance, but its exact meaning can be assessed only if one knows the frequency and the circumstances of this interaction—the time, the place, the occasion, the particular role relationship involved. Even intimacy does not necessarily signify class equality. A man may tell a "perfect stranger" things he wouldn't tell his wife. Domestic servants are sometimes allowed to know intimate family secrets, not because they are socially equal to the members of the family but because they are treated, in their status, as "nonpersons" (Goffman, 1959, pp. 151-53, 229n.). To some extent, also, persons of high rank offer morsels of intimacy to their inferiors in return for services.[4]

Sexual relations are usually regarded as intimate, yet they by no means always imply social equality. Apart from relations with prostitutes, there occur secret relations between persons of greatly differing social rank:

> . . . when we study service occupations, especially lowly ones, inevitably we find that practitioners have anecdotes to tell about the time they or one of their colleagues redefined the service relation into a sexual one (or had it redefined for them) [Goffman, 1959, p. 194].

With regard to intimacy, we must note, finally, that it is functionally necessary in any society that permits a considerable amount of social climbing for social-class lines to be treated as irrelevant in many situations. Of particular importance is the fact that people ordinarily continue to have intimate, though intermittent, interaction with their parents and siblings after leaving the parental household. Since fathers and sons are sometimes in very different social classes, the kinship system could hardly coexist with the class structure if all intimate social interaction could take place only between class equals (Parsons, 1940).

SOCIAL CLASS AND "STYLE OF LIFE"

One's acceptability to another for different kinds of social interaction will depend upon a wide variety of qualities and performances. As a first approximation, we can say that every social class tends to have a total "style of life" of its own, distinguishing it more or less sharply from the other classes in the same society. (At the same time, the existence of a common social system, of which the several classes are subsystems of a certain kind, presupposes that the classes, however different from one another in style of

---

[4] We have already noticed a similar phenomenon; namely, that in formal organizations higher officials may win better morale and cooperation from lower officials by seeming to give them a voice in making joint decisions.

life, all share to some degree the same norms and standards of judgment. Although we shall from time to time use the expression "class culture" to mean "style of life," the two are not exactly the same. Some relatively distinctive aspects of a class style of life are cultural, but some are simply due to the situation in which the members of the class typically find themselves. The poverty of lower classes, for example, is not entirely cultural, and if lower-class persons live in hovels the main reason is that they are poor.)

The term "style of life" must be understood in a comprehensive sense. The style of life of a particular social class might be more or less distinctive with respect to all the following points (and the list is not exhaustive): prenatal care; amount and kind of facial and body decoration; characteristic standards of personal grooming; posture, gestures, and general physical bearing; speech patterns; kinds and quality of clothing; type of residence and its location in the community; items of house furnishings and their style; type of occupation for men and type for women (if any); amount and kind of education, and the schools at which it is obtained; patterns of family life, including husband-wife relations and the training of children; religious beliefs, church membership, and amount and kind of participation; taste in reading, radio programs, and other modes of communication; recreational patterns; participation in formal organizations other than school and church; contributions of money and services to civic enterprises; political affiliations and opinions; standards of sexual morality and of interpersonal conduct in general; and funeral customs. The sweep of this incomplete list shows that the term "style of life" is not inappropriate.

It is of course impossible to deal here with the styles of life of all classes in all societies. Some of the more important components of class cultures will be discussed briefly in later sections of this chapter. At this point, however, we shall mention a few examples, as preparation for some rather general remarks about class styles of life.

Miller's description of lower-class culture shows that there are indeed cultural differences from one class to another in our own society, in both "important" and "unimportant" respects. For example, lower-class men are frequently tattooed. To take a more "important" pattern: in the lower class we often find, instead of a stable family consisting of husband and wife and their children, a less stable pattern of "serial polyandry," in which two or more women, often a mother and her adult daughter, live together with the daughter's children by a succession of men. At any particular time, the daughter may also have, or be on the lookout for, a man, not exactly her husband, who lives with her and takes little responsibility for bringing up the children. This pattern, while not regarded as ideal even in the lower class, is a common one, to which many lower-class women know they have to adjust, despite early romantic fantasies of a very different course of events. Miller refers to the pattern as "the female-based household." Not all female-based households are due to this "serial polyandry."

Speech is often somewhat distinctive for a social class:

> The hallmark of the English "cockney" is his distinctive mode of speech. The "old school tie" may well be a hackneyed music-hall joke, but a misplaced "h" is sufficient to betray a man's breeding, his education, his social class [Pieris, 1951, p. 500].

There are more important speech differences between social classes than is indicated by our example. Schatzman and Strauss (1955) made a careful analysis of tape-recorded interviews with persons who had been in or close to areas ravaged by a tornado in Arkansas. From approximately 340 interviews, the investigators selected twenty. Ten were with persons who had not gone beyond grammar school and whose annual family income was less than $2000; these constituted the "lower class" sample. The ten "upper class" interviewees all had had one or more years of college, and all had incomes of $4000 or more. (The "lower class" interviewees in this sample were probably of the lower class in a fairly well-accepted sense, but the so-called upper-class interviewees probably belonged to a stratum that most sociologists would label "middle class." They were "upper" only relative to the lower ten.) All twenty interviewees were adults, white, and native to Arkansas, with more than three years' residence in the community they were in when the tornado struck. All the interviewees were judged to have cooperated well during the interview. Finally, to minimize the effect of interviewers' structuring of the interviewees' accounts, each selected interview contained fewer than eight probes per page (a "probe" is a question the interviewer asks to elicit a clearer or more detailed statement about something the interviewee has said). The two investigators coded the recorded interviews with "virtually perfect" agreement. They found that the upper-class respondents *without exception* presented their accounts in a more highly organized form; seemed to be more aware of the listener's need for orientation that could not reasonably be taken for granted; combined more points of view in their narratives, not confining their accounts to what had happened to themselves; used many more classificatory (abstract) terms, summarizing many particular details; and more often referred to the activities of organizations, with a greater awareness, apparently, of the interrelatedness of diverse activities. At worst, the lower-class respondents were not able to give a coherent account at all: they seemed to forget that the interviewer had not been present at the events described; they seemed unaware of the many frames of reference within which the same events may be viewed and talked about; in their reports, concrete images of actions and persons (often mentioned by name, meaningless to the interviewer) sometimes seemed to "float" dreamlike in the stream of what they said, so that the investigators were hard put to it to make sense of them.

This investigation is of more than passing interest, for it gives us a glimpse of the more subtle reasons for the relative lack of informal intimacy between persons of different social classes. The fact is that the life experience of persons in one social class may be different enough to make comfortable communication impossible with persons of another class. In saying this, we are assuming, of course, that the differences between the upper-class and lower-class respondents were not entirely differences in sheer linguistic ability. Some of them are attributable to the fact that the lower-class respondents spoke from a different background of daily experience (for example, their experience of organizations was different); some to the fact that these respondents undoubtedly were used to speaking in situations in which they could take much for granted, without having to be aware that people are always talking within more or less limited, variable frames of reference. Concerning the "naive" concreteness of their lower-class interviewees, the investigators were reminded of a comment in another research report:

> The lower class is even more concrete in its outlook than the lower-middle class. For example, a question . . . where chewing gum is usually purchased will be answered by an upper-middle person: "At a cashier's counter or in a grocery store." By the lower-middle: "At the National or the corner drugstore." By the lower class: "From Tony" [*Marketing Chewing Gum* . . . , 1950].

We should also note that the general findings of this study of social-class differences in communication patterns are unaffected by the fact that the investigators were themselves middle-class persons and may not have perceived certain organizing principles in the interviews with lower-class persons. Nor are the results affected by the fact that the interviewers also were from the middle class. The fact remains that the investigators were able to understand the so-called upper-class respondents more easily than they could understand the lower-class respondents. An important motive for associating more often and more intimately with one's social equals may be that one is more comfortable doing so. We can see what people mean when they say, "So-and-so speaks my language." The kind of motivation implicit in such a remark is probably more important than snobbery, to which social-class exclusiveness is sometimes unduly attributed.

> It is not snobbery to eschew things or company one finds vulgar (even though they be popular); or to prefer to associate with high status groups or with "highbrow" things. Attachments and slights are snobbish only when spurious and motivated by the wish for prestige, the concern for status and not by a genuine judgment or a true personal preference. Snobbishness always involves status pretension—a wish for unearned reputation—or, at least, exclusive concern with others in status terms [van den Haag, 1956, p. 215].

As we have remarked, the ten persons designated "upper class" by Schatzman and Strauss were "upper" only within the framework of the Arkansas sample; they were probably not members of a social class that sociologists would call "upper" when thinking of the total society. Writing of "genuinely" aristocratic classes, Adam Smith makes the following observation:

> As all his words, as all his motions are attended to, [the young nobleman] learns a habitual regard to every circumstance of ordinary behavior, and studies to perform all those small duties with the most exact propriety. As he is

> conscious of how much he is observed, and how much mankind are disposed to favor all his inclinations, he acts, upon the most indifferent occasions, with that freedom and elevation which the thought of this naturally inspires. His air, his manner, his deportment, all mark that elegant, and *graceful sense of his own superiority, which those who are born to inferior stations can hardly ever arrive at.* . . . These arts, *supported by rank and pre-eminence,* are, upon ordinary occasions, sufficient to govern the world [A. Smith, 1853, p. 75; italics added].

Some patterns in a class style of life are easy to imitate, others are relatively difficult.

> In *Great Expectations* the sensitive and impressionable Pip was humiliated by Estella's slighting remarks: "He calls the knaves, Jacks, this boy! . . . And what coarse hands he has! And what thick boots!" . . . [Pieris, 1951, p. 500].

It would have been easier for Pip, if he had had the money, to change his thick boots and his coarse hands than to change his speech, and, as Adam Smith suggests, it is difficult indeed for the Pips of the world to acquire those many habits of social self-assurance which are said to be not rare among aristocrats. Moreover, some patterns of a class style of life are both difficult to acquire or imitate and also important; for example, education and type of occupation. From these facts it follows that adherence to the various patterns of an admired style of life may have different significance for different persons, depending upon the particular patterns and the total configuration presented by a person who exemplifies them. Adherence to some of the "easy" patterns may be superficial; it may win for the sedulous social climber only ridicule or a precarious acceptance from ignorant people in a few situations. Adherence to other patterns (speech, occupation), though hard won after the formative years of childhood, may win for the ambitious adult a fairly secure place in a higher social class than the one into which he was born. Adherence to still other patterns—for example, whatever is involved in the "graceful sense of [one's] own superiority"—may seem to flow from long and intimate association with "socially superior" people and may therefore betoken a secure upper-class position (membership in some class I core group). Nevertheless, in general we can never draw a firm line between the *criteria* of class position (the marks by which people find one another acceptable or not acceptable and grant or withhold prestige) and the *symbols* of class position (the marks, genuine or spurious, by which people seek to create for others the impression that they belong to a particular social class). In all our social interaction we are forced, to some extent, to judge "reality" from appearances, and even efficiency and moral virtue can sometimes be successfully simulated (Goffman, 1959). For this reason we spoke of prestige as respect and deference commanded by virtue of *imputed* qualities and performances. It is perhaps significant that the word "prestige" comes from a Latin word, *praestigium,* meaning "delusion," "illusion." This remark, however, must not be taken too serously. The impression conveyed in casual contacts is sometimes illusory, no doubt, but illusion is seldom the main basis of the prestige people command from others who know them well.

THE PARTLY ARBITRARY NATURE OF SOCIAL CLASSES

In any society there are so many different bases of prestige that we might wonder whether social classes are definite groups, with definite membership, or whether they are only social categories whose defining characteristics and membership are somewhat arbitrarily determined by sociologists. No sociologist denies the existence of cliques—informal groups of friends who see one another frequently and freely—and there are cliques of families, or at least of couples, as well as of individuals (Warner and Lunt, 1941, pp. 110-12, 350-55). A social class, however, is never so well knit as a clique. It is doubtful whether anyone has defined "social class" so narrowly as to imply that all members of a particular class must even be acquainted with one another. When strangers do meet, however, they appraise signs of each other's style of life, often very quickly, and they decide how much intimacy, and under what circumstances, they will permit each other to have. In widely separated parts of the United States at least, there are cliques whose general styles of life are similar in many respects.

There is also some evidence that marriages do tend to take place between couples very close to each other in style of life. In July 1945, the Office of Public Opinion Research of Princeton University asked a representative cross-section of white males to specify their occupation and the occupation of wife's father. The results of this investigation, given in Tables 12 and 13, show that most marriages do occur between social equals or near-equals. They also show, as we should expect (see pp. 168-69), that more men than women marry "down" (Centers, 1949).[5] (Note, however, that the proportion of men marrying "down" would be smaller if we were comparing occupation of husband's *father* with that of wife's father.)

Other studies support the common-sense impression that social classes, broadly defined in terms of life-styles, tend to be endogamous. Hollingshead, for example, studying the residence areas of New Haven, Connecticut, divided them, according to technical criteria, into six classes, from "best" to "worst." Of all persons married in New Haven in 1948 and still living there in February 1949, 58.2 per cent had come from a residential area of the same class as their spouse. When we include residential areas of adjacent classes, the figure rises to 82.8 per cent. The tendency for marriage and residential class to be associated held good when religion and education were

---

[5] Similar results were obtained in earlier studies—e.g., one by D. M. Marvin, 1918, of marriages contracted in Philadelphia between 1913 and 1916, and one by T. C. Hunt, 1940, of marriages contracted in Norwood, Mass., between 1923 and 1937. The study by Centers is superior to these in that it involves a national sample, covers marriages taking place within a much longer time-span, and compares the occupation of husband with that of wife's *father* rather than with that of *wife*.

TABLE 12

*Urban marriages of urban males, U.S.A., reported 1945 **

Occupational stratum of male	*No.*	*Percentages married to women of various occupational strata (as determined by wife's father's occupation)*						
		BUSINESS EXECUTIVE	PROFESSIONAL	SMALL BUSINESS	WHITE-COLLAR	SKILLED MANUAL	SEMI-SKILLED MANUAL	UNSKILLED MANUAL
Business executive	40	15	15	33	13	20	2	2
Professional	44	7	25	30	2	23	13	—
Small business	78	3	8	40	8	25	10	6
White-collar	88		5	32	23	24	13	3
Skilled manual	81		1	14	9	46	24	6
Semiskilled	85		2	12	8	27	41	10
Unskilled	33			3	12	9	36	40

* Slightly adapted from R. Centers, "Marital Selection and Occupational Strata," *Amer. J. Sociol.*, May 1949, v. 54, p. 6, Table 1, p. 532.

TABLE 13

*Percentages of males married to females of their own or a contiguous occupational stratum, U.S.A., 1945 **

Occupational stratum of male	*Per cent*	*Strata included in each case*
Business executive	30	Business executive and professional
Professional	62	Business executive, professional, and small business
Small business	56	Professional, small business, and white-collar
White-collar	79	Small business, white-collar, and skilled manual
Skilled manual	79	White-collar, skilled manual, and semiskilled
Semiskilled	78	Skilled, semiskilled, and unskilled
Unskilled	76	Semiskilled and unskilled

* Slightly adapted from Centers, 1949, Table 2, p. 532.

held constant. In this study too it was found that men marry "down" more often than women do (Hollingshead, 1950).[6]

Although these studies show that married couples tend to come from the same class, as defined by certain aspects of "style of life," they also show that there are many exceptions. Not all social classes, therefore, can be regarded as *rigorously* endogamous groups. As far as the United States is concerned, the prevalent emphasis on the ideal of romantic love may tend to weaken class endogamy.

Estates

In the Middle Ages and roughly down to the French Revolution, there was in Europe a system of "estates" recognized in law, consisting of the clergy, the nobility, and the people, or commoners. These historical estates had affinities with social classes in at least two respects. Each estate was to some extent characterized by a distinctive style of life; and the three estates were thought of as composing a hierarchy, from the clergy at the top to the commoners at the bottom. Actually, however, the three estates were not a hierarchy of social classes in any acceptable sense. The clergy was called the First Estate only in deference to the medieval idea that the State is subordinate to the Church; although the relative rank and power of Church and State varied at different points in history, on the whole the secular power won out. This fact by itself would not disqualify the estates as social classes, for we might say that ideology simply distorted the facts, that in reality there *were* three classes, but with the *nobility* (including royalty) at the top. Certainly the royal family was at the apex of any national system of prestige, and the rest of the nobility came just below. We could perhaps reconcile with the hierarchy theory the fact that some higher bourgeois (i.e., upper-middle-class commoners) married *high* nobles, and even the fact that almost all the higher clergymen were at the same time nobles. But we can hardly reconcile with this theory the fact that many other clergymen were of far lower social rank than many bourgeois who could in no sense be regarded as nobles-without-titles. Many parish priests were essentially of the same class as the peasants they served. Another reason for not regarding the estates as social classes is that the clergy, being celibate, was not composed of families, the normal units of a social class; it would be stretching our conceptions too far to treat a whole class as composed of "one-member families."[7]

Not only are there nobles without legal titles of nobility; there are also nobles *with* titles who are not members of a predominantly noble social class. It is one thing to count as nobles the persons who have the accredited right to use a title of nobility, and it is another thing to count the persons

[6] The same study showed (as others have) that married couples tend to be alike in age, race, ethnic group, and religion.

[7] For an excellent and vivid treatment of the estate system of France, and a criticism of the use of *estate* as a class concept, see E. G. Barber, 1955.

who actually compose a fairly definite social stratum—exchange hospitality, provide one another with marriage partners, and otherwise treat one another as social equals. In France before World War II, for example, there was a stratum of nobles in the latter sense, but many persons with accredited titles were not members of it, and there were many persons without titles who did belong to it (*notables assimilables*) (Ferré, 1934, p. 144). In general, formal titles of rank do not necessarily reflect accurately the actual social rank of their holders (for an army example, see Goffman, 1959, pp. 28-29).

A further remark about the prewar French nobility will emphasize the fact that "social class" is almost always a matter of an indefinite number of prestige gradations, and any division of a population into definite social strata is somewhat arbitrary. Accredited titles of nobility were not of equal social value. As every reader of Proust knows, the nobility itself punctiliously distinguished between noble families according to the historical origin of their titles. There were (and are) nobles who traced their titles to the *ancien regime*, and among these some were of royal blood and some not. There were other nobles whose titles went back only to the Empire. Those whose ancestors were ennobled in the period from the sixteenth century to the Revolution were distinguished according to whether their ancestors were of nonbourgeois or of bourgeois origin.

Caste

Of societies with rather clearly defined status groupings of families, one of the best examples is India, with its hierarchical system of castes.[8] Each caste has a name, a fairly definite membership, and in many respects a clearly defined style of life. In a broad sense, the term "caste system" as applied to India takes in the main features of the social structure of the society. In the more restricted sense that we adopt here, a caste (*jat* or *jati*) is an endogamous group of families which recognize the degrees of ritual purity and pollution that the Brahmans have rationalized over the centuries. (In Chapter 19 we shall modify this conception slightly when we explain the practice of hypergamy in India, but for the moment we shall do no great violence to the facts if we adopt the narrow definition of caste given above: certainly, in its "ideal" form the *jat* is endogamous.) As far as religion is concerned, castes may differ in the extent to which they participate in Hinduism or retain non-Hindu beliefs and practices that are closely connected with particular tribes. The nature of these beliefs helps to determine the prestige rank of the caste. "Persons who worship the *avatars,* or incarnations of the Absolute Power—Vaishnavites (Vaishnavs), Saivites (Saivas), Buddhists, Christians—are regarded as superior to those who worship nature

---

[8] Unless another source is explicitly mentioned, the main source for our statements on Indian caste is H. C. N. Stevenson's excellent article "Caste (Indian)" in the *Encyclopaedia Britannica,* 1957 printing, v. 4, pp. 977-86.

spirits" (Stevenson, 1957, p. 983). As Stevenson makes clear, such beliefs are less important, however, than practices guided by the pollution concept. The arbiters of both belief and practice are the Brahman priests of high caste. In other aspects of its life as well as religion a caste may have more or less distinctive features. For example, there is great variety in India in forms of the family and rules of descent.

The endogamy of a caste is connected with its prestige rank in the system, for if the issue arises whether or not a caste should amalgamate with another or should split up into two castes, the issue will be decided on the basis of the relative ritual purity of the two castes or the two parts of a caste, and the endogamous group will consist of families whose degree of purity in ritual practices is about the same. One of the main tasks of the caste council (*panchayat*) is judging cases in which the caste *dharma* is alleged to have been broken. The council metes out punishment if this seems necessary to safeguard the purity or other interests of the caste. There are other organizations—for example, village councils and caste associations uniting several castes for specific purposes—but the existence of the *jat* council is another indication of the formal distinctiveness of the social classes we are calling castes.

No one knows precisely how many castes there are in India, in this sense of caste. The number is certainly in the thousands. Despite the fact that endogamy and ritual practice are related, there are many cases of two or more castes roughly equal in prestige rank—that is, in ritual purity (or degree of pollution)—that nevertheless do not compose a single endogamous group. Moreover, there are different castes bearing the same name or similar names but with their centers in different communities. The Brahmans are especially heterogeneous. They do not constitute a single caste, and although the castes at the apex of prestige are Brahman, other Brahman castes are close to the base. It is contrary to the basic ideas of the system to regard all these "Brahmans" as belonging to the same caste, but their heterogeneity is no doubt due in part to caste splits in the past. Some rising schismatic castes have adopted a name of generally higher prestige (at first hyphenating it with their old name, then dropping the old name); other castes have fallen in purity and prestige but have retained a famous name. Little confusion is caused by this similarity in name and disparity in status, since approximately 80 per cent of the population of India live in rather small villages, where the local castes are well known and clearly ranked. The claims made by strangers are investigated if anything important, such as marriage, is involved.

There is no need to repeat here what has been said in our chapters on religion concerning the principles of purity and pollution and their connection with the ranking of occupations and the rules of intercaste behavior ("interdining," touching, avoiding shadows, and the rest). Clearly these rules of intercaste behavior not only manifest the "Hindu pollution concept" (as Stevenson calls it) but indicate the gradations of caste ranking.

Western education, especially British, introduced Western science and democratic ideals (if not always practice) into India. Many Indian leaders have little real sympathy for many Hindu ideas (see Nehru 1946, pp. 12-22). Thus the present independent government of India is attempting reform of the caste system. At the same time, urbanization is making impracticable some of the old rules of avoidance. Industrialization has brought many new occupations.

Yet caste has by no means disappeared, and its future is not altogether certain. Persons who migrate from the villages to the city often abandon the traditional occupations of their castes, but they tend to choose new occupations that are somehow connected with the old and that have, if possible, an equal or higher degree of ritual purity (Niehoff, 1959). Moreover, despite the urban influences that are breaking down some aspects of caste, the rule of caste endogamy is still quite strong. In 1951–52, only nine out of some 2000 married household heads who were interviewed in the metropolis of Bangalore admitted that they had married outside their caste (Gist, 1954). Gist believes that few of the respondents lied about their marriages, but in any case even lying, in an attempt to conceal marriage across caste lines, would have been a tribute to caste endogamy. There can be no question that the rate of marriage between castes is even lower in the villages.

Within a caste there are frequently great differences in wealth and secular prestige. These no doubt affect the choice of marriage partners within the caste. Nevertheless, the ritual prestige (or lack of it) of a person's caste is important for his daily life, and he cannot escape it unless he withdraws into the life of a recluse. No social-class system of Western society has such formalized hereditary, rigorously endogamous, and clearly ranked social classes as the castes of India.

The caste system also shows in extreme form the tendency of social classes to attempt to monopolize certain advantages, often economic. Many of the castes have taken organized action to do this. The social classes of the United States (as distinguished from some kinds of economic class) are hardly organized, if at all, for such purposes. Yet to some extent they have the same effect. We may suppose that "social" preferences easily pass over into business preferences. Social class undoubtedly operates informally to restrict job opportunities, investment opportunities, and opportunities to buy land and houses. Class endogamy tends to keep the rich rich and the poor poor. (There are other factors, of course, which partly counteract the influence of class exclusiveness on economic opportunities.) Finally, we all recognize the fact that, as compared with children born into lower-class families, children born into the upper class have greater opportunities to learn the manners, techniques, and perspectives that are requisite for success in the upper reaches of the occupational hierarchy.

The Ranking of Occupations

A system of social stratification rests in part on a value system. Since performance capacities are among the things valued, we should expect occupation of family head to be an important basis on which families are stratified. The concept of "occupation" as it applies in the United States is more or less appropriate for most modern industrialized societies. As we have seen (Chap. 10), it is less appropriate in many primitive and traditionalistic societies; nevertheless, in every society there is some degree of role differentiation according to function, whether this differentiation is "occupational" in the narrow sense or not. (Indeed, the word "role" is often used to mean function.) It is a striking fact that most attempts to describe the class structure of any particular society place great emphasis on occupation or its equivalent.[9]

One of the best-known attempts to rank occupations in the United States was made by the National Opinion Research Center, using plans made by Paul K. Hatt and Cecil C. North (National Opinion Research Center, 1947, and Hatt, 1950). Interviewers asked a cross-section of the American public in 1947 to rate ninety occupations. After a preliminary explanation, they handed to each respondent a card bearing the words:

> For each job mentioned, please pick out the statement that best gives *your own personal opinion* of the *general standing* that such a job has:
> 1. *Excellent standing.*
> 2. *Good* standing.
> 3. *Average* standing.
> 4. *Somewhat below average standing.*
> 5. *Poor* standing.
>
> X. I don't know where to place that one.

On the basis of replies, North and Hatt gave each occupation a score. The highest score (96) was obtained for the occupation *U. S. Supreme Court Justice,* and the lowest (33), for *shoe shiner*. These are composite scores, taking into account all responses of those interviewed. There was by no means perfect agreement between the interviewees. For example, 83 per cent rated *U. S. Supreme Court Justice* as excellent and 15 per cent as only good. At the other extreme, 13 per cent rated *shoe shiner* as average, 28 per cent as somewhat below average, and 56 per cent as poor.

---

[9] See, among many other examples, Fei Hsiao-T'ung, "Peasantry and Gentry: An Interpretation of Chinese Social Structure and its Changes" (1946); Tomašić, "The Structure of Balkan Society" (1946); Inkeles, "Stratification and Mobility in the Soviet Union: 1940-1950" (1950a); all reprinted in Bendix and Lipset, eds., 1953, pp. 631-50, 622-31, 609-22, respectively. See also R. L. Beals, "Social Stratification in Latin America" (1953); van der Kroef, "The Changing Class Structure of Indonesia" (1956); and Svalastoga *et al.*, "Differential Class Behavior in Denmark" (1956). In no one of these studies is occupation the only focus of concern. In his review of current literature on stratification, Pfautz remarks that "the most popular single criterion of class placement is occupation" (1953, p. 395).

For some occupations fairly large percentages of the respondents felt unable to give a rating since they had too hazy an idea of what the occupational title meant. This was true for *nuclear physicist* (51%), *sociologist* (23%), and *biologist* (16%). Moreover, it turned out that many persons who *had* been willing to rate *nuclear physicist* had a wrong (7%) or a vague (17%) idea of that occupation (cf. Hutchinson, 1957). Finally, different categories of respondent (e.g., from different sections of the country, of different occupations or ages) tended to rate the same occupation differently. Thus the resulting composite rank-order is far from perfect. If it constituted a true scale, then every respondent who ranked *architect* (score value 86), *civil engineer* (84), and *railroad engineer* (77) would have had to rate them at least in that same order, from high to low; but of course this did not happen. Comparing five different studies of the ranking of occupations, Adcock and Brown (1957) found minor discrepancies from one study to another in the ranking of particular occupations, although an occupation ranking high in one study tended in general to rank high in the others. They found no tendency, however, for occupations to be grouped in anything resembling a clear-cut set of social classes.

The North-Hatt rank-order of occupations, obtained in the United States, has been compared with the results of similar investigations made in five other industrialized countries: Great Britain, Germany, U.S.S.R., Japan, and New Zealand (Inkeles and Rossi, 1956). Since these studies were designed somewhat differently, such a comparison has to be made with caution; nevertheless, these results, given in Table 14, do show a remarkable degree of agreement between these six countries in the ranking of occupations. The number of occupations with respect to which any two of the countries could reasonably be compared varied from seven to thirty.

TABLE 14

Correlations between prestige scores (or ranks) given to comparable occupations in six national studies *

	U.S.S.R.	*Japan*	*Great Britain*	*New Zealand*	*U.S.*	*Germany*
U.S.S.R.		.74	.83	.83	.90	.90
Japan			.92	.91	.93	.93
Great Britain				.97	.94	.97
New Zealand					.97	.96
United States						.96
Av. correlation	.84	.89	.93	.93	.94	.94

* A. Inkeles and P. H. Rossi, "National Comparisons of Occupational Prestige," *Amer. J. Sociol.*, Jan. 1956, v. 61, no. 4, p. 332, Table 2. The studies on which this table is based are described and credited to their authors in Inkeles and Rossi. All coefficients are product-moment correlations, with the exception of those involving Germany, which are rank-order coefficients.

Another study reported a rank-order correlation of 0.916 between the ranking of occupations in the British study and the ranking of occupations in São Paulo, which is the center of industrialization in Brazil (Hutchinson, 1957).

PRIMARY FACTORS AFFECTING OCCUPATIONAL PRESTIGE

Each of these studies provides us with a more or less rough *index* of the prestige of various occupations in one or more countries. For the more general theory of social stratification, we must ask what factors affect the prestige of an occupation. The tentative answer given by K. Davis and Moore (1945) and independently by Barnard (1946) apparently goes beyond common sense, for it has aroused a certain amount of controversy (Tumin, 1953; K. Davis, 1953; W. E. Moore, 1953). Two factors seem to account for greater prestige, especially if they are taken together: first, the functional importance of an occupation to the social system in which it is rated; and second, the scarcity of personnel for the occupation relative to demand.

In broad outline, this explanation is easy to accept; in detail, it raises problems. For one thing, many different degrees of talent, knowledge, and skill are often covered by the same occupational title—for example, "engineer." Obviously, therefore, the explanation of prestige in terms of relative functional importance and relative scarcity must be applied, not to concrete occupational categories, but to occupational qualities and performance-capacities viewed more analytically.

Another difficulty must be handled in similar fashion. There are many different positions, or jobs, in the same occupation, and these positions vary in ways that are important for prestige. For example, a "school superintendent" may have a position in a small town or a large city; he may be responsible for a small or a large budget; he may have authority over a small or a large school system; his staff may consist of persons poorly or well trained on the average; and, independently of all these factors, the community he serves may have a small or a high proportion of families high in prestige (Mason and Gross, 1955). To take another example: apart from his technical skill, a doctor is rated to some extent by the average prestige of his patients. In assessing functional importance and scarcity of personnel, one would have to either abstract from particular occupational *positions* of a given category or take their variable aspects into account systematically (These points show once again the crudity of scales used to rate occupations.)

Another difficulty arises from the fact that the same position can be filled with varying degrees of success. Just as we must distinguish between *role* and *role performance,* so we can and must distinguish between the *prestige* of role occupants as such and the *esteem* given to particular role occupants for their particular role performances (K. Davis, 1942a, p. 312).

Even after we have allowed for all these complications, functional importance and scarcity of personnel are still not easy to assess. Relative functional importance is usually easier to appreciate in a small social system than in a total society. If a task is at all complex, certain skills will be indispensable, and others will not be. As far as total societies are concerned. it seems that considerable variation is possible in "functional emphasis" (Davis and Moore, 1945). Most observers would agree that religious functions have relatively higher prestige in India than in the United States. Parsons (1953) has suggested that every society in effect ranks the four functional subsystems that he distinguishes, stressing one above the other three, giving another subsystem second place, and so on. Thus we could imagine a limited number of theoretically possible "profiles," each characterized by a particular rank-ordering of the four functional subsystems. It would be possible, of course, for two of the functional subsystems to be given about equal emphasis. Whether this way of handling the problem of "functional emphasis" will be helpful we do not know yet; much more research will be necessary. We must remember that the functional significance of an activity is not given in a description of the activity itself, and we must also remember that the four functional subsystems distinguished by Parsons are highly abstract. In general, the four functional subsystems are all so important that in every society there are high-ranking occupations in each of them. But the relative emphasis on the four subsystems in any particular society would determine subtle differences in the ranking of occupations. Thus most executive roles would outrank most roles requiring narrow technical skill. but of two executive roles the one whose functions lay in the higher-ranking subsystem would presumably rank somewhat higher than the other.

The relative functional importance of an activity varies from time to time, according to changes in the (internal) structure and (external) circumstances of a social system. One of the most obvious examples of change in external circumstances from the American point of view is the rather sudden emergence of the Soviet Union after World War II as a threat to the security of the United States. The tendency of the world to become polarized around two power centers has made it seem more important whether a particular country can be regarded as a potential ally or not. Therefore the function of diplomacy seems more important than it did earlier. Consequently we find in the United States, in both major political parties, a growing tendency to demand high qualifications for ambassadorships that once were given to amiable amateurs as reward for their financial support in domestic political campaigns.

This example also brings out the fact that prestige can attach to occupations only when their functions are somehow recognized or understood. It is quite possible that at any given moment certain occupations might be overrated or underrated, but occupations are ranked not according to their functional importance in an "absolute" sense but according to their importance in the eyes of men in a particular social system.

The criterion "scarcity of personnel" is not a simple one There are several possible reasons for scarcity of personnel in a given field. Presumably some fields require unusual innate capacities. Scarcity could also be due to the fact that unusual training, in kind or in amount, may be required to gain competence. "Unusual" training is itself a variable. The ability to write is virtually taken for granted in the United States and by itself has no market value, but in Egypt or China it is a marketable skill. A certain kind of training may be scarce because some organization, such as a labor union, restricts entrance to the field. Training may take a long time because the knowledge and skill to be mastered are difficult, but it may take a long time simply because training methods are poor (Froomkin and Jaffe, 1953), or because some organization has made the standard of competence unnecessarily high or the period of training unnecessarily long. According to Goffman (1959), the United States Army during World War II innocently trained pharmacists and watch repairers in six weeks, to the embarrassment of the professionals.[10]

SECONDARY FACTORS

At least three factors have a secondary effect on the prestige of occupations: the average income, the prestige, on other grounds, and the publicity given to those who engage in it.

To some extent, the prestige of an occupation is affected by the average income of those who pursue it. We must remember, however, that a high average income is often due, in part, to the functional importance of the occupation and the relative scarcity of qualified personnel. Since money income is one of the chief rewards of an occupation, we should expect income to be high if personnel are scarce and the function is important. But these are not the only factors that affect the average income of an occupation. Another important factor is the source of remuneration of those who follow a particular occupation. We observed in Chapter 12 that salaries in private business, which of course is run for profit, are on the whole higher than salaries derived from taxes or from philanthropic contributions. Income from fees is often higher than fixed salaries. These differences are to some extent "accidental" in relation to functional importance and scarcity of trained personnel. To some extent, people in the United States recognize the "accidental" character of some high average incomes; that is, people do not regard even the greatest baseball player as more important than the president, despite the fact that the baseball player may have a higher salary. Roughly speaking, income as an independent factor in determining prestige —independent of functional importance and scarcity of personnel—is more

[10] In the business of watch repairing, according to Strodtbeck and Sussman (1956), more skill goes into fooling the customer and, in a high proportion of cases, cheating him than into repairing watches, which has become so utterly routine that very little skill is required for it—a fact that watch repairers carefully conceal from the public.

important within a given occupation than between different occupations. Within an occupation, size of income is only a *rough* index of achievement in role performance.

Another secondary factor affecting the prestige of an occupation is the prestige on other grounds of those who choose it. In the long run, however, we must suppose that the opposite relationship is more important—that men of high prestige (for example, men born into upper-class families) choose certain occupations because these have high prestige.

The very nature of certain occupations requires that the people engaged in them be given unusual publicity, another secondary factor. Politicians who run for office are usually more widely known than government bureaucrats, who are typically appointed to their offices. Public entertainers get more publicity than school teachers. As Bernard Barber (1957) points out, participants in certain other occupations, notably advertising and journalism, are in a good position to give themselves favorable publicity. Whether favorable publicity that is not due to unusual functional importance creates prestige and, if so, to what extent it creates prestige are hard to say. As we shall see below, it is possible for people to be ignorant to some extent of the stratification in their own society; this means, in part, that publicity is not necessarily a very important independent factor in prestige. Most people probably could not name the chief of the Bureau of the Census, yet this personage would be acceptable in quite high social circles.

In a survey conducted by the National Opinion Research Center (1947), respondents were asked, "When you say that certain jobs have excellent standing, what do you think is the *one main* thing about such jobs that gives this standing?" For reasons we have already given, some of the answers can be regarded as essentially nonresponsive to the question. For example, 18 per cent of the respondents said, "The job pays so well"; 14 per cent said, "The job carries social prestige"; and small percentages mentioned other rewards or advantages to those who are engaged in the occupation in question. If we ignore these essentially "useless" answers, however, most of the respondents mentioned the factors that we have singled out as the most important determinants of relative prestige of occupations—namely, functional importance and scarcity of qualified personnel. Such answers are the following: "It serves humanity; it is an essential job" (16 per cent), "Preparation requires much education, hard work and money" (14 per cent), "It requires high moral standards, honesty, responsibility" (9 per cent), "It requires intelligence and ability" (9 per cent).

THE IMPORTANCE OF OCCUPATION FOR SOCIAL CLASS

A rough idea of the importance of occupation for social-class positions may be obtained by comparing names in the *Social Register* with names in *Who's Who in America* (Baltzell, 1953). The *Social Register,* published in twelve volumes, covers fourteen large cities. These cities are important enough in the life of the United States for one to say that the families included in the *Social Register* constitute at least the nucleus and more likely the large majority of the upper class in the country as a whole. The information given for the families listed tells us what some of the criteria of upper-class membership are. The husband's college and class are given. Presumably the class is a helpful indication of age to users of the *Social Register*. Also, achievements, including club memberships perhaps, have to be judged with age in mind. The college is likely to be one of the older Eastern colleges, particularly Harvard, Yale, or Princeton. The husband's clubs are named. The names of the children are given, with the schools or colleges they are attending. The younger children are attending exclusive private schools; the older ones are attending either one of the men's colleges with great prestige or one of a few women's colleges or junior colleges. The address of the family is also given; it is in a fashionable and expensive residence area. Upper-class emphasis on the continuity of family tradition is reflected in the fact that many of the men listed, and many of their sons, bear first and second names that their ancestors have had, so that they are so-and-so II or III. The occupation of the head of the family is not given, but it is important nevertheless, as we shall see. Another important piece of information is given only indirectly; namely, the fact that the family is by no means poor. It may not be very rich, but the probability that it has a good deal more money than the average family is shown in the fact that it can afford to live in an expensive neighborhood, pay high club fees, and send its children to expensive schools and colleges. The fact that the head of the family went to one of the "better" colleges is in itself an indication that his earnings are probably well above average. A national survey of college graduates made in 1947 showed that the median income for graduates of "the big three" (Harvard, Yale, and Princeton) was $7365, as against $4235 for the graduates of "minor" Eastern colleges (that is, colleges other than the big technical schools, the Ivy League colleges, and twenty famous Eastern colleges such as Amherst and Bowdoin) (Havemann and West, 1952, Chap. 15). Many of the *Social Register* families are much better off than these figures indicate.

Unlike some other observers, Baltzell maintains that there is a fairly self-conscious *national* upper class in the United States, the families in which are fairly closely connected with one another, and that the twelve volumes of the *Social Register* give us a fairly good list of its members. His contention is plausible, for, as he points out, the children of these families get to know one another by attending a limited number of schools and colleges and by restricting their dating and courtship circle fairly narrowly to upper-class people. A casual glance at the society columns of the New York *Times* will show that engagements are frequently made between young men and women from widely separated parts of the country.

Whereas the *Social Register* emphasizes acceptability in exclusive "social" circles—as shown above all in club memberships—*Who's Who in America* is primarily a list of people whose occupational achievement has been outstanding. Many of the persons listed are of humble origin, and more of them belong to the upper-middle class than to the upper class. Since *Who's Who* probably overemphasizes certain fields, notably education and the clergy, it is not a perfect index of achievement. Neither is the *Social Register* a perfect index of upper-class membership; in Washington, D.C., for example, all senators are automatically listed (but not all representatives). Nevertheless, these two lists are probably the best indices we have, one to upper-class membership and one to outstanding occupational achievement. It would be interesting, therefore, to ask what the relationship between them is. Roughly speaking, we may assume that the *Social Register* stresses the occupational achievements of past generations while *Who's Who* stresses achievement in the present; some persons now listed in *Who's Who* but not in the *Social Register* will later be reckoned as the "founders" of *Social Register* families (more strictly, of *Social Register* lineages). A study confined to Philadelphia shows, however, that a high proportion of *Social Register* men are also listed in the current *Who's Who* and that these men are prominent in occupations with high prestige and power.

> . . . of the Philadelphians listed in *Who's Who* in 1940, the members of some occupational categories were more likely to be listed in the *Social Register* than those in other categories. One of the functions of upper class solidarity is the retention, within a primary group of families, of the final-decision-making positions within the social structure [as far as possible]. As of the first half of the twentieth century in America, the final-decisions affecting the goals of the social structure have been made primarily by members of the financial and business community. Thus the contemporary upper class in Philadelphia is a business and financial aristocracy. . . . [T]he bankers, lawyers, engineers, and businessmen—the business elite—are more likely to be drawn from the upper class than those persons in other occupational categories. While . . . 75 per cent of the members of the banking elite in Philadelphia are upper class members, the presidents, and over 80 per cent of the directors, of the six largest banking establishments in the city are upper class members. Moreover, of the 532 directorships in industrial and financial institutions reported by *all* the Philadelphians listed in *Who's Who*, no less than 60 per cent are reported by individuals also listed in the *Social Register*. Finally, while 51 per cent of the lawyers listed . . . are upper class members, over 80 per cent of the partners of the six leading law firms in the city are upper class members [Baltzell, 1953, p. 183].

It is extremely unlikely, of course, that the occupational prominence of men in the *Social Register* is due to a concentration of favorable genes in the upper class. Obviously the advantages of upper-class position gave most of them a big head start in any competition that they may have been part of, and many of them hardly had to compete at all for their positions. The present members of the Ford family are no doubt very able, but there was little doubt when they were in the cradle that if they lived long enough they would eventually be in the saddle. Even so, the amount of effort required to learn how to ride and how to stay in the saddle is far from negligible. We are not, however, considering the question of the ultimate justice of things—a question, in any case, to which no objective answer is possible. It is not necessarily "just" that Henry Ford II is president of the Ford Motor Company; he may or may not "deserve" all the prestige he has. It is quite certain, however, that his occupational position is functionally important to the society. We may note, in passing, that what has been said about the relation between personal deserts and the prestige of occupations is equally true, although less obviously so, of the relation between personal deserts and the *esteem* an individual role occupant may have for his particular role performance; for if there are unusual opportunities to get into high positions, there are also advantages by which one may excel in them. Wealth and favorable social contacts are, of course, not the only possible advantages.

The Ranking of Ethnic and Religious Groups

Ethnic groups and religious groups are somewhat like social classes in that they tend to be composed of families; they tend to be endogamous; to some extent they have their own subcultures; they are more than statistical categories, their members being conscious of belonging to status groups at least; in all cases group consciousness and group interests lead to considerable interaction and special organizations among the members, and in some cases the group is fairly well organized; and, finally, groups of each of these kinds tend to be stratified relative to one another in any given society. It is conceivable that a religious group, and especially an ethnic group, might actually be a social class also; more often, however, religious and ethnic affiliations enter into the determination of social-class status but are not decisive criteria by themselves. The main thing that ordinarily precludes our regarding either an ethnic group or a religious group as a distinctive social class is that within a group of either type, unless it is very small, there are sets of families belonging to different social classes within the wider society.

This is notably true of societies that are ethnically relatively homogeneous; in such a society, of course, ethnic-group affiliation could not be a basis of class differentiation. If India were entirely Hindu in the religious sense, it would be an example of a society religiously homogeneous, broadly speaking, but with social classes differentiated on the basis of religious rank. As it is, there are several Moslem castes as well as many Hindu castes. The Moslem castes, however, are Hinduized to the extent that they are conscious of the Hindu pollution concept, in terms of which they are ranked in the caste system as a whole.

In the United States there is considerable intermarriage between the main religious groupings—Protestants, Catholics, and Jews—but these broad religious groupings are so nearly endogamous that each of them constitutes something like a separate class hierarchy of its own, if we stress lack of connubium as the basis for differentiating classes. With respect to intimate social interaction apart from courtship, the situation is more complex, but it is clear that many social clubs restrict their membership to persons of one religious group. Some of these religiously homogeneous social clubs also confine their membership to social equals.

However, if in our conception of social class we play down endogamy and intimate social interaction and emphasize *style of life,* then our characterization of the American system will have to be different, for clearly there are large subgroups of Protestants, Catholics, and Jews all of whom have the same style of life (apart from religion).

There are some ethnic groups, however, that have a tenacious separateness roughly comparable to that of the three broad religious groups. These are the ethnic groups that are highly visible as such because of their relatively distinctive "racial" characteristics. The most important example in the United States is the large group of Negroes, but there are others—for example, Mexicans, others of Indian ancestry, Puerto Ricans, Chinese, and Japanese. If a group is "racially" distinct to any great extent, we may assume that it was once culturally distinct also, although it may no longer be. As contacts between different racial groups become more frequent and extensive, their culture can and often does change more rapidly than the "racial" traits that separate them. Thus American Negroes are more Negroid in appearance than they are African in culture. Culturally, their distinctiveness as a group has very little to do with Africa—partly because whatever African cultural traits have been retained have been widely diffused among the whites and have fused with American culture in general. Yet racial visibility remains important in social interaction.

There are at least two fundamental reasons for this fact. The first is that racial traits acquire a kind of emotional value as powerful symbols of good and bad (see Chap. 4). The second reason shows once again the similarity between ethnic groups and social classes. If an ethnic group has ranked low in a particular society, and if it is to any extent physically distinctive ("visible"), then these physical or so-called racial traits will continue to mark out their possessors as of low social origin whatever their qualities and achievements may be at present. Thus, to the extent that a racial group as a whole tends to have a low status, all those who can be identified with it share in that low status even if they as individuals have been culturally assimilated and are superior by accepted cultural standards. It is as if the two racial groups lived together in a small town and the dominant racial group regarded the socially inferior one as just one big clan; however much individuals from that clan stand out as individuals, the dominant group cannot forget that they still belong to the "low" clan.

From the foregoing broad remarks about resemblances between ethnic groups and religious groups, we turn now to a few more details about ethnic groups in particular.

ETHNIC GROUPS

Wherever different ethnic groups come in contact, there seems to be a tendency for one of them to establish dominance over the others. In fact, as far as ethnic groups are concerned, the distinction between dominant group and subordinate groups is probably more important sociologically than the distinction between majority and minority. In referring to ethnic groups, many sociologists use the term "minority" to mean subordinate group, without necessarily implying that the subordinate group is less numerous than the dominant group.

The subordination of some ethnic groups to others is by no means confined to the United States. It is not too much to say that it occurs, with varying intensity, on every continent and in virtually every country of any great size. The past and present colonial societies of Asia, Indonesia, Africa, and Latin America are good examples. India prides itself on its lack of ethnic-group prejudice, but we must remember that Indian tolerance, such as it is, is the product of a long process of assimilation, in the earlier stages of which ethnic-group domination and subordination were not lacking. Moreover, the many tribes that have a low position because of religion are in effect separate ethnic groups in the process of assimilation. Other countries in which ethnic-group prejudice is sometimes supposed not to exist will be found on closer scrutiny to have some after all. This is true, for example, of Brazil (see Willems, 1949, but also Bastide and van den Berghe, 1957), of the rest of Latin America (see Beals, 1953), of Jamaica (see Broom, 1954), of Haiti (see G. E. Simpson, 1941), and of Hawaii (see Marden, 1952).

Relations between ethnic groups thus tend to assume an ingroup-outgroup character. Ethnocentrism, greed, hostility, and fear on the part of the dominant group manifest themselves in exploitation, discriminatory practices in competition, and enforced assimilation. The intensity of ethnocentrism, greed, hostility, and fear varies with many other variables. Some of the more important are the extent of visibility, the nature of initial contacts between the groups (relatively friendly and cooperative, or the reverse), the rate of influx of a minority over time, the degree to which the minority is dispersed or concentrated, the relative size of the minority and the dominant group, whether the minority is ethnically related to a friendly nation or a hostile nation or no other nation, and the extent to which the minority attempts to compete economically with the dominant group. In Chapter 21 we shall deal briefly with two other phenomena that are relevant to the degree of hostility and fear the dominant group may have toward the minority.

In short, there is abundant evidence of "unfair" treatment of ethnic minorities. The process of assimilation may have ups and downs. And the intensity of prejudice probably never diminishes in a straight line. The factors that determine it are themselves too erratic. If we could control all these factors, however, we should probably find that a minority is more nearly accepted as equal the closer its culture approximates that of the dominant group. Because of discrimination against them, minorities are often objectively inferior to the dominant group in many ways. But the negative attitude that the dominant group has toward minorities is not simply the product of unfair discrimination. For example, the dominant language of the United States is English, and the Puerto Ricans who come to New York in many cases speak objectively inferior English. They are to this extent objectively inferior by American standards. Unfair discrimination, strictly speaking, occurs when members of a minority are refused equal treatment even though they do compare favorably in culture from a dominant-group point of view.

Somewhat distinctive ethnic-group cultural patterns, including patterns of socializing children, are known to affect chances for upward mobility (Lipset and Bendix, 1959, pp. 255-56). Groups such as the Japanese and the Chinese are trained to respect learning, endure relative privation, and work hard toward distant rewards. American Jews whose ancestors came from eastern Europe have had a higher rate of mobility than American Italians whose ancestors came from southern Italy. Comparatively speaking, the Jews show more interest in individual rather than group credit, are more likely to believe that by rational planning people can control their destiny, and are more ambitious (less easily satisfied in occupational achievement) (see also Strodtbeck, McDonald, and Rosen, 1957). Jews in America and Scots in the British Isles tend to have relatively high intelligence-test scores "regardless of what social factors are controlled" (Lipset and Bendix, 1959, p. 255)—that is, presumably, regardless of what gross factors, such as amount of education and wealth of family, are controlled. Both the Jews and the Scots have a great drive for learning, which seems to be related to their interest in religious education. When the Anglo-Saxon Americans encountered the French-speaking Creoles in New Orleans, the Americans fairly soon achieved dominance although the Creoles were originally in power there. The aristocratic Creoles, who stressed hereditary wealth, were no match for the brash Americans whose "sun god [was] the self-made man" (Gilmore, 1944). Similarly, in Hawaii the native Hawaiians are culturally easygoing and therefore are no match, on the average, in competition with the Chinese and Japanese, to say nothing of the *haoles,* the whites in Hawaii (whose dominance, however, rests partly on more or less suave discrimination). The Mexicans are commonly exploited in the United States, but their low position and slow rise are due in part to cultural handicaps for which discrimination is not responsible.

Assimilation is accompanied by a higher rate of upward mobility for the minority. However, the fact that the dominant group and other groups assimilated earlier have a head start means that the ethnic minority will tend to remain toward the base of the class structure for some time.

The tendency for ethnic groups as such to be roughly ranked was shown in the Yankee City research conducted by W. L. Warner and P. S. Lunt (1941, p. 225, Table 7). The dominant ethnic group in Yankee City is the Yankees, whites of Anglo-Saxon ancestry, who are also Protestants. Warner and Lunt identify nine other ethnic groups and six social classes.

> From the viewpoint of the ethnic composition of each class, we find that the upper-upper class is the only one which is homogeneous, comprising only natives [Yankees: some members of the other ethnic groups were also native Americans]. The lower-upper, on the other hand, includes a few Irish [but no other members of minorities]. In the upper-middle class, all ethnic groups save the two most recent ones and the Negroes have a representation. The lower-middle class and the upper-lower include members of every ethnic group except the Negroes. In complete contrast to the top class in the society, the lower-lower contains members of every ethnic group to be found in the city [p. 224].

This quotation also illustrates the point that, at least in the United States, an ethnic group is not a social class, although it is similar in some ways.

RELIGIOUS GROUPS

In a San Joaquin Valley town, Goldschmidt (1944) found nine relatively large religious groups. In keeping with the universalistic character of an ecclesia, the Roman Catholic Church cuts across the social strata of the town. The Protestant denominations and sects are more differentiated according to social class. If the population of the town is categorized according to occupation, we find that five different occupational ranks are unequally represented in the eight Protestant groups. The Congregational church, at the "top," has the largest proportion of professionals, managers, and entrepreneurs (about 50 per cent of the membership); a tiny proportion of unskilled laborers; and, in between, somewhat larger proportions of farm operators and managers, clerks and other white-collar workers, and skilled laborers. At the other end of the range, the Pentacostal sect has no professionals, managers, entrepreneurs, or farm operators and managers at all; about 80 per cent of its members are unskilled laborers. Two other groups have no professionals, managers, or entrepreneurs, but more farm operators and managers, and more skilled laborers. It is possible, therefore, to rank the eight Protestant groups from predominantly upper class to predominantly lower class, as follows: Congregational, Methodist, Baptist, Seventh-day Adventist, Nazarene, Assembly of God, Church of God, and Pentacostal. By this criterion of occupational distribution of members, the Roman Catholic Church in this town has about the same rank as the Seventh-day Adventist group. The lower-ranking individual members of the Roman Catholic parish are Mexican unskilled laborers; but it is significant that, according to the priest in charge, they do not attend the card parties and socials in the parish church. In other words, the Catholic group is differentiated within itself according to class, while the Protestant groups are differentiated not only each within itself but also, to some extent, one from another.

Our information about the class composition of the chief religious groups in the United States as a whole is not very extensive. Moreover, the social prestige of any particular denomination varies somewhat from one part of the country to another. In large cities, where a large denomination may have several congregations, there may be a tendency for these congregations to vary in the average social-class rank of their members. Informal class segregation is made possible, without Christian embarrassment, by the fact that social class and place of residence within the city tend to be associated. We may assume, moreover, that within a very large denomination, such as the Southern Baptist Convention (with nearly eight million members), there are undoubtedly some congregations close to the lower-class sect type as well as congregations more denominational in tone. The prevailing tone of a particular congregation would reinforce the influence of relative convenience of location. As we have noted, when a congregation becomes denominational in tone, the sectarians tend to drop out.

These points should be borne in mind in the interpretation of Table 15, which shows the class composition of religious bodies in the United States. In other breakdowns of the same data (L. Pope, 1948), on the relation between religious affiliation and (1) education, (2) occupation, and (3) voting, we find that Congregationalists, Episcopalians, and Presbyterians do not maintain the same rank order relative to one another but always rank first, second, or third. The Methodists are in fifth position in all four lists.[11]

The relatively low average social-class position of Catholics in the United States is due, of course, to the fact that the majority of Catholics here are descendants of recent immigrants. In France, for centuries a predominantly Catholic country, the degree of observance is associated with social-class position: in general, the higher the class, the more strongly it supports the Church. Some Catholics are devout (Mass every Sunday, regular confession); some are Easter Catholics, so to speak; some are indifferent; and some are hostile to the Church. There are so many possible religious observances that many degrees of adherence can be distinguished.

The rigor of Catholic observance in France depends upon many things besides class position. Local traditions, the presence of a monastery, the attitude of local notables, the degree of isolation from new currents of thought—all these affect the religious tone of a particular area. Nevertheless,

---

[11] The order of the eight religious groups with respect to educational attainment was exactly the same as the order with respect to social class generally. The data on occupation are too ambiguous to reproduce here. Voting preferences are influenced by many factors that vary within the same broad social class, but the data given by Pope bear out the general impression that the Republican Party is the preferred party of the upper groups, while the Democratic Party is the preferred party of the minorities and lower-class voters. The Methodists, in an intermediate position, were divided almost perfectly: 38 per cent for Dewey and 37 per cent for Roosevelt in 1944. We should note, however, that all these statistical associations, including that between religious group and social class, change considerably even in short periods of time. No one should take the exact figures given in this section too seriously.

TABLE 15

Class composition of religious bodies, 1945-46 (per cent distribution) *

Body	*Upper class*	*Middle class*	*Lower class*
ENTIRE SAMPLE	13	31	56
Congregational	24	43	33
Episcopalian	24	34	42
Presbyterian	22	40	38
Jewish	22	32	46
Methodist	13	35	52
Lutheran	11	36	53
Catholic	9	25	66
Baptist	8	24	68

* Slightly adapted from L. Pope, "Religion and the Class Structure," *Annals Amer. Acad. Polit. Soc. Sci.*, March 1948, v. 256, pp. 84-91, Table 2, as reproduced in M. L. Barron, ed., 1957, p. 356. The data were derived from four polls taken by the American Institute of Public Opinion in 1945-46, covering approximately 12,000 cases. Each poll covered a "voting sample" of approximately 3,000 cases. These polls were probably not exactly representative of religious groups. "Further, classification of interviewees into social classes generally rests on rather superficial and subjective methodology; in most cases, the interviewer makes the classification in terms of general impressions as to the type of neighborhood, occupation, house furnishings, dress, and so on" (Pope, 1948, p. 355 n. 3, in Barron's pagination).

broadly speaking, the evidence seems clear that the most important single determinant of the strength of religious attitudes in France has been social-class position or closely associated economic interests.

During the eighteenth century both the nobility and the bourgeoisie were becoming more and more critical of religion and therefore less strict in religious observance. After the Revolution, the bourgeoisie continued to fall away, but the nobility, finding in the Church an ally against the revolutionaries, became more pious. After the early revolutionary stage of repression of the established religion, the workers and peasants (the *peuple*) also returned to the Church. But as the doctrines of socialism and class struggle spread, toward the end of the nineteenth century, the bourgeoisie tended to grow more faithful, more like the nobility, and the urban workers moved in the opposite direction. During the twentieth century, the rural masses have been gradually becoming less strict in observance and therefore closer to the urban workers. With the strictures mentioned above concerning the multiplicity of factors that affect religious attitudes in France, we can say roughly that the propertied classes have been strong supporters of the Church in recent decades, while the classes without property have been either indifferent or hostile. The Communists in particular are the nucleus of the hostile group (Le Bras, 1942, v. 1, pp. 108-09; 1945, v. 2, pp. 62-65, 145-46).

Indicators and Indices of Social Class

Obviously it is very difficult to study social classes directly by observation. One has to investigate the complex networks of informal relations between families, study the meaning of social gestures of all kinds to see whether or not they imply equality, note the marriages that occur and ask what social characteristics of brides and bridegrooms made them possible. This last question is part of a broader question that would have to concern the investigator; namely, what are the systems of values, avowed and unavowed, that seem to underlie the various degrees and kinds of social intimacy observed? To put the same question in another form: what criteria are people evidently following in accepting and rejecting one another socially?

Since this kind of investigation is extremely time-consuming, it is desirable to have some indicator or index that will enable the investigator to place families in the class structure quickly. An index, to be of use, has to be fairly simple. It also has to be reliable (which means that different persons using it will come up with the same results). And it should be valid (which means that the results obtained by using it are fairly close to those one would obtain by making a detailed investigation of the phenomena in question). The validity of an index is a complex matter. It involves clear definition of concepts. For example, there are different meanings of "class." An indicator or an index (combination of indicators) that might satisfactorily indicate a stranger's class in the Marxist sense might or might nor serve equally well to indicate his class in the sense we have intended. Indicators and indices cannot be validated—that is, one cannot determine whether they are valid—unless one knows what they are to be valid for.

But here another difficulty arises. In validating an index, one gathers evidence to show to what extent the results obtained by using it are correlated with the more complex, less easily observed phenomena to which it is supposed to be an index. In the process of validation, however, one necessarily gathers only a sample of all the relevant evidence. Therefore one can easily make a mistake in assuming that an index valid for some tested range of application would be equally valid outside that range.

An early attempt to devise an index of social class was cleverly based on the assumption that the various items in a family's living room would be correlated with its prestige standing in the community, style of life, and participation with others in various activities (Chapin, 1933). The presence or absence of a certain item in a living room was given a weighted numerical value, and the total score for the family indicated its class position. For example, a hardwood floor was given a value of 10 whereas a softwood floor received only 6. The resulting index was easy to use and reliable. It was validated by studying samples of families in Minneapolis. One of the questions raised about such indices, however, is whether they will be equally valid when used in another place and another time. In general, any indicator or index of social class would have to be revised from time to time and validated by checking a sample of the population in which it is to be used (see Lazarsfeld and Rosenberg, eds., 1955).

"SUBJECTIVE" AND "OBJECTIVE" INDICATORS AND INDICES

Indicators and indices of social class are usually described as either "subjective" or "objective." The self-rating indicator, which may be "open-ended" or "closed," is an example of the subjective type. In so-called open-ended self-rating, the respondent states what social class he thinks he is in, without having been asked to choose from a list of named possibilities.[12] In the "closed" approach to self-rating, the respondent is presented with a list of social classes and asked to state which of them he belongs to. In both types of self-rating, the answer may be treated as an indicator of the respondent's social class. A defect of these methods is that the investigator cannot be sure that two respondents mean the same thing if they say they belong to "the middle class." As Rogoff says, people place themselves in relation to different reference groups (1953, p. 352). N. Gross (1953) gave two different closed questions to the same sample of respondents in Minneapolis and obtained different results. When the respondents were asked to choose from among four classes (middle class, lower class, working class, and upper class), 42 per cent said they belonged to the middle class; but 76 per cent of the same respondents said they belonged to the middle class when they were asked to choose from among three classes (upper class, middle class, and lower class). Before being asked either of these closed questions, the same respondents had been asked an open-ended question about the class they belonged to: the results of this question were different still; 31 per cent spontaneously said that they belonged to the middle class.

Is there any value to self-ratings? As Gross points out (1953, p. 403), self-ratings in answer to open-ended questions give us a clue to class self-consciousness. If the differences are small between answers to open-ended questions and answers to closed questions, this is evidence of a kind that the class structure or part of it is relatively clear-cut. In France, for example, members of the peasant class, which is rooted in tradition, probably are aware of their membership (see Rogoff, 1953). It is probably better to treat self-ratings as evidence concerning the class structure as a whole than as an indicator of the classes to which individual respondents actually belong. That is, the investigator can ask people not only to place themselves but to state on what basis they do so, how many classes they think there are in the society (or local community), and how these classes differ. The answers to these questions provide one kind of evidence concerning the class structure.

Another short-cut method of "placing" families in social classes is to

---

[12] A somewhat different version of the open-ended question is described in Hetzler, 1953.

ask persons in the community to rate the families they know personally or by reputation. Here again, the judges can be given an open-ended or a check-list (closed) question, and the objections to either procedure are similar to the objections that can be made to self-rating. If several judges are asked to rank the same families but are not told how many ranks they are to distinguish, they do not agree concerning the total number of classes; consequently they do not agree in the exact placing of particular families (see, e.g., Hollingshead, 1949, p. 30). Lenski (1952, p. 142) found, in his study of Danielson, Connecticut, that the few judges who did agree on the number of classes disagreed on their relative size, as they indicated by assigning different numbers of families to, say, the third class down. When judges are given a frame of reference, their agreement is a little better. Hollingshead (1949) asked his thirty-seven raters or judges to tell everything they knew about the families included in his total sample of 535. The raters were also asked to compare each of the families they knew in the sample with twenty families in a "control list," indicating which of the control families the sample family most closely resembled in social rank. Hollingshead had previously decided that there were five social classes in Elmtown and he had selected for the control list well-known families that were representative of all five classes. The class of each family in the control list had been determined to the investigator's satisfaction. Consequently the thirty-seven raters were classifying the sample families into five classes without knowing it. Their agreement was not perfect, but it was high. A particular family was placed in one of the five classes by averaging the ratings of all judges who had rated it.

In a later study, two sociologists familiar with New Haven (Hollingshead and J. K. Myers) acted as raters of the sample families, using as a basis the information contained in a 200-item interview schedule. Each family was placed independently by the two sociologists into one of five classes. When they disagreed in placing a family, the extent of their disagreement was never greater than a difference of one class: in other words, if Hollingshead placed the family in Class III, Myers might place it in Class II or in Class IV. However, there was perfect agreement in 96 per cent of the cases (Hollingshead and Redlich, 1958, p. 389).

Self-ratings and ratings by community judges are sometimes called "subjective" indicators mainly because the criteria used by the raters are not clear-cut. (They might also be called subjective for a quite different reason; namely, that they depend on attitudes existing in the population being studied, rather than on attitudes of the observer, which are "objective." The ratings of Hollingshead and Myers were both subjective and objective in this sense.) The basis of self-ratings is only as subjective (in the sense of vague) as the investigator permits it to be. It would be theoretically possible for the respondents to be given exact instructions for rating themselves. This would be impractical, however, since the instructions would have to be so complex that the investigator might as well make his own ratings in the first place.

So-called objective indicators and indices of social class include such things as amount of education, size of income, rental value of house, and occupational category. Hollingshead and Myers devised an objective index after using a subjective one (see Hollingshead and Redlich, 1958).

OTHER QUESTIONS ABOUT INDICATORS AND INDICES

The basic purpose of an indicator or an index is to enable us to predict something with a certain degree of probability and with relative dispatch. One of the questions that some investigators therefore ask about an indicator or an index is: By using it what can we predict? It is possible to forget about the complex concept of "social class" entirely and try to find out, for example, what behavior or other characteristics can be predicted, with what rate of success, if we know the amount of someone's income, the number of years he attended school, or what category his occupation falls in. It is possible that income is a better indicator of some things than education is, but that education is a better indicator for certain other things. Haer (1957) studied the relative predictive power of five indicators or indices: (1) the answers to the question, "If you were asked to use one of these names for your social class standing, which would you say you belong to: the middle class, lower class, working class, or upper class?"; (2) answers to the open-ended question "Which social class are you in?"; (3) occupation (U. S. Census classification); (4) education (twenty-three categories); and (5) Index of Status Characteristics (an index of social class devised by W. L. Warner, in which a total score is obtained for certain weighted items; namely, type of occupation, dwelling area, house type, and source of income). These indicators or indices were compared for their power to predict twenty-two variable forms of behavior or attitudes—e.g., total amount of participation in voluntary organizations, frequency of church attendance, listening to news broadcasts, travel outside the United States, accuracy of information about a Supreme Court case in which a decision was pending.

The results of this research tend to show the superiority of an index over an indicator. The Index of Status Characteristics (no. 5 in the series above) was superior to all the others in eighteen of the twenty-two comparisons. Occupation (no. 3) was superior to all the others in one comparison; namely, attitude toward possible results of the Supreme Court decision on desegregation. The best *indicator* was education (no. 4), which was second to ISC in twelve comparisons.

Another question that is gaining attention is the effect of inconsistency in status characteristics. There is a broad tendency for people with higher education to have higher-ranking occupations and to live in higher-ranking neighborhoods. It is interesting to ask in what other ways, if any, people are different, on the average, if they have higher education, for example, but have a relatively low-ranking occupation and live in a relatively low-ranking neighborhood. The study of such questions is still rather new, and the results are somewhat controversial, but the field appears to be promising (see Lenski, 1954; Broom, 1959).

The Usefulness of the Concept of Social Classes

In our consideration of social class, we have stressed three things: (1) hierarchies of values in terms of which individuals and families are judged and may be roughly grouped according to rank; (2) the expression of values in a more or less comprehensive and integrated style of life for each class, with some values central and others peripheral; and (3) actual and potential intimate social interaction that is symbolic of mutual acceptability as social equals or near-equals. In all these respects, the lines between social classes are not sharply drawn. In any complex society there are likely to be various hierarchies of values, not just one. There are many components of a style of life, and it is doubtful whether any two families may be said to have exactly the same style of life. Finally, there are many kinds and degrees of intimacy, and the extent to which individuals and families consciously identify with any group that might be called a social class varies considerably, both within a particular society and from one society to another. For these reasons, many sociologists deny the objective existence of social classes.

Some sociologists regard the actual social ranking of families as a continuum rather than a hierarchy of discrete strata. We have given reasons for holding the opinion that any conception of a society as a single pyramid with a definite number of steps is to some extent arbitrary. The conception of a continuum, however, is equally arbitrary. If social class is conceived of as a matter of style of life, of ranking, and of the possibility of intimate social interaction, then obviously the class structure is not a continuum such as the theoretical distribution of the population according to height or age. The reason is that the class structure is not a matter of variation in a single dimension, and the several dimensions in terms of which we characterize it do not vary exactly together. This fact we shall confirm in more detail below.

There are several reasons for finding out and emphasizing the *degree* to which social classes actually exist. Social-class consciousness, a common way of life, and intimate social interaction—the things that at least tend to transform a social class from a statistical category into a social group—imply relative ease and frequency of communication, and they can facilitate joint action for a common cause. This fact is probably continuously important, as we shall see in Chapter 19. At the moment, however, we wish to stress the importance of class cohesion in the type of situation with which Marxist theory deals.

The Marxist conception of class is not exactly the same as the one we have been discussing. Briefly, it differs from ours in its relatively greater emphasis on the "objective" basis of class in a common economic position, and on the inherent conflict of interest between different classes. For example, wage earners in modern capitalist society constitute a Marxist-type class in the sense that they all have essentially the same place in the system of production—they do not own the tools of production and they are all selling their strength and their relatively small degree of skill in return for the same type of income, namely wages. Moreover, they have an objective common interest in raising their income, and this interest brings them into objective conflict with capitalists (those who own the means of production), who would like to keep the wage level down. These two classes are only particular historical examples—in other times and places, in which different systems of production prevail, classes would be based on somewhat different economic interests, and the nature of the class struggle would be somewhat different. In general, however, there tends to be conflict between those with property and those without (that is to say, between those whom the existing institution of property protects and those whom it essentially keeps relatively deprived). In a sense the two main classes in capitalist society objectively exist whether or not the members of them fully understand the situation (are aware of both the community and the conflict of interest); but at the same time these classes are not fully developed, and their mutual opposition cannot have its full effects in history, until the members of each class are conscious of their membership and their common cause, and on the basis of this class consciousness organize to struggle against the common enemy, the other class. In general, class consciousness is important for all class struggles.

The foregoing statement of Marxist theory is inadequate and perhaps misleading, in particular because it does not convey fully the sense in which Marxist theorists regard class struggles as the main instruments and vehicles of institutional change. From a Marxist point of view, it is wrong to think that the class struggle in capitalist society is a mere effort on the one side to keep wages low and on the other side to force them higher. As time goes on, many changes take place in the factors of production. For example, the size of the population changes, some natural resources become depleted and others are discovered, and science and technology advance and make new productive processes possible. According to Marxist theory, a time comes when the existing institutional order underlying the whole system of production, and in particular the existing institution of property, must be changed if the potentialities for greater production are to be realized; moreover, the existing institutional order gradually ceases to serve the needs of the population even as well as it has in the past. According to this theory, the propertied class, which was once the bearer of fruitful innovation, is now merely defending its vested interests and resisting the changes that would be desirable. Meanwhile the relatively disadvantaged class or classes become more and more acutely aware of their common interest in putting down the ruling class and changing the institutions of society—the institution of property in particular but not only that. Thus the class struggle eventually becomes a struggle between those whose interest is in changing social institutions and those whose interest seems to lie in resisting such change.[13]

To Marxists, there is a kind of inevitable progress in history, one set of classes in one system of production giving way to a more progressive system of production with a different set of classes, and so on, until the culmination of the whole process of history in the classless communist society of the future, the attainment of a secularized Kingdom of God on earth. It is not necessary to accept Marxist evaluations, the Marxist conception of inevitability, the conception of conflict as the basic relation between social classes, or the conception of class struggle as *the* key to institutional change or even to revolution. However, there have been societies in which division of sentiment concerning the justice of social arrangements has gone so far as to produce civil war and revolution. In such struggles, relatively cohesive social classes, in the broader sense we began with (not in the narrower Marxist sense), help to develop the solidarity of each side and widen the gulf between the two sides. Marx considered the question of what factors tend to produce class consciousness (in the Marxist sense of class, which may be provisionally called "economic class"). One of the most important conditions for the growth of class consciousness in this sense is easy and frequent communication between those whose objective economic situations are similar. Among the factors that facilitate such communication is the tendency toward *social*-class formation. As we showed earlier, members of the same social class "speak the same language."

Lest this whole train of thought be misunderstood, we should state explicitly that conflict between social classes is not always—probably not usually—the most important aspect of their mutual relations. It is certainly possible for a stratified society to be fairly well integrated—for the various strata to accept the same basic standards of evaluation and to regard as just, in the main, the actual ranking of families. When this is true, the chief kind of relation between social classes is cooperation. Not every stratified society is on the brink of revolution.

The first reason, then, for noting tendencies toward social-class formation in the ranking of families is that in certain conditions these tendencies

---

[13] Karl Marx never worked out his theory of social class and class struggles in detail. Partly for this reason, the theory is rather vague in important respects. Our brief exposition would not be a fair statement if the object were to criticize the theory. It will serve our present purpose, however, which is to indicate that in situations broadly similar to the ones Marx contemplated tendencies toward social-class cohesion and division between classes on the basis of style of life, if they happened to coincide to any great extent with conflicting interest groups, could contribute to the development of a revolutionary movement. For this rather general point, the controversy over details of Marx's theory is not important. For a more detailed account of the Marxist conception of classes, see Bendix and Lipset, "Karl Marx' Theory of Social Classes," in Bendix and Lipset, eds., 1953, pp. 26-35.

can be divisive. The second reason is that under other conditions the same tendencies can contribute to the integration and efficiency of society. (We shall develop this point in Chap. 19.) The third reason for emphasizing the group or quasi-group character of social classes is that it is convenient to do so. The conception of distinct groups is accompanied by the conception of subcultures. Even if few families perfectly exemplified "lower-class culture" ("style of life"), the concept would still be valuable as an ideal type. Social workers, policemen, school teachers, missionaries, psychiatrists, and others who need practical understanding of the culture of the people they are trying to help would not find it useful to be told that every family is culturally unique (even though this is true in a sense). On the other hand, it would be useful to have a small set of carefully formulated descriptions ("profiles") of class cultures—provided, of course, that one recognized the tentative and approximate character of such descriptions and did not make stereotypes of them.[14] Although brief, such descriptions could warn against stereotyping by indicating ranges of behavior and belief as well as averages or modal forms. Moreover, descriptions of class cultures (subcultures of the society) could be adjusted to the particular purposes for which they are to be used; policemen, clergymen, and psychiatrists might need to be aware of somewhat different aspects of a class culture.[15] Finally, since such descriptions would admittedly be simplifications for practical purposes, it would be possible to treat the class structure of a small community or of a single city to some extent as if that place were a self-contained society; the "upper class" of Prairieville might be "lower middle" or "upper middle" in the country as a whole, but the point would not be vital for practical purposes if the scope of any description is indicated.[16] A descrip-

---

[14] For examples of ideal-typical descriptions of social classes, see Warner and Lunt, 1941, Chaps. 20-22 (six classes in "Yankee City," a New England town, pop. 17,000; data for 1930-34); Davis, Gardner, and Gardner, 1941, Chaps. 4-6 (three white classes in "Old City," a Deep South town, pop. 10,000; data for 1936); Drake and Cayton, 1945, Chaps. 19-22 (three Negro classes in "Bronzeville," the Negro section of Chicago, Ill.; time, about 1940); Hollingshead, 1949, Chap. 5 (five classes in "Elmtown," a Midwestern town of 6,000; data for 1941-42); and Hollingshead and Redlich, 1958, Chap. 4 (five classes in New Haven, Conn.; time, about 1950). Kahl, 1953, using six variables (personal prestige, occupation, possessions, interaction, class consciousness, and value orientations), gives profiles of six American classes; his data are drawn from various sources.

[15] See, for a good example, W. B. Miller, "Implications of Urban Lower Class Culture for Social Work" (1959a).

[16] This does not mean that for all purposes the place of a community in the larger society can be neglected. For example, the class structure of the society as a whole misleadingly seems static if one neglects to consider the fact that many persons migrate to larger cities from small communities and improve their class position. As we have pointed out, small communities also tend to emphasize ancestry and length of residence as criteria for ranking families much more than larger communities do. The work of W. Lloyd Warner and his associates has been criticized for neglecting these limitations of study of small communities, as well as for other methodological defects. See especially Kornhauser, 1953, pp. 224-55. Hochbaum *et al.*, 1955, have shown that the variables considered by Warner are not interrelated in Minneapolis (a 1948 sample) in the same way they are in "Jonesville" (the same Midwestern town of 6,000 that

tion intended to be valid for a whole society would have to give great attention to the ranges of behavior and belief.

Allison Davis (1946) provides us with a good example of a brief description of a social class, the "lower lower" class of Chicago. ("Lower lower" is the term that many or most American sociologists would use, following the usage of W. Lloyd Warner; Davis uses the term "working class" or refers to "underprivileged workers," probably because his sketch is intended in part for business managers who are concerned with the absenteeism, lack of skill, and apparent lack of ambition of the men and women workers of the lower-lower class. This brief sketch, therefore, illustrates the fact that a class profile can be focused to some extent on some problem of practical interest.) Though short, this sketch shows that many features of lower-lower-class life tend to reinforce one another and form a kind of pattern (what we have called a style of life or class subculture). In reality, Davis' description refers in part to two subdivisions of the lower-lower class, the Negro and the white; but we shall largely ignore this fact. In general, if the social situation and cultural level of the whites are thought of as "bad," those of the Negroes are worse; for example, the average length of education of the whites is low, as we shall see, but that of the Negroes is lower still. The reader should pay more attention to the general pattern than to exact figures, for the exact statistics change rather rapidly from year to year. Moreover, our focus here will be on the results of research rather than on the methods by which these results were obtained. Nevertheless, the description by no means rests on vague impressions.

The white working-class mothers had had an average of 8.6 years of schooling, as against 14.2 years for the white middle-class mothers. The white working-class fathers had had an average of 8.3 years of education, as against 16 years for the white middle-class fathers. The married couples in the working class tended to have relatively large families. The average number of children in the white middle class was 2.2; in the white working class, 3.3. One sample of three hundred Negro working-class families had an average of 4.9 children. One of the persistent problems of the working class was poor housing. Several families often shared the same cramped living quarters. People had to take turns sleeping, several to a bed. A sample of working-class Negroes in 1944-45 had an average of less than five hours of sleep a night. Children had to play in the street. Partly because of these crowded conditions, the children received from their parents and older siblings very little if any help or encouragement in their school work. The housing problem was so serious that many young men and women who wished to marry felt unable to do so.

Both the men and the women who were employed worked at exceedingly hard physical labor. Partly because of relative lack of education,

Hollingshead called "Elmtown"); see Hochbaum *et al.*, 1955, p. 34, Table 3, "Comparison of Minneapolis and 'Jonesville': Correlation of Selected Socioeconomic Variables." The data for Jonesville were taken from Warner *et al.*, 1949.

partly because of lack of the incentive to get ahead which in the middle class is derived to some extent from concern to maintain and improve a stable family life and provide for the education of children, the working-class men and women could not realistically look forward to any improvement in their work situation. Hard work and lack of sleep, among other things, resulted in high rates of disease and rapid aging, but the working-class men and women regarded general physical deterioration as normal; although their objective need for medical care was greater than that of the middle class, they seldom saw a doctor.

Economic insecurity was also regarded as normal; the working-class men and women had "adjusted" to it. They could not be frightened by the threat of loss of a job. In many cases, two or more families shared not only living quarters but also clothes, cooking utensils, food, drink, and money. Unmarried adults participated in the same basic pattern. A man out of work or temporarily out of money did not hesitate to share in the temporary prosperity of some relative or friend who had just received a pay envelope. The kind of personal and family pride which in the middle class makes it difficult for a man in financial difficulty to appeal to relatives for help was not present in the lower-lower class. On the contrary, the cultural pattern required people to help one another without reserve or deprecation. It was understood that a man who was a benefactor today might need help himself a week or so later. Since they were already at or near the bottom of the prestige scale, these families had no prestige to lose by acknowledging their dependence on others.

Living in crowded conditions, working very hard when they were on the job, and having little education or means to provide themselves with other kinds of recreation, the lower-lower-class men took their pleasure in sexual adventures, heavy drinking, gambling, and the luxury of sitting around loafing. The week-end "binge" was a common pattern. The resulting hangovers contributed to absenteeism.

Many aspects of a class style of life were not touched upon in the foregoing sketch. For example, we said little or nothing about so-called communication behavior, about diet, about political attitudes and behavior, about beliefs and practices in the rearing of children, or about religious beliefs and practices. Nevertheless, our sketch includes enough to show that the various aspects of lower-lower-class life tend to reinforce one another. Poor education leads to poor jobs and poor prospects, and poor jobs are partly responsible for poor housing. Poor housing in turn is related to lack of sleep, lack of family independence, lack of supervision of children's recreation, poor facilities for studying, difficulty in getting married. Lack of prospects, lack of family pride, the pattern of sharing, the poor health due to hard work, little sleep, and general neglect—all these contribute to the relative absence of "ambition" and to unreliability on the job. A sufficient sense of well-being is provided by sex, drinking, gambling, and loafing. Moreover, the whole pattern is regarded not as a problem but as normal.

Both in what it includes and in what it does not include, it tends to reproduce itself in succeeding generations. The children will drop out of school early and drift into essentially the same pattern of life their parents have.

This sketch provides little positive guidance to personnel managers and social reformers, but it shows the futility and emptiness of comfortable moralizing. It shows that "ambition," as Davis says, is a kind of luxury, that it is possible only when a certain level of living has been attained and is to some extent secure. It shows that reform presupposes not only better housing and provision of realistic prospects for a "higher" way of life but also training to "unlearn" a pattern that is not inborn or willful but cultural—learned and socially sanctioned.

Some sociologists accept the idea that there are local classes but deny the existence of society-wide classes. Whether they are correct or not depends partly upon facts and partly upon the definition of "social class." If one were to insist that the members of a "social class" must all know one another and interact intimately, then obviously there are no nationwide classes in the United States. But if one places the emphasis, as we have, on similarity of culture and on acceptability as social equals, then obviously there are, broadly speaking, nationwide social classes. This conception includes the fact of intimate association between class equals but does not require that a member of a class should associate intimately with every other member of the same class. In an earlier section we noted Baltzell's reasonable opinion that there exists a fairly self-conscious nationwide upper class in the United States. In the sense of "social class" that we have adopted, there is an urban lower-lower class in the United States, as is shown in the similarities between the sketch by Davis and the sketches by Warner and Lunt (1941) and Hollingshead and Redlich (1958), among others, of lower-lower-class groups in other American communities. We might also recall our earlier references to the articles by W. B. Miller (1959a and no date), who has pointed out that many features of American urban lower-class culture may be found in other countries as well (see also Knupfer, 1947).

RECOMMENDED READING

The most comprehensive work on social stratification is B. Barber, *Social Stratification: A Comparative Analysis of Structure and Process*, Harcourt, Brace, 1957, which is clear and enlivened by numerous quotations. See also R. Bendix and S. M. Lipset, eds., *Class, Status and Power: A Reader in Social Stratification*, Free Press, 1953. Several of the best articles are original, and many of the others are also excellent. A good elementary work on social classes in the United States is J. A. Kahl, *The American Class Structure*, Rinehart, 1953.

For additional reading on the theory of social stratification, see in particular H. M. Brotz, "Social Stratification and the Political Order," *Amer. J. Sociol.*, May 1959, v. 64, no. 6, pp. 571-78.

Most brief descriptions of the caste system of India convey some misconceptions. Ours is probably not free from the same fault. For an authoritative, highly compact, beautifully organized introduction to the subject, with bibliography, see the article "Caste (Indian)," by H. N. C. Stevenson, in *Encyclopaedia Britannica*, 1957 printing, v. 4, pp. 977-86. A longer treatment of a different caste system is presented in B. Ryan, *Caste in Modern Ceylon: The Sinhalese System in Transition*, Rutgers University Press, 1953.

Two books on history can be recommended as excellent from a sociological point of view. E. G. Barber, *The Bourgeoisie in 18th Century France*, Princeton University Press, 1955, gives in brief compass an amazing amount of well-ordered information about the relative prestige, styles of life, and channels of mobility of the whole class structure (not only of the bourgeoisie). Another well-written work is J. J. Hecht, *The Domestic Servant Class in Eighteenth-Century England*, London: Routledge and Kegan Paul, 1956. Here again, despite the title, one learns a good deal about the whole class structure; but this well-documented work is especially interesting as a study of the great heterogeneity of an occupation and the opportunities for upward mobility that it provided.

All the works mentioned contain good bibliographies, but see also H. W. Pfautz, "The Current Literature on Social Stratification: Critique and Bibliography," *Amer. J. Sociol.*, Jan. 1953, v. 58, no. 4, pp. 391-418.

19. The Functions and Dysfunctions of Social Stratification

In the preceding chapter our emphasis, on the whole, was on the ways in which social classes are alike. Here we shall take up some of the ways in which they differ—themes that were largely implicit in Chapter 18. Although the functions and dysfunctions of class stratification are to an important extent the same in all systems, we shall find that systems vary in the functions they stress and in the degree to which they achieve a favorable balance between functions and dysfunctions. Functional variation, however, depends to a large extent on structural variation, and it is to this that we turn first.

Variations in Social-class Systems

There are several ways in which systems of social classes may differ from one another. We shall list and comment briefly on some of the more important and then comment on three variables at somewhat greater length.

1. *Differences in the value systems on which the systems of stratification in part rest.* Davis and Moore (1945, pp. 244-48), who introduced the concept of functional emphasis, noted that any one of the following functions might be emphasized in a given society to the relative neglect of the others: religion; government; wealth, property, and labor; and technical knowledge. More recently, Parsons (1953) has treated variation in values as a matter of the relative weight given to the four functional subsystems of society that he distinguishes—the systems of pattern maintenance and tension management, adaptation, goal attainment, and integration.

The actual class position of particular families and individuals in any society is determined only in part by the system of values and norms. In particular, the rules of ascription or competition are sometimes violated successfully—that is, without detection or effective social control. Apart from such violations, we must remember that competitors are almost never evenly matched, even if they all abide by the rules. Differences of wealth are only the most obvious inequalities.

2. *The number of classes* (see pp. 514-16).

3. *The span of the system*—that is, the difference in prestige and style of life between the highest-ranking families and the lowest. Although it would be difficult to assign comparable index numbers to different systems, it is obvious that so-called civilized or advanced societies—for example, India, pre-Communist and Communist Russia and China, Ottoman Turkey, the contemporary United States—have far greater spans of prestige and style of life than most primitive societies, such as the Navaho Indians or the Lovedu of South Africa.

4. *The shape of the system.* This refers to the proportion of the population of a society in each of the social classes. As we have seen, it is misleading, although fairly common, to refer to a class system as a "pyramid," if this term is intended to suggest that the population is always divided in the same proportions among the various classes. For rough purposes, societies are frequently divided into upper, middle, and lower classes. The upper class in most societies is relatively small, but whereas in the United States and Sweden, for example, the middle class is rather large, a characteristic of so-called backward societies is that the middle class is small in relation to the population as a whole. Indeed, this is one of the symptoms of "backwardness." Examples of societies with very small middle classes in the North American sense are Colombia and pre-Castro Cuba (Beals, 1953, p. 337).

In neither India nor Ceylon is caste the only basis of class prestige, but if we confine ourselves to caste it is striking that the highest caste in Ceylon, the Goyigama, is also the most numerous: it includes 50 per cent of the population (Ryan, 1953, p. 19). In India, by contrast, the highest caste, the Brahman, includes perhaps 6 per cent of the population. (Note, however, that this is not a comparison of social-class structures but only of one element in them, and note that caste is much less important in Ceylon than in India.) The terms "span" and "shape" are used by B. Barber (1957, pp. 67-93). For the same concepts, P. A. Sorokin uses the terms "height" and "profile," which are perhaps more suggestive (1927, *passim;* e.g., Chap. 4).

5. *Ideology with respect to vertical social mobility.* We shall deal with ideology in greater detail in Chapter 21; for the present we shall say that the term refers to the values and beliefs people have about social systems in which they participate. "Vertical social mobility," treated in detail on pages 516-35, refers here to passage from one social class to another, higher or lower in the hierarchy. In some class systems (India is the best example), it is not legitimate for an individual family to strive for upward social mobility; theoretically (i.e., in people's ideology), upward mobility does not occur. Ideology has considerable influence on behavior, as we shall see, but social reality never conforms perfectly to ideology. As for India, ideology with respect to social mobility is changing in that country. Moreover, it has always been legitimate for a caste as a whole to seek to improve its relative position by purifying its religious practices.

6. *The amount and net direction of vertical mobility.* Regardless of

ideology, a certain amount of vertical social mobility is always going on. We could express the *rate* of vertical mobility as the proportion of men in a generation who have a higher or lower class position than their fathers had. To determine the *amount* of vertical mobility, we should have to consider not only the rate but also the average "social distance" up or down the class system the mobile men go; some move only to the next class up or down, others move two or more classes.

In any generation some men's families of procreation are higher in rank than their families of orientation, while other men's families of procreation are lower. The first set of men have been upward mobile; the second set, downward mobile. The *net direction* of vertical mobility would of course be the ratio of the upward mobile to the downward mobile. In studying mobility, it is also possible to consider family lines over several generations.

7. *The channels of mobility.* This refers to the activities and organizations in which people find opportunities to move up in the class structure. Typical channels vary from one society to another. In the United States today, the systems of public education are by far the most important channels of mobility, at least at the beginning of individual careers; at a later point, the colleges and universities are important. The great bureaucracies of business and government open careers to talent. In France before the Revolution business activity *per se* was less important as a means of reaching the top than as a means for the purchase of honorific public offices and, in effect, of noble husbands for one's daughters by offering large dowries. Money-making was also important in that it permitted the adoption of a noble style of life. The Church was relatively more important as a channel of mobility than it is in the United States today: The army was also important, education less so (E. G. Barber, 1955, Chap. 6).

8. *The degree of normative integration.* Briefly, this refers to the degree to which the values and norms of the system are institutionalized. There may be conflicting criteria of evaluation: to this extent the system is malintegrated and the "upper" classes are in a morally ambiguous position, with their "superiority" due in unusual degree to force and the threat of force. We shall give more attention below to the integration of systems of class stratification.

THE NUMBER OF CLASSES

The question of how many classes a stratification system has is not always easy to answer, for essentially the same reason that it is difficult to answer the question of whether or not there *are* social classes. We pointed out in Chapter 18 that there are what might be called significant discontinuities in the culture and in the complex web of interaction that joins people from the top of a society to the bottom; that it is somewhat arbitrary to say in a given case that these discontinuities are great enough to warrant our speaking of two classes rather than one; but that for several reasons it is desirable as well as defensible to think in terms of relatively distinct social classes.

One kind of distinctiveness is social-class consciousness, in a sense wider than that which Marx gave to the term. If people think of themselves as belonging to a certain class and if other people agree in placing them in that class, these facts are fairly good evidence that they *do* belong to a distinct class. Yet we noted that in India caste consciousness, as indicated by the rather unusual development of formal names, formal councils, and other formal marks of group identity, may to some extent blur or blot from awareness important differences *within* a particular caste, differences based perhaps on wealth. In general, however, we should attach much more weight to social-class consciousness than to the absence of it. Simple ignorance of the nature of the existing class system is not at all uncommon: a person can belong to a class in our sense without being aware of it. This springs in part from the tendency to associate with class equals, which might lead to the idea that we are all equals. More important, however, is the reluctance of some people to accept the fact of social inequality, due partly to ideological distortion. Especially in the United States, there is an ideological tendency to deny the existence of social classes, as in the Soviet Union there is for other ideological reasons a tendency to play down the great differences in style of life and the inequalities of opportunity that exist.

Greater weight should be given to cultural differences and to relative breaks in the web of social interaction. Seldom, however, do we find cleavages so clear-cut as the cleavage in Latin American countries between people who work with their hands and people who do not. This difference in style of life is accompanied by a social gulf. The following quotation refers to Argentina and Chile, where the development of a middle class similar to that in the United States has gone further than it has in most of South America.

> . . . there is still no real break in the fundamental distinction between those who work with their hands and those who do not. It is difficult for either North Americans or Latin-Americans to realize the depth of the cleavage involved. The middle-class family with two cars and no servants, the banker who washes windows in preparation for his wife's tea party, the professor in overalls wielding a shovel in his garden—all are incomprehensible in Latin America. Unless an individual occupies an impregnable social position, there are certain manual activities which may *never* be engaged in even for recreation, certain implements which must never be touched [Beals, 1953, p. 339].

Presumably a girl whose father did no manual work would find it difficult, perhaps "unthinkable," to marry a manual worker.

Unfortunately, most descriptions of class systems are based on less evidence than we should like. For example, few investigators have made a study of the social characteristics of grooms as compared with those of the brides' fathers, although this kind of evidence is probably taken into account impressionistically. The question of the distinctiveness of social classes is also related to patterns of social mobility; but, again, this kind of evidence is rarely gathered systematically. We have mentioned vertical mobility, upward and downward. There is also another kind; namely, "horizontal" mobility—that is, change in social position that has no significance for social prestige or for invidious social interaction.[1] If in a study of mobility we found that many men in one generation whose fathers were lawyers are themselves doctors and that many of their sons in turn are lawyers, we should have to conclude that this particular movement is merely horizontal movement, that without further qualification there is no class difference between doctors and lawyers.

Since different writers are likely to use different kinds of data for their descriptions of class systems, it is rather difficult to give a good example of two systems differing in number of classes. Perhaps we are on relatively safe ground, however, if we take two descriptions by the same investigator (see Tables 16 and 17). In setting the boundaries of a social class, and thus deciding on the number of classes in a system, Beals used the criteria "cultural definition" (class culture, style of life), "self-identification" (social-class consciousness), and "participation" (differential intimate social interaction, mutual social acceptability) (Beals, 1953, p. 332).

VERTICAL SOCIAL MOBILITY

The study of vertical social mobility is of interest for at least two reasons. First, in democratic countries a high rate of vertical social mobility is commonly regarded as a good thing, since it is taken as an indication that the ideal of equality of opportunity is realized to some extent. Secondly, we shall see that the closing of hitherto open channels of mobility may in certain circumstances generate instability in the social order.

In studying mobility, we could focus attention on either individuals or groups. (In the course of time certain occupational groups may attain greater prestige.) For the most part, however, we shall confine our attention in this section to individual mobility. Moreover, we shall largely ignore the study of intragenerational mobility and confine ourselves to mobility as measured by the difference between the occupations of father and of son.[2]

Ideology of mobility

Downward mobility is ideologically permitted in every society. This arises from the fact that loss of prestige, varying from lowered reputation to ostracism or banishment, is a negative social sanction in every society. If a

---

1 Both vertical and horizontal social mobility are to be distinguished from migration, which is movement in geographical space. Mobility and migration are, of course, often related.

2 Unless we indicate otherwise, "mobility" will mean vertical social mobility. We shall refer to a few other works, but for the most part this section is based on Lipset and Bendix, 1959, which is a summary of numerous studies made in the United States and other countries.

TABLE 16

The class structure of Brazil *

Rural	*Urban* [a]
Uppermost elite tends to define self racially [it is white], but [is] ideologically opposed to discrimination in economic and political matters	
Landholders turning to industry, banking, commerce. High government officials, heads of church, army, many professional men, declining number of intellectuals	
Managerial, including some former upper-class landholders [b] Middle bureaucracy Professionals, lower church and army officials, teachers, small landholders, storekeepers	Managerial Middle bureaucracy Storekeepers Some professionals and intellectuals Teachers Some service personnel and technicians White-collar workers
(Increasing breaching of barriers)	
Negro, mulatto, and mestizo [c] with few barriers to marriage; little discrimination	
Small traders Independent small farmers Farm laborers	Petty civil servants Small shopkeepers Artisans Working-class groups
Large groups of extremely impoverished in both rural and urban settings	

* R. L. Beals, "Social Stratification in Latin America," *Amer. J. Sociol.*, Jan. 1953, v. 58, no. 4, p. 334. Continuous horizontal lines mean effective barriers to vertical movement; broken line means considerable ease of mobility.

[a] "Distinctions of significance exist between rural and urban. They are of greater importance for the lower status groups. Free movement between rural and urban is possible in most countries today but was not so free in the past except for those of relatively high status" (p. 333).

[b] "Hierarchical differences exist within each class, crudely represented by the relative vertical positions of the listed occupational groups" (p. 333).

[c] A mulatto is "racially" half white, half Negro. A mestizo is of mixed Indian and white ancestry.

member of an upper class falls too far below the standard of conduct expected in his class, he will lose his status. In India, a person may be excluded from his caste for marrying someone of another caste, especially a lower one.

Probably no society absolutely forbids all upward mobility, but there are great differences from one society to another in attitude toward it. As

TABLE 17

The class structure of Peru *

Rural	*Urban*
Racially defined elite [white]: wealthy landowners, high government officials, heads of army and church, professional men of proper family, industrialists, heads of large commercial interests, some intellectuals	
(Barriers almost completely impenetrable)	
Racially defined "Cholo" [a] or mestizo middle class oriented toward upper-class and elite goals:	
Hacienda managers,[b] shopkeepers Small independent landowners Some technical, professional, church, and army personnel	Managerial: middle bureaucracy Storekeepers, some professionals and intellectuals Teachers, middle church, and army personnel White-collar workers
Rural Cholos, often with marked local cultures: Small farmers Farm workers Small-town craftsmen, nonagricultural workers, traders	Cholos: Small shopkeepers Working-class groups Artisans Petty civil servants Domestic servants Lowest groups, often extremely impoverished
Indians—two main cultural groups locally organized	Indian migrants from rural areas engaged in lowest-paid factory work and forming lowest ranks of army and police

* Beals, 1953, p. 334. See notes to Table 16, p. 517.

[a] "Cholo" is the Peruvian term for mestizo (roughly).
[b] A hacienda is a landed estate, often very large.

we have noted, in India one's caste is determined by birth and in principle is fixed for life. Since caste is an important part of one's total social status, India comes close to exemplifying the theoretical polar type of "closed" class system. At the opposite pole ideologically is the "open" society, exemplified imperfectly by the United States. Whereas in a closed society fixed status is regarded as just and attempts to change class status are regarded as wrong or unthinkable, in an open society the fixation of status by law or by informal barriers is ideologically regarded as immoral, and personal ambition to rise is encouraged. We are speaking now of ideal types; actual societies are never perfectly open or perfectly closed in either their ideals or their practices. Every society allows some scope for personal ambition, and every society cherishes some institutions that inevitably prevent equality of opportunity. We have seen, for example, that the institution of the family, with its fostering of family solidarity, inevitably gives certain advantages to children whose families of orientation happen to be favorably placed in the social system.

The two extreme ideal types are sometimes called "caste" and "open class" societies. We avoid the term "caste" in this sense because it is somewhat ambiguous. In the broadest sense, as we have seen, a caste is a fairly large hereditary group of families that is strictly endogamous, one of two or more such groups composing a hierarchy within the society. In this sense, Negroes in the United States come close to being a caste, as do the whites as a whole. In a narrower sense such a group is not a caste unless the chief ideology of the society supports the idea of fixed class status. In this sense, the Negroes and the whites in the United States are not castes, for discrimination against Negroes is widely regarded as a deplorable practice. There is enough moral opposition to it to warrant our saying that the inferior social position of Negroes as such is not institutionalized. On the other hand, there is also a secondary ideology supporting discrimination. Although it is not intellectually respectable and is on the defensive, it nevertheless has enough believers and practitioners to preclude our calling the United States a fully open society, even ideologically. We follow those writers who inadequately suggest the complex ambiguities of the situation by calling the whites and the Negroes "quasi-castes."

India and the United States have been mentioned as ideological opposites with respect to mobility, although neither society is a perfect example of its type and India especially has been changing in recent years toward the "open" end of the continuum. Most societies probably fall, ideologically, somewhere closer to one or the other extreme, but closer to the middle than India or the United States.

Factors hindering mobility

Regardless of ideological differences, in all societies there are factors hindering social mobility and other factors facilitating it. Most of the factors hindering mobility are connected with the existence of the family. In some of the socialist collective farms (*kibbutzim*) of Israel, children do not live with their parents, but they do have affectionate relations with them; presumably the better-educated or more intelligent parents are able to communicate some advantages to their children (Spiro, 1956, 1958). In other words, wherever the family is a recognized group there will be inequality of opportunity at least to the extent that some children will be more favorably socialized than others.

The other inequalities associated with families are negligible in the Israeli *kibbutzim* but are important elsewhere, including Israel apart from the *kibbutzim*. In stratified societies with families—for all practical purposes, in all civilized societies—upper-class children have the great advantage of associating with better-educated friends and relatives than lower-class children. These friends and relatives outside the family itself are often able to provide opportunities for good careers, in addition to the general influence they exert through their values.

Some families are able to give their children the further advantage of wealth. The extent of inequality caused by differences in wealth and income obviously depends in the first place upon how great these differences are. It also depends upon the degree to which a society provides public services to all. Tax-supported education and medical services, for example, help to ensure that gifted children from the poorer classes will be better able to compete and thus reduce somewhat the advantage of wealth. Even then, however, private wealth will enable some families to give advantages to their less gifted children.

Finally, the existence of social classes as we have defined them depends of course on the existence of the family, and one aspect of social class is the tendency toward class endogamy. This means in general a tendency to keep advantages in a relatively small group from generation to generation.

In some societies legal arrangements reinforce some of the advantages due to family and add others. For example, in the United States children without scholarships have to pay fees even in the state colleges and universities. In civil-service examinations war veterans are given an advantage. In the Union of Soviet Socialist Republics too the law has ensured inequality of opportunity since 1940 at least (Inkeles, 1950a). Not only has the institution of the family been strengthened by law but fees have been introduced for higher education. The sons of army officers are favored for careers in the army. Although the Soviet educational system comes closer than the American to providing equal opportunity for all, the Soviet system of income and inheritance taxation is surprisingly "reactionary" by American standards. In the Soviet Union whatever advantages may be involved in the vast differences in income are perpetuated by the tax laws. For example, although in most Western countries the inheritance taxes on large estates are virtually confiscatory, in the Soviet Union the tax may in no case exceed 10 per cent of valuation. Furthermore, on top of a regressive tax system the classless society also provides additional sums to the widows *and children* of prominent persons (who presumably are in less need of additional sums than most other people are). There are many other legal guarantees of inequality of opportunity, but this one is particularly interesting.

> Perhaps even more striking [than certain other inequalities] has been the recent practice of providing large cash grants and substantial annuities for the widows and heirs of prominent Soviet officials, scientists, and artists. To choose some examples more or less at random: the wife of Peoples' Artist of the U.S.S.R. A. V. Aleksandrov was given 50,000 rubles and a personal

> pension of 750 rubles per month, and his son Yuri a pension of 750 rubles per month until completion of his higher education; the widow of Lt. General of Engineering Troops D. M. Karbshev was granted a pension of 1,000 rubles a month, and his daughter and son each 700 rubles per month until the completion of their education. No instances are known to this writer of comparable grants made to persons of lesser social rank who made outstanding contributions at the level of *their* occupational skill [Inkeles, 1950a, p. 470; see also Timasheff, 1944, pp. 17-21].

The point of recording such phenomena is not to decry them. Presumably the system of differential rewards for achievement has much the same effect in the Soviet Union that it has in the more old-fashioned capitalist countries; namely, to stimulate achievement in certain fields. The Soviet government has simply seized upon the powerful motive of concern for the future welfare of one's family. The chief difference from the capitalist system is in the *kinds* of achievement that are most rewarded; and this difference is not without interest. The point here, however, is that both systems tend to ensure inequality of opportunity, hence to foster the perpetuation of class status; and this fact is not without ironic interest either.

In general, there is a tendency for the advantages of upper-class status to be cumulative. The following quotation applies mainly to the United States, but a similar statement could be made about almost any other country.

> . . . the poverty, lack of education, absence of personal "contacts," lack of planning, and failure to explore fully the available job opportunities that characterize the working-class family are handed down from generation to generation. The same cumulation of factors, which in the working class creates a series of mounting disadvantages, works to the advantage of a child coming from a well-to-do family [Lipset and Bendix, 1959, p. 198].

Before leaving the subject of restrictions on equality of opportunity, we should make some more general points about the relation between social class and money. Contrary to much slipshod thinking, the amount of money a high-ranking family has is almost never the main basis for its high rank. It is hardly an exaggeration to say that in the United States money alone is the measure of man only in the so-called shady hierarchy, composed mostly of gamblers, and in the underworld, where, respectability having been renounced, almost the only thing left is money and what money can buy. Almost: even in the underworld there is a hierarchy of criminals according to the types of crime they specialize in; a skillful forger or "con man" is admired, but a molester of children is despised. In this respect, the underworld is not essentially different from the legitimate world, except in the kind of achievement admired; in both, people are interested in what a man *does* as well as in what he *has*. The underworld as a whole suffers opprobrium in comparison with the legitimate world not because criminals are poor (many are not) but because what they do is not regarded as a contribution to society.

But once the foregoing qualifications have been stated, we must admit that money is enormously important to social class. In the first place, in a highly stratified society the maintenance of the upper-class style of life, including its pattern of achievement, requires, for the class as a whole, a relatively large and secure financial base. Once this base is lost, the upper class is on its way out unless it can find some other financial resources. Secondly, although possession of money is not in itself honorific, "bad" money can easily be transformed into higher status in successive generations. Balzac's Pere Goriot himself is forever soiled with business; he is only rich. But his money has provided his daughters with an upper-class education and large dowries, so that they can marry into the upper class and snub their poor old father. Thus money is not only a means for maintaining high class position but also a means for upward mobility. The maintenance of high social status without money is so difficult that many people understandably but mistakenly speak of money as if it were the chief *basis* of prestige (criterion for giving or withholding prestige), whereas money is actually one of the chief *means* of acquiring and maintaining it, *provided that the money is properly used*. This difference is not slight.

Factors ensuring mobility

Despite inequality of opportunity, a great deal of mobility occurs in every society. Even India is no exception. Downward mobility occurs whenever a family fails conspicuously to live up to the requirements of its caste. We noted that one of the chief activities of a caste council (*panchayat*) is to chastize and, if necessary, expel delinquent members. Expulsion means that a man's family must accept lower status with him unless they are willing to ostracize him. But, more important, upward mobility also occurs in India, although it probably is rarer than in Western countries. (In speaking of India, we shall confine our attention to the modern period, in which the caste system has been more rigid than in ancient times, although as we have mentioned it is becoming looser again. We shall also confine our attention to legitimate channels of mobility, neglecting the cases in which, no doubt, some people, today as in the past, rise by fraud.)

Stevenson points out (1957, p. 981) that we must distinguish between secular rank and ritual rank. From the point of view of any individual, the ritual rank of his caste is for all practical purposes fixed, but he may improve his secular rank. The system of religious ideas is not inflexible on that score. Although what has been called the "trade union" tendency of caste restricts the opportunity for occupational mobility somewhat, the restriction is not absolute even in principle. It varies from caste to caste. The caste *dharma* may or may not require that caste members follow a specific occupation. Stevenson cites with approval Ghurye's generalization that the members of any caste can enter agriculture, trade, or military service without losing their caste standing. Industrialization has opened new occupations. Government careers are open to all castes. Since religious principles leave many occupational variations religiously indifferent, there is nothing contrary to the Hindu tradition in the political activity that some castes have undertaken to open up new occupational opportunities for their members.

> The first caste conference was that of the Kayasths or accountants in 1887. Since then hundreds of castes have met and organized themselves to perpetuate and extend their special privileges, to raise their social status by reforms, to provide for the education of their needy and deserving children, to help their poor, and to petition for larger employment in government service. Most provinces have been forced by such pressures to pass rules that a definite proportion of the posts in the various services shall be filled from members of different castes, provided that they have the minimum qualifications. Sometimes even those who have failed in the examinations are admitted to office [Olcott, 1944, pp. 652-53].

In principle, however, the caste ritual rank of an individual is fixed. This is important, for it limits the desirability of acquiring a higher secular rank. Although he has gained more secular prestige, the "successful" individual will continue to be faced with whatever commensal and connubial restrictions his caste rank imposes. He *can* gain higher individual ritual rank, but only at the cost of giving up "the world" altogether and withdrawing into a lonely ascetic life. Such a course is no threat to the prestige hierarchy of the caste system or to the prevailing distribution of material goods.

This limitation on purely individual mobility makes all the more important the means whereby a caste as a whole may rise in ritual rank. A caste council may decide to make the caste *dharma* more strict, so that it will come closer to the Brahman ideal. Thus the council might decide to restrict caste members henceforth to "purer" occupations. If the caste splits on such an issue, it is likely that part will form a new caste. True, it may take the "purer" group several generations of tireless effort to get its claim to higher rank recognized. The castes just above it are not going to grant equality to it in any sudden fashion. The upward mobility of a caste necessarily requires a transitional period during which its status is intermediate between what it was before the stricter rule of purity was introduced and what it will be when the claim to higher rank is fully recognized. We must observe, however, that this intermediate stage is already higher than the early stage; and if the ritual rank of the group is higher, then of course the ritual rank of its members is higher.

The transitional status is clearly marked by "hypergamy," or "marriage up" from the woman's point of view. The "purer" group (now a new caste) marks its aspirations by limiting intermarriage of its members with the less pure caste from which it separated. Henceforth it may take women from the old group, but it refuses to allow its own women to marry the men from the old caste. The older caste accepts this arrangement because it acknowledges the superiority of the group that split off. How can the old group do otherwise when the new has adopted a purer style of life? The transition is easy since the two castes have recently been one thoroughly endogamous caste (or else a tribe). In time, a higher caste than both may accept the claim of the new caste and show its acceptance, no doubt, by accepting the daughters of the new caste as wives. At first these marriages will be hypergamous, but gradually they will be accepted as marriages between equals.

Hypergamy occurs only between groups that have little disparity in status. Thus we see that upward mobility in India tends to occur by small degrees. But it does occur. To be sure, Ghurye states that hypergamy is rare, but his sense of "caste" is more restrictive than the one we have adopted:

> Recent practice of hypergamy as between caste and caste, and not between subgroups of a caste, is very restricted in its distribution. It is practiced in parts of the Punjab, where caste system is notoriously lenient and lax, and on the southwest coast, where marriage is matrilocal and descent matrilineal [Ghurye, 1949, p. 467].

From these words we may infer that if so-called subcastes were called castes, then hypergamy could be described as more common. (There is no little confusion about just which groups are called "castes." We have confined the term to endogamous groups that accept the Hindu system of evaluations with regard to ritual purity, except that we also call a group a caste if it permits its men to take wives from slightly lower groups or gives some of its women in marriage to men of slightly higher groups.)

If upward mobility can occur in India, it is difficult to imagine a stratified society in which it could not occur. Among the general factors that make some amount of mobility inevitable in any society, the following are perhaps most important:

1. Social prestige ultimately depends upon the accepted value system. If certain qualities or achievements are socially valued, some people will strive for them; and if newcomers attain these values they must eventually be recognized, whether or not they "ought" to have striven for them. Thus, a system with a caste ideology cannot be perfectly maintained in practice (K. Davis, 1949, p. 384).

2. There is no constant tendency for intelligence and other kinds of native capacity—notably sheer energy—to be confined to upper classes; consequently many individuals are unable to maintain the high status won by their ancestors, and other individuals push their way to the top. It has not been at all uncommon for the sons of farmers, laborers, and slaves to rise to the very highest positions in their societies (see Sorokin, 1927, Chap. 7).

3. At varying rates of speed, changes are always occurring in the demand for different kinds of skill; innovation and market changes open up new opportunities.

4. The birth rate of each class never exactly fills all the positions in the class; sometimes there are too many people and some must move up or down; sometimes there are too few people and positions are left open

for people from classes below. Of less *general* importance, but of tremendous importance when it occurs, is the opening up of opportunities through deaths in war, or through mass emigration.

5. Finally, although birth into the upper classes brings many advantages, as we have seen, it also seems to foster complacency in many persons. Many countries have adages similar to the one with which we are all familiar: "From shirtsleeves to shirtsleeves in three generations."

> Charles McArthur's study of the personality characteristics of upper- and middle-class men at Harvard [1955] shows that the latter are much more likely to be work oriented and to reject both strong family ties in general and in particular their father, whom they desire to surpass in status. The men from upper-class families, on the other hand, will tell stories in response to the unstructured pictures of the TAT (Thematic Apperception Test) that suggest they are less oriented toward work as a field of accomplishment, that they respect their father, and that they have a strong positive family feeling [Lipset and Bendix, 1959, pp. 245-46]

These findings are in keeping with other well-known facts—for example, that boys from public schools do better in their studies in college than boys from private schools, and that college performance records vary inversely with economic advantage when intelligence is held constant (Lipset and Bendix, 1959, p. 246.)

Amount of mobility

In considering the amount of mobility, we could focus on a society as a whole, on the comparison of different groups within a society—for example, religious and ethnic groups—or on individual characteristics that determine which persons are most likely, and which least likely, to be mobile. We shall give our greatest attention here to the amount of mobility in society as a whole, but first we shall consider briefly some of the individual differences that are significant for mobility. All the relationships to be mentioned are supported by varying amounts of research.

Some of these relationships are easy to understand; for example, high intelligence, having parents who urged striving for achievement, coming from a small family, and late marriage are all correlated with a relatively high rate of upward mobility. Other relationships are more obscure; for example, upward mobility is also associated with deferring sexual relations until relatively late in growing up, having parents who were downward mobile, and having a "weak" father and a "strong" mother. It may be that the inhibition of sexual behavior somehow makes energy available for learning about the environment or is a sign that the growing personality is preoccupied with useful learning. The association between upward mobility and having parents who were downward mobile can be plausibly explained: downward-mobile parents invest their wishes for upward mobility in their children and encourage them more vigorously than parents who have not "failed" in life. That the combination of "weak" father and "strong" mother should lead to upward mobility can also be plausibly explained on a somewhat speculative basis. It may be that the strong mother shifts to her son both the ambition she may have suppressed in herself and the ambition, sharpened by disappointment, that she had for her husband. The combination of weak father and strong mother also resembles somewhat the impelling and fruitful situation of the middle-class Harvard boys studied by McArthur, as compared with the complacency-producing situation of the upper-class boys. In general, we should observe that the study of "individual" differences is not sharply distinguishable from the study of group differences, for certain individual characteristics may be more common in a particular group because of its social situation and its culture.

When we said above that the relationship between upward mobility and coming from a small family is "easy to understand," we were laying a trap for the reader in order to point up the desirability of carefully controlled research. One might guess that parents imbued with values that make them ambitious for their children would also be likely to follow the middle-class pattern of having small families. One might also guess that lower- or middle-class parents who want their children to rise or upper-class parents who want their children to remain in the upper class might decide to have few children so that they could provide better for them. But there is evidence that these reasonable hypotheses (which are supported by the known facts) may not be enough to account for the positive relationship between high upward mobility and origin in a small family. "Only children" and other children in small families have more interaction with adults and thus learn more than children in larger families. Eldest and youngest children have an advantage over middle children. Intelligence-test scores reflect such environmental influences as well as native endowment. Two national surveys, one conducted in Scotland (J. Maxwell, 1954), the other in France (Institut National . . . , 1950), show that children from small families achieve higher intelligence-test scores than children from larger families, *when father's occupation is held constant* (Lipset and Bendix, 1959, p. 243).

Turning now to the amount of mobility in a total society, we must note first of all that the amount varies a great deal from one society to another and from time to time. One of the outstanding characteristics of those social upheavals we call class revolutions is that many who were high are struck down and many who were low are elevated (Sorokin, 1927, pp. 143-44; Timasheff, 1944). This is probably especially true at the very top of society. Politically prominent families and others who symbolize the old regime are most likely to lose their positions in the upheaval. The need for educated and experienced men is so great in the period of reconstruction, however, that many persons who had fairly high positions in the old regime also have better than average positions in the new. It is virtually certain that the French nobility are unusually prominent today in proportion to their number. Even in Russia, the old class of "exploiters" have done very well since the Revolution (see Feldmesser, 1953).

Many laymen have the impression that the rate of mobility is declining in the United States. They point to "the closing of the frontier" and the decline in immigration. Sociologists are not so sure that there is any less mobility today than there was fifty years ago. The question is not easy to answer. Indeed, the question itself is somewhat ambiguous. The whole social structure is constantly changing. For example, new industries rise and old ones decline. Consequently the class structure is changing all the time too. Thus, if we make periodic comparisons of sons and fathers with respect to social status and find an increasing (or decreasing) amount of vertical mobility, we must ask whether this change in mobility is due mainly to a change in the shape of the class structure or mainly to a greater (or lesser) approximation to equality of opportunity. If the class structure is such that the upper class (however defined) is small, then few people would be in it even if we had perfect equality of opportunity. Only one player can win a golf tournament, yet the tournament might be quite fair. Thus a high rate of mobility is not by itself proof of openness in the class structure, nor is a low rate proof that the structure is closed.

Rapid change in the occupational structure may also raise the question of whether a particular movement is vertical or merely horizontal. For example, how do the sons of small independent farmers feel when they come to the city and take a factory job? Have they moved up or down, or neither? This question is closely related to the point that the shape of the class structure is changing, but we see that it might not be easy to decide from year to year just what the shape is.

A further difficulty is that the information we have about social mobility in earlier times is less than exact and is not easy to compare with our knowledge of the amount of mobility in more recent times. Part of the difficulty can be appreciated if we reflect that for both early and late periods we must content ourselves, for the most part, with some crude index of social class, usually occupation. Thus if we want to know whether there was more mobility or less in 1950 than in 1900, we compare a representative sample of fathers and sons in 1950 with a representative sample of fathers and sons in 1900. Then if we are interested in the effect of changes in the *shape* of the class structure we have to compare the actual rate of occupational mobility for each sample with what its rate would be if there were perfect equality of opportunity. At best, this comparison would be difficult to make because for each historical period the number of occupational classes, the cutting points, and therefore the shape of the occupational structure would have to be decided somewhat arbitrarily. Moreover, if we had a larger number of occupational classes for one period than for the other, then automatically we should be increasing the chances for vertical mobility in the first period, since any change in occupation would be more likely to be a vertical movement. Therefore, to make the two periods comparable we should have to decide to have the same number of occupational classes for both periods. Yet this might be a distortion of the situation in one or both periods. As a matter of fact, we do not have for any early period a representative sample in which the occupation of each man is compared with that of his father. The information we have, then, is not very satisfactory.

The question of equality of opportunity is extremely complex. In general, there is probably a closer approximation to equality of opportunity in the United States today than there was in earlier times. There is a slow trend toward equalization of wealth (although we do not mean to suggest that this trend will go on indefinitely). There is a trend, gradual, and painfully slow, toward treating Negroes without discrimination. Other minorities are numerically less important, but in the aggregate they are more numerous than the Negroes, and there is no question that the assimilation of most of these other minorities has been going on with great rapidity. Much remains to be done toward equalizing opportunity for medical service and education, both of which are vital to general equality of opportunity. Although in both these fields there are great regional and rural-urban differences, there is little reason to think that these differences are greater today than in the past. Moreover, increase in the average amount of education is significant partly because education tends to make people more ambitious (Lipset and Bendix, 1959, p. 281). Finally, if anything the *ideal* of equality of opportunity is stronger today than in the past, for it is rapidly becoming an international ideal and a standard by which countries are judged in world opinion.

Before presenting some of the information we do have on the rate of mobility in the United States, let us summarize some of the conclusions to which it leads:

1. In all times boys from upper-class families have had a distinct advantage.

2. At no time has the number of "spectacular" rises—cases of mobility from the lower class to the "top" of society—been negligible, but on the other hand there were fewer such cases in the nineteenth century and earlier than is widely supposed.

3. Most vertical mobility, both upward and downward, is slight within any one generation and more impressive over several generations.

4. The rate of upward mobility in the United States has changed very little over the past fifty or a hundred or a hundred and fifty years.

5. The rate of downward mobility, which is somewhat independent of the rate of upward mobility, has also remained about the same or has declined slightly.

6. The rates of upward and downward mobility are due in large part to economic progress, which has both shaken the sieve, so to speak, and changed the shape of the occupational structure favorably for upward mobility. In determining the rate of mobility in any country, economic progress is probably more important than ideology.

Studying top business leaders in the United States, Mabel Newcomer (1955) took a sample of the largest railroad, public-utility, and industrial corporations for each of three periods: 1899–1903, 1923–1925, and January 1, 1948–June 30, 1953. For each corporation in a given sample, only the president and the chairman of the board were included in the sample of business leaders for that year. Note that such high officials in any year would have been born not less than fifty years earlier, on the average; thus most of the leaders of 1900 must have been born around 1850 or earlier. From a variety of sources, Newcomer gathered certain information about each business leader—for example, his religion, his ethnic group, and his father's occupation and income. For each of the three periods, she took the largest nonfinancial corporations; the total assets of the corporations in the sample amounted to about a third of the total assets of all nonfinancial business firms listed in that year. ("Nonfinancial" firms are those other than banks and insurance companies.) Thus she allowed for secular change in the average size of firms and in the relative importance of business itself. And since she defined "business leader" precisely and sought the same kinds of information for all her leaders, her three samples are truly comparable. The results of her study show little change in the rate of mobility over the long period of time (see Tables 18 and 19).[3]

Bendix and Howton (1959) obtained similar results by a different method. They took a random sample consisting of every ninth businessman who was born between 1771 and 1920 and whose biography is given in the *National Cyclopedia of American Biography*.[4] Somewhat different results were obtained by C. W. Mills in a study similar in type to that of Bendix and Howton. Mills took *all* businessmen born between 1570 and 1879 for whom there is in the *Dictionary of American Biography* an entry giving adequate information. His results

> . . . show first a marked decline in the proportion of business leaders coming from upper-class families from 1715 (69 per cent) to 1835 (20 per cent) and, secondly, a marked increase of that proportion from the low of 20 per cent in 1835 to 41 per cent in 1865, with indications that this upward trend has continued since then [Bendix and Howton, 1959, p. 135, summarizing Mills, 1945, p. 30].

Biographical dictionaries are a somewhat uncertain basis for a study of trends in the rate of social mobility; the editorial policy of such dictionaries is not devised with trend studies in mind, so that the data are only roughly comparable.

---

[3] Several similar studies have yielded similar results; see, in particular, S. Keller, 1953, which made use of data collected, in part, by William Miller and associates and published in previous reports; and W. L. Warner and J. C. Abegglen, 1955, which in part made use of the pioneering study by F. W. Taussig and C. S. Joslyn, 1932. Warner and Abegglen, incidentally, found that 24 per cent of the top American business leaders in 1952 had never entered college—a remarkable fact (B. Barber, 1957, p. 396). It is safe to say that the percentage will be much smaller in studies made henceforth.

[4] Bendix and Howton supplemented this sample in a systematic way; for details, see their text (1959), p. 121, including n. 11.

TABLE 18

Occupations of the fathers of corporation officials *

Occupation [a]	*Number of executives*			*Percentage distribution*		
	1900	1925	1950	1900	1925	1950
HEAD OF SAME CORPORATION AS SON [b]	24	43	100	7.8	13.4	11.6
INDEPENDENT BUSINESS [c]						
Finance	17	21	48	5.5	6.7	5.5
Manufacturing, mining, and transportation	52	33	77	16.9	10.2	8.9
Mercantile	44	41	136	14.2	12.8	15.8
Farming	64	48	115	20.8	15.0	13.4
Craft	9	11	29	2.9	3.4	3.4
Other	4	3	28	1.4	0.9	3.3
TOTAL INDEPENDENT	190	157	433	61.7	49.0	50.3
EMPLOYEE						
Official [d]	8	13	63	2.6	4.1	7.3
Sales	2	2	16	0.7	0.6	1.9
Clerical and minor administrative	2	11	32	0.7	3.4	3.7
Skilled labor	9	10	46	2.9	3.1	5.4
Semiskilled and unskilled labor	4	10	18	1.3	3.1	2.1
TOTAL EMPLOYEE	25	46	175	8.1	14.4	20.4
PROFESSIONAL						
Lawyer	16	21	44	5.2	6.6	5.1
M.D.	15	7	23	4.9	2.2	2.7
Clergyman	19	18	19	6.2	5.6	2.2
Teacher	6	9	20	1.9	2.8	2.3
Engineer	2	7	12	0.7	2.2	1.4
Public official [e]	5	8	11	1.6	2.5	1.3
Other	6	4	24	1.9	1.2	2.8
TOTAL PROFESSIONAL	69	74	153	22.4	23.1	17.8
Total	308	320	861			
No information	8	10	21			

* M. Newcomer, *The Big Business Executive,* Columbia University Press, 1955, p. 53-54. Small errors in the addition of columns have been allowed to stand.

[a] When more than one occupation was found, the occupation in which the father was engaged at the time that the son was launched on his business career was used.

[b] In some instances the business was not incorporated when the father headed it, so that this group includes both independent entrepreneurs and corporation officials. The number of these is smaller than the cases of inheritance owing to the fact that inheritance from other members of the family is not included here unless the other relative was also responsible for the individual's upbringing.

[c] In addition to individual entrepreneurs, this includes corporation presidents who were the founders of the business. It does not include corporation officials who did not start the business or founders whose sons succeeded them.

[d] This includes only the upper ranks of corporation officials, such as presidents, vice presidents, general managers, and treasurers.

[e] Mostly army officers.

TABLE 19

*Economic status of fathers of corporation officials (percentage distribution)**

Economic status of father	*1900*	*1925*	*1950*
Wealthy	45.6	36.3	36.1
Medium	42.1	47.8	51.8
Poor	12.3	15.8	12.1

* Adapted from B. Barber, *Social Stratification,* Harcourt, Brace, 1957, p. 462, which in turn is adapted from M. Newcomer, *The Big Business Executive,* Columbia University Press, 1955, p. 63.

> . . . Mills has commented that the business leaders included in his sample were above average in income, but not necessarily rich; some were founders of enterprises which became prominent only after their deaths; and many were probably prominent because of their political roles rather than because of their success in business [Bendix and Howton, 1959, p. 119, citing Mills, 1945, p. 20].

The discrepancies between the results of these two studies may be due in part to the fact that the investigators may have had slightly different biases in judgment when assessing ambiguous evidence in any given case; they had to decide whether the evidence was adequate, and whether to call the father upper class or middle, middle class or lower. But probably the main cause of discrepancy is the tremendous difference in editorial policy between the *Dictionary* (*DAB*), which Mills used, and the *National Cyclopedia* (*NCAB*), used by Bendix and Howton.

> Thus, the *DAB* has an estimated total of 1,830 entries for businessmen born after 1570; the *NCAB* comprises an estimated total of 9,000 to 10,000 entries for businessmen born after 1771 [note the date]. This contrast confirms the statement by the editors of the *NCAB* that they placed a heavy emphasis on prominent businessmen–our reason for choosing this source for our study [Bendix and Howton, 1959, p. 129].

Thus we see that the implicit definition of "business elite" in one of these studies is quite different from that in the other, and that both are exceedingly vague in this respect. In any event, other studies of particular American elites—United States senators, prominent lawyers, prominent scientists—as well as studies of "eminent men" from diverse fields, give better support to the conclusion that the rate of mobility has remained about the same (as Bendix and Howton; Newcomer; Keller; and Warner and Abegglen contend) than to Mills's tentative conclusion that the rate of mobility is declining (see B. Barber, 1957, pp. 373-74, 463-67).

Although all these studies—including Mills's—show a considerable amount of vertical mobility in every period, they all tend to underestimate the actual amount. This is inevitable for at least two reasons. First, they are studies of elites, and it is at the top of the occupational system, of course, that one would expect the exclusiveness of upper-class status to manifest itself most clearly. Secondly, since available data are not always ample and clear, the investigator dare not divide the cases in his sample among a large number of "classes," for to do so would involve making discriminations that the data do not permit; but making do with a small number of classes inevitably obscures the presumably numerous cases of relatively small movement up or down from one generation to the very next. For example, a majority of the sons will be adjudged to be in the same social class as their fathers; yet almost every distinguished man is either more distinguished or less than his father, and this will be the more strikingly true the more narrowly we define distinction.

A valuable study by N. Rogoff (1953), though limited in other ways, is free from the limitations of studies of elites. Rogoff compared two periods in the history of Marion County, Indiana, which includes Indianapolis. From all applications for marriage licenses made by white males during 1905–12 and 1938–41 she took information on the applicant's occupation and that of his father. All the occupations were classified in ten large categories, which were prestige-ranked. Comparing the distribution of father-son shifts for the two periods, Rogoff found a somewhat higher rate of mobility in the later period.

Using data obtained by the Survey Research Center of the University of Michigan in its study of the presidential election of 1952, G. E. Lenski (1958) was able to derive certain rough and tentative conclusions concerning trends in occupational mobility in the country as a whole. He confined his attention to male respondents but included Negroes as well as whites. For each respondent he had occupation and father's occupation. Since the sample was small, he used only three occupational categories, which he called "white collar," "blue collar," and "farmer." These categories are admittedly crude. Lenski assumed that a father-son shift from either farmer or blue collar to white collar is upward mobility, that a shift from white collar to blue collar or farmer is downward, and a shift from blue collar to farmer or from farmer to blue collar is horizontal. Since he could not compare *samples* of respondents from different periods, he compared five "age cohorts" in his one 1952 sample. Each age cohort consisted of the men who were born within a particular ten-year period. Lenski adjusted the relative size of the age cohorts to take into account the important fact that men in college were underrepresented in the total sample. To allow for the fact that the younger men had not yet attained their final occupational positions, he adjusted the distributions of father-son shifts from one occupational category to another within the later age cohorts. This adjustment he made by extrapolating to the later age cohorts the trend of father-son shifts manifested in the successive age cohorts that had "completed" their respective shifts.

Having performed these calculations, Lenski found, among other results, that there was a slightly rising over-all trend in the rate of upward mobility and a slightly falling over-all trend in the rate of downward mobility. The curve in the rate of downward mobility varied somewhat independently of the curve in the rate of upward mobility. This is possible, of course, because *three* curves are involved—the curve of upward mobility, the curve of downward mobility, and the curve in the successive age cohorts which is made by fathers and sons in the same occupational category combined with the cases of merely horizontal father-son shifts.

For each of the five time periods represented by the age cohorts in his sample Lenski estimated as well as he could the relative proportions of white-collar workers, blue-collar workers, and farmers in the changing occupational structure of the United States. On the basis of these estimates he concluded that during the whole time within which the total sample had been born (roughly, 1873 to 1932) the occupational structure had changed in such a way as to increase the opportunities for upward mobility—in effect, that the number of white-collar jobs had increased relative to the number of blue-collar jobs and jobs in farming. He concluded, further, that if these changes in the occupational structure had not taken place, then the over-all trend in the rate of upward mobility would have fallen and the over-all trend in the rate of downward mobility would have risen. In short, the stability or slight improvement in the actual rate of mobility was due more to economic progress than to any trend toward equality of opportunity. This finding is not very different in its general significance from a finding Rogoff made in her study of mobility in the metropolitan area of Indianapolis. As we have noted, in that study Rogoff found that there was a rising trend in the rate of upward mobility from 1910 to 1940. When she converted her figures, however, from what they were to what they would have been if the shape of the occupational hierarchy had remained the same over the thirty-year period, she found that the rate of vertical mobility showed little change. If Rogoff's findings show slightly more favorable trends than Lenski's, the probable reason is that her study was confined to whites and she used ten occupational categories rather than three.

On the basis of several studies of varying scope in which a variety of approaches were used, we may tentatively conclude, therefore, that the rate of vertical mobility in the United States has shown no tendency to decline over a long period.

It is generally agreed that the ideology of equality of opportunity is especially pronounced in the United States. It is also widely believed, more by laymen than by sociologists, that the actual rate of vertical mobility is greater in the United States than in most other countries. The supposed class rigidity of England and France, for example, is often mentioned. Lipset and Bendix (1959, Chap. 2) have reviewed many of the studies of mobility in the United States and other countries. Comparison of the results of these studies is rather difficult, since the concepts and methods employed in one study are seldom exactly the same as those employed in another. For the most part Lipset and Bendix were obliged to use a rather crude indicator of mobility. They regarded as upward mobility any father-son shift from a manual to a nonmanual occupation, and as downward mobility any shift from nonmanual to manual. They were aware, of course, that not every nonmanual occupation outranks all manual occupations, but they felt that the errors entailed in the use of this indicator neutralized one another to some extent. Furthermore, it is *broadly* true that nonmanual occupations outrank manual ones.

The data on rates of mobility are reasonably comparable for the United States, France, Germany, Japan, Sweden, and Switzerland. In interpreting Table 20, which presents the results of ten studies covering these six countries, note especially that the mobility taken into account for each of the countries is only the mobility that occurred *within the nonfarm part of the population*. If the whole population had been taken into account, the over-all rates of mobility for the several countries might have been different. This is especially important in the case of France, which has a much higher proportion of its population on farms than the United States has.

Allowing for the unavoidable crudity of the indicator of mobility, for the inexact comparability of the data, and for the limitation to the nonfarm population, the results of this comparison are still not without interest. The table shows that the rate of upward mobility varies somewhat from one country to another, that the rate of downward mobility also varies, but that the over-all rates for all the countries are about the same. It would be hazardous to attach much importance to the slight differences. At the same time, we cannot conclude that there are no differences in patterns of mobility among these countries. More detailed investigation shows that movement into and out of particular occupational categories—e.g., civil servants, politicians, business executives—is different for various countries (see Lipset and Bendix, 1959, pp. 39-41).

We should also call attention once again to the fact that the over-all similarity in rates of mobility shown in Table 20 does not mean that all these countries have the same degree of approximation to equality of opportunity. Concerning this question, we can reach no conclusion from the data presented in the table. What the table does at least tend to show is that the actual rate of mobility tends to be similar in industrialized countries. Although the data for Italy as a whole—a less industrialized country—are not directly comparable with those for the six countries in Table 20, we do have more nearly comparable data for the city of Rome, and they tend to show that the rate of vertical mobility in Italy is lower than that in the more industrialized countries (Lipset and Bendix, 1959, pp. 32-33).

What we call "economic progress" is associated with industrialization; and industrialization, with a higher rate of vertical mobility. In this connection, the opinion of a sociologist of the University of Warsaw is especially interesting:

> A socialist system needs economic development even more than a capitalist one. . . . Therefore one of the immediate aims of the leaders of the socialist

states was to reach the level of more advanced capitalist countries in industrialization, urbanization, development of communications, and mass education. All these processes imply an increase in social mobility in socialist countries as well as elsewhere. . . . But it is the "social-economic expansion" and not the revolutionary introduction of a socialist order which can be considered a necessary condition of this increase. Increased mobility of this type could have been accomplished also if the capitalist system had persisted: it could have been done, e.g., with the help of schemes like the Marshall plan [Ossowski, 1957, as quoted in Lipset and Bendix, 1959, p. 282; italics omitted].

TABLE 20

*Comparative indices of upward and downward mobility, nonfarm populations only (percentage distribution)**

Country	*Upward mobility (Nonmanual sons of manual fathers)*	*Downward mobility (Manual sons of nonmanual fathers)*	*Total vertical mobility (Of all sons, those who moved either up or down)*
Germany	29	32	31
United States	33	26	30
Sweden	31	24	29
France	39	20	27
Japan	36	22	27
Switzerland	45	13	23

* Adapted from S. M. Lipset and R. Bendix, *Social Mobility in Industrial Society*, University of California Press, 1959, Table 2.1, p. 25. The percentages for Germany are the averages of three studies; so also are the percentages for the United States. The ten original studies on which the table is based are listed in Lipset and Bendix, pp. 19-21, 25.

DEGREES OF INTEGRATION

The integration of the class system of a society is almost synonymous with the integration of the society itself. Few subjects connected with social class are more complex and involve more danger of misunderstanding. The very concept of society implies that to some appreciable extent the various social classes share certain standards of evaluation. The relative emphasis on different values may be different for different classes, but if the values themselves were entirely different we could hardly speak of a *system* of classes. Nevertheless, the degree of integration varies widely from one society to another and within the same society from time to time.

As we have pointed out, the existence of somewhat different styles of life for different social classes does not necessarily mean that these classes disagree in their evaluations. For example, on the basis of a study of family budgets, Maurice Halbwachs found that in the French working class there was relatively little concern for the quality of housing. In the upper classes, on the other hand,

> . . . rather clear intervals separate the prices of lodging [and] to each figure for rental expense are found associated, in the social mind, definite figures for each of the other expenses [food and clothing]. To these determined standards of living correspond distinct social strata [Halbwachs, 1913, p. 450, as quoted in Pfautz and Duncan, 1950, p. 211].

Here, to be sure, are different styles of life, even different standards in a sense, but they do not mean that we are dealing with entirely different and mutually incompatible scales of evaluation. Presumably the members of the working class would acknowledge that a *hôtel* in the city or a *chateau* in the country is preferable to a run-down apartment. Halbwachs' findings simply show that there are several sets of families distinguished by their incomes and the ways in which they budget their resources. This is a very different situation from the one Beals describes for Peru (see Table 17, p. 518). At the bottom of the class hierarchy of Peru he places "two main cultural groups [of Indians] locally organized" with an "internal prestige system." (He does not indicate whether the two groups have the same system.) Here we are dealing with a class system imperfectly integrated normatively. These Indians simply do not share the values of the upper classes in the same society. They live by their own system of values as enclaves in the society. They stand at the bottom of the class structure, not because they fall short by standards they themselves appreciate, but because the other groups—the whites and the Cholos—are more powerful than they are. The culture of the more powerful groups is not necessarily "better"—it simply prevails. It prevails so clearly that in describing the class structure of Peru as a social system one can ignore the internal stratification of these Indian groups: *vis-à-vis* the dominant groups, the Indians are "all alike."

In a normatively integrated class system, acceptance of low status and low level of living is common. The Śūdras (Shudras) in India are the lowest of the four *varnas* (groupings of castes); only the "outcastes" or untouchables are below them. Yet we read that "orthodox Śūdras of the old school will not break their fast until they have sipped water which a Brahman has sanctified by dipping his toe into it" (Gait, 1928, p. 236). No doubt this is an extreme example. Yet even in the United States, where social ambition is not only accepted but urged and where in dress and other outward signs there are no clear-cut traditional differences between one class and another, the day-to-day round of living accustoms most people to their social level so thoroughly that even in their dreams and fantasies they do not ask for much more than they have.

> In a recent *Fortune* poll, a cross-section of the American people was asked what income they would like to have, if there were no limits to their demands. The average person gave a figure less than 25 per cent above what he was at the moment making; the mean figure was less than $4,000. See "Portrait

of the American People," *Fortune* (1947) 35:10 [Riesman, 1954, p. 328, n. 70].[5]

Fundamental acceptance of the stratification system is not incompatible with a good deal of complaining. Indeed, to a certain extent it is perfectly normal for the members of *each* social class to stress the respects in which it is *superior* to all the other classes. Self-esteem requires that those in a low position should stress two things: whatever is "good" about their way of life, especially whatever is *morally* good, worthy of pride, and, secondly, the "bad fortune" (not moral unworthiness) that caused them to be in a relatively low position. (The second line of thought does implicitly acknowledge a certain kind of social inferiority, but it absolves the self from blame.) The point we are stressing here is that such claims and absolutions serve self-esteem; they are functional for personalities. The point is not that the claims are untrue, for indeed there may be a good deal of truth in them.

Thus each class is to some extent a reference group for at least some other classes, in particular for the class directly above and the class directly below, if any. Practically everyone will remind himself of the inferiority of those below. Persons who have hope of getting into the class above will be less inclined to criticize it than those who feel stuck where they are. The latter will adjust, in part, by feeling that despite appearances and despite the "breaks" of life and birth they are just as good as those above—indeed, when you come right down to it, better. Such compensatory feelings are undoubtedly more "necessary" in a relatively open competitive system, in which social ambition is fostered and ideology stresses (and exaggerates) the existence of equality of opportunity. As we have noted, the compensatory feelings may have a solid basis in fact, but little discernment is needed to see that they are also expressions of envy; their very intensity is a tribute to the felt, but grudgingly acknowledged, superiority of those with greater prestige

Some of these points are illustrated in a field study of Prairieton, a small town in South Dakota. The highest-ranking families in the town were locally known (c. 1940) as "the Tops," and the lowest-ranking families were known as "the Bottoms" (Useem, Tangent, and Useem, 1942, p. 332). As is often true in local communities, these two classes were largely segregated residentially; the Bottoms were indeed concentrated "on the flats" and the Tops lived "on top of a bluff." The investigators interviewed a sample of twenty-two families from each of the two classes. The Tops tended to emphasize the ignorance, improvidence, and shiftlessness of the Bottoms. "Furthermore, two thirds believe the Bottoms are mentally dull, have low

5 In the text, Riesman refers to "the 'damned wantlessness of the poor,' against which Lassalle [a socialist] protested" (p. 328). On the tendency for women in the United States, regardless of class, to adopt the same fashions, see B. Barber and Lobel, 1952; as these authors point out, there are, of course, subtle differences according to age and social set, but there is nothing approaching the class costumes that in some societies have been established by law or custom.

moral standards, drink too much, are irreligious, behave in an ill-mannered fashion, and fail to appreciate those who try to help them" (p. 338). Although the Bottoms are more ambivalent, as we shall see, they are also critical of the Tops. "Parents of both strata make it a point to their young to avoid intimacy with children from the other stratum" (p. 339)

> While there is no single trait which all the lower class feels the Tops possess, two thirds declare they "try to show off," act as if they were inherently better than others, drink to excess, fail to live up to the religious teachings of their churches, use too much profanity and have easy jobs. More than half also claim that the elite are not well-behaved, are unkind and unsympathetic to the less fortunate, "try to run everybody else's business," and discriminate against Bottoms people [p. 338].

No doubt many of these points are sound, but the fact remains that the Tops families were much better educated than the Bottoms, and the family heads had positions of much greater responsibility in the town (they were landowners or "entrepreneurs" while the Bottoms family heads were "common laborers").

Class conflict

Class conflict, properly speaking, is much more serious and rare than this kind of mutual invidious comparison between adjacent classes, which is more or less normal (Marshall, ed., 1938). Economic competition and bargaining over the terms of cooperation in contractual relationships both involve some degree of conflict of interest, but they also imply an overriding common interest: an interest in maintaining the institutional rules of the game, an interest in seeing that the game itself goes on—the "game" of buying and selling in peaceful markets, the "game" of producing goods and services under the agreed-upon terms of labor contracts. Class conflict is much bitterer than economic competition and bargaining. In class conflict, the very rules of the game are questioned, and in extreme cases the protesting classes are ready to stop the game altogether and begin another one, with different rules. In short, the extreme form of class conflict occurs in a prerevolutionary and revolutionary period. Marx of course stressed this fact; one of his errors, indeed, was to treat class conflict as almost the *only* source of institutional change. According to R. M. MacIver (1947, p. 271), the class revolution is one of the *two* main types of revolution; the other is the national revolution in which a more or less unified nation throws out its foreign rulers.

Brinton's study of four great revolutions (1938) brings out certain tentative uniformities in class revolutions.[6] Among these uniformities is a

[6] In *The Anatomy of Revolution* (1938), Brinton analyzes and compares the English revolution of the 1640's, the American, the French, and the Russian revolutions. His uniformities do not hold so well for the American Revolution as for the others, but this reflects the fact that, as MacIver (1947, p. 471) points out, Brinton did not distinguish between the two major types of revolution. The American Revolution certainly involved class interests, but it was predominantly a national revolution.

sense of frustration in some class below the top. Many members of the frustrated class may have great economic achievements to their credit, and many have acquired wealth, but the entrenched upper class will not give them access to top public positions of power and prestige—in effect, will not admit them to the upper class. This element of status frustration was particularly pronounced in the French Revolution (see E. G. Barber, 1955, esp. Chap. 6). The upper bourgeoisie of financiers, shipbuilders, and large-scale merchants had been able for two centuries or more to buy its way into high positions in the army and in the courts (the *noblesse de robe*), but rather suddenly in the middle of the eighteenth century these channels of mobility were cut off. This stoppage of mobility, which is known as "the feudal reaction," affected most strongly the middle bourgeoisie, "composed of merchants, manufacturers, lawyers, and doctors" (E. G. Barber, 1955, pp. 143-44). The bourgeois were indignant. It was not only or mainly their economic interests that were involved, however. Perhaps of equal or greater importance was the fact that they felt themselves to be morally equal or superior to the upper class; they felt that their merit was not being recognized; they felt that the *privileges* of the upper class were unjust. They drifted into revolution, however, only very gradually.

Their sentiment of moral superiority went far beyond such "petty" notions as that they did not drink so much or use so much profanity as the upper class.

> We need hardly labor the point that both the French and the Russian middle classes hated, and envied, and felt morally superior to their aristocracies, and that their writings are filled with passages indicative of the strength and spread of these sentiments. At fourteen years Manon Phlipon, later as Madame Roland something more than Egeria to the Girondin party, told her mother after a week spent with a lady of the suite of the Dauphiness, "Another few days and I shall detest these people so much that I shan't be able to control my hatred." And to her mother's question as to what harm these aristocrats did her she answered, "It's just feeling the injustice, thinking every moment about the absurdity of it all." The higher the French bourgeois rose, the closer he came in his way of life to the aristocracy, the more vividly in some respects he felt the gap which separated him from his neighbor with four quarters of nobility. "It wasn't the taxes," wrote Rivarol in his memoirs, "nor the *lettres de cachet*, nor all the other abuses of authority; it wasn't the vexations of the *intendants*, nor the ruinous delays of justice which most irritated the nation; it was the prejudice of nobility. What proves this is that it was the bourgeois, the men of letters, the financiers, in fine all those who were envious of the nobility, who raised against the nobility the petty bourgeois of the towns and the peasants in the country" [Brinton, 1938, pp. 72-73].

In a prerevolutionary situation, the feeling of frustration and injustice goes well beyond the envious carping that is more or less normal in interclass relations. Possibly the upper class becomes more snobbish, more resistant to talent from below, the more insecure it becomes economically and the more incompetent in those functions for the performance of which it was originally given power and prestige. If so, its pretentiousness and exclusiveness would be the more galling to the new class of ambitious people conscious of their achievements, their real power, and their moral worth. In any case, a uniformity in prerevolutionary situations is unusual incompetence in the government. Such a statement admittedly comes close to being an unscientific value judgment, but at least the feeling is widespread in a prerevolutionary society that the governing class is incompetent. And objective evidence is not lacking. Both radicals and conservatives, for example, agree that the Russian conduct of World War I was not brilliant. Defeat in war is always bad for the prestige of a government. Moreover, another uniformity in prerevolutionary situations is that the government is having grave financial difficulties. It seems likely that the frustrated class below, although better able than ever to pay taxes, is less willing to do so because of its being excluded from positions of public prestige and because of its consciousness that the upper class is incompetent.[7] The government is losing its authority.

All these questions need further study. In particular, it would be desirable to know which is more important in a prerevolutionary situation—the personal incompetence of the decaying upper class, or the inadequacy of existing political institutions to meet internal and external changes. It is possible that the "need" for political reform is greater than the "need" for economic reform. More important is the fact that the two are interrelated. The reader may have wondered about our wobbling between the terms "upper class" and "governing class." We use the term "governing class" (or "ruling class") with great misgiving, for it has been used very loosely indeed by propagandists. Nevertheless, it has some justification. What we have said about political power in Chapters 13 and 14 may serve as a sufficient indication of both the appropriateness and the inappropriateness, in some situations, of the term "governing class." We have noted that the "political" subsystem of society is not exactly the same thing as the government, although the government is primarily political. In addition, the following comment seems very judicious:

> When conflict breaks out, the attack is made against a group of persons wielding power. They may be referred to as "the governing class." This phrase is loosely used. The feudal aristocracy was literally a governing class. The modern capitalists are not. And yet the words express a truth. The implication is that the capitalist is using in the economic field a power that is partly political, in that it is derived from the laws and institutions of the society. If a class is strong enough to secure or to preserve those institutions that favour its activities, it may be said to be "governing" to that extent [Marshall, 1953, p. 85].

From the point of view of an upper class, one of the most ominous signs of its loss of moral authority is the all but unanimous alienation of the

[7] In his study of six sixteenth-century revolutions occurring in six different countries, R. B. Merriman (1938) found that in each case the revolution began as a protest against taxation.

intellectuals. The term "intellectuals" is here used loosely, to mean articulate molders of opinion, especially in influential circles: writers, teachers, preachers. Indeed, in the prerevolutionary situation the incompetence or at any rate the inadequacy of the ruling class has gone so far that some of its own members defect and join the chorus of satirists and other critics (Brinton, 1938, pp. 64-70).[8] But as we have noted, a large part of the upper class remains intransigent or vacillates unskillfully.

Revolutionary sentiments are bitter and violent when they arise, but they do not arise easily. Despite the incompetence of the "old regimes"—the prerevolutionary government and ruling class—it may be that their refusal to share their prestige with talent from below is more damaging to them than their personal incompetence. Here is a comment on the French Revolution:

> Strikingly enough, there were few expressions of egalitarian sentiments by bourgeois writers of the 18th century. The vast majority . . . supported the anti-egalitarian presuppositions of the structure of French society and of the French government. The bourgeois made no explicit assertion of the equal dignity of all men, nor of the equal right of all men to opportunity for advancement. Only implicitly did he claim for himself the right to change his inferior status to one that did have dignity; and once he became a nobleman, he tried to identify himself completely with his new social "equals." But when the limited opportunities for mobility were denied, he gradually swung over his predominant allegiance to the universalistic values on which his all-important claim to mobility depended [E. G. Barber, 1955, p. 144].

Criticism of the upper class may go very far, the class system may be malintegrated, but there is perhaps seldom any doubt as to which class *is* the upper class at any given time. In Prairieton, South Dakota, the Bottoms families were critical of the Tops, as we saw. Yet their criticism did not prevent them from being willing to join the reprehensible idlers at the top. The critical ratios (C.R.'s) given in the following quotation all indicate that the numerical differences are almost certainly not due to chance variation in the samples.

> . . . while all twenty-two of the Tops desire their children to marry within their own class, only five of the Bottoms express a similar wish (C.R = 8.46). ["Fifteen others had no decided preference and two hoped to have their children marry into Tops families"–authors' footnote.] Nineteen of the high status class and only four of those of low status say they do not want members of the other stratum in their clubs (C.R. = 6.00). Fifteen of the former and but six of the latter do not enjoy companionships of persons from the outgroup (C.R. = 2.91) [Useem, Tangent, and Useem, 1942, p. 339].[9]

---

[8] It seems to the present writer that Brinton in these pages is not sufficiently critical of Pareto's "loaded" view that the moral self-doubt of some members of the ruling class is an unmanly symptom of effeteness. It seems more likely that such doubt reflects their sense of the personal or institutional "inadequacy" we have been discussing.

[9] The authors point out that "E. T. Hiller [1939, p. 134] found a similar pattern in another low status rural group."

To return to the prerevolutionary situation, in which class conflict is at its most intense until the revolutionary period itself: the intransigence of the governing class finally drives the frustrated to make greater demands than they would have dreamed of making only a few years earlier. People whose forebears had borne poverty perhaps for centuries suddenly decide that they are intolerably oppressed. The old regime is painted as entirely black, while a utopian vision takes hold of the ideologists' imaginations. Idealistic fervor eventually leads to the "reign of terror and virtue."

We began by saying that mutual invidious comparison is virtually normal in the relations between adjacent social classes. In an abnormal situation this normal comparison changes its character:

> Comparison does not make contacts, it breaks them. It leads to isolation rather than to conflict. But if conflict is brewing, the attitudes born of comparison will stimulate it, and, when it matures, embitter it, and they are always there, ready to convert into a class struggle a dispute which is in essence no more than a disagreement about the terms of cooperation [Marshall, 1953, p. 84].[10]

The Functions and Dysfunctions of Social Stratification

The functional significance of social class is to some extent implicit in much that we have already said. Here we shall devote our attention to a more explicit functional assessment of the various aspects of class that we have stressed: the basis of stratification in a hierarchy of values and in role differentiation; the fact of prestige ranking; the fact that the unit of social class is the family, and more generally the fact that class implies some differential association between the families of which a society is composed; and the tendency of social classes in the same system to have different styles of life, apart from the differences implied in role differentiation. Functional assessment in this field as in others is not a simple matter. We shall find that to some extent functions and dysfunctions are bound up together, but we shall also find that there are various possible kinds of functional balance. We have already caught a glimpse of the important fact that some class systems seem to have a relatively unfavorable balance between functional and dysfunctional characteristics. But we must also allow for the possibility that different systems are not necessarily capable of being ranked on a simple scale according to their adequacy in meeting the functional requirements of a society. It can probably be said of class systems, as of organisms, that somewhat different combinations of characteristics may all be functionally

---

[10] After the French Revolution, although the nobility lost corporate influence, the prestige of old titles remained so great that the high bourgeoisie continued to regard marriage into the nobility as desirable. For many examples, see Hamon, 1936, v. 1, pp. 50, 118-21, 183, 202 n.2, 225, 296-97.

"favorable." Certain things can be said, however, about the functions and dysfunctions of class systems in general.

FUNCTIONS

One of the principal functions of class stratification is to induce people to work hard to live up to values (K. Davis and Moore, 1945, pp. 242-43; K. Davis, 1953, p. 396). Those who best fulfill the values of a particular society presumably are given the rewards of greater prestige, social acceptance by others who are rated high and are presumably worth knowing, and money (or comfort and diversion in some more direct form). Money of course is also a symbol of prestige. All these rewards are at the same time incentives. We have noted that occupations tend to rank high if their functions are important and the requisite personnel is scarce. Among the reasons for scarcity of personnel, we pointed out, is that relatively hard work may be necessary to acquire the necessary training. Another reason may be that the position in question involves a heavy burden of responsibility. To the extent that hard work and responsibility are involved, there must be compensations for undertaking them. In thinking about this problem, people sometimes make comments on the prestige and comfort of priests and doctors, for example, but forget about the arduous training that may have been required. In the *kibbutz* described by Spiro (1956), the ideology stressed the value of manual labor and distrust of authority. The planning and executive positions involved no greater prestige and in many cases no privileges. In consequence, nobody wanted these positions. People had to be drafted for them. The work and responsibility involved were not adequately compensated for.

If a society offers a high degree of prestige and other rewards for certain positions, there will be some competition for them. To the extent that the more valued positions involve talent and training, presumably competition helps to ensure that the more able rise to the top, where their ability can best be used. In other words, to some extent class stratification (in its differential-reward aspect) helps to ensure what is often called "the circulation of the elite."

So far we have said, in effect, that differential rewards have a pattern-maintenance function to the extent that they provide incentive for hard work and open up a career for talent. The competitive aspect has a kind of economic (adaptive) function also in that it helps to ensure the rational use of available talent (part of one of the "factors" of production, namely, "land"). But it is important to see that differential rewards are functional even if positions at the top are largely ascribed—in other words, if competition is severely restricted, as in a caste system. For even in such a system those at the top can lose their positions (downward mobility is always possible); differential rewards therefore provide the incentive for the upper classes to work at maintaining their positions. There may be a tendency in the United States to think of aristocracies as corrupt, lazy, and incompetent.

These qualities may indeed be common in a decaying aristocracy, but on the other hand a decaying aristocracy is in a vulnerable position; eventually it will cease to be an aristocracy if there are other people in the society who are actually doing the work that requires talent and training. *Noblesse oblige* is not a meaningless phrase.

Moreover, some of the privileges enjoyed by elites—for example, extra comfort and immunity from tiring menial labor—are functionally justified to the extent that men in the elite *actually possess* scarce and socially valued abilities and qualities, whether these are partly innate or wholly acquired, and whether the society is close to having equality of opportunity or far from it. It would be wasteful to pour the scarce resources of society into the training of surgeons, let us say, and then to require the surgeons to wash the floors. Differential rewards and inequality of opportunity are not the same thing (Davis and Moore, 1945). Even in a caste system, which has *systematic* inequality of opportunity, the great prestige of a high-caste man is not entirely explained by his birth into a high-caste family (K. Davis, 1953, p. 395). As for why the caste has a high position (receives differential rewards), the explanation lies in functional importance and relative scarcity of personnel, not in birth. The point is that immunity from menial labor is not only a reward, it is also a kind of economic facility in some cases. In a way, competition is more rational than ascription, but no matter how people are chosen in the first place, once they have been trained for certain difficult positions it would be dysfunctional to waste their time and energy on tasks for which there is no scarcity of personnel.

Relatively frequent and intimate association with fellow class-members, which we have treated as an aspect of class, also has a double function. In the first place, for the upper classes at least, it is a kind of differential reward. Secondly, however, it tends to stabilize and reinforce the attitudes and skills that may be the basis of upper-class position. Having similar values and interests tends to enable people to associate comfortably with one another, to draw them together; but the frequent association also confirms their common values and interests.

Since all societies have a family institution (not necessarily the same one), there will be in every society, as we have noted, some tendency toward inheritance of status. Children from the beginning will ordinarily begin associating more frequently and more intimately (in some ways) with class equals. In the United States this will be so even if some people are ideologically opposed to such discrimination. To some extent, no discrimination is necessary: differential association will take place automatically as a result of residential segregation by class. Differential social interaction thus makes possible the inculcation and cultivation of somewhat different values, qualities, and skills in different social classes (W. B. Miller, 1959a). Up to a point, this differentiation is functional for society, for the fact is that society needs manual as well as nonmanual workers, that many jobs are not attractive to highly trained or "refined" people, and therefore that the different kinds and results of socialization connected with the several social classes of a society are all functional to some extent. It is because this truth seems harsh that the economist Galbraith, among others, regards as an important social goal the development of more and more jobs that permit their occupants to be interested in them and that are done in clean and pleasant physical and social surroundings (1958, Chap. 24).

To the extent that "lower class" cultural characteristics are necessary to society, they are of course functional, and differential class interaction and socialization are functional—and, we may add, a certain amount of mutual antagonism between social classes is functional. To some extent, an upper class and a lower class (we mention only two to make the point simply) are negative reference groups for each other. Useem, Tangent, and Useem discerned the rationalizing function of mutual deprecation by the Tops and the Bottoms of Prairieton: they saw, that is, that the Bottoms in particular safeguarded their self-esteem by criticizing the Tops. To this point we add that as long as there must be Top and Bottom positions it is functional for society that the Tops and the Bottoms reject each other's ideals to some extent.

> Boys and girls from Tops families by the age of ten think Bottoms children their own age are "tough, stink, and dumb"; the latter label upper class children as "sissies, smart-alecks, and stuck up" [1942, p. 339].

This pattern that each class has of using the other as a negative reference group may be regarded as having both a pattern-maintenance and a social-control (integrative) function.

Class stratification has another social-control function. We mentioned earlier that only in the "shady" world of gamblers and in the underworld of lower criminals is money taken as the main criterion of success and prestige. One reason that illegal services are likely to be expensive (or profitable, from the seller's point of view) is that the buyer has to pay the seller for the unusual risk he is taking and for the loss of prestige he suffers. In a way, money here is not so much a criterion of prestige as a substitute for it, a compensation for renouncing it. The legitimate class structure, however, continues to attract the shady classes and the underworld. This attraction exerts a social-control function. Instead of continuing in a profitable shady career, racketeers wish to gain respectability for their money and for their children. They enter legitimate fields and become philanthropists and patrons of the arts.

DYSFUNCTIONS

The dysfunctions of class stratification are probably more obvious than the functions. They stem largely from the fact that the unit of class is the family. The tendency toward inheritance of class position, which is revealed in every study of the relation between fathers' occupations and those of their sons, inevitably means that to some extent the circulation of the elite is hampered, there is some waste of talent, and presumably some social positions are filled less efficiently than they would otherwise be. Family loyalty is not the only cause of this. To whatever extent social-class consciousness exists (not necessarily in the rather narrow Marxist sense) there is inevitably a tendency toward class favoritism. In the caste type of system, constriction of the circulation of the elite is elevated into a principle.

Another tendency inherent in the castelike aspect of a class system—and we must remember that this tendency exists in every system: what we call a caste system is only an extreme type, sanctified in religion or ideology—is the tendency for the upper classes to accumulate wealth: "To them that have shall be given. . . ." The distribution of wealth in all forms probably never fulfills perfectly the function of giving greater rewards to those whose contributions to society are the more important. From a sociological point of view, the dysfunction involved in this "maldistribution" lies not in its abstract injustice but, rather, in the *sense* of injustice, in the danger to morale involved in the spread of the feeling that effort is not rewarded according to desert, and in the strain put upon the integration of society. The distribution of good things in general, which is to some extent controlled by the sheer power aspect of upper-class position, is dysfunctional, in other words, if it begins to undermine the value system and transform "normal" criticism from below into class rancor. In this case, the differential-reward aspect of class does not fulfill its pattern-maintenance and integrative functions; instead, it creates a "problem" in the areas of pattern-maintenance and integration.

A special aspect of "maldistribution" of rewards in this sense is implicit in much that we have said. In some cases, as for example in the growing rancor of the bourgeoisie before the French Revolution, the maldistribution that caused complaint was not so much maldistribution of material rewards. Nor was there great danger that the bourgeoisie would through apathy cease to perform its functions for society. The trouble, it appears, was that the bourgeoisie felt that it was not given adequate public recognition for the functions it was in fact performing. Inadequate public recognition was no doubt partly a matter of restricting business activities unnecessarily (as if they were unimportant); and it was partly a matter of not permitting members of the bourgeoisie to gain the social distinction of nobility. This feeling of injustice led to, or was involved in, class conflict; when circumstances were ripe the growing strength of the frustrated classes overcame the weakness of the "ruling class," but only at the great cost of revolution.

The dysfunctions of social class, then, are the prevention of talent from reaching certain top positions where it would be socially most useful, the hampering of talented persons in the positions they do occupy, and the withholding of social rewards from functionally important people and unduly confining these rewards to people whose contributions to society seem less important. These dysfunctions are always present to some degree, but they are not always so pronounced as to outweigh the functions we have mentioned. In other words, a certain amount of "injustice" and inflexibility can exist without creating universal cynicism and destroying the integration of society. We shall see in Chapter 21 that it is one of the normal functions of the prevailing ideology of a society to gloss over or play down "injustice," which to some extent is inevitable. The *spread* of a revolutionary ideology decrying the "official" one is a symptom that the sense of injustice has broken through the beliefs that ordinarily keep it in check.

THE DEFECTS OF VIRTUES

At first glance, the foregoing analysis of the functions and dysfunctions of class stratification may seem self-contradictory. We may seem to have said that differential rewards are both functional and dysfunctional, that class loyalty is both functional and dysfunctional, and that differential interaction based on social class is both functional and dysfunctional. Where does all this leave us?

The truth seems to be that in every society prestige, power, and other desirable things are to some extent rewards for unusual contributions and at the same time means whereby functionally important persons can better carry out their functions. But to some extent in every society prestige, power, and other desirable things are mere privileges, enjoyed by people who have unusual access to them but who make no unusual contribution to society and may even be a drag upon it. Prestige, power, and comfort are facilities—but they facilitate either functional contributions or retention of privilege. To the extent that they are rewards for actual valued ability actually used, and as facilities are accompanied by recognized responsibilities, to that extent class is functional in the ways we have specified. To the extent that prestige, power, and comfort are based on privilege alone and are used to facilitate retention of mere privilege, to that extent class is dysfunctional. If prestige, power, and comfort are hereditary by recognized right, as in a caste system, then there must be a great emphasis on accompanying responsibility; they must be thought of as anticipatory rewards, as facilities granted in the expectation that the recipients will contribute ability and energy to society. If the hereditary lower castes are to be expected to settle for less prestige, power, and comfort, they must be able to expect something in return, some services from above.

Although these statements sound moralistic, they are not necessarily wrong on that account. It is possible to devise empirical tests or indices of the relation between prestige, power, and comfort on the one hand and responsibility and unusual functional contributions on the other. It would also be possible to test empirically the hypothesis that the association between prestige and functional responsibility is closer in some social systems than in others. Finally, it would be possible to test empirically the hypothesis that when the association becomes weaker than it has been in the same social system, then prestige tends to lose its moral authority—that is, tends to cease being prestige. To this extent, if the hypothesis is true, the dysfunctional aspect of differential reward tends to be self-correcting.

We should make a few qualifications explicit. One is that a system can apparently become stabilized at a point at which the upper classes may seem to be contributing rather little to those below. We have already noted that through conquest a group can establish itself over another, and we early called attention to "the normative tendency of the actual"—the tendency for people to come rather quickly to expect that an interaction pattern once established will be maintained, and "expect" in the sense that they feel it ought to be. For this reason we suggested that prestige is weakened only when those who have it do *less than they have been doing* to deserve it.

Another point is that what seems like small functional responsibility from one point of view might not from another. There is great danger that our judgments will be ethnocentric. For example, to a Westerner it might seem that the Brahmans do little for all their prestige. But we saw in our study of religion that the Brahmans are chiefly responsible for the system of values that provides some degree of integration to an extremely heterogeneous society. Moreover, any Brahman who ceases to uphold the system by exemplifying these values to an unusual degree loses prestige and may lose his formal status.

Finally, we should note that we are here discussing the relation between prestige and power on the one hand and functional contribution on the other. We are not discussing the abstract justice or injustice of some particular degree of approximation to the Western ideal of equality of opportunity. Here again the danger of ethnocentrism is great, and the Hindu system is instructive. From a naive American point of view, the ascription of caste status in India is grossly unjust, but we must remind ourselves that from a Hindu point of view it is not unjust at all. It would be unjust, rather, if the unusual merit an individual has earned in his earlier incarnations were not appropriately rewarded by his caste status in the present. We must also remind ourselves that from a purely rational and empirical point of view the system of religious ideas underlying such a sense of justice is at least as respectable and subtle as any religious ideas that are common in the West.

Although our discussion certainly leaves many questions unanswered, we shall turn away from them to another point. It seems that the open type of society has a certain set of characteristic advantages and disadvantages and that the closed type has a different characteristic set. The advantages of *institutionalized* caste—morally approved caste—seem to derive from the fact that the course of individual lives can be foreseen to a greater extent than in an open-class system. Consequently individuals can begin to prepare early for their responsibilities. Furthermore, they can be relatively serene, for they are relieved of the burden of proving to themselves that they can achieve a higher status; no one expects them to do so, not even they themselves. They can be serene for another reason also: being relatively settled in life, they are assured that their family relationships and friendships will remain relatively stable. Some of the disadvantages of caste are obvious: It impedes, although it cannot prevent, the circulation of the elite. Since responsibilities are fixed by tradition, it is presumably somewhat inflexible, even though the conception of an utterly static caste system is a kind of myth. Finally, the danger of abuse of power—if only negatively, by not doing anything to justify having it—must be great.

The advantages and disadvantages of an open-class system seem to be the reverse of those of a caste system. The open-class system is presumably more flexible, encourages the circulation of the elite, and makes prestige more strictly dependent upon performance. The disadvantages are also great, however. Competition makes the problem of maintaining self-esteem more difficult. Ambitions are inevitably due to be disappointed in many cases. At the same time, those who have prestige must feel somewhat insecure, since in a competitive order full of ambitious people they can easily be displaced. Finally, with a great deal of social mobility, relations with family and friends are much less stable. Many people achieve a higher class status, or drop to a lower one, and in either case they leave some friends behind and weaken kinship ties. Moreover, there is a good chance that they will be somewhat uncomfortable, even ambivalent, in their new class associations. An open society must have a higher proportion of marginal men in it.

RECOMMENDED READING

S. M. Lipset and R. Bendix, *Social Mobility in Industrial Society*, University of California Press, 1959, is especially valuable for its critical summary of recent European and Japanese studies. Many of the works recommended for Chapter 18 are also relevant for this chapter. On channels of mobility and studies of the varying amount of mobility, see P. A. Sorokin, *Social Mobility,* Harper, 1927 and B. Barber, *Social Stratification,* Harcourt, Brace, 1957, Chaps. 14-16. Chapter 11 gives a fairly detailed review of social-class differences in the socialization of children. For a good example of research in this field, see B. C. Rosen, "The Achievement Syndrome," *Amer. sociol. Rev.*, April 1956, v. 21, no. 2, pp. 203-11.

On revolution, see C. Brinton, *The Anatomy of Revolution*, W. W. Norton, 1938, which also contains a good annotated bibliography. See also L. Gottschalk, "The Causes of Revolution," *Amer. J. Sociol.*, July 1944, v. 50, no. 1, pp. 1-8. In the same issue of *Amer. J. Sociol.*, pp. 9-21, see N. S. Timasheff, "Vertical Social Mobility in Communist Society," which incidentally offers a pertinent criticism of Brinton's phase theory of the course of revolutions.

On the functions and dysfunctions of class systems, see K. Davis and W. E. Moore, "Some Principles of Stratification," *Amer. sociol. Rev.*, April 1945, v. 10, no. 2, pp. 242-49. This article is especially valuable for its analysis of the factors that give great prestige to religious, political, and economic leaders and of the factors that prevent any one of these types of leader from monopolizing prestige and power. A criticism of Davis and Moore is presented in M. M. Tumin, "Some Principles of Stratification," *Amer. sociol. Rev.*, Aug. 1953, v. 18, no. 4, pp. 387-94. They satisfactorily answer Tumin's criticisms in the same issue of the *Review*: K. Davis, "Reply," pp. 394-97, and Moore, "Comment," p. 397.

part eight

SOCIAL DEVIATION AND SOCIAL CHANGE

20. Social Conformity, Social Deviation, and Social Control

The three related concepts to be discussed in this chapter are not new to us. They are inherent in the conceptual framework of modern sociology—at least, of the so-called structural-functional theory. They all focus on social norms and social action.

"Conformity" and "deviation," in the present context, have meaning only in relation to the fact that the actors in social systems are oriented to social norms that are internalized as part of their personality. "Conformity" is action that (1) is oriented to a social norm (or norms) and (2) falls within the band of behavior permitted by the norm. Conformity, in other words, does not just happen to fall within the range of permitted behavior. The relevant norm or norms are part of the actor's motivation, although he is not necessarily conscious of them at all times or at any time. Modern legal systems, for example, are so complex that we require specialists to tell us what our specific rights and obligations are. There is, however, in every field of social interaction the general knowledge that some legal norms apply to it and the generally recognized obligation to find out what those norms are. But we are not necessarily conscious at all times or at any time of legal or other social norms that are in fact "known" to us. We may implicitly accept a norm without being able to put it into words.

Corresponding statements can be made about social deviation. Deviant behavior is not merely behavior that happens to violate a norm; it is behavior that violates a norm to which the actor is oriented at the time; it is motivated violation.[1] This does not necessarily mean that the actor is alienated from the norm. He may wish to conform but be unable to do so because of implicit or explicit coercion. For example, not all persons are prejudiced

[1] Note that we are defining deviation, not making a factual statement about it. People do sometimes break rules of whose existence they are unaware. The "deviant" aspect of such cases requires no scientific theory to explain it. Such cases are of little empirical interest either, although they do occur (mostly in relation to recent or minor laws). The legal stand was explained by the seventeenth-century scholar John Selden: "Ignorance of the law excuses no man; not that all men know the law, but because 'tis an excuse every man will plead, and no man can tell how to confute him" (*Table Talk,* 1696, under "Law").

who violate the norms of fair play by discriminating against Negroes; some of them might prefer to treat Negroes according to universalistic standards but are afraid to do so because of the prejudice of others around them (see Merton, 1948a). More often perhaps, the deviant actor not only knows the norm to which he is oriented but to some degree accepts its validity.

Social control consists in the operation of all mechanisms that counteract deviant tendencies, either by preventing outward deviation or, more important, by checking or reversing the elements of motivation that tend to produce deviant behavior.

Virtually no act is normatively indifferent. We shall regard as conforming behavior all behavior that does not violate any of the norms to which the actor in question is oriented. An implication of this definition is that not all novel behavior is deviant. Innovation is often possible within the social norms to which the actor is committed. Social change may of course occur as a result of the failure of social-control mechanisms to check or reverse deviant tendencies, but much social change has other sources, as we shall see in Chapter 22.

On the whole, deviant behavior is dysfunctional for the group in which it occurs. The smoothness and success of individual activity as well as of cooperative activity depend to a great extent on the predictability of other people's actions, and this predictability in turn depends in part on the system of norms to which the members of the group are presumed to be oriented. We have called attention to the instructive ambiguity of the words "expect," "expectation." Behavior in conformity with group norms is expected in the sense that it is obligatory; being obligatory, it is also expected in the sense that others are implicitly predicting that it will occur in the relevant circumstances. When behavior that is counted on does not occur, the deviation is of course typically disruptive to some extent. Indeed, it is this disruption that arouses negative feelings and ordinarily sets in motion negative sanctions intended to punish the deviant, to restrain him, and possibly to restore him to the "expected" path. In short, disruption and social control are two sides of the same coin.

Yet deviant behavior is not necessarily dysfunctional. We noted in Chapter 3 that norms are sometimes dysfunctional; when they are, it is presumably conformity and not deviation that is dysfunctional. In Chapter 12 we cited the study of an enforcement agency in which the officials were by formal rule expected to report to higher authorities any attempt that might be made to bribe them, and we noted that if the officials had complied with this rule they would have had a more difficult time accomplishing the official purpose for which the agency was set up. Their deviation from the rule was functional for achieving the purpose of the agency. However, the *informal* rule in the agency was *not* to report the proffering of bribes. In other words, "deviant" behavior in that situation was equivocal, for the actor's immediate associates in the agency—his colleagues—expected it. In general, in considering whether behavior is deviant we must be careful to specify the group whose point of view we are taking, and in considering whether it is dysfunctional we must specify the group whose activities we have in mind. Conforming behavior in a subgroup—for example, a criminal gang—may be deviant in the larger society; it can be functional for the subgroup and dysfunctional for the society.

Here we must recall another caveat we made earlier; namely, that "functional" does not necessarily mean ethically good, and "dysfunctional" does not necessarily mean ethically bad. Nor can we equate "conforming" and "good," "deviant" and "bad." Merton has made this point and gone on to quote Gilbert Murray's remark about the second book of Plato's *Republic:*

> No one who has read it can easily forget the account of the righteous man [who has deviated] in the evil or mistaken society, how he is to be scourged and blinded and at last impaled or crucified by the society that misunderstands him, because he is righteous and seems the reverse, and how after all it is better for him so to suffer than to follow the multitude in doing wrong [Murray, 1946, p. 75; quoted in Merton, 1957, p. 183].

In this time when a few people are rightly calling attention to the danger of a slavish conformism in public life, it is perhaps necessary to make explicit the fact that "conformity," as the term is used in this chapter, is not necessarily bad either.

Causes of Conformity

The following list is undoubtedly not complete, but it includes the most important general causes of widespread conformity to the social norms of a group. Behind these causes lie more complex causes, some of which we have treated earlier in this book. There is no logical end, of course, to the analysis of the causes of anything.

1. *Socialization.* In Chapter 5 we examined some of the processes by which social norms (as well as other parts of culture) are inculcated so that they become part of the personality.

2. *Insulation.* We noted in Chapter 2 that role conflict—more generally, any conflict in the norms that apply to the same actor—inevitably results in deviation. Any built-in arrangements that tend to reduce normative conflict thereby contribute to conformity. Among such arrangements one of the most important is the fact that social norms that might conflict are largely prevented from doing so by applying to different times and places. Thus "incompatible" expectations cause no trouble unless for some reason the actor fails to allocate his time properly, so that action appropriate for one occasion encroaches upon another. Another important kind of insulation is provided in the fact that, to a large extent, a given actor carries out the activities of his various roles with, or *vis-a-vis,* different role-sets.

3. *Hierarchy.* Another built-in arrangement is the fact that to a considerable extent the norms that apply to a particular actor are ranked

in some order of precedence. Thus if expectations conflict (or might otherwise conflict) the actor has grounds for making a choice. The hierarchy of norms, as well as the time-and-place aspect of norms, is part of culture. Thus it is not a device peculiar to each personality but permits intermeshing of the expectations of an indefinite number of persons who share in the culture and are cognizant of the facts of particular situations. Socialization is incomplete unless the time-and-place and hierarchical aspects of norms are inculcated along with the expected forms of behavior. These are important aspects of the integration of a cultural system. However, any system of norms is likely to be imperfectly integrated in this sense, and when this is so, not socialization but the culture itself is at fault.

4. *Social control.* In Chapter 2 we pointed out that social control works in part through the fact that a socialized actor is able to anticipate in imagination what would happen to him if he violated the legitimate expectations of others. Thus sanctions lead to conformity largely without being actually applied. The mechanism of social control will be discussed further below.

5. *Ideology.* Chapter 21 is devoted entirely to ideology, but we may anticipate it a little by saying that the willing participation of group members, including their conformity to group norms, depends to some extent upon the ideas they hold concerning the place of the group in a larger social setting and the way in which the group functions and ought to function. There are at least two ways in which an ideology is connected with institutionalized norms. First, the norms partly express broader values that in the ideology are likely to be emphasized in purer form. Secondly, the ideology is likely to exaggerate the extent to which social institutions actually fulfill the ideals or values of the group. Thus in general the ideology strengthens faith in the existing system and therefore presumably helps to motivate people to conform to its norms. Ideology adds to the norms themselves a kind of cognitive framework, an "intellectual" support.

Even in these brief comments we must make two qualifications. Roughly speaking, the larger the group, the more likely it is to have ideological conflict within it. We have been describing the conservative ("official") ideology of the group, temporarily ignoring the fact that many groups, especially many large-scale societies, also have dissident subgroups and movements with ideologies that in various ways and degrees attack the official ideology. Secondly, although the official ideology largely supports the social structure, motivating people to conform to it, there are cases in which the official ideology to some extent helps to bring about nonconformity in some elements of the population. We shall describe an example later in this chapter.

6. *Vested interests.* Conformity to social norms does not depend upon idealistic motives alone, nor upon these motives plus sanctions. We must remember that social norms define rights as well as obligations. Many rights—property rights are a good example—inherently protect certain ad-

vantages that some members of the group enjoy to the relative exclusion of other members. Those who enjoy such advantages are likely to be well satisfied with the norms that protect them; hence they are likely to support these norms with a greater sense of conviction than the disadvantaged can have.

The term "vested interests" is often used in a pejorative sense, but not here. Here the term is perfectly neutral. How particular vested interests are to be judged depends upon various circumstances. Vested interests are not just any advantages whatever; they are advantages that are legitimized and hence sanctioned by the social order. Thus landlords' rents are vested interests because the institution of private property makes it quite legitimate to own houses and rent them for a profit. The income from rents is an "advantage" because not everybody owns houses.

By extension, the term "vested interests" may refer to advantages that depend upon existing social institutions without being legitimized by then For example, during Prohibition bootleggers (manufacturers and distributors of illegal alcoholic liquor) had a vested interest in the Prohibition law in the sense that their profits depended upon it. But of course the Prohibition law itself did not sanction the illegal manufacture and sale of liquor.

Vested interests may be of the most various kinds. All legitimate possessions and rewards are vested interests, as are certain potential possessions and rewards. It might be said, for example, that legitimate heirs have a vested interest in the laws on illegitimacy, since by virtue of these laws they have advantages in inheritance. A man may be said to have a vested interest in his wife's affection and in various specific symbols of it. The editors of foreign-language publications have a vested interest in all organizations that maintain and promote the use of the language in question.

Vested interests, therefore, are not necessarily sinister. It is perfectly normal, indeed inevitable, that vested interests develop around all social institutions. The support of social institutions depends to some extent on vested interests in them, as well as on moral sentiments. In this sense, the stability of society depends upon vested interests. By the same token, however, vested interests are the nucleus of resistance to social change. From the point of view of reformers, vested-interest groups stand in the way of "progress," and social stability is in some aspects social rigidity.

Vested interests are only the *nucleus* of resistance to social change. Social institutions are also supported by people who have no vested interests in them. Not only the rich but also the poor support the laws against theft. One might say that the extent to which a pattern is supported by people who have no vested interests in it is an index of the degree to which that pattern is institutionalized. In the study of social problems, the main reason for focusing attention on vested-interest groups is that they tend to be the only or the chief *organized* resistance to social change; hence they are the most effective resisters.

Anomie and Social Deviation

An important step toward classifying the forms of social deviation and explaining variation in the rates of their occurrence was made by R. K. Merton in "Social Structure and Anomie" (1938a). This paper has stimulated fruitful research as well as controversy. We shall not be able to present more than a sample of the results.

Every case of deviant behavior has its own history. There are many possible paths by which a person can become deviant. The chief interest of Merton's paper, however, lies in the fact that he identifies a social and cultural situation that tends to generate a high *rate* of deviant behavior. His theory is sociological; it is not directed toward solving the psychological (or socio-psychological) problem of why certain individuals become deviant and others do not. There is some knowledge about this problem too, but it is not our immediate concern.

"Anomie" literally means normlessness.[2] The term can be and has been applied to the state of mind of individuals regardless of the state of the society. (The state of an individual's personality is, of course, always bound up with the state of society, and even more intimately with the state of the smaller social systems in which he participates.) We shall use the term, however, to refer solely to a certain condition in a social system, large or small. Quite adequate and less recondite terms already exist to refer to the personality states for which the term "anomie" has been used. Anomie, then, is a condition in which many persons in a social system have a weakened respect for some social norm or norms, and this loss of legitimacy is traceable in part to something about the social structure itself.

Anomie is not the same thing as the absence of norms (even though this is the literal meaning of the term). Anomie is not even lack of clarity in norms—vague definition of what behavior is required. If there were no norms at all, we could not speak of deviant behavior; and if the norms were not clear, we should be almost equally embarrassed to call any specific action deviant. In the condition called anomie, norms are present, they are clear enough, and the actors in the social system are to some extent oriented to them. But this orientation, on the part of many, is ambivalent; it either leans toward conformity, but with misgivings, or leans toward deviation, but with misgivings. Furthermore, anomie is not any condition whatever in which there is a high rate of deviation from a social norm or from a system of norms; anomie is not merely the statistical resultant of many particular deviations springing from a multitude of heterogeneous

---

[2] Merton took the concept of anomie from Émile Durkheim, who revived the old term for his own purposes in 1893 and used the concept especially in his sociological study of suicide rates (1897, trans. 1951). For a good secondary treatment of Durkheim's ideas, see Parsons, 1937, esp. Chap. 8.

causes. Not *merely* that, we say: for it is true that any high rate of deviation is due in part, and at a very concrete level of analysis, to various causes. Anomie, however, is due in part also to some structural factor in the social system, a factor that must impinge upon nearly every member of it, although its precise effect is not the same for all.

We do not know how many different factors can produce anomie. We shall mention only two here. One is role conflict or, more generally, conflict of norms. A good example, to which we have referred earlier, is the conflict in the United States between universalistic and particularistic standards in the treatment of Negroes. The anomic character of this conflict is especially clear in the South. Southerners *feel* the moral obligation to be fair, and there is little real question, despite a fog of rationalizations produced by the conflict itself, about what *is* fair. On the other hand, Southerners also have a sentimental "patriotic"—to that extent, moral—obligation to the distinct South, for whose quasi-national self-consciousness, symbolized in the myth-like grandeur of the Confederacy, the North is a negative reference group. In this frame of reference, the North hypocritically stands, in theory, for emancipation of the Negroes, and the South stands for slavery (although no longer by so harsh a name). There would be no anomie if Southern whites were simply and wholeheartedly Southerners, but they are not. They are also Americans. Their role conflict results in deep ambivalence, the symptoms of which are obvious to anyone who is capable of not being defensive about them. It also results in widespread reduction of the legitimacy of the norms of fair play when Negroes are concerned. This condition is anomie because the norms have not disappeared; Southern whites are still acutely aware of them, still troubled by them.

In the paper referred to earlier, Merton identified another source of anomie.[3] In its most clear-cut form this anomic factor would be a situation in which many persons in a social system are *required* to strive for some goal but are not provided with adequate legitimate means to reach it, but the goal Merton chose as an example—the goal of competitive occupational success in the United States—is, strictly speaking, not a prescribed goal, it is only preferred. Nevertheless, "the American dream," the ideology of individual success in a system that theoretically provides equality of opportunity, is so pervasive, so much emphasized, that it poses a problem of self-esteem for virtually every man in the society. "Success," of course, is a relative goal. To be sure, the idea that *any* ambitious man can rise to the top is very common in the United States, but it is possible that an ideolog-

[3] The ideas that follow in this section are highly selective in their emphasis. There are fairly important differences of emphasis among the several papers in which Merton himself has dealt with his theory. His 1938 paper was revised in 1949 and printed in Anshen, ed., 1949 (reprinted in Merton, 1949 and 1957, Chap. 4). Other important sources are Merton, 1955; Merton, 1957, Chap. 5: "Continuities in the Theory of Social Structure and Anomie"; and Merton, 1959: "Social Conformity, Deviation, and Opportunity-Structures: A Comment on the Contributions of Dubin and Cloward." Our account most closely follows Merton, 1955.

ically favored goal somewhat less extreme might be an equally anomic or even more anomic factor. The goal of moving from a blue-collar to a white-collar position can seem frustratingly difficult to lower-class boys who for various reasons are not doing well in school, have no money, and are bogged down by other internal and external conditions.

As we have seen, there is probably about as much actual upward mobility in England as there is in the United States, but England is (or has been until recently) ideologically different. There is less obligation in England to strive to get out of the social class into which one is born. Many people can more easily regard those who rise as simply ambitious, talented, or lucky individuals, without necessarily feeling a loss of self-esteem if they themselves follow in the footsteps of their fathers. Differences in this respect between modern industrialized societies are of course relative, but in the United States it seems true that individual rise from low status to "success" is more often regarded as to some extent a reflection on those who, being presumed to have had a chance also and having been urged to take it, nevertheless do not distinguish themselves. Moreover, every ambitious person, in the American sense, is a reflection on those who are not ambitious (who are said to lack "get-up-and-go").

Here we have an example of an ideology that to some extent indirectly encourages deviant behavior. The source of anomie identified by Merton may be described as a frustrating gap between a culturally favored goal and the actual possibility of attaining it. Virtually all adults know what the culturally favored goal is, although not all strive to reach it. The considerable proportion of those for whom the culturally favored goal *is* personally important find that the institutionally permitted means for achieving it are not distributed evenly throughout the social structure

One result of this gap is anomie with respect to the goal of success, the norms that define and confine the means permitted to achieve it, or both. The attenuation of the legitimacy of norms and ideals can express itself in any one of the possible forms of deviant behavior. One general direction is juvenile delinquency and crime. From one point of view, "crime" and "delinquency" are intolerably broad terms—blanket terms that conceal important differences within the categories they name. However, we are concerned at the moment with *rates* of crime and delinquency, and criminologists think that, after making all allowances for the difficulty of drawing precise international statistical comparisons, the United States has a high rate of juvenile delinquency and adult crime.

In relation to the culturally defined goal of success, many forms of delinquency and crime have an ambiguous character. True, it is difficult to separate the goal of success, as presented in the many versions of the American dream, from the means used to attain it; most criminals seem to have abandoned not only the confinement of the law but the goal of success as it is ordinarily understood. Yet it is also true that many versions of the American dream stress monetary success, and this is a possible link between the culturally favored goal and the goal of much crime and some delinquency. It had been observed before Merton that poverty is not always associated with a high crime rate: among peasants, for example, the crime rate is usually low. Merton points out that the anomie widespread in American society, and perhaps especially in the lower classes, does not exist when there is no great gap between what people are expected to do and what they *can* do legitimately. A peasant may be greedy, but he is not constantly lured by his culture to accept the idea that he too can be rich if he will only put his mind to it as he should.

In appraising Merton's theory of anomie, we should keep in mind that the vast majority of Americans do adjust themselves more or less to the realities of the occupational structure. They are certainly not fabulously rich or famous, nor are they criminals. Most of them are factory workers, small farmers, mill workers, school teachers, minor white-collar workers, postmen, policemen, firemen. As H. Hyman (1953) has shown, most lower-class Americans do not *aspire* to become rich or famous. Hyman seems to be wrong, however, in believing that this fact disconfirms Merton's theory. Among his data, Hyman presents the results of a 1937 Roper survey of a national sample of adults. They were asked the question, "Do you think that today any young man with thrift, ability, and ambition has the opportunity to rise in the world, own his own home, and earn $5000 a year?"[4] Merton seems to be right in asserting that we should pay less attention to the fact that a *smaller* proportion of "poor" adults than of "prosperous" adults answered yes, and more attention to the fact that a *considerable* proportion of even "poor" adults said yes: "Among the prosperous, 53% affirmed the belief that this was so, compared with what Hyman describes as 'only' 31% among 'the poor'" (Merton, 1957, p. 172). It remains a question whether the high rate of crime is due mainly to those who believe in the possibility of success or mainly to those who do not. It seems likely that more of the disbelievers than of the believers would become "professional" criminals. The main point seems to be that widespread vaulting ambition puts a strain on those who feel themselves incapable of rising in respectable channels. The most usual reaction, evidently, is to ignore the American dream and take whatever legitimate job is actually available. *One* reaction, however, is to throw over the whole system and become a criminal.

To the extent that the American ideology produces anomie, note that there is an inherent spiraling effect. If the norms are weakened for some people, these people are likely to influence others. At a certain point, there is widespread ambivalence toward the norms, and presumably the very process of socialization is subtly changed in that part of the population

---

[4] This was in 1937. In judging the distribution of answers to the question, we might bear in mind that in 1935-36 the average income of the highest fifth of the families in the United States was $4,216; the average income of the top 5 per cent of the families was only $8,654 (*Statistical Abstract of the United States, 1957*, p. 307, Table No. 374).

most affected. Crime and juvenile delinquency become more nearly normal in the statistical sense and morally less reprehensible in the view of the anomic population. This spiraling process cannot go on forever without engendering a counteractive process. In so-called delinquency areas and areas of high crime rates we find something like a stable equilibrium between the forces making criminal deviation "normal" and the forces counteracting it, but the equilibrium is at a fairly high level of anomie. We shall return to this analysis when we discuss juvenile delinquency.

Recently there has been a significant extension of Merton's theory of anomie (Cloward, 1959). E. H. Sutherland had long held the theory that criminal behavior is largely learned subcultural behavior, and that a person typically becomes a criminal by "differential association"—that is, by unusual exposure to the influence of persons and groups who are already criminal.[5] Merton had emphasized that persons variously located in the social system have unequal access to legitimate means for achieving occupational success, that they hold different positions in the opportunity structure. Cloward essentially brought Sutherland's theory and Merton's together. Those for whom there is a big gap between the American dream and realistic legitimate opportunity do not have equal access to *illegitimate* channels of opportunity. Moreover, success in criminal activity is not something to be taken for granted. Not only must the potential criminal have the opportunity to learn from others but he must "make good" in a highly competitive field. Not all who try succeed. Cloward's insight has helped to clarify some of Merton's findings. For example, Merton had noted that one deviant reaction to anomie is "retreatism"—a kind of passive rejection of the goal of success and of respectable occupational activities. "In this category fall some of the adaptive activities of psychotics, autists, pariahs, outcasts, vagrants, vagabonds, tramps, chronic drunkards and drug addicts" (Merton, 1957, p. 153). Cloward notes that many "retreatists" are evidently double failures; they have abandoned hope of legitimate success, but they have also failed as criminals.

> This does not mean that retreatist adaptations cannot arise precisely as Merton suggests: namely, that the conversion from conformity to retreatism takes place in one step, without intervening adaptations. But this is only one route to retreatism. The conversion may at times entail intervening stages and intervening adaptations, particularly of an innovating type. This possibility helps to account for the fact that certain categories of individuals cited as retreatists–for example, hobos–often show extensive histories of arrests and convictions for various illegal acts. It also helps to explain retreatist adaptations among individuals who have not necessarily internalized strong restraints on the use of illegitimate means. In short, retreatist adaptations may arise with considerable frequency among those who are failures in both worlds, conventional and illegitimate alike [Cloward, 1959, p. 175].

---

5 For a summary of Sutherland's theory, see Clinard, 1959, p. 510.

The focus on *both* legitimate and illegitimate "opportunity structures" is a step toward explaining not only the rates of deviant behavior in different classes, ethnic groups, and other social divisions but also the rates of different *kinds* of deviant behavior.[6]

The Directions of Deviation

In discussing the possible adaptations to anomie, Merton noted in passing that ambivalence is probably common to all forms of deviant behavior. He also noted that some forms of deviation—for example, hoboism—are relatively passive and other forms, such as rebellion, are active. But, Merton was primarily interested in another basis for classifying deviant behavior. Parsons (1951, Chap. 7) made ambivalence and the active-passive distinction basic to his classification and he added a third factor; namely, whether the deviant person's main target of negative feeling was the norm or norms from which he deviated or the person or persons whom he would hurt through his deviation.

AMBIVALENCE

As we have noted, by definition all deviation involves violation of norms to which the actor is oriented. Parsons assumes that unless the deviation is unwitting or is committed under duress or is otherwise unavoidable, the actor always feels ambivalent. This means that he feels the moral validity of the norm but is also alienated from it for one reason or another. It is also possible to be indifferent to the norm, but, as Merton had already noted, once a norm is internalized it is extremely unlikely that all attachment to it will be extinguished. The attitude of indifference to the norm is of negligible importance, for if such an attitude is at all widespread in a group then the "norm" simply is not normative in that group.

Ambivalence toward norms is extremely common. Indeed, it is possible that acceptance combined with some degree of alienation is more common than pure acceptance, and it is plausible that traces of alienation are more common the more important the norm. This is speculative, but it rests on the assumption that "important" norms will at times be frustrating, just as "important" persons (persons to whom one is strongly attached) are inevitably frustrating at times. Most of us would agree that in the United States property rights come close to being sacred, and that stealing is not nice at all. Yet consider the following story from the experience of John Edward Reid, whose business is lie-detecting and who has interviewed over 25,000 persons.

> In support of his belief [that no one is absolutely honest] Reid cites the time he had lunch with the owner of a jewelry supply house that employed

---

[6] A compact analysis of an anomic process is given by Cloward in Witmer and Kotinsky, eds., 1955, Session 4.

140 people. The owner, who had had some experience with lie detectors in Army Intelligence, thought Reid might help him screen his employees for honesty. . . .

After questioning the employees and administering tests, Reid found that 95% had been stealing wrist-bands, rings and other items from the company. They were even using the company's automatic postage-paying facilities to send the loot to relatives. One man had got away with $3,400 worth of material. The only employees who proved to be honest were office workers who had no opportunity to get their hands on the stock. . . .

Reid does admit that while everybody is dishonest to some degree, there is a vast difference between major and minor dishonesty. *His own dividing line is $1,000*. People who will steal more than $1,000 are major league crooks, in Reid's opinion [Brean, 1958, p. 70; italics added].

The lie-detector, which Reid helped to improve, depends upon the fact that virtually everyone is ambivalent about lying. In the act of lying, one's physical reactions to the guilt and strain involved are virtually impossible to control. Changes in breathing, the pulse rate, blood pressure, body temperature, and salivation give the liar away.

An ancient Oriental lie-detecting method consisted of giving the suspect some rice to chew. If he had difficulty spitting it out, presumably because his mouth was dry, he was judged guilty [Brean, 1958, p. 73].

The lie-detector is not regarded as infallible, and Reid's experience does not prove, of course, that everyone lies and steals. However, other studies provide further evidence that most otherwise respectable persons have committed various crimes.[7]

If some degree of alienation from a norm is a settled element in a person's motivation, he is likely to deviate from it more frequently. With respect to that norm, he can fairly be called a deviant person. An ambivalent person may "permanently" repress the negative or alienative side of his motivation, may repress the conformative side, or may vacillate, one side being regnant for a time and the other breaking through. But whichever of these "solutions" prevails, settled ambivalence toward a norm often leads to deviation when the opportunity exists. If the conformative side is repressed, the ambivalent person will tend toward *under*conformity. If the alienative side is repressed, he will tend toward *over*conformity. Alternative names for the same phenomena are compulsive alienation and compulsive conformity. Parsons also speaks of "conformative dominance" and "alienative dominance." Assuming for the moment that the concept of overconformity makes sense (we shall return to this question), it is easy to see how ambivalence might lead to overconformity. Repressed elements in motivation may be thought of as trying to break through to expression. One of the personality defenses against this danger is known as reaction formation. We encountered an example in our analysis of the incest taboo. It

---

[7] For example, see Porterfield, 1943; Wallerstein and Wylie, 1947. With regard to Reid's experience, it is probably true that people have less compunction about stealing from an "impersonal" organization than from an individual. See Smigel, 1956.

will be remembered that sexual feelings toward tabooed persons are ordinarily repressed and that the repression is often (perhaps usually) backed up by a conscious feeling of revulsion at the thought of a violation of the taboo. This abhorrence or shrinking away is interpreted by psychologists as a reaction formation protecting the subject from his unconscious desire to violate the taboo. If it were not for the unconscious desire, the subject would presumably be sexually indifferent to the tabooed object. Were it not for the fact that reaction formation in this case and the actions to which it leads are extremely common, it is conceivable that we could speak of a kind of overconformity to the incest taboo. It is possible that some bizarre behavior—some kinds of cruelty, for example—can be interpreted in this way.

We encountered a more obvious example of overconformity in Chapter 12, where we touched upon Merton's study of a common type of bureaucratic personality. Fearful of sticking his neck out, the bureaucrat may in effect transform the organizational rules from means to ends in themselves and cleave to them even when doing so prevents attainment of the goals for which the rules were devised. This kind of bureaucrat is an example of a larger class of overconformers—namely, the perfectionists who never get anything done. Since we do not ordinarily label such disruptive behavior overconformity, we might have to reflect for a moment in order to persuade ourselves that it is indeed a kind of deviation and, moreover, that when people detect it they apply negative sanctions to it.

ACTIVE AND PASSIVE FORMS OF DEVIATION

We hardly need to stress that alienation can express itself by avoidance or withdrawal as well as by more vigorous acts. One way of expressing a deviant tendency is to put yourself in a situation in which the norm applies, then to violate it flagrantly. Another way is to avoid studiously the situations in which you would have to conform. Such an alienative attitude is likely to lead to overt deviation in the form of "forgetting" to do something expected or of half-doing it or of making "mistakes." These forms of deviation are relatively passive. They are likely to provoke negative sanctions only when they are repeated often enough for people to sense the underlying alienative motivation.

Parsons called attention to the fact that much sickness is a form of passive deviant behavior. Since the psychological and sociological conception of motivated sickness has not yet quite become part of common sense, a word or two of explanation would perhaps be helpful.

We all recognize that mental illness is a disturbance of the personality, hence that it involves unconscious motivation. Perhaps few psychologists would maintain that ordinary injuries and sicknesses are *always* motivated; but when a patient breaks a leg or has a cold that confines him to bed, a psychiatrist would be inclined to look for some motivation that might have contributed to the "accident" or sickness. There is a growing list of psychosomatic illnesses recognized in psychiatry. (Incidentally, criminologists with a psychological bent have also pointed out that some, not necessarily many, of the *victims* of some kinds of crime—notably rape, swindling, and homicide—contribute to the crime by "stupid" behavior that is unconsciously motivated; that is, they unconsciously cooperate with the criminal. See, for example, von Hentig, 1948.)

It is an easy step from this psychological insight to the recognition that many cases of sickness and injury should be considered in the sociology of deviant behavior. One obvious aspect of much sickness and injury is that it provides the patient with an acceptable excuse for not performing many of the duties he would otherwise be expected to perform. In some cases the patient unconsciously became sick or suffered injury *in order* to be relieved of his responsibilities. This essentially passive form of deviation Parsons classifies as *evasion*. To recognize explicitly the intimate involvement of some sickness and injury in the role relationships of social systems is, of course, to point out a field for research. (Is "evasion" of this kind more common for men or for women? Is there any tendency for this path of deviation to be found more frequently in some social situations than in others? Why?) To avoid misunderstanding, we should note explicitly that it is extremely implausible that all forms of sickness and injury are motivated. Moreover, not all motivated sickness and injury are deviant in the technical sense. For example, a person might unconsciously wish to get injured not to evade responsibility but to punish himself for something he has done.

THE TARGET OF NEGATIVE FEELING

As we have repeatedly stressed, all forms of deviation involve violation of a norm. Nevertheless, some deviant behavior seems to be motivated more by alienation from persons than by alienation from norms. The deviant expresses his negative attitude toward persons either in the *form* of his deviant act—assault and battery, for example—or merely through the fact of deviation itself, as when a person violates a norm mainly because it was laid down or is upheld by someone toward whom he feels aggressive. Psychologists often say of a person that he has a negative attitude toward authority. This statement means that an alienative attitude originally directed, presumably, toward a particular person in authority—say, the father—has spread, more or less unconsciously, to all persons whose status-role is somewhat like that of the original authoritative figure. This process of spreading by unconscious association or symbolic connections is sometimes called *generalization*. Any ambivalent structure in the personality—whether it involves persons primarily or norms primarily—can be relatively focalized or relatively generalized. This means that the object of ambivalence, personal or normative, may range from something very specific to a very broad class of objects (such as all persons having any kind of authority). The conditions that determine whether alienation will be focal or general are sociologically relevant, of course, but the problem is essentially psychological and need not detain us.

This question is closely related to another. Table 21, which reproduces the directions of deviation as distinguished by Parsons, should be interpreted primarily as a classification of deviant behavior rather than of deviant persons. Most individuals conform most of the time to the vast majority of the norms to which they are subject. We should not lose sight of this fact. Moreover, if a person's deviation in one area—perhaps under one kind of stress—takes one direction, his deviation in some other area may take another direction. However, it does seem possible to characterize some personalities as passively inclined rather generally, or as compulsively conforming, and so forth.

TABLE 21

Possible directions of deviant behavior *

	Activity		*Passivity*	
	FOCUS ON SOCIAL OBJECTS	FOCUS ON NORMS	FOCUS ON SOCIAL OBJECTS	FOCUS ON NORMS
Conformative dominance	Compulsive performance orientation		Compulsive acquiescence	
	Dominance	Compulsive enforcement	Submission	Perfectionistic observance (Merton's "ritualism")
Alienative dominance	Rebelliousness		Withdrawal	
	Aggressiveness toward social objects	Incorrigibility	Compulsive independence	Evasion
	Revolutionary activity		Noninterference with revolutionaries (non-cooperation with agents of suppression)	

* Adapted from T. Parsons, *The Social System,* Free Press, 1951, p. 259. "Revolutionary activity" and the corresponding passive form have been added to the table. The fact that the vertical lines are not extended to the base of the table indicates that revolutionary activity and its passive form cut across the distinction of focuses.

Juvenile Delinquency

That juvenile delinquency is a serious social problem needs no emphasis today. Each state has its own precise definition of the age range covered by "juvenile"; seventeen, or eighteen, and so on up to twenty-one.

The range of behavior legally covered by the term "delinquency," however, is not precisely defined. For example,

> A Massachusetts law defines a juvenile delinquent as "a child between seven and seventeen who violates any city ordinance or town by-law or commits an offense not punishable by death." Under this law nearly every child within this age range is, or will be, a delinquent-by-definition [Vedder, 1954, p. 2].

In the same state, a child of eight can be branded a juvenile delinquent if his parents complain that they cannot manage him. Although most children have committed offenses that are technically punishable, we ordinarily regard as juvenile delinquents only those who have been officially convicted of delinquency. Moreover, the juvenile delinquents in whom both criminologists and the general public are most interested are those who commit many offenses—that is, children and especially adolescents in whose behavior patterns delinquency figures rather prominently. It is these offenders, who usually belong to "gangs," that we shall be discussing here.

The extent of juvenile delinquency is not precisely known. Some idea can be obtained from the following quotation:

> During 1948, 94,236 children's cases were handled by 399 juvenile courts reporting from seventeen states. About one-half the cases were conducted without formal judicial action. According to the United States Children's Bureau, if the volume of delinquency continues at the 1948 level, 275,000 delinquents may be expected to come before the juvenile courts of the United States each year [Vedder, 1954, p. 27].

It is fairly generally, although not unanimously, accepted by professional students of juvenile delinquency that the vast majority of delinquents come from the lower class and that they commit their offenses as members of gangs. Many observers have pointed out that middle-class offenders may be dealt with informally and hence do not appear in official statistics. It is also true, however, that the vast majority of delinquent acts committed by lower-class offenders are not officially punished. The few writers who think that the percentage of serious offenders in the upper classes is at least as great as the percentage in the lower class do not make their opinion convincing. A. K. Cohen has reviewed the evidence carefully (1955, pp. 36-44). It may be that an understandable ideological bias has led some writers to be uncritical of the evidence they have uncovered. For example, one writer shows that the average number of offenses that middle-class "nondelinquents" admit to having committed is greater than the average number of similar offenses *officially charged* to delinquents. As Cohen remarks, such a comparison is virtually meaningless. The delinquents have no doubt committed many offenses in addition to those officially charged against them.

Cohen cites one study (E. E. Schwarz, 1945) indicating that, small as it is, the percentage of middle- and upper-class boys officially brought to court may exaggerate the true percentage of delinquents from the upper classes.

Some cities keep a central register of children "known to the police, the school, social and recreational agencies and other community agencies because of delinquent or 'bothersome' behavior. . . . It is generally assumed that such register data are more representative than court data, which are the result of a long selective process of complaint, arrest, arraignment and prosecution" (Cohen, 1955, p. 40). Schwarz's study of the central register of Washington, D. C., showed that "the children from the higher income residential areas appeared relatively more frequently in the court cases than they did in the central register. If any conclusion can be drawn from this, it is that the court cases *exaggerate* the proportions of delinquents from the upper social levels" (Cohen, 1955, pp. 40-41). It would be hazardous, however, to draw this conclusion. What Schwarz's study does show is that lower-class boys have a good chance of escaping official punishment for their juvenile delinquency. Such studies as that of Hollingshead (1949) show that school teachers (and no doubt the personnel of recreational agencies, etc.) are "easy" on upper-class boys, partly because they fear retaliation from parents.

It seems more likely that an upper-class boy has a better chance of escaping the *label* "juvenile delinquent" than a lower-class boy has. This assumption should of course not be taken for granted either. If it is true, its importance rests in the possibility that having an official record of delinquency will contribute to a boy's self-conception, and therefore a lower-class boy may have a handicap in growing out of the pattern of delinquent behavior (Merton, 1955, p. 32). For an experiment showing that a boy's conception of himself (for example, as one who will never be taken to a juvenile court, or as one who might be) is probably important for his subsequent behavior, see Reckless, Dinitz, and Kay, 1957.

One of the most important differences between lower-class delinquent adolescents and their age peers in college, who are not infrequently guilty of destroying property and otherwise committing acts for which they are legally liable to punishment, is in the subjective meaning of their acts. A college boy as such can hardly help having a different self-conception from that of a lower-class boy who typically leaves school at the age of sixteen. Roughly speaking, the general stream of behavior of which delinquency is an important part is the serious business of the lower-class boy's life, whereas the college boy seems to view his delinquency as a holiday respite from the serious business of *his* life, which is to study (not necessarily very hard) to prepare himself for a reasonably well-assured respectable and profitable adult role. Not only sociologically but according to the philosophy of the juvenile courts, the two types of delinquency do not have the same meaning and should not be handled in the same way. (This comment should not be taken to mean that lower-class delinquency is for the most part being intelligently treated.)

For every girl delinquent, there are at least four or five boy delinquents. There are girls' gangs too, but they faintly imitate those of the boys. Apart from sexual offenses, in which the boys of course cooperate, the delinquency of girls is almost negligible. If a theory of juvenile delinquency can account for the delinquency committed by gangs of boys, it accounts for all but the fringes of delinquency in general.

Some idea of the population from which most juvenile delinquents come is conveyed in Table 22, which might be regarded as a table of various indicators of the size of the "lower class." Walter B. Miller, from whom we borrow this table, is of course well aware of the crudity of these indicators, and we have said enough in Chapters 18 and 19 to make further comment unnecessary here.

The best study of lower-class boys' delinquency is that of A. K. Cohen (1955). The basic idea of Cohen's book is an application of Merton's theory of anomie, and he uses the case analyzed by Merton, although he states it a little more cautiously and describes some of the effects of anomie in what is perhaps a more acceptable way.

Cohen's analysis begins with the fairly well-supported assumption that although the American dream of occupational success (not necessarily of

TABLE 22

Proportion of United States population in selected educational, occupational, and income categories *

Category	*Approximate per cent of population*	*Year or period*
Household heads in large Northern cities who did not enter high school	42	1950
Adults over 25 years old who did not *complete* high school	60	1953
Adults in U. S. civilian labor force in "unskilled" positions	25-30	1930-40
Adults in U. S. civilian labor force in "semiskilled" and "unskilled" positions	40-50	1910-50
Consumer units in U. S. with annual incomes under $2000	30	1954
Consumer units in U. S. with annual incomes under $3000	42	1952
Household units in large U. S. cities reporting female household head	20	1950

* Slightly adapted from W. B. Miller, "Implications of Urban Lower-Class Culture for Social Work," *Social Service Rev.*, Sept. 1959, v. 33, no. 3.

affluence) is basically the ideal of the middle class, it is shared to a large extent by *all* classes in American society. Napoleon is supposed to have impressed upon his adoring army the idea that every foot soldier carries a marshal's baton in his knapsack. Since at no time have there been a great many marshals of France, the idea was hardly less romantic than the American dream, which every American boy of the humblest ranks has been told he ought to dream if he is going to be as American as possible. The middle class is said to be the backbone of America, the most typical American class, partly because the American goal of individual success is most characteristic of the middle class. But, as Cohen suggests, few American boys of any class have never heard or read the ideology of success in some form, and many lower-class boys are affected by it.

Lower-class boys are extremely handicapped in competition with middle-class boys. At school, for example, the teachers are likely to be middle-class women, slightly insecure themselves, having typically risen from a somewhat lower status. They favor the boys from middle-class homes, who are obviously headed for college and whose verbal ability, while not necessarily better than that of the lower-class boys (although the teachers do not know this), seems better from a certain middle-class point of view. The verbal ingenuity widely admired in the lower class (see W. B. Miller, 1958) takes a form that middle-class school teachers would not appreciate. In manners and dress the middle-class boys also seem to be superior from a middle-class teacher's point of view. The upshot is that lower-class boys, who would be handicapped even if they were made welcome and treated sympathetically, are often alienated from school; yet without success in school their chance of occupational success in legitimate fields dreamt of in the American dream is slim indeed.[8] According to Cohen, lower-class boys can react to their somewhat handicapped situation in any one of three possible ways:

1. A small proportion decide to buck the system regardless of their handicap. They try to "pull themselves up by the bootstraps," carefully screen their speech, become sedulous apes to middle-class models as far as they can. Cohen appropriately calls these the "college boys," after the ambitious Italian-American boys in the slum studied by W. F. Whyte (1943).[9]

2. Presumably the great majority of lower-class boys mark time

---

[8] For a good study revealing differential treatment in school, see Hollingshead, 1949.

[9] Robert Louis Stevenson set himself to be a "sedulous ape" to master writers. It is hard to speak of the different reactions to the lower-class situation without seeming to evaluate them. Whyte admitted in the second edition of his book (1955) that the "college boys" complained to him that his treatment of them in the first edition had been unsympathetic. This charge may be true. In any case, it is perhaps worth remarking that from a broad humane point of view people sometimes do the "right" thing for the "wrong" reasons. It is even conceivable that one reason some lower-class boys might try the "college boy" solution is their relative inability to compete comfortably in the *lower*-class situation. It is part and parcel of the whole theory of anomie that *any* course of behavior is likely to be somewhat ambivalent.

through the ordeal of school, leave when the law permits (if not before), and take a respectable dead-end lower-class job. Cohen calls this the "corner boy" solution, after the heroes of Whyte's slum study.

3. Juvenile delinquency is the third "solution." Cohen's thesis is that the lower-class juvenile delinquent rejects middle-class standards, although with ambivalence; joins with others in a similar situation; bases his self-esteem on his success in the bold activities of the gang (a standard he *can* live up to); and becomes a kind of compulsive nonconformist, his reaction formation against his own repressed conformative tendency leading him to "burn his bridges behind him"—that is, to cut himself off so completely from middle-class society that he will not be tempted or able to yield to the repressed side of his personality.[10]

It is, of course, this third solution that we are interested in here. Cohen is modifying the anomie theory slightly and giving it psychological depth by applying to it the insights of Parsons with regard to ambivalence and reaction-formation.

Ever since a classic work by Thrasher (1927), a series of sociologists have documented the thesis that juvenile delinquency of the type we are discussing is a subculture within the lower class, passed on from one generation to another through a constantly replenished series of age-graded gangs.[11] It will be remembered that E. H. Sutherland held that the most important cause of crime is "differential association": a person becomes a criminal by associating intimately with criminals. More recently, W. B. Miller has stressed the subcultural aspect of juvenile delinquency and related it to lower-class culture in general. He points out that the concern with physical courage is basic in the lower class and that many lower-class jobs require essentially the same toughness and courage for which the delinquency subculture helps to prepare lower-class boys (Miller, 1958, 1959a, and no date). Bloch and Niederhoffer (1958) develop the thesis that passage through the series of age-graded gangs is functionally similar to *rites de passage* in primitive societies. The adults impose restrictions, and adolescents in particular chafe because they are not recognized as adults. According to this view, gang activity (of which delinquency is only the more spectacular part) is a somewhat shortsighted but subculturally approved

---

[10] This classification of possible reactions to the anomic gap between middle-class goals and lower-class legitimate opportunities is a good first approximation. The rest of this section is in effect a commentary on it. We should note at once, however, that the third possibility is presented too starkly. Many lower-class boys *vacillate* between legitimate and illegitimate behavior. The "bridge-burning" type is probably relatively rare. For the same reason, the difference between Cohen's second and third possibilities is not a rigorous one in practice.

[11] Among the most important of the sociologists in this field are F. Zorbaugh, L. S. Cottrell, and especially C. R. Shaw and H. D. McKay. For references to their work, see Jonassen, 1949, and see the rejoinder by Shaw and McKay in the same issue of *Amer. sociol. Rev.* The pioneering work is now largely accepted as "given," and we are concerned with somewhat more recent ideas.

and regularized attempt to prove masculine qualities, and a protest against the adult world.

There is no doubt some truth in this view, especially as it applies to boys who see for themselves no career in school leading to a career afterwards. The corner "boys" whom Whyte studied were beyond the age of juvenile delinquency (Doc, the leader, was in his early thirties), but it is clear from the very first pages of Whyte's book that these corner boys had once been members of tough gangs which in their day would have been regarded as delinquent. Doc reminisces about the "rallies" of his youth and about what a walloper he had been while keeping control of his gang and defending his "street" against rival gangs. The young toughs of today, equally anxious not to appear "chicken," equally concerned with the "rep" of their gang, have "rumbles" and defend their "turf." In short, there is no doubt that "juvenile delinquency" is for many lower-class boys a fairly normal transitional stage, and presumably most of them do not emerge from it as hardened criminals, although some of course do. Most of them probably come out very much as Whyte's "corner boys" did.

To emphasize the lower-class subcultural aspect of gang delinquency is not to dismiss the thesis about anomie developed by Cohen from the theories of Merton and Parsons. After all, the "lower class" is not a self-contained social system. It is not only surrounded by the middle class in a physical sense; its life is controlled, hampered, and helped by middle-class people. Middle-class ideals are constantly paraded for emulation. Cohen's thesis and Miller's are not incompatible. On the contrary, if Cohen is right, we should expect to find just the sort of thing Miller describes. The delinquent subculture does exist and it does reveal ambivalent attitudes toward the norms of "respectable" society—*ambivalent* attitudes, not indifference: Miller's papers make this point clear although not explicit. Cohen explains the content of the subculture as determined in part by compulsive opposition to middle-class norms. The middle class values property: the delinquent subculture shows its contempt for property. The middle class places value upon working toward the deferred goal of success: the delinquent subculture despises school and abandons the goal of middle-class success, along with all the discipline and decorum required to achieve it.

We shall not describe the delinquent subculture in detail, but there seems to be no doubt that delinquent gangs do go in for wanton destruction, do have a kind of puerile hatred and defiance of the conventional world. Cohen's point is that such attitudes and behavior are not simply passed down like the ritual of the Shriners; they are a meaningful "solution" to the problem of self-esteem produced for the lower-class boy by the gap between what seems to be expected of him in the middle-class world and what he thinks he can do. The "solution" is admittedly precarious; that is one reason that so much affect goes into it. Cohen shows how and why the delinquent subculture might arise today, full blown and fully nourished by the conditions of today, even if the subculture did not already exist. And he maintains that the subculture is not transmitted by inertia but is continuously supported by the social structure of the society as a whole, not of the lower class alone.[12]

To be sure, once anomie has become widespread it is part of a subculture and affects socialization. There is some evidence that lower-class mothers are less interested in virtue for its own sake than they are in training their children to keep out of trouble and not make a nuisance of themselves. At least this is the conclusion of a careful study of lower- and middle-class families in Washington, D. C. (Kohn, 1959). Kohn's major conclusion, which he italicizes, is as follows:

> Working-class parents are more likely to respond in terms of the immediate consequences of the child's actions, middle-class parents in terms of their interpretation of the child's intent in acting as he does [Kohn, 1959, p. 364].

Kohn makes it clear that this difference is fairly subtle. He is not saying, for example, that lower-class parents are indifferent to whether their children are really honest or not. But if his interpretation is correct, it seems likely that for the lower-class child middle-class morality is, *relatively speaking,* an external set of rules, not so deeply internalized as they would be in a middle-class child. Miller's papers on the lower class show the pervasiveness of lower-class ambivalence toward the law. Thus Miller speaks not of the "value" of law-abiding behavior for the lower class but, rather, of "trouble" as a lower-class "focal concern" with the "perceived alternatives" of law-abiding behavior and law-violating behavior (1959a, 1960).

The anomie of the lower class might help to explain the not uncommon ambivalence toward middle-class people and the uncertain feeling that middle-class people aren't much anyway.

Cohen is quite explicit about the fact that he is attempting to explain the high *rate* of juvenile delinquency in the lower class; he is not explaining the delinquency of any individual boy. Only an intensive psychological investigation, preferably carried out with full awareness of the social and cultural situation we have been describing, could do that.

> Consider . . . that membership, as such, in a social group [for example, a juvenile gang] may yield all sorts of benefits and satisfactions sufficient to motivate people to want to belong. The distinctive creed of such a group may be a matter of indifference to a particular individual; it is not the creed but the other benefits of membership which attract him to the group. Acceptance of that creed, however, may be a condition or by-product of his membership. In such a case, the motivation for his participation in the subculture may throw little light on the reasons for its distinctive content. Conversely, the needs and problems which make intelligible this distinctive content may have little to do with why this particular individual has taken it over [Cohen, 1955, pp. 148-49].

---

[12] Cohen's analysis of how a subculture might arise (1955, Chap. 3) has been misunderstood. Kitsuse and Dietrick (1959, p. 213) erroneously believe that Cohen is theorizing only about the ambivalence of past populations. Not at all: he is theorizing about the anomie of today, with the ambivalence of today.

It is easy to take anomie for granted and thus to overlook it and the causes of it. Nevertheless, the problem does remain of why some lower-class boys keep getting into fairly serious "trouble" while others do not. Miller suggests that the problem of "proving" masculinity is greater for boys from "female-based households," and he points out that homosexuality is a pervasive although largely unconscious concern of boys' gangs (W. B. Miller, 1958; see also Bloch and Niederhoffer, 1958, pp. 103-04). As we indicated earlier (see p. 128), homosexuality may result from failure to identify securely or wholeheartedly with one's proper sex-role. Many boys in so-called female-based households are, of course, handicapped by having no adult male role-model. This suggestion is not intended, of course, to explain all delinquency. It is merely an example of a selective factor.

If the foregoing analysis of juvenile delinquency is correct, there is little hope for a sharp reduction of it in a short time. We cannot ask lower-class people to teach their children to strive for lower-class jobs only. Most Americans would disapprove of a social order in which adult positions were largely ascribed, as in a caste system. It would be difficult to institutionalize such a system in the United States. There seems also to be little hope in attempting to level all occupations, according them nearly equal prestige. Such a leveling would reduce the strain on those at the bottom of the hierarchy but would create the problem of motivating people to try for the difficult positions of responsibility at the top. Moreover, attempts to equalize opportunity, while desirable for their own sake within the American value system, would not necessarily reduce the competitive strain for those whose native endowments or unusual personal experiences unfit them for successful competition. Further, the social structure itself has a limited number of places at the top, and some people would have to "fail" even if all were equally able.

We must remind ourselves, however, that deviant behavior, including juvenile delinquency, has many causes. It should be clear that the widespread popular view that "parents are the real delinquents" is shortsighted. The family, the church, and the school are much influenced and limited by the structure of the total society of which they are but parts. Yet it is extremely probable that a more general understanding of the causes of delinquency could reduce the strain on lower-class adolescents in our society. The sense of inadequacy or insecurity has to be generated, if anywhere, in the particular small social systems—home, church, school, play groups, and so on—to which individuals belong. While all these groups affect one another and are affected by the occupational system and the class structure, still men are not helpless to affect their social milieu. It is not necessary, for example, for school teachers to be ignorant of the possible harm they can do to lower-class boys by subtly making them ill at ease at school. It is not necessary for lower-class corner groups to be without competent adult direction. Social control *is* possible. The best methods, however, require understanding and a good deal of money.

Factors Facilitating Deviation

As we have noted, the violation of norms is not evenly spread in a population, nor is the violation of all norms equally likely. We can reinforce these points by listing some of the factors that make it more likely either that a particular norm will be violated or that particular persons will violate a given norm, or both.

1. *Faulty or lacking socialization.* The term "faulty" is evaluative, of course, and we should note that socialization is faulty only from the point of view of those who accept the norm or norms in question. We mentioned the probability that many lower-class persons, although not necessarily criminals, are ambivalent toward norms that largely protect the rights of the upper classes. If this is so, it is not difficult to imagine that they communicate their sometimes repressed alienation to their children. Parsons (1951, Chap. 7) gives a subtle analysis of the genesis of deviant behavior, and in it he points out that socializing agents often condemn deviant behavior overtly but reward it covertly and perhaps half-consciously.

2. *Weak sanctions.* If the positive sanctions for conformity and the negative ones for deviation are weak, the actor gets the idea that perhaps "they don't mean it."

3. *Poor enforcement.* The sanctions may be strong enough, but if they are frequently not applied at all, perhaps because of too small an enforcement staff, the validity of the norm is weakened.

These three factors account for a good deal of "white-collar crime." This term was first used by E. H. Sutherland (1940) to refer mainly to certain illegal acts committed by persons not ordinarily regarded as criminals: namely, by business and professional men in the more or less normal course of their work. Many if not most large corporations have been found guilty of offenses such as violation of the antitrust laws, false advertising, and infringement of patent rights. Most of the acts Sutherland had in mind are treated not in the criminal but in the civil courts, and there has been some controversy as to whether they should be called crimes (see, e.g., Sutherland, 1945; Tappan, 1947; Hartung, 1950; Burgess, 1950; Aubert, 1952). It is certainly true that many of the offenses in question are declared by law to be "socially injurious," that violations are punishable by fines and sometimes by imprisonment, and that enforcement agencies could if they wished bring action against offenders in the criminal courts. But it is no accident that the enforcement agencies seldom do take these cases to the criminal courts. They would have to show that the offenses were "willful," which might be difficult to do. Moreover, the offenders are often highly respected and important. Most important, however, is the fact that the moral sentiment behind the laws in question is not very strong, or is not strong in all quarters. The category of so-called white-collar offenses is not defined in the same way by different writers, to be sure; but all writers who use the term agree that there is a large class of offenses that some businessmen and professional men regard as minor or even as excusable (although in general they admit—and feel—the obligation to abide by the law). Violations of price controls are a good example of the type of offense we have in mind. The laws may be technical and new (hence businessmen have not been socialized to regard violation as serious), violations are widespread and there is a feeling that many people are getting away with them (poor enforcement), and, because the people involved are respectable citizens and the laws are not among the Ten Commandments, sanctions are weak (the fines are often negligible). It is a characteristic of some of these laws—again, price-control laws are a good example—that they run counter to widely held ideology. Price controls violate the sacred principle of freedom of competition.

Despite the fact that many white-collar offenses probably go unpunished, many are taken to court; no doubt many business firms regard such cases as part of the normal cost of doing business.

> Total violations of OPA [Office of Price Administration] regulations by business concerns, both retail and pre-retail, has undoubtedly been a large figure. Violations of this type uncovered during 1944 alone numbered 338,-029. This figure represents violations by approximately 11 per cent of the business firms of the United States [Clinard, 1946, p. 264].

It should be clear from what we have said that one of the more general causes lying behind "faulty" socialization, weak sanctions, and poor enforcement is the fact that the norms in question are only barely recognized as legitimate, if at all. They are legitimate in the sense that most of the people who violate them would prefer to keep within the law and consequently must feel at least a twinge of ambivalence when they violate even a law of which they do not approve. Some of the laws themselves are not "meant" to be obeyed strictly; they are symbolic of political and class attitudes not unanimously felt. At least, this seems to be true of Norway:

> Most of the laws and a very significant part of the enforcement machinery that make up the legal background of economic regulations in Norway aim specifically at the business group, which contains at least a large segment of people with high socio-economic status. It seems justified to interpret the growing number of *legally defined* crimes in this area as a symptom of a slow change in Norwegian social structure, where two partly competing social hierarchies, each with its own marks of distinction, are existing peacefully side by side. Of these, the labor movement and the government agencies it controls represent the ascendant hierarchy, while the business group and its fringes represent the descendant hierarchy. It seems that the definition of new legal crimes of the white-collar brand has served an important social function by giving the ascendant group a feeling of possessing the economic power corresponding to its political supremacy. We do, on the other hand, find traces of resistance to implementation in the social structure in general and in the enforcement machinery. The result is slowness and inefficiency which creates a feeling of harmlessness among the violators. This

may then serve the function of pacifying the businessmen and in that way insure the social peace which Norway has enjoyed after the war [Aubert, 1952, p. 269].

These white-collar crimes, which occur close to the "top" of the social system, have some resemblance to certain crimes that occur close to the "bottom." In particular, illegal gambling is often morally condemned by one part of the population and highly valued by another. This situation affects the enforcement of laws against gambling. To some extent the lower-class racketeers involved regard the occasional light fines they have to pay as a normal cost in their business (see Whyte, 1943, Chap. 4)

4. *Ease of rationalization.* When we remember that most people have internalized social norms and are ambivalent about violating them, we should expect that violators must soothe their conscience by inventing more or less plausible rationalizations.

> . . . the individual who violates the .orms of society is an individual who has constructed an intricate system of ego defenses which he uses to ward off the reactions of the social groups to which he belongs. *They're picking on me; I couldn't help myself; I didn't do it for myself; They asked for it; It's a deal; It's all a matter of luck*: these become the slogans, the attitudes which the individual uses to deflect or neutralize the praise and blame of significant others [Sykes, 1956, pp. 89-90].

Cressey (1953) found that embezzlers must first reconcile their deviant behavior with their self-image as persons worthy of trust; a typical rationalization is that they are "borrowing" the money and will soon pay it back.

The social situation sometimes provides rationalizations so handy that they acquire a kind of cultural currency. During World War II some women and girls were able to persuade themselves that the young men going off to war and possibly to death deserved the comfort of sexual relations. These girls were known as "Victory girls." "A 25-year-old woman arrested on her fourth charge of vagrancy (prostitution) in almost as many months said in explanation of her behavior since the war began, 'It is our part to cheer them up'" (Bromberg, 1943, p. 689). Cabdrivers have a special term ("Live Ones") for out-of-town conventioneers and night-time revelers, whom they regard as fair game: "Knowing that Live Ones are out to 'blow their money' anyway, many drivers believe they are justified in seeing to it they are not deprived of a small portion" (F. Davis, 1959, p. 163). Hayner found that the pay of policemen in Mexico City in the 1940's was so low "that the *mordida,* literally 'bite,' has become more of a custom than a crime." He continues:

> This refers to the practice on the part of the police of supplementing their income by extracting petty fines for minor infractions of the law, these "fines" being paid directly to the policeman. For example, the owner of a grocery store accidentally closes at 8:30 P.M. rather than 8:00 P.M. as required by law. He gives a peso to the policeman, who notices that the store is open,

and the policeman passes a *tostón* (50 centavos) to his superior who happens to pass by. Unless the grocer wishes regularly to keep open late, with this *mordida* the incident is forgotten [Hayner, 1946, p. 429].

5. *Indefinite range of the norm.* Parsons (1951, p. 293) points out that deviation of the radical political type (see Chap. 21) usually finds a bridge to the legitimate values of society. The scope of patriotism or freedom, for example, is not clearly defined, and behavior that is or might be regarded as deviant is often defended as more truly legitimate than the expected behavior. Here we might recall that beliefs as well as outward behavior are often institutionalized.

6. *Secrecy of violations.* The chief significance of secrecy of violations is that the alienative attitude underlying them may become confirmed before the ordinary processes of social control can come into play to reverse it. Merton (1957, pp. 319-20, 374-75) has frequently emphasized the importance of observability of behavior for both conformity and social control.

7. *Unjust or corrupt enforcement.* It seems likely that police corruption and illegal violence do much to undermine respect for the law in those parts of the population most affected. Lincoln Steffens, the famous journalist of "muckraking" days, pointed out that the police often maintain informal relations (understandings, implicit deals) with the underworld (Steffens, 1931). Such relations in effect condone the activities the police are supposed to suppress. Presumably the extent of police corruption reported for Mexico City is rare in the United States and most European countries.

> One factor accounting for the relatively low percentage of registered crimes against property for adults is the lack of confidence in, or even fear of, the police which results in failure to report many cases of stealing. Citizens hesitate to report a burglary lest the investigating detectives make additional thefts. Policemen who serve as night watchmen are especially feared because of a tendency to connive with thieves. The extent to which thieves are known to the police is unique for such a large city. As soon as a theft is reported the thieves may be warned by a dishonest policeman and have an opportunity to move to an unknown location [Hayner, 1946, p. 436].

American criminologists attribute the high crime rate among Negroes in part to the fact that many cities have no Negro policemen, and the white policemen treat lightly or ignore crimes of Negroes against other Negroes.[13] Both lacking the protection of the law, relatively speaking, and being actively discriminated against to some extent by white policemen (the representatives of the law whom Negroes as well as others are most likely to meet), many Negroes presumably lose some of their respect for "white man's law" and therefore violate it relatively more often than whites do. As for police violence, it is common and has several causes (Westley, 1953).

---

[13] An earlier tradition in criminology sought to show that criminality is to some extent biologically determined. Few if any authorities accept such theories today. For a refutation of such theories, see Merton and Ashley-Montagu, 1940.

The legal safeguards of justice are a heavy handicap to the police in their job of apprehending and convicting offenders. Public pressure upon them to get quick results encourages third-degree methods.

The New York City Council voted, 21 to 3, with one member not voting, to ask the Police Commissioner to order patrolmen on the 8 A.M. to 4 P.M. shift to carry a nightstick instead of the regulation billy for daytime use. The City Council thought that a "get tough" policy was in order against young hoodlums. The nightstick is twenty-two inches long and is made of wood, whereas the billy, although just as thick (one and a quarter inches), is only half as long and is made of "moderately hard rubber." In a statement issued the following day, the Police Commissioner called the proposal "phony" and suggested that the City Council was making it for reasons of political expediency (The New York *Times,* Oct. 28, 1959, p. 1, col. 4, and Oct. 29, 1959, p. 26, col. 8)

Public indignation, combined with the attitudes common among the police themselves, results in the use of informal methods against certain types of offender, notably sex offenders. The police are also extremely sensitive concerning their prestige and the ambivalent attitude much of the public has toward them. Westley found that a show of disrespect toward a policeman is often informally regarded as sufficient justification for teaching the offending citizen a rough lesson. Moreover, the policemen's code forbids their reporting one another's illegal use of violence, even if on occasion they disapprove of it. No doubt public attitudes and the reactions of the police constitute a vicious circle to some extent.

8. *Cooperation of the victim.* This facilitation of crime has already been mentioned.

9. *Ambivalence of the agents of social control.* This is similar to ambivalence in the socializing agent. Psychoanalysts use the term "seduction" to refer to attempts by the patient (who is, of course, the deviant) to make an accomplice of the therapist. Such attempts may be largely unconscious. A female patient, for example, may play upon the sympathy or even the sexual susceptibility of the male therapist and persuade him, if he is not careful, that the world is at fault, not she, that she is being put upon by people who do not understand her. Such attempts are more likely to be successful if the therapist himself is ambivalent about the norms in question. What is here said about professional therapists is far more likely to be true of ordinary persons, who have not had the benefit of the therapist's professional training. The purpose of such training, in part, is to give the therapist enough self-insight to enable him to guard against his own deviant tendencies. Policemen, teachers, parents, business superiors, all have complex personalities with unconscious deviant tendencies which may lead them unconsciously to abet certain kinds of deviation rather than to counteract it. When Studs Lonigan, in James T. Farrell's novel *Young Lonigan,* makes his sister furious by occupying the bathroom for a quite

unnecessarily long time, keeping his sister from her preparations for school, their father rebukes Studs quite properly; but soon afterward, perhaps expressing the bond between males who must put up with the silly complaints of women, the father slips Studs a dollar as the boy leaves for school.

There is another possibility. If the agent of social control—or, rather, the person who in normal situations would be the agent of social control—has a fairly deep-seated alienative attitude that he has repressed and counteracted by means of reaction formation, so that he is a compulsive conformist of the active, dominating type, then he may punish others for the same alienative tendency, and his excessive sanctions, being regarded as unduly harsh or as unjust, may drive the deviant to an even more alienative attitude (Parsons, 1951, pp. 274ff.). Thus interaction that would ordinarily check deviant tendencies may involve a vicious spiral confirming them.

10. *Subcultural legitimation of deviation.* One of the most important factors encouraging deviation is the reinforcement of alienative attitudes and nonconforming behavior in a group. What is nonconforming in the outside world becomes conforming in the group. We have seen an example of this in delinquent gangs. Parsons (1951, p. 286) points out that in a deviant group a person is able to act out both the conformative and the alienative sides of his ambivalent motivation. This he does by splitting them; the alienative side is satisfied in the deviant activities of the group *vis-à-vis* the wider society, and the conformative side is satisfied by conformity to the standards of the deviant group. Moreover, as Parsons points out, an organized group is much better able than an individual to cope with the counteracting efforts of agents of social control.

11. *Sentiments of loyalty to deviant groups.* This factor, which Parsons also mentions, is closely bound up with the preceding one but is not quite the same. The point is that once a person is involved in a deviant group, so that the other members of it are depending upon his cooperation, he will find it hard to let them down and suffer their disapproval and rejection even if he no longer believes in their activities. The cruder aspect of such pressure is often shown in grade B crime movies, in which the erring hero sees the light but is threatened with reprisals from the mob if he leaves them. The more subtle aspect is that the hero who finally wants to go straight feels pangs of conscience about his disloyalty to his partners in crime. As Parsons also points out, deviant groups deal harshly with disloyal members not only because they fear exposure to enforcement agencies but also because defection is a threat to the stability of their own ambivalent motive-structure. The defection of one member acts like an appeal to the repressed conformative side in the personalities of the others. That is to say, for some members of the group who do not defect, the example of a defecting member may renew a bothersome temptation of their own. Defection thus destroys the very solidarity that made the deviant group so satisfying in the first place.

Social Control

Most social control is exerted with so little fanfare that it goes largely unnoticed. Parsons, whose account of social control (1951, pp. 297ff.) we follow here, calls it "nipping deviant tendencies in the bud." We have discussed it as the application of informal sanctions. The most inconspicuous form is the self-control exerted by individuals either because of their ability to imagine the negative reactions of others or because of their own conscientious censorship.

Sometimes, however, deviant tendencies are not checked until they get well beyond the bud stage, and it is with the mechanisms of social control that then come into play that we must now deal. The most important of them may be regarded as forms of therapy, although they are not always known as such. One of the most general statements that can be made about deviant behavior is that it is a reaction to strain of some kind. We have noted many examples of this fact. Role conflict is a kind of strain. Being required to do something one seemingly cannot do imposes a strain. Therapy, therefore, if it is to be successful, has to cope with the causes of strain and with the reactions to it.

We may distinguish four principal kinds of reaction to strain, all of which are well known (Parsons, 1951, pp. 298-99). They have in common the fact that they express a wish—and, in a sense, are an attempt—to create a situation in which the particular strain does not exist, perhaps to restore some state of affairs that existed before the strain set in, or at least to prevent the present provocative situation from getting worse. All four reactions may occur in the same case. When the cause of strain has been stabilized and has therefore already been adjusted to in part, the only reaction may be *fantasy*—the fulfillment in daydreams of the wish that things were different. When the cause of strain might or might not continue or get worse, *anxiety* will occur in addition to fantasy. Anxiety leads to distortion of perception, to misinterpretation, and to exaggerated needs for reassurance. Another common reaction to strain is *aggression*—hitting back or hitting out. This reaction, however, may be prevented by the wish to regain or create a more favorable situation. For example, aggressive feelings may be repressed lest they further endanger a relationship whose deterioration caused the strain. In general, the fourth possible reaction to strain, *defensiveness,* is residual—it includes whatever is not covered by fantasy, anxiety, and aggression but has the purpose of removing the source of strain. An increased attempt to be ingratiating or an attempt to dominate may be such a reaction.

A person in therapy is in a learning situation very similar to the one involved in socialization (see Chap. 5). It will be remembered that the socializing agent has to cope with the learner's being under strain, with his typical reactions. Upon analysis it appears that therapeutic social control, like socialization, requires that the controlling agent follow four rules:

1. Provide emotional support, reassuring the learner that he is not cast out even though his present behavior may not be entirely acceptable. Support copes with the learner's anxiety.

2. Be somewhat permissive with respect to the subject's hostility and other signs of strain. Persons known to be under strain should not be pushed any harder than is necessary.

3. Although permissive, do not reciprocate in just the way the subject might wish. For example, the controlling agent or "therapist" will "not accept either dominance or submission" from the subject (Parsons, 1951, p. 300). The danger of excessive permissiveness is that it will create a vicious circle in which the subject's deviant behavior will get worse and worse. Successful therapy, therefore, requires a balance between permissiveness and the refusal to reciprocate. Just what behavior on the therapist's part will maintain the proper balance cannot be stated in general. The therapist must take into account the cause or causes of strain. He must also consider the "total" social situation of the subject; other persons, for example, might be providing too much or too little permissiveness and perhaps should be counteracted. The "rules" we are outlining are merely rough guides, indicating the general features of what is desirable and what is to be avoided.

Decisions with respect to both permissiveness and refusal to reciprocate are legitimized in terms of the institutionalized patterns that the controlling agent is trying to restore respect for. The controlling agent often has at least one advantage over the socializing agent: he can presume that the subject already has a conformative (as well as an alienative) attitude toward these patterns, whereas relatively speaking the socializing agent, especially when dealing with a child, has to cope with the fact that the subject may not recognize the legitimacy of the patterns being inculcated and may even regard the demand to conform to them as a violation of a tacit contract. For the therapist, however, there are often disadvantages that more than counterbalance this advantage.

4. Finally, reward the learner appropriately when he does the right thing or in any way manifests the right attitude: "right" meaning, of course, in line with the norm being restored to vigor in ego's personality (which may or may not be a "good" norm in unanimous opinion).

These psychological considerations are unavoidable if our treatment of social control (as of socialization) is to be better than superficial. In both cases, however, psychology is brought in to help us understand how social systems work. We must emphasize that what is called "therapy" above is not confined to psychoanalysis and other forms of psychiatry. Much of it is built into role relationships that we ordinarily do not view in these terms. For example, Parsons (1951, Chap. 10) shows how the treatment of the physically sick embodies the same principles of social control. The patient is expected to regard his condition as undesirable; is accepted, however; is permitted to be less cheerful and responsible than usual, but is not allowed to regard his condition as permanent (if his physical condition *is* permanent, then his *attitude* is not to be regarded as permanent); and, finally, is rewarded and encouraged when he cooperates and shows signs of improving. For another example of social routine in which the principles of social control are implicit, we have only to recall our earlier analysis of the function of mourning and funeral rituals (pp. 465-66).

Another example of social control of the therapy type is not yet widely institutionalized in the United States. In several large cities, however, including New York and Chicago, there are or have been delinquency-prevention programs, and they are promising although rather expensive. The program we shall use as an illustration is the so-called Roxbury Project, which was conducted in a high-delinquency area of Boston, Massachusetts, from June 1954 to June 1957 (W. B. Miller, 1957, 1959). This was both a service and a research project. Seven trained social workers worked full time with delinquent corner groups. Each of the workers spent most of his time with one group over the three-year period.

> It took between one and two years for the new role of "social worker" to become generally familiar and acceptable. A social worker came to be seen as someone who spends a great deal of time in the neighborhood, who helps youngsters to form clubs and find jobs, who serves as a liaison between children and parents, teachers, and other authorities, and who can be turned to in times of trouble.
>
> The establishment of this new role has important implications for future service in the community. It means that a new worker who comes into the area and is identified as a social worker will be accepted and turned to without having to undergo the long and difficult initial period of antagonism, suspicion, and "testing" that persons filling an unfamiliar role must undergo. The activities of Program area workers resulted in establishing among the youth and many of the adults of the community the conception of a new role–that of "social worker"–which came to be almost as familiar and well understood as that of policeman or priest [Miller, 1957, p. 397]

The purpose of the service aspect of the program was to reduce the amount of law-violating behavior and to establish and confirm in each boy or girl included in the program the personal resolution to live within the law. In place of "horsing around" and delinquency the groups were encouraged and guided to form clubs and engage in competitive athletics.

> Two things necessarily involved in setting up a club made it very difficult for members to keep under the surface a commitment as to which side they were on. One was the necessity of specifying in the constitution the purposes of the club, and the other, and more important, the necessity of setting up qualifications for membership. It was a striking experience for Program workers to watch the struggles of the newly forming clubs trying to come to a decision as to who should and who should not be a member. As names were proposed, one by one, the group would engage in a heated discussion as to whether or not this person was acceptable–and acceptability was decided primarily on the basis of which path of life the boy was known to favor, although this was not the way the group phrased it. The basic issue was forced to the surface: Will this club and those in it follow the law-abiding or law-violating path of life? In no case was this issue resolved at the outset,

> and the membership list usually included boys with inclinations toward both paths of life, but a conflict heretofore vaguely defined and hidden was now brought much more sharply into focus. As the clubs developed, the presence and activities of the workers constituted a subtle but persistent force in support of the law-abiding way of life [Miller, 1957, p. 404].

This project did succeed in reducing delinquency, but unfortunately it had to be discontinued. (It was a demonstration project with limited funds.) Table 23 is a summary of some of the evidence that the project was successful (see Miller, 1957, 1959). As Miller points out, in estimating success, one has to consider cost as well as results.

One difficulty the program encountered toward the end is another indication of its success. Gangs that did not have an attached social worker became envious and attacked the groups that did have social workers. These envious gangs were apparently acting on the quite reasonable idea that they might be given a social worker too if they showed they needed one (Miller, 1957, p. 399).

This brief description shows how support, permissiveness, refusal to reciprocate, and reward are judiciously combined in such a program. The key figure, of course, is the social worker. He must be the kind of person the boys can respect and trust (for example, he does not report delinquent acts known to him, although of course he does not indicate approval of them). To the extent that the group members have lacked a suitable male role model—as, for example, many of those from "female-based households" do—the social worker fills this need. We can imagine that in time the tone of a neighborhood might change rather markedly—anomie might be reduced. But so long as the basic conditions that seem to produce anomie

TABLE 23

*Correctional institutional rates: project area compared with rest of district **

Areas	*All offenses: both sexes*		*All offenses: boys*		*"Serious" offenses: boys*	
	BEFORE PROJECT	DURING PROJECT	BEFORE PROJECT	DURING PROJECT	BEFORE PROJECT	DURING PROJECT
Project area	6.8	7.5	10.4	10.7	7.8	6.7
Rest of district	6.8	9.8	10.7	17.5	8.4	12.3

* W. B. Miller, "Preventive Work with Street-corner Groups: Boston Delinquency Project," *Annals Amer. Acad. Polit. Soc. Sci.*, Mar. 1959, v. 322, p. 101, Table 1. Figures represent number of commitments of individuals aged 13 to 17 divided by number of individuals 14 to 17 in each area. "Before Project" figures represent averaged rates for the years 1952 and 1953; "During Project," averaged rates for 1955 and 1956. 1954 is omitted because service operations were not started until June, and all workers were not in the field until late October. "Serious" offenses comprise seven categories of offense: grand and petty larceny, theft, assault and battery, arson, murder, and property destruction, eliminating such categories as "stubborn child."

persist, it seems likely that such a program as the one we have briefly described cannot have a lasting effect unless it is carried on for a long time, perhaps permanently.

In addition to "nipping in the bud" and "therapy" there is another form of social control that needs our attention. This is the branding and isolation of deviant persons so that they will not be able to spread their deviant attitudes or establish any claim to legitimacy for them. We seldom acknowledge frankly that we use this method, but it is essentially what we do with "criminals" whom we put away in prisons. The claim is sometimes made and occasionally is justified that rehabilitation (successful therapy) is accomplished by this method, but on the whole it seems likely that many or most of the persons subjected to it are essentially lost to society (see Weinberg, 1942; Schrag, 1954; Sykes, 1956, Chap. 6). What the method accomplishes is to affirm symbolically the community's insistence on law-abiding behavior. In other words, this method presumably has a more important social-control function for those who are not subjected to it than for those who are.

If certain kinds of deviant behavior spiral and spread to many people without being successfully checked, social change occurs. That is to say, what has been deviant becomes legitimate. In the next chapter we take up systems of beliefs and values that are important for social conformity, social deviation, and social change.

RECOMMENDED READING

For recent research on deviant behavior, see A. K. Cohen, "The Study of Social Disorganization and Deviant Behavior," and M. B. Clinard, "Criminological Research," both in R. K. Merton, L. Broom, and L. S. Cottrell, Jr., eds., *Sociology Today: Problems and Prospects,* Basic Books, 1959, Chaps. 21, 23. For a treatment of the genesis of alienative attitudes, the possible directions of deviation, and the mechanisms of social control, see T. Parsons, *The Social System,* Free Press, 1951, Chap. 7. Chap. 10 analyzes medical practice as a kind of social control. On anomie, see R. K. Merton, *Social Theory and Social Structure,* rev. ed., Free Press, 1957, Chaps. 4, 5. The most important extension of Merton's theory, in one direction, is contained in a paper by R. A. Cloward, "Illegitimate Means, Anomie, and Deviant Behavior," *Amer. sociol. Rev.,* April 1959, v. 24, no. 2, pp. 164-76.

Perhaps the most well-balanced treatment of "white-collar crime"—at any rate, an excellent introduction to the topic—is V. Aubert, "White-Collar Crime and Social Structure," *Amer. J. Sociol.,* Nov. 1952, v. 58, no. 3, pp. 263-71.

The best introduction to the study of juvenile delinquency is A. K. Cohen, *Delinquent Boys: The Culture of the Gang,* Free Press, 1955. The student should also read three papers by W. B. Miller, in the order given here. For a good statement of Miller's essential position, that delinquency arises from lower-class culture (as opposed to Cohen's position, that the delinquent subculture is primarily a response to middle-class society), see "Lower-class Culture as a Generating Milieu of Gang Delinquency," *Social Issues,* 1958, v. 14, no. 3, pp. 5-19. On the delinquency-prevention program, see "The Impact of a Community Group Work

Program on Delinquent Corner Groups," *Social Service Rev.*, Dec. 1957, v. 31, no. 4, pp. 390-406. On the difficulty of obtaining full cooperation between churches, schools, and social agencies, partly on account of different conceptions of the nature and causation of juvenile delinquency, see "Interinstitutional Conflict as a Major Impediment to Delinquency Prevention," *Human Organization*, 1958, v. 17, no. 3, pp. 20-23. On delinquency, illegal gambling, and the tie-in of racketeers, police, and politicians, see W. F. Whyte, *Street Corner Society: The Social Structure of an Italian Slum*, University of Chicago Press, 1943; the second edition (1955) has a long and fascinating account of Whyte's field-work methods and experiences.

On the role and status of the police, see W. A. Westley, "Violence and the Police," *Amer. J. Sociol.*, July 1953, v. 59, no. 1, pp. 34-41. On prisons, see G. M. Sykes, *Society of Captives: A Study of a Maximum Security Prison*, Princeton University Press, 1958, and *Crime and Society*, Random House, 1956, Chap. 6.

21. Ideology

The members of every society are of necessity "amateur sociologists." That is to say, they have ideas about the structure of their society, its social processes, and its place in the world. If they did not have ideas on these matters, their social life would be without meaning to them; they would lack a cognitive framework within which to fit the multitude of specific social events touching themselves and the wider circles of people they know and know about. Thus everyone has some idea of the internal differentiation of the society—for example, of the social classes it contains, how they differ from one another, why there *are* different classes, what the typical paths are by which individuals and families "get ahead" or fall behind. Everyone has some image of the leaders of the society—who they are, what they are like, how they came into their important positions. As for the international setting, many political questions have meaning only on the basis of certain cognitive assumptions: for example, some other countries are thought to be friendly; others, less friendly; and still others definitely hostile in their intentions.

People not only have ideas about these matters, but they also have feelings about them, and make evaluations. Certain foreign countries are feared; others are liked. In the United States, most people regard private enterprise, competition, the independent nuclear family, literacy, and many other aspects of the culture and social structure as good or even necessary. On the other hand, communism is regarded as bad.

In short, people have ideas about how things *are,* how things *are tending,* and how things *ought* to be—what the society should be aiming toward. Everyone "knows" that things are not quite perfect; but this judgment implies at least a rough conception of the ideal society and the ideal international community.

A Definition of Ideology

We shall say, to begin with, that the ideology of a society consists of (1) popularly accepted ideas about the structure, the internal processes (including the changes taking place), and the world situation of the society; (2) popularly accepted ideas about its history; (3) popular evaluations of the accepted facts; and (4) popularly approved values and goals for the society. This definition is not meant to suggest that "the" ideology of a society is a perfectly definite, coherent, and universally approved system of beliefs and values. Many qualifications and elaborations will be necessary as we go along.

Every group in society has its own ideology. The A.F.L.–C.I.O. has a conservative labor ideology, and the N.A.M. (National Association of Manufacturers) has a conservative business ideology. Each stresses the values and interests of one segment of the population, yet the two ideologies have far more in common than they have in opposition to each other. The A.F.L.–C.I.O. strongly supports the principle of private enterprise, and the N.A.M. recognizes the legitimacy of unions.

Countless more examples could be given. Every political party, pressure group, professional organization, and social club has an ideology. Feuding families in Burma develop different stories about the origins of the feud; the different versions, which of course seek to justify conflicting claims, disagree on the facts but appeal to the same structural norms and values of the society. In the same group (the Kachins of Highland Burma), an upward-mobile lineage seeks to legitimize its higher rank by manipulating the complex genealogical tradition; the result, of course, may be regarded as part of the ideology of the lineage (see Leach, 1954, pp. 89ff., 164).

With reference to the prevailing social structure of a total society, we must distinguish between the conservative ideology and its variants (if any) and a revolutionary ideology or ideologies. The terms "conservative" and "revolutionary" refer not to the content of ideologies but to their relation to prevailing social institutions. Marxism-Leninism is the conservative ideology of the Soviet Union and a revolutionary ideology in the United States. From this example, we can see that in general a conservative ideology explains and defends existing institutions, especially those having to do with government, the economy, and the class structure, whereas a revolutionary ideology attacks the existing social order.

A special form of revolutionary ideology may be called "reactionary." The terms "conservative," "revolutionary," and "reactionary" should not be regarded as evaluative in the present context. A reactionary ideology is not necessarily bad or good; it is simply an ideology supporting the restoration of some institutional features of the past. Following any revolution, it is perhaps normal for surviving representatives of the defeated side to favor a return to the institutional forms that were overthrown by the revolution.

In a looser sense, every revolutionary ideology appeals to the past. A revolutionary movement must use some existing bridges to the minds of the people whose allegiance it seeks to gain, and the most important of these bridges are established values and interests. The Nazi ideology, for example, appealed to German nationalism, which was certainly not something the Nazis invented. But this bridge to the past is not enough to justify calling the Nazi ideology reactionary in our sense, for nationalism is not a specific social institution. Nor is it enough that the Nazi leader, Hitler, aimed to make himself an autocratic ruler like the Kaisers of German history, for institutionally speaking the resemblance between the status-role of the Kaisers and the status-role of the Fuehrer (Hitler's personal role) is rather superficial.

We must be careful, moreover, to distinguish between revolutionary ideology and revolutionary achievement. The Nazi ideology promised socialism (although rather vaguely), and the movement attracted no small part of its following through its ideological hostility to "commercial-mindedness," "international capitalism," "selfishness," and the like. The Communist ideology promised the abolition of government and the family in Russia. The fact that the government and the institution of the family are stronger than ever in Russia today does not mean that Communism, in its revolutionary phase, was reactionary. The fact that the Nazi movement did not succeed in its avowed purpose of doing away with capitalism but instead "saved" capitalism by transforming it less than the Communists would have done if *their* revolutionary movement had been successful in Germany does not make the Nazi movement reactionary either. We shall later take up some of the reasons for the gap between ideologies and the actual performance of the groups that hold them.

The varying ideologies of the subgroups of a society are normally to some extent alike in their basic premises. This is true even of groups that are opposed to each other. For example, although a revolutionary group seeks to overthrow the existing system, or many aspects of it, we have noted that the revolutionary ideology stresses some values that are already widely accepted and seeks to show that the revolutionary program will realize these accepted values better than the existing institutional patterns do. The differences between a conservative and a revolutionary ideology in the same society are, of course, much greater than those between the competing versions of the origins of a feud in Highland Burma. In one sense the competing versions are two different ideologies, one for each of the feuding families. At a somewhat more abstract or general level, however, the two versions might be regarded as evidence that the two families share the same broader ideology, since the two versions contain the same conceptions of the "right" and "wrong" working of Kachin society in Highland Burma.

A "counter-ideology," as we use the term, is an ideology that justifies the patterns of a deviant group but without seeking to change the society as a whole.

> Here, as illustrated by the case of the delinquent gang, there is an explicit lack of appeal to legitimation in terms of the values and ideology of the wider society, there is an open "state of war." But within the deviant collectivity

> there is very definitely a value-system and hence an ideology. This ideology will always include a diagnosis of the basis for the break with the main society and its value system. For example, there will be such beliefs as that "you can't win" in the wider society, that "they're out to get you" and the like. It will also involve an ideology of the relationship system within the deviant collectivity, as for instance to why leadership and discipline should be accepted, and as to why "ratting" cannot be tolerated. In such cases of an open break with the value-system and ideology of the wider society we may speak of a "counter-ideology" [Parsons, 1951, p. 355].[1]

Every ideology is institutionalized in the group for which it is an ideology. But there are great differences from one group to another in the elaboration and sanctions of the group ideology. It seems plausible that elaboration of ideology and severity of sanctions are greater when there is more conflict in a society, hence when there are competing ideologies; or when there is greater conflict between societies (see Mannheim, 1936; Merton, 1957, Chaps. 12, 13, 15).

So much speech and writing is partly ideological that one must not expect perfect agreement concerning the details of a conservative ideology for a whole society. One must rely, moreover, on a sampling of public utterances and on statements that for some good reason can be taken as authoritative. A well-known study of the ideology of American business, which of course forms a large part of the ideology of American society, is based on analysis of five kinds of material:

> 1. pamphlets, leaflets, journals, and other material distributed by business firms or by business organizations such as the National Association of Manufacturers; (2) statements of businessmen and business spokesmen in Congressional hearings; (3) advertisements by business firms or associations of business firms in periodicals of general circulation; (4) articles and editorials in business periodicals and in the financial sections of newspapers; (5) speeches, books, pamphlets, and other forms of public utterance by individual businessmen [Sutton *et al.*, 1956, p. 406].[2]

Novels, plays, and even history textbooks have been examined as sources of ideological statements.[3]

---

1 Sutton, Harris, Kaysen, and Tobin, in *The American Business Creed* (1956), use the term "counter-ideology" to refer to a minor variant of the most widely held conservative ideology of a society; we shall describe an "alternative conservative ideology" later in this chapter.

2 These investigators did not use a formal sampling procedure or formal techniques of content analysis (such as counting the occurrences of specific ideas, images, and symbols), but they found impressive agreement in their sources. According to them, the most elaborate and representative statement of the "classical" form of the American business ideology is National Association of Manufacturers, Economic Principles Commission, *The American Individual Enterprise System, Its Nature and Future,* 2 vols., McGraw-Hill, 1946; of the newer form of conservative business ideology (the "managerial ideology"), *USA, The Permanent Revolution,* by the Editors of *Fortune,* with the collaboration of Russell Davenport, 1951.

3 A well-known contributor to the sociology of technology has remarked, only half facetiously, that history books used in the elementary schools ought to be catalogued under "myth" and "legend." Literary works might perhaps be studied by sociologists

The relation between ideology and science is complex and variable. According to the usage we have adopted here (which is not universal), an ideology is not necessarily unscientific as a whole. Every ideology must distort social reality to some extent; nevertheless, popular impressions are never wholly incorrect. The proportions of "truth" and "error" vary from one case to another; each ideology must be considered separately. An especially rich fusion of truth and distortion is to be found in the works of Karl Marx, which not only have been an ideological bible for socialists and communists but also have been of great value to social science. Much of the work of Max Weber, for example, seems to have been a conscientious attempt to find out what qualifications are necessary to the sometimes dogmatic statements of Marx (see Weber, 1946)

The standard of truth, deficient as it may be, is the best available knowledge in the social sciences and, where relevant, in the other sciences. Sometimes the distortion in an ideology is striking and easy to show; but more often, perhaps, the difference between an ideological statement and a scientific statement in the same field is that the scientific statement is less sure of itself, subject to more qualifications. Science is tentative; ideology is dogmatic. Ideally at least, science is skeptical and is not satisfied with casual evidence, whereas ideology often contains, as "proof," highly selected facts. The ideologist seeks facts (if at all) in order to "prove" a belief he has already accepted; the scientist, ideally, suspends judgment until he has deliberately looked for facts that might not be in agreement with his tentative hypotheses. It is nevertheless implicit in this formulation that the difference between science and ideology is a relative one.[4]

The relative skepticism and affective neutrality of social science, however, make it vulnerable to suspicion and attack from the orthodox ideolo-

---

more than they are. No literary work can be regarded, without other evidence, as a faithful reflection either of social structure or of ideology; but great creative works, as well as works that are merely popular, might well provide suggestions for further study. We should expect, in particular, that literary works (including plays) must often provide clues to (1) the mutual reinforcement, as well as conflict and strain, produced by the four functional subsystems of society as they affect the occupants of particular roles and (2) typical ideological and other adjustments. It should not be taken for granted, however, that even the greatest artists are necessarily reliable sociologists: for one thing, the purposes of art are to some extent incompatible with the purposes of sociology.

4 ". . . the newspaper editor or columnist, faced with a column of empty space . . . can speak with finality and authority on any social topic, however complex. He might not attempt to diagnose what is wrong with his sick cat; he would call a veterinarian. But he knows precisely what is wrong with any social institution and the remedies" (Stouffer, "Some Observations on Study Design," 1950, p. 355). Every would-be sociologist, if not every student, should read Stouffer's article, which is a plea for methodological rigor in sociology. On the other hand, in the present state of sociology, the student should also read the wise words of Talcott Parsons in his Introduction to *Essays in Sociological Theory,* rev., 1954, esp. pp. 12-18. Stouffer's article and Parsons' Introduction represent two different emphases, both valuable. Despite their different emphases, both essays recognize that in the long run methodological precision is sterile without scientific imagination, and *vice versa.*

gists of society, who see in bloodless objectivity a possible threat to the true faith and to conformity. Indeed, the organized pressure for ideological conformity is sometimes strong enough to override the institutional safeguards of science, such as academic freedom. At other times, social scientists, being participating members of their societies, have temporarily and unconsciously allowed social pressures to influence their scientific results. A good instance is the state of scientific opinion with regard to "race" in the late nineteenth and early twentieth centuries. So great was popular prejudice that most social scientists accepted surprisingly meager (and largely irrelevant) evidence in favor of the doctrine that some "races" are biologically "superior" to others (for examples, see Handlin, 1957, Chap. 4). Equally striking, however, is the fact that social scientists have long since given up this error, while many ideologists continue to spread it and show no interest in contrary evidence.

Ideology is similar to religion in some respects, and what is called "religion" often contains ideological elements. Analytically, however, religion and ideology are distinct. Ideology is concerned with social systems in their social setting. Religion is concerned with a supernatural order which has relevance for human action. From this difference comes another: cognitive ideological statements are in principle capable of being confirmed or disconfirmed by reference to empirical facts, but the most distinctive religious statements, since they are about a supernatural (nonempirical) order, are not.

There is of course an actual social structure of norms, roles, subgroups, functional subsystems—all of which the participants in their own terms know about to some extent. We have noted, however, that it is not necessary for participants to have an exact and comprehensive knowledge of the social systems in which they participate. They know a little more clearly the zones of interaction in which they participate most directly and frequently; but even here it is possible for them, in good faith, to behave in one way and yet, if asked, to give an account of their behavior that is inconsistent with observable fact. To some extent, ideology is a substitute for exact knowledge. But it is an important part of the institutionalized culture of society

Ideology is a relatively stable complex of beliefs and values. It is to be distinguished, therefore, from flexible opinions expressed from day to day about passing events. Even propaganda is not always entirely ideological, for often a propagandist says things he does not believe, in order to make a specific point expediently or to disarm opposition. From a series of propagandistic documents we could distill the ideology by eliminating these shifting tactical points and keeping only the residue of statements, values, and symbols that constantly recur. For example, the "line" taken by communist parties on various specific issues has been quite flexible, but underneath there has been a stable ideology. A rigorous technique for extracting ideology exists in the modern methods of "content analysis" (see Berelson, 1951).

Functions and Dysfunctions of Ideology

No society, as we have seen, is perfectly integrated. Nagging moral dilemmas, conflicts between morality and interest, conflicting demands made upon the occupants of the same role, conflicts of interest between subgroups—all these are as common as the "faults" geologists find in rock structures. These "faults" in social structure are foci of problems, both for individual personalities and for cooperation between individuals and subgroups. They are also the foci of a great part of ideology.

SOURCES OF IDEOLOGICAL DISTORTION

Psychologists have shown that personality conflicts often produce rationalizations, more or less compulsive behavior, and *idées fixes.* If the occupants of a social role are subject to conflicting demands, they are likely to develop similar symptoms. In one aspect, ideology consists of such symptoms. Ideological distortions, then, are to some extent rationalizations. Being socially enforced to some extent, and widely held, they are sometimes even more impervious to rational criticism than are the private rationalizations peculiar to individual personalities.

Social malintegration is not the only source of ideological distortion. Another source is the fact that the members of a group need some sort of common cognitive orientation in order to cooperate; since social reality is complex, this common cognitive orientation is likely to be oversimplified from a scientific point of view. One has only to imagine what paralyzing confusion—or, more likely, apathetic boredom—would take possession of the electorate if political campaigners made a determined effort to expound the difficult economics of the national debt or the farm problem, the intricacies of balancing conflicting interests in foreign policy, the extremely complex state of affairs in the Soviet Union. Having to deal with so many complex questions, the campaigners themselves must be content, even in their own thinking, with many oversimplifications. These distortions are in the nature of the case largely unwitting.

Ideology may be said to have two social functions. With regard to individuals in their capacity as role occupants, ideology has a tension-management function. Problems of moral conflict, which might lead to loss of morale and of self-esteem, are to some extent handled by means of ideological distortion. With regard to groups, ideology has an integrative function. We have already touched upon one aspect of this function: the provision of a common cognitive orientation. Another aspect, as we shall see below, is the ideological "bridging" of some social conflicts, in the interest of enhanced social integration. The resulting social solidarity may be precarious, but it provides a basis upon which cooperation can work toward a firmer solidarity.

The various kinds of distortion are often found together. The need for simplification, in particular, always operates, whether or not other sources of distortion exist. Ideology tends to be expressed in slogans and slogan-like sayings: "Manifest Destiny," "the White Man's Burden" (or the French *"mission civilisatrice"* in colonial countries), "Competition weeds out the inefficient," "What we need in government is more hard-headed businessmen, who have had the experience of meeting a payroll." Our examples in this section are taken largely from familiar conservative ideologies, but in later sections we shall see that revolutionary ideologies also contain a good deal of distortion.

Morale is likely to be enhanced if harsh facts are to some extent glossed over. Thus a conservative ideology tends to select pleasant facts about the existing order, ignore the unpleasant, and overemphasize the importance of certain features of the social structure.[5] Ideals are always imperfectly realized, but from many statements of business ideologists one would never learn that there are many families in the United States without streamlined kitchens, tiled bathrooms, and outdoor fireplaces. From these ideologists, moreover, we learn that our economic prosperity (which does exist, of course, in a comparative sense) is entirely due to the "democratic free-enterprise system." Little or no mention is made of our vast natural resources, the contributions of millions of immigrants, or our freedom over a long period from the necessity of maintaining an expensive military establishment. Needless to say, no mention is made of the social costs of private enterprise or of its undemocratic features.

The most interesting source of ideological elaboration and distortion is the existence of moral dilemmas and conflicts of interest in the social system. For example, business legitimizes the pursuit of self-interest to a much greater extent than do the professions; yet businessmen in every society have some obligation also to have concern for the people with whom they deal and for the general welfare. The businessman's dilemma has produced various ideological distortions, not always consistent with one another—e.g., "The pursuit of self-interest results in the greatest welfare of all," and "Business is service." We could hardly take such slogans literally even if advertisers had the practice of informing us carefully about the defects of their products and the greater merits of some of the competing products.[6]

---

[5] To this generalization we must add a small qualification. The conservative ideology may even exaggerate certain trends in the existing system which the ideologists regard as dangers. For example, business ideologists sometimes grossly exaggerate the size, growth, and "peril" of the national debt. (See Sutton *et al.*, 1956, pp. 196-97ff.)

[6] Our examples of business ideology come from Sutton *et al.*, 1956. As these authors point out, businessmen are not the only ideological exaggerators. Academic men, for example, are reluctant to admit that the pursuit of truth may not always have good

POSITIVE AND NEGATIVE SYMBOLS: SCAPEGOATING

In oversimplifying, ideologists make much use of positive and negative symbols. Some business ideologists, for example, like to represent the gigantic corporation as a "team" or even as a "family." These images evoke extremely favorable attitudes, and no doubt they do symbolize one aspect of business; but of course they hardly do justice to the complex reality. On the other hand, "government spendthrifts" and intellectuals in their "ivory towers" ("dreamers," "eggheads") are negative symbols. A corresponding term of abuse in the Soviet Union would be "bourgeois reactionary" or "deviationist."

Sometimes the negative symbols in ideology are scapegoats. A scapegoat is an object upon whom (or upon which) anger or resentment is irrationally displaced. "Displacement," like all the other Freudian mechanisms, is an unconscious process. The scapegoater is of course often aware that he feels anger or resentment, and he is aware that he feels it toward a particular object; what he is not aware of is the fact that this consciously disliked object is a substitute for some other object, or for a complex source of frustration that, in rational terms, might be difficult to identify as a single culprit. Scapegoating occurs when three conditions are fulfilled:

1. For some reason the true source of frustration and resentment cannot be attacked.

2. Some other object exists that is symbolically connected with the source of frustration and is therefore a psychologically appropriate substitute as an object of aggression.

3. For some reason this substitute is less well protected against attack than the true source of resentment.

It is difficult to say whether these three conditions are sufficient as well as necessary for scapegoating to occur. At any rate, the syndrome is common.[7]

The term "frustration" has to be given a wide meaning. In particular, we should include a feeling of guilt as well as the feeling associated with being thwarted in some manner. The true source of frustration may be, in part, the scapegoater himself, who feels guilty about something. In that case, he is displacing resentment from himself to the substitute outside himself. It is also theoretically possible for a person to displace anger *upon* himself. In that case, the scapegoater and the scapegoat are the same. Displacement simply involves the wrong choice of an object for certain feelings

---

social consequences. It is easy to discover distortion in radical as well as in conserv tive ideologies.

There is no *necessary* intention of debunking in pointing out the existence of ideological distortion. However, pointing out distortion is one of the favorite tech niques of ideological conflict. Indeed, for many people the very words "ideology" and "ideological" are terms of abuse.

[7] By far the best analysis of scapegoating is Parsons, "The Sociology of Modern Anti Semitism (1942c), although several inferior treatments of anti-Semitism and of scape goating generally are cited more often.

Scapegoating frequently involves projection as well as displacement. Projection is an unconscious mechanism in which certain feelings or intentions—in general, "subjective" states—are erroneously attributed; the true location of the feelings is in the person projecting, not in the person (or group) to whom the feelings are attributed.[8] Thus when guilt is the "frustration," the feelings or intentions that occasion the guilt are first projected upon another person or group, then that other person or group is made a scapegoat.

Projection and displacement are primarily mechanisms of defense. Their function is to enable the subject to remain unaware of something he does not wish to face directly. Projection enables him to remain unaware of his own feelings by locating them in someone else. Displacement enables him to remain unaware of his feelings in another way: by choosing the wrong object, he remains unconscious of the true object. He might unconsciously wish to do this because, for example, it might for one reason or another be dangerous for him to express his feelings toward the object that has in fact occasioned them.

These comments on the function of displacement and projection put us in a position to see more clearly the sense in which these mechanisms are irrational. The point is not that the person to whom certain feelings are attributed does not have those feelings. He may or may not. The point is that the one who is projecting derives satisfaction from the attribution of feelings, not from its objective accuracy, but from the fact that he can thus avoid facing his own feelings. The same is true of displacement. Here again, the scapegoat may actually "deserve" a certain amount of anger. But the scapegoater remains irrational in the sense that he remains unaware of the fact that the true object also "deserves" anger. This element of irrationality leads to another: Whatever may be the true state of affairs with regard to the victim of projection or displacement—whether he does or does not have the attributed feelings, whether he does or does not "deserve" to be the object of resentment—he will be treated to some extent irrationally, for in addition to the treatment that may be objectively "justified" by his own feelings or actions, he will be the victim of misdirected treatment. In one case, he will be blamed in part for having feelings that someone else has (as well as for his own); in the other case, the anger directed against him will be more intense because some of it, at least, was generated by someone else. And in some cases, of course, the same person (or group) is the victim of both projection and displacement.

If we understand the defense function of displacement, we shall be able to avoid the common error of assuming that the primary function of displacement is necessarily the release of anger. The scapegoat does indeed

---

8 Note, however, that the subject may project complementary feelings instead of his own feelings. Thus, if he is hostile, his projection may take the form of attributing *fear* to another.

provide an outlet for anger, but this is only one aspect of scapegoating. The defense function may be successfully performed, moreover, whether or not the venting of aggression upon the scapegoat diminishes the sense of frustration.[9]

We must correct one oversimplification in what we have already said. It is true that the scapegoater frequently diverts his aggression from its "real" object onto a substitute. But perhaps more frequently there *is* no "real" object: the frustration was produced by many causes, so that it would be straining reason to blame any one man or group. If "justice" means anything, we could hardly blame a depression or a lost war on the malignity of any one person without making him a scapegoat. Indeed, in a wide perspective, whoever diverts blame upon himself, however much he may from a narrow point of view "deserve" blame, is only "choosing" one scapegoat rather than another: for all actors, including one's self, are at the same time "victims" in that they are acted upon by external events.

When the "real" occasion of frustration is complex and essentially impersonal, scapegoating still has a function. It provides a meaning for events; it defines the situation of action; it shows the way to what "must" be done. The fact that the "meaning" is somewhat delusory does not prevent it from being psychologically satisfying. Scapegoating, then, is another example of ideological oversimplification.

There is such a thing as a private idiosyncratic ideology, but of course ideology, including scapegoating, is more interesting sociologically when it becomes part of the culture of a group. The *social* function of ideology, as we have pointed out, is integrative as well as tension-managing. By providing a socially accepted definition of the situation, ideology makes cooperative action possible. Both the tension-management function of providing meaning and the integrative function of making cooperation possible may be more important than the fact that scapegoating provides an outlet for aggressive feelings. In many examples of scapegoating the victim suffers little more than verbal abuse. There are, however, notable cases in which social meaning, solidarity, and the possibility of cooperation are achieved only at dear cost to the scapegoat.

In many expositions of scapegoating the emphasis is placed upon the relative helplessness of the victim, to the neglect of another factor that is equally important both psychologically and sociologically. The victim is chosen irrationally, but he is not chosen at random; his actual characteristics are not irrelevant. As we noted above, there is always at least a symbolic connection between the victim and the scapegoater's frustration. If this is important for individual cases of displacement, it is more important still

---

9 The irrationality of scapegoating may or may not prevent it from removing the sense of frustration. Scapegoating can produce satisfactions besides those of defense and release, and may actually end up by changing the whole situation that occasioned frustration in the first place.

for a social movement in which many people are deluded in the same way. Although the victim is "innocent," his place in the social structure does have something to do with his being victimized.

An example of scapegoating: the American Negro about 1900

To turn from the general to the particular, the American Negroes were the victims of scapegoating on a national scale in the period extending roughly from 1890 to 1910. The result of the white-supremacy ideology of that time was the ramified system of humiliating, degrading segregation known as Jim Crow.[10] That system, being protected by law, produced vested interests of various kinds, which have supported it long after the occasion for scapegoating had passed. It was not until the 1930's that the system began to crumble under the impact of new events and interests, and since then the position of Negroes has been steadily improving. We have no objective standard by which to say whether this improvement is "rapid" or "slow." In the present context, however, we wish to focus attention on the scapegoating episode of the 1890's and early 1900's.

The so-called Compromise of 1877 marked the end of the Reconstruction period, yet the Jim Crow system did not come into being until many years later. It was not, as is sometimes thought, simply a reaction to the Reconstruction period itself.

> In 1878 Colonel Thomas Wentworth Higginson went south to investigate for himself. . . . One of the most militant abolitionists . . . [h]e compared the tolerance and acceptance of the Negro in the South on trains and street cars, at the polls, in the courts and legislatures, in the police force and militia, with attitudes in his native New England and decided that the South came off rather better in the comparison. . . . Six years later, in a review of the situation in the South, Higginson found no reason to change his estimate of 1878 [Woodward, 1957, pp. 16-17].

In 1885 the Negro journalist T. McCants Stewart, after a prolonged journey in the South, wrote glowing reports for the New York *Freeman*. He went down expecting to be discriminated against, and he was determined to make a fuss about it.

> Nothing of the sort happened, however, nor was there any unpleasantness when Stewart complained of a request from a white Virginian that he shift his baggage so that the white man could sit beside him [Woodward, 1957, p. 20].

---

[10] Since in the following paragraphs we are going to have to say many unpleasant things about the South, we had better make it clear that Northern whites have little to brag about in comparison with Southern whites. With an admirable restraint not always matched in the North, this fact is gently hinted by the Southern historian C. Vann Woodward, upon whose work we shall heavily depend. Woodward is certainly right: the white North has started many race riots, discriminates in employment, segregates Negroes residentially by restrictive covenants which perpetuate crowded ghettoes such as Harlem and Bronzeville, tolerates state laws against intermarriage, and in intimate social interaction hardly acknowledges the existence of Negroes. If the situation in the South is worse still, the fact is due to relatively peculiar circumstances, for which, as we shall make clear, the North is partly responsible.

To be sure, from the point of view of virtually all whites, in the North as well as in the South, the Negroes were an outgroup. Even the "radical" white Populists, who tried to join with the freed Negroes politically in order to achieve economic reforms from which both could benefit, did not associate with Negroes in intimate social life. They carefully emphasized their white purity by declaring that their alliance with the Negroes was solely for economic interests. As we shall see, this limited attitude was a weakness in the Populist movement in the South. The Southern conservatives took a paternalistic attitude toward Negroes: Negroes were not the equals of whites, of course, but they were all right in their place and there was no need to humiliate them needlessly. Many of the poor whites in the South—the so-called "crackers"—were violently anti-Negro, but their attitude was not considered respectable even in the South.[11] Thus Negroes were not living in paradise even before the scapegoating period, but their situation was much better than it later became.

The later scapegoating of Negroes was made possible only by the general consensus among whites that Negroes are biologically inferior. The social and cultural causes of that consensus are not well understood, either abroad or in the United States. When the Negroes were first brought by force from Africa, the cultural differences between them and the whites from Europe led to ethnocentric reactions. The failure of missionaries to make any significant progress in the assimilation of the Indians reinforced the suspicion that these strange peoples were simply incapable of being "civilized." Even Thomas Jefferson, who was as liberal and almost as learned as any other man of his time, feared that the Negroes and the Indians might create an insuperable problem for democracy. The Swiss naturalist Louis Agassiz, after seeing the Negroes in the South around 1846, reluctantly abandoned his objections to the theory that the human species might have had multiple origins (Handlin, 1957, p. 65).

Economic and other interests tended to strengthen the belief in Negro inferiority and confirm a system of exploitation. Slavery was profitable, and there was a tremendous vested interest in the slaves as property. The white colonists preferred to have white servants from Europe but found it hard to attract them. At first the Negro slaves had a status similar to that of the white indentured servants, but in order to attract more whites from Europe the white colonists began to treat the white indentured servants with much more consideration. The Negroes in Africa did not have to be attracted

---

[11] In one perspective, the behavior of the "crackers" may be regarded as scapegoating; in another, not. If we regard the crackers' whole social situation as given, then they were realistic in regarding the Negroes as a threat to them, for the Negroes *were* at the bottom of the society and the crackers were in danger of being pushed down there with them. On the other hand, if the crackers had not been deluded by their racist ideology, they might have joined with the Negroes politically to extract concessions from the white upper class, which was benefiting from the poverty of both Negroes and poor whites. In this perspective, the crackers made a scapegoat out of the Negroes instead of attacking the white upper class, the "real" source of their frustration.

since they were brought by force. By the time of the Civil War, the Negroes were slaves in the full sense most of us have in mind when we use the term.

After the Civil War and the emancipation of the slaves, the whites were unwilling to give up their superior status. They were also unwilling to admit to themselves that the terrible war in which brave fathers, brothers, and sons had been killed had been fought largely to protect crass material interests. They had to believe that the South had fought for civilization.

In all these developments, there were facilitating factors. The invention of the cotton gin, at a time when slavery was hardly profitable any more, had suddenly created a demand for more slaves and enhanced the economic value of those already here. The different color of the Negroes made them socially "visible" for generations, and also made it possible to believe that every Negro had recently been a slave or was the descendant of slaves. Because of the presence from early times of white women in the colonial population, there had been little intermarriage between whites and Negroes; therefore it did not happen in the United States, as it did in Brazil, that white men had legitimate children of mixed "blood" to whom they wished to bequeath their possessions and their status. The numerous illegitimate children of mixed blood were therefore simply treated as Negroes.

Vicious circles were also involved. Discrimination against Negroes kept many of them illiterate and most of them poorly educated. Continued discrimination and exploitation created more and more fear that the Negroes would retaliate if they were given the chance to do so.

Ironically, the racist ideology developed in part because of the very strength of democratic values in the United States, including the South. In order to reconcile the interests and sentiments outlined above with the contrary values of democracy, the whites "had" to regard Negroes as less than human and hence not worthy of equal treatment.[12] This ideological distortion, at first developed to justify slavery, was later resurrected to justify the Jim Crow system of segregation. The ideology was of course perpetuated to some extent by the ordinary processes of socialization. Nevertheless, the Jim Crow system, as we have mentioned, did not arise until twenty years after the Reconstruction period, and it was essentially a case of scapegoating.

As Woodward makes clear, the Compromise of 1877, which ended the period of Reconstruction, was itself the prelude to a progressive relaxation of Northern liberalism. Both the North and the South were tired of their struggle; the desire for national union was strong. But a conciliatory attitude on the part of the North meant condoning discrimination against Negroes, although it did not necessarily mean approving of the Southern anti-

---

[12] For most of these points, see Handlin, 1957, Chaps. 1, 2. On the moral conflict between various unacknowledged interests and the "American creed," see Myrdal, 1944, v. 1, Part I. On the understandable tendency of Southerners to romanticize the Civil War, see the sympathetic comments by Cash, 1941, pp. 127-28.

Negro extremists, whose behavior was to a large extent held in check by the paternalistic conservatives.

The Supreme Court cooperated in the spirit of conciliation. In order to show that the Court became more and more conciliatory as time went on, we shall cite only three of the long series of anti-Negro decisions from 1873 to 1898. In the *Civil Rights Cases* of 1883 the Court

> held that the Fourteenth Amendment gave Congress power to restrain states but not individuals from acts of racial discrimination and segregation. . . . [T]he Court in 1890 (*Louisville, New Orleans, and Texas Railroad* v. *Mississippi*) ruled that a state could constitutionally *require* segregation on carriers. . . . [I]n 1898 [perhaps the climactic year in the scapegoating period], in *Williams* v. *Mississippi* the Court completed the opening of the legal road to proscription, segregation, and disfranchisement by approving the Mississippi plan for depriving Negroes of the franchise [Woodward, 1957, pp. 53-54].

Following the Compromise of 1877, the upper-class conservatives controlled the politics of the South. In order to get the Northern carpetbaggers thrown out, they had played up to the extremist anti-Negro sentiment of the crackers, but after 1877 these conservatives restrained the extremists and, as we have mentioned, took a paternalistic attitude toward the Negro. Indeed, this protective attitude was one of the political weaknesses of the conservatives, since it alienated the so-called straightout white supremacists. The conservatives were also weakened politically by a series of financial scandals that were worse than any of the depredations of the carpetbaggers. These scandals were especially damaging since the conservatives had been the great crusaders against corruption. The most persistent and basic political weakness of the conservatives, however, was their policy of cooperating with Northeastern railroad and financial interests. Politically, therefore, in the long run the poorer whites had nothing to gain from the conservatives, and even the Negroes, whom they patronized, had nothing to gain except protection against the white racists. The conservatives reminded the Negroes that their position could be much worse—a point that later events bore out.

The political tide turned against the conservatives during the agrarian depression of the 1880's and 1890's. Although the Populist movement was strongest in the West, it was also very strong in the South. The popular upheaval due to economic discontent was, according to Woodward (1957, p. 60), greater than that of the depression in the 1930's.

> "I call that particular change a revolution," wrote the Alabama historian William Garrott Brown, who lived through it, "and I would use a stronger term if there were one." . . . The Populists defied not only the conservative leaders but pretty much all they stood for, including the one-party system, the Eastern alliance, and white solidarity [Woodward, 1957, p. 60].

The white Populist leaders appealed to Negro voters with so much success that the conservatives "lost their heads" and abandoned their policy of protecting the Negroes. They deliberately made the Negro the scapegoat for lower-class-white discontent. The conservatives now gave the signal to the cracker racists that they could go all out against the Negroes. At the same time, the conservatives were able by fraud to defeat the white majority in elections. They counted nonexistent Negro votes in favor of white supremacy. Many of the white Populists understood clearly what was going on, but others, defeated by force and fraud, blamed the Negroes for their disillusionment. Here the great weakness of the Populist position was displayed. Even these "radical" friends of the Negro were friends only for expediency. Their solidarity with the Negroes was only the solidarity of class in the Marxist sense and had to contend with irrational ethnic-group ("racial") prejudice. By 1895 the Negro leader Booker T. Washington was counseling the Negroes to accept a policy of humble submission to white supremacy.

We have said that 1898 might be regarded as the climactic year in the scapegoating episode. In that year the United States, partly as a result of the Spanish-American War, acquired control over Cuba, Hawaii, and the Philippines—with eight million colored people. Racists in the South gleefully asserted that the ideology of "the White Man's burden," espoused by the North as well as the South, differed little from their own ideas concerning the Negroes at home. Thus the Negroes were the victims of a heightened need for national unity in the face of external problems. Very soon they also became the victims of a renewed feeling that the terrible breaches that had occurred in the white population of the South should be healed. National unity and sectional unity were achieved partly at the expense of the Negro.

> Economic, political, and social frustrations had pyramided to a climax of social tensions. No real relief was in sight from the long cyclical depression of the 'nineties, an acute period of suffering that had only intensified the distress of the much longer agricultural depression. Hopes for reform and the political means employed in defiance of tradition and at a great cost to emotional attachments to effect reform had likewise met with cruel disappointments and frustration. There had to be a scapegoat. And all along the line signals were going up to indicate that the Negro was an approved object of aggression. These "permissions-to-hate" came from sources that had formerly denied such permission. They came from the federal courts in numerous opinions, from Northern liberals eager to conciliate the South, from Southern conservatives who had abandoned their race policy of moderation in their struggle against the Populists, from the Populists in their mood of disillusionment with their former Negro allies, and from a national temper suddenly expressed by imperialistic adventures and aggressions against colored peoples in distant lands [Woodward, 1957, p. 64].

The Reconstruction period was ideologically "reconstructed." [13] By

---

[13] "It is instructive to compare the picture of the Negro painted by . . . authors who lived through Reconstruction themselves with the picture of the Negro during Reconstruction that emerges in the pages of Thomas Dixon, who was born the last year

law in the Southern states the Negroes were segregated in public carriers, restaurants, hotels, restrooms, waiting rooms, theatres, swimming pools, playgrounds, and cemeteries. In majestic courtrooms Negro witnesses kissed a Jim Crow copy of the Bible. More important, the Negroes were barred from most forms of lucrative employment and were deprived of the suffrage.[14]

If it is clear that the Negroes served as a scapegoat, it is not equally clear who the "real" object of aggression was or whether there was one. The Spanish-American War was clearly not a national crisis great enough to produce a need for a scapegoat. The war and "imperialism" were only facilitating factors. The people who were most frustrated and who chiefly had to be appeased were the lower-class Southern whites, whether racists or radicals; they were suffering from economic depression, low status, and lack of hope. But we shall leave it to others to decide whether or to what extent the Eastern financiers and railroad magnates and their Southern conservative allies were "really" to blame for the depression.

In the discussion thus far, we have stressed the functions of ideology. We should note, however, that ideology also has dysfunctions. Technically, perhaps, the suffering of Negroes is no more dysfunctional than the loss of men in a victorious battle. Everything, including the integration of social systems, is achieved at a cost. But we are all victims of the racist ideology. We all suffer from the fact that the talents of one tenth of the population are not used so well as they might be. It is *American* foreign policy, not Negro foreign policy, that suffers on account of our well-known and much-despised racism. In fact, it can hardly be doubted that the Supreme Court, in its 1954 decision on the desegregation of schools, was influenced by the international situation. The lawyers for the Negroes explicitly pointed out that discrimination against Negroes weakens our appeal to the colored peoples of Asia and Africa. Moreover, the "New Reconstruction" that is taking place in the South for this reason and others will undoubtedly do much to change the brutality, backwardness, poverty, and hostility to the intellect which, with notable exceptions, have characterized the South; and these changes will certainly benefit whites as well as Negroes. In the long run, we tend to pay a price for any considerable distortion of reality. In this respect, a scapegoating ideology is like a private neurosis, which is

---

of the Civil War. . . . His trilogy: *The Leopard's Spots: A Romance of the White Man's Burden—1865-1900* (1902); *The Clansman: An Historical Romance of the Ku Klux Klan* (1905); and *The Traitor: A Story of the Fall of the Invisible Empire* (1907) was the perfect literary accompaniment of the white-supremacy and disfranchisement campaign, at the height of which they were published" (Woodward, 1957, p. 78).

[14] Minorities are of course not the only scapegoats. We need only mention "witches," "communists," "capitalists," the United States (for many foreign countries), even the Devil. Foreigners who feel superior to white Americans are probably no less (nor more) guilty of scapegoating, which appears to be a fundamental process in social interaction. Scapegoats differ according to the particular frustrations and circumstances. At the same time, we are free, of course, to think that a scapegoater, like a rotten apple, is still rotten, even though he cannot help being so.

functional only within confining limits. A scapegoating ideology is also like a private neurosis in another respect, however: it may be the only mode of integration available to the total system at a particular time.

Conservative Ideologies

It is impossible to give an adequate conception of the ideology of a great society in a short space. In dealing with the United States we have touched upon the ideological elements in romantic love, democracy, the belief in equality of opportunity, and racism. In the present section we shall deal briefly with the ideological defense of private enterprise, which is of course one of the basic institutional features of American society. Our chief aim here is to illustrate the fact that there is not necessarily only one conservative ideology in a given society, even with regard to so basic a thing as capitalism. There are variants, and they may indicate a gradual shift in the conservative ideology to bring it more nearly in line with changed social conditions.

The "classical" ideology of American business is built on the image of small owner-run firms, oriented to profit-making in a competitive economy. The impersonal competition among these firms keeps prices low and eliminates the inefficient, so that society as a whole benefits. The chief dangers to the system are monopoly and "excessive" government intervention. Partly in answer to radical ideological criticism, partly in response to the changed reality of American capitalism, there has grown up, however, an alternative conservatism defending the existing system. This has been called the "managerial ideology." It recognizes the preponderant influence of big business and acknowledges the characteristic separation between management and ownership as a whole. While still insisting that competition plays a large part in the system, it also exaggerates another mechanism that allegedly ensures efficiency and justice in the allocation of the benefits of the economy. This other mechanism is the professionalization of the managers. According to this ideological conception (which is a distortion only in part), the modern "professional" business executive uses his power in the interests of society as a whole. He recognizes a responsibility not only to the stockholders who employ him but also to the employees of the company and to consumers.

Although the managerial ideology seems to be gaining ground, it is not likely to replace the classical version altogether, for at least three reasons:

1. The so-called professionalism of the managers does not provide clear-cut directions to business managers. *How* are they supposed to compromise between the conflicting demands and interests of stockholders, labor, and consumers? In contrast, the classical ideology justifies running the business, as far as possible, in the interests of its owners.

2. The managerial ideology provides no answer to the problem of the efficiency of the economy as a whole. Even if all the managers were professional-minded, they would hardly be able to coordinate all their independent decisions so as to achieve the best over-all results. In contrast again, the classical version, by exaggerating the importance of the wholly impersonal mechanism of competition, can maintain that maximum efficiency is achieved automatically.

3. The managerial ideology unintentionally highlights the passivity of the stockholders ("absentee owners"). Since the stockholders take little risk and have no part in making decisions, the question of how their good fortune can be socially justified becomes more acute. The classical ideology emphasizes that the investor in a small competitive business risks the loss of his hard-earned savings. Not only that, but he is a bold entrepreneur, and he thoroughly deserves the profits he receives, for his role is indispensable to the progress and functioning of the system.[15]

Revolutionary Ideologies

Revolutionary ideologists have special problems. Having been socialized according to the values and beliefs of the conservative ideology, they have to contend with the lingering attachment to it which remains a part of their personalities. This attachment must be repressed. There may be repressed guilt feelings also. Moreover, if the revolutionary movement is to be successful, it must of course proselytize among people who are still presumably believers in the old ideology. These problems are obviously less acute for reactionary revolutionists. Unless they are so few as to classify as crackpots, they presumably have considerable psychological support in the continued legitimacy, for some people, of the institutions they are seeking to restore. (We must bear in mind that we are speaking rather abstractly. There are reactionaries and reactionaries, some of whom we like while disliking others, depending upon our point of view. For example, both the republicans and the royalists in Spain are reactionaries in a technical sense.) We shall occasionally use the word "radical" to refer to revolutionaries who are not reactionaries.

By this time, it is hardly necessary to point out that the inner struggle of conscience that the revolutionary ideologist must undergo is not carried on in a social vacuum. He may have friends and relatives to whom he is attached and whose opinion, if it is contrary to his own, he will not be able to shake off easily. He will thus be subject to a double strain: first, from his own inner struggle over principles and programs, and second, from his

[15] This embarrassment of the managerial ideology probably accounts, in part, for the gross (and deliberate, in this case) understatement of the actual amount of profits. See Sutton *et al.*, 1956, Chap. 4. All the points in the present section are taken from this book.

intimate social difficulties. This double strain is not all he must bear. In addition, the more radical his views are, and the more openly and vigorously he expresses them, the more he will be subject to reprisals from people he does not know intimately—from the various ideological watchdogs that every society has.

We may note, in passing, that certain typical features of the organization of radical movements are traceable to the strains and pressures we have just mentioned. The typical radical movement fiercely emphasizes loyalty, to the radical program and to fellow members of the movement. As proof of his loyalty, a member of a radical movement must be willing to give up former friends, even to repudiate his wife if necessary. There is an obvious resemblance to the following of a charismatic religious leader. Another typical feature of radical movements is secrecy. Clearly, if the movement is utterly secret, it will tend to defeat its purposes; nevertheless, unusual care must be taken to circumvent the established authorities. For this purpose in part, the Communists have evolved the cell system. Each cell elects a representative to the next higher body, so that any one member of the total organization, unless he is at a high level, will not necessarily know who many of the other members are. Another device is the use of pseudonyms. These and similar devices have some disadvantages, but they help to reduce the danger of exposure.

Since the radical ideology is in part an attack on certain aspects of the existing social structure, it must offer both a critique of those aspects and a program for substituting something else. The ideologist has of course been disaffected or he would still be a more or less devoted conservative. His disaffection, if it is shared with a large number of people, is itself a symptom of social malintegration. Somehow the established social order is not working as well as it might, at least for these people. We must assume, that is to say, that the primary determinant of both critique and program lies in the existing social structure. This does not mean that the critique is entirely rational or that the program is entirely realistic. Nevertheless, we must assume that a social movement has social starting points. The radical critique and the radical program are determined in part by the ideologist's own disaffection from the existing order and by his conception and hope that other segments of the population, though not yet disaffected, can become so if the "right" criticisms are made and the "right" program is held out to them. The radical ideologist does not assume, of course, that he can win over *all* segments of the population by persuasion alone; he merely assumes that certain segments are particularly susceptible.

The radical ideology is shaped, therefore, not only by the ideologist's own social problems but also by his conception of the social situation of others. Moreover, if the radical movement survives long enough, its ideology will to some extent be adjusted to the ideologist's *changing* conception of his followers and potential followers. Part of the ideology, to be sure, will be relatively resistant to change for the sake of expediency, but many lesser elements will be dropped or added in order to neutralize potential opposition or win peripheral support.

The problem of ambivalence (the ideologist's continuing attachment to the old social order) and the problem of converting people who are still to some extent "blind" supporters of that order affect the content of the ideology as well as the form and spirit of organization. The ideologist must attempt to show that the radical program will actually express some existing values better than the existing social structure expresses them. Further, the problems mentioned lead to considerable distortion in the radical critique of the existing order. Finally, the need to justify a break with the past leads to utopian elements in radical ideologies—that is, to promises that can hardly be fulfilled in reality.[16]

The Communist ideology, which of course is by far the most important radical-revolutionary ideology in the world today, promises that Communism will establish "true" democracy—namely, "economic democracy"—in place of the "sham" that "so-called democratic" countries now have. This particular promise is rhetorical to some extent, since it involves a verbal trick: "economic democracy" has little to do with "democracy" as that concept is ordinarily understood. This fact, however, only emphasizes our point that the radical ideology maintains continuity with what is good in established values and promises to fulfill them. Communism also promises peace and plenty for all—again, values that almost everyone already accepts.

The radical critique of the existing order tends to be distorted in that it is highly selective; it tends to emphasize the points that conservative ideologists play down or omit and to glide over the valid aspects of the conservative ideology. Some of the same symbols appear, but with the opposite value. Whereas for the conservative ideology private enterprise is the source of all good, it is the source of all evil for Communism. The radical ideology, like the conservative, tends to see things as black or white.

Closely akin to distortion is the tendency to adopt a closed system of thought. In Communism, for example,

> Gradualism is excluded because dialectical development proceeds by discrete jumps. You cannot have half a negation. And since by definition communism negates capitalism, there can be no compromise between them. More precisely the ideas of capitalism and communism are fundamentally opposed. It is therefore impossible for capitalists even if they want to do so to satisfy the inevitable claims of the workers. Hence it follows that social security legislation and welfare states must be swindles. They must be just camouflage behind which the progressive exploitation of workers by

---

[16] It is perhaps necessary to mention again that our analysis of ideology is not meant as debunking. As we have noted, conservative ideologies also distort. They do so unavoidably, and so do radical ideologies. One might choose between them on the basis of the *relative* truth and realistic promise they seem to contain. The fact that a radical ideology cannot be entirely fulfilled in reality does not mean, logically, that it has no value at all. On the other hand, the fact that it can be partly fulfilled does not necessarily recommend it.

> capitalists goes on unabated, and the more they look as if they were the real thing the more detestable they are. It takes a good deal of natural piety to make this sound plausible, but the foundations are such that the effort has to be made [Weldon, 1953, p. 13–].[17]

A closed system of thought, then, is one in which certain assumptions are so dogmatically held that any facts whatever will be tortured till they yield support.

Among the utopian promises of communism, perhaps the one most often mentioned by its opponents is the "withering away of the State." What exactly Marx meant by this is not known. But he almost certainly had some conception of human beings so much purified by communism that the repressive activities of government would become unnecessary. This conception could be criticized in general terms, but it is enough for the enemies of Soviet Communism to point to the "totalitarian" state of the Soviet Union.

Utopian hopes are, of course, functional. They not only help to justify the break with the past but also justify and compensate for the often terrible sacrifices the radicals must make for the movement. These, of course, are tension-management as well as integrative functions.

The importance of symbols is illustrated in the utopian ideology of some of the collective settlements (*kibbutzim*) of Israel. Most of these *kibbutzim* are strongly oriented toward Orthodox Judaism, but a few are antireligious and Marxist. In a Marxist *kibbutz* studied by Spiro (1956) some of the principles of radical communism are carried out much more rigorously than they are in the Soviet Union. The members are better able to endure their hardships, some of which are caused by the system itself, because they have a bright vision of a secular heaven-on-earth to come. Their faith is sustained by their much-exaggerated idea of the extent to which the Soviet Union has already realized the utopian dream. The "Soviet Union" is of course a symbol in the ideology. The corresponding negative symbol is the "United States," the source of evil in the world. It is of no consequence that the people of the United States help to keep Israel alive. How important for morale a positive symbol can be—a symbol "proving" that one's utopian hopes are realistic—and also how far ideological distortion can go are both shown in the following passage, which gives the ideological explanation of facts that unenlightened people might misunderstand:

> The Soviet Union has seemed to be anti-Zionist because Zionist activities in the past had taken place within the context of Turkish and British imperialism, and have often been dominated by American Jewish capitalists. That these are the grounds for its anti-Zionist attitude is evident from the fact that when the British were about to abandon Palestine in 1947, Andrei Gromyko, the delegate from Russia, delivered a speech in the United Nations, referring

[17] We should note, however, that some ideologists derived from Marx *are* gradualist. This is true of the Fabians in England the American socialists, and "social democrats" generally, all of whom the Communists despise.

> to the "rights" of the "Jewish People" to a homeland in Palestine. Furthermore, in the Israel War of Liberation, it was Czechoslovakia which supplied the Jews with arms [Spiro, 1956, pp. 189-90].

In a footnote to this passage, Spiro remarks:

> That Gromyko's speech might have been motivated by a desire to weaken the position of the British, rather than by sympathy with the Zionist cause; and that Czechoslovakia, as a Soviet satellite, was motivated by a desire to create unrest in the Near East, as well as by a need for American dollars (the arms were not given as a gift, and only dollars were accepted as payment) are considerations which the kibbutz refuses to entertain as possible motives. That the Soviet Union had not changed its policy is best indicated by the fact that the Communist Party in Israel which, presumably, was closer to the Soviet Union than is the Federation [of Marxist kibbutzim], continued its policy of virulent anti-Zionism.[18]

From a conservative point of view, one of the most irritating traits of the radical is his tendency to *want* things to be bad. He is chagrined to learn that the present system may not be quite so unjust as he had thought. We might suggest that this tendency comes from some of the strains and ideological adjustments we have been discussing. If things as they are are bad, then the radical is reassured, for he need not (he keeps telling himself) feel guilty about his defection from the existing order and his treasonable loyalty to the radical ideology. And if things get worse, then presumably more and more people will see the light, and the day of fulfillment will be closer at hand.

Despite these marks of sociopsychological tension, the main content of radical ideologies derives from societal malintegration. In Chapter 13, it will be remembered, we pointed out that the concept of charisma does not so much solve as it does identify a sociological problem. The analysis of two examples of revolutionary ideology will help us to see how charismatic leaders are able to win followers.

NAZISM IN GERMANY

Our first example is the Nazi ideology, which "justified" the overthrow of the Weimar Republic, carried Adolf Hitler to the mastery of Germany and much of western Europe, and helped to plunge the whole world into war.

Many writers have described Hitler's hypnotic power. They emphasize,

---

[18] The question might be asked whether we are justified in regarding the Marxist ideology of the *kibbutz* as radical, in view of the fact that it is official. If we consider the *kibbutz* alone as our social system, then its ideology is certainly conservative according to our definition. If we regard the *kibbutz* as part of Israel, then its ideology is radical. However, a conservative ideology can have utopian elements in it. Strictly speaking, the American ideal of equality of opportunity is utopian. Marxism, which with modifications is the conservative ideology of the Soviet Union, also has utopian elements, as we have noted. In the United States, however, the "official" ideology tends to play down the extent to which equality of opportunity has not yet been attained; in this sense, the ideal is not really utopian (a promise for the future). And in the Soviet Union, little mention is made these days of the withering away of the state.

in particular, his eyes and his voice. An English historian, speaking of Hitler's last days, writes that

> The fascination of those eyes, which had bewitched so many seemingly sober men—which had exhausted Speer, and baffled Rauschnig, and seduced Stumpfegger, and convinced an industrialist that he had direct telepathic communication with the Almighty—had not deserted them [Trevor-Roper, 1947, p. 70].

His voice, in his prime, could enthrall a mass audience, could express cajolery, irony, humor, indignation, wrath; it was sometimes shrill, sometimes vibrant-deep, sometimes thunderous. Without underrating this personal magnetism, however, we must assume that what Hitler had to say had something to do with his success. Many an actor on the stage has a thrilling voice, but we cannot imagine him as a spellbinder in politics. Probably Hitler's eyes and his voice came to symbolize his message, which in turn had a powerful emotional appeal on account of the social situation.

From early in modern history to the defeat of the Axis powers in 1946, the Germans were justly proud of their military prowess, and in Germany military officers had great prestige. The loss of World War I, therefore, after tremendous sacrifices, was a bitter humiliation.[19] One of the aims of all German governments after World War I was revision of the Treaty of Versailles, which the Germans claimed—with some justification—kept Germany in an inferior position quite incommensurate with her population, technical accomplishments, and potential power. The main object of French foreign policy was to keep Germany down. The object of English foreign policy was to maintain a balance of power on the Continent. This meant to the English not allowing *either* France or Germany to become much stronger than the other. In practice the English policy was to restrain France and support Germany's complaints. The conflict between the French and English policies resulted in the failure of both (Wolfers, 1940). French policy in particular was provocative.[20] In any case, one cannot emphasize too strongly the expansionist aim of the Nazi movement. Whatever may have been the "true" ideological aims of the movement in economic arrangements, there is no doubt whatever about its aggressive nationalism.

---

[19] In their propaganda, the Nazis made special appeals to war veterans. After the Battle of France in 1940, Hitler received the French generals, to accept their surrender, in Marshal Foch's railway carriage in the Forest of Compiègne, where in 1918 the French had dictated harsh armistice terms to Germany. Outside the railway carriage Hitler did an ecstatic little dance, which can be seen in a newsreel.

[20] This point is documented in Wolfers, 1940, as well as in other works. It is obvious that the success of the Nazi movement in capturing control of Germany depended in part upon the whole political situation in Europe; however, the virtual paralysis of France, due to many social, economic, and cultural factors, was perhaps most important. We have called French foreign policy provocative not at all because it was aggressive: from the point of view of French interests, it was not aggressive enough on important occasions. But French "paper" alliances were provocative, and so was French intransigence on the question of revision of the Versailles Treaty—intransigence arising almost entirely from fear. That is to say, French weakness was provocative.

The military defeat of 1918 and Germany's subsequent humiliation were not the only sources of frustration. Inflation and depression ruined the lower and lower-middle classes or made them insecure. The conservative government, which represented the interests of the big industrialists and the big landlords, had little popular support, despite the prestige of the rather senile president, von Hindenburg, the "great" victor of Tannenberg. The two strongest parties in Germany were the Nazis, led by Adolf Hitler, and the Communists. Although still quite strong, the Nazis were losing ground and the Communist Party in Germany became the strongest in Europe outside the Soviet Union itself. In desperation, von Hindenburg, who detested and feared the Nazis only less than the Communists, called the upstart Hitler to the chancellorship, hemming him in, as he thought, by making certain other appointments at the same time. But the conservatives, who thus sought to make use of Hitler, soon found that they were helpless in his hands.

Many lower-class war veterans belonged to the Nazi private army, which the Hindenburg government tolerated in defiance of the Treaty of Versailles. But the chief political strength of the Nazi movement lay in the lower-middle class.

> The bureaucratic aspect of the party appeals greatly to those potential recruits with a bureaucratic background. It attracts especially the teaching profession, the more so as the unpolitical hero-worship and moralistic character of the propaganda allows for an interpretation which presents the conquest of power as the education of a misguided nation.
>
> The teachers—mostly elementary-school teachers—are the best represented of all professional groups composing the Nazi party—97 per cent of all German teachers are members of the party or its affiliates. . . . The relatively heavy representation of the middle classes (58 per cent of the total) becomes even more evident if we compare the composition of the party with the composition of the total gainfully employed. The manual workers were underrepresented in the party by 14.8 per cent, the white-collar employees overrepresented by 8.6 per cent, and the peasants underrepresented by 8.5 per cent. The party membership amounted at that time (January 1, 1933) to 849,009.
>
> The common element in the situations of all these different strata was their despair and lack of social and economic security, the wide differential between self-esteem and actual status, between ambition and accomplishment, between subjective claims for social status and the objective possibility of attaining these goals through competitive orientation toward "market chances," or opportunities for social ascent through bureaucratic careers [Gerth, 1940, pp. 104-05, 106; see also Heiden, 1944; and Kotschnig, 1937].

This quotation certainly exaggerates the "bureaucratic" aspect of the Nazi movement, but Gerth is correct in calling attention to the hero-worship and moralism characteristic of Nazism. The emphasis on soldierly qualities—discipline, courage, self-sacrifice, dedication—was partly due to expansionist ambitions, but it was partly a reaction against the impersonal "selfish" competitiveness of the modern world. There was a mystique of nature and natural nobility, of simplicity of character as opposed to commercial-minded trickery. To some extent the peasantry was exalted, and this was associated with emphasis on purity of blood. These two themes were expressed in the slogan *Blut und Boden* (blood and land). The common element is a mystical sense of "community." The emphasis on belonging, on giving for the good of the whole, and on sharing in the glory as well as in the trials of the national community (mystically symbolized in "racial" terms) offered a kind of compensation to many lower- and lower-middle-class persons (especially: there were recruits from all classes) who had not succeeded in the individualistic competitive struggle of a modern industrialized society and who did not understand the values on which such a society is based. These people were told, in effect, that success in that jungle of selfishness was really a mark of inferiority anyway, that they, the plain, honest, self-sacrificing Germans, were really the salt of the earth. Although anti-Semitism was not peculiar to the Nazi movement and had a long history, especially in Germany, it would be a mistake to treat the Nazi movement as primarily the outcome of the history of ideas. Similar ideas were available in all Western countries. Presumably they were especially attractive in Germany because of some features of its social structure and the depth of its frustration. In any case, the following quotation sums up some of the points already made and also indicates the chief function of anti-Semitism in the Nazi movement:

> . . . first, perhaps, is the conception of the German national community, the *Volksgemeinschaft,* pseudo-biologically defined as a "race," as having a special historic role, a mission to purge the world of the great evils and impurities of the time—of "materialism," "corruption," plutocracy, bolshevism. This purge is to usher in an eschatological millennium, the New Order or *Tausendjaehriges Reich* in which all men will be blissfully happy and noble.
>
> A major aspect of the corrupt world which is to be purged is capitalistic materialism, commercial-mindedness. Over against this is set the "heroic" ideal which serves to rationalize a conspicuous readiness to resort to force in order to execute the providential mission—and thus to idealize "militarism."
>
> The sense of a special mission is also closely associated with the "master race" idea. Since the Germans are the heroic people, it is to be expected that their superiority should be manifested in a position of dominance attained by force and perpetuated that way. All other peoples are thus inferior and to be subordinated—for their own good, of course. The development of democracy, capitalism and bolshevism among the most important of these other peoples demonstrates their decadence and unfitness to perform a role of leadership in the world.
>
> The Jew has of course served as the master symbol of the adversary of the German people and their mission. One of his most important functions is to unify the different evils which beset them in a single tangible symbol—above all to bring capitalism and bolshevism together. The Jew is not only a group enemy but is also a semi-magical source of "infection." So far as the Nazis attack anything, it becomes "Jewish" in sovereign disregard of the alleged biological race doctrine. Thus both American capitalism and Russian communism are essentially Jewish, although J. P. Morgan and Henry Ford,

> like Lenin and Stalin, would appear to have no Jewish antecedents whatever. Even the British people as a whole have become "white Jews" to certain radical Nazi circles [Parsons, 1954, pp. 266-67].

As this quotation makes clear, the Jews were a negative symbol in the ideology, a scapegoat. The conception of the Jews as a source of "infection" made it possible for many non-Jewish people and things to be regarded as "essentially" Jewish.

As is true of less severe cases of scapegoating, the Nazis' "choice" of the Jews as scapegoat was not accidental or random. Anti-Semitism has *personality* functions if it bolsters self-esteem—that is, keeps the individual from being painfully aware of his own sense of inadequacy—or if it serves to cover up some other conflict. Self-esteem comes into question most often in relation to achievement: the individual feels (underneath) that he is a failure, or that his position is at least insecure. If he feels resentment toward some other person or persons in his own group, perhaps because of their relative success, he is likely at the same time, to feel that his own resentment is a threat to him, for if he expresses it he may suffer retaliation or he may break up relationships that for other reasons he wishes to maintain. In short, anti-Semitism may be said to have a personality function if it is a cover for other deep-seated feelings; momentary irritations hardly qualify.[21]

To say that anti-Semitism sometimes has personality functions does not, however, explain it adequately. In the first place, there are personalities in whose makeup anti-Semitism is peripheral—it does not affect the core of their self-esteem, and it does not cover up a deep conflict. Despite their anti-Semitism, they may be said to be within the range of normality. The clearest cases of this kind are people who have simply accepted a cultural stereotype without reflection or serious interest in it. These cases shade off into cases in which anti-Semitism is felt because of a wish to be socially acceptable to other people who are anti-Semitic. The need to be socially accepted is so general that one can hardly call it abnormal unless it is strong enough to override deep moral scruples. Finally, conventional anti-Semitism may be used to rationalize economic or political interests, and it may be so used by people who suffer from no special sense of inadequacy.

In the second place, the personality-function theory does not account adequately for the anti-Semitism of even those persons to whom it applies. Personality functions do not account for the definition of the ingroup. The Jews are an outgroup, a "minority," because they are religiously different from the dominant group. Neither do personality functions account

---

21 See Ackerman and Jahoda, *Anti-Semitism and Emotional Disorder* (1950). Perhaps the most elaborate study of the anti-Semitic personality is Adorno *et al., The Authoritarian Personality* (1950). Unfortunately, this study is marred by ideological distortion. See the criticism by Kecskemeti, "Prejudice in the Catastrophic Perspective" (1951); see also Shils, "Authoritarianism: 'Right' and 'Left'" (1954), and Glazer, "New Light on 'The Authoritarian Personality'" (1954).

for the frequency with which among outgroups the Jews are selected as a target, or for the intensity of the prejudice felt against them. In order to explain these aspects of anti-Semitism we must consider the factor of symbolic appropriateness in scapegoating, and this inevitably leads us to a consideration of the actual place the Jews have in the social structure, a place that is not due to the personality needs of any particular anti-Semite. Finally, the very needs of the typical anti-Semite can be understood only in relation to the competitive aspect of the social structure and to that rapid process of social and cultural change which comprehensively has been called "the process of rationalization."

The basic thesis of the scapegoat theory of Nazi anti-Semitism is that the Jews were a negative symbol of three things: (1) capitalism (commercial-mindedness), (2) the rationalistic left (socialists and Communists), and (3) outgroups (from the national point of view); and that the Jews, though "selected" irrationally (hence the term "scapegoat"), were nevertheless "selected" on account of facts that made them symbolically "appropriate," hence vulnerable, as a scapegoat.[22] (Incidentally, wherever we mean to imply that communist ideology is specifically of the Soviet Russian variety we write "Communist.")

That Jews are "disproportionately" engaged in retail trade has been well established. In Europe they also have had a "disproportionate" role in banking. Thus, although Jews were far from controlling the economy of Germany, they were a not wholly inappropriate symbol of capitalism and of success in competitive occupations.[23] There is, of course, nothing sinister about the uneven spread of the Jews in the various branches of the economy. For special historical reasons, different in each case, every minority is unevenly spread in the economy. The Jews' special position was due to many factors, among them the facts that in times past they had been prevented from owning land, the occupations connected with money and trade were

---

[22] Our discussion of anti-Semitism as scapegoating is based mainly on Parsons, 1954, Chap. 7, and 1942c; and on Valentin, 1936. Valentin gives the essential facts about the cultural, economic, and social position of Jews in western Europe and also traces the history of anti-Semitism. One factor in Nazi anti-Semitism to which we give little attention is pre-Nazi anti-Semitic ideology. This has roughly the same importance for Nazi scapegoating that the racist ideas developed in the United States before the 1890's had for the later Jim Crow period.

[23] In the United States also, Jews, as a symbol of success, have been the object of the displaced aggression of people who are frustrated by a sense of failure or of social insecurity. In their study of veterans of World War II, Bettelheim and Janowitz (1950) found a higher level of anti-Semitism among veterans who (1) had recently experienced a shift downward in their job status or (2) were pessimistic about the prospects for the country as a whole. The pessimism seemed to be an expression of feelings about the subjects' own position. (The finding that veterans who had recently made relatively great shifts *upward* were even more anti-Semitic is not incompatible with the hypothesis. Such persons may, as Bettelheim and Janowitz suggest, be more "aggressive" in general than others, but this fact is probably less important than the known status-insecurity of rapid social climbers.) The sample included no officers, no Jews, and no members of any colored minority.

stigmatized, the Jews had no religious objection to commerce and money-lending, and they had many enemies, so that it was some advantage to have their possessions in some compact form, ready if necessary for flight. The need for flight had long been absent in Germany, but the Nazi movement brought it again.

In Europe especially, Jews have also been associated with socialism and communism. The Nazi ideology on this point too was a distortion of the facts: the vast majority of socialists and Communists in Europe have been non-Jews. It is true, however, that Jews have been "disproportionately" represented in the socialist and Communist movements,[24] and that a large number of the leaders, beginning with Karl Marx, have been Jewish.

The Nazi movement was in part a reaction against "the process of rationalization"—the development of science and technology, producing cumulative change in men's occupational roles and entire life patterns; the development of highly impersonal modes of organization, in broader markets and larger productive units, with new patterns of property and other rights and liberties; and the progressive application of "critical rationality" to philosophical thought and religious tradition, rapidly undermining important bases of the feeling of security, especially for people who, being half-educated, have not really grasped the nature of science and the other universalistic values of the modern world. The Nazi movement was in part a passionate revolt of the half-educated, a violent blind reassertion of particularism in the form of militaristic nationalism—a "fundamentalist reaction," analogous to the blind fundamentalism that, in Tennessee, led to the Scopes trial against the teaching of evolution in the public schools.[25]

This aspect of the Nazi ideology is extremely complex, and so is its relation to Nazi practice. Of two things there can be no doubt. First, the Jews have made outstanding intellectual and rational contributions to culture ever since their emancipation from the physical and cultural ghettoes of Europe (see Valentin, 1936, p. 251). Secondly, the Nazi movement was fundamentally anti-intellectual. This can be seen from Hitler's *Mein Kampf* itself or from a description of "a model Nazi library" (Ebenstein, 1943, pp. 135-39). Although almost all the masterpieces of European literature were excluded, there was still room for the works of the pre-Nazi anti-

---

[24] On this problem, see Valentin, 1936, and Heiden, 1944, pp. 64-66. Marx was Jewish only in the sense that his ancestors were. The identification of Jews with leftist revolution is found also in France, and there are both pre- and post-Nazi examples. Strong (1941) found the same themes of Jews as capitalists and, especially, Jews as Communists in the anti-Semitic "literature" in the United States. He also found that the anti-Semites came disproportionately from the insecure lower-middle class of self-righteous, thwarted strivers. This conclusion was based on such evidence as occupations mentioned in newspaper accounts, checking reported residence against census tracts, and the nature of advertisements in anti-Semitic publications.

[25] The concept of "fundamentalist reaction" comes from Talcott Parsons. It provides one key to the fascist movements, including Nazism. Note that the fundamentalist reaction to the process of rationalization was against the rational and universalistic aspects of capitalism, communism, and impersonal scholarship.

Semites Theodor Fritsch and Richard Wagner. Ironically, Fritsch's book lists hundreds of Jews who have made notable contributions in literature, the other arts, and science. The listing of "Jewish" *accomplishments* by an anti-Semite may be regarded as primarily an example of treating the Jews as a symbol of success rather than as a symbol of intellectualism.[26] However, Nazi anti-intellectualism was clearly manifested in the official attitudes toward science. In order to make war, the Nazis had to be interested in technology, but they had contempt for scientific theory as such (see Merton, 1957, Chap. 15).[27]

The inclusion of the works of Richard Wagner in the model Nazi library brings us to the Nazi attitude toward religion. If the Nazi movement was indeed a reaction against rationalism, one might expect to find that religion was exalted (just as one finds that in rationalistic Communism religion is attacked). Actually this expectation was fulfilled, but somewhat indirectly. The Nazi movement, once in power, tolerated *no* really independent group in Germany. Conflict with religious groups was inevitable, especially since the Nazi glorification of military virtues for their own sake was not in harmony with Christian doctrines. Moreover, Christianity was too universalistic for the intensely "patriotic" particularism of the Nazis. The more zealous Nazis therefore attempted, with official support, to revive the ancient Germanic religion as it is celebrated in the operas of Wagner. The most extreme development was a plan for a new "National Reich Church." "Points 18 and 19: The National Reich Church will remove from the altars of all churches the Bible, the cross, and the religious objects. In their place will be set *Mein Kampf* and a sword" (quoted in Ebenstein, 1943, p. 204).

In relation to this apotheosis of German nationalism the Jews were as vulnerable ideologically as they were in relation to the more rationalistic objects of Nazi rage. For, as we noted in our discussion of religion, Judaism is the religion of a "people," a kind of nationalistic religion. This same aspect of Judaism, as manifested in modern Zionism, has led the Soviet government to come perilously close to abrogating its avowed ideological tolerance for minorities.

---

[26] Robert K. Merton (1957, Chap. 11) points out that the members of a minority, who are supposed to be inferior, present a problem and a threat to the dominant group when their achievements are actually superior. The reaction is partly simple jealousy, partly a devaluation of the outgroup achievements. There is apparently an unexpressed expectation that achievements should be commensurate with social status. According to Merton's theory (which seems to be correct), the upward mobility of minority members produces insecurity in some members of the dominant group. The scapegoat theory, in one aspect, regards the Jews as a symbol of success for people whose status insecurity exists *regardless of the presence of minorities;* the Jews, of course, did not produce the frustration and aggression manifested in the Nazi movement.

[27] As Merton makes clear, the Nazi attitude toward science was complex. First of all, most of the Nazis knew nothing about it, and they certainly did not understand the ethos of science. At the same time they were impressed by the prestige of science, as they showed by elaborating a pseudo-science of race. This was another example of their preference for the "practical" in "science."

The merit of the scapegoat theory of anti-Semitism is that it helps to explain the lack of a sense of proportion. Nothing that Jews have said or done could possibly warrant the tremendous hatred that was directed against them and the fantastic ideas that were held about them. The disproportion seems less great when we realize that the hatred was largely displaced, that for the anti-Semite a complex, rapidly changing, bewildering world was made to seem understandable and his shaky place in it was enhanced or explained away, so that he could continue to think well of himself after all. Moreover, once anti-Semitism was accepted as part of the ideology of a mass movement, the Nazis could enjoy the comforting warmth of a strengthened ingroup and could conscientiously and, so they thought, constructively release their stored resentment on Jews and on other nations.

The function of the ideology, then, for Germany as a whole, was to strengthen integration and morale. It could do both the more easily as it presented a simplified view of a complex situation, a view that all could "understand." Moreover, the specific simplification gave hope for the future, for it presented, apparently, a single enemy to be subdued. As Hitler recognized, the Germans might have lost confidence if they had been fully aware of the multiplicity of forces arrayed against them.[28]

A popular idea about ideology is that it is merely a cover for "self-interest," conceived of in materialistic terms. According to this inadequate conception of ideology, the Nazis might have picked on the Jews in order to despoil them of their wealth. As a matter of fact, from the point of view of crude self-interest Nazi anti-Semitism was a serious handicap, for it deprived Germany of much of its talent and aroused the determined opposition of much of the world. Once in power, the Nazis had no need of Jewish money in particular, yet it was after this point that the worst atrocities against the Jews were committed. The spoils taken from the Jews were used, in large part, to pay for the anti-Semitic program itself. We can only agree with the following criticism of the "interest" theory:

> The "interest" theory contains important elements of truth. It is easy to understand why the ideology of the domestic watch industry, both management and labor, features support of tariff protection and includes all the venerable arguments and symbols which might persuade the Tariff Commission, the Congress, and the public of the protectionist case. . . . Actually the relationship between specific ideologies and economic interest is seldom so clear. A more typical example is provided by the passionate support a businessman gives to the principle of a balanced federal budget. . . . Assessing the ultimate effects of alternative budgetary policies on the profits of a specific business firm is a formidable econometric problem. Yet businessmen speak on the subject with such confidence, emotion, and

---

[28] A careful reading of *Mein Kampf* and of many other books on the Nazi movement would convince most people that Hitler was "sincerely" anti-Semitic; we must remember that for him the Jews were a symbol and anti-Semitism a kind of *idée fixe*. Yet at the same time Hitler was fully aware of the socio-psychological advantage of anti-Semitism to his political movement. He was also aware of the fact that the "Aryan race" was to some extent an ideal to be realized in the future.

> unanimity that, in the "interest" theory of ideology, we would be forced to conclude that they have no trouble knowing on which side of the issue their interests lie, and that varying effects on different groups of businessmen are never to be anticipated.
>
> It is true that with sufficient ingenuity one can construct a chain which reconciles practically any ideological position to the economic interest of its holder. Or one can make the task easier by attributing to the ideologist a mistaken or unduly certain conception of his own interest. One can make the task still easier by widening the notion of self-interest to encompass psychological satisfactions other than economic returns. But these expedients are really the end of the theory they are designed to salvage. They reduce it to a tautology: "Men act in their own interests" becomes "Men act as they are motivated to act" [Sutton *et al.*, 1956, pp. 12-13].[29]

COMMUNISM IN ASIA

For our second example of a revolutionary ideology, we shall deal briefly with the appeal of Communism to the "underdeveloped" countries of Asia—e.g., China, India, and the countries of the southeast. In order to account for the success of Communism, in China particularly, we have to ask, among other questions, why a capitalist ideology has had little appeal.

In all these countries, the peasants are a large part of the population. They labor, or have labored, under a heavy burden of rents, taxes, and high prices. As we have seen, what industrialization has taken place under private capitalist auspices has tended to disrupt village life to a considerable extent. The Communists, in appealing to the peasants, must of course face the opposition of landlords and industrialists. The landlords, however, are not organized and are far less numerous than the peasants they "oppress." As for the industrialists, whose skills the revolutionaries need for the future development of the economy, they fear socialization of industry, but to some extent they have been bought off by promises of good jobs and by the assurance that, on account of their superior education and opportunities, they will be able to help their sons to do well in the new regime (Watnik, 1952).

The leaders of revolution in Asia are "intellectuals." They associate capitalism with the hated colonial status under Western countries. Moreover, when Asia was under the domination of the West, these intellectuals, though often well trained, were not allowed to have social positions commensurate with their abilities. As a result they became fiercely nationalistic, and one of their chief goals has been to throw out the Westerners.

The leaders of India are hardly less nationalistic than the leaders of China, but India has not yet succumbed to Communism, for at least three reasons: (1) Although the leaders were cramped under British rule, they were educated, many of them, in England, and they became strongly imbued with democratic ideals. (2) England withdrew from India voluntarily and,

---

[29] To be sure, much of the business concern about balancing the federal budget is due to simple ignorance, but many of the statements of businessmen suggest that this concern is part of a more general tendency to make the federal government a scapegoat. See Sutton *et al.*, 1956, pp. 368-79.

in the end, fairly gracefully, so that the bitterness of earlier years was somewhat allayed. (3) During World War II India not only freed herself from British economic control but became, to a considerable extent, a creditor to England. A fairly important group of native Indian industrialists arose.

The native industrialists and financiers of China, on the other hand, were identified with a conservative regime that had been unable to prevent the Japanese invasion and had been strongly and openly supported by the hated West, especially the United States. In China private enterprise on a large scale would have to be financed by foreign investment, but the nationalism and anti-Western sentiment of the revolutionary intellectuals inclines them to prefer forced capital-formation under a centralized "totalitarian" government. The example of the Soviet rulers, who had to work in a "backward" country, has been an inspiration. The Soviet government is also attractive because it is relatively free of ethnic prejudice. Moreover, although the Soviet Union has helped the Chinese Communists, it has taken care to do so with much less fanfare than the United States displayed in helping the Chinese government of Chiang Kai-shek. In turn, the Chinese Communists have taken care to obviate the charge of foreign domination by dramatically asserting their independence of Russia.

Western influence in China has been extremely disruptive in that it has undermined the ancient religious and ideological foundation of Confucianism. It is somewhat speculative to say so, but it is probable that the Communist ideology, which provides an elaborate theory, with an "answer" for everything and with the cachet of "science," at once fills the void left by the moribund Confucianism and has the appeal of seeming to be modern and progressive.

For there is little doubt that, in China especially, one of the deepest sources of frustration is the fact that for some time now Asia has not been in the forefront of world "progress."

> By defying the United Nations and waging war successfully [in Korea] against the expeditionary forces of the principal Western nations, the Communists have restored to the Chinese that attitude of arrogant superiority which marked their dealings with foreigners up until the 40's of the last century. . . .
>
> The anti-Western and pan-Asian propaganda now emanating from Peking owes its appeal throughout the East to a factor far deeper than any specific resentment against Western colonial rule or economic penetration. Asia's fundamental grievance is something that is nobody's fault and that nobody can help; it is the plain historical fact that Asia stayed behind during the three or four centuries when the West was creating the modern world. The sense of frustration instilled in Asians by their "backwardness" is ultimately a feeling of dissatisfaction with themselves. . . . There is just enough evidence to render plausible the [erroneous] idea that everything wrong in the world is due to imperialism. . . . If America is rich, it can only be because the Americans have plundered other countries; if Western money has endowed schools and hospitals in Asian lands, it must have been for imperialist ends (or in the case of Catholic orphanages, according to the

> official Peking version, for the purpose of murdering children!). Are we not faced here with a paranoid construction as crazy and as impervious to reason as the anti-Semitism of the Nazi Reich? [Hudson, 1952, p. 418].

Here again we have an example of scapegoating "justified" by ideological distortion.

The Influence of Ideology on Behavior

No one can doubt that ideology, by providing an interpretation of the social world and a direction for action, has a great deal of influence on men's behavior. Once the American racist ideology, with Negroes as the scapegoat, gained a precarious regnancy [30] around the turn of the present century, the South proceeded to build, by state and local laws and by tacit agreement, a system of segregation so detailed and nearly complete that it has been matched only in South Africa. The Nazis systematically killed approximately six million Jews, as well as many other "inferior" people. The Communists in Russia have indeed abolished private industry and established a kind of socialism.

Concerning Russian, and now Chinese, Communism in particular, certain oversimplifications are rather common in our journalism. One of these is the belief that the totalitarian dictators do not believe in anything, that they are purely cynical. An American authority on the Soviet Union, however, after agreeing that the Soviet leaders have often been cynical and have frequently lied and manipulated, goes on to say the following (in which for the term "mystique" substitute the term "ideology"):

> The questions are what makes them cynical and what are they cynical about? The mystique dictates their morality, indeed it stands above ordinary human morality and places its adherent outside the demands normally to be made of a man and leader. Hence the totalitarian may be cynical about and manipulate "law," "loyalty," "truth," "honesty," and so on. For as long as he manipulates these in the service of the mystique, his action is beyond question —it is law, truth, honesty, loyalty, unto itself [Inkeles, 1954, p. 92].[31]

The same author criticizes another common error, closely related to the foregoing. This is the belief that totalitarian dictators act solely for the sake of expediency: they do whatever will increase their power. There is

---

[30] "Precarious" not only because the ideology is already breaking up but because it is and always has been fundamentally in conflict with basic American values; it has been only "semi-institutionalized."

[31] The term "mystique" adds to the concept of ideology the idea that the totalitarian leader (e.g., Stalin, Hitler) has a peculiar kind of personality, one element in which is his conviction that he has a direct ("mystical") apprehension of some inner truth about the social world; this conviction gives him great self-confidence and self-righteousness, despite the appearance of cynicism. Inkeles sometimes writes (e.g., pp. 88-89) as if he thinks of the mystique as distinct from the ideology, but usually (e.g., pp. 91, 92, 94) he writes as if he regards ideology as part of the mystique.

a great deal of evidence that this belief is a gross oversimplification. The best evidence is the fact that the dictators, motivated by their faith in their ideology, have often done things quite unnecessary for the enhancement of their power. Indeed, they have done unnecessary things that made them unpopular.[32] The Soviet leaders early tried to eliminate the stability of marriage and the family (in those days, the family as such was a "bourgeois" institution). And, to consolidate their power, there is absolutely no need for the Soviet leaders to impose such burdens as they do on religious groups. The fact is that from their point of view religion is irrational and evil, an obstacle to the attainment of the good society. It is their "mystical" vision that enables charismatic political leaders to endure so bravely the sacrifices of others. Suffering is given a meaning and is incidental in the larger scheme of things.

It is often thought in the West that censureship of art, in Nazi Germany and in the Soviet Union, has been in the interest of suppressing criticism or serving some esthetic ideal ("realism"). There is no evidence that the Soviet leaders are interested in esthetic ideals, and as for suppressing criticism (presumably in order to safeguard their power) they actually make themselves less popular (and to that extent endanger their power) by insisting that novels and plays and paintings should do more than refrain from criticism: they should create images of "ideal" men and women, symbols of the future good society: in short, they should not be realistic at all, in the usual sense.

In Nazi Germany, the program for the literal extermination of the Jews was a severe political handicap to the Nazis abroad, and they were aware of this, for they tried to keep it secret. Even at home, the actual executioners in the concentration camps were a small group of selected psychopaths. The soldiers who took part in shooting Jews in occupied countries regarded their task with horror and had to be fortified with alcohol. Although there is fairly good evidence that most of the German population at least suspected what was going on and were not concerned enough to protest, they obviously did not want to know about it (see Poliakov, 1951). Himmler, who, though not the author of the program, was in charge of it, was known, not ironically, as "the gentle Heinrich," and he was a rather hesitant, mild man, much liked by his associates. He was one of the former

---

32 Inkeles goes further and says that their mystique drives them to do things that endanger their power. Hitler was an outstanding example of Inkeles' point, partly because Hitler's mystique was personal, partly because he came closer than most dictators to having absolute power over his subordinates. These two factors make the study of Hitler's personality especially important, although of course not to the exclusion of studying the factors that caused people to accept him. In addition to the references given in other footnotes and in Chapter 13, where we considered charismatic leaders, see Bloom, 1957. It is perhaps worth making explicit that the more a dictator believes in a mystique in Inkeles' sense, the less he is likely to think he is taking chances and the more he is actually likely to take chances from an objective (nonmystical) point of view.

schoolteachers. He was saddened and even shocked by the reputation for sadistic cruelty that he had acquired. Actually his trouble was not sadistic cruelty; it was that he believed—profoundly, ridiculously, tragically—in the Nazi racist ideology (see Trevor-Roper, 1947, pp. 17-25; and Poliakov, 1949).

However great may be the fanaticism of the leaders, they nevertheless have to make compromises in order to stay in power. Hitler gave up his "secret" program of killing the inmates of mental hospitals on account of popular opposition to it. In fact, this opposition is one piece of evidence that the Germans must have known (underneath) about "the definitive solution of the Jewish problem," which was also secret. (This fact is also a rough indication of the *ambivalence* the German gentiles felt about the Jews: they wanted no direct complicity in the horrid program, but few protested against it.)

A better-known compromise the Nazis made with their ideology was their continued tolerance of capitalism—a capitalism, to be sure, modified almost beyond recognition and subordinated ruthlessly to the "needs" of the state. At a crucial point in the rise of the Nazi movement, Hitler played down the anticapitalist part of his ideology in order to disarm the German industrialists, who otherwise would have prevented his accession to government power. The truth is that Hitler was not interested in the form of the economy so long as it served his main value, which was militaristic nationalism.

The Communists in Russia have also made compromises with their ideology. The state has not noticeably withered away, nor are people paid according to "need." (They are paid according to an incentive system.) An American student of the Russian Communists concluded his study of ideological fulfillment and compromise with the following temperate statement:

> The transfer of the means of production to the society as a whole is the only aspect of Marxist-Leninist doctrine about which one can say with considerable plausibility that the goal has been achieved. For many Marxists this was not an important goal in itself, but a means to the end of creating a society free from the oppressions believed to be inherent in the capitalist system. Some of the Marxist-Leninist ends appear to have been achieved, particularly the elimination of recurring cycles of unemployment with their corrosive effects on human personality. Yet it would be difficult to maintain that the other goals of liberation have been won [B. Moore, 1950, pp. 424-25].

The various factors that shape the actions of revolutionary leaders—ideology, power struggles, and the necessity of making compromises in order to carry on—are all shown in the "purges" that have taken place in the totalitarian countries. Many are purged for [illegible] insufficient evidence of loyalty to the leader or to the program; but some, like Gregor Strasser who was not only an idealistically socialist Nazi but almost as popular as

Hitler, are purged for *excessive* attachment, one might say, to the ideology.[33] Most of the old Russian Bolsheviks have been liquidated. They were unable to compromise.

RECOMMENDED READING

On ideology in general, the treatment in the present chapter is much indebted to Talcott Parsons, *The Social System*, Free Press, 1951, pp. 348-59. For an excellent analysis of American conservative ideologies, which emphasizes distortion and the reasons for it, see F. X. Sutton, S. E. Harris, C. Kaysen, and J. Tobin, *The American Business Creed*, Harvard University Press, 1956.

On Hitler and the Nazi movement, see Konrad Heiden, *Der Fuehrer: Hitler's Rise to Power*, trans. by Ralph Manheim, Houghton Mifflin, 1944. Heiden has not settled upon a firm sociological interpretation of the Nazi movement, but his book contains a wealth of details. For descriptions of the impression that Hitler's personality made on various individuals and for an account of the purges, look in the index under "Hitler," "Strasser, Gregor," and "Röhm, Captain Ernst." For a study of some of the possible sources of Hitler's ideas and goals, see S. F. Bloom, "The Peasant Caesar," *Commentary*, May 1957, pp. 406-18. Talcott Parsons, "Some Sociological Aspects of the Fascist Movements," in Parsons, *Essays in Sociological Theory*, rev. ed., Free Press, 1954, Chap. 7, is a remarkably concise and original sociological contribution to the understanding of fascism (including Nazism). In discussing the question of how to deal with Nazi Germany, the same author, in "The Problems of Controlled Institutional Change," *Essays*, Chap. 12, throws additional light on the nature of the Nazi movement. H. R. Trevor-Roper, *The Last Days of Hitler*, Macmillan, 1947, is interesting here mainly as a vivid description of the "sincerity" of Nazi ideologists and the extreme loyalty Hitler was able to inspire in many members of his administrative staff.

By far the best available treatment of modern anti-Semitism is Talcott Parsons, "The Sociology of Modern Anti-Semitism," in Isacque Graeber and S. H. Britt, eds., *Jews in a Gentile World*, Macmillan, 1942, pp. 101-22. This paper points out significant similarities and differences between the American and the Nazi-German social conditions. As far as the United States is concerned, factual data which support various points in Parsons' analysis are presented in Nathan Glazer, "What Sociology Knows About American Jews," *Commentary*, March 1950, v. 9, pp. 275-84; A. C. Ivy and I. Ross, "Religion and Race: Barriers to College?" Public Affairs Pamphlet No. 153, published in cooperation with the Anti-Defamation League of B'nai B'rith, 1949, esp. pp. 6-7; W. M. Kephart, "What Is the Position of Jewish Economy in the United States?" *Social Forces*, Dec. 1949,

---

[33] Such a judgment, of course, is somewhat arbitrary. Strasser and, later, Roehm were by definition wrong since the charismatic leader is always right. Underneath, however, there may be differences of opinion within the revolutionary movement as to which are its chief aims and which are secondary (and therefore dispensable). For Hitler the main thing was the aggrandizement of Germany. He had always emphasized that he did not like ordinary socialism any better than he liked capitalism; his was a national German "socialism"—that is, a subordination of private interests to political goals. Compare Parsons: "This reaction against the 'ideology' of the rationalization of society is one principal aspect at least of the ideology of fascism. It characteristically accepts in essentials the socialist indictment of the existing order described as capitalism, but extends it to include leftist radicalism and the whole penumbra of scientific and philosophical radicalism" (1954, p. 143).

v. 28, pp. 153-64; S. M. Robison, "How Many Jews in America?" *Commentary*, Aug. 1949, v. 8, pp. 185-92; and Ernest Havemann and P. S. West, *They Went to College: The College Graduate in America Today*, Harcourt, Brace, 1952.

C. Vann Woodward, *The Strange Career of Jim Crow*, new and rev. ed., Oxford University Press, 1957, though short, is extremely enlightening not only on the development of segregation but also on the process of desegregation now going on. Bernard Berelson and P. J. Salter (P. S. West), "Majority and Minority Americans: An Analysis of Magazine Fiction," *Pub. Opin. Quart.*, 1946, v. 10, pp. 168-90 (reprinted, with a few omissions, in M. L. Barron, ed., *American Minorities: A Textbook of Readings in Intergroup Relations*, Knopf, 1957, pp. 114-32), analyzes a sample of short stories from such popular magazines as *The Saturday Evening Post* and *The Ladies' Home Journal* and shows their tendency toward subtle stereotyping and discrimination against the non-Anglo-Saxon characters. Perhaps of equal interest is the fact that the minority problems of the United States receive very little direct attention in the stories. This reflects the ideological picture of America as the land of opportunity and fair play. This article is a good example of modern techniques of content analysis.

22. Social Change

Although we have dealt with many specific problems of social change in previous chapters—for example, in our analysis of change in kinship systems (Chap. 8) and in political systems (Chap. 13), in our treatment of the transformation of certain kinds of sect into denominations (Chap 16), and in our analysis of the routinization of charisma (Chap. 13)—it is desirable, at the end of our introduction to sociology, to take a more general view of the problem of social change.

Broadly speaking, there are two kinds of process going on in a social system: processes that maintain or tend to maintain the structure of the system, and processes that tend to change it. Examples of the first kind of process are socialization and social control. The line between such processes and the processes of change is not fixed. For example, in a society undergoing revolution, parents, in socializing their children, deliberately teach them values and patterns of behavior that are oriented more to the future structure of society than to its present structure—at least, the parents are not teaching everything that *their* parents taught *them*. In this case, the parents are transmitting or maintaining culture but they are also helping to reshape the social system.

Moreover, although processes of change by definition change the social system, they may also help to maintain it. In the face of new circumstances a social system may need to adapt its structure to some extent in order to survive. Change in the structure of the system may enable it to maintain its integrity as a distinguishable system, whereas if it maintains the same structure too long it may lose its integrity as a system altogether.

Our first task here is to explain as carefully as we can what we mean by "social change."

Kinds of Social Change

In the most concrete sense of "change," every social system is changing all the time. This follows from the fact that at the very least its members are growing older and are therefore undergoing physiological transformations, some of which affect their role performance. Changes due to aging may not be very important in the short run, but there are other short-run changes going on continuously. For example, in the very process of interacting with one another, the members of a social system subtly affect one another's attitudes, including their mutual expectations. If the social system is a subsystem of a larger one, then its members are also being subtly changed in their abilities and attitudes by their participation in social systems other than the system of reference. These are only a few examples of the myriad changes going on in a concrete sense. Perhaps it is enough to point out that the very definition of social action implies some change in the concrete state of a social system.

Despite the existence of such continuous change, we often speak of a social system as being relatively stable, and we may even speak of it as unchanging. Such judgments (which may be valid within a certain frame of reference, as we shall see) imply that some kinds of change are regarded as more important than others and that for certain purposes some changes may be ignored. It will be the purpose of this section to specify the various kinds of social change and the contexts in which each may be important.

As we have frequently indicated, in this book we have been developing a *structural-functional* theory. Without repeating in detail the definition of social structure, we may recall two points about it. First, structure is something stable relative to some point or points of reference. For example, a child's mother behaves somewhat differently from day to day; yet she maintains a certain kind of relationship to the child—she continues to protect, guide, encourage, and care for him. Ignoring minor variations in the way in which she carries out these activities, we can say that her role as mother remains fairly stable. It is part of the structure of the relationship. Secondly, we related structure to functions. For example, in the family (a social system) the role of mother has functions such as socializing children and maintaining harmony and morale. (Technically, the mother role has goal-attainment, integrative, and tension-management functions for the family and pattern-maintenance and tension-management functions for wider social systems.) In a narrow sense, social change is change in the structure of a social system; what has been stable or relatively unchanging changes. Moreover, of structural changes the most important are those that have consequences for the functioning of the system—for attaining its goals more (or less) efficiently or for fulfilling more (or less) efficiently the conditions that must be met if the system is to survive at all.

In its basic sense, then, social change means change in social structure. Later in this chapter we shall see that "structural change" is itself a relative concept in at least two ways. Before attempting to explain it, let us list the possible kinds of change that might be regarded as "structural." The following list proceeds roughly from more important to less important kinds of change. The criteria of "importance" will emerge in the course of our discussion. Since change has been defined as structural change, this list is of course parallel to our treatment of social structure in Chapter 3. The only difference is that some of the items treated separately in Chapter 3 are combined here for convenience.

CHANGE IN SOCIAL VALUES

The most important kind of structural change is change in the comprehensive standards that we have called values. It will be recalled that values are a kind of norm but that we use the term "value" when we wish to imply that the norm in question affects or is expressed in more specific norms. "Fair play" is a value. The rule that a judge should disqualify himself in certain cases is a norm. The values we have in mind here are, of course, values that directly affect the content of social roles and social interaction, not purely cultural values, such as classicism in art. It is the relatively comprehensive character of change in social values that leads us to regard this kind of change as the most important. It is likely to have far-reaching consequences for the more detailed aspects of social structure and for the over-all functioning of social systems.

On a concrete level, we might give as an example of value change the transition from a feudal type of society to an industrial-commercial type. Such changes do not occur in a short space of time but may take generations; they manifest themselves in a gradual long-term trend, with ups and downs in the short run.

On a more analytical level, this change in values may be viewed as a change in the relative emphasis upon different system problems, or different functional subsystems of society. In a feudal society, the highest social positions, those that manifest the chief values, are in the goal-attainment and integrative subsystems predominantly. (In more concrete terms, warriors and priests are at the top of society.) Economic functions, while important because they are necessary (as always), are not valued so highly as the others. In the industrial-commercial type of society, however, economic production is more highly valued and leaders in this field of activity have greater prestige.

Some changes in values are changes in the relative scope of the "pattern variables" discussed in Chapter 5. For example, India seems to be undergoing a gradual transformation which can be broadly characterized as an increasing emphasis on "universalism" as against "particularism." Universalism has never been entirely absent from India or any other society. In India, for example, any man who lives a "holy" life, whatever his origins, is admired and praised. For the holy life (withdrawn from worldly ambitions), the standards are universalistic: they apply regardless of the particular social positions a man may have, regardless of the groups he may belong to. The caste system, however, is intensely particularistic as a whole. We saw that the *dharma,* or religiously prescribed set of duties, for one caste is often quite different from the *dharma* of another caste. Men are judged and treated for the most part not according to the same standards but according to the caste (particular group) to which they belong. In modern India, however, the scope of universalistic standards is gradually increasing, and men are being judged more often than in the past according to standards that have nothing to do with their particular caste.

INSTITUTIONAL CHANGE

Under "institutional change" we mean to include change in all more definite structures, such as forms of organization, roles, and role content. A change from a polygynous to a monogamous system, from an absolute monarchy to a democracy, from private enterprise to socialism—these are examples of society-wide institutional changes. With respect to smaller social systems, comparable changes occur. For example, in a business organization a new method of calculating wages may be introduced, or a labor union may acquire certain new rights in the determination of company policy.

As with changes in values, so with changes in particular patterns such as norms and roles, a change may consist in the introduction of something new or in a shift in the relative importance of patterns already existing. The change from a dictatorship to parliamentary government in a particular society is the introduction of something new, accompanied, of course, by the disappearance of an older form. Changes that affect many groups within a society may involve some innovation that at first is not important so far as the structure of the whole society is concerned but becomes important as it gradually spreads and establishes itself as the normal pattern for groups of the relevant type. The change from polygyny to monogamy, for example, is not likely to take place all at once. At any given point of time during the transition, the change occurring is a change in the relative number of monogamous and polygynous households and in the public attitudes toward the two forms. The change will have been completed on the societal level only when polygynous households are widely regarded as deviant, so that social-control mechanisms come into play to break them up or punish the non-conforming persons involved.

CHANGE IN THE DISTRIBUTION OF POSSESSIONS AND REWARDS

In discussing social structure, we distinguished between structural and quasi-structural aspects of the social system. For example, without change in the *institution* of property a change can occur in the distribution of property rights. The growth of monopoly is a good example. Here the change is not merely a change in the particular location of particular rights, as when a man takes over the rights his father had, but a change in the number of productive firms in a particular field, a change in the quantitative distribution of possessions in the population composing the social system. Such changes are likely to have profound effects on the operation of the system. In the first place, they constitute a redistribution of power. Thus in the example just cited, the growth of monopoly affects the process by which prices are determined. In the second place, great changes in the distribution of possessions, even though they may occur within an institutionalized pattern for the transfer of property, are likely to have repercussions on the institutionalized pattern itself. Thus measures for the regulation of large corporations—a change in the *institution* of property—were introduced in the United States only after the process of concentration within the old pattern had reached a certain stage of development.

We have already pointed out the close connection between possessions and "rewards." In some particular cases, the distinction between the two is only analytical. Wages, for example, are a reward for services, a symbol of approval, and at the same time a possession. But there are also intangible rewards—what we ordinarily refer to as prestige, reputation, love, affection, resentment, and many shades of attitudinal attachments—and such rewards are constantly shifting, although usually the shifts are so gradual that we tend to think of reputations and the like as fairly stable. Like property rights, rewards may be redistributed over time not only in the sense that different persons and groups give and receive them but in the more important sense that different kinds of person and group may receive them and they may be more widely diffused or more concentrated. Since rewards, like possessions, constitute a kind of power, they also affect processes of decision-making and possibly the level of functioning of the social system.

CHANGE IN PERSONNEL

Independently of any changes in the value patterns, institutional patterns, and quantitative distribution of possessions and rewards, changes may occur in the particular persons occupying the roles of a social system. Over a long period of time, such changes are of course inevitable since people grow old and retire or die.

The importance of these changes varies. At a very concrete level of analysis, it is always important who occupies a particular social position. At this level, everyone is unique in his capacities and developed abilities. In a subtle way, the normative system itself—the detailed expectations with regard to quality and kind of role performance—is affected by the unique personality of the role occupant. However, taking all the roles of a large social system as a whole, the change effected by a turnover in personnel alone is ordinarily not great, and not great enough to be regarded as structural change. It is usually regarded as an aspect of the endlessly varied flow of interaction *within* a given social structure.

We are here speaking about turnover as if it occurred within relatively stable conditions; that is, we are considering the effect of turnover that is caused by retirement, death, and the "normal" processes of dismissal from positions for incompetence or other revealed defect. The quality of personnel will be affected, however, if the conditions of selection change. For example, if the criteria governing recruitment of personnel change, then of course the average quality of role performance is also likely to change. This type of change is covered under institutional change: the rules of the system are different, for whoever has responsibility for selecting personnel is expected to behave in a new way. But change in the rules for recruitment is not the only way in which the average quality of personnel may be affected. Especially in social systems within the "total" society, the average quality of personnel is affected by impersonal competitive processes beyond the control of the recruiting agents. In an employers' market the turnover may improve the average quality of personnel. In a market favoring those who are offering their services the average quality of personnel may suffer. Change in the sources of personnel may be in part a side-effect of changes in social values, institutions, or the distribution of possessions and rewards. But other factors may also be involved. For example, the rates of immigration and emigration change not only with internal changes in a society but also with changes in opportunities outside, and these rates affect various labor markets.

Apart from changes in the rules or sources of recruitment, "normal" turnover of personnel is likely to affect the functioning of a social system under other conditions as well. It is probably safe to say that the smaller a social system is, the greater will be the relative part played in it by any one member; consequently, a change in personnel is likely to require relatively great adjustments. It is also safe to say that changes in personnel are likely to be more important toward the top of an organization than toward the bottom, for reasons too obvious to dwell upon. Both these generalizations (which are statistical in nature although we are not able to cite actual statistics) are more likely to hold true the less the recruitment process is governed by criteria that are relevant to the demands of the position to be filled. For example, turnover in a university presidency is likely to make less difference to the university if the board of trustees is free to search out a competent person than if the rules require that the position be given to the closest living kinsman of the last president. In general, the average quality of personnel is likely to be higher when positions are achieved than when they are ascribed. But even this generalization could be qualified.

The basic reason for our assertion that changes in personnel are in general less important in themselves than the previously mentioned kinds of change—relatively so unimportant, indeed, that we do not regard change in personnel as a structural change at all—is that turnover in personnel, if it is sociologically important, will bring about changes in values or in institutional patterns. If the mechanisms of social control are not adequate to keep a role occupant's performance up to normative expectations—perhaps because the role occupant *cannot* live up to expectations—then either the role occupant must go or the expectations must change and role adjustments be made in the occupant's role-set within the system. If the system goes on much as it did before the new role occupant came in, then obviously no structural change has occurred. In other words, mere turnover in personnel is not a structural change in itself, but it may cause structural change under some circumstances.

CHANGE IN THE ABILITIES OR ATTITUDES OF PERSONNEL

What we have said about turnover applies equally to changes in the same personnel. They do not constitute structural change, but they may cause it. If we were to regard changes in the personality or physical constitution of a role occupant as social change, we should have to give up the distinction between change and stability. If the structure of a system remains the same, the system is to that extent stable, and changes within but not *of* the structure are regarded as the simple operation of the system.

Broadly speaking, social change is either change in the structural or quasi-structural aspects of a system or change in the relative importance of coexisting structural patterns. Change is qualitative when something structurally new is added to the system (and hence brings about adjustments in other parts of the system). Change is quantitative in that certain new elements bring about more structural adjustment than others, and also in the sense that a new pattern may replace an older pattern to a greater or less extent. For example, the change in the American economy that Berle and Means (1932) called "separation of ownership and control" has occurred to such an extent that in describing the process of decision-making in the economy as a whole we should have to regard the professionally managed corporation as the structurally basic type. We could support such a judgment by setting forth statistics on such matters as the number of persons employed by corporations of different types, the relative value of their products, and their relative influence on general price levels. But at some early point the separation of ownership and control was quantitatively a less important pattern of corporate organization, although it existed; moreover, this pattern has not yet stopped spreading in the economy.

The Relativity of Social Change

We may now turn to two senses in which structural change is relative, apart from qualitative and quantitative relativity. Social change is relative to the system level we are considering. Parsons (1951, pp. 503-05) provides a good example. A socialization process within a particular family is a process of orderly change in the structure of that family, but it is not an example of social change in the society as a whole. The process by which children are taught to speak, walk, respect property rights, refrain from clobbering each other, and so forth goes on according to patterns established in the culture of society. When these patterns become relevant in a particular family, as when a child is born, the adults in the family typically conform to the patterns, thus merely acting out established societal roles; but in doing so they of course bring about very important structural changes in the particular family.

There is another sense in which social change is relative. We have already suggested it in speaking of the fact that changes in personnel in roles close to the top of any social system are likely to be especially important. On one level of analysis, the presidency of the United States has remained very much the same over the years, in the sense that the institutional definition of the office has always been broad enough to accommodate both "strong" and "weak" presidents. (By "strong" presidents we mean, here, presidents who tended to assert vigorously their rights of leadership—if anything, straining them a little.) Another way of putting this is to say that some of the differences between successive presidents are merely differences in role performance, not changes in the presidential office itself. At another level of analysis, however, we might regard each president's characteristic relations with his cabinet, with congressional leaders, with military leaders, and so on as having a structure of their own within the rather broad permissive limits of the presidential office. The differences we have in mind are not differences in role performance as this is ordinarily understood. When we compare the role performance of two incumbents, we usually have in mind the comparative degree to which they live up to the norms and values that institutionally define their status-role. Given these standards, we are making a judgment regarding conformity and deviation, a judgment of performance along some explicit or implicit scale of merit by conventional criteria. But consider the following different kind of case. In important negotiations during World War II, President Franklin D. Roosevelt did not consult his Secretaries of State, War, or the Navy but relied chiefly upon military men (S. P. Huntington, 1957, pp. 320ff.). This amounted to a pattern in his relations with the other important officials of the government; in that sense, it was a kind of structural constant in his administration. In his official acts, however, he did not overreach any of the rights given to the president in the Constitution—at least, no one suggested that he should be impeached, and none of these Secretaries threatened to resign, although in his *Memoirs* Secretary of State Hull expresses restrained resentment. According to Huntington, however, the structural pattern that Roosevelt established at the highest level of government had profound consequences not only for the conduct of the war but for the position of the United States in the international situation ever since.[1]

Social change, then, is relative to system level and also to analytical

---

[1] The present writer is not competent to judge whether Huntington's theses are sound or not. Huntington does not consider several extremely important questions that would have to be answered satisfactorily before one could accept his analysis of this particular historical case. For the present purpose, however, it is enough to note that some particular role performances may be distinctive enough to warrant our speaking of structural change.

level. Whether Presidents Roosevelt, Truman, and Eisenhower occupied the "same" role or different roles depends upon how concrete or abstract our analysis is, and the level of analysis will probably depend upon the problems we are trying to illuminate. In any analysis at the more microscopic (although not necessarily more trivial) level—the level at which we are regarding the distinctive constants of a set of related role performances as structural—it is probably wise to keep in mind the "macroscopic" structural limits within which role performance as ordinarily understood is allowed to vary. In terms of the case we mentioned, however distinctive President Roosevelt's performance may have been and however pervasively, characteristically, and definitely he may have established a certain structure of role relationships at the top, he had to consider always what the Constitution permits American presidents to do. We know, for example, that President Roosevelt, if he wished to continue as president, could not avoid an election campaign in 1944, however inconvenient such a campaign might have been for his conduct of the war.

Some Causes and Patterns of Social Change

There are many possible causes of social change, but they can all be regarded as belonging to three types: (1) There are causes of change inherent either in social systems in general or in particular kinds of social system; (2) change may be due to some impact from the social environment of the social system of reference; (3) change may be due to some impact from the nonsocial environment. These three types are, of course, often combined in various ways. A change from one source may set in motion a sequence of changes, with continual feedback affecting earlier "causes" in the sequence. Perhaps the fundamental aspect of a system is that component parts are so interrelated that any change in one causes adjustive changes in the others. This means that if we arbitrarily regard any process of change as starting, let us say, from some impact from the social or nonsocial environment, the resulting change in the social system will itself be the "start" of more social change. Moreover, a social system makes efforts to control both its social and its nonsocial environment. For this reason, it is sometimes arbitrary to attribute social change to external causes, either social or nonsocial, since these causes have often been shaped to some extent by the social system of reference.

In Chapter 4 we noted that cultural change is of interest to sociologists only to the extent that it produces social change. Since culture can be produced and borne only in social systems, a cultural change is a result either of the internal processes of the social system of reference or of the impact of some other social system. Nevertheless, for convenience we shall regard certain inherent aspects of culture as a fourth source of change, even though this may not be strictly logical.

INTERNAL SOCIAL PROCESSES: STRAIN AND CONFLICT

Conflict of interests is always present to some extent in social systems. The area of politics is the struggle of competing and conflicting groups to realize their goals against opposition. The concept of power virtually implies the idea of conflicting purposes.

In stable social systems conflicts of interest are settled largely within institutionalized rules. In modern societies, for example, we have legislatures and courts, although not all conflicts by any means are confined to those precincts.

The normal processes of decision-making gradually produce change in the structure of the system in which they occur (Lowell, 1937). For example, the Revolution of 1688 in England legally established the independence of the courts and the separation of the executive and legislative branches of the government. The king was empowered to appoint his ministers, and Parliament was empowered to consider proposals for new legislation, pass on them, and make financial appropriations for carrying on the affairs of government. In order to ensure the separation of the executive and legislative branches, it was provided that the ministers of the crown could not sit in Parliament. Early in the reign of Queen Anne, however, this rule was found inconvenient, for it was desirable that the ministers of the crown should be able to explain proposed legislation to Parliament. Here we see that conflict had to be reckoned with, for the crown could not simply take it for granted that Parliament would accept all its proposals. As soon as the minister or ministers of the crown were installed in Parliament, they had to contend for parliamentary support for proposed legislation. Parliament came to be divided into various blocs or factions contending for control. In time the prime minister, although still appointed technically by the crown, became in fact the man who could win a majority of the members of Parliament to support his leadership, and in time the contending factions within Parliament evolved into disciplined political parties that contend in election campaigns throughout the country.

These fundamental changes took place so gradually that in a sense they were not noticed. Some time after the so-called separation of the executive and legislative branches had become only a legal fiction, such distinguished writers on government as Montesquieu, DeLolme, and Blackstone were still praising the English system for this wonderful "separation of powers."

> . . . the parliamentary system as it now stands was by no means contemplated by the men who brought it about; . . . it was in fact quite contrary to their theories of government; . . . the steps they took were consciously and rationally taken to meet certain immediate needs without a thought of possible ultimate consequences; but . . . they naturally led to the system finally evolved [Lowell, 1937, p. 121].

The system is "finally" evolved, of course, only in a relative sense. But this evolution of the English system after the Revolution of 1688 is a good example of the gradual crystallization of a new set of rules, under the impact of specific decisions made in the course of power struggles.

Another example of how conflict, this time less peaceful, gradually evolves new institutions is to be found in the history of labor unions. Disputes between employers and workers may arise over such matters as wages, hours of work, working conditions, vacations, and hiring policy. In the earlier period of the labor movement, relations between employers and workers resembled warfare—to the extent that employers used tear gas, clubs, and even firearms to break strikes, and the workers retaliated. Gradually the workers established the right to have unions. In England this was accomplished mainly by strikes and demonstrations; in the United States, by the same methods and by voting strength (it has become illegal for employers to prevent workers from joining unions). During the prolonged conflict, both employers and workers have formed larger and larger associations in order to be able to put more pressure on each other. But the conflict has not become more and more violent. On the contrary, an impressive set of normative working agreements has been built up in every industrialized country. Rules for hiring and rules governing the relations between employers and employees are established by negotiation, mediation, arbitration, or inquiry; all these methods are established patterns by which disputes are settled. In England most of these methods have no legal sanctions behind them. They are within the "private" sphere, but they are no less binding. Moreover, the agreements in England are not contracts valid only for a certain period of time, as in the United States; they have an indefinite duration of validity, and there are provisions for continual adjustment as economic conditions change.

These complex patterns of collective bargaining could not have been established, and would not be effective today, if the unions had not had, and did not still have, the power to strike. But it would be a mistake to assume that the present structure of relations is nothing but a balance of naked power, with no real normative validity—no "legitimacy." On the contrary, once unionization in an industry has gone far enough, employers' associations often seek to increase the number of workers belonging to unions and to strengthen the hold of unions over their members, and the unions seek to extend the membership of the employers' associations. Moreover, in the interest of preventing strikes and lockouts maintaining predictability in employer-employee relations, and equalizing the conditions of competition, for employers with one another and for workers with one another, both employers and union officials press the same rules (the results of collective bargaining) upon employers who have not joined the employers associations and upon workers who have not joined the unions or confederations of unions. The common system is now strong enough to have developed vested interests on both sides. Out of conflict and the latent possibilitity of conflict (which is inherent in all social life and is not peculiar to labor relations) has grown a complex of organized groups, with their internal norms, and a complex of rules governing individual employer-worker relations and relations between the groups.[2] The generalization has been established for four countries that the wider is the membership of nonagricultural workers in unions, the fewer are the workers involved in strikes and the shorter is the duration of strikes.[3]

The issues and interests involved in conflict of course vary from one situation to another. There are certain rather broad causes of conflict, however, that to some extent exist in every social system. In dealing with some of the causes of class conflict in modern industrial societies, Parsons (1949) has in effect listed some causes of conflict in every complex society:

1. The exercise of authority (the legitimate right to give commands) always generates some opposition. There is virtually always some question whether or not authority is being abused.

2. There is a general tendency, variable only in degree, for power of all kinds (not only authority in the narrow sense) to be used to exploit people. Almost every social system has some safeguards against exploitation, as also against abuse of authority, but probably every system has loopholes. This statement does not mean, of course, that "one system is as good as another." In any case, abuse of authority and exploitation generate alienation and conflict.

3. When a social system is large and highly differentiated, it is virtually inevitable that subcultures will arise that are to some extent mutually incompatible or, at least, are different enough from one another to make intercommunication difficult. In some cases, a subculture is brought into the society from the outside, as when a large group of ethnically different people immigrate. Groups bearing different subcultures are likely to discriminate against one another to some extent and to develop distorted ideas of one another.

4. Virtually every society has some competitive processes within it, and every competition produces losers as well as winners. The disappointment of losers sometimes leads them to question the fairness of the competition.

The next two causes of conflict mentioned by Parsons are especially important in the United States, which ideologically emphasizes equality of opportunity.

5. The full attainment of equality of opportunity is probably impossible. We have referred above to the particularistic tendencies of ethnic groups—and, we might add, of religious groups. In Chapter 19 we discussed the fact that the institution of the family also to some extent makes inequality of opportunity inevitable.

---

[2] For a good analysis, touching upon the somewhat different systems of England, France, Germany, Australia, and the United States see Kahn-Freund, "Intergroup Conflicts and Their Settlement" (1954).

[3] For the relation between unionization and strikes, see H. L. Sheppard, "Approaches to Conflict in American Industrial Sociology" (1954).

6. We have also discussed the fact that the existence of class subcultures affects socialization. The same is true of ethnic subcultures. Some subcultures are an advantage, others a handicap, in competition for power and prestige.

As far as conflict of interests is concerned, perhaps the most general thing about every large-scale social system is that its institutionalized structure never benefits all participants in the system equally. As we noted in Chapter 20, broadly speaking (there are individual exceptions) we may expect the strongest support for social institutions to come from those who have vested interests in them. But for various reasons an institutional order is supported also by many people who have relatively little at stake in it. Even in a quite nonegalitarian society there are few people who have absolutely nothing to lose if the system is overthrown. More important, once a system is more or less stabilized, people tend to be immersed in it and do not seriously consider whether some other system might be possible. In such a system, people are like fish who, swimming around in water all their lives, presumably are unaware that there is or could be any other milieu in which to live.

One reason that the social order tends to be taken for granted is that normally those who benefit most from it are also most active in creating and polishing the ideology that explains and defends it. In fact, the promulgation of the official ideology (under the name "education") may be one of the special provinces of the upper class or of people close to it.

Sjoberg (1952) has pointed out that many of the societies of the world have been and still are in a broad sense "feudal." In this broad sense, a "feudal" society, such as India or China or Europe until modern times, has two main social classes. The great majority of the people are peasants or craftsmen. They support a small upper class of governors and educators, who may also be religious leaders. The upper class often includes warriors as well. Although each of these two "classes" may be differentiated internally to some extent, this differentiation is socially unimportant compared with the gulf between the two main classes. The religious or scholarly members of the upper class may be the only persons who can write, and they elaborate a complex system of thought that in effect explains why everything in the world is as it is. The system of writing may be difficult to master and the body of thought subtle. The mass of the population "understand" only certain basic ideas and are assured that what they do not understand can be perfectly explained by the scholars. The system of education—open to few—is controlled by the official ideologists. Since all members of the upper class are educated in the same sacred classics, that class is more homogeneous than the mass of the population, whose members, tied to their villages, may develop local subcultures that prevent effective communication between one small group and another. As Sjoberg points out, the upper classes of such "feudal" societies have shown a remarkable ability to resist change or to survive close to the top if change comes. Writing in 1952, Sjoberg doubted whether the Chinese Communist regime would substantially change the "feudal" system of China. It is conceivable that the new drastic system of communes, in which parents and children are separated, may have been considered necessary partly in order to break down the old regime. In traditional China, as we have seen (Chap. 7), the upper class maintained its power in part through the strong coherence of upper-class families.

Although not all societies are of the stable "feudal" type we have just described, it is probably normal for most conflict to take place within the institutionalized rules. Institutionalization has the effect of stabilizing expectations, and this helps to explain why the less advantaged members do not more often or more intensely complain about the justice of the social order itself. For, as Parsons (1951, pp. 513-14) points out, the sense of frustration is always relative to expectations.

To this extremely important point, two qualifications are necessary. Some institutionalized expectations are inherently more likely than others to encourage a sense of frustration, hence conflict, and hence social change. The cultural emphasis in the United States on equality of opportunity "invites" minorities and other disadvantaged groups to complain and agitate and fight for improvement of their situation. Moreover, however disillusioned any observer may feel about the sincerity with which the dominant group and other advantaged groups profess belief in equality of opportunity, it must be admitted that the difference between profession and practice is a great source of embarrassment and a fulcrum for change. Our whole institutionalized system of political parties, electoral campaigns, and legislative sessions—compared, say, with a traditionalistic system—is also an invitation to try to change the rules in favor of this interest or that.

The second clarification of the point that frustration is relative to expectations is that the term "expectations" is slightly ambiguous, as we have pointed out before. Institutionalized expectations are rights. People also sometimes "expect" things to which they have no established right. For example, if a revolutionary movement manages to gather enough momentum to give it the apparent assurance of success, or even a fairly realistic hope of success, then we may expect that some humble people, hitherto innocent of subversive thoughts, will perceive new possibilities and develop a sense of frustration in their lives, an alienation from things as they are; yet things may be objectively no worse than they have been for some time and may even be better. This statement follows from the fact that the institutionalized order is most strongly supported by groups with vested interests. There is, in other words, at all times a latent conflict between those whom the existing system is benefiting and those whom it is benefiting less. This conflict will become manifest if the disadvantaged are made to feel that the existing order is not the only realistically possible order.

Social problems

Problems such as prejudice and discrimination against minorities, juvenile delinquency, the inadequate provision of medical care for a large part of the population, the need for improving the system of public education, the need for slum clearance—to name some of the most widely discussed social problems in the United States—always involve a good deal of social conflict, in the course of which social change occurs.

What do the problems named have in common? They are all situations that many people deplore. These people think that something should be done to change the situation in question—that is, something more than is being done. The second thing these problems have in common is obvious once it is mentioned, yet it is frequently not appreciated in its implications. These are *social* problems: they arise, presumably, from some aspects of the existing social structure. Therefore, if they are to be solved or reduced, the existing social order will have to be changed to some extent. For example, the social problem of inadequate medical care is not the same thing as the fact that doctors do not know as much as they would like to know about disease. On the contrary, medical care is seen as a problem and is described as inadequate partly because the medical knowledge that we already have is not being applied to enough people. The third thing these problems have in common is closely related to the second. It is that the state of affairs regarded as undesirable is not regarded as inevitable. There is agitation against it because some people think that social changes could be brought about that would reduce or eliminate the problem.

Some writers (e.g., Fuller and Myers, 1941) have distinguished between social problems and natural problems, but this distinction is not very useful. Destructive floods, for example, arise from "nature," to be sure, but they give rise to a social problem as soon as a considerable number of people realize that floods can be prevented or controlled and feel that the necessary social steps should be taken. After all, "natural" causes are present in all social problems, from overpopulation in India to traffic congestion in American cities. It is worth noting, however, that if a problem is viewed as "natural" in the sense that it seems somehow to be in the nature of things, so that people are sorrowfully resigned to it, then it is not a social problem in our sense, however unpleasant the condition may be and no matter how remediable it may be from some outsider's objective point of view. No doubt many people in India still think of famine exclusively in terms of food shortage and not in terms of overpopulation. Overpopulation in India cannot be regarded as a significant *social* problem until a politically significant number of Indians come to feel that social resources should be mobilized to convince men and women that they ought to have fewer children; this feeling would lead to cooperative effort in such fields as public education and birth-control clinics.

Why are social problems ordinarily difficult to solve? The answer is implicit in what we have already said. The existing social structure is supported by powerful sentiments and vested interests. Solving a social problem always involves costs in a broad sense. Sometimes those with vested interests are among the very people who deplore the state of affairs regarded as a social problem (Waller, 1936). This is strikingly true of racial discrimination in the United States (Myrdal, 1944). Many of the same people who at least feel shame and guilt concerning racial discrimination, since discrimination is incompatible with their professed belief in democracy, are also reluctant to give up the advantages they enjoy in social prestige, cheap labor, and job monopolies. These advantages are vested interests protected by all legal, semilegal, and informal provisions for discrimination.

The resistance to proposed solutions of social problems takes several forms. One of the most common tactics of vested-interest groups is to deny the existence of the problem. In the late nineteenth century, child labor was a social problem, but some employers of children professed to think that child labor is good in that it toughens the character and inculcates habits of thrift and industry. Such arguments are sometimes psychological rationalizations and sometimes plain attempts to deceive the public.

Probably more common than outright denial that a problem exists is the argument that the remedies proposed would cause greater evils than the problem they are designed to solve. On the whole, this is the line taken by the American Medical Association in its fight against proposals for improving the social arrangements for providing medical care. This type of opposition may also be "sincere" or "insincere" or both in varying proportions.

The third type of opposition might be called rear-guard action or a slow retreat. For example, the AMA at one time refused to recognize that any medical-care problem exists and opposed even voluntary health-insurance plans. Now that such plans are fairly well established, the AMA accepts them but opposes compulsory health insurance, although reformers do not agree that voluntary plans are an adequate solution of the economic problem of providing medical care to the whole population. It may be doubted whether compulsory health insurance would be an adequate solution either, but if it comes we may be sure that further proposals will also be vigorously attacked.[4]

Although rationalizations and deliberate distortions are common in conservative efforts to resist the loss of vested interests, we must not assume out of hand that all arguments advanced against any proposal for reform are mere rationalization and propaganda. One of the problems of legislators is that they cannot make any such easy assumption. Every proposal and every argument against it must be examined on its own merits, regardless

---

4 On the tactics of the American Medical Association see the remarkable collection of documents in S[illegible]ler *et al.*, eds., 1952, pp. 504-33.

of the special interests it may serve; and this is true even if the proposal or the criticism is advanced rather obviously in order to serve special interests. Special interests are not necessarily incompatible with broader social interests.

One of the broadest facts about human action is that it almost always brings about unanticipated consequences, some of which may be undesired (see Merton, 1936a). It seems probable that some undesirable consequences of action can be forestalled if the groups that will be most directly affected can receive a sympathetic hearing in advance.

Revolution and retreat

The most intense conflict in a society occurs during a revolution. Although students of revolution (e.g., Brinton, 1933; Gottschalk, 1944; Parsons, 1951, pp. 520ff.; and many others upon whom these writers have depended) use somewhat different terms in discussing causes, there is broad agreement in substance. The success of a rebellion depends upon the presence at one time or close together in time of several factors. Many rebellions fail because only one or two of these factors are present.

First of all, there must of course be fairly widespread alienation from the existing social order, or some aspects of it.

> The first cause of revolution . . . may be called "provocation" if it results in dissatisfaction sufficiently general to create not merely a certain slough of subjective despair but an epidemic desire for action. Such provocation came in the American Revolution, the French Revolution, and the Russian Revolution from such things as land hunger; taxation; high fees for services rendered or not rendered; exclusion from certain kinds of prestige or from certain kinds of office; misgovernment; bad roads; commercial restrictions; corruption; military or diplomatic defeat; famine; high prices; low wages and unemployment [Gottschalk, 1944, p. 5].

As Gottschalk goes on to say, however, we should be in perpetual revolution if frustration alone were sufficient to cause it. There must also be "solidified public opinion" and leadership. A part of the alienated population must be organized in a revolutionary group. This means that the mechanisms of social control have not been strong enough to dissipate or to reverse alienation. A dissident group strengthens alienation by giving alienated persons mutual support and by subjecting them to mutual pressure for conformity to the group itself. Dispositions that were once only alienative are now at the same time conformative.

Accompanying the formation of a group, and partly making it possible, is the development of a revolutionary ideology, which both crystallizes sentiments and ideas against the existing order and provides a program that offers hope and guidance for action to various alienated parts of the population—to potential active and passive supporters of the revolutionary movement. As we have mentioned, the revolutionary ideology has a better chance of catching on if it incorporates, in slightly adapted form, some of the values of the existing social structure than if it is entirely new.

Even if all these conditions are fulfilled, a revolution will not be successful unless the conservative forces, and especially the government, are weak. Defeat in war and depletion of financial resources are typical signs of weakness as well as causes of frustration. Particularly important is the state of opinion and morale in the armed forces.

We mentioned in another connection that the weakness of a prerevolutionary government is not merely "material." Typically there is considerable withdrawal of moral support by the upper classes. some members of which no longer believe in the rightfulness of the regime. Many scholars have noted that many of the important leaders of revolutions do not come from the bottom of the society.

> The English Revolution, for example, had its Lord Fairfax; the French Revolution, Lafayette, Mirabeau, and Talleyrand; the American Revolution, Washington and Lord Stirling; the Russian Revolution, Prince Lvov and Lenin. Although such upper-class leaders do not provide all leadership, they frequently provide so important a part that it is incorrect to say that they are only the exceptions that prove the rule. The exceptions are so many collectively and so important singly that they raise doubt as to whether any rule about the lower-class origin of leaders does in fact exist [Gottschalk, 1944, p. 6].

We have also dealt with some aspects of what Parsons (1951, pp. 525ff.) calls "the adaptive transformation of a revolutionary movement." By this phrase he means, in part, that after it has achieved power a revolutionary movement retreats to some extent from its avowed program. There are various causes of this retreat.

The ideology of the movement almost inevitably includes utopian promises—that is, promises that cannot be fulfilled in the actual world. Such promises should not be regarded as primarily deceitful lures employed by cynical leaders in order to gain a following. Study of actual revolutions shows that the principal leaders are dedicated men with more than the usual amount of idealism in their personalities. If we bear in mind the powerful moral forces that bind people to a social order, we must realize that an intense vision of something not only better but much better is helpful and perhaps necessary in enabling people to take the drastic step of throwing over the more or less sacred past. As we noted in Chapter 20, all truly deviant action (and revolutionary action is of course deviant) involves ambivalence. In common-sense terms, the utopianism of revolutionary leaders accounts for the zeal with which they carry out the revolution, often with tremendous sacrifices. But we must remember that the revolutionary leader is also a deviant. He is alienated from the old order, but there is also present in his personality a repressed conformative tendency with respect to the old order. His alienation is merely dominant; it is not the sole magnet of his feelings. If we remember this, then it will seem likely that revolutionary utopianism in part testifies indirectly to the strength of the repressed loyalty to the old regime. In order to justify abandoning the old, it is necessary to idealize the new.

Another source of utopianism is the fact that fantasy is one of the reactions to frustration. The frustration caused by the old regime gives rise to wish-fulfillment fantasies, some of which are embodied in the revolutionary ideology.

We stress the "sincerity" of utopianism for more than one reason, but most important is that it helps to account for the conflicts that typically occur within the top leadership of the revolutionary movement once it has established itself in power. The utopian hopes must be abandoned—more likely, deferred to some vague future time—but they are not abandoned easily, and some of the leaders are more flexible than others. "Utopian" is a relative term. The more strictly utopian hopes are those that conflict with deep-seated functional requirements of large-scale social systems. For example, the idea of doing altogether without coercion is probably utopian in this sense. Although the promise "from everyone according to ability, to everyone according to need" is too vague to be criticized very safely, it probably "means," in fantasy, a system of rewards that could hardly meet the requirements of a large-scale society. It is therefore probably utopian.

Just what adjustments a revolutionary movement will have to make to "reality" depend, of course, upon the precise nature of its utopian promises. Other revolutionary ideals, although not strictly utopian, must be abandoned or modified because of the persistence of sentiments deriving from the past as well as from strong if not immovable factors inherent in human societies. The Soviet Union has had to abandon the revolutionary ideas about marriage and the family and modify the revolutionary opposition to religion. Outside opposition to the revolutionary regime may provide an excuse for the "temporary" abandonment of some utopian ideals.

The assumption of governmental responsibility brings problems markedly different from those of the movement in its revolutionary phase. We need only recall our discussion of the routinization of charisma (Chap. 13).

The fact that a revolutionary movement in power adapts itself to apparent necessity does not necessarily mean that the utopian promises are forgotten. The American Declaration of Independence declares that "all men are created equal"—a promise that citizens would have equal rights. This "promise" has never been perfectly fulfilled, but it has never ceased to be a source of social change, for people have always pointed with indignation to the gaps between the ideal and the reality. Similarly, it is not likely that the Communist promise to abolish coercion in government can simply be forgotten, with no further consequences (Parsons, 1951, p. 530).

CULTURAL CHANGE

Cultural innovation is occurring constantly, although not all new forms survive. An innovation is a new combination of old elements, which may come from the innovator's own society or from some other. The diffusion of culture within society and from one society to another has been a great source of cultural and social change in every society. Borrowed elements are "new" in the sense that they have not been seen before in the new setting. As we saw in Chapter 4, borrowed culture objects often acquire new meaning in a new social setting—that is, strictly speaking they become new culture. Apart from that, borrowed culture provides additions to the total cultural base from which innovations come. Roughly speaking, the larger the available cultural supply, the greater the possibility of new combinations, or innovation.

A theme that concerned Max Weber in much of his work was the so-called process of rationalization. As he used this term, it was broad enough to include both the systematization of rules in bureaucracy and the systematization of notation in Western music. To him, "rationalization" meant progress toward greater standardization and consistency.

According to Weber, the process of rationalization is one of the most important trends in human history (see the discussion in Parsons, 1951, pp. 352, 505ff.). The field in which the process of rationalization is most clearly revealed is empirical knowledge, especially science (see our discussion of cultural progress, in Chap. 4). As Parsons makes clear, the rationalization of knowledge is only a tendency, not an undeviating line of development. There are reversals, historical cases of lost knowledge. There are also cases in which individuals and whole groups seem to prefer inadequate beliefs when beliefs that are better by rational scientific standards are available to them. We assume, however, that, other things being equal, people everywhere prefer truth to error. Therefore, whenever people conspicuously prefer error to truth, we look for something that, from their point of view (perhaps unconscious), compensates them for the dissatisfaction and strain involved in accepting beliefs that are inferior by standards of logic and empirical evidence. The false beliefs, we assume, must serve important personal, and possibly social, needs.

It is still a broadly true generalization, however, that in the field of empirical knowledge at least, and perhaps in other fields as well, such as expressive symbolism, there is a progressive trend, a linear development. The development of science in turn affects the development of ideas of other kinds—philosophical, ideological, and religious. The influence is in no case one-sided, although for various reasons science, or empirical lore in primitive societies, probably plays a leading role in influencing the entire body of beliefs. In any case, there is a broad tendency for men to strive to make their various ideas mutually consistent. This tendency is an aspect of the process of rationalization and is subject to the qualifications we have made. If group cohesion or alleviation of anxiety or some other need supervenes, men are able and willing to some extent to compartmentalize their ideas of different kinds, scientific, religious, and ideological. Nevertheless, these other needs must contend with "the strain toward consistency."

It is implicit in what we have said that new ideas are not accepted without conflict. The history of the reception of the theory of evolution is only one of the more striking illustrations of this fact. Opposition to new scientific ideas comes not only from religion or from ideology (as in the government decree concerning biological theory in the Soviet Union). It comes from scientists also. In all fields of culture, including science, there are vested interests in the broad sense of that term. As institutionalized patterns protect the vested interests of landlords and shareowners, so prevailing scientific theories, artistic fashions, and theological systems protect the reputations for achievement and competence of scientists, artists, and religious leaders. They have a stake in established ideas, and they are not able to consider new ideas on their merits without an inner struggle. In the case of science, however, the only legitimate vested interests are validated claims to have discovered or stated some idea first (Merton, 1957b). In priority disputes, however, the legitimate vested interest is not that people accept the idea itself as eternally valid. A scientist may legitimately wish to have credit for ideas that, though now outdated, once played a part in the development of currently accepted ideas. But since there can be no *legitimate* vested interest in the continued acceptance of outmoded scientific ideas, the resistance that disgruntled scientists sometimes make to new scientific ideas eventually crumbles. (We should not think, of course, that all opposition stems from jealousy or envy; scientists often have doubts based on unanswered questions, and when they do they perform a service to science by resisting the new until it has been tested further.)

As we have stated, cultural change and social change are not quite the same thing, but cultural change often has a tremendous impact on social structure. Technological change is, of course, behind the process of industrialization, increasing division of labor, and growth of large-scale formal organization.

The impact of technology on social structure is also resisted. Management resists some innovations in part because of the threatened loss of money invested in existing plant. Labor resists some innovations because of the threatened loss of time invested in acquiring existing skills and also, sometimes, because of fear of the prospect of unemployment. The analysis of the impact of technology on social structure is not essentially different from the analysis of social problems—in fact, resistance to innovation is often regarded as a social problem. In each case, one has to ask what vested interests would be adversely affected, and what groups stand to gain, by the acceptance of the specific innovation. What kinds of power can these two sides use in the conflict? In what ways can each side appeal to a wider public for support? What bridges to accepted values are available?

The resistance to change is not necessarily direct. As we saw in Chapter 21, people are not always aware of the causes of their frustration. It is common in ideology to focus the blame on one or more scapegoats. Following Parsons, we suggested that anti-Semitism in Nazi Germany was in part a symbolic reaction against the effects of the process of rationalization. Although the Nazi program was not specifically reactionary in the sense that it proposed restoration of some particular institutions of the past, it was reactionary in one of the accepted meanings of the term: it was a revolt against what is usually regarded as progress.

Although we are primarily concerned here with the influence of culture on social systems, we should remind ourselves that social systems also influence culture. Science and technology do not arise spontaneously. At any given time, to be sure, the cultural base—the whole store of existing culture—has inherent possibilities for development, and also inherent limitations. But whether any of the possibilities will be developed depends, of course, upon human activity, and since most human activity is part of social systems, the development of science and technology, as of other aspects of culture, depends upon the structure of social systems. Presumably not all the possibilities inherent in a cultural base are realized. Which ones are realized depends upon which lines of endeavor are socially encouraged. For example, governments in the world today are giving massive encouragement to the development of ideas that promise military advantage. This encouragement takes many forms, but one of the most important is allocation of research funds to projects of certain kinds. Any theory that traces social change to technological change alone is one-sided.

THE IMPACT OF THE ENVIRONMENT

As we saw in Chapter 4, environment, whether social or nonsocial, influences culture. It also affects social structure. As far as social change is concerned, the impact of the social environment is probably more important than the impact of the nonsocial environment, except possibly over vast stretches of time, such as glacial and interglacial periods. For any period likely to be analyzed sociologically, the nonsocial environment of land, water, air, fauna, and flora will usually be much the same at the end of the period of change as at the beginning. Therefore, the nonsocial environment will have had its greatest effect on the social system before social change begins, and any new effect creating social change is likely to be relatively slight. Moreover, changes due to the nonsocial environment—for example, the presence or depletion of some resource—are frequently due to social action, to cultural change, or to change in the social environment. For example, prolonged farming without crop rotation or wind screens or use of fertilizers may deplete or erode the soil; science may reveal a new use for cobalt or tungsten; an economic blockade may cut off the supply of some raw material. Nevertheless, changes in the nonsocial environment, however they themselves were caused, do sometimes require adaptive social changes.

The influence of the social environment is ordinarily much more important in bringing about change in a particular social system (not in determining its structure in the "first" place) Shifts of political alliances, military invasions, peaceful immigration, trade shifts—all these influences and others can of course present difficult problems of adjustment to social systems. Any one of these changes is likely to affect some parts of the social structure first and then have effects in other parts later

Social systems may be to some extent interdependent, even though their members are unaware of the fact. Teggart says that the disturbance of trade in the period from 58 B.C. to 107 A.D. due to wars in the eastern parts of the Roman Empire and even due to wars in the western part of the Chinese Empire was great enough to produce uprisings in Europe. The connection was so close that every uprising in Europe was preceded by one of the disturbances in the rather remote East, and every war in the East was followed (presumably fairly soon) by an uprising in Europe. Yet the Romans were unaware of this connection (Teggart, 1939, pp. 46-52).

The restructuring of the social system, whatever its cause or causes, may be temporary or permanent; more likely, some effects will be temporary and others more enduring. In general, mechanisms for resisting change are implicit in the social structure at any time. These mechanisms are broadly functional in the sense that they maintain the independence of the system. If the mechanisms for resisting change are too weak, the system may disappear as a distinguishable entity. If the mechanisms for resisting change are too strong (so that the system is inflexible), the system may also disappear. In any case, the impetus to structural change, from whatever source, is always resisted. The new structure of the system, if the system survives, will show the effects of the resistance as well as of the impetus to change.

The Structural-Functional Analysis of Change

The conceptual framework employed in modern sociology is rather cumbersome as compared with that in physics or chemistry. Sociologists do not have a small number of variables composing a neatly defined system so that when a quantifiable change occurs in one of the variables they can mathematically calculate, by means of equations, the exact kinds and amounts of change that will occur in the other variables (Parsons, 1951, pp. 481ff.). However desirable such a theoretical system would be, at present we must be content with the concepts of structure and function, and with the related concept of system problems, or "needs." We cannot deal simultaneously with all the changes that are going on in a social system. We are obliged to consider the impact of some impetus to change—a "disturbance" of the system, a strain or conflict, or a cultural or environmental impetus of some kind—upon some part of the total system, and while doing so we temporarily regard the rest of the system as fixed or constant. Then we must progressively consider further repercussions of the initial change throughout the system, including those repercussions that modify the original impetus to change and its initial effects on the system. Cumbersome as this approach is, it is much better than no theoretical approach at all. The concept of structure enables us to define the system that is subject to change. The concepts of functional "problems" and functional interdependence indicate for us the significance of particular interaction processes. Finally, the concept of structure enables us also to define the changes that have occurred or that are to be explained.

We have no general scientific laws of change in or of social systems. (This does not mean that such laws might not be discovered eventually.) The theoretical framework that we do have enables us, however, to define fairly precisely the relevance of all other scientific knowledge to both the processes that maintain and those that change systems of action. Since the participants in these systems are human beings, the laws of motivation are especially relevant. Another advantage of the structural-functional approach, therefore, is that the cumulative knowledge of psychology can be drawn upon in the explanation of social processes. This does not mean that sociology is a branch of psychology or that it is applied psychology alone, any more than application of the knowledge of chemical processes to the explanation of bodily functioning makes biology a branch of chemistry. But just as the concepts of structure and function in biology are useful partly because they guide the application of chemical knowledge, so in sociology the concepts of structure and function, defined somewhat differently since social systems are not the same as organisms, are useful partly because they guide us in the application of psychology.

It has often been remarked that progress in science depends upon fruitful formulation of problems. Such concepts as social norm, social role and status, culture, socialization, social institution, vested interests, social conformity, social deviation, and social control are sociological, not biological or psychological, and they have proved fruitful both in organizing knowledge about social systems and in organizing other kinds of knowledge in such a way that they can be useful to sociology. There seems good reason to expect that these and other sociological concepts, and still others that will be invented to supplement them, will continue to be fruitful in sociological research for some time to come.

RECOMMENDED READING

The basic outline for this chapter is taken from Talcott Parsons, *The Social System*, Free Press, 1951, Chap. 11, although Parsons is not to be held accountable for any departures or errors there may be in the chapter. Parsons has also written a valuable comment on the merits and limitations of Karl Marx's theory of social change; see "Social Classes and Class Conflict in the Light of Recent Sociological Theory," Papers and Proceedings, *Amer. econ. Rev.*, May 1949, v. 39, no. 3, pp. 16-26. David Lockwood, in "Some Remarks on 'The Social System,'" *Brit. J. Sociol.*, June 1956, v. 7, no. 2, pp. 134-46, maintains that an adequate theory of social change must combine the views of Parsons and Marx. Lockwood's paper is in part a criticism of Parsons. Whether this criticism is justified or not depends upon one's interpretation of Parsons, but in any case Lockwood's paper will be valuable to the student of sociological theory.

An early paper by Willard Waller, still worth reading, states without marked ideological bias the basic relation between vested interests and social problems; see "Social Problems and the Mores," *Amer. sociol Rev.*, 1936, v. 1, pp. 922-23. A good analysis of resistance to technological innovation is V. H. Whitney, "Resistance to Innovation: The Case of Atomic Power," *Amer. J. Sociol.*, Nov. 1950, v. 56, no. 3, pp. 274-54. This article not only analyzes one timely case but in effect shows how economic factors work in many similar cases. Unlike some other analysts, Whitney sees nothing necessarily sinister in resistance to innovation.

For a good analysis of the interrelations of religion, social structure, and cultural innovation, see R. K. Merton, *Science, Technology, and Society in Seventeenth Century England*, in *Osiris*, ed. by George Sarton, v. 4, part 2, Bruges, Belgium: The Saint Catherine Press, 1938. Among other things, Merton's study shows that at any given time various factors favor the growth of some branches of culture (even particular branches of a particular science) more than others. A less intensive but more extensive study, A. L. Kroeber, *Configurations of Culture Growth*, University of California Press, 1944, shows that in many societies and many periods of history geniuses tend to cluster in particular fields. Kroeber suggests that this may be due in part to the changing inherent possibilities of particular fields, which at times are many and great and at other times are close to exhaustion in a particular cultural tradition.

H. G. Barnett, *Innovation: The Basis of Cultural Change*, McGraw-Hill, 1953, is a carefully written analysis of many cases of innovation of many kinds, from primitive and from advanced societies, with an attempt to state the conditions under which innovation occurs. This book brings out the fact that innovation is not rare. We are all innovators, but of course most of our "innovations" are new only to ourselves and most of them have little influence on cultural and social change.

The writer regrets that he was not able to read Neil Smelser, *Social Change in the Industrial Revolution: An Application of Theory to the Lancashire Cotton Industry, 1770-1840* London: Routledge & Kegan Paul, 1959; it was published too late to be consulted for the present book.

The same is true of Kingsley Davis' presidential address read at the annual meeting of the American Sociological Association, Chicago, September 1959 ("The Myth of Functional Analysis as a Special Method in Sociology and Anthropology," *Amer. sociol. Rev.*, December 1959, v. 24, no. 6, pp. 757-72), in which Davis argues persuasively that structural-functional theory is not just one kind of sociological theory but the only kind we have. He shows, for example, that "some of the best analyses of social change have come from people labeled as functionalists," but that these analyses "do not differ in any basic way from many studies of social change by persons opposing functionalism or at least not wearing the functionalist label." We have repeatedly warned the reader against certain misunderstandings of functional theory, some of them due to semantic difficulties. Davis believes that these misunderstandings are troublesome enough to warrant abandoning the term "functional theory" in favor of the simple term "sociological theory."

Bibliographical Index

Acknowledgment is made to authors and publishers for permission to quote from some of the following works. References are listed alphabetically by date of publication. Boldface numbers following each entry identify the pages of this text on which the reference is cited.

Abegglen, J. C. *See* Warner and Abegglen, 1955.

Aberle, D., 1950. Shared values in complex societies. *Amer. sociol. Rev.*, v. 15, pp. 495-502. **97.**

Ackerman, N. W., and M. Jahoda, 1950. *Anti-Semitism and Emotional Disorder*. Harper. **613*n*.**

Adam, K., 1954. *The Spirit of Catholicism,* rev. ed., trans. Dom Justin McCann, O. S. B. Doubleday Image Books. **409, 420*n*.**

Adams, I. B. *See* Queen and Adams, 1952.

Adcock, C. J., and L. B. Brown, 1957. Social class and the ranking of occupations. *Brit. J. Sociol.,* v. 8, no. 1, pp. 26-32. **486.**

Adnan, A. A., and G. Lewis, 1957. Turkey: history. *Encyclopaedia Britannica,* v. 22, p. 595. **330.**

Adorno, T. W., E. Frenkel-Brunswik, D. J. Levinson, and R. N. Sanford, 1950. *The Authoritarian Personality*. Harper. **613*n*.**

Albrecht, R., 1954. The parental responsibilities of grandparents. *Marriage and Family Living,* v. 16, pp. 201-04. **182.**

Albrecht, R. *See also* Havighurst and Albrecht, 1953.

Allen, F. L., 1952. *The Big Change: America Transforms Itself, 1900-1950*. Harper. **275, 277, 278.**

Allport, G. W., 1954. *The Nature of Prejudice*. Addison-Wesley. **41*n*.**

Amory, C., 1947. *The Proper Bostonians*. Dutton. **473*n*.**

Anshen, R., ed., 1949. *The Family: Its Function and Destiny*. Harper. **558*n*.**

Arensberg, C. M., and S. T. Kimball, 1940. *Family and Community in Ireland*. Harvard University Press. **158*n*., 163, 175.**

Arensberg, C. M. *See also* Polanyi, Arensberg, and Pearson, 1957; Polanyi, Arensberg, and Pearson, eds., 1957.

Armstrong, R. C., 1912. *Just Before the Dawn: The Life and Works of Ninomiya Sontoku*. Macmillan. **90*n*.**

Arnold, R., 1957. A port of trade: Whydah on the Guinea coast. In Polanyi, Arensberg, and Pearson, eds., 1957, pp. 154-76. **207*n*., 247.**

Asakawa, K., 1931. Feudalism: Japanese. *Encyclopedia of the Social Sciences,* v. 6, pp. 214-19. **234*n*., 264.**

Ashley-Montagu, M. F. *See* Montagu, M. F. A.

Aubert, V., 1952 (Nov.). White-collar crime and social structure. *Amer. J. Sociol.,* v. 58, no. 3, pp. 263-71. **575, 577, 585.**

Baber, R. E., 1953. *Marriage and the Family,* 2nd ed. McGraw-Hill. **172.**

Bailey, S. K., and H. D. Samuel, 1952. *Congress at Work*. Holt. **355, 358*n*., 360, 390.**

Bakke, E. W., 1940. *The Unemployed Worker: A Study of the Task of Making a Living Without a Job*. Yale University Press. **262.**

——, 1940a. *Citizens Without Work: A Study of the Effects of Unemployment upon the Workers' Social Relations and Practices*. Yale University Press. **262.**

Bales, R. F., 1949. *Interaction Process Analysis: A Method for the Study of Small Groups*. Addison-Wesley. **53*n*., 78.**

——, 1953. The equilibrium problem in small groups. In Parsons, Bales, and Shils, 1953, Chap. 4. **67.**

——, 1955. Adaptive and integrative changes as sources of strain in social systems. Excerpt from R. F. Bales. 1949. Reprinted in Hare, Borgatta, and Bales, eds., 1955, pp. 127-31. **56, 78.**

——, and P. E. Slater, 1955. Role differentiation in small decision-making groups. In Parsons and Bales, 1955, Chap. 5. **124.**

Bales, R. F. *See also* Hare, Borgatta, and Bales, eds., 1955; Parsons and Bales, 1953; Parsons and Bales, 1955; Parsons, Bales, and Shils, 1953.

Baltzell, E. D., 1953. "Who's Who in America" and "The Social Register": elite and upper class indexes in Metropolitan America. In Bendix and Lipset, eds., 1953, pp. 172-85. **490, 492.**

Barber, B., 1948. *"Mass Apathy" and Voluntary Social Participation in the United States.* Unpublished Ph.D. dissertation, Harvard University. **367*n*.**

——, 1950. Participation and mass apathy in associations. In Gouldner, ed., 1950, pp. 477-504. **367.**

——, 1952. *Science and the Social Order.* Free Press. **243*n*., 451*n*.**

——, 1954. The three human females. In Geddes, ed., 1954, pp. 49-61. **144.**

——, 1957. *Social Stratification: A Comparative Analysis of Structure and Process.* Harcourt, Brace. **490, 510, 513, 529*n*., 531, 549.**

——, and L. S. Lobel, 1952. "Fashion" in women's clothes and the American social system. *Social Forces,* v. 31, pp. 124-31. **537*n*.**

Barber, E. G., 1955. *The Bourgeoisie in Eighteenth-Century France.* Princeton University Press. **481*n*., 511, 514, 539, 541.**

Barber, H. W., 1947. Religious liberty *vs.* police power: Jehovah's Witnesses. *Amer. polit. Sci. Rev.,* v. 41, no. 2, pp. 226-47. **427.**

Barnard, C. I., 1938. *The Functions of the Executive.* Harvard University Press. **280*n*., 283, 285, 297, 302, 311, 318*n*.**

——, 1946. Functions and pathology of status systems in formal organizations. In Whyte, ed., 1946, Chap. 4. **25*n*., 65*n*., 79, 308*n*., 311, 487.**

——, 1949. The entrepreneur and formal organization. In *Change and the entrepreneur,* 1949, pp. 7-11. **260.**

Barnes, H. E., H. Becker, and F. B. Becker, eds., 1940. *Contemporary Social Theory.* D. Appleton-Century.

Barnett, H. G., 1953. *Innovation: The Basis of Cultural Change.* McGraw-Hill. **649.**

Barron, M. L., ed., 1957. *American Minorities: A Textbook of Readings in Intergroup Relations.* Knopf. **499.**

Barton, A. H., 1955. The concept of property-space in social research. In Lazarsfeld and Rosenberg, eds., 1955, pp. 50-52. **13.**

Barton, A. H. *See also* Lipset *et al.,* 1954.

Bastide, R., and P. van den Berghe, 1957 (Dec.). Stereotypes, norms and interracial behavior in São Paulo, Brazil. *Amer. sociol. Rev.,* v. 22, no. 6, pp. 689-94. **495.**

Bates, A., 1942. Parental roles in courtship. *Social Forces,* v. 20, pp. 483-86. **167, 168.**

Bates, M., 1953. Human ecology. In Kroeber, ed., 1953, pp. 700-13. **100, 103, 109.**

Bateson, G., and M. Mead, 1942. *Balinese Character: A Photographic Analysis.* Special Publications of the New York Academy of Sciences, v. 2, Dec. 7, 1942. **95*n*., 129-30, 235.**

Bauer, R. A., A. Inkeles, and C. Kluckhohn, 1956. *How the Soviet System Works: Cultural, Psychological, and Social Themes.* Harvard University Press. **207*n*.**

Beach, F. A. *See* Ford and Beach, 1951.

Beals, R. L., 1953. Social stratification in Latin America. *Amer. J. Sociol.,* v. 58, no. 4, pp. 327-39. **485*n*., 495, 513, 515-18, 536.**

Bean, L., 1940. *Ballot Behavior: A Study of Presidential Elections.* Washington, American Council on Public Affairs. **388*n*.**

——, 1948. *How to Predict Elections.* Knopf. **388*n*.**

Becker, C., 1932. *Heavenly City of the Eighteenth-Century Philosophers.* Yale University Press. **452, 462.**

Becker, F. B. *See* Barnes, Becker, and Becker, eds., 1940.

Becker, H., 1933. The sorrow of bereavement. *J. abnorm. soc. Psychol.,* v. 27, pp. 391-410. **398*n*.**

——, and R. Hill, eds., 1942. *Marriage and the Family.* Heath.

——, 1948. *Family, Marriage and Parenthood.* Heath.

Becker, H. *See also* Barnes, Becker, and Becker, eds., 1940; Von Wiese and Becker, 1932.

Beigel, H. G., 1951. Romantic love. *Amer. sociol. Rev.,* v. 16, pp. 326-34. **165, 176.**

Bellah, R. N., 1957. *Tokugawa Religion: The Values of Pre-Industrial*

Japan. Free Press and Falcon's Wing Press. **88, 89*n*., 90.**

Bendix, R., and F. W. Howton, 1959. Social mobility and the American business elite. In Lipset and Bendix, 1959, Chap. 4. **529-31.**

Bendix, R., and S. M. Lipset, 1953. Karl Marx' theory of social class. In Bendix and Lipset, eds., 1953, pp. 26-35. **506*n*.**

——, eds., 1953. *Class, Status and Power: A Reader in Social Stratification*. Free Press. **506*n*., 510.**

Bendix, R. *See also* Lipset and Bendix, 1952; 1959.

Benet, F., 1957. Explosive markets: the Berber Highlands. In Polanyi, Arensberg, and Pearson, eds., 1957, Chap. 10. **208.**

Berelson, B., 1951. *Content Analysis in Communications Research*. Free Press. **593.**

——, and P. J. Salter, 1946. Majority and minority Americans: an analysis of magazine fiction. *Pub. Opin. Quart*., v. 10, pp. 168-90. **624.**

Berger, M., 1957. *Bureaucracy and Society in Modern Egypt: A Study of the Higher Civil Service*. Princeton University Press. **309, 310.**

Berle, A. A., Jr., and G. C. Means, 1933. *The Modern Corporation and Private Property*. Macmillan. **231*n*., 631.**

Berliner, J. S., 1957. *Factory and Manager in the USSR*. Harvard University Press. **303.**

Berry, B., 1958. *Race and Ethnic Relations*. Houghton Mifflin. **323.**

Berry, G. L., 1947. *Religions of the World*. Barnes and Noble. **396, 429.**

Bettelheim, B., and M. Janowitz, 1950. *Dynamics of Prejudice: A Psychological and Sociological Study of Veterans*. Harper. **614*n*.**

Betts, G. H., 1929. *The Beliefs of 700 Ministers*. Abingdon. **401.**

Bierstedt, R., 1950. An analysis of social power. *Amer. sociol. Rev*., v. 15, no. 6, pp. 730-38. **318*n*.**

Bird, C. *See* Hochbaum *et al*., 1955.

Birnbaum, N., 1953. Conflicting interpretations of the rise of capitalism: Marx and Weber. *Brit. J. Sociol*., v. 4, pp. 125-41. **466-67.**

Bishlawy, S., 1948. Islam. In Ferm, ed., 1948. **412.**

Blau, P. M., 1955. *The Dynamics of Bureaucracy*. University of Chicago Press. **289, 290, 302, 304, 312.**

——, 1957. Formal organization: dimensions of analysis. *Amer. J. Sociol*., v. 63, no. 1, pp. 58-69. **290.**

Bloch, H. A., and A. Niederhoffer, 1958. *The Gang: A Study in Adolescent Behavior*. Philosophical Library. **571, 574.**

Bloch, M., 1931. Feudalism: European. *Encyclopaedia of the Social Sciences*, v. 6, pp. 203-10. **234*n*., 264.**

——, 1949. *La Société Féodale*, series *L'Évolution de l'Humanité*, 34. Paris: Albin Michel. V. 1: *La Formation des Liens de Dépendance*. **228, 234*n*.**

Bloom, S. F., 1957 (May). The peasant Caesar. *Commentary*, pp. 406-18. **621*n*., 623.**

Boas, F., ed., 1938. *General Anthropology*. Heath.

Boeke, J. D., 1948. *The Interests of the Voiceless Far East: Introduction to Oriental Economics*. Leiden: Press Universitaire. **213, 214.**

Boisen, A. T., 1939. Religion and hard times: a study of the H ly Rollers. *Social Action*, v. 5, no. . . pp. 8-35. **426*n*.**

Borgatta, E. F. *See* Hare, Borgatta, and Bales, eds., 1955.

Bossard, J. H. S., 1954. *The Sociology of Child Development*, rev. ed. Harper. **47, 143, 168*n*.**

Bradley, Phillips, ed., 1954. *Tocqueville's "Democracy in America."* 2 vols. Vintage Books. **69*n*.**

Bradley, P. D., 1949. Entrepreneurship in Latin America. In *Change and the Entrepreneur*, 1949. **211, 225.**

Brean, H., 1958 (Nov.). Everybody is dishonest. *Life*, v. 45, no. 21, pp. 70-76. **563.**

Bredemeier, H. C. *See* K. Davis, Bredemeier, and Levy, eds., 1948, 1949.

Brinton, C., 1938. *The Anatomy of Revolution*. Norton. **461*n*., 538, 539, 541, 549, 641.**

Britt, S. H. *See* Graeber and Britt, eds., 1942.

Brogan, D. W., 1954. *Politics in America*. Harper. **351*n*., 354, 355, 376*n*.**

Bromberg, W., 1943 (Dec.). The effects of the war on crime. *Amer. sociol. Rev*., v. 8, no. 6, pp. 685-91. **577.**

Brookover, W. B., 1955. *A Sociology of Education*. American Book. **139.**

Brookover, W. B. *See also* Schuler *et al*., eds., 1952.

and his fare: facets of a fleeting relationship. *Amer. J. Sociol.*, v. 65, no. 2, pp. 158-65. **577.**

Davis, K., 1942. Changing modes of marriage: contemporary family types. In H. Becker and Hill, eds., 1942. **163, 165, 175.**

——, 1942a (June). A conceptual analysis of stratification. *Amer. sociol. Rev.*, v. 7, no. 3, pp. 309-21. **487, 510.**

——, 1944. Children of divorce. *Law and contemp. Problems,* v. 10, pp. 700-10. **174, 176.**

——, 1949. *Human Society*. Macmillan. **112***n*.**, 140***n*.**, 233, 264, 340, 417, 524.**

——, 1950. Statistical perspective on divorce. *Annals. Amer. Acad. polit. soc. Sci.*, v. 272, pp. 15-21. **172, 176.**

——, 1953 (Aug.). Reply. *Amer. sociol. Rev.*, v. 18, no. 4, pp. 394-97. (*See* Tumin, 1953.) **487, 510, 543, 544, 549.**

——, 1959. The myth of functional analysis as a special method in sociology and anthropology. *Amer. sociol. Rev.*, v. 24, no. 6, pp. 757-72. **649.**

——, H. C. Bredemeier, and M. J. Levy, Jr., eds., 1948, 1949. *Modern American Society: Readings in the Problems of Order and Change.* Rinehart.

Davis, K., and W. E. Moore, 1945. Some principles of stratification. *Amer. sociol. Rev.*, v. 10, no. 2, pp. 242-49. **487, 488, 510, 512, 543, 544, 549.**

De Coccola, R., and P. King, 1956. *Ayorama*. Oxford University Press. **87***n*.**, 109.**

Denney, R. *See* Riesman, 1955.

Deutsch, M. *See* Selltiz *et al.*, 1959.

Dewhurst, J. F., and assoc., 1955. *America's Needs and Resources: A New Survey*. Twentieth Century Fund. **276, 278, 318.**

Dibble, B., 1957. Electric power: national and regional schemes: United States. *Encyclopaedia Britannica,* v. 8, p. 284. **211.**

Dickson. *See* Roethlisberger and Dickson, 1939.

Dietrick, D. C. *See* Kitsuse and Dietrick, 1959.

Dinesen, Isak (Baroness Karen Blixen), 1938. *Out of Africa*. Random House. **95.**

Dinitz, S. *See* Reckless, Dinitz, and Kay, 1957.

Dornbusch, S. M., 1955. The military academy as an assimilating institution. *Social Forces*, v. 33, pp. 316-21. **42, 141.**

Drake, St. C., and H. R. Cayton, 1945. *Black Metropolis: A Study of Negro Life in a Northern City*. Harcourt, Brace. **196, 473***n*.**, 507***n*.

Dreyfuss, C., 1938. *Occupation and Ideology of the Salaried Employee*. Trans. E. Abramovitch. Columbia University Press. **301.**

Duncan, O. D. *See* Pfautz and Duncan, 1950.

Duprat, G. -L., 1924. *Le Lien familiale: causes sociales de son relachement*. Paris: F. Alcan. **164.**

Durkheim, E., 1933. *On the Division of Labor in Society*. Trans. G. Simpson. Macmillan. Originally published in Paris: F. Alcan, 1893. **26.**

——, 1947. *The Elementary Forms of the Religious Life*. Trans. J. W. Swain. Free Press. Originally published in Paris: F. Alcan, 1912. **408***n*.**, 409, 417, 457***n*.

——, 1951. *Suicide: A Study in Sociology*. Trans. J. A. Spaulding and G. Simpson. Free Press. Originally published in Paris: F. Alcan, 1897. **557***n*.

Duverger, M., 1954. *Political Parties: Their Organization and Activity in the Modern State*. Trans. B. North and R. North. Foreword by D. W. Brogan. Methuen and Wiley. **343***n*.**, 361, 363, 376, 389.**

Easterbrook, W. T., 1949. Some comments on the nature of entrepreneurial history. In *Change and the Entrepreneur,* 1949, p. 33. **212.**

Ebenstein, W., 1943. *The Nazi State*. Farrar & Rinehart. **615, 616.**

Eckard, E. W., 1947. How many Negroes "pass"? *Amer. J. Sociol.*, v. 52, pp. 498-500. **47.**

Editors of *Fortune,* 1951. *USA, The Permanent Revolution*. Prentice-Hall. **590***n*.

Eells, K. *See* Warner, Meeker, and Eells, 1949.

Efron, D., 1941. *Gesture and Environment*. King's Crown Press. **95***n*.

Eggan, F., 1956. Review of Homans and Schneider, 1955. *Amer. sociol. Rev.*, v. 21, pp. 402-03. **79.**

Ehrmann, W. W., 1954. Non-conformance of male and female reports on premarital coitus. *Social Problems*, v. 1, pp. 155-59. **149.**

Eisenstadt, S. M., 1954. Reference group behavior and social integration: an explorative study. *Amer. sociol. Rev.*, v. 19, pp. 175-85. **41.**

Eldersveld, S. J. *See* Eulau, Eldersveld, and Janowitz, eds., 1956.

Eliot, T. D., 1948. Bereavement: inevitable but not insurmountable. In H. Becker and Hill, eds., 1948. **398*n*.**

Ellsworth, J. E., Jr., 1952. *Factory Folkways: A Study of Institutional Structure and Change*. Yale University Press. **271*n*.**

Elwin, V., 1947. *The Muria and Their Ghotul*. London: Oxford University Press. **148*n*.**

Embree, J. J., 1941 (Sept.). Some social functions of religion in rural Japan. *Amer. J. Sociol.*, v. 47, pp. 184-89. **459.**

Eulau, H., 1955. Perceptions of class and party in voting behavior: 1952. *Amer. polit. Sci. Rev.*, v. 49, pp. 364-84. **376*n*., 377.**

——, S. J. Eldersveld, and M. Janowitz, eds., 1956. *Political Behavior: A Reader in Theory and Research*. Free Press. **389.**

Factors Determining Human Behavior, 1937. Harvard Tercentenary Publications.

Fales, E., 1937. *Genesis of Level of Aspiration in Children from One and One-Half to Three Years of Age*. Unpublished manuscript. Reported in Child, 1954, p. 674. **119.**

Fanfani, A., 1935. *Catholicism, Protestantism, and Capitalism*. Sheed & Ward. **445-46, 447, 466.**

Faris, E., 1937. *The Nature of Human Nature and Other Essays in Social Psychology*. McGraw-Hill. **431.**

Fauset, A., 1944. *Black Gods of the Metropolis: Negro Religious Cults of the Urban North*. University of Pennsylvania Press. **437-38, 439.**

Fedotov, G. P., 1948. The Eastern Orthodox Church. In Ferm, ed., 1948. **411.**

Fei Hsiao-T'ung, 1939. *Peasant Life in China*. Dutton. **27, 186.**

——, 1946. Peasantry and gentry: an interpretation of Chinese social structure and its changes. *Amer. J. Sociol.*, v. 52, pp. 1-16. **157*n*., 175-76, 449*n*., 485*n*.**

Feld, M. D., 1959. Information and authority: the structure of military organization. *Amer. sociol. Rev.*, v. 24, no. 1, pp. 15-22. **293, 296.**

Feldmesser, R. A., 1953. The persistence of status advantages in Soviet Russia. *Amer. J. Sociol.*, v. 59, no. 1, pp. 19-27. **526.**

Ferm, V., ed., 1948. *Religion in the Twentieth Century*. Philosophical Library.

Ferré, L. M., 1934. *Les Classes sociales dans la France contemporaine*. Paris: Librairie Philosophique, J. Vrin. **472, 482.**

Fiero, M. L. *See* Schuler *et al.*, eds., 1952.

Firth, R., 1936. *We, the Tikopia: A Sociological Study of Kinship in Primitive Polynesia*. American Book. **94*n*.**

——, 1955. Function. In W. L. Thomas, Jr., ed., 1955, pp. 237-58. **78.**

Flanner, J., 1944. *Pétain: The Old Man of France*. Simon & Schuster. **317.**

Folsom, J. K., 1934. *The Family*. Wiley. **165.**

Ford, C. S., and F. A. Beach, 1951. *Patterns of Sexual Behavior*. Harper and Paul B. Hoeber. **99*n*., 148, 150*n*., 176.**

Fortes, M., 1949. Time and social structure: an Ashanti case study. In Fortes, ed., 1949, pp. 54-84. **186.**

——, ed., 1949. *Social Structure: Studies Presented to A. R. Radcliffe-Brown*. Oxford: Clarendon Press.

Fortune, R. F., 1932. Incest. *Encyclopaedia of the Social Sciences*, v. 7, pp. 620-22. **67.**

——, 1932a. *Sorcerers of Dobu*. London: George Routledge. **154*n*., 186, 416.**

Fox, R. C., 1957. Training for uncertainty. In Merton, Reader, and Kendall, eds., 1957, pp. 207-41. **143.**

Frampton, M. E. *See* Zimmerman and Frampton, 1935.

Franke, O., 1931. Feudalism: Chinese. *Encyclopaedia of the Social Sciences*, v. 6, pp. 213-14. **234*n*., 264.**

Frazier, E. F., 1939. *The Negro Family in the United States*. University of Chicago Press. **197, 200.**

——, 1957. *Race and Culture Contacts in the Modern World*. Knopf. **206.**

Freedman, R., A. H. Hawley, W. S. Landecker, and H. M. Miner, 1952. *Principles of Sociology*. Holt.

Frenkel-Brunswik, E. *See* Adorno *et al.*, 1950.

Friedeburg, L. von, 1953. *Die Umfrage in der Intimsphäre*. Stuttgart: Ferdinand Enke Verlag. Reported in *Sociolog. Abstracts*, July 1956, v. 4, no. 3, p. 157. **147*n*.**

Friedrich, C. J., 1952. Some observations on Weber's analysis of bureaucracy. In Merton *et al.*, eds., 1952, pp. 27-33. **290*n*.**

——, ed., 1954. *Totalitarianism*. Harvard University Press.

Froomkin, J., and A. J. Jaffe, 1953. Occupational skill and socioeconomic structure. *Amer. J. Sociol.*, v. 59, no. 1, pp. 42-48. **489.**

Fuller, R. C., and R. R. Myers, 1941 (Feb.). Some aspects of a theory of social problems. *Amer. sociol. Rev.*, v. 6, pp. 24-32. **639.**

Gait, E. A., 1928. Caste. In Hastings, ed., 1928, v. 3, pp. 230-39. **536.**

Galbraith, J. K., 1954. *The Great Crash: 1929*. Houghton Mifflin. **277.**

——, 1956. *American Capitalism: The Concept of Countervailing Power*, rev. ed. Houghton Mifflin. **218, 266*n*., 273-76, 278.**

——, 1958. *The Affluent Society*. Houghton Mifflin. **274, 278, 545.**

Garceau, O., and C. Silverman, 1954. A pressure group and the pressured: a case report. *Amer. polit. Sci. Rev.*, v. 48, pp. 672-91. **386*n*., 390.**

Gardner, B. B. *See* A. Davis, Gardner, and Gardner, 1941.

Gardner, M. R. *See* A. Davis, Gardner, and Gardner, 1941.

Garrard, L. H., 1938. *Wah-to-Yah and the Taos Trail*. Glendale. **236.**

Garrison, W. E., 1928. *Catholicism and the American Mind*. Willett, Clark & Co. **422.**

Geddes, D. P., ed., 1954. *An Analysis of the Kinsey Reports on Sexual Behavior in the Human Male and Female*. Mentor.

Gelhorn, W. *See* McKeon, Merton, and Gelhorn, 1957.

Georgopoulos, B. S., and A. S. Tannenbaum, 1957 (Oct.). A study of organizational effectiveness. *Amer. sociol. Rev.*, v. 22, no. 5, pp. 534-40. **287, 288.**

Gerth, H. H., 1940. The Nazi Party: its leadership and composition. *Amer. J. Sociol.*, v. 45, pp. 517-41. **611.**

——, and C. W. Mills, 1953. *Character and Social Structure*. Harcourt, Brace. **318*n*.**

Gesell, A., and F. L. Ilg, 1946. *The Child from Five to Ten*. Harper. **121, 127.**

Getzels, J. W., and E. G. Guba, 1954. Role, role conflict, and effectiveness: an empirical study. *Amer. sociol. Rev.*, v. 19, pp. 164-75. **30, 32, 46.**

Ghurye, G. S., 1949. Review of O. C. Cox, *Caste, Class and Race: A Study in Social Dynamics* (Doubleday, 1948). In *Amer. J. Sociol.*, v. 54, no. 5, pp. 466-69. **522, 524.**

——, 1955. Nomenclature of kin. *Sociol. Bull.* (Bombay, India), v. 4, pp. 45-84. **190*n*., 191*n*., 194*n*.**

Gibson, D. L. *See* Schuler *et al.*, eds., 1952.

Gilfillan, S. C., 1953. Social implications of technical advance: a trend report and bibliography. *Current Sociol.*, v. 1, no. 4. **103.**

Gillin, J., 1948. *The Ways of Man*. Appleton-Century-Crofts. **427.**

Gilmore, H. W., 1944 (Aug.). The old New Orleans and the new: a case for ecology. *Amer. sociol. Rev.* As reprinted in L. Wilson and Kolb, 1949, pp. 414-24. **496.**

Gilson, E., 1948. *Dante the Philosopher*. Trans. D. Moore. Sheed & Ward. **422.**

Gist, N P., 1954 (April). Caste differentials in South India. *Amer. sociol. Rev.*, v. 19, no. 2, pp. 126-37. **484.**

Glazer, N., 1950 (March). What sociology knows about American Jews. *Commentary*, v. 9, pp. 275-84. **623.**

——, 1954. New light on *The Authoritarian Personality*. *Commentary*, v. 17, no. 3, pp. 289-97. **613*n*.**

Glazer, N. *See also* Riesman, 1955.

Glick, P. C., 1947. The family cycle. *Amer. sociol. Rev.*, v. 12, pp. 164-69 **154.**

Goffman, E., 1956. Embarrassment and social organization. *Amer. J Sociol.*, v. 62, no. 3, pp. 264-71. **84.**

——, 1959. *The Presentation of Self in Everyday Life*. Doubleday Anchor Books. **474, 478, 482, 489.**

Goldhamer, H., and E. A. Shils, 1939.

Types of power and status. *Amer. J. Sociol.*, v. 45, no. 2, pp. 171-82. **318*n*.**

Goldschmidt, W. R., 1944. Class denominationalism in California churches. *Amer. J. Sociol.*, v. 49, pp. 348-55. **435, 497.**

Goode, W. J., 1951. *Religion Among the Primitives*. Free Press. **412*n*.**

——, 1956. *After Divorce*. Free Press. **171, 173, 174, 176.**

——, and P. K. Hatt, 1952. *Methods in Social Research*. McGraw-Hill. **14.**

Goodsell, W., 1935. *A History of Marriage and the Family*, rev. ed. Macmillan. **165, 178*n*., 442.**

Goss, M. E. W., 1959. *Physicians in Bureaucracy*. Unpublished doctoral dissertation, Columbia University Department of Sociology. **294.**

Gottschalk, L., 1944. Causes of revolution. *Amer. J. Sociol.*, v. 50, no. 1, pp. 1-8. **549, 641-42.**

Gouldner, A. W., 1952. Red tape as a social problem. In Merton *et al.*, eds., 1952, pp. 410-18. **308*n*.**

——, 1954. *Patterns of Industrial Bureaucracy*. Free Press. **291.**

——, ed., 1950. *Studies in Leadership: Leadership and Democratic Action*. Harper.

Graeber, I., and S. H. Britt, eds., 1942. *Jews in a Gentile World*. Macmillan.

Graham, S., 1957. *American Culture: An Analysis of Its Development and Present Characteristics*. Harper. **271.**

Grampp, W. D., 1951. The facts about "capitalist inequality." *Commentary*, v. 11, pp. 513-24. **276.**

Gray, A. P. *See* Merton, *et al.*, eds., 1952.

Green, A W., 1956. *Sociology: An Analysis of Life in a Modern Society*. McGraw-Hill. **448.**

Greenblum, J., and L. I. Pearlin, 1953. Vertical mobility and prejudice: a socio-psychological analysis. In Bendix and Lipset, eds., 1953. **40.**

Groethuysen, B., 1927. *Origines de l'esprit bourgeois en France*. Paris: Gallimard. V. 1: *L'Église et la Bourgeoisie*. **448.**

Gross, N., 1953. Social class identification in the urban community. *Amer. sociol. Rev.*, v. 18, no. 4, pp. 398-404. **501.**

Gross, N. *See also* Mason and Gross, 1955.

Grousset, R., 1931. *The Civilization of India*. Trans. C. A. Phillips. Tudor. **408*n*.**

Guba, E. G. *See* Getzels and Guba, 1954.

Guest, R. H. *See* Walker and Guest, 1952.

Gurvitch, G., and W. E. Moore, eds., 1945. *Twentieth Century Sociology*. Philosophical Library.

Haer, J. L., 1957. Predictive utility of five indices of social stratification. *Amer. sociol. Rev.*, v. 22, no. 5, pp. 541-46. **503.**

Haggard, H. W., 1929. *Devils, Drugs, and Doctors: The Story of the Science of Healing from Medicine-Man to Doctor*. Blue Ribbon Books. **415.**

Halbwachs, M., 1913. *La Classe ouvrière et les niveaux de vie*. Paris: F. Alcan. **536.**

Hall, O., 1948. The stages of a medical career. *Amer. J. Sociol.*, v. 53, pp. 327-36. **21.**

Hall, T. C., 1930. *The Religious Background of American Culture*. Little, Brown. **447.**

Hallowell, A. I. *See* Spier, Hallowell, and Newman, eds., 1941.

Halpin, A. H., ed., 1958. *Administrative Theory in Education*. University of Chicago Press.

Hamon, A., and "X. Y. Z.," 1936, 1937, 1938. *Les maîtres de la France*. 3 vols. Paris: Éditions Sociales Internationales. **448, 542*n*.**

Handlin, O., 1957. *Race and Nationality in American Life*. Doubleday Anchor Books. **205, 592, 599, 600*n*.**

Harding, L. W., 1957. Illiteracy. *Encyclopaedia Britannica*, v. 12, p. 94. **93.**

Hare, A. P., E. F. Borgatta, and R. F. Bales, eds., 1955. *Small Groups: Studies in Social Interaction*. Knopf.

Harris, S. E. *See* Sutton *et al.*, 1956.

Hartung, F. E., 1950 (July). White-collar offenses in the wholesale meat industry in Detroit. *Amer. J. Sociol.*, v. 56, no. 1, pp. 25-32. **575.**

Hastings, J., ed., 1928. *Encyclopaedia of Religion and Ethics*. Scribner's.

Hatt, P. K., 1950. Occupation and social stratification. *Amer. J. Sociol.*, v. 55, no. 6, pp. 533-43. **485.**

Hatt, P. K. *See also* Goode and Hatt, 1952.

Hauser, A., 1951. *The Social History of Art*. 2 vols. London: Routledge and Kegan Paul. **17.**

Howton, F. W. *See* Bendix and Howton, 1959.

Hsu, F. L. K., 1943. The family in China. In Anshen, ed., 1949, Chap. 4. **157*n*.**

——, 1949. The myth of Chinese family size. *Amer. J. Sociol.*, v. 14, pp. 559-62. **157*n*.**

——, 1949a. Social mobility in China. *Amer. sociol. Rev.*, v. 14, pp. 764-71. **158*n*.**

——, 1952. *Religion, Science, and Human Crisis: A Study of China in Transition and Its Implications for the West*. London: Routledge and Kegan Paul. **415, 418.**

——, 1953. *Americans and Chinese*. Schuman. **157*n*.**

Huberman, L., and P. M. Sweezy, 1956 (May). Capitalism and agriculture. *Monthly Review*, v. 8, no. 1, pp. 1-12. **268*n*.**

Hudson, G. F., 1952 (May). Why Asians hate the West. *Commentary*, v. 13, pp. 411-18. **620.**

Huitt, R. K., 1954. The congressional committee: a case study. *Amer. polit. Sci. Rev.*, v. 48, pp. 340-65. **360*n*., 387.**

Hunt, T. C., 1940. Occupational status and marriage selection. *Amer. sociol. Rev.*, v. 5, pp. 495-504. **479*n*.**

Huntington, E., 1945. *Mainsprings of Civilization*. Wiley. **102.**

Huntington, M. J., 1957. The development of a professional self-image. In Merton, Reader, and Kendall, eds., 1957, pp. 179-87. **46, 143.**

Huntington, S. P., 1957. *The Soldier and the State: The Theory and Politics of Civil-Military Relations*. Harvard University Press. **308, 312, 632.**

Hutchinson, B., 1957 (June). The social grading of occupations in Brazil. *Brit. J. Sociol.*, v. 8, no. 2, pp. 176-89. **486, 487.**

Huxley, J., 1939 (March). The uniqueness of man. *Yale Rev.*, v. 28, no. 3, pp. 473-500. **111.**

Hyman, H., 1953. The value systems of different classes: a social-psychological contribution to the analysis of stratification. In Bendix and Lipset, eds., 1953, pp. 426-42. **560.**

Ilg, F. L. *See* Gesell and Ilg, 1946.

Ingram, J. K., and F. D. Lugard, 1957. Slavery. *Encyclopaedia Britannica*, v 20, pp. 773-87. **205.**

Inkeles, A., 1950. *Public Opinion in Soviet Russia: A Study in Mass Persuasion*. Harvard University Press. **319.**

——, 1950a. Stratification and mobility in the Soviet Union: 1940-1950. *Amer. sociol. Rev.*, v. 15, no. 4, pp. 465-79. **485*n*., 520-21.**

——, 1954. The totalitarian mystique: some impressions of the dynamics of totalitarian society. In Friedrich, ed., 1954, pp. 88-108. **344, 620, 621*n*.**

——, and P. H. Rossi, 1956 (Jan.). National comparisons of occupational prestige. *Amer. J. Sociol.*, v. 61, no. 4, pp. 329-39. **486.**

Inkeles, A. *See also* Bauer, Inkeles, and Kluckhohn, 1956.

Institut National d'études démographiques, 1950. *Le Niveau intellectuel des enfants d'âge scolaire*, No. 13. Paris: Presses Universitaires de France. **526.**

Ivy, A. C., and I. Ross, 1949. *Religion and Race: Barriers to College?* Public Affairs Pamphlet No. 153, Anti-Defamation League of B'nai B'rith. **623.**

Jacobson, P. H., 1950. Differentials in divorce by duration of marriage and size of family. *Amer. sociol. Rev.*, v. 15, pp. 235-44. **173, 174.**

——, 1959. *American Marriage and Divorce*. Rinehart. **176**

Jaffe, A. J. *See* Froomkin and Jaffe, 1953.

Jahoda, M. *See* Ackerman and Jahoda, 1950; Christie and Jahoda, 1954; Selltiz *et al*., 1959.

James, W., 1890. *Principles of Psychology*. 2 vols. Holt. **85*n*.**

Janowitz, M., 1959 (Mar.). Changing patterns of organizational authority: the military. *Admin. Sci. Quart.*, v. 3, no. 4, pp. 473-93. **293.**

Janowitz, M. *See also* Bettelheim and Janowitz, 1950; Eulau, Eldersveld, and Janowitz, eds., 1956.

Jonassen, C. T., 1947. The Protestant ethic and the spirit of capitalism in Norway. *Amer. sociol. Rev.*, v. 12, pp. 676-86. **445*n*., 466.**

——, 1949 (Oct.). A re-evaluation and critique of the logic and some methods of Shaw and McKay. *Amer. sociol. Rev.*, v. 14, no. 5, pp. 608-14. **571*n*.**

Konow, S., and P. Tuxen, 1949. *The Religions of India*. Trans. S. Konow. Copenhagen: G. E. C. Gad. **405*n*., 425*n*., 450.**

Kornhauser, R. R., 1953. The Warner approach to social stratification. In Bendix and Lipset, eds., 1953, pp. 224-55. **507*n*.**

Kotinsky, R. *See* Witmer and Kotinsky, 1955.

Kotschnig, W. M., 1937. *Unemployment in the Learned Professions*. London: Oxford University Press, Humphrey Milford. **611**

Kreps, T. K., 1957. Trade organization. *Encyclopaedia Britannica*, v. 20, pp. 360-68. **267.**

Krige, E. J., and J. D. Krige, 1943. *The Realm of a Rain-Queen: A Study of the Pattern of Lovedu Society*. Oxford University Press. **107, 108, 249. 251, 264, 329*n*.**

Krige, J. D. *See* Krige and Krige, 1943.

Kroeber, A. L., 1944. *Configurations of Culture Growth*. University of California Press. **85, 649.**

——, 1948. *Anthropology: Race, Language, Culture, Psychology, Prehistory*, rev. ed. Harcourt, Brace. **98, 106*n*., 108.**

——, ed., 1953. *Anthropology Today: An Encyclopedic Inventory*. University of Chicago Press.

Kroeber, A. L., and C. Kluckhohn, 1952. *Culture: A Critical Review*. . . . Papers of the Peabody Museum of Harvard University. **83*n*.**

Krogman, W. M., 1945. The concept of race. In Linton, ed., 1945. **100*n*., 109.**

Landecker, W. S. *See* Freedman *et al*. 1952.

Landis, B. Y., ed., 1954. *1955 Yearbook of American Churches*. National Council of the Churches of Christ in the U.S.A. **458.**

Landis, J. T., 1947. Social action in American Protestant Churches. *Amer. J. Sociol*., v. 52, pp. 517-22. **395.**

——, 1952. Marriages of mixed and non-mixed religious faith. In Landis and Landis, eds., 1952. **173.**

——, and M. G. Landis, 1948. *Building a Successful Marriage*. Prentice-Hall. **167, 199.**

——, 1953. *Building a Successful Marriage*, 2nd ed. Prentice-Hall. As quoted in Rosten, ed., 1955, p. 268. **443.**

——, eds., 1952. *Readings in Marriage and the Family*. Prentice-Hall. **175.**

Landis, M. G. *See* Landis and Landis, 1948; 1953; Landis and Landis, eds., 1952.

Lang, O. 1946. *Chinese Family and Society*. Yale University Press. **150, 157-59, 170, 175, 183, 272, 278.**

Langer, S. K., 1942. *Philosophy in a New Key: A Study in the Symbolism of Reason, Rite, and Art*. Harvard University Press. **91, 108, 417.**

——, 1953. *Feeling and Form: A Theory of Art Developed from* Philosophy in a New Key. Scribner's. **50*n*., 91*n*., 94, 108, 408*n*., 417.**

Larsen, O. N. *See* Lundberg, Schrag, and Larsen, 1954.

Lazarsfeld, P. F., and M. Rosenberg, eds., 1955. *The Language of Social Research: A Reader in the Methodology of Social Research*. Free Press. **14, 285*n*., 501.**

Lazarsfeld, P. F. *See also* Lipset *et al*., 1954; Merton and Lazarsfeld, eds., 1950.

Leach, E. R., 1954. *Political Systems of Highland Burma: A Study of Kachin Social Structure*. Harvard University Press. **162, 588.**

Le Bras, G., 1942, 1945. *Introduction à l'histoire de la pratique réligieuse en France*. 2 vols. Paris: Presses Universitaires de France. **499.**

Lee, Shu-Ching, 1953. China's traditional family, its characteristics and disintegration. *Amer. sociol. Rev*., v. 18, pp. 272-80. **157*n*., 169, 175.**

Lehman, M., 1953. The watchful Congressman and the wasteful Army. *The Reporter*, July 7, 1953, pp. 23-25. **295*n*.**

Lekachman, R., 1954. Economics: science or visionary art? *Commentary*, v. 18, pp. 260-65. **210.**

Lenski, G. E., 1952. American social classes: statistical strata or social groups? *Amer. J. Sociol*., v. 58, no. 2, pp. 139-44. **502.**

——, 1954. Status crystallization: a non-vertical dimension of social status. *Amer. sociol. Rev*., v. 19, no. 4, pp. 405-13. **504.**

——, 1958. Trends in intergenerational occupational mobility in the United States. *Amer. sociol. Rev*., v. 23, no. 5, pp. 514-23. **532-33.**

vard educ. Rev., v. 24, pp. 256-61. **525.**

McArthur, C., 1955. Personality differences between middle and upper classes. *J. abnorm. soc. Psych.*, v. 50, pp. 247-58. **525.**

McCarthy, M., 1956. The revel of the earth. *The New Yorker,* July 14, 1956, p. 30. **420*n*.**

Maccoby, E., R. E. Matthews, and A. S. Morton, 1954. Youth and political change. *Public Opin. Quart.*, v. 18, pp. 23-39. **382.**

McDonald, M. R. *See* Strodtbeck, McDonald, and Rosen, 1957.

McGee, R. J. *See* Caplow and McGee, 1958.

McGinnis. *See* Winch and McGinnis, 1953; Winch and McGinnis, eds., 1953.

MacIver, R. M., 1947. *The Web of Government*. Macmillan. **333*n*., 340, 349*n*., 389, 538.**

——, and C. H. Page, 1949. *Society: An Introductory Analysis*. Rinehart. **106*n*., 109.**

MacIver, R. M., ed., 1948. *Discrimination and National Welfare*. Institute for Religious and Social Studies.

Mack, R. W., R. J. Murphy, and S. Yellin, 1956 (June). The Protestant ethic, level of aspiration, and social mobility: an empirical test. *Amer. sociol. Rev.*, v. 21, pp. 295-300. **448.**

McKay, H. D. *See* Shaw and McKay, 1949.

McKeon, R., R. K. Merton, and W. Gelhorn, 1957. *The Freedom to Read: Perspective and Program*. National Book Committee by R. R. Bowker Co. **347*n*.**

McNeill, J. T., 1951. *A History of the Cure of Souls*. Harper. **410.**

MacRae, D., Jr., 1952. The relation between roll-call votes and constituencies in the Massachusetts House of Representatives. *Amer. polit. Sci. Rev.*, v. 46, pp. 1046-55. **390.**

McSorley, J., 1947. State aid to parish schools. *Catholic World,* v. 165, pp. 131-35. **458.**

Madariaga, S. de, 1929. *Englishmen, Frenchmen, Spaniards: An Essay in Comparative Psychology*. London: Oxford University Press. **164.**

Malinowski, B., 1932. *Argonauts of the Western Pacific: An Account of Native Enterprise and Adventure in the Archipelagoes of Melanesian New Guinea*. London: Routledge. **261*n*., 264.**

——, 1937. Culture as a determinant of behavior. In *Factors Determining Human Behavior,* 1937. **414.**

——, 1954. *Magic, Science, and Religion*. Doubleday Anchor Books. **398*n*., 418.**

Mandelbaum, D., 1949. The family in India. In Anshen, ed., 1949, Chap. 5. **163.**

Mannheim, K., 1936. *Ideology and Utopia*. Harcourt, Brace. **590.**

March, J. G., and H. A. Simon, in collaboration with H. Guetzkow, 1958. *Organizations*. Wiley. **282, 287, 292, 311.**

Marden, C. F., 1952. *Minorities in American Society*. American Book. **495.**

Marketing Chewing Gum in New England: A Research Study, 1950. Social Research, Inc. **477.**

Marshall, T. H., 1953. The nature of class conflict. In Bendix and Lipset, eds., 1953, pp. 81-87. Originally in T. H. Marshall, ed., 1938, pp. 97-111. **540, 542.**

——, 1956. Anthropology today. *Brit. J. Sociol.*, v. 7, pp. 59-64. **69.**

——, ed., 1938. *Class Conflict and Social Stratification*. Ledburg, England: Institute of Sociology, Le Play House. **538.**

Martin, W. E., and C. B. Stendler, eds., 1954. *Readings in Child Development*. Harcourt, Brace. **108, 143.**

Marvin, D. M., 1918. Occupational propinquity as a factor in marriage selection. *Pub. Amer. Statist. Assoc.*, v. 16, pp. 131-56. **479*n*.**

Masland, J. W., and L. I. Radway, 1957. *Soldiers and Scholars: Military Education and National Policy*. Princeton University Press. **312.**

Mason, W. S., and N. Gross, 1955 (June). Intra-occupational prestige differentiation: the school superintendency. *Amer. sociol. Rev.*, v. 20, no. 3, pp. 326-31. **487.**

Matthews, D. R., 1954. United States Senators and the class structure. *Pub. Opin. Quart.*, v. 18, pp. 5-22. **349.**

Matthews, R. E. *See* Maccoby, Matthews, and Morton, 1954.

Matthiessen, P., 1958. Annals of crime: peut-être un peu excessif. *The New Yorker,* Nov. 1, 1958, pp. 119 ff. **326*n*.**

Maurer, H., 1955. *Great Enterprise: Growth and Behavior of the Big Corporation*. Macmillan. **266, 275.**

Mauss, M., 1954. *The Gift: Forms and Functions of Exchange in Archaic Societies*. Free Press. **248.**

Maxwell, A. S., 1955. What is a Seventh-Day Adventist? In Rosten, ed., 1955. **426*n*.**

Maxwell, J., 1954. Intelligence, fertility and the future: a report on the 1947 Scottish mental survey. *Proc. World Population Conference, 1954*. United Nations. **526.**

Mayo, E., and G. F. F. Lombard, 1944. *Teamwork and Labor Turnover in the Aircraft Industry of Southern California*. Harvard Business School, Business Research Studies No. 32; as summarized in Broom and Selznick, 1955, pp. 152-54. **239.**

Mead, G. H., 1934. *Mind, Self, and Society from the Standpoint of a Social Behaviorist*, ed., with introduction, C. W. Morris. University of Chicago Press. **93, 116*n*., 139.**

Mead, M., and N. Calas, eds., 1953. *Primitive Heritage: An Anthropological Anthology*. Random House. **148*n*.**

Mead, M. *See also* Bateson and Mead, 1942.

Means, G. C. *See* Berle and Means, 1933.

Medical Survey of the Bituminous-Coal Industry, A, 1947. Government Printing Office. **263*n*.**

Meeker, M. *See* Warner, Meeker, and Eells, 1949.

Melton, A. W., 1950. Learning. *Annual Rev. Psychol.*, v. 1, pp. 9-30. **143.**

Merrill, F. E., 1949. *Courtship and Marriage: A Study in Social Relationships*. William Sloane. **165.**

Merrill, F. E. *See also* Truxal and Merrill, 1947.

Merriman, R. B., 1938. *Six Contemporaneous Revolutions*. Oxford: Clarendon Press. **540*n*.**

Merton, R. K., 1936. Civilization and culture. *Sociol. soc. Research*, v. 21, pp. 103-13. **106*n*.**

——, 1936a. The unanticipated consequences of purposive social action. *Amer. sociol. Rev.*, v. 1, pp. 894-904. **641.**

——, 1938. *Science, Technology, and Society in Seventeenth-Century England*. In *Osiris*, ed. by George Sarton, v. 4, Part 2. Bruges, Belgium: Saint Catherine Press. **450-52, 466, 649.**

——, 1938a (Oct.). Social structure and anomie. *Amer. sociol. Rev.*, v. 3, no. 5, pp. 672-82. **557, 558.**

——, 1940. Bureaucratic structure and personality. *Social Forces*, v. 17, pp. 560-68. **290*n*., 304*n*.**

——, 1941. Karl Mannheim and the sociology of knowledge. *J. liberal Relig.*, v. 2, pp. 125-47. **96.**

——, 1945. The sociology of knowledge. In Gurvitch and Moore, eds., 1945. **96.**

——, 1948. Discussion of Parsons' "Position of sociological theory." *Amer. sociol. Rev.*, v. 13, pp. 164-68. **78.**

——, 1948a. Discrimination and the American creed. In MacIver, ed., 1948, pp. 99-126. **553.**

——, 1949. Social structure and anomie: revisions and extensions. In Anshen, ed., 1949, pp. 224-57. **451, 462, 558*n*.**

——, 1955. In Witmer and Kotinsky, eds., 1955. **558*n*., 568.**

——, 1957. *Social Theory and Social Structure: Toward the Codification of Theory and Research*, rev. and enlarged ed. Free Press. **13, 14, 18, 35, 36, 45-47, 63, 65, 66, 68, 69*n*., 71*n*., 75, 77*n*., 78, 109, 243*n*., 318*n*., 389, 390, 467, 554, 558*n*., 560, 561, 578, 585, 590, 616.**

——, 1957a. The role-set: problems in sociological theory. *Brit. J. Soc.*, v. 8, no. 2, pp. 106-20. **295*n*.**

——, 1957b. Priorities in scientific discovery: a chapter in the sociology of science. *Amer. sociol. Rev.*, v. 22, pp. 635-59. **243*n*., 645.**

——, 1958 (Jan.). The functions of the professional association. *Amer. J. Nursing*, v. 58. **37, 294.**

——, 1958a. Issues in the growth of a profession. *Proc.* 1958 Convention, American Nurses' Association, pp. 2-12. **37.**

——, 1959 (April). Social conformity, deviation, and opportunity-structures: a comment on the contributions of Dubin and Cloward. *Amer. sociol. Rev.*, v. 24, no. 2, pp. 177-89. **558*n*.**

——, L. Broom, and L. S. Cottrell, Jr., eds., 1959. *Sociology Today: Problems and Prospects*. Basic Books.

Labor: Social Aspects of Economic Development. Cornell University Press. **213.**

——, 1953. Comment [on Tumin, 1953]. *Amer. sociol. Rev.*, v. 18, no. 4, p. 397. **487, 549.**

Moore, W. E. *See also* K. Davis and Moore, 1945; Gurvitch and Moore, eds., 1945.

Moos, M., 1956. *The Republicans: A History of Their Party*. Random House. **372.**

Morris, R. T., 1956 (Oct.). A typology of norms. *Amer. sociol. Rev.*, v. 21, pp. 610-13. **13.**

Morton, A. S. *See* Maccoby, Matthews, and Morton, 1954.

Mowrer, O. H., 1947 (Oct.). Discipline and mental health. *Harvard educ. Rev.*, v. 17, pp. 284-96. **120.**

——, 1950. *Learning Theory and Personality Dynamics: Selected Papers*. Ronald. **128, 130*n*., 143.**

Murdock, G. P., 1949. *Social Structure*. Macmillan. **66, 67, 79, 147, 148, 150, 151, 153-56, 175, 177, 179, 182, 191, 192, 194*n*., 195, 196, 200, 443.**

Muret, C. T., 1936 (Aug.). Marriage as a career. *Harper's*. **164.**

Murray, G., 1946. *Greek Studies*. Oxford: Clarendon Press. **554.**

——, 1955. *Five Stages of Greek Religion*, 3rd ed. Doubleday. **400, 407.**

Muzumdar, H. T., 1951. The teaching sociologist's frame of reference. *Amer. sociol. Rev.*, v. 16, no. 5, pp. 713-18. **83.**

Myers, R. R. *See* Fuller and Myers 1941.

Myrdal, G., with the assistance of R. Sterner and A. Rose, 1944. *An American Dilemma: The Negro Problem and Modern Democracy*. 2 vols. Harper. **47, 94, 100, 600*n*., 640.**

National Association of Manufacturers, 1946. *The American Individual Enterprise System, Its Nature and Future*. 2 vols. McGraw-Hill. **590*n*.**

National Opinion Research Center, 1947. Jobs and occupations: a popular evaluation. *Opinion News*, v. 9, pp. 3-13. As reprinted in Bendix and Lipset, eds., 1953, pp. 411-26. **485, 490.**

National Resources Committee, 1939. *The Structure of the American Economy*. Government Printing Office. As reprinted in part in Bendix and Lipset, eds., 1953, pp. 129-54. **266.**

Neale, W. C., 1957. Reciprocity and redistribution in the Indian village: sequel to some notable discussions. In Polanyi, Arensberg, and Pearson, eds., 1957, pp. 218-36. **249, 250, 264.**

Needham, J., 1954. *Science and Civilization in China*, V. 1, *Introductory Orientations*. Cambridge: Cambridge University Press. **449*n*.**

Nehru, J., 1946. *Discovery of India*. John Day. **484.**

Newcomb, T., 1950. *Social Psychology*. Dryden. **111, 112*n*.**

Newcomer, M., 1955. *The Big Business Executive: The Factors That Made Him, 1900-1950*. Columbia University Press. **528-31.**

Newman, S. S. *See* Spier, Hallowell, and Newman, eds., 1941.

New York Stock Exchange, 1959. *Shareownership in America: 1959*. **265.**

Niebuhr, H. R., 1929. *The Social Sources of Denominationalism*. Holt. **428, 430, 431, 440, 455.**

Niederhoffer, A. *See* H. A. Bloch and Niederhoffer, 1958.

Niehoff, A., 1959 (March). Caste and industrial organization in North India. *Administrative Sci. Quart.*, v. 3, no. 4, pp. 494-508. **484.**

Nock, A. D., 1933. *Conversion: The Old and the New in Religion from Alexander the Great to Augustine of Hippo*. Oxford: Clarendon Press. **401.**

Nottingham, E. K., 1954. *Religion and Society*. Doubleday. **419*n*., 439.**

Noyes, C. R., 1936. *The Institution of Property: A Study of the Development, Substance and Arrangement of the System of Property in Modern Anglo-American Law*. Longmans, Green. **229*n*., 234.**

Olcott, M., 1944 (Dec.). The caste system of India. *Amer. sociol. Rev.*, v. 9, no. 6, pp. 648-57. **523.**

Olds, J., 1955. *The Growth and Structure of Motives: Psychological Studies in the Theory of Action*. Free Press. **114, 115*n*., 118*n*., 143.**

Olds, J. *See also* Parsons and Olds, 1955.

Oliver, D. L., 1951. *The Pacific Islands*. Harvard University Press. **205.**

Opler, M. K., 1943. Woman's social status and the forms of marriage.

Amer. J. Sociol., v. 49, pp. 125-46. **152n., 153, 175.**

Orlansky, H., 1949. Infant care and personality. *Psychol. Bull.*, v. 46, pp. 1-48. **143.**

Ossowski, S., 1957. Social mobility brought about by social revolution. Paper presented at Fourth Working Conference on Social Stratification and Social Mobility, International Sociological Association, Geneva, Dec. 1957. As quoted by Lipset and Bendix, 1959, p. 282, n. 42. **535.**

Page, C. H. *See* MacIver and Page, 1949.

Pareto, V., 1935. *The Mind and Society.* Ed. A. Livingston, trans. A. Bongiorno and A. Livingston with the advice of J. H. Rogers. Harcourt, Brace. **325n.**

Parsons, T., 1937. *The Structure of Social Action.* McGraw-Hill. (Free Press ed. 1949.) **26, 466, 557n.**

——, 1939. The professions and social structure. *Social Forces,* v. 17, pp. 457-67. **243n.**

——, 1940. The motivation of economic activities. *Canad. J. econ. polit. Sci.*, v. 6, pp. 187-203. **264, 474.**

——, 1942. Age and sex in the social structure of the United States. *Amer. sociol. Rev.*, v. 7. **199n., 200, 245.**

——, 1942a. Max Weber and the contemporary political crisis. *Rev. Politics,* v. 4, pp. 61-76, 155-72. **340.**

——, 1942b. Democracy and social structure in pre-Nazi Germany. *J. Legal polit. Sociol.*, v. 1, pp. 96-114. **340.**

——, 1942c. The sociology of modern anti-Semitism. In Graeber and Britt, eds., 1942, pp. 101-22. **595n., 614n., 623.**

——, 1942d. Some sociological aspects of the Fascist movements. *Social Forces,* v. 21, pp. 138-47. **340, 623.**

——, 1943. The kinship system of the contemporary United States. *Amer. Anthropologist,* v. 45. **169, 175, 181.**

——, 1948. The position of sociological theory. *Amer. sociol. Rev.*, v. 13, pp. 156-71. **78.**

——, 1949 (May). Social classes and class conflict in the light of recent sociological theory. *Amer. econ. Rev.*, v. 39, no. 3, pp. 16-26. **636, 648.**

——, 1951. *The Social System.* Free Press. **19n., 21n., 25n., 33, 46, 51n., 61, 78, 87n., 393, 417, 450n., 452, 457n., 461, 466, 562, 566, 575, 577, 580-82, 585, 590, 623, 631, 638, 641-44, 647, 648.**

——, 1951a. *Religious Perspectives of College Teaching in Sociology and Social Psychology.* Edward W. Hazen Foundation. **417.**

——, 1953. A revised analytical approach to the theory of social stratification. In Bendix and Lipset, eds., 1953. **53n., 78, 87n., 90n., 108, 468, 488, 512.**

——, 1953a. The theory of symbolism in relation to action. In Parsons, Bales, and Shils, 1953, Chap. 2. **93n.**

——, 1954. *Essays in Sociological Theory,* rev. ed. Free Press. **46, 78, 243n., 340, 412n., 417, 591n., 613, 614n., 623.**

——, 1954a. The incest taboo in relation to social structure and the socialization of the child. *Brit. J. Sociol.*, v. 5, no. 2, pp. 101-17. **67, 79, 131.**

——, 1955. The American family: its relations to personality and to the social structure. In Parsons and Bales, eds., 1955. **34.**

——, 1955a. Family structure and the socialization of the child. In Parsons and Bales, eds., 1955, Chap. 2. **126n., 128n., 132n., 135, 136n.**

——, 1955b. The organization of personality as a system of action. In Parsons and Bales, eds., 1955, Chap 3. **136n.**

——, 1955c. "McCarthyism" and American social tension: a sociologist's view. *Yale Rev.*, pp. 226-45. **417.**

——, 1956. Suggestions for a sociological approach to the theory of organizations. *Admin. Sci. Quart.*, v. 1, no. 1 (June), pp. 63-85; no. 2 (Sept.), pp. 225-39. **285, 311.**

——, 1957. The distribution of power in American society. *World Politics,* v. 10, pp. 123-43. **386n., 389.**

——, 1958. Some ingredients of a general theory of formal organization. In Halpin, ed., 1958, Chap. 3. **283, 286, 295, 311.**

——, and R. F. Bales, 1953. The dimensions of action-space. In Parsons, Bales, and Shils, 1953, Chap. 3. **87n., 241n.**

——, 1955. *Family, Socialization and Interaction Process.* Free Press. **143.**

——, and E. A. Shils, 1953. *Working*

Redlich, F. C. *See also* Hollingshead and Redlich, 1958

Reynolds, C. N. *See* Hayner and Reynolds, 1937.

Riesman, D., 1954. *Individualism Reconsidered and Other Essays.* Free Press. **537.**

——, with N. Glazer and R. Denney, 1955. *The Lonely Crowd: A Study of the Changing American Character,* abridged by the authors. Doubleday Anchor Books. **238*n*.**

Robertson, R. M., 1955. *History of the American Economy.* Harcourt, Brace. **218, 267, 271, 272, 275, 276, 277*n*., 278.**

Robison, S. M., 1949. How many Jews in America? *Commentary,* v. 8, pp. 185-92. **624.**

Roethlisberger, F. J., and W. J. Dickson, 1939. *Management and the Worker.* Harvard University Press. **6*n*.**

Rogoff, N., 1953. *Recent Trends in Occupational Mobility.* Free Press. **501, 532-33.**

——, 1958. Social stratification in France and in the United States. *Amer. J. Sociol.,* v. 58, no. 4, pp. 347-57. **501, 532, 533.**

Rose, A. M. *See* Myrdal, 1944.

Rosen, B. C., 1956 (April). The achievement syndrome. *Amer. sociol. Rev.,* v. 21, no. 2, pp. 203-11. **549.**

Rosen, B. C. *See also* Strodtbeck, McDonald, and Rosen, 1957.

Rosenberg, B. *See* L. A. Coser and Rosenberg, eds., 1957.

Rosenberg, M. *See* Lazarsfeld and Rosenberg, eds., 1955.

Ross, A. M., 1948. *Trade Union Wage Policy.* University of California Press. **270.**

Ross, I. *See* Ivy and Ross, 1949.

Rossi, P. H. *See* Inkeles and Rossi, 1956.

Rosten, L., ed., 1955. *A Guide to the Religions of America.* Simon and Schuster.

Rowland, B., 1953. *The Art and Architecture of India: Buddhist, Hindu, Jain.* Penguin. **408*n*., 417.**

Ryan, B., 1953. *Caste in Modern Ceylon: The Sinhalese System in Transition.* Rutgers University Press. **511, 513.**

Sales, de, R. de R., 1938 (May). Love in America. *Atlantic Monthly.* **164.**

Salter, P. J. *See* Berelson and Salter, 1946.

Samuel, H. D. *See* Bailey and Samuel, 1952.

Samuelson, P. A., 1951. *Economics: An Introductory Analysis,* 2nd ed. McGraw-Hill. **266*n*., 269, 277-78.**

Sanford, R. N. *See* Adorno *et al.,* 1950.

Schapiro, M., 1953. Style. In Kroeber, ed., 1953, pp. 287-312. **108.**

Schatzman, L., and A. Strauss, 1955 (Jan.). Social class and modes of communication. *Amer. J. Sociol.,* v. 60, no. 4, pp. 329-38. **476, 477.**

Schild, E. *See* Svalastoga *et al.,* 1956.

Schneider, D. M. *See* Homans and Schneider, 1955.

Schrag, C. C., 1954 (Feb.). Leadership among prison inmates. *Amer. sociol. Rev.,* v. 19, no. 1, pp. 37-42. **585.**

Schrag, C. C. *See also* Lundberg, Schrag, and Larsen, 1954.

Schuler, E. A., D. L. Gibson, M. L. Fiero, and W. B. Brookover, eds., 1952. *Outside Readings in Sociology.* Crowell. **640*n*.**

Schumpeter, J. A., 1947. *Capitalism, Socialism, and Democracy,* 2nd ed. Harper. **277, 344*n*.**

——, 1949. Economic theory and entrepreneurial history. In *Change and the Entrepreneur,* 1949. **218.**

——, 1957. Capitalism. *Encyclopaedia Britannica,* v. 4, pp. 801-07. **277.**

Schwartz, H., 1950. *Russia's Soviet Economy.* Prentice-Hall. **207*n*.**

Schwarz, E. E., 1945. A community experiment in the measurement of juvenile delinquency. In *Yearbook of the National Probation Association,* National Probation Assoc., pp. 156-81. **567-68.**

Sears, R. R., 1951. Social behavior and personality development. In Parsons and Shils, eds., 1951, pp. 474-76.

Seligman, B. Z., 1929. Incest and descent. *J. Royal anthrop. Inst.,* v. 59, pp. 243-45. **67*n*.**

Sellin, T., ed., and J. C. Charlesworth, assoc. ed., 1952. *Social Contribution by the Aging.* Special issue of *Annals Amer. Acad. polit. soc. Sci.,* v. 279, no. 1. **199*n*.**

Selltiz, C., M. Jahoda, M. Deutsch, and S. W. Cook, 1959. *Research Methods in Social Relations,* rev. ed. Holt. **14.**

Selvin, H. C. *See* Merton, Gray, Hockey, and Selvin, eds., 1952.

Selznick, P., 1949. *TVA and the Grass-*

roots. University of California Press. **297.**

Selznick, P. *See also* Broom and Selznick, 1955.

Shabat, O. E. *See* Weinberg and Shabat, 1956.

Sharp, W. R., 1931. *The French Civil Service: Bureaucracy in Transition*. Macmillan. **306*n*.**

Shaw, C. R., and H. D. McKay, 1949. Rejoinder. *Amer. sociol. Rev.*, v. 14, no. 5, pp. 614-17. (*See* Jonasson, 1949.) **571*n*.**

Sheppard, H. L., 1954. Approaches to conflict in American industrial sociology. *Brit. J. Sociol.*, v. 5, pp. 324-41. **636*n*.**

Sherif, M., 1948. *An Outline of Social Psychology*. Harper. **136*n*.**

Shih Kuo-Heng, 1944. *China Enters the Machine Age*. Harvard University Press. **301*n*.**

Shils, E. A., 1954. Authoritarianism: "right" and "left." In Christie and Jahoda, eds., 1954. **613*n*.**

——, 1956. *The Torment of Secrecy: The Background and Consequences of American Security Policies*. Free Press. **296, 312.**

Shils, E. A. *See also* Goldhamer and Shils, 1939; Parsons, Bales, and Shils, 1953; Parsons and Shils, 1951; Parsons and Shils, eds., 1951.

Shu-Ching Lee. *See* Lee, Shu-Ching.

Siegfried, A., 1913. *Tableau politique de la France de l'Ouest sous la Troisième République*. Paris: Armand Colin. **381*n*.**

Sills, D. L., 1957. *The Volunteers: Means and Ends in a National Organization*. Free Press. **284-85.**

Silverman, C. *See* Garceau and Silverman, 1954.

Simmel, G., 1950. *The Sociology of Georg Simmel*. Trans. K. H. Wolff. Free Press. **318*n*.**

Simon, H A., 1945. *Administrative Behavior: A Study of Decision-Making Processes in Administrative Organization*. Macmillan. **280*n*., 283, 287, 291, 298, 306*n*., 311.**

Simon, H. A. *See also* March and Simon, 1958.

Simpson, G. E., 1941 (Oct.). Haiti's social structure. *Amer. sociol. Rev.*, v. 6, no. 5, pp. 640-49. **495.**

Sjoberg, G., 1952 (Nov.). Folk and "feudal" societies. *Amer. J. Sociol.*, v. 58, no. 3, pp. 231-39. **637-38.**

Slater, P. E. *See* Bales and Slater, 1955.

Slotkin, J. S., 1952. *Personality Development*. Harper. **111.**

Smelser, N. J., 1959. *Social Change in the Industrial Revolution: An Application of Theory to the Lancashire Cotton Industry, 1770-1840*. London: Routledge & Kegan Paul. **649.**

Smelser, N. J *See also* Parsons and Smelser, 1956.

Smigel, E .O., 1956 (June). Public attitudes toward stealing as related to the size of the victim organization. *Amer. sociol. Rev.*, v. 21, no. 3, pp. 320-27. **563*n*.**

Smith, A., 1853. *The Theory of Moral Sentiments*. London: Henry Bohn. **477-78.**

Smith, M. B., 1949. Combat motivations among ground troops. In Stouffer *et al.*, eds., 1949, v. 2, pp. 172-91. **414, 464.**

Sorokin, P. A., 1927. *Social Mobility*. Harper. **513, 524, 526, 549.**

——, 1937. *Social and Cultural Dynamics*. American Book. **340.**

Sperry, M. *See* Hollenberg and Sperry, 1955.

Spier, L., A. I. Hallowell, and S. S. Newman, eds., 1941. *Language, Culture, and Personality*. Sapir Memorial Fund.

Spiro, A. G. *See* M. E. Spiro, 1958.

Spiro, M. E., 1951. Culture and personality: the natural history of a false dichotomy. *Psychiatry*, v. 14, pp. 19-46. **98, 108.**

——, 1956. *Kibbutz: Venture in Utopia*. Harvard University Press. **147, 519, 543, 608-09.**

——, with the assistance of A. G. Spiro, 1958. *Children of the Kibbutz*. Harvard University Press. **110, 147, 519.**

Starkey, M. L., 1949. *The Devil in Massachusetts: A Modern Inquiry into the Salem Witch Trials*. Knopf. **417.**

Steffens, L., 1931. *Autobiography of Lincoln Steffens*. Chautauqua Press. **578.**

Steiger, G. N., 1936. *A History of the Far East*. Ginn. **329, 332.**

Stendler, C. B. *See* W. E. Martin and Stendler, eds., 1954.

Stern, B. J. *See* A. Locke and Stern, eds., 1946.

Stevenson, H. C. N., 1957. Caste (Indian). *Encyclopaedia Britannica*.

1957 printing, v. 4, pp. 977-86. **397, 482-84, 511, 522.**

Stoke, S. M., 1950. An inquiry into the concept of identification. *J. genet. Psychol.*, v. 76, pp. 163-89. **130*n*.**

Stonequist, E. V., 1957. *The Marginal Man*. Scribner's. **47.**

Stouffer, S. A., 1949. An analysis of conflicting social norms. *Amer. sociol. Rev.*, v. 14, pp. 707-17. **23, 29, 46.**

——, 1949a. A study of attitudes. *Sci. Amer.*, v. 180, pp. 11-15. **47.**

——, 1950. Some observations on study design. *Amer. J. Sociol.*, v. 55, pp. 355-61. **14, 591*n*.**

——, 1955. *Communism, Conformity, and Civil Liberties: A Cross-Section of the Nation Speaks Its Mind*. Doubleday. **388*n*.**

——, *et al.*, eds., 1949. *The American Soldier*. 2 vols. Princeton University Press. **40, 42, 43, 307.**

Strauss, A. *See* Schatzman and Strauss, 1955.

Strodtbeck, F. L., M. R. McDonald, and B. C. Rosen, 1957 (Oct.). Evaluation of occupations: a reflection of Jewish and Italian mobility differences. *Amer. sociol. Rev.*, v. 22, no. 5, pp. 546-53. **496.**

Strodtbeck, F. L., and M. B. Sussman, 1956. Of time, the city, and the "one-year guaranty": the relations between watch owners and repairers. *Amer. J. Sociol.*, v. 61, no. 6, pp. 602-09. **489*n*.**

Strong, D. S., 1941. *Organized Anti-Semitism in America: The Rise of Group Prejudice During the Decade 1930-40*. American Council on Public Affairs. **615*n*.**

Stroup, H. H., 1945. *The Jehovah's Witnesses*. Columbia University Press. **427, 428, 432.**

Sugimoto, E. I., 1953. Old love and new. In Winch and McGinnis, eds., 1953, pp. 45-47. **176.**

Summerson, J., 1949. *Heavenly Mansions and Other Essays on Architecture*. London: Cresset. **408*n*., 417.**

Sumner, W. G., 1906. *Folkways: A Study of the Sociological Importance of Usages, Manners, Customs, Mores, and Morals*. Ginn. **13, 21*n*.**

Sussman, M. B., 1953. The help pattern in the middle-class family. *Amer. sociol. Rev.*, v. 18, pp. 22-28. **181, 182.**

——, ed., 1955. *Sourcebook in Marriage and the Family*. Houghton Mifflin. **175.**

Sussman, M. B. *See also* Strodtbeck and Sussman, 1956.

Sutherland, E. H., 1940 (Feb.). White collar criminality. *Amer. sociol. Rev.*, v. 5, pp. 1-12. **575.**

——, 1945 (April). Is "white collar crime" crime? *Amer. sociol. Rev.*, v. 10, no. 2, pp. 132-39. **575.**

Sutton, F. X., S. E. Harris, C. Kaysen, and J. Tobin, 1956. *The American Business Creed*. Harvard University Press. **590, 594*n*., 605*n*., 618, 623.**

Svalastoga, K., W. Høgh, M. Pedersen, and E. Schild, 1956. Differential class behavior in Denmark. *Amer. sociol. Rev.*, v. 21, no. 4, pp. 435-39. **485*n*.**

Sweezy, P. M. *See* Huberman and Sweezy, 1956.

Sykes, G. M., 1956. *Crime and Society*. Random House. **585, 586.**

——, 1958. *Society of Captives: A Study of a Maximum Security Prison*. Princeton University Press. **586.**

Tangent, P. *See* J. Useem, Tangent, and Useem, 1942.

Tannenbaum, A. S. *See* Georgopoulos and Tannenbaum, 1957.

Tappan, P. W., 1947 (Feb.). Who is the criminal? *Amer. sociol. Rev.*, v. 12, no. 1, pp. 96-102. **575.**

Taussig, F. W., and C. S. Joslyn, 1932. *American Business Leaders*. Macmillan. **529*n*.**

Tawney, R. H., 1922. *Religion and the Rise of Capitalism*. Harcourt, Brace. **446*n*.**

Tax, S., 1945. The problem of democracy in Middle America. *Amer. sociol. Rev.*, v. 10, pp. 192-99. **334.**

Taylor, E., 1947. *Richer by Asia*. Houghton Mifflin. **98.**

Teggart, F. J., 1939. *Rome and China*. University of California Press. As reprinted in A. Locke and Stern, eds., 1946, pp. 46-52. **647.**

Terman, L., *et al.*, 1938. *Psychological Factors in Marital Happiness*. McGraw-Hill. **443.**

Thomas, F., 1940. The role of anthropogeography in contemporary social theory. In Barnes, Becker, and Becker, eds., 1940, pp. 143-211. **103.**

Thomas, W. I., 1923. *The Unadjusted Girl*. Little, Brown. **136*n*.**

——, and F. Znaniecki, 1927. *The Polish Peasant in Europe and America*.

171, 174, 176, 398*n*., 399.

Wallerstein, J. S., and C. J. Wyle, 1947 (March-Apr.). Our law-abiding lawbreakers. *Probation,* v. 25, pp. 107-12. **563*n*.**

Wallin, P. *See* Burgess and Wallin, 1943.

Wallis, W. D., 1926. Geographical environment and culture. *Social Forces,* v. 4, pp. 702-08. **103.**

Waln, N., 1933. *House of Exile.* Little, Brown. **157*n*.**

Warner, W. L., 1937. *A Black Civilization.* Harper. **187, 411, 417.**

——, and J. C. Abegglen, 1955. *Occupational Mobility in American Business and Industry.* University of Minnesota Press. **529*n*., 531.**

Warner, W. L., and J. O. Low, 1947. *The Social System of the Modern Factory.* Yale University Press. **271.**

Warner, W. L., and P. S. Lunt, 1941. *The Social Life of a Modern Community.* Yale University Press. **472, 479, 497, 507*n*., 510.**

Warner, W. L., M. Meeker, and K. Eells, 1949. *Social Class in America: A Manual of Procedure for the Measurement of Social Status.* Science Research Associates. **508*n*.**

Warriner, C. K., 1956. Groups are real: a reaffirmation. *Amer. sociol. Rev.,* v. 21, pp. 549-54. **13.**

Watnik, M., 1952. *Economic Development and Cultural Change.* University of Chicago Press. **618.**

Waugh, E., 1956. An open letter. In Mitford, ed., 1956. **473.**

Weber, M., 1922. *Gesammelte Aufsätze zur Religionssoziologie,* v. 1. Tübingen: J. C. B. Mohr (Paul Siebeck). Unpublished trans. H. Johnson. **423.**

——, 1930. *The Protestant Ethic and the Spirit of Capitalism.* Trans. T. Parsons. Scribner's. **444, 466.**

——, 1946. *From Max Weber: Essays in Sociology.* Trans. and ed. H. H. Gerth and C. W. Mills. Oxford University Press. **69, 290, 311, 315, 316, 318*n*., 346*n*., 396, 405*n*., 418, 591.**

——, 1947. *The Theory of Social and Economic Organization.* Trans. A. M. Henderson and T. Parsons. Ed. with introduction by Parsons. Oxford University Press. **62, 204*n*., 206, 207, 222, 234*n*., 264, 290, 311, 315*n*., 324*n*., 328, 330, 332, 338, 340, 349*n*.**

——, 1950. *General Economic History.* Trans. F. H. Knight. Free Press. **226, 450.**

——, 1950a. *The Hindu Social System.* Trans. H. H. Gerth and D. Martindale. University of Minnesota Sociology Club Bulletin No. 1. **424, 425, 442.**

——, 1951. *The Religion of China: Confucianism and Taoism.* Trans. and ed. H. H. Gerth. Free Press. **183*n*., 423*n*., 439, 442, 449, 466.**

——, 1952. *Ancient Judaism.* Trans. H. H. Gerth and D. Martindale. Free Press. **455, 466.**

——, 1954. *Max Weber on Law in Economy and Society.* Trans. E. Shils and M. Rheinstein, ed. and with introduction and annotations by M. Rheinstein. Harvard University Press. Originally published in 1925. **327*n*.**

——, 1958. *The Religion of India: The Sociology of Hinduism and Buddhism.* Trans. H. H. Gerth and D. Martindale. Free Press. **466.**

Weiler, E. T., 1952. *The Economic System: An Analysis of the Flow of Economic Life.* Macmillan. **273, 276, 278.**

Weinberg, M., and O. E. Shabat, 1956. *Society and Man.* Prentice-Hall. **239, 344, 350, 367*n*.**

Weinberg, S. K., 1942 (March). Aspects of the prison's social structure. *Amer. J. Sociol.,* v. 47, no. 5, pp. 717-26. **585.**

Weldon, T. D., 1953. *The Vocabulary of Politics.* Penguin. **608.**

West, P. S. *See* Havemann and West, 1952.

Westley, W. A., 1953 (July). Violence and the police. *Amer. J. Sociol.,* v. 59, no. 1, pp. 34-41. **578, 586.**

Whatmough, J., 1956. *Language: A Modern Synthesis.* St. Martin's Press. **109.**

White, R. W., 1948. *The Abnormal Personality: A Textbook.* Ronald. **112, 127, 128.**

Whiting, B. B., 1950. *Paiute Sorcery.* Viking Fund Publications in Anthropology, No. 15. **122.**

Whiting, J. W. M., and I. L. Child, 1953. *Child Training and Personality: A Cross-Cultural Study.* Yale University Press. **121, 122.**

Whitney, V. H., 1950 (Nov.). Resistance to innovation: the case of atomic power. *Amer. J. Sociol.,* v. 56, no. 3, pp. 247-54. **649.**

Subject Index